C000157967

Anglo-Saxon England 33

Her mon mæg giet gesion hiora swæð

ANGLO-SAXON ENGLAND
33

Edited by
MICHAEL LAPIDGE
University of Cambridge

MALCOLM GODDEN
University of Oxford

SIMON KEYNES
University of Cambridge

CAMBRIDGE
UNIVERSITY PRESS

Published by the Press Syndicate of the University of Cambridge
The Edinburgh Building, Cambridge CB2 2RU, United Kingdom
40 West 20th Street, New York, NY 10011-4211, USA
47 Williamstown Road, Port Melbourne, VIC 3207, Australia
Ruiz de Alarcón 13, 28014 Madrid, Spain
Dock House, The Waterfront, Cape Town 8001, South Africa

First Published 2004

Typeset by
Servis Filmsetting Ltd
Manchester

Printed in the United Kingdom by
the University Press
Cambridge

ISBN 0 521 84905 5
ISSN 0263-6751

COPYING

SUBSCRIPTIONS: Anglo-Saxon England (ISSN 0263-6751) is an annual journal. The subscription price (excluding VAT) of volume 33, which includes print and electronic access is £85 for institutions (US$135 in the USA, Canada and Mexico), £52 (US$80 in the USA, Canada and Mexico) for individuals ordering direct from the Press and certifying that the annual is for their personal use. EU subscribers (outside the UK) who are not registered for VAT should add VAT at their country's rate. VAT registered subscribers should provide their VAT registration number. Japanese prices for institutions are available from Kinokuniya Company Ltd., P.O. Box 55, Chitose, Tokyo 156, Japan. Orders, which must be accompanied by payment, may be sent to a bookseller, subscription agent, or direct to the publishers: Cambridge University Press, The Edinburgh Building, Shaftesbury Road, Cambridge CB2 2RU, UK. Orders from the USA, Canada or Mexico should be sent to Cambridge University Press, Journals Fulfillment Department, 100 Brook Hill Drive, West Nyack, New York 10994-2133, USA. Prices include delivery by air.

Back volumes: £80.00 (US$125.00 in the USA, Canada and Mexico) each available from Cambridge or the American Branch of Cambridge University Press.

A catalogue record of this book is available from the British Library.

Contents

Illustrations

PLATES

between pages 150 and 151

between pages 246 and 247

Illustrations

FIGURES

ACKNOWLEDGEMENTS

By permission of the Trustees of the British Museum the design on the cover is taken from the obverse of a silver penny issued to celebrate King Alfred's occupation and fortification of London in 886.

Permission to publish photographs has been granted by the Staatliches Konservatoramt of the Saarland (pl. I); the Bibliothèque Nationale de France, Paris (pl. II); the Somerset Archive and Record Service (pls. III and IV); T. Pestell (pl. V*a*); the St Edmundsbury Museums Service (pl. V*b* and *c*); the administrators of the Haverfield Bequest, University of Oxford (pl. VI*c*); the Dean and Chapter, Chichester Cathedral (pl. VII*a*); Frank Green (pl. VII*b*); the Trustees of the Museums and Galleries of Northern Ireland (pl. VII*c*); the National Museum of Ireland (pl. VIII*a*); the Derby Museums and Art Gallery (pl. VIII*b*); Canon Nicholas Horton (pl. VIII*c*); Philip A. Rahtz (pl. IX*a*); Pre-Construct Archaeology Limited (pl. IX*c*); Jane Beale (pl. X*a*); the Portable Antiquities Scheme (pl. X*b*); the Trustees of the British Museum (pls. X*c* and XI*c*); the Norfolk Museums & Archaeology Service (pl. XI*a*); Kevin Leahy, North Lincolnshire Museum (pl. XI*b*); English Heritage (pl. XII*a*); the Visitors of the Ashmolean Museum, Oxford (pl. XII*b*); David Guyatt (pl. XII*c*); Christie's Images Ltd (pl. XII*d*).

CONTRIBUTIONS FOR FUTURE EDITIONS ARE INVITED

Material should be submitted to the editor most convenient regionally, with these exceptions: an article should be sent to John Blair if concerned with archaeology, to Mark Blackburn if concerned with numismatics, to Richard Gameson if concerned with art history, to Simon Keynes if concerned with history or onomastics, and to Michael Lapidge if concerned with Anglo-Latin or palaeography. Whenever a contribution is sent from abroad it should be accompanied by international coupons to cover the cost of return postage. A potential contributor is asked to get in touch with the editor concerned as early as possible to obtain a copy of the style sheet and to have any necessary discussion. Articles must be in English.

The editors' addresses are:

Dr M. A. S. Blackburn, Fitzwilliam Museum, Cambridge CB2 1RB (England)

Dr W. J. Blair, The Queen's College, Oxford OX1 4AW (England)

Professor M. Clayton, Department of Old and Middle English, University College, Belfield, Dublin 4 (Ireland)

Professor R. Frank, Department of English, Yale University, New Haven, Connecticut 06520 (USA)

Dr R. Gameson, Faculty of Humanities, Rutherford College, University of Kent at Canterbury, Canterbury, Kent CT2 7NX (England)

Professor H. Gneuss, Institut für Englische Philologie, Universität München, Schellingstrasse 3, D-80799 München (Germany)

Professor M. R. Godden, English Faculty, St Cross Building, Manor Road, Oxford OX1 3UQ (England)

Professor M. Gretsch, Seminar für Englische Philologie, Universität Göttingen, Käte-Hamburger-Weg 3, D-37073 Göttingen (Germany)

Professor N. Howe, Department of English, University of California, Berkeley, 322 Wheeler Hall, Berkeley, California 94720 (USA)

Professor S. D. Keynes, Trinity College, Cambridge CB2 1TQ (England)

Professor M. Lapidge, Clare College, Cambridge CB2 1TL (England)

Professor P. Lendinara, Cattedra di Filologia Germanica, Università degli Studi di Palermo, Facoltà di Magistero, Piazza Ignazio Florio 24, 90139 Palermo (Italy)

Professor K. O'Brien O'Keeffe, Department of English, University of Notre Dame, Notre Dame, Indiana 46556 (USA)

Professor A. Orchard, Centre for Medieval Studies, University of Toronto, 39 Queen's Park Crescent East, Toronto, Ontario M5S 1A1 (Canada)

Professor P. G. Remley, Department of English, Box 354330, University of Washington, Seattle, WA 98195–4330 (USA)

Professor F. C. Robinson, Department of English, Yale University, New Haven, Connecticut 06520 (USA)

Contributions for future editions are invited

Professor D. G. Scragg, Centre for Anglo-Saxon Studies, University of Manchester, Manchester M13 9PL (England)

Professor P. E. Szarmach, The Medieval Institute, 102 Walwood Hall, Western Michigan University, Kalamazoo, Michigan 49008 (USA)

St Aldhelm's bees (*De uirginitate prosa* cc. IV–VI): some observations on a literary tradition

AUGUSTINE CASIDAY

Although the classic comparison of monks to bees owes its enduring success chiefly to the *Vita S. Antonii*, one of the most interesting developments of that simile is found in the prose treatise *De uirginitate* by Aldhelm of Malmesbury. In his writings, Aldhelm demonstrates familiarity with most of the conventional similes – monks are like bees in their industry, their intelligence, their chastity, and so on – but he also insists that monks are like bees in their 'voluntary solidarity' and obedience to leadership. This is a novel claim, one that I will argue Aldhelm makes by introducing a theme known from other Christian (and pagan) literature into his advice to nuns. The present article will describe the traditions incorporated by Aldhelm into his claim that monks, like bees, are obedient to a fault. In this way, this article will offer a broad view of the literary heritage to which Aldhelm's treatise belongs and in which it should be interpreted. This will entail an assessment of which sources Aldhelm likely knew. While this assessment is indebted to the excellent notes by Rudolf Ehwald (as indeed all scholarship subsequent to Ehwald must be), it will not be bound by Ehwald's conclusions.[1] In some instances, I will posit sources not mentioned by, and perhaps not detected by, Ehwald; in others, I will with trepidation suggest refinements to Ehwald's work. It is hoped that on these grounds the article will be useful to students both of late antique monasticism and of Anglo-Saxon England. Since this is the goal of the article, it will be convenient to begin each section with an excerpt from Aldhelm and follow it with the relevant antecedents; each section will then be concluded with a return to Aldhelm; this will allow us to appreciate the distinctiveness of Aldhelm's contribution. The article itself will be concluded with an overview of the comparisons and of the relationship between the earlier writings and Aldhelm's.

INDUSTRY

Aldhelm's *De uirginitate* is an *opus geminatum*, a 'twinned' work, so called because it consists of a prose version and a poetic version. That the versions are not

[1] *Aldhelmi Opera*, ed. R. Ehwald, MGH Auct. antiq. 15 (Berlin, 1919).

identical is evident, for example, from the fact that the simile about bees that concerns us here is lacking from the poetic version. The prose treatise is in the form of a letter addressed to Hildelith, abbess of a monastery in Barking, Essex, and the sisters with her (an establishment mentioned by Bede).[2] Aldhelm first brings his readers' attention to the bees in the elaborate – indeed, overly elaborate – compliment that he pays to the dedicatees of the treatise. He congratulates them on their devotion to study of scripture and their discipline. First, he likens them to athletes, with an eye to I Cor. IX.24 ('all run indeed, but one wins the prize') and to Vergil (quoting *Aeneid* XI.875). It is not unusual for Aldhelm, whose knowledge of Vergil was considerable,[3] to pair secular and sacred literature in this way. Then, with an extremely tenuous transition, Aldhelm adds to his convoluted salutation the figure of the bee.[4] Or, to be more precise, he adds the simile of the bee's industry: '. . . the richest experience of life clearly declares that the industry of the highly industrious bee might be adapted to the aforementioned schemes of examples'.[5] He adduces three examples. First, bees pour out across the fields to 'gather honeyed moisture drop by drop in their mouths and, as if with the treacly must of the sweet wine made for royal feasts, they struggle eagerly to fill the greedy receptacles of their stomachs'. Second, they take from the blossoms of the willow and the broom 'their fertile booty' from which 'they build waxen castles'. Third, from the ivy and lime tree, they derive the substances needed to build the honeycomb. Aldhelm amplifies the last point with two learned quotations (the first, he points out rather pedantically, in catalectic verse; the second, in a brachicatalectic) from Caelius Sedulius's *Carmen paschale*, praef. 13 and 14.

With this much said, it is high time for Aldhelm to explain himself. The nuns, he writes, are similar because they, too, roam 'widely through the flowering fields of scripture'. He mentions in particular the prophets who foretold the coming of the Saviour; the Mosaic laws; the gospels – together with the commentaries of the catholic Fathers, who used the methods of *historia*, *allegoria*, *tropologia* and *anagoge*; and finally the historians and the grammarians. This five-fold curriculum is predicated on the gospels. The gospels provide the

2 Bede, *Historia ecclesiastica* IV.6–10 (ed. B. Colgrave and R. A. B. Mynors (Oxford, 1969), pp. 354–64); see also the introduction to Lapidge's translation of *De uirginitate prosa*, in M. Lapidge and M. Herren, *Aldhelm: the Prose Works* (Cambridge, 1979), pp. 51–8. Unless otherwise noted, all quotations of *De uirginitate* will be taken from this translation (*ibid.* pp. 59–132). All other translations are my own.

3 Cf. T. J. Brown, 'An Historical Introduction to the Use of Classical Latin Authors in the British Isles from the Fifth to the Eleventh Centuries', *SettSpol* 23 (1975), 237–93, esp. 274–5.

4 But for his reference to Vergil, Aldhelm's transition compares very closely to the one made by Gregory Nazianzen, *Oratio XV*: *In Macchabeorum laudem* (PG 35, col. 933).

5 This quotation, and the others in the same paragraph, is from Aldhelm, *De uirginitate prosa*, c. iv (ed. Ehwald, pp. 231–2).

norms for selecting and interpreting what is relevant in the prophets and the Law, and the commentaries (theological, historical and grammatical) provide the techniques needed for making sense of the gospels. The last two items, the historians and the grammarians, are included because (at least from the time of Augustine's *De doctrina christiana*) competence in these subjects had been expected of would-be biblical scholars.[6]

That bees are hardworking animals is platitudinous. In a declamation by ps.-Quintilian, we are told that the three chief natural characteristics of bees are thriftiness, loyalty and industry.[7] Roughly three centuries later, Ambrose draws the attention of nuns to bees, 'for worthy is that virginity which can be compared to bees – so industrious, so modest, so temperate'.[8] And, in the fifth century, Salvian upbraids his fellow Christians by appealing to the natural industry of the bees and contrasting this to the habitual shiftlessness of his peers.[9] The simile about industry recurs in the form of exhortations to one's reader to produce a meaningful compound out of what has been gleaned from experience (not least the experience of reading). Thus, Seneca exhorts Lucilius to separate out 'whatever we have collected from diverse readings' and 'to mix these juices together into a single delicacy' – just as bees do.[10] In arguably the most influential monastic *uita*, the *Life of St Antony*, Antony is portrayed as seeking out ever-more-advanced disciplines 'like a clever bee'.[11] In a treatise ascribed to Ephrem the Syrian which circulated in Greek, the author was similarly moved by consideration of the bee, hard at work, and invoked her example to spur on the monk to diligence: 'Have a care for yourself, lest you should lapse into carelessness: for the tyranny of carelessness is the source of destruction. Recall the bee and behold her wondrous mystery, how from the flowers scattered throughout the earth she accomplishes her work. Consider, then, her thriftiness . . .'[12] The impact of this conceit is evident in the considerably later Greek anthology of monastic lore, the *Pratum spirituale*, the very title of which depends upon that simile.[13] But it influenced Latin Christian

[6] E.g., Augustine, *De doctrina christiana* II.xxviii.42.105 (for history), III.xxix.40.87–8 (for grammar) (ed. R. Green, Oxford Early Christian Texts (Oxford, 1995), pp. 104 and 170).

[7] Ps.-Quintilian, *Declamationes XIX maiores* XIII.iii, lines 16–17: 'Nam quid apibus inuenit natura praestantius? Parcae, fideles, laboriosae' (ed. L. Håkanson (Stuttgart, 1982), p. 267).

[8] Ambrose, *De uirginibus* I.viii.40 (ed. F. Gori, Biblioteca Ambrosiana 14.1 (Rome, 1989), p. 140).

[9] Salvian, *De gubernatione Dei* IV.ix.43 (ed. G. Lagarrigue, SChr 220 (Paris, 1975), p. 268).

[10] Seneca, *Epistulae morales ad Lucilium* LXXXIV.v: 'quaecumque ex diuersa lectione congressimus . . . in unum saporem uaria illa libamenta confundere' (ed. O. Hense (Leipzig, 1938), p. 332).

[11] Athanasius, *Vita S. Antonii* III.iv (ed. G. J. M. Bartelink, SChr 400 (Paris, 1994), p. 136).

[12] Ephrem graecus, *Sermo asceticus* (*Ὁσίου Ἐφραίμ τοῦ Σύρου ἔργα*, ed. K. G. Phrantzoles (Thessalonica, 1988) I, 122–84, at 152). How much of the Greek corpus – if indeed any of it at all – should be attributed to Ephrem himself has not yet been established; but, for the sake of convenience, in what follows I will simply refer to this material by Ephrem's name.

[13] John Moschus, *Pratum spirituale*, prologue (PG 87, col. 2852).

writers no less. This is particularly evident from the theme of 'spiritual honey' that we often meet and to which we shall soon turn.

Before turning to that topic, we would do well to note that Aldhelm has modified the traditional monastic simile that bees and monks are industrious, by introducing the topic of scriptural exposition. When Aldhelm mentions this topic, he does so by invoking terms and techniques that indicate his familiarity with traditional methods of exegesis. What makes this stand out is that the authors we have considered so far typically regarded mundane physical activities (for example, manual labour or pilgrimage) as evidence for monastic industry. By contrast, Aldhelm emphasizes reading and interpreting scripture and holy tradition as a form of industry; this hearkens back to Seneca's advice to Lucilius when he encouraged him to cull worthwhile bits from his reading. It is certainly appropriate that Aldhelm should begin his florilegium on virginity by expressing his approval for hard work in the form of collecting, presenting and thereby interpreting monastic lore for the benefit of others. Even if he cannot echo John Moschus's claim to have personally visited the people about whom he writes and witnessed the fruits of their extraordinary commitment to God, Aldhelm can nevertheless take some satisfaction in having culled choice passages about their lives to edify the nuns of Barking.[14] The distinctiveness of Aldhelm's use of the industrious bee is also evident when we consider a subset of this simile – the 'spiritual honey' that the bees' industry produces.

'Spiritual honey'

Several late antique authors wrote about 'spiritual honey', though Aldhelm differs from all of them because he takes the bee to represent the religious who are extracting spiritual sense from scripture. By contrast, the bees in question are variously treated in the antecedent literature. In one instance, they are explicitly identified as bishops, distilling the sense of scripture for the benefit of the laity; in two others, it appears that the bees should be understood as the laity themselves; and in other cases, though it is clear that the bees stand for monks, it is not at all clear whether the monks are distilling scripture. Since this last type can be disposed of quickly, we will consider it first. It is found in Fortunatus's *Carmen* IV.xi, his 'Epitaph for Victorian', and in the *Paraenesis ad ascetas* in the Greek corpus of Ephrem's writings. In the latter, we read, 'A monk should speak chiefly in sweet phrases: for honey has no bitterness. Let not the chief worker of righteousness be careless: for the bee works ceaselessly.'[15] As for Fortunatus's epitaph, Victorian was the abbot of the monastery of St Martin in Asan, Spain and died in 558. With regard to the success of Victorian's abbacy, Fortunatus says that he 'established many examples for the

[14] Cf. Aldhelm, *De uirginitate prosa*, c. xix (ed. Ehwald, p. 249).

[15] Ephrem graecus, *Paraenesis ad ascetas* (ed. K. G. Phrantzoles, p. 350).

monks; the bee made honey from eternal flowers'.[16] Fortunatus regrettably does not tell us more about this honey 'made from eternal flowers', leaving us to wonder from which flowers Victorian made it. Perhaps he was like Gregory of Nyssa, who writes that he extracted spiritual honey from the writings of Ephrem the Syrian;[17] but this is conjecture.

By contrast, the other cases are explicit: the spiritual honey is produced from scripture. The longest of them is from Maximus of Turin, even though it is almost certainly fragmentary.[18] What we have is basically an exordium but it is particularly interesting because in it Maximus reflects on how bishops are like bees:

> I ought, brethren, to preach something richer after these several days, and refresh you with a sweet sermon now that I have returned from such a swarm of bishops. I said 'swarm of bishops' rightly, since like the bee they make sweet honey from the blossoms of Divine scriptures, and whatever pertains to the medicine of souls they compound by the skill of their mouth. Bishops are justly compared to bees since like the bee they display chastity of the body, they offer the food of heavenly life and they exercise the sting of the law. For they are pure in order to sanctify, sweet in order to refresh and severe in order to punish. They should obviously be compared to bees who are kept, as it were, in a sort of beehive by the grace of Mother Church, in which they produce many swarms of Christians from the one swarm of the Saviour and by their most sweet preaching make little cells of various merits.[19]

By contrast, the other sources attest that this form of bee-like industry is not the exclusive domain of bishops. About a century and a half earlier, Ambrose had written: 'The bee is fed by the dew, knows no intercourse, and compounds honey. The virgin's dew is likewise divine discourse, since the words of God fall like the dew. [. . .] The virgin's offspring is the fruit of her lips, which lacks any bitterness and is rich with sweetness.'[20] Although Ambrose adds the exceptional remark that the bees feed on dew, rather than blossoms,[21] he nevertheless affirms that they extract sweet spiritual honey from the words of God. In

[16] Fortunatus, 'Epitaphium Victoriani abbatis de monasterio Asane' (ed. M. Reydellet (Paris, 1994), I, 143–4). The biographical details for Victorian given above are taken from Reydellet's notes *ad loc.* [17] Gregory Nyssen, *In sanctum Ephraim* (PG 46, col. 825).

[18] This is almost certainly a fragment because it does not relate Maximus doing precisely what he has announced he would do: preach a sweet sermon, drawn from scripture.

[19] Maximus of Turin, *Collectio sermonum antiqua* LXXXIX (ed. A. Mutzenbecher, CCSL 23 (Turnhout, 1962), p. 364).

[20] Ambrose, *De uirginibus* I.viii.40 (ed. F. Gori, p. 140); cf. his *Expositio psalmi cxviii*, XIII.xxiii (ed. M. Petschenig, CSEL 62 (Vienna, 1913), p. 294).

[21] It should be noted that at *De uirginibus* I.viii.41 and 43, Ambrose does say that the bee feeds on *flos* rather than on *ros*. In his edition of the text, E. Cazzaniga emended *flos* to *ros* at I.viii.41, but this is a questionable emendation because *flos* recurs at I.viii.43. Ambrose's description at I.viii.40 depends on *ros* and at I.viii.41–3 it depends on *flos*, so it would appear that he simply preferred a stylish transition to slavish consistency.

his warning to monks against the dangers of nodding off during the reading of scripture or during the sermon, Ephrem appeals to a very similar image: 'Pluck from them remedies for the soul, just like a wise bee collecting honey from the flowers.'[22] Here, the monk is intended to extract medicine for the soul from the readings he hears in church.

Likewise, in one of his sermons Caesarius says to his audience that, 'like most prudent bees, [you] faithfully hasten to Christ's beehive so that you can partake of the sweetness of spiritual honey from the holy readings'.[23] While it could be argued that Caesarius is calling the listeners to receive the honey he has derived from scripture, this seems implausible: he has, after all, just likened them to the bees and honey is made by bees. In other words, Caesarius is not suggesting that in his capacity as bishop he has extracted spiritual honey for the benefit of the faithful; instead, he is calling them to make spiritual honey from the holy readings that are provided for them. In a comparable passage, Caesarius upbraids all Christians, lay, clerical and monastic, for failing to produce spiritual honey.[24] Because Ambrose and Ephrem had made monastic Christians (and not necessarily only those in orders) out to be the bees who derive honey from spiritual reading, Aldhelm's call for the nuns of Barking to emulate bees in just this way is not unprecedented. Even as he praises their intelligence and diligence for having 'subtly investigated bit by bit and stage by stage' such abstruse questions as the scriptural distinction of the 'inner man' and 'outer man',[25] he encourages them to continue in this good work.

WISDOM

The praise Aldhelm gave to his nuns' intellectual vigour points up another salient aspect of the simile from bees: bees, and monks, are intelligent. We have already encountered this characteristic of the bees when we read, in the excerpt from Caesarius's sermons, his description of bees as *prudentissimae*. That bees are 'most prudent' is evident from the skill they display in producing honey. Skill is one of the signal attributes of the prudent person. But *prudens* also designates intelligence. Although Aldhelm does not make a sharp or clear distinction between *prudentia* as intelligence and *prudentia* as skill, his description of how the nuns read scripture nevertheless makes it quite obvious that he has in

22 Ephrem graecus, *De recta uiuendi ratione* 36 (ed. K. G. Phrantzoles).

23 Caesarius, *Sermo* CCVII.ii (ed. D. Morin, CCSL 104 (Turnhout, 1953), pp. 829–30): 'Magis enim de uestra deuotione confidens credo uos uelud apes prudentissimas ad aluearium Christi fideliter festinare, ut dulcedinem spiritalis mellis ex diuinis lectionibus possitis accipere, et cum propheta dicere: quam dulcia faucibus meis eloquia tua, Domine, super mel et fauum ori meo.'

24 Caesarius, *Sermo* CLVI.v (ed. Morin, p. 638).

25 Aldhelm, *De uirginitate prosa*, c. iii (ed. Ehwald, p. 231).

mind both senses of the word. The interpretative gymnastics they are capable of undertaking attest to intellectual subtlety, and also intellectual skill.[26] He makes several statements about the interpretative process, all of which stress the high level of intellectual activity characteristic of interpretation, within his extended analogy of bees flying through a glade. Let us return to the passage just examined and note the several references to intelligence and understanding that it features. In the first instance, it is the nuns' 'remarkable mental disposition' that Aldhelm likens to bees. This disposition leads them to plumb 'the divine oracles of the ancient prophets foretelling long in advance the advent of the Saviour with certain affirmations' and to engage in the four-fold interpretation of scripture under the headings of literal, allegorical, topological and anagogic sense. Finally, he claims that the nuns have been motivated in their precocity to consult historians and grammarians so as to facilitate their understanding of scripture. Such extensive measures attest to a considerable theoretical foundation no less than to an impressive practical aptitude.[27]

Once more, in the matter of bees' intelligence, Aldhelm is treading well-worn ground. One might even call it battle-scarred ground, for the question of whether or not bees could be meaningfully considered intelligent was widely debated. Vergil initiated the discussion by referring to the 'divine intelligence' of bees.[28] This was well within his prerogatives as a poet; but it is somewhat surprising to find that the naturalist Hyginus entertained similar beliefs.[29] On the other hand, the rather more pragmatic Columella considered it a topic not worthy of serious discussion: with an all but audible scoff, Columella notes that farmers have more important things to do than propagate fairy tales and pore over literature.[30] But if the topic did not merit the attention of practical agronomists, it certainly detained the attention of philosophers. For instance, in rebutting Celsus, Origen stipulates that bees are not reasoning creatures and therefore they cannot be praised for their actions (or, more to the point, the significance of humans' rational actions cannot be minimized by comparing

[26] See Aldhelm, *De uirginitate prosa*, c. iii: '. . . ita interioris qualitatem, qui caelesti afflatus spiraculo iuxta Geneseos relatum creditur, *a uestra prudentia* membratim et particulatim subtiliter inuestigatam reor' (ed. Ehwald, p. 231). In this passage, he also praises the nuns' discipline and industry – which point to the skill involved in *prudentia* – and their sagacity and subtlety – which point to the intelligence involved in *prudentia*. Note that he does not mention *uirgines sapientes* until *De uirginitate prosa*, c. xlviii (*ibid.* p. 302).

[27] Aldhelm, *De uirginitate prosa*, c. iv: 'uestrum . . . memoriale mentis ingenium'; 'diuina priscorum prophetarum oracula certis adstipulationibus iamdudum saluatoris aduentum uaticinantia enixius inuestigando'; etc. (*ibid.* p. 232).

[28] Vergil, *Georgics* IV.219–21 (ed. O. Ribbeck (Leipzig, 1894), p. 186).

[29] Hyginus *ap.* Columella, *Res rustica* IX.ii.2–3 (ed. V. Lundström, A. Josephson and S. Hedberg (Leipzig, 1897–1968), p. 640).

[30] Columella, *Res rustica* IX.ii.5 (ed. Lundström *et al.*, p. 640)

them to what bees do).[31] According to Origen, bees act according to their providential design – a view also found in a homily by one of Basil's disciples and indeed in one of Aldhelm's letters.[32] On a comparable note, Seneca assigns the skills exhibited by bees and particularly their co-operation to a natural desire for self-preservation.[33]

Despite this dismissive treatment by philosophers and naturalists, the image of the 'wise bee' persists in the literature. The great poet and theologian, Gregory Nazianzen, concluded one of his homilies with a florid, quasi-architectural description of bees' cells; then he added, 'So it befits us, too – Christ's apiary – and let us take this example of wisdom and industry.'[34] Wisdom is evident in the well-ordered proportions of the cell, but also in the forethought demonstrated by bees who store up honey for the future. (In Gregory's hands, this becomes an occasion to exhort his audience to hospitality: like bees, good Christians ought to make provisions for entertaining guests!) Furthermore, Evagrius of Antioch's Latin translation of the *Life of St Antony* tells us that the great hermit was 'like a wise bee' when he went from ascetic to ascetic, learning and perfecting his ascetic skills.[35] Even if for different reasons, Ambrose likewise thought virgins should emulate 'that wise bee'.[36]

These cases have in common an extremely practical sensibility. In all of them, the primary evidence for wisdom and intelligence is moral know-how. As we have seen, Aldhelm emphasizes both the practical skill of the nuns and their intellectual acuity – both at the same time by referring to the example of a swarm of bees seeking out the right flowers and compounding honey from them. But, to reiterate a theme, Aldhelm's decision to correlate the nuns' exegetical acumen with the symbol of the bee is a new departure. The well-established (if, in some quarters, controversial) precedent for appealing to the wisdom and intelligence of the bees notwithstanding, Aldhelm reworks the tradition in a strikingly original way by appealing to the figure of speech in order to connote a very sophisticated level of intellectual culture.

[31] Origen, *Contra Celsum* IV.lxxxi (ed. M. Borret, SChr 136 (Paris, 1968), II, 384–8).

[32] Origen, *Contra Celsum* IV.lxxxii (ed. Borret II, 388); ps.-Basil, *Sermo in illud, Ne dederis somnum oculis tuis et c.* (PG 31, cols. 1502–4); Aldhelm, *Epistulae* XII, 'Ad Wilfridi abbates' (ed. Ehwald, p. 501).

[33] Seneca, *Epistulae morales ad Lucilium* CXXI.xxii (ed. Hense, p. 593).

[34] Gregory Nazianzen, *In nouam dominicam* (PG 36, col. 620); cf. Basil, *Homiliae in hexaemeron* VIII.iv.47–55 (ed. S. Giet, SChr 26, 2nd ed. (Paris, 1968), pp. 450–2).

[35] Evagrius of Antioch, *Vita Antonii latine* III.iv.18: 'ut sapiens illa apis' (ed. G. Bartelink, *Vite dei Santi* 1, 6th ed. (Milan, 1998), p. 12).

[36] Ambrose, *De uirginitate* XVII.cvii (ed. Gori, p. 84). Ambrose encourages his readers to emulate the dynamic stability of bees who are not blown off course 'per inania . . . nubila' (a phrase which he owes to Vergil, *Georgics* IV.191 (ed. Ribbeck, p. 184)); his readers similarly ought not be 'in tantis mundi fluctibus iactantiae'.

CHASTITY

By comparing the nuns to bees, Aldhelm has offered an elaborate compliment to their industry, practicality and intelligence. As we have seen, these associations are time-honoured and when he thus compliments the nuns, Aldhelm appeals to a literary tradition that he may well have expected the nuns to appreciate. However, it comes as a surprise that Aldhelm makes little of a far more obvious aspect of the metaphor – the chastity of bees. Because the ancients never observed sexual reproduction among bees, many assumed that bees must reproduce asexually. As Pliny notes, 'How they produce offspring was a major and subtle question among the learned – for bees' intercourse has never been seen. Previously, most believed they were produced from the mouth by blending reed and olive flowers; others, from the intercourse of that bee in the swarm who is called the king . . .'[37] The belief that bees reproduce asexually had been advanced by no less an authority than Vergil.[38] This was a thoroughly useful device for Christian polemicists, since it provided a ready example of virgin birth.[39] Sometimes, though, Christians simply mention the asexual reproduction of bees in passing, without imputing any obvious significance to it. In such a case, one suspects that the reason this claim is inserted into a discussion where it is completely irrelevant, is simply so the author can demonstrate a knowledge of Vergil.[40]

By contrast, St Ambrose integrated this belief into his presentation of consecrated virginity.[41] In a passage we have already met twice from his treatise *De uirginibus*, Ambrose praises the virtues of the anthropomorphic bee and encourages the Christian virgin to attain these virtues: 'How I wish, O daughter, that you would imitate this little bee, whose food is the flower, whose offshoot is collected and composed by its mouth. Imitate this bee, O daughter!'[42] In this account, the figure of the bee attains almost mythic status, for Ambrose intricately relates every convention we have encountered so far and incorporates them under the claim that bees are virginal creatures.

Aldhelm's rationale and approach appears to be more straightforwardly Pauline: those who are chaste have fewer cares for the world; in connection with the bees at least, Aldhelm shows little or no interest in chastity as such.[43]

37 Pliny, *Historia naturalis* XI.xvi.46 (ed. L. Ian and C. Mayhoff (Leipzig, 1892–1909), p. 297).

38 Vergil, *Georgics* IV.197 (ed. Ribbeck, p. 184).

39 Thus, John Cassian, *De incarnatione Domini* VII.v.4 (ed. M. Petschenig, CSEL 17 (Vienna, 1888), p. 360); Augustine, *De bono conjugali* II.ii (ed. P. Walsh, Oxford Early Christian Texts (Oxford, 2001), pp. 2–4).

40 E.g., Salvian, *De gubernatione Dei* IV.ix.43 (ed. Lagarrigue, p. 268).

41 See P. Brown, *The Body and Society: Men, Women and Sexual Renunciation in Early Christianity* (New York, 1988): pp. 341–66.

42 Ambrose, *De uirginibus* I.viii.41 (ed. Gori, p. 140).

43 Cf. I Cor. VII.29–38.

For the nuns at Barking, being disentangled from the cares of the world means that they have more time to pursue Christian learning. And we know from Jerome and Augustine that there is a long and venerable tradition of retirement from the cares of the world for the sake of Christian learning.[44] In other words, Aldhelm shows surprisingly little interest in praising the nuns' chastity as such: he shows more interest in particular virgins than in abstract virginity. Aldhelm's relative lack of interest in virginity as such is perhaps attributable to the status of his addressees as married women who had retired into chastity – 'born-again virgins', so to speak.[45] Aldhelm's circumspection in praising virginity and his sensitivity in praising chastity are evidently related to their status.[46] There is no compelling reason to suppose that the aforementioned passages from Christian literature had any particular impact upon Aldhelm's thought; it is more economic to suppose that he got his belief in the asexual reproduction of bees immediately from Vergil, whose works he knew.

The virginal church

But an interesting aside that Aldhelm makes when writing about bees' chastity deserves some further consideration. He writes, 'The bee, I say, by virtue of the special attribute of its peculiar chastity, is by the undoubted authority of the scriptures agreed to signify a type of virginity and the likeness of the church . . .'[47] It is curious, given how slight is Aldhelm's interest in the bee-like chastity of nuns, that he should incorporate this not particularly intuitive comparison of the 'chaste bee' to the church. One might suppose that the conjunction of 'virginal bees' and 'virginal church' – the latter a very widely attested

[44] E.g. Augustine, *Confessionum libri tredecim* VI.xii.21 and VI.xiv.24 (ed. L. Verheijen, CCSL 27 (Turnhout, 1981), pp. 87 and 89–90), regarding his plan and Alypius's to retire with friends into a community of learned men; Jerome, *Epistula* CVIII.xxvi (ed. J. Labourt (Paris, 1955) V, 194–6), regarding Paula's and Eustochium's asceticism and knowledge of Hebrew.

[45] See the analysis of Lapidge in Lapidge and Herren, *Aldhelm: the Prose Works*, pp. 51–2.

[46] See Aldhelm, *De uirginitate prosa*, cc. ix–xi (ed. Ehwald, pp. 236–40). It would not be amiss in this context to note that the status of the nuns at Barking is not a uniquely Anglo-Saxon phenomenon. Examples of marriages set aside for the pursuit of consecrated 'virginity' are known in eastern ascetic literature (e.g. *Apophthegmata Carion* 2 (PG 65, cols. 249–51); Cassian, *Conlationes* XXI.ix *passim* (ed. Petschenig, pp. 581–4)). Ambiguous parallels are available in the west: e.g. the celebrated chaste marriages of Paulinus and Therasia (note his description of the common life that she and he share with eight others in Nola, and also his praise of a chaste marriage in the *epithalamium* for Julian of Aeclaum: *Carm.* XXI.272–93 and XXV (ed. W. Hartel, CSEL 30 (Vienna, 1894), pp. 167 and 238–45) and of Melania and Pinianus (see Anon., *Vita s. Melaniae* I–VI (ed. D. Gorce, SChr 90 (Paris, 1962), pp. 130–8); and Palladius, *Historia lausiaca* LXI.i–iii (ed. G. Bartelink, *Vite dei Santi* 2, 4th ed. (Milan, 1990), pp. 264–6)).

[47] Aldhelm, *De uirginitate prosa* c. v (ed. Ehwald, p. 233).

image[48] – suggested this remark to Aldhelm. Granting this possibility, it is still worth noting that a precedent for explicitly comparing the virginal church to virginal bees is found in a sermon by Peter Chrysologus.

Let no one wonder if the holy church – a virgin mother – produces numerous offspring with heavenly fertility, personally bears pastors for herself and personally begets rectors. For the bee – knowing no intercourse, ignorant of unchastity and set apart from corruption; as a model of modesty, an exemplar of chastity and a symbol of virginity – who from mere heavenly dew conceives by the mouth, [also] delivers by the mouth, compounds chaste seeds by the mouth, makes leaders for itself by the mouth and personally generates and produces kings for itself by the mouth . . .[49]

One seldom finds the church mentioned at all in connection with the bee-simile. When this connection is made, the church is often peripheral. A good example, and helpful contrast to Chrysologus and Aldhelm, is found in a homily by Caesarius of Arles. Caesarius talks of 'Christ's beehive', a curious term that he later glosses as 'the beehive of the church'.[50] This is unexceptional. Since the bees are conventionally understood to represent Christians, it is easy to imagine the church as a kind of beehive. But the church itself is almost never compared to a bee. So it is Chrysologus's (and, later, Aldhelm's) use of this vivid comparison that is surprising. Although no citations of Chrysologus are recorded in R. Ehwald's excellent index of Aldhelm's written sources,[51] the fact that both Chrysologus and Aldhelm employ the conventional types in this unconventional way, indicates that further examination of Aldhelm's possible use of Chrysologus's sermons would be well worthwhile.

48 E.g. Novatian, *De Trinitate* XXIX.xxvi.172 (ed. G. Diercks, CCSL 4 (Turnhout, 1972), p. 72); Ambrose, *De Isaac uel anima* VIII.lxiv (ed. J. Scheckl, CSEL 32 (Vienna, 1897), p. 687) and *De uirginibus* I.vi.31 (ed. Gori, p. 132); Zeno of Verona, *Tractatus* I.i.3 (ed. B. Löfstedt, CCSL 22 (Turnhout, 1971), p. 8); Chromatius of Aquileia, *Sermo* X.ii (ed. R. Étaix-J. Lemarié, CCSL 9A (Turnhout, 1974), p. 44); Augustine of Hippo, *Quaestionum in Hectateuch libri septem* VII, quaestio Judicum, qu. XLIX.xxvi (ed. I. Fraipont, CCSL 33 (Turnhout, 1958), p. 372) and *In Iohannis euangelium tractatus* XIII.xii (ed. R. Willems, CCSL 36 (Turnhout, 1954), p. 137); Quodvultdeus, *Sermones tres de symbolo* II.iv.28 and III.iv.24 (ed. R. Braun, CCSL 40 (Turnhout, 1976), pp. 341 and 355–6); *et al.*

49 Peter Chrysologus, *Sermo* CXXX *bis* (ed. A. Olivar, CCSL 24B (Turnhout, 1982), p. 801): 'Nemo miretur si sancta ecclesia, si uirgo mater que numerosas suboles caelesti fecunditate diffundet, ipsa sibi pastores generet, pariat ipsa rectores, quando apes concubitus nescia, obscoenitatis ignara, corruptionis expers, ad formam pudicitiae, ad castitatis exemplum, ad uirginitatis insigne, quae solo rore caelesti ore concipit, ore parturit, ore germina casta componit, ore sibi duces format, ore sibi reges ipsa generat et producit . . .'

50 Caesarius of Arles, *Sermo* CCVII.iv (ed. Morin, p. 831): 'Iterum atque iterum rogo, ut qui ad ecclesiae aluearium, sicut iam dixi, quasi ad dulcissimum christi fauum plena deuotione concurrunt, uelud apes prudentissimae de diuersis diuinarum scripturarum floribus intra se cellulas praeparent, ubi sancta et caelestia mella suscipiant.'

51 See *Aldhelmi Opera*, ed. Ehwald, p. 545.

SOCIAL ORDER

When we turn to traditional views of bees' social ordering and structure, we find that Aldhelm is amongst the proponents of a strongly anthropomorphic account. We will have occasion to note that this account is consistently used by authors who seek to promote some particular vision of society. After a marvellously convoluted account of how bees are willing to abandon a perfectly cosy home at the command of 'that bee who among the others discharges the office of magistrate', Aldhelm adds the following rhetorical question: 'What, I ask, in the nature of visible things can be seen, that obeys the command of its begetter and strives to fulfil the order of its king with such great desire . . . ?'[52] The lengthy question that follows – like the lengthy statement that preceded it – is intended to delight the reader while simultaneously edifying her. The reader's delight is enhanced by the recognition that Aldhelm has cleverly redirected the ancient perception that bees are orderly by finding in their orderliness a close correspondence with the monastic virtue of obedience.

Although it is true that the ancients without exception found bees to be orderly animals, it is worth noting that they did not therefore necessarily subscribe to an anthropomorphic view of insects. Some ancient authors were content to observe order without deducing from it a moral lesson. For instance, Aristotle and Celsus both advanced straightforwardly naturalistic observations about bees and how bees live.[53] Other authors resort to anthropomorphic language to describe bees' behaviour, but we know from other contexts that these authors are strongly disinclined to perpetuate literary whimsy or political agendas. Varro is a good example: although he draws his vocabulary from the stock of political language ('these cities', he writes, 'are like men's, for here there are king, commands and society'), he does not seem to be unduly influenced by that choice of terms.[54] Columella himself, whose own views about the worth of literature for farmers were extremely trenchant,[55] indulges in some remarkable political metaphors to describe what can transpire in beehives. Thus, he advises against replacing the 'king bee' because the older bees, 'like a kind of Senate', might not be willing to obey their juniors and so might be put to death by the younger bees; elsewhere, he warns of 'sedition' erupting

[52] Aldhelm, *De uirginitate prosa*, c. vi: 'ille, qui inter ceteras magistratus officio fungitur'; 'Quid enim, quaeso, in rerum uisibilium uideri ualet natura, quod tam ingenti studio auctoris sui praecepto pareat et regis imperium implere contendat. . . ?' (ed. Ehwald, pp. 233–4).

[53] Aristotle, *Historia animalium* VIII.lx, 623b26 (ed. D. M. Balme (London, 1991), p. 334); Celsus *ap.* Origen, *Contra Celsum* IV.lxxxi (ed Borret II, 384–6).

[54] Varro, *Res rusticae* III.xvi.16, 'Haec ut hominum ciuitates, quod hic est et rex et imperium et societas'; cf. *ibid.* III.xvi.4: 'Apes non sunt solitaria natura, ut aquilae, sed ut homines' (ed. G. Goetz (Leipzig, 1929), p. 144).

[55] See above, p. 7, n. 30.

in beehives due to inept bee-handling.[56] In this matter, Pliny follows Varro and Columella, although it must be admitted that Pliny's descriptions (while expansive) are not as compelling as Columella's.[57] On the other end of the spectrum we might place Vergil, whose poetic presentation occasionally makes it unclear when observation leaves off and imagination takes over.[58] Again, it is unclear what lessons Vergil might have hoped to impart to his readers by portraying bees as social animals.

In other authors, however, the application of this political language is not far to seek. Seneca appeals to the case of bees to show that kingship is a naturally occurring phenomenon.[59] Noting, as he thought, that 'king bees' have no sting, Seneca draws the moral that it is natural for kings to show clemency (a message he is keen to put across to Nero).[60] A similar anecdote is preserved in Greek, for Dio Chrysostom relates that Diogenes addressed Alexander the Great with precisely the lesson of the 'king bee's' clemency.[61] Both messages were no doubt timely. Dio's peer, Plutarch, takes another lesson from the bee. He tells us that the Spartan ambassadors could, by their very presence, restore order to a throng of turbulent Hellenes – 'like bees who, when their leader appears, swarm together and put themselves in order'.[62] The connection between the moral drawn by Seneca and Dio on the one hand, and Plutarch's story on the other, is that bees obediently adhere to the order of their society. The implication of this claim, sometimes made explicit, is that order and obedience are natural phenomena. A fourth-century commentary on creation, spuriously attributed to Eustathius of Antioch, elegantly makes the connection: 'Bees have a king, and they fly together and together they dwell; none of them tries to leave before the king himself has taken to flight.'[63]

[56] Columella, *Res rustica* IX.xi.2 and IX.xiii.9; this sort of description is also found, in less quotable form, at IX.ix.1–8 (ed. Lundström *et al.*, pp. 662, 668 and 672).

[57] Pliny, *Naturalis historia* XI.iv.11: 'Sed inter omnia ea principatus apibus et iure praecipua admiratio . . . Rempublicam habent, consilia priuatim et duces gregatim, et quod maximus mirum sit, mores habent praeter cetera, cum sint neque mansueti generis neque fieri.' He further describes the social order of bees at XI.x.20–xii.29, and the 'king bee' at XI.xvii.53–4 (ed. Ian and Mayhoff II, 287, 290–2 and 299–300).

[58] Vergil, *Georgics* IV.149–96 (description of bees' social order) and lines 210–18 (anthropomorphic description of the 'king bee') (ed. Ribbeck, pp. 182–6).

[59] Seneca, *De clementia* I.xix.2 (ed. C. Hosius (Leipzig, 1914), p. 235).

[60] *Ibid.* I.xix.2–4; cf. Ambrose, *Exameron, dies V*, VIII.xxi.68 (ed. K. Schenkl and G. Banterle, Bibliotheca Ambrosiana 1 (Rome, 1979), 320): 'nam etsi habet aculeum, tamen eo non utitur ad uindicandum'.

[61] Dio Chrysostom, *Oratio* IV.lxi–lxiv (ed. J. W. Cohoon (London, 1961), p. 196).

[62] Plutarch, *Lycurgus* XXX.ii.14 (ed. B. Perrin (London, 1967), p. 296).

[63] Eustathius of Antioch, *Commentarius in hexaemeron* (PG 18, col. 736); cf. Basil, *Homiliae in hexaemeron* VIII.iv.5–9 (ed. Giet, pp. 446–8). This theme is also found in Aldhelm, *Epistulae* XII, 'Ad Wilfridi abbates' (ed. Ehwald, p. 501).

These trends come together very effectively in a discrete reference to bees found in a letter by Cyprian of Carthage, who noted that 'bees have a king'.[64] It makes very good sense that Cyprian, whose tenure as primate of Africa coincided with great turmoil in the African churches, would seize upon the combination of good order and obedience so readily.[65] Cyprian's mention of the 'king bee' is in the context of an astringent letter in which he calls a certain Puppianus to obedience.[66] The rigorist Puppianus was apparently fomenting unrest by claiming that Cyprian was tainted by consorting with sinful clergy and that this taint was contagious. Cyprian responded by heaping scorn on Puppianus. He asserted that even dumb animals (such as bees) and thieves display more obedience and loyalty than Puppianus was doing. In other words, he berates Puppianus with the example of the bee precisely because Puppianus's behaviour is less dignified than an animal's. It is unclear how much can be made of Cyprian's thinking on the basis of this *ad hominem* attack. But implicit in Cyprian's claim is the identification of the bishop with the 'king bee'. This fits neatly within Cyprian's efforts to secure the integrity of a fissiparous Christian community by insisting on proper order. Cyprian demonstrated sensitivity in doing this, but he also was prepared (like the bishops described by Maximus of Turin) to be 'severe in order to punish'. Regardless of Seneca's and Dio's fine beliefs and tolerant advice, Cyprian clearly had a sting and was prepared to use it.

The flavour of Ambrose's remarks on bees' social order is very different. He begins by noting the amazing extent to which bees share everything in common. In his list, Ambrose includes their offspring, dwelling-place, work, food, activity, effort and its reward, will, procreation, virginal chastity and, rather more abstractly, the limits beyond which they do not fly.[67] Ambrose goes on to note, however, that 'they nominate a king for themselves, make themselves into a people and, though they may be under a king, they are free'.[68] He expands upon this seemingly paradoxical claim by insisting that the king's rule is predicated on respect and devotion. Yet even though he states that the king is nominated and rules at the good pleasure of those he rules, Ambrose acknowledges that the 'king bee' is marked from birth with 'distinct signs' ('he is eminent by the dimensions of his body and his face and, what is chiefly important in a king, the meekness of his manner.')[69] How such congenital fea-

[64] Cyprian, *Epistula* LXVI.vi (ed. G. F. Diercks, CCSL 3C (Turnhout, 1996), p. 440).

[65] See now J. P. Burns, *Cyprian the Bishop* (London, 2002), pp. 1–12.

[66] See the excellent notes of G. W. Clarke, *The Letters of St Cyprian of Carthage* (New York, 1986) III, 321–33.

[67] Ambrose, *Exameron, dies V*, VIII.xxi.67 (ed. Schenkl and Banterle, p. 318).

[68] *Ibid.* VIII.xxi.68 (*ibid.* p. 320)

[69] *Ibid.* VIII.xxi.68 (*ibid.* p. 320): 'Apibus autem rex naturae claris formatur insignibus, ut magnitudine corporis praestet et specie, tum quod in rege principuum est, morum mansuetudine.'

tures are consistent with this noble democratic ideal, which was politically salient, is a problem Ambrose does not resolve.[70] The contrast with Basil's *Homiliae in hexaemeron* is instructive. In his *Homiliae*, which were much used by Ambrose, he flatly states that 'the king is not elected (χειροτονητός) by them (for often the masses lack of discernment puts the worst in power)'.[71] Quite apart from the interest generated by Basil's more pessimistic remark, his claim is significant because the sharp difference between it and Ambrose's claim goes to show that precisely what an author makes of the perceived social order of bees is arbitrary. Furthermore, what the author makes of this order can provide some evidence of his social and political ideals.

Bearing this in mind, we may well find it curious that, although monastic sources valued good order and obedience, and although we frequently meet the simile of bees in monastic literature, we rarely find any applications of the simile to monastic society. There is merely a single reference in Palladius's *Lausiac History* that points in the general direction of what we might expect. In his account of Elpidius of Cappadocia, an ascetic who dwelt in one of the caves of Mt Douka near Jericho, Palladius tells how Elpidius's reputation garnered him many followers – including Palladius himself. In language redolent of the *Life of St Antony*, Palladius writes that 'A full measure of brethren assembled to live there (I too was there, for a time) just like bees around their king, and thus made a city of the mountain; and different ways of life were to be found in that place.'[72] Palladius's remark is limited in scope. The monks may well have assembled around Elpidius like bees, but nothing in Palladius's testimony justifies the inference that the community was rigidly structured after the manner of a beehive: he makes no claims regarding Elpidius's authority over the assembled brethren. While it should not therefore be assumed that Palladius is uninterested in the proper ordering of monastic society, it is nevertheless strange in light of what we found in Cyprian, Basil and Ambrose that Palladius does not exploit the opportunity he made by invoking bees to make a point about monastic life.

More promising for our purposes is Jerome's letter to Rusticus about the monastic life. In this letter, Jerome categorically likens the monastery to a beehive, and he does so with particular reference to order and obedience. Along with other advice about how Rusticus might pass his time in an edifying fashion, Jerome writes, 'Construct an apiary for bees, to which Proverbs refers

[70] Cf. G. Banterle's note *ad loc* regarding Valentinian II (*ibid.* p. 321). Pliny also notes that 'king bees' are distinguished from birth but, in contrast to Ambrose's political sensibilities, he allows that inferior specimens are destroyed in their youth: *Historia naturalis* XI.xvi.51 (ed. Ian and Mayhoff II, 299). [71] Basil, *Homiliae in hexaemeron* VIII.iv.9–11 (ed. Giet, p. 448).

[72] Palladius of Hellenopolis, *Historia lausiaca* XLVIII.ii (ed. Bartelink, p. 238); cf. Athanasius, *Vita s. Antonii* VIII.ii (ed. Bartelink, p. 156): καὶ τὴν ἔρημον πολίσῃ τῆς ἀσκήσεως.

you, and learn the order and royal discipline of monasteries from small animals.'[73] Jerome later elaborates on how he thinks this is to be done and what he anticipates will be learnt:

No art is learnt apart from a teacher. Even dumb animals and packs of beasts follow their leaders. *There are princes among the bees*; cranes follow one of their number in the shape of a letter [the letter 'Y']. There is one emperor, one provincial judge . . . the bishops of the churches are singular, the archpriests singular, the archdeacons singular – and every ecclesiastical order relies upon its rectors . . . And, lest I should disgust the reader by including too many examples, my speech tends for all this to one point: I would not teach you to be left to your own will, but rather that you ought to live in the monastery under the discipline of one father and in dealing with many. In this way, you will learn humility from one and patience from another; this one will teach you silence, that one, meekness.[74]

For many reasons, this is a significant passage. Jerome follows the precedent set by Seneca and Dio for extracting a principle of society from observations about natural order. Like Cyprian, he applies this principle within the Christian community. He is unlike Cyprian, however, in that his observation is propaedeutic rather than polemic. When Jerome urges Rusticus to consider the bee, he follows this up with instruction on what this consideration ought to show. Furthermore, Jerome differs from Cyprian in that he is writing specifically about life in the monastery rather than about more general ecclesiastical polity. And when Jerome encourages Rusticus to learn the virtues that his confreres have personally developed to a high degree, we may detect an allusion to Athanasius's account of St Antony, bee-like, going from ascetic to ascetic in order to distil the honey of monastic life. However, it should not escape our attention that the great Antony was father of the hermits; and what Jerome has in mind is definitely cenobitic. This letter contains not even the slightest hint that Jerome envisages a day when Rusticus will have learnt enough from the community to strike out on his own.[75] What is chiefly remarkable about this letter is Jerome's synthesis of several identifiable but disparate strands within the literary tradition, which brings to light a new facet of the traditional simile: monks are like bees because they are obedient.

Jerome merely sheds light on this new facet of the simile; Aldhelm celebrates it. 'This also is to be remembered, I suggest, concerning the harmonious fellowship of the bees, and to be admired as some theatrical spectacle – I mean the spontaneous inclination to voluntary servitude which they are

[73] Jerome, *Epistula* CXXV.xi (ed. Labourt VII, 124); he refers to Prov. VIII.6a–b (LXX).

[74] *Ibid.* CXXV.xv (ed. Labourt VII, 126–7).

[75] This perspective can be contrasted to John Cassian, *De institutis* V.iv.1–2 (ed. Petschenig, CSEL 17 (1888), pp. 83–4), on which see below.

known to exercise in obedience to their rulers.' The foregoing analysis of classical and Christian literature should convince us that, just as Aldhelm has said, bees were thought to be inclined spontaneously to voluntary servitude. This far, Aldhelm might simply be following Jerome. But immediately hereafter, he strikes out on a rather more ambitious course than Jerome had done. 'In respect of this sort of consideration, are not all the disciplines of the monastic way of life and the regular practices of monasteries indicated by an extremely close comparison?'[76] It is convenient for us to forego Aldhelm's 'extremely close comparison' and in its place substitute a drier and conciser summary. Like ps.-Eusthatius, Aldhelm observes that bees do not depart the hive without direction and while they remain in the hive, they care for it. If, on the other hand, the king bee should decree that 'their ancient dwellings' ought to be abandoned, they set off in swarms (much as Palladius's monks did) in search of a new home and so forsake the domestic comforts of familiarity. The bee, Aldhelm writes, exemplifies obedience for us 'mortals living in this vale of tears' by its 'spontaneous acceptance of devout servitude'.[77] As he draws these reflections to a close, Aldhelm also recapitulates the bee's appropriateness as a symbol of unspotted virginity, and as the distiller of honey. At the mention of honey, he tirelessly sets off again – this time by comparing the virginal life to the angelic life, both of which are incomparably sweeter than the usual fare of life. With this, his attention decisively turns from bees. But we would do well to dwell a bit longer on what he has written in his last flourish.

The only real precedent for Aldhelm's extraordinary remarks about the effectively monastic obedience of bees, is the aforementioned letter by Jerome. This very naturally leads one to pose the question of influence. Was Aldhelm following Jerome in this instance? Although that possibility cannot be ruled out, it seems to me a somewhat remote possibility. In the first place, there are no direct borrowings in Aldhelm's account, and in fact no parallels so close that one might propose literary dependence. Secondly, though Aldhelm was broadly familiar with Jerome's work, we do not have any evidence that he knew any of Jerome's letters.[78] Third, even though we have found Jerome's lesson from the obedient bee to be evident across the relevant passage from the letter, by the close of the passage it has died away to an echo of the *Life of St Antony*. While the simile is an arresting way to introduce his calls for obedience (just as it was for Cyprian), Jerome was not sufficiently beguiled by the simile that he developed it in any significant way. This is altogether different from Aldhelm's extended meditation on the obedience of bees. Fourth, it is *prima facie* unlikely

76 Aldhelm, *De uirginitate prosa*, c. vi (ed. Ehwald, p. 233). 77 *Ibid.*

78 Cf. Ehwald, *Aldhelmi Opera*, p. 545, *sub nomine* 'Hieronymus'.

that Jerome would have been able to express his enthusiasm for good order and obedience as crisply as Aldhelm did. After all, Aldhelm wrote after the celebrated work of Benedict had exerted a considerable influence along the lines of structuring Western monasticism.[79] Due to the impact of Benedict's Rule, we may well suppose that Aldhelm would have been more attuned to 'natural' evidence for order and obedience than Jerome was. Accordingly, even if Aldhelm did know Jerome's letter, intervening circumstances would have enabled Aldhelm to refine the point quite dramatically. Finally, as this article has shown and as we will note again in concluding, Aldhelm appears to have had at his disposal a considerable number of other sources for the tradition about bees. It is possible to account for what Aldhelm has written, even if Jerome's letter was not among those sources. In sum, so great is the difference between their accounts that one may doubt whether Aldhelm owes anything to Jerome at all, and suppose instead that the two of them arrived at this insight on different tracks.

ALDHELM'S SOURCES AND HIS USE OF THEM

This examination of Aldhelm's use of the bee as a type for the Christian nun has sought to uncover the broad literary antecedents of that simile. There is a considerably greater number of sources, both classical and Christian, wherein some mention of bees is made than what we have seen here. But, limiting ourselves to works that directly bear on Aldhelm's appropriation of the simile, we are still left with an impressive dossier. We will proceed by quickly recapitulating which sources are relevant to which broad theme in Aldhelm's treatment. Then we will want to make some judgement regarding which sources likely had a direct impact on Aldhelm's writing, and which (helpful though they may be for appreciating what Aldhelm was up to in this knotty passage) were only part of the tradition.

Among the sources that are helpful for background, but unlikely to have contributed directly to Aldhelm's writing, are the following: Aristotle, *Historia animalium*; Varro, *Res rusticae*; Columella, *Res rustica*; ps.-Quintilian, *Declamatio XIII*; Seneca, *De clementia* and *Epistulae morales*; Plutarch, *Lycurgus*; Celsus, *Alethes Logos*; Origen, *Contra Celsum*; Dio Chrysostom, *Orationes*; Eustathius of Antioch, *Commentarius in hexaemeron*; ps.-Basil, *Sermo in illud: 'Ne dederis somnium oculis tuis' et c.*; Gregory Nazianzen, *In Machabaeorum laudem*; Gregory Nyssen, *In sanctum Ephrem*; Cassian, *De incarnatione Domini*; and Salvian, *De gubernatione Dei*. These sources contribute to a stock of images from which Aldhelm draws. But, although they are valuable for coming to grips with the nuances of Aldhelm's use of the simile, I find no reason to suppose that Aldhelm consulted any of

[79] For Aldhelm's assessment of Benedict, see *De uirginitate prosa*, c. xxx (ed. Ehwald, pp. 268–9).

them or consciously referred to any of them. It need not surprise us that the two late ancient agricultural handbooks would not have had a direct impact upon Aldhelm, particularly in as much as Aldhelm seems to have been versed in Pliny and Vergil – who could well have supplied all the details regarding bees that we have considered. Apart from the works of Vergil and Pliny, Aldhelm's knowledge of classical Latin literature is not comprehensive. We have no strong reason to suppose he knew Seneca or ps.-Quintilian.[80] Although Aldhelm cites Rufinus's prologue to his translation of some of Gregory Nazianzen's *Orationes*, the *In Machabeorum laudem* is not among them.[81] Cassian's *De incarnatione Domini* did not enjoy a wide circulation;[82] and the slight relevance of an aside in Salvian's *De gubernatione Dei* hardly instils confidence that Aldhelm had read it. With respect to the Greek literature, even though Aldhelm passed some time in Canterbury during the extraordinary archiepiscopacy of Theodore, when Greek books were available, none of the aforementioned titles feature prominently in the reconstructed 'library catalogue' for the Canterbury school.[83]

In the case of a few of the other passages considered above, we can be more confident that Aldhelm knew the works in which they appeared and so we can reasonably suppose that they might have directly influenced him. The two most obvious such cases are the various excerpts from Pliny's *Naturalis historia* and Vergil's *Georgics*. But it is also known that Fortunatus's *Carmina* were popular in Anglo-Saxon England.[84] His poem for Victorian may have been known to Aldhelm. Other works that figure into the literary convention, such as the works of Greek Ephrem (*De recta uiuendi ratione*, *Paraenesis ad ascetas* and *Sermo asceticus*) and the *Homiliae in hexaemeron* of Basil the Great, may well have been available in Theodore's Canterbury. (Michael Lapidge has advanced this claim on the basis of material present in the Canterbury biblical commentaries.)[85] Indeed, Aldhelm mentions a translation of Basil's *Hexaemeron*

[80] See the discussion by T. J. Brown (above, p. 2, n. 3).

[81] Aldhelm, *De uirginitate prosa*, c. xxvii (ed. Ehwald, p. 263); Rufinus, *Tyrannii Rufini Orationum Gregorii Nazianzeni nouem interpretatio* (ed. A. Engelbrecht, CSEL 46 (Vienna, 1910)). It should be noted that Engelbrecht opted not to include the *De fide* (for his argument, see *ibid.* pp. ix–xvi), which means that the following are available in a critical edition: *Orationes* II (*Apologeticus*), XXXVIII (*De epiphaniis*), XXIX (*De luminibus*), XLI (*De Nicena fide*), XXVI (*De semetipso ex agro reuerso*), XVII (*De dictis hieremie*), VI (*De reconciliatione*), XVI (*De grandinis uastatione*), XXVII (*De arrianis*), according to the order in which they appear in Rufinus.

[82] This is adduced from the sparse manuscript tradition, as described by M. Petschenig in his *Iohannis Cassiani De institutis coenobiorum et De octo principalium uitiorum remediis, libri XII; De incarnatione Domini contra Nestorium, libri VII*, CSEL 17 (Vienna, 1888), pp. lxxi–lxxviii.

[83] See B. Bischoff and M. Lapidge, *Biblical Commentaries from the Canterbury School of Theodore and Hadrian*, CSASE 10 (Cambridge, 1994), 205–42.

[84] See M. Lapidge, 'Appendix: Knowledge of the Poems in the Earlier Period', ASE 8 (1979), 287–95.

[85] See Bischoff and Lapidge, *Biblical Commentaries*, pp. 232–41.

and, though this does not guarantee that Aldhelm actually read it, we cannot preclude the possibility that he did.[86] These works might therefore be regarded as possible sources.

This leaves us with a handful of ambiguous passages. For instance, in the matter of bees reproducing asexually, numerous Christian authors express that belief; but since Aldhelm knew Vergil (in whose *Georgics* that belief was clearly stated), it is difficult to claim with any conviction that the Christian authors had any direct impact upon Aldhelm with respect to this claim. Indeed, since Aldhelm is not particularly disposed to make much of the supposed virginal reproduction of bees – something most of the Christians who attest to this belief were quite keen to do – I think it is highly unlikely that Aldhelm owes his knowledge of this ancient belief to them.

It is opportune in this connection to point out that, even though we have repeatedly made reference to the *Life of St Antony*, there is no conclusive evidence that Aldhelm had any significant knowledge of that work. I do not argue that the *Life* was unavailable to him; it probably was.[87] However, it must be acknowledged that his mention of Antony in the roster of notable virgins is replete with generalities and invokes Antony's reputation in very vague terms before any mention is made of the written version.[88] The only concrete details he offers about Antony are either totally banal (Aldhelm knows that Antony was Egyptian) or totally baffling (Aldhelm inexplicably associates Antony with the cenobitic movement). Because Aldhelm refers his readers to Athanasius's work, or rather to Evagrius's translation of that work, for specific details, one may doubt whether Aldhelm actually knew much about the details of Antony's life. I would offer two conjectures on the provenance of Aldhelm's information about Antony. First, Aldhelm's mention of Evagrius as the translator suggests that he might have cribbed his information from Jerome. Certainly, Jerome's incisive entries for Athanasius, Antony and Evagrius are sufficient to account

86 Aldhelm, *De uirginitate prosa*, c.xxvii (ed. Ehwald, p. 263). It may be noted in this connection that Aldhelm may well have known the work in Eustathius's Latin translation, rather than in Rufinus's (as Ehwald supposed: *ibid.* p. 263, n. 8). Aldhelm merely says the homilies *in latinum translata leguntur*, but does not tell us who translated the version he has in mind. Furthermore, Rosalind Love has shown that Bede's *Commentarius in Genesim* is based in part on Eustathius's work (R. C. Love, 'The Sources of Bede, *Commentarius in Genesim (Libri I et II)* (L.F.2.1.105, L.F.2.1.035, L.F.2.1.030, L.F.2.1.019, L.F.2.1.018)', *Fontes Anglo-Saxonici: World Wide Web Register*. http://fontes.english.ox.ac.uk/ (2000), accessed October 2002). Might it not have been available to Aldhelm as well? This Eustathius is not to be confused with 'Eustathius of Antioch', mentioned above (see p. 13, n. 63).

87 This view can be advanced on the basis of glosses to the Latin translation of the *Vita S. Antonii* in the 'Leiden Glossary'; see J. H. Hessels, *A Late Eighth-Century Latin–Anglo-Saxon Glossary preserved in the Library of the Leiden University* (Cambridge, 1906), pp. 22–3.

88 Aldhelm, *De uirginitate prosa*, c. xxviii (ed. Ehwald, pp. 264–5).

for the information Aldhelm relays about Antony.[89] Second, his strange remark about Antonian cenobitism may be attributable to a faulty recollection of a passage by John Cassian. Cassian attributes to Antony a dictum about how the spiritually accomplished cenobite is justified in leaving the cenobium in order to pursue the virtues by emulating virtuous hermits, wherever they may be found.[90] Cassian's point has very little to do with Aldhelm's bizarre suggestion about Antony, but the juxtaposition of cenobitism and eremitism with regard to Antony is nevertheless closer in Cassian than in the *Life of St Antony*. Cassian's anecdote is far more in keeping with the consistent tradition about Antony's attitude toward the cenobia than is Aldhelm's fleeting remark. In any event, there is more evidence that Aldhelm knew Cassian's writings than that he knew the *Life of St Antony*.

More interesting than these cases, though, are the instances where Aldhelm's treatment of the simile closely parallels the earlier writings of Jerome and Peter Chrysologus. Ehwald has noted Aldhelm's familiarity with a number of Jerome's exegetical works, his *Lives* of SS Hilarion, Malchus and Paul the Hermit, his *Chronicon* and his *Letter to Eustochium*.[91] We have just considered that Aldhelm's vague account of Antony can be attributed to his reliance upon Jerome's *De uiris inlustribus*. Since Aldhelm was evidently knowledgeable of a broad swathe of Jerome's writings, and since Aldhelm and Jerome are the only authors to draw the bee-imagery into a discussion of monastic obedience, it is undeniably possible that Aldhelm also knew Jerome's *Letter to Rusticus*. However, it must be acknowledged that Aldhelm's treatment of that theme is considerably more profound that Jerome's. Indeed, Jerome mentions it very briefly before passing on to other edifying pastimes that Rusticus might profit from undertaking. If Aldhelm was in fact inspired by Jerome's letter, he certainly improved upon what he found there. As for Chrysologus's homilies, Ehwald did not detect any references to them in Aldhelm's works. Indeed, for clear evidence of Chrysologus's impact upon Anglo-Saxon authors, we must turn to Ælfric's *Catholic homilies*, written roughly two centuries after Aldhelm flourished.[92] However, the striking parallel comparison of the church to the

89 Cf. Jerome, *De uiris inlustribus*, cc. lxxxvii–lxxxviii and cxxv (ed. E. Richardson, Texte und Untersuchungen 14(1)A (Leipzig, 1896), pp. 44–5 and 53). That this was available to Aldhelm in Canterbury is probable on the evidence from the Leiden glosses; see Hessels, *Latin–Anglo-Saxon Glossary*, pp. 27–9.

90 John Cassian, *De institutis* V.iv.1–2 (ed. Petschenig, pp. 83–4); for other references to Cassian's *Institutes* in Aldhelm, see Ehwald, *Aldhelmi Opera*, p. 544, *sub nomine*.

91 Ehwald, *Aldhelmi Opera*, p. 545, *sub nomine*.

92 See M. R. Godden, 'The Sources of Ælfric, *Catholic homilies* (C.B.1.1.6.009.01, C.B.1.1.6.012.01)', *Fontes Anglo-Saxonici: World Wide Web Register*: http://fontes.english.ox.ac.uk/ (1997), accessed September 2002.

bee (advanced only by Chrysologus and Aldhelm) justifies further research into Chrysologus's influence in Anglo-Latin literature.

Having now considered the sources at Aldhelm's disposal, we shall conclude this article with a few remarks on how Aldhelm handled this traditional theme. Two features are chiefly notable. The first is the shift in the bee simile that Aldhelm brings about, by stressing the intellectual culture of the nuns. This is not an entirely unprecedented feature of the tradition, but Aldhelm nevertheless brings it about in a noteworthy way. By heavily stressing the exegetical skills of the nuns and especially by likening the nuns' intellects to bees, Aldhelm redirected a simile initially formed to praise ascetic work so that it could be used to praise intellectual work. His esteem for the nuns' intellectual prowess indicates Aldhelm's high valuation of literacy and the liberal arts.

The second transformation of the simile is evident in Aldhelm's decision to use it in order to praise the social coherence of the nuns' life and their obedience. We have seen that bees' social order is a widely attested perception among ancient authors. But, curiously, this aspect of secular literature was not adopted by the monastic authors who were otherwise so keen to appropriate the image of the bee. Even Jerome, who makes the first reference to bees' obedience within the context of discussing monastic life, has relatively little to say about the aptness of the simile. Once we read Aldhelm's strong claims about how bees exemplify monastic obedience, it seems like such an obvious remark that one feels mildly shocked that no one had noticed the parallel before. This is perhaps a mark of the brilliance which Aldhelm exhibited in his fascinating digression about bees: although it is in many respects highly original, the description has in the end a familiarity akin to inevitability.[93]

[93] I undertook this study while working over Aldhelm's *De uirginitate prosa* for the Fontes Anglo-Saxonici register. I would like to express my gratitude to Dr Rosalind Love for encouraging me to pursue this line of enquiry.

Poetic words, conservatism and the dating of Old English poetry

DENNIS CRONAN

Although the lexicon has frequently been used in discussions of the dating of Old English poetry, little attention has been paid to the evidence that poetic simplexes offer.[1] One exception is an article by R. J. Menner, who noted that *Beowulf* and *Genesis A* share three poetic words, apart from compounds, that are not found elsewhere: *freme* 'good, valiant', *gombe* 'tribute', and *secg* 'sword'.[2] Menner used these words as part of an argument for an early date of *Genesis A*, an argument which hinged, in part, on lexical similarities between this poem and *Beowulf*, which he assumed was early. Although such an *a priori* assumption is no longer possible, evidence provided by the limited distribution of certain poetic simplexes is nonetheless useful for demonstrating the presence of a connection between two or more poems. Such a connection may be a matter of date or dialect, or it may indicate that the poems were the products of a single poetic school or subtradition. Unfortunately, we know little, if anything, about poetic subtraditions, and the poetic *koiné* makes the determination of the dialect of individual poems a complex and subtle matter that requires a much wider variety of evidence than poetic words can provide.[3] However, the limited distribution of certain poetic simplexes can serve as an index of the poetic conservatism of the poems in which these words occur. This conservatism could be due to a number of factors: genre, content (that is, heroic legend vs biblical or hagiographical), style, or date of composition. As will emerge in the course of this discussion, the most straightforward explanation for this conservatism is that the poems which exhibit it were composed earlier than those which do not. Other explanations are, however, possible, and the evidence of poetic words is hardly sufficient by itself to determine the dating of Old English poems. But by focusing on patterns of distribution that centre upon

[1] For an overview of the use of lexical evidence in dating, see A. C. Amos, *Linguistic Means of Determining the Dates of Old English Literary Texts* (Cambridge, MA, 1980), ch. 3.

[2] R. J. Menner, 'The Date and Dialect of *Genesis A* 852–2936 (Part III)', *Anglia* 70 (1952), 285–94, at 286–7. Menner also notes that *missere* 'half-year' appears only in *Genesis A*, *Beowulf* and *Exodus*, and that *bresne* 'mighty' occurs only in *Genesis A* and *Daniel.* All citations from Old English poetry, with the exception of those from *Beowulf*, are taken from G. P. Krapp and E. V. K. Dobbie, ASPR, 6 vols. (New York, 1931–53). *Beowulf* is cited from *Beowulf and the Fight at Finnsburg*, ed. F. Klaeber, 3rd ed. (Lexington, MA, 1950).

[3] See R. D. Fulk, *A History of Old English Meter* (Philadelphia, 1992), ch. XI, for a thorough discussion of dialect indicators in Old English verse.

Beowulf, we can examine what certain words may tell us about the conservatism of this poem and of those poems which are connected to it.

METHODOLOGY

Poetic simplexes are more reliable than compounds for such an investigation because the restriction of a compound to two or three poems may be no more than a coincidence. Working on their own, poets could (and in many cases, probably did) form the same word from common elements, since compounding was dynamic. This quality of compounds can be easily perceived in their distribution: of the 840 poetic compounds which occur in two or more poems, 451 (54%) are found in only two. Even more striking is the presence of 2,604 poetic compounds in only one poem, a situation which demonstrates just how productive and idiosyncratic compound formation was in the poetic tradition. In contrast, of 264 poetic simplexes, only forty-four (16.7%), are found in only two poems. Similarly, there are relatively few simple *hapax legomena* in the verse – only 193. Some of these *hapax* were probably coined by the poets, others may be poetic words not otherwise attested, and the rest are probably ordinary words which were not recorded elsewhere. Thus, while the usage of poetic compounds was essentially innovative, with the poets following typical patterns to generate new compounds, the usage of poetic simplexes was predominantly conservative, with the poets drawing on the stock of words they had inherited from other poets. This difference in the usage of compounds and simplexes in verse is illustrated quite concisely by a comparison of their average distributions: leaving aside the *hapax legomena*, poetic compounds appear in an average of three poems, with an average occurrence of four times; poetic simplexes appear in an average of eight poems, with an average occurrence of nineteen times.

However, compounds do provide solid evidence when they are of a rare or unusual type, or when the distribution of one of the elements of a compound is restricted. *Suhter(ge)fæderan* (*Beo* 1163, *Wid* 46), for example, is a dvandva, or copulative compound, a type which was very rare in the early Germanic languages. Other compounds include elements such as *-hyðig* (*unhyðig, And* 1078, *GuthB* 1328) and *-scerwen* (*ealuscerwen*, *Beo* 769; *meoduscerwen, And* 1526), which do not occur outside of these compounds.[4]

The definition of a 'poetic simplex' for this study is based entirely upon distribution: a poetic simplex is any simple word found in two or more poems whose occurrence is either completely restricted to poetry, or whose use in prose or glosses seems to be exceptional in some way. Poetic simplexes can also

[4] Elements such as *-hyðig* and *-scerwen* which occur only in poetic compounds are included among the poetic simplexes for this study.

appear as elements of compounds. Since both the frequency of occurrence and the distribution of the words discussed here are limited, it is likely that some of them were not actually part of the poetic wordhoard. Their restriction to poetry could be due to any one of a number of causes: chance, the conservatism of the poetic tradition relative to prose, the loss of the word in question before the surviving prose texts were written, or the unusual use of an otherwise unrecorded colloquialism. In many cases there is some indication one way or the other about the status of a word, but certainty in such matters cannot always be achieved.

The simple listing of lexical items does not necessarily prove anything. Of course, an accumulation of items can be significant in itself, but the precise nature of this significance can be determined only after the evidence offered by each word has been carefully scrutinized. Systematic scrutinization is especially important in an investigation such as this, which focuses on a limited number of words, each with a very limited distribution. In her analysis of the evidence that vocabulary offers for the determination of the authorship of the 890 *Chronicle*, Janet Bately observes that the presence of a word in a given text is significant only if it was used at the expense of another word.[5] Thus, for example, the restriction of *fær* 'ship, vessel' to *Beowulf* and *Genesis A* is potentially significant because the poets could have used any one of a number of synonyms instead. In contrast, the restriction of *trem* 'space, step' to *Beowulf* and *Maldon* is probably not signficant because there do not appear to have been any synonyms for this word.

Studies such as Bately's draw upon a relatively large body of evidence and are thus able to focus on the usage of the particular text(s) they are examining. When evidence is limited, as it is here, demonstrating that one word was used in a particular poem at the expense of another is not enough to establish that the presence of that word is significant. It is also necessary to show that the word could have been used in other poems where it does not appear. That is, it is not enough to establish that there existed one or more synonyms that might have been used in *Beowulf* and *Genesis A* instead of *fær*; we must also demonstrate that there are poems which actually contain these synonyms, poems which had a need for a word meaning 'ship', and yet used another word. Thus, in determining the significance of the restriction of any given word to two or three poems, the absence of that word from poems where it could have been used is every bit as important as its presence in the texts in which it occurs.

The Old English poetic corpus contains 181 poems (counting each riddle as a separate poem, *Solomon and Saturn* as two poems, multiple attestations of

[5] J. Bately, 'Old English Prose Before and During the Reign of Alfred', *ASE* 17 (1988), 93–138, at 95.

poems such as *Cædmon's Hymn* as a single poem, and the works of Cynewulf as one poem), many of which are quite short. The absence of a particular word or its synonyms from the short poems is clearly irrelevant, although the presence of synonyms in such poems can be significant. A length of 300 lines provides a useful if somewhat arbitrary cut-off point for identifying poems in which the absence of a particular word and the presence or absence of its synonyms are of potential significance. In addition to *Beowulf*, there are sixteen such poems: *Andreas*, *Christ I*, *Christ III*, *Christ and Satan,* the works of Cynewulf, *Daniel*, *Exodus*, *Genesis A*, *Guthlac A*, *Guthlac B*, *Judith*, *Maldon*, the *Meters of Boethius*, the *Paris Psalter*, *Phoenix* and *Solomon and Saturn B*.[6] Given the average distribution rate of the poetic simplexes, which is eight poems per word, the presence of the synonyms of a particular word in eight or more of these poems can be regarded as strong synonym support, and an indication that the restriction of the word in question to two (or in some cases three) poems is significant. The presence of synonyms in at least five poems can be regarded as moderate synonym support; if synonyms occur in fewer than five poems, then the synonym support is weak. The words discussed below are thus all evaluated in terms of the strength of the evidence they provide. The restricted distribution of words with strong or moderate synonym support is clearly significant. The presence of words with weak synonym support is less decisive; in the absence of other evidence, such as that drawn upon in the discussion of *suhtriga*, below, these words can only play a supporting role. In certain cases, when appropriate evidence is available, words can be characterized as 'early' or 'archaic'. Such earliness or archaicism is of course relative to the rest of the tradition, although in the case of *suhtriga*, its archaicism can be placed, chronologically, in relationship to the Old English vocabulary as a whole.

The conclusion that the presence of a particular word in only two poems is significant does not in itself establish a connection between the two poems: The inference of such connections must be based on an accumulation of significant items. Thus there is little to be gained by examining every word whose distribution is limited. For example, the restriction of *hwearf*, 'troop', to *Guthlac A* and *Judith* is of little consequence in the absence of other similar connections between the poems, despite the presence of synonyms and near-synonyms for this word throughout the corpus. It is much more profitable to focus on patterns of limited distribution in which poems are linked by the presence of two or more words not found elsewhere. It is precisely such a pattern that we find centred upon *Beowulf*, which shares a number of items with

[6] *Genesis B* is omitted since it is a translation from Old Saxon. *Judgment Day II* is omitted because it contains only eleven poetic words. Of the thirteen synonym groups examined here, it participates in only two, 'king, lord' and 'sin, evil'.

only *Genesis A* on the one hand, and with only *Maxims I* on the other. This pattern then radiates outward to include words restricted to *Beowulf* and/or *Genesis A* and one of a small group of other poems: *Daniel*, *Exodus*, *Widsith* and the works of Cynewulf.

Studies such as this one are conducted against the backdrop of the invisible presences of unrecorded oral compositions and lost poetic texts. The patterns of distribution and usage we examine here would be different if more poems had survived. This knowledge alone demands a certain diffidence towards both the analyses and their results. Attempting to discern Old English poetic history by analysing word distributions is like attempting to map a submerged valley by correlating the positions of protruding hill tops: although we would learn some facts about the hidden contours, it is highly unlikely that this method alone would produce a clear picture of the entire valley. Now that the debate over the date of *Beowulf* (and, by implication at least, the date of much of the rest of the corpus) is almost twenty years old, it appears unlikely (but not impossible) that a single decisive piece of evidence will emerge. In the absence of such evidence, any conclusions we reach about the dating of Old English poems need to be based on the joint witness of numerous pieces of evidence, none of which is completely convincing on its own. Viewed together, however, these fragments of evidence may form a coherent and decisive picture of at least part of the history of Old English verse. The analyses and conclusions presented here are intended as a contribution to the delineation of this picture.

BEOWULF AND *GENESIS A*

In addition to the three words listed by Menner as appearing only in *Beowulf* and *Genesis A*, *freme*, *gombe* and *secg*, there are three others found only in these two poems: *fær* 'ship, vessel', *dyhtig* 'strong' and *heore* 'safe, pleasant, mild'.

Secg 'sword' (*GenA* 2001; *Beo* 684) occurs elsewhere in its literal meaning as the first element of compounds: *secgplega* 'sword-play' (*And* 1353) and *secgrof* 'bold with a sword' (*Rui* 26). While it is possible that these two words are traditional compounds in which *secg* was preserved in ossified form, it is much more likely, given the readiness with which poets combined and recombined the elements of compounds (for example, there are fourteen distinct compounds built upon *-plega*, eight of which are *hapax legomena*, eighteen built upon *-rof*, nine of which are *hapax*), that the presence of these words in *Andreas* and *Ruin* indicates that the poets were familiar with the simplex *secg* 'sword'. Thus *secg* occurs in a total of four poems, not only in *Beowulf* and *Genesis*, and provides no evidence for a connection between these poems.

Although *heore* 'safe, pleasant, mild' occurs only in these two poems in Old English (*GenA* 1468; *Beo* 1372), it also has little value as evidence. Two derivatives, *unheore* (*unhire*, *unhyre*, *unhere*) 'horrible, monstrous' and *unheorlic* (*unhirlic*, *unhyrlic*, *unherlic*) 'wild, fierce, savage' occur more widely in the surviving records (*unheore*: 7× poetry, 4× prose, 10× glosses; *unheorlic*: 1× poetry, 4× prose).[7] Furthermore, the simplex appears several times in Middle English texts such as Layamon's *Brut* and *The Destruction of Troy*.[8]

Fær 'ship, vessel' (*GenA* 1307, 1323, 1394(?), 1419, 1544; *Beo* 33) appears to be a narrowed meaning of *fær* 'way, journey, passage'. Since Old Icelandic *far* exhibits a similar semantic range, the meaning 'ship, vessel' was probably inherited from Common Germanic. Icelandic *far* 'ship' occurs in prose as well as poetry, and it is possible that the Old English word was not originally poetic either. On the other hand, the word belongs to a fairly robust synonym group (*bat*, *ceol*, *cnear*, *fleot*, *flota*, *lid*, *naca* and *scip*), four of which (*fleot*, *flota*, *lid*, and *naca*) are poetic. In any case, the restriction of this meaning of the word to these two poems is significant, since synonyms occur 126× in the poetic corpus (simplexes 85×; compounds, or elements of compounds, 41×), and are fairly widespread, occurring in eight of the other fifteen poems that are longer than 300 lines.[9]

There is strong evidence that *freme*, 'vigorous, flourishing, excellent', was a word in colloquial use from the earliest times. The *English Dialect Dictionary* gives copious citations that include practically all dialects. The *Middle English Dictionary* lists two occurrences in the fourteenth and fifteenth centuries, in the *Pearl* and the *Liber Cocorum*. The *OED* ('frim') classifies the word as obsolete except in dialects and gives citations from every century up to the nineteenth.[10] The word itself is thus by no means a poetic word. However, its appearance in both *Beowulf*

[7] These figures are derived from A. diP. Healey and R. L. Venezky, *A Microfiche Concordance to Old English* (Toronto, 1980). J. Bosworth and T. N. Toller, *An Anglo-Saxon Dictionary* (Oxford, 1898), lists an occurrence of *heore* in *Guthlac A* which the most recent editor of the poem rightly takes as the comparative of *heah*: 'þær se hyra gæst/ þihð in þeawum' (397–8): 'where the higher spirit prospers in its ways'. *The Guthlac Poems of the Exeter Book*, ed. J. Roberts (Oxford, 1979).

[8] See H. Kurath *et al.*, *A Middle English Dictionary*, in progress (Ann Arbor, 1952–), for citations.

[9] For the meanings and distribution of OI *far*, see R. Cleasby and G. Vigfusson, *An Icelandic–English Dictionary* 2nd ed., with a supplement by Sir W. A. Craigie (Oxford, 1957). Unless otherwise indicated, information about the meanings and distribution of Old Icelandic words are derived from this work. Synonyms of *fær* appear in *And*, Cynewulf, *Ex*, *GuthB*, *Met*, *Mald*, *MSolB*, *PPs*. The figures for the various synonyms are as follows: *bat* 6×; *ceol* 29×; *cnear* 1×; *fleot* 1×; *flota* 6×; *lid* 8×; *naca* 10×; *brimhengest* 3×; *brimþissa* 3×; *brimwudu* 2×; *hringedstefna* 3×; *lidmann* 2×; *merehengest* 2×; *sæbat* 4×; *sæmearh* 4×; *sundwudu* 3×; *wægþel* 4×; *wæterþissa* 2×; *yþbord* 2×; *yþmearh* 2×; and 38 compound *hapax legomena*, which I do not list due to space considerations. The synonym groups drawn upon in this article are taken primarily from my own research. I have also consulted J. Roberts and C. Kay, *A Thesaurus of Old English*, 2 vols. (London, 1995).

[10] J. Wright, *The English Dialect Dictionary*, 6 vols. (Oxford, 1898–1905); J. A. H. Murray *et al.*, *The Oxford English Dictionary*, 13 vols. (Oxford, 1933), a corrected re-issue, with an introduction, supplement and bibliography, of *A New English Dictionary on Historical Principles* (1884–1928).

(1932) and *Genesis A* (2332), which are the only recorded occurrences in Old English, appears to be a specialized poetic use of the word. Only in these occurrences is the word used to describe a person; only here, as the *OED* observes, is it used in a non-physical sense. The only word that can be regarded as a close synonym is *geþungen* 'full-grown, thriven; excellent, distinguished', which occurs in five poems longer than 300 lines. In addition, however, both *god* and *til*, which are partial synonyms when they refer to people, occur with such a reference in another five of these poems.[11] Thus ten of the fifteen poems in the comparison group contain a close or partial synonym of *freme*.

Gombe 'tribute' occurs in the formula *gomban gyldan* (*Beo* 11; *GenA* 1978: *gombon gieldan*). It is cognate with Old Saxon *gambra* 'tribute', which occurs in the *Heliand*, line 355, where it is collocated with *gelden*, the equivalent Old Saxon cognate of *gyldan*.[12] Its appearance in a formula only in these poems and the restriction of its sole cognate to an Old Saxon verse passage in which it is collocated with the same verb as in Old English suggest that the word was obsolete in the colloquial language, if it had ever been used there, and was on its way to becoming obsolete in poetry as well. These factors also suggest that the word had been inherited from the West Germanic poetic tradition and that its occurrence in only *Beowulf* and *Genesis A* is an indication of the conservatism of these poems. Two synonyms appear in verse, *gafol* and *gafolræden*, which were used to refer to various types of payments such as tax, rent and interest as well as tribute. *Gombe* and its synonyms are thus not entirely interchangeable. *Gafol* could be used instead of *gombe*, and, indeed, in *GenA* the two words are used together: 'gombon gieldan and gafol sellan' (1978). But *gombe* could not always be used instead of *gafol* or *gafolræden*, since its meaning is more restricted. In the meaning 'tribute', these two words appear in only four poems where their presence or absence can be considered significant.[13] With such weak synonym support, only limited weight can be placed on the evidence of *gombe*.

Dyhtig 'strong' (*Beo* 1287, *GenA* 1993) has cognates in Middle Low German, *düchtich*, and Middle High German, *tüchtec*. In Old English there is another form of the word, without umlaut, *dohtig* (ModE *doughty*), found only in late prose texts: *The Anglo-Saxon Chronicle*, MS C, 1030, and an eleventh-century charter (S 1461).[14] According to Campbell §204(7), the suffix-*ig* represents both Prim OE

[11] *Geþungen*: *And*, Cynewulf, *Jud*, *Met* and *Phoen*. *God* and *til*: *Dan*, *GuthA*, *Mald*, *PPs* and *Sat*.

[12] *Heliand und Genesis*, O. Behagel, Altdeutsche Textbibliothek 4, 9th ed. rev. B. Traeger (Tübingen, 1984). All subsequent references to Old Saxon poetry are to this edition.

[13] *Gafol:* Cynewulf, *Mald; gafolræden*: *And, GuthB* .

[14] *Two of the Saxon Chronicles Parallel*, ed. C. Plummer (Oxford, 1892–9) I, 157. The charter is a marriage agreeement, no. 77 in *Anglo-Saxon Charters*, ed. A. J. Robertson, 2nd ed., (Cambridge, 1956). S = P. H. Sawyer, *Anglo-Saxon Charters: an Annotated List and Bibliography*, R. Hist. Soc. Guides and Handbooks 8 (London, 1968).

-æg (> *-eg*) and *-ig*. There is thus fluctuation between mutated and unmutated vowels before *-ig*, just as we see in these two forms.[15] *Dyhtig* occurs only as part of a formula, *ecgum dyhtig*, (*Beo*; *GenA: ecgum dihtig*) 'strong in edges', used as an epithet of a sword. Given the narrow use of this word, there are no equivalent synonyms.[16] However, the formula is a sword-epithet, and there are frequent references to swords throughout the poetry. Thus this formula, and *dyhtig*, could potentially have occurred in the twelve longer poems which include words for 'sword', as well as in many of the shorter works. Words for 'sword' appear 229 times in the poetic corpus.[17] The word is thus strong evidence for a connection between *Beowulf* and *Genesis A*.

BEOWULF AND *MAXIMS I*

Four words appear only in *Beowulf* and *Maxims I*. Although both *Genesis A* and *Beowulf* are regarded as unified works today, the case of *Maxims I* is rather different. The most recent editor of the *Exeter Book*, Bernard Muir, believes that we have three separate poems here.[18] Furthermore, whether *Maxims I* is one or three poems, according to general consensus it is primarily a collection of maxims, many of which may have been in oral circulation, or perhaps in written form, for quite some time before the compilation was made.[19] *Maxims I* would thus appear to be a poor subject for a vocabulary study such as this one.

Although there is no space here for an extended consideration of this issue, there is some evidence which suggests that, on some level at least, *Maxims I* is a unified composition:

1. Despite Muir's inclination to view it as three separate poems, the evidence of the scribe's use of capitalization, spacing and punctuation is inconclusive.[20] Muir's excellent textual notes enable us to compare these elements of *Maxims I* with the way the scribe identified the commencement of sections in other

15 A. Campbell. *Old English Grammar* (Oxford, 1959), p. 84.

16 Except for *þyhtig* 'strong, firm', which occurs in the same formulaic system: *ecgum þyhtig*, *Beo* 1558. But this word occurs nowhere else.

17 *And*, Cynewulf, *Dan*, *Ex*, *GenA*, *GuthA*, *Jud*, *Mald*, *Met*, *MSolB*, *PPs* and *Sat*. The 229 occurrences of words meaning 'sword' are divided as follows: *bill* 25×; *ecg* 25×; *heoru* 2×; *iren* 16×; *mece* 24×; *secg* 2×; *brand* 1×; *sweord* 82×; *bradsweord* 2×; *brogdenmæl* 3×; *ecghete* 3×; *heardecg* 4×; and 40 compound *hapax*.

18 *The Exeter Anthology of Old English Poetry*, ed. B. J. Muir (Exeter, 1994) II, 530.

19 See, e.g., the observations in *The Exeter Book*, ed. G. P. Krapp and E. V. K. Dobbie, ASPR 3 (New York, 1936), xlvi–xlvii.

20 As Krapp and Dobbie, p. xlvi, observe, 'So far as the indications in the manuscript go, therefore, it is impossible to tell with any certainty whether the three sectional divisions indicated in the manuscript were intended by the scribe to be taken as three parts of a single poem, or as three separate poems.'

poems, particularly *Juliana* and the *Husband's Message*, whose unity is not in doubt, despite similar use of capitalization, spacing and punctuation.

2. The first three lines of the poem, which use direct address, serve as the introduction for all three sections; B and C begin with nothing even remotely similar, commencing instead with simple gnomes.[21]

3. Given the general consensus that *Maxims I* and *II* are collections of traditional gnomic sayings, it is surprising that there is no duplication of gnomes whatsoever. This lack of duplication would be even more surprising if *Maxims I* were three poems instead of one, especially since there is thematic overlap among the sections. Formulæ there are, and formulaic verses, but no repeated gnomes. The striking uniqueness of each gnome, coupled with the frequent use of extended, almost narrative passages in *Maxims I*, suggests that these poems are much more than the compilations of traditional materials they have been assumed to be. Perhaps there is more creativity in these poems than we have been willing to credit, or perhaps there was a guiding hand which either avoided or edited out duplicated gnomes.

These factors suggest that there is some kind of unity here, whether it be provided by the editorial work of an anthologist or by the composition of a poet. Moreover, three of the four words examined here appear in extended passages: *umbor* is found in a five-and-a-half line passage on God's control of human population through disease (29b–34); *eodor* occurs in the frequently quoted passage about the relationship and responsibilities of a king and queen (81–92); and *heoru* appears in the conclusion of the poem which traces feud and conflict back to Cain's murder of Abel (192–204). Such passages are more likely to have been composed than collected. Only *wlenco* (60) appears in a brief maxim.

Heoru 'sword' appears as a simplex only in these two poems (*Beo* 1285, *Max I* 200). It also appears as the first element of twenty compounds (thirty-eight total occurrences), where it almost always has intensive, instead of literal force, for example, *heorogifre*, 'fiercely ravenous' (*Beo* 1498, *Jul* 586, *ChristB* 976), or has been generalized to mean 'war, battle' as in *heorosceorp*, 'battle-garments' (*DHl* 73), or *heoruwulf*, 'war-wulf, i.e. warrior' (*Ex* 181; cf. *hildewulf*, *GenA* 2051, and *herewulf*, *GenA* 2015). In *Beowulf* there are two compounds in which the word retains its literal force: *hiorudrync* 'sword-drink' (2358), and *heorosweng* 'sword-stroke' (1590). However, when this latter compound appears in *Andreas* 952, *heoru-* serves as an intensifier, and the word means 'fierce stroke'.[22] Andreas is

[21] For a well-balanced discussion of the implications of these opening lines, see E. T. Hansen, *The Solomon Complex* (Toronto, 1988), pp. 157–63.

[22] Given the high frequency of compound formation in the poetic tradition, the appearance of some compounds with different meanings in two poems was probably inevitable. Other compounds with two meanings include *deaþcwalu*, *niðhete*, *randburg*, *searunet* and *þrohtheard*.

not struck by swords but is dragged along the ground. Similarly, in *Judith*, when the Hebrews fight the Assyrians, they are armed with *heardum heoruwæpnum* 'hard battle-weapons' (263). *Wæpen* is compounded with words meaning 'battle' or 'war', eg. *beaduwæpen* (*R15* 3, *R17* 8), *compwæpen* (*R20* 9), *herewæpen* (*F34* 3), *hildewæpen* (*Beo* 39, *R92* 5), but never with words for particular kinds of weapons.

All the evidence indicates that the literal meaning of *heoru* was in the process of becoming obsolete, and was archaic even in poetry. It was a common Germanic word, with cognates in Gothic (*hairus*), Old Icelandic (*hjörr*, which occurs only in poetry), and Old Saxon. The Old Saxon form, *heru-*, occurs only as the first element of compounds, with a semantic range similar to that found in Old English. In the light of the Old Saxon evidence, it would appear that the meaning of *heoru* had already begun to be generalized in West Germanic. It was presumably the pressure of these secondary meanings which drove the original meaning 'sword' into obsolescence. Words meaning 'sword' occur 229 times in the poetic corpus and are distributed quite widely, occurring in twelve of the poems in the comparison group as well as many of the shorter works.[23] The appearance of the literal meaning of *heoru* only in *Beowulf* and *Maxims I* is thus strong evidence of a connection between the two poems and an indicator of their conservatism.

Eodor 'edge; fence, boundary, enclosure; protector' appears in five poems, but only in *Beowulf* and *Maxims I* does it occur as the base word of a *kent heiti* for 'king, lord': *eodor Scyldinga* (*Beo* 428, 663), *eodor Ingwina* (*Beo* 1044), and *eodor æþelinga* (*Max I* 89). The appearance of the Old Icelandic cognate *iaðarr* in similar expressions, such as *fólks iaðarr* 'protector of the troop' (*Helgaqviða Hundingsbana önnor* 42), *hers iaðarr* 'protector of the army' (*Fáfnismál* 36) and *ása iaðarr* 'protector of the Æsir' (*Locasenna* 35), indicates that this usage of *eodor* was inherited from the earlier Germanic period.[24] Words and expressions which are closely or approximately synonymous occur throughout the poetry, in all of the poems with 300 or more lines and in most of the shorter poems.[25]

[23] See above, p. 30, n. 17, for a list of the twelve poems and the various words for 'sword'.

[24] Words and quotations from the Poetic Edda are cited from *Edda: die Lieder des Codex Regius nebst verwandten Denkmälern*, Gustav Neckel, 4th ed. rev. Hans Kuhn (Heidelberg, 1962). For a discussion of *eodor* and its Germanic cognates, see G. Neckel, '*Under Edoras*', *Beiträge zur Geschichte der deutschen Sprache und Literatur*, 41 (1916), 163–70.

[25] By my count there are a total of 3,086 words and expressions for 'king, lord, ruler'. 2,645 simplexes: *bealdor* 10×; *brego* 32×; *brytta* 36×; *cyning* 363×; *dryhten* 1,114×; *ealdor* 104×; *eodor* 4×; *fengel* 4×; *frea* 177×; *fruma* 9×; *hearra* 30×; *healdend* 6×; *helm* 38×; *hlaford* 57×; *hleo* 26×; *hyrde* 32×; *ord* 8×; *ræswa* 18×; *ðengel* 2×; *þeoden* 171×; *weard* 120×; *wealdend* 260×; *wine* 11×; *wisa* 13×; and 381 compounds: *æþelcyning* 3×; *anwealda* 3×; *beaggyfa* 8×; *bregoweard* 2×; *dryhtenbealu* 2×; *ealdhlaford* 2×; *ealdorduguð* 2×; *eorðcyning* 7×; *eðelweard* 6×; *folccyning* 5×; *folctoga* 15×; *frea-*

The restriction of this word to *Beowulf* and *Maxims I* is certainly significant and provides strong evidence of a connection between these two poems. The absence of this word from other poems, all of which had a great demand for words and expressions meaning 'lord, king', strongly suggests that this usage of *eodor* became obsolete during the historical period and that its presence in these two poems is an indication of their conservatism.

Wlenco is attributed the poetic meaning 'bravado' by Clark Hall and 'high spirits' by Klaeber; both definitions are apparently attempts to distinguish the poetic meaning of the word from the pejorative 'pride, arrogance', which is more common in the surviving texts and which appears to have developed under Christian influence. Of the fourteen occurrences of *wlenco* in poetry, only four have the poetic sense: three occurrences in *Beowulf* (338, 508, 1206) and one in *Maxims I* (60). The clearest occurrence of this meaning is found in *Beowulf*, where the coastguard tells Beowulf:

'Wen' ic þæt ge for wlenco, nalles for wræcsiðum,
ac for higeþrymmum Hroðgar sohton.' (338–9)[26]

'High-spirits' or 'bravado'' are acceptable if somewhat vague translations of *wlenco* here. We also find this meaning in a martial gnome in *Maxims I*:

þrym sceal mid wlenco, þriste mid cenum,
sceolun bu recene beadwe fremman.[27] (60–1)

In other contexts, such as when Unferth uses the word to describe Beowulf's swimming match with Breca in line 508, the word includes the connotation of 'recklessness', even 'foolhardiness'. The word is used with a similar sense during the first account of the death of Hygelac in Frisia:

dryhten 4×; *freawine* 3×; *freodryhten* 7×; *frumgar(a)* 15×; *goldgyfa* 3×; *goldwine* 9×; *guðcyning* 6×; *guðweard* 2×; *heafodweard* 2×; *heahcyning* 19×; *heahfrea* 2×; *heretema* 2×; *heretoga* 3×; *herewisa* 2×; *hildfruma* 6×; *hordweard* 9×; *leodfruma* 10×; *leodgebyrga* 3×; *liffrea* 8×; *mægencyning* 5×; *mægoræswa* 4×; *mandryhten* 21×; *manfrea* 3×; *ordfruma* 9×; *ræsbora* 3×; *rodorcyning* 3×; *sigedryhten* 18×; *sincgyfa* 6×; *soðcyning* 11×; *sweglcyning* 2×; *þeodcyning* 11×: *þeodenhold* 5×; *ðrymcyning* 4×; *wigfruma* 2×; *wilgyfa* 5×; *winedryhten* 12×; *wuldorcyning* 44×; *woruldcyning* 3×; and 40 compound *hapax*.

Strictly speaking, *brytta*, *eodor*, *helm*, *hleo*, *hyrde*, *weard* and *wine* do not mean 'lord, king', but function as base words in expressions with these meanings. I have included the base words alone for the sake of brevity.

The overwhelming majority of these words refer to God, not to earthly kings. This is true, for example, of the occurrences of *dryhten*, nearly half of which (532) appear in the *Paris Psalter*. I have excluded words which are used only in reference to God, such as *rædend* and *reccend*.

26 'I think that it is because of *wlenco*, not at all because of exile, but for greatness of heart that you sought Hrothgar.'

27 'Might together with bravado, daring together with the bold, both must engage in battle quickly.'

þone hring hæfde   Higelac Geata,
nefa Swertinges,   nyhstan siðe,
siðþan he under segne   sinc ealgode,
wælreaf werede;   hyne wyrd fornam,
syþðan he for wlenco   wean ahsode,
fæhðe to Frysum. (1202–7)[28]

Both here and in line 338 *wlenco* denotes a daring bravado which shades into the recklessness that can impair a person's judgement. *Wlenco* thus appears to have been a great-spirited courage which could lead one to daring undertakings for the good of others or to reckless endeavours that produce unnecessary risk. It thus may be useful to distinguish two pejorative meanings of the word: the heroic/poetic 'recklessness' seen in these two passages, and the Christian 'pride, arrogance'. As in the case of other heroic words that implied an aggressive self-assertiveness, such as *gylp*, *beot* and *lofgeorn*, the meaning of *wlenco* was probably devalued under the influence of Christianity.[29] In the first glossary in London, British Library, Cotton Cleopatra A. iii, for example, it glosses *insolentiam* 'pride, arrogance' and *fastus* 'pride, haughtiness'.[30] This meaning also occurs in poetry, as in *GenA* 2581: 'Hie þæs wlenco onwod and wingedrync . . .'[31]

Beowulf and *Maxims I* have thus preserved the heroic meaning of the word. However, synonym support for this word is weak, with only two partial synonyms occurring in two poems: *noð* 'daring' in *Juliana* (343), and *byldu* 'boldness' in *Christ I* (113).

Umbor 'child, infant' occurs in the compound *umborwesende* 'being a child', which appears twice in *Beowulf* (46, 1187). As a simplex it is found only in line 31 of *Maxims I*: *Umbor yceð* 'he [God] increases children'. There are no known

[28] 'Hygelac of the Geats, Swerting's grandson, had that necklace for the last time when he defended treasure beneath his banner, protected the spoils of battle; the course of events destroyed him when he, on account of *wlenco*, sought woe, enmity from Frisians.'

[29] For a discussion of *gylp* and *beot*, see B. Nolan and M. W. Bloomfield, '*Beotword*, *Gilpcwidas*, and the *Gilphlæden* Scop of *Beowulf*', *JEGP* 79 (1980), 499–516, at 501–2. On *lofgeorn*, see D. Cronan, '*Lofgeorn*: Generosity and Praise', *NM* 92 (1991), 187–94. The argument for the devaluation of *wlenco* assumes that the heroic meaning is the orginal meaning of the word. But in the absence of cognates in the other Germanic languages (and in Indo-European, for that matter), such an assumption is at best probabilistic, and leans heavily upon analogy with other words which show a similar dichotomy between heroic and Christian meanings. Given the range of meanings, 'bravado, pride, pomp, wealth, riches', and the meanings of the closely related *wlanc*, 'boastful, proud, splendid, magnificent, rich', and *wlencan*, 'to enrich, exalt', it seems likely that these words descend from a (non-Indo-European?) root that meant something like 'to increase, expand, swell'. It is possible that the use of the word in Christian contexts to mean 'pride, arrogance' is more a product of semantic narrowing than of devaluation.

[30] W. G. Stryker, 'The Latin–Old English Glossary in MS. Cotton Cleopatra A.III' (unpubl. PhD dissertation, Stanford Univ., 1951), glosses 3061, 2445.

[31] 'Pride and wine-drinking penetrated them . . .'

cognates of this word, and the etymology is uncertain. Lehmann hesitantly suggests a connection with *wamb*.[32] Given the meaning of this word, it is unlikely that it was ever part of the poetic wordhoard. These two poems have apparently both used an otherwise unrecorded colloquial word. The synonyms *cild, cniht* and *bearn* (only when it is clear that the reference is to a young child) occur in eight of the poems longer than 300 lines.[33] The presence of *umbor* in these two poems is thus strong evidence.

BEOWULF , *GENESIS A*, AND OTHER POEMS

Before considering the significance of the distribution of these words, let us broaden the evidence a bit by examining, first, words which occur only in *Beowulf*, *Genesis A* and one other poem, and second, words whose occurrence is restricted to *Beowulf* or *Genesis A* and one other poem.[34] In order to ensure that this second group remains a tightly focused body of evidence, and does not dissolve into a mere catalogue of vocabulary items, it is necessary to add one other qualification: the other poem must share restricted words with both *Beowulf* and *Genesis A*, even though each word occurs in only one of these poems. Thus, for example, this qualification excludes consideration of two words found only in *Beowulf* and *Andreas, gifeðe* (noun) and *-scerwen*, because *Andreas* does not share any restricted words with *Genesis A*. On the other hand, *lufen* and *wæfre*, which appear only in *Beowulf* and *Daniel*, will be discussed, because *Daniel* and *Genesis A* share another restricted word, *bresne*.

Suhtriga, *suhterga*, 'brother's son, nephew; cousin', is probably the most complex of all the cases examined here. It occurs in *Widsith* and *Beowulf* in the compound *suhterfædren* (*Wid* 46), *suhtergefæderen* (*Beo* 1163). In *Genesis A* it occurs four times as a simplex (1775, 1901, 2071, 2029). The occurrences of the compound in *Beowulf*,

þær þa godan twegen
sæton suhtergefæderan; þa gyt wæs hiera sib ætgædere,
æghwylc oðrum trywe. (1163–5),[35]

and in *Widsith*,

Hroþwulf ond Hroðgar heoldon lengest
sibbe ætsomne suhtorfædran . . . (45–6)[36]

[32] W. P. Lehmann, *A Gothic Etymological Dictionary* (Leiden, 1986). See entry W28, *wamba*.

[33] These poems are *ChristA*, Cynewulf, *Ex*, *GenA*, *GuthB*, *MSolB*, *PPs* and *Phoen*.

[34] There are no such words in *Beowulf* and *Maxims I*.

[35] 'The two good ones, uncle and nephew, sat there; they were still united in peace, each one true to the other.'

[36] 'Hrothwulf and Hrothgar, uncle and nephew, kept their peace together for the longest time . . .'

appear to be derived from a common source. Both passages are referring to Hrothgar and Hrothulf. Both exhibit the alliterative collocation of the compound with *sibb* and the presence of either *ætsomne* or *ætgædere*, each of which means 'together, united'.

Even more significant is the fact that *suhtergefæderan* is a dvandva, or a copulative compound, a type that was all but extinct by the time of the surviving written texts. The only other example in Old English of such a compound occurs in *Beowulf* 84: *aþumsweoran* 'son-in-law and father-in-law', emended from *aþum swerian*, which is also a possible form of the word, since a form *sweri(g)a*, with a suffixal extension like that seen in *suhtriga*, *suhterga*, is possible. But as Klaeber observes, the scribe probably mistook the word and blundered.[37] Only two other copulatives occur in the early Germanic languages: Old Saxon *gisunfader* 'son and father' (*Heliand* 1176) and Old high German *sunufatarungo* 'son and father' (*Hildebrandslied* 4). As Carr observes, such compounds were inherited older formations which were no longer productive when they were recorded.[38]

Suhtriga also occurs in a number of glosses, once in the Corpus Glossary, 'Fratuelis' *suhterga*, twice in the first glossary in Cleopatra A. iii, 'fratuelis i filius fratris' *suchtyrga*, and 'fratres patrueles' *suctyrian* 'sic dictus est ad patres eorum si fratres inter se fuerunt', and once in the Harley Glossary, 'Fratruelis i filius fratris uel martertere filius' *sihterge*.[39] Three of these glosses, the Corpus, the Harley and the first from Cleopatra A. iii, are related and are ultimately derived from the same source. The first glossary in Cleopatra A. iii contains about half the glosses from Corpus in batches that follow almost the same order;[40] the Harley glossary contains about two fifths of the Corpus material.[41] The simplest way to illustrate the connections between these three glossaries, and between the three *suhtriga* glosses, is to examine a sequence that includes ten glosses to either side of the gloss 'Fratuelis i filius fratris' *suchtyrga* in Cleopatra A. iii, listing the corresponding glosses in Corpus and Harley.[42]

37 *Beowulf*, ed. Klaeber, p. 130 (note on line 84).

38 *Hildebrandslied* is cited from W. Braune, *Althochdeutsches Lesebuch*, 16th ed. rev. E. A. Ebbinghaus (Tübingen, 1979), pp. 84–5. On copulative compounds in the early Germanic languages, see C. T. Carr, *Nominal Compounds in Germanic*, St Andrews University Publications 41 (London, 1939), pp. 40–2.

39 J. de Hessels, *An Eighth-Century Latin–Anglo-Saxon Glossary* (Cambridge, 1890), F. 319; Stryker, gll. 2514, 2750; R. T. Oliphant, *The Harley Latin–Old English Glossary*, Janua linguarum, series practica 20 (The Hague, 1966), gl. 5216.

40 J. D. Pheifer, *Old English Glosses in the Épinal–Erfurt Glossary* (Oxford, 1974), p. xxxi.

41 Ibid. p. xxxv.

42 Cleopatra A. iii is the most economical choice as a base for this comparison because, unlike the two other manuscripts, it is strictly a Latin–Old English glossary. Choosing Corpus, the oldest of the manuscripts, as a base would greatly extend the amount of material to be compared, since it includes Latin–Latin glosses which Cleopatra A. iii omits.

2504 Fouit bredeþ, feormaþ. = Corpus 6.264; Harley F606 (fomet feormeþ)
2505 Formido onoþa. = Corpus 6.277
2506 Forfix isernfetor. = Corpus 6.279, 2.38; Harley F646 (no gloss)[43]
2507 Fornaculæ cylene, heorþe. = Corpus 6.289
2508 Foros bolca. = Corpus 6.293
2509 Fortex edwielle. = Corpus 6.300
2510 Follis blastbelg. = Corpus 6.305; Harley F625 ('blaedbylig')
2511 Folliginis bylgum. = Harley F624 (belgum)
2512 Fornaculum here. = Corpus 6.306
2513 Fronulus linetwige. = Corpus 6.314
2514 Fratuelis i filius fratris suchtyrga. = Corpus 6.319; Harley F683
2515 Frugus uncystig vel heamol, fercuþ. = Corpus 6.324; Harley F802[44]
2516 Frixum afigen. = Corpus 6.325; Harley F762
2517 Fraxinus æsc. = Corpus 6.327
2518 Fraga ofet. = Corpus 6.326; Harley F656
2519 Fringella finc. = Corpus 6.331
2520 Framea sweord vel ætgare. = Corpus 6.344; Harley F675
2521 Fretus confidens presumptus bald. = Corpus 6.347
2522 Fragor cirm, sweg, gebrec. = Corpus 6.348; Harley F653
2523 Fraudulenter facenlice. = Corpus 6.356; Harley F686
2524 Frutina fultumend. = Corpus 6.365; Harley F834

Of the twenty-one entries in Cleopatra A. iii, twenty correspond to glosses in Corpus, and twelve correspond to glosses in Harley. Thus, despite the presence of these *subtriga* glosses in Cotton Cleopatra A. iii, from the mid-tenth century (Ker 143), and BL, Harley 3376, from the late tenth or early eleventh century (Ker 240), it is clear that these glosses stem from a much earlier period. The original collection of *glossae collectae* that appears in the Leiden family of glossaries,

[43] Despite the peculiar glossing of *Forfex* 'shears' with the gloss *isernfetor* 'iron fetter' (which is the interpretation of Cleopatra 645 'Balus isenfetor') instead of with *isern sceruru*, as in Corpus 6.279, it is clear that the entry in Cleopatra A. iii comes from the same tradition as Corpus. The lemma in Harley lacks a gloss; it is the third in a series of 'shears' lemmata:

H F644 Forfices ræglsceara.
H F645 Forpices fexsceara.
H F646 Forfex.

Again, the connection with the Corpus tradition is readily apparent.

[44] The compiler of the Harley manuscript had a habit of translating the Old English interpretations into Latin, which then either preceded or replaced the Old English (Pheifer, *Old English Glosses*, p.xxxvi). I am thus including several lemmata with Latin glosses as probable equivalents of OE glosses in Corpus and Cleopatra A. iii:

F802 Frugus auarus = CCl 2515; Corpus 6.324
F762 Frixum i coctum assatum = CCl 2516; Corpus 6.325
F675 Framea rumphea gladius = CCl 2520; Corpus 6.344
F834 Frutina i auxiliator = CCl 2524; Corpus 6.365

in Épinal–Erfurt and in the second glossary in Corpus, is now regarded as having been compiled during the second half of the seventh century.[45] The Corpus Glossary combined the common original of Épinal–Erfurt with new material from the same sources.[46] It is therefore possible that the original use of *suhtriga* as a gloss occurred in the seventh century. However, it is better to be cautious, and simply date this original use as predating Corpus, a manuscript of the late eighth or early ninth century (Ker 36).[47]

The other gloss in Cleopatra A. iii, 2750: 'fratres patrueles' *suctyrian* 'sic dictus est ad patres eorum si fratres inter se fuerunt', is a bit more difficult to place, since there are no corrresponding glosses in other manuscripts. However, glosses in this manuscript sometimes preserve archaic forms among its more normal late West-Saxon orthography. Pheifer takes such spellings as an indication that the exemplar of the *ab* batches corresponding to Corpus was at least as old as Corpus itself.[48] Both occurrences of *suhtriga* in Cleopatra A. iii exhibit archaic spellings: *suchtyrga* (2514); *suctyrian* (2750). These spellings with *cht* and *ct* indicate an early exemplar, whose spellings the scribe mechanically reproduced, cf. *dryctin* (2×) and *allmectig* in the Northumbrian version of *Caedmon's Hymn* in the Moore manuscript (*c.* 737). Such spellings (instead of *ht)* occurred only as late as the *Liber Vitae Dunelmensis* (first half of the ninth century). According to Campbell, §57.3, 'Before *t*, . . . the normal symbol of a velar or palatal spirant was *c* in early OE, though *ch* is also found . . . But here also *h* gradually replaces *c*: while *ct* is universal in the Moore Bede [*c.* 737], it gives way rapidly to *ht* in the glossaries, though it returns in L[iber]V[itae], where both *ct* and *cht* are more frequent than *ht*'.[49] With the exception of the *Liber Vitae*, *ct* and *cht* spellings were replaced by *ht* during the course of the eighth century; thus the spelling *suctyrian* makes it likely that behind this gloss there also lies an eighth-century exemplar. The preservation of earlier spellings in *suchtyrga* and *suctyrian*, and the misspelling *sihterge* in the Harley Glossary, suggest that the scribes did not recognize the word: these glossaries not only preserved glosses from the eighth-century (or even earlier), they preserved a word which was no longer part of everyday speech.

Further evidence for this conclusion is provided by the distribution of the synonyms of *suhtriga* in prose and glosses: *nefa* (25×),[50] *broþorsunu* (8×), and *broðor sunu* (17×). These words occur in a large number of texts that cover the entire period, ranging from the Corpus Glossary, through works of Alfred's reign (the Old English Bede, *Gregory's Dialogues*, the early *Chronicle*) and the writ-

[45] M. Lapidge, 'The School of Theodore and Hadrian', *ASE* 15 (1986), 45–72, at 58.

[46] J. D. Pheifer, 'Early Anglo-Saxon Glossaries and the School of Canterbury', *ASE* 16 (1987), 17–44, at 18.

[47] N. R. Ker, *Catalogue of Manuscripts Containing Anglo-Saxon* (Oxford, 1957).

[48] Pheifer, *Old English Glosses*, p. xxxii.

[49] Campbell, *Old English Grammar*, p. 24.

[50] This figure omits the nine occurrences in the *Peterborough Chronicle* during the twelfth century.

ings of Ælfric, to texts of the eleventh century (*Apollonius of Tyre*, the later *Chronicle*).[51] Ælfric used *broðor sunu* to refer to Lot, Abraham's nephew, in several passages in the portions of Genesis which he translated (Gen XIV.12, 13, 16; XIX.1), precisely the purpose for which the *Genesis A* poet used *suhtriga*.[52] Were it not for the peculiarity of the distribution of *suhtriga*, this synonym alternation could be seen as the product of a series of independent stylistic choices. But the complete absence of *suhtriga* from prose of any period coupled with its use in poetry and its preservation in a series of archaic glosses makes it clear that this is a word which became obsolete early in the Anglo-Saxon period.

In verse, these synonyms are found only in *Beowulf* (*nefa* 4×), *Riddle 46* (*nefa* 1×), and *Genesis A* itself (*broðor sunu* 1×). But the presence or absence of synonyms in verse is not as important in this case as it is in others, since *suhtriga* is not a poetic word, and its appearance in verse is contextualized for us by a gloss which first occurs in a manuscript dated to the late eighth or early ninth century, a gloss which reflects the usage of an earlier period – perhaps as early as the second half of the seventh century. This word thus points decisively towards a connection between the eighth century and the composition of *Genesis A*. The evidence of this word is quite different from the evidence provided by the presence of *heoru* in the meaning 'sword' in *Beowulf* and *Maxims I*: *heoru* indicates that these poems are conservative in diction, but this conservativeness is relative to the rest of the poetry, since there are no occurrences of *heoru* in early texts or glosses to provide an external dating context.

Although *suhtriga* is not poetic, the copulative *suhter(ge)fæderen* is. The evidence provided by this compound is similar to that of *heoru*, but more complex. Its presence in *Widsith* and *Beowulf* (along with that of *aþumswerian*) is an indication that these poems are more conservative than poems without such compounds. But this indication is qualified by the connection of these compounds with a specific theme: the relation of Hrothgar and Hrothulf, and their conflict with Ingeld and the Heathobeards. These compounds are thus evidence of the age of the theme itself, whose preservation may be due more to genre and subject matter than to the age of the poems in which it occurs. Yet the meaning of these compounds must have been transparent to the original 'scribes/composers' of these poems. In contrast, the first scribe of the Nowell Codex, writing at the beginning of the eleventh century, clearly failed to understand either of the copulative compounds and erred badly in his transcription of

[51] See diPaolo Healey and Venezky, *Microfiche Concordance*, for individual citations.

[52] Ælfric translated chapters 1–3, 6–9 and 11–24. S. B. Greenfield and D. G. Calder, *A New Critical History of Old English Literature* (New York, 1986), p. 84.

both.[53] Line 65 of Cynewulf's *Juliana* is also relevant here, since it utilizes the phrase *sweor ond aþum*, instead of the copulative *aþumsweoran*. Perhaps this phrase was used merely for the sake of its alliteration on *s*; on the other hand, its use could be an indication that by the time of Cynewulf, whose works are usually dated to the ninth century, copulative compounds were obsolete even in verse.[54] However we view this evidence, there is no denying that *Beowulf* and *Widsith* contain two of the only four copulatives preserved in the early Germanic languages. The presence of these compounds is thus strong evidence for the conservative nature of the diction of these poems.

The obscured compound *missere* (<*mis-jari) 'half-year', originally 'changing year', appears only in *Beowulf* (4×: 153, 1498, 1769, 2620), *Genesis* (3×: 1168, 1743, 2347), and *Exodus* (49). Since the Old Icelandic cognate *missari* appears in both prose and poetry, it is possible that *missere* once had a wider distribution as well and was not originally a poetic word. However, seven of its eight occurrences are formulae, *misserum frod* (2× in *GenA*), *fela missera* (3×), and *hund missera* (2×), a circumstance which suggests that word was well embedded in the diction of these poems, with a depth of usage behind it, so the word probably was poetic. The synonyms *gear* and *winter* occur in eleven of the other fourteen poems which are 300 lines or longer.[55] These three factors – the cognate in Icelandic, the wide-spread use of synonyms in other poems, and the heavy formulaic use of this word – indicate that *missere* is not only strong evidence that these three poems are connected but also evidence of their conservative diction. Given the high demand for words in this semantic field (they appear in a total of twenty-four poems), the simplest explanation of the restriction of *missere* to these three poems is that at some point it disappeared from use.

þengel 'prince, lord, king' occurs only in *Beowulf* (1507) and *Exodus* (173). Synonymous simplexes occur in all of the poems in our comparison group and

[53] The scribe's confusion of *aþumsweoran* with *aþum swerian* in l. 84 is obvious. On the form *suhtergefæderen* in l. 1164, Carr, p. 41, observes, 'That this mode of composition appeared unusual to the Beowulf scribe is shown by the fact that he reolved the compound into *suhtorgefædran*.' OE *gefædera*, a loan-translation from Latin *compater*, means 'godfather'.

[54] See, for example, K. Sisam, 'Cynewulf and his Poetry', in his *Studies in the History of Old English Literature* (Oxford, 1953), pp. 1–28. P. W. Conner, 'On Dating Cynewulf', *Cynewulf: Basic Readings*, ed. R. E. Bjork (New York, 1996), pp. 35–47, has argued for the dependence of *The Fates of the Apostles* on the 'Usuardian' recension of the *Martyrologium*. Cynewulf would therefore have worked after 875, the date of Usuard's dedication of his recension to Charlemagne. Conner favours a date for the works of Cynewulf in the tenth century. J. M. McCulloh has more recently argued that the evidence for Cynewulf's use of a martyrology is not as strong as Conner claims. See his 'Did Cynewulf Use a Martyrology? Reconsidering the Sources of *The Fates of the Apostles*', *ASE* 29 (2000), 67–84.

[55] *And*, Cynewulf, *Dan*, *GuthA*, *GuthB*, *Mald*, *Met*, *MSolB*, *PPs*, *Phoen* and *Sat*. They also appear in ten of the shorter poems.

in the overwhelming majority of the shorter poems.[56] Given the tremendous usage of words in this semantic field in the poetry and the distribution of these words throughout the entire corpus, the restriction of *þengel* to *Beowulf* and *Exodus* is clearly significant and provides very strong evidence of a connection between these two poems. The poetic status of the Old Icelandic cognate *þengill* suggests that *þengel* was inherited as a poetic word from earlier Germanic tradition. It appears to be an old poetic word which was obsolete except for its use in the conservative diction of *Beowulf* and *Exodus.*

Genesis A shares one word with the works of Cynewulf, *gnyrn* (*GenA* 2422, *Ele* 422, 1138; *gnyrnwræc Ele* 359) which is not found elsewhere. The meaning of this word ranges from 'grief' to 'sin, evil'. This latter meaning appears to be a secondary development, since related words such as *gnorn, gnornung* and *gnornian* all belong to the semantic field 'grief, sorrow and lamentation'. In any case, it is the meaning 'sin, evil' which is relevant here since only this meaning occurs in both poems (*Ele* 422). The synonyms *firen*, *leahtor* and *synn* appear in thirteen poems in the comparison group.[57] This word is thus strong evidence for a connection between these two poems.

Geatolic 'ornamented, splendid', appears only in *Beowulf* (215, 308, 1400, 1562) and *Elene* (258, 331). The frequent collocation of this word with *guð* 'war, battle' (*Beo* 215, 2154, both occurrences in *Elene*) indicates that it was firmly embedded in the poetic tradition. It is difficult, however, to identify either complete or partial synonyms. Although *A Thesaurus of Old English* lists it among words meaning 'shining, splendid, radiant, beautiful' (07.10), there does not seem to be any component of 'shining' or 'radiance' in its meaning. Words meaning 'adorned, ornamented' (07.10.03) are another possible synonym group, but closer inspection reveals that the words in this semantic field which occur in poetry, such as *gehroden, (ge)hyrsted* and *geweorðod,* are frequently accompanied by a noun in the dative case, as in *golde geweorðod* (*Ex* 581, *Wld2* 19), *hringum gehrodene* (*Jud* 37), and *golde gehyrsted* (*Ele* 331). The meaning of such phrases are compatible with the meaning of *geatolic*, and indeed, the last phrase occurs in apposition to *geatolic* in *Ele* 331: 'geatolic guðcwen golde gehyrsted'. But the differences in usage and form (all these words were originally past participles) indicate that *geatolic* does not belong in this synonym group.

However, as in the case of *dyhtig*, an adjective could potentially occur wherever the type of noun it modifies occurs. *Geatolic* modifies nouns designating war-gear, swords, a hall, a king (Hroðgar) and a queen (Elene). It thus seems fair to say that this adjective would not have been out of place in any one of the poems in the comparison group. Its presence in these two poems is thus significant.

[56] See above, p. 32, n. 25, for a list of the synonyms of *þengel.*

[57] *And*, *Beo*, *ChristA*, *ChristC*, *Dan*, *Ex*, *GuthA*, *GuthB*, *Met*, *MSolB*, *PPs*, *Phoen* and *Sat.*

Beowulf and *Daniel* share two words not found elswhere: *lufen* 'joy?, hope?' (*Beo* 2886, *Dan* 73), and *wæfre* 'restless, wandering, wavering' (*Beo* 1150, 1331, 2420, *Dan* 241). The precise meaning of *lufen* is uncertain. Grein–Köhler and Bosworth–Toller incline toward 'hope', as do Holthausen and Lehmann who regard it as a cognate of Gothic *lubain* 'hope'. If this is the meaning, then nine of the poems in our comparison group have synonyms.[58] On the other hand Klaeber and Farrell, in an appendix to his edition of *Daniel and Azarias*, incline toward 'joy'. In this case, twelve of the poems in our comparison group include synonyms.[59] However, the potential value of this word as evidence is weakened by the uncertainty about its meaning.

Given the semantic range of *wæfre*, it is difficult to find comparable synonyms. *Waðol* 'wandering' (*Fnb* 8) could perhaps be a synonym of the occurrence of *wæfre* in *Beo* 1331, where Hrothgar uses the word to describe the *wælgæst* who has just slain Æschere. Certain adjectives plus *lig/fyr* can be regarded as rough equivalents of *wæfran lige* in *Dan* 241: *lacende lig* (*Ele*, *ChristB*), and *weallende lig* (*ChristB*), *weallende fyr* (*GenA*). Otherwise synonym support for the word is weak.

Bresne 'powerful, mighty' is found only in *Genesis A* (2802) and *Daniel* (173, 448). The synonyms *mihtig* and *rice* appear in eleven of the comparison poems.[60] It is thus significant evidence for a connection between these two poems, although the nature of this connection is difficult to characterize without a clear context in which to place the word – it has no equivalent cognates, and there is no way to tell whether the word is poetic or not.

LIMITED DISTRIBUTION IN THE POETIC CORPUS AS A WHOLE

Context is indeed the key to our understanding of the significance of the limited distribution of the words discussed here. For some words little context is available: they have no cognates, there is nothing to indicate whether they are poetic or nonpoetic, and in the case of a word such as *wæfre*, even the context most essential for our purposes, the presence of synonyms in other poems, is lacking. But other words, such as *eodor*, *heoru*, *suhtriga* and *þengel*, have abundant context, and it is the context of such words that makes their restricted distribution understandable.

However, there is another kind of context which also needs to be considered,

[58] C. W. M. Grein, *Sprachschatz der angelsächsischen Dichter*, unter mitwirkung von F. Holthausen, neu herausgegeben von J. J. Köhler (Heidelberg, 1912). F. Holthausen, *Altenglisches etymologisches Wörterbuch* (Heidelberg, 1934). *Hopa, hyht*: *And*, *ChristA*, Cynewulf, *GuthA*, *GuthB*, *Jud*, *PPs*, *Phoen*, *Sat*.

[59] See Klaeber's glossary. *Daniel and Azarias*, ed. R. T. Farrell (London, 1974), pp. 137–8. *Dream*, *wynn*: *And*, *ChristA*, *ChristC*, Cynewulf, *Ex*, *GenA*, *GuthA*, *GuthB*, *Mald*, *PPs*, *Phoen*, *Sat*.

[60] *And*, *Beo*, *ChristA*, *ChristC*, Cynewulf, *GuthA*, *GuthB*, *Jud*, *Met*, *PPs*, *Phoen*.

that of the limited distribution of poetic simplexes in the corpus as a whole.[61] *Beowulf*, at 3,182 lines, and *Genesis A*, at 2,319 lines, are the two longest Old English poems. One could therefore argue that they provide more scope than any other two poems for the occurrence of words not found elsewhere, and that the restriction of such words to these two poems proves little. But no such argument is possible in the case of *Beowulf* and *Maxims I*, since the latter contains only 204 lines. And when we consider the case of the poems of Cynewulf, it becomes difficult to dismiss the restriction of *fær*, *gombe*, *dyhtig* and *freme* to *Beowulf* and *Genesis A* as simply a consequence of the length of these poems. Taken as a group, the signed poems of Cynewulf constitute 2,601 lines of verse – almost 300 lines longer than *Genesis A*. Yet only *geatolic* is restricted to Cynewulf and *Beowulf*, and only *gnyrn* is restricted to Cynewulf and *Genesis A*.[62] Length alone is not a sufficient explanation for the restriction of these four words to *Beowulf* and *Genesis A*.

The appendix lists the remaining poetic simplexes which are found in only two poems. As is the case with the words already examined, it is likely that not all of these words were actually poetic, despite their restriction to poetry. As a group, these thirty-two words have a wide distribution, appearing in twenty-eight poems, a ratio of eight words for every seven poems, or roughly one to one. This distribution contrasts sharply with that of the thirteen words discussed above, which appear in only six poems, or slightly more than two words for every poem. Even more striking is the fact that, with only one exception, none of these poems share more than one word of restricted distribution. Like the patterns already examined, the exception involves *Beowulf*: *gifeðe* 'fate' and *-scerwen* '?' appear only in *Beowulf* and *Andreas*.

It is not surprising that *Beowulf* participates in so many limited distribution patterns; of the 264 simplexes that occur only in verse, 187 are found in *Beowulf*. Moreover, *Beowulf* has one of the highest proportions of words with a limited distribution: 19 of the 187 poetic simplexes (10.1 per cent) found in *Beowulf* appear in only one other poem. The figures for other relevant poems are:

[61] For the sake of conciseness, I restrict my observations here to words appearing in only two poems; as already seen, my discussion as a whole at times depends on words appearing in three poems, such as *missere* and *suhtriga*(-).

[62] Menner, 'Date and Dialect', 287, makes a similar comparison with the *Paris Psalter* and the *Meters of Boethius*. However, as M. S. Griffith has demonstrated, the Psalter uses only a limited subset of the poetic vocabulary. Thus, although the Psalter is comparable in terms of length, the comparison of its vocabulary to that of *Beowulf*, *Genesis A*, or the poems of Cynewulf is neither useful nor fair. See 'Poetic Language and the Paris Psalter: the Decay of the Old English Tradition', *ASE* 20 (1991), 167–86. Given that the *Meters* contains only fifty-two poetic words, none of which is restricted to two poems, its use in such a comparison would also be irrelevant.

Andreas: 4 out of 152 words (2.6%)
Christ I: 1 out of 42 words (2.4%)
Christ III: 0 out of 47 words (0%)
Christ and Satan: 2 out of 28 words (7.1%)
Cynewulf: 9 out of 152 words (5.9%)
Daniel: 3 out of 60 words (5%)
Exodus: 5 out of 86 words (5.8%)
Genesis A: 9 out of 120 words (7.5%)
Guthlac A: 3 out of 39 words (7.7%)
Guthlac B: 4 out of 66 words (6%)
Judith: 2 out of 68 words (2.9%)
Maldon: 2 out of 38 words (5.3%)
Maxims I: 5 out of 44 words (11.4%)
Meters of Boethius: 0 out of 52 words (0%)
Paris Psalter: 0 out of 54 words (0%)
Phoenix: 2 out of 67 words (3%)
Solomon and Saturn II: 0 out of 19 words (0%)
All poems: 44 out of 264 words (16.7%)

Although *Beowulf* has by far the most poetic simplexes, it is worth noting that both *Andreas* and the poems of Cynewulf contain twenty-six more simplexes than *Genesis A*.

The poems of Cynewulf and *Genesis A* both contain nine words which appear in only one other poem. The differences in the distribution of these nine words are, however, quite telling:

GenA	*Cynewulf*
Beo: dyhtig	*And*: þroht
Beo: fær	*Beo*: geatolic
Beo: freme	*Exo*: (-)hlence
Beo: gombe	*GenA*: gnyrn
Cyn: gnyrn	*GuthB*: flacor
Dan: bresne	*Phoen*: æppled
Deo: gesihð	*Rid93*: gehleþa
Jud: bælc 'pride'	*Rim*: grorn
Rid3: engu	*Run*: hearding

Four of the words in *Genesis A* (44 per cent) also occur in *Beowulf*. In contrast, the nine words in Cynewulf are found in nine different poems, an apparently random distribution.

The distribution in other poems of words of limited distribution found in *Beowulf* is even more telling:

And: gifeðe 'fate'	*GenA*: gombe
And: -scerwen	*GuthB*: bleat
ChristA: hoðma	*Mald*: trym
Cyn: geatolic	*Max I*: eodor 'protector'
Dan: lufen	*Max I*: heoru
Dan: wæfre	*Max I*: wlenco 'daring'
Exo: þengel	*Max I*: umbor(-)
GenA: dyhtig	*Sea*: -floga
GenA: fær 'ship'	*Sat*: fyren 'pain, violence'
GenA: freme	

Eight of these nineteen words (42 per cent) appear in *Genesis A* or *Maxims I*. Twelve (63 per cent) occur in poems which include at least one other word from this list.

The participation of *Beowulf* in all the restricted distribution patterns can be explained in several ways. Part of the explanation is, of course, the sheer weight of poetic simplexes appearing in this poem, which are due to the poem's heroic content. But neither *Andreas* nor the poems of Cynewulf, with 152 simplexes each, exhibit even remotely similar distribution patterns. And the case of *Maxims I*, which contains only forty-four poetic simplexes and shares four out of five words of restricted distribution with *Beowulf*, is clear evidence that while poem length and the number of poetic simplexes a poem contains are factors at work here, they clearly are not the decisive ones. Indeed, even without the detailed examination of particular words already presented, the differences in restricted distribution patterns seen here are evidence that something more substantial than random distribution influenced by poem length has shaped these patterns.

CONCLUSIONS

When the evidence provided by the words of limited distribution discussed above is viewed in the context of these distributional patterns in the corpus as a whole, the following conclusions emerge:

1. The distribution of *dyhtig*, *fær*, *freme* and *gombe* (all except *gombe* with strong synonym support) are evidence of a connection between *Beowulf* and *Genesis A*; *eodor*, *heoru*, *wlenco* and *umbor* (all except *wlenco* with strong synonym support) are evidence of a connection between *Beowulf* and *Maxims I*. Given that poem length plays some role in these patterns, the evidence for the connection with *Maxims I* is stronger than that for the connection with *Genesis A*.

2. The evidence for a connection with *Genesis A* is, however, further strengthened by the distribution of *suhtriga* (*Beo*, *GenA*, *Wid*; synonym support irrelevant) and *missere* (*Beo*, *GenA*, *Exo*; strong synonym support). Further evidence

for a connection between *Beowulf* and *Exodus* is provided by *þengel* (strong synonym support). *Lufen*, *wæfre* (*Beo*, *Dan*) and *bresne* (*GenA*, *Dan*) are perhaps yet more evidence of a connection between *Beowulf* and *Genesis A* and of a connection between these poems and *Daniel*. But the evidence these words provide is weaker: there are no words found only in these three poems, *wæfre* has no real synonym support, and the meaning of *lufen* is debatable. Similarly, although *gnyrn* (*GenA*, Cynewulf) and *geatolic* (*Beo*, Cynewulf) could potentially have occurred in most of the major poems, these two words are, in the absence of any corroborating evidence, insufficient to establish a connection between these three poems.

3. A number of these words are evidence of the conservative diction of these poems. The nature and strength of this evidence varies from word to word:

Suhtriga connects *Genesis A* with an eighth-century (perhaps even earlier) glossary collection, and appears in *Beowulf* and *Widsith* as the first element in a copulative compound, an archaic type of compound which was all but extinct in the Germanic languages during this period. Although the precise significance of *suhtor(ge)fæderen* is debatable, it is thus doubly conservative. On the other hand, the significance of the connection that *suhtriga* establishes between *Genesis A* and eighth-century glossary materials is straightforward: the connection points toward an eighth-century context for this poem and, on the strength of the interconnections established by other shared lexical items of restricted distribution, perhaps for *Beowulf* and *Maxims I* as well.

The loss of the literal meaning of *heoru* in a tradition which has a high demand for this literal meaning indicates that *Beowulf* and *Maxims I* are distinctly more conservative than poems which do not use this word in the primary, literal sense 'sword'. It thus serves as a clear indicator of lexical conservatism.

The cases of *eodor* and *þengel* are similar to that of *heoru*, insofar as they are members of a semantic group which is used very frequently in the poetic corpus. Moreover, these two words also have poetic cognates in Old Icelandic verse, a situation which suggests that they were poetic words of considerable antiquity. Given the great demand throughout Old English verse for words and expressions meaning 'lord, king', the simplest explanation of their absence from other poems is that at some point they disappeared from the poetic vocabulary, and that *Beowulf*, *Exodus* and *Maxims I* are thus more conservative than poems which do not contain these words.

Similarly, given the frequent occurrence of words meaning 'year' throughout the corpus, the presence of *missere* in only *Beowulf*, *Exodus* and *Genesis A* is likewise an indicator of conservatism. *Missere* almost always occurs in a formula, a usage which suggests that if the word was not actually poetic, it was well embedded in the tradition. Its absence from other poems is most easily explained by its disappearance from the tradition at some point after the composition of these three poems.

Although its presence in the same alliterative collocation in both Old English and Old Saxon verse suggests that *gombe* was probably an old poetic word, the lack of synonym support weakens its value as evidence.

What, then, is the significance of the conservative diction of these poems? Although the sheer number of poetic words in *Beowulf* is due, at least in part, to its heroic content, archaic vocabulary also appears in the biblical verse of *Genesis A* and *Exodus*. The heroic poetic vocabulary appears in nearly all Old English poems, regardless of their subject. The density of this vocabulary is lower in some poems than in others, and one might argue that this lower density, due to the non-heroic subject matter of such poems, decreases the chance of archaic words occurring in them. But neither *suhtriga* nor *missere* is heroic, and *eodor* and *þengel* belong to a semantic field, 'lord, king', whose presence is almost universal in Old English verse. Content cannot explain the distribution of these words.

Genre is an equally unsatisfactory explanation. The poems in question belong to a range of genres, including heroic epic, gnomic verse, catalogue verse and biblical history.

It is possible that these poems belong to a local tradition or school of poetry which was more conservative in its diction than other schools, preserving words that otherwise disappeared. But we know nothing of such schools – not even if they existed – and explaining this conservative diction through an unknown is poor methodology.

The most straightforward explanation is that these poems used more conservative diction than other poems because they are older. While it is reasonable to assume that some poems, for whatever reason, may be more conservative than others, it is important to remember that the poetic tradition as a whole is innately conservative. This conservatism is purely functional, preserving only those elements that play a significant role in the tradition; it does not indiscriminately preserve every word that drops out of colloquial speech, even if these words have occasionally been used in verse.

The case of *suhtriga* is a good illustration of the issues involved here. The compound *suhter(ge)fæderen* demonstrates how the use of a word may be due to the conservatism of a particular theme, instead of the age of the poems the word appears in. This word may thus have been preserved long after copulative compounds ceased to be generated and *suhtriga* disappeared from the language. Although the double conservatism of this word – its formation and the initial lexical component – makes such a case unlikely, it is nonetheless plausible. In the case of the simplex *suhtriga*, on the other hand, where the simplex appears only in *Genesis A* and a set of glossary entries dating from the eighth century or earlier, we see a nonpoetic word used in a specific and nontraditional context – the relationship between Abraham and his nephew Lot, characters from biblical history, not from the native tradition. Since neither the status nor the usage of this word marks it as a significant element of the poetic tradition, there is no functional motivation for the tradition to preserve this word after it became obsolete in the colloquial language. The presence of this word in *Genesis A* is thus strong evidence of a link between this poem and the period of the other attested occurrences of *suhtriga*, the eighth century.

Given this link, and the links established among *Genesis A*, *Beowulf*, *Exodus*, *Maxims I* and *Widsith* by the restricted distribution of a small number of words, the most reasonable explanation of the conservative diction found in these poems is that the poems were composed in or around the eighth century. The words examined here would be a remarkably slender foundation if the goal were to establish such a dating on the basis of their evidence alone. But their evidence does contribute to the current debate over the dating of Old English poems. In particular, it is worth noting the correlation between the conclusions reached here and those in R. D. Fulk's *A History of Old English Meter*. Fulk's study of metrical variations in the poetic corpus confirms a chronology presented by Thomas Cable in 1981:[63]

657–80	*Cædmon's Hymn*
735	*Bede's Death Song*
700s	*Leiden Riddle*
700s	*Genesis A*
700s	*Daniel*
–	*Beowulf*
700–800	*Exodus*
800s	*Elene*
800s	*Fates of the Apostles*
800s	*Juliana*
800s	*Andreas*
890–9	*Preface* and *Epilogue*, *Pastoral Care*
897	*Meters of Boethius*
937	*The Battle of Brunanburh*
942	*Capture of the Five Boroughs*
900s	*Judith*
973	*Coronation of Edgar*
991	*The Battle of Maldon*
1066	*Death of Edward*
1110	*Durham*

[63] Fulk, *History*, pp. 60–5. T. Cable, 'Metrical Style as Evidence for the Date of *Beowulf*', *The Dating of Beowulf*, ed. C. Chase (Toronto, 1981), p. 80.

As Fulk observes, the precise ordering of this chronology must not be insisted upon, since his chronological and dialectical criteria are not delicate enough to produce precise distinctions in date or sequence. Fulk's dating has recently been further strengthened by Michael Lapidge, who has recently argued that the patterns of letter confusion in the *Beowulf* manuscript indicate an archetype in 'Anglo-Saxon set minuscule script, written before *c.* 750'.[64]

The words examined here confirm the presence of the chronological connection between *Beowulf* and *Genesis A* seen in this list, and to a lesser extent they also confirm the connection between these poems and *Exodus*, and perhaps *Daniel*, although in this latter case the evidence is not as reliable. The distribution of *suhtriga*, *heoru*, *eodor*, *þengel* and *missere* indicate that these poems are probably early; the restriction of *suhtriga* to *Genesis A* and *Beowulf* (as well as *Widsith*) and to glossaries derived from a seventh- or eighth-century collection indicates an eighth-century date for *Genesis A*, and, by implication, for *Beowulf*, *Maxims I*, *Exodus* and perhaps *Widsith*. In the case of *Maxims I* it is uncertain whether the evidence points toward an eighth-century date for some of the materials in the poem, for the editorial work of an anthologist, or for the poem itself.[65]

APPENDIX

POETIC WORDS FOUND IN ONLY TWO POEMS[66]

Word	Occurrences	Poems
æppled 'like an apple'	3×	Cynewulf (*Elene*, *Juliana*), *Phoenix*
anad 'solitude'	3×	*Guthlac A* (2x), *Riddle 60*
bælc 'pride'	2×	*Genesis A*, *Judith*
bleat 'wretched'	2×	*Beowulf*, *Guthlac B*
bytla 'builder'	3×	*Gifts of Men*, *Guthlac A* (2×)
-dryhtu 'nobleness'	2×	*Seafarer*, *Phoenix*
engu 'narrowness, confinement'	3×	*Genesis A*, *Riddle 3* (2×)
færing 'journey, wandering'	2×	*Riddle 73*, *Widsith*
-felo (*-fælo*) 'harmful'	2×	*Andreas*, *Riddle 23*
-floga 'flier'	6×	*Beowulf* (5×), *Seafarer*
flacor 'flying, flickering'	2×	Cynewulf (*Christ B*), *Guthlac B*
flah 'wily, deceitful, hostile'	2×	*Exodus*, *Whale*
fyren 'pain, violence'	11×	*Beowulf* (10×), *Christ and Satan*
geatolic 'adorned, splendid'	7×	*Beowulf* (5×), Cynewulf (*Elene* 2×)
gifeðe 'fate, lot'	2×	*Andreas*, *Beowulf*

[64] M. Lapidge, 'The Archetype of *Beowulf*, *ASE* 29 (2000), 5–42, at 34.

[65] I wish to thank R. D Fulk for his careful reading of a draft of this article, and for his many useful suggestions.

[66] This list includes only those words which have not been examined in the discussion.

gnyrn 'grief, sin evil'	4×	Cynewulf (*Elene* 3×), *Genesis A*
(-)*grorn* 'sorrow, sadness;	2×	Cynewulf (*Juliana*, *Riming Poem*)
hearding 'bold man, hero'	3×	Cynewulf (*Elene* 2×), *Rune Poem*
(-)*hlence* 'mail, byrnie'	3×	Cynewulf (*Elene*), *Exodus* (2×)
gehleða 'comrade'	2×	Cynewulf (*Elene*), *Riddle 93*
hoðma 'grave'	2×	*Beowulf*, *Christ A*
hwearf 'troop'	2×	*Guthlac A*, *Judith*
-*hyðig* 'having booty'	2×	*Andreas*, *Guthlac B*
lærig 'shield rim'	2×	*Exodus*, *Maldon*
(-)*mæcga* 'man'	2×	*Fates of Men*, *Solomon and Saturn II*
geneah 'sufficiency, abundance'	2×	*Homiletic Fragment I*, *Maxims I*
-*scerwen* '?'	2×	*Andreas*, *Beowulf*
gesiðð 'company, retainers'	3×	*Deor*, *Genesis A* (2×)
swice 'escape'	2×	*Guthlac B*, *Whale*
trym 'step, space'	2×	*Beowulf*, *Maldon*
þroht(-) 'suffering, affliction'	6×	*Andreas* (2×), Cynewulf (*Elene* 2×)
wealic 'woeful, sorrowful'	2×	*Christ and Satan*, *Fates of Men*

The several compilers of Bald's *Leechbook*

RICHARD SCOTT NOKES

The critical history of the Old English charms is replete with examples of scholars claiming that the charms are pagan remnants with a thread-bare Christian garment covering ancient pre-Christian rituals. Other scholars, more interested in combing the charms for magical elements, have viewed them as even more primitive than a pre-Christian religion and have instead treated them as Germanic magic. The first two of three texts found in London, British Library, Royal 12. D. XVII, more commonly known as Bald's *Leechbook*,[1] certainly do not fit this description. In this manuscript, we find medical reference-books produced by a team of compilers, perhaps as part of the intellectual renaissance sponsored by King Alfred. Evidence in the manuscript also suggests that the Anglo-Saxons had considerable access to Latin sources of medical learning and also had a well-developed native medical knowledge.

The above reference to the team of 'compilers' requires explanation of the creation and transmission of Bald's *Leechbook*. As this study will demonstrate, the creation of the *Leechbook* and its subsequent transmission to Royal 12. D. XVII is complex, requiring clear definition of terms. The first stage in the genesis of the text was of compilation. Here the term 'compiler' or 'compilers' will refer to those involved in collecting and organizing the remedies found in the *Leechbook*. The second stage of creation of the text was the copying out of the text. Presumably the compilation of the text involved keeping remedies from various sources on scraps of parchment. Someone had to take those organized scraps and copy them all out in the coherent chapter forms which we see in Bald's *Leechbook*. The person or persons involved in this part of creation are here called the 'writers'. In terms of stylistic features and issues of rhetoric, the voices of the writers are most prominent. The writers may or may not have been the same persons as the compilers, although presumably the two groups overlapped to some degree. The original text was designed to be in two transportable volumes which were intended as a unit. After this original text was created, the two books of Bald's *Leechbook* went through a period of transmission, during which they were separate volumes of a single text. At some

[1] In this study, 'Bald's *Leechbook*' will refer to the first two texts of Royal 12. D. XVII, '*Leechbook III*' will refer to the third book of Royal 12. D. XVII and '*Leechbook*' will refer to all three texts, when discussing them as a whole.

point, the two texts became separated. To some degree their histories of transmission must be considered separately. As Books I and II were transmitted, alterations and corruptions crept into the texts. Some corruptions may have been accidental omissions through eye-skip and other scribal errors, but others were intentional additions of other remedies that had not been included in the original compilation. Other omissions may have been intentional, as the holder of the text discarded a particular remedy as not being efficacious. These people who made changes in the text during transmission, whether the changes were intentional or not, are referred to here as 'redactors'. Finally, the term 'scribe' will be used here to refer only to the person who actually put quill to parchment on the manuscript Royal 12. D. XVII, as well as other incidental hands found in the margins. Books I and II were reunited and *Leechbook* III was tacked on by the scribe of Royal 12. D. XVII.

While some students of the Old English charms have used the study of the material text as their primary approach, to a lesser or greater extent various scholars have described this manuscript in at least a passing manner. Royal 12. D. XVII is described in N. R. Ker's *Catalogue* (1957). While more detail has been uncovered since 1957, Ker's basic description still stands. Ker's description pertains to the entire manuscript, whereas we are only concerned here with Leechbooks I and II, occupying fols. 1–109 of the Royal 12. D. XVII manuscript. The remainder of the manuscript, *Leechbook III*, fols. 109–27, will be treated elsewhere. Ker identifies the manuscript as '[t]hree collections of medical recipes'.[2] He also uses the word 'Recipes' as the titular head of the entry, probably in deference to Oswald Cockayne, who used the word 'recipes' in his own edition. Most recent scholars have avoided that term because of the potential misunderstanding that these books might deal with matters of food preparation.

Ker identifies four hands in the text, three of which are marginal hands. The main text is written in a single hand, which he assigns to the middle of the tenth century (s. x^{med}), although as we shall see subsequent scholars have refined that date. He also dates *nota* signs and some Latin marginalia as having been added around the end of the twelfth and beginning of the thirteenth centuries (s. xii/xiii), as well as an additional 'recipe' added in the eleventh century (s. xi) 'in a poor hand'.[3] The only other hand is a thirteenth-century hand (s. xiii) found on the binding entitling the manuscript 'Medicinale anglic'. Ker also notes that the primary hand of the manuscript is 'a decorative and practised Anglo-Saxon minuscule identical with that of the annals for 925–55 in the Parker Chronicle', and that both the Parker Chronicle and this manuscript were written at Winchester.[4] Ker points out that manuscripts called 'Medicinale

[2] N. R. Ker, *A Catalogue of Manuscripts Containing Anglo-Saxon.* (Oxford, 1957), p. 332.
[3] *Ibid.* [4] *Ibid.* p. 333.

anglicum' are found in the medieval catalogues of both Rochester and Glastonbury, but that no evidence demonstrates that this manuscript is the one referred to in either. As we will see, the evidence found in the *Leechbook* suggests that a wide body of Anglo-Saxon medical knowledge existed, proving Ker correct in being cautious in assuming that references to 'Medicinale anglicum' must refer to this particular manuscript.

In 1955 C. E. Wright produced a facsimile edition of all three *Leechbooks*.[5] The introduction to this edition contains his findings regarding the text. Wright comes to most of the same basic conclusions as Ker about the manuscript, but his exclusive focus allows him to be more detailed. Wright considers this manuscript, along with the *Lacnunga* manuscript (BL, Harley 585) to be 'the two central works for the study of Anglo-Saxon medicine and medico-magic'.[6] Wright assumes that Bald is 'the practitioner for whom the original text of Books I and II was written', because of the colophon and its placement, a view to which I will return.[7] Implicit in this assumption is the further assumption that Bald was a leech 'practitioner'. In trying to determine Cild's role in the creation of the text, Wright looks closely at the reference to him in the colophon on 109r:

> Bald habet hunc librum cild quem conscribere iussit;
> Hic precor assidue cunctis in nomine Xristi.
> Quo nullus tollat hunc librum perfidus a me.
> Nec ui nec furto nec quodam famine falso.
> Cur quia nulla mihi tam cara est optima gaza.
> Quam cari libri quos Xristi gratia comit.

> Bald is the owner of this book, which he ordered Cild to write (compile?);
> earnestly here I beg everyone in the name of Christ
> that no deceitful person should take this book from me,
> neither by force nor by stealth nor by any false statement.
> Why? Because no richest treasure is so dear to me
> As my dear books which the grace of Christ attends.[8]

Focusing on the word 'conscribere', Wright examines the ambiguity in the role of Cild. This word may indicate simply 'to write', or perhaps also 'to put together in writing, to draw up, to compose'. The difference between the two is apparently that between a compiler and a simple scribe. In the end, Wright concludes that Cild was probably only a scribe.[9]

[5] C. E. Wright, *Bald's Leechbook: British Museum Royal Manuscript 12.D.xvii*, EEMF 5 (Copenhagen, 1955). [6] *Ibid.* p. 12. [7] *Ibid.* p. 13.

[8] The translation is from Wright, *Bald's Leechbook*, p. 13.

[9] *Ibid.* p. 13. Here you will note ambiguity in the way Wright thinks of a scribe, compiler and writer.

Wright was also able to make some conclusions based upon the positioning of the colophon in the manuscript. The main text of Book II ends at the bottom of 108v. The colophon is entered at the top of 109r and is immediately followed on the same leaf by the beginning of Book III. The number of lines found on 108v is twenty-two, at variance with the twenty-one line leaves that are standard elsewhere in the book. This deviation is explained by the fact that the bottom line is not a complete line and simply contains the last three words of Book II in an ornamented bracket. Furthermore, fols. 108 and 109 are the conjoint middle leaves of the gathering and no change in handwriting occurs between Books II and III. From this evidence, Wright concluded that the scribe of our extant manuscript (not to be confused with Cild, who was the scribe of an exemplar) had separate copies of both texts. He endeavoured to finish the text of Book II at the bottom of a leaf through the artifice of the bracketed twenty-second line, copied the Book II colophon at the top of 109r, then switched to a new exemplar for Book III. Furthermore, Wright makes the point that the subject matter of Book III is in many ways redundant to Books I and II and therefore likely had a separate genesis.[10]

Manuscript evidence suggests that the compilers of Bald's *Leechbook*, whether among them were Bald and Cild or not, were working as a team of at least two persons. The cooperation of a team of people on a project of this scope implies institutional support of the type one might find King Alfred providing. Therefore, while it is not possible to prove conclusively that the compilers put together Bald's *Leechbook* as part of Alfred's educational and intellectual policies, the sum of the evidence very strongly suggests that Bald's *Leechbook* was produced in the intellectual climate of the Alfredian renaissance, perhaps at the instigation of King Alfred himself. Audrey Meaney has suggested that the original copies of Books I and II were compiled during the reign of Alfred. She went even further and suggested that the original fair copy was also produced during Alfred's reign, by Cild for Bald.[11]

In discussing the production of Bald's *Leechbook*, I have consistently referred to the 'compilers' in the plural, rather than to a singular 'compiler'. Scholars have generally worked under the assumption, arising perhaps from the post-medieval notion of authorship, that the text is the product of a single compiler, often identified as Bald or Cild. Another factor sustaining this assumption is one of the burden of proof; as the text exists, we know that it had to have at least one author, or in this case, compiler and writer. The existence of other compilers and writers is supposition in the absence of evidence.

[10] *Ibid.* p. 14.

[11] A. L. Meaney, 'Variant Versions of Old English Medical Remedies and the Compilation of Bald's *Leechbook*', *ASE* 13 (1984), 235–68, at 236.

Two-fold evidence for other compilers is found in the books themselves. First, the project is one of a wide scope, involving the collecting, translating and organizing of hundreds of remedies from various sources. While such a project is certainly possible for a single man, the time and effort necessary to complete this project would have been immense. Unless we assume that this single compiler was Bald or Cild, we cannot assign a name to the text, despite the months of effort that a single individual would have to have put into it. This lack of a named 'author' is not especially strong evidence (since medieval notions of authorship were quite different from ours and we cannot absolutely rule out Bald or Cild as the compiler), but it is certainly suggestive.

The strongest evidence for a team of compilers and writers comes from an examination of the stylistic features of the person who wrote Book I against the style of the writer of Book II. Each of these texts was written principally by a different person, demonstrating that at least two people had to be involved in writing the remedies out after they had been compiled. Stylistic evidence demonstrates that at least two people, who may or may not have been involved in the compilation process, wrote out the remedies in a clear and organized fashion once they had been assembled. The content of individual charms was frequently composed by someone not involved in the compilation process, since many of these remedies have been copied or translated directly from other sources. The stylistic features of the source texts need not be a problem, however, given that the evidence for different stylistic features in writing comes not in the main text of the remedies, but in the transitional phrases at the beginnings and endings of groups of remedies. The second of the writers often tried to position himself within a broader community of leeches, whereas the first of the two appears uninterested in thus positioning himself.

Scholars have noted some differences between Books I and II, but have not taken those differences to be indicative of more than one mind working on the text. As was mentioned above, Wright noted several differences. The most obvious difference is one of content. Book I deals mostly with external medicine, though as Wright notes, its organization begins to break down after ch. XXX.[12] Book II, on the other hand, deals more with internal afflictions. Wright characterizes Book II as being more 'learned' because it includes 'the recognition of signs of disease and occasional attempts at diagnosis', and also because it contains remedies from Greek and Latin writers.[13] Wright correctly perceives differences between the books, but the attempts at diagnosis may have less to do with how learned the compilers were and more to do with the nature of

12 Wright, *Bald's Leechbook*, p. 14.

13 *Ibid.* p. 15. Very possibly the Greek writers came to the compilers in translated form, either through Latin or Old English.

internal medicine versus external medicine. Very many of the afflictions mentioned in Book I have no need for mention of diagnosis, such as broken bones, animal bites, or open wounds. Book II does, however, have a slightly different orientation in this regard. While we cannot accept Wright's evaluation without the caveat that the diagnoses for external afflictions are often more obvious, his evaluation may have some merit. Perhaps the 'learned' quality of Book II reflects a greater understanding of diagnosis by the compilers, or if not a greater understanding, then at least a greater interest.

Other scholars have also noted some difference between the two books, beyond the difference in types of remedies found therein. Godfrid Storms, who was interested in finding magical elements in the charms, describes the beginning of Book I as having 'little in it connected with magic', but writes that 'from section XLV onwards we find directions against poisons, worms and fevers, three diseases that were supposedly caused by magic'.[14] Here we should note that Wright too found the end of Book I as being qualitatively different from the previous text, though he puts the demarcation line at ch. XXX. As for Book II, Storms notes (as did Wright) that a great part of this book is taken over from the work of Alexander of Tralles.[15] The last three chapters contain subjects other than internal medicine. The table of contents shows that these last three chapters were at one time preceded by six other chapters, now missing, which also dealt with non-internal medical topics.[16] While on the surface Book II appears to be more unified, we see that at one time many chapters were included by later redactors that did not fit the original paradigm of the book as constructed by the original compilers.

These few exceptions aside, most scholars have tended to treat Books I and II as a unit, with Book III as the outsider. This position is justifiable, as Book I and Book II are apparently the two halves of a single project to compile medical knowledge, whereas Book III is a later addition, as evidenced both by the placement of the colophon after the second book and by the repetition of content from Books I and II. Very little has been said about the differences between the first two books. Scholars have noted that one deals with external medicine and the other with internal. Wright, as noted above, has argued that Book II is more learned. Storms finds that Book II uses Alexander of Tralles as its major source, while Book I uses a wider variety of sources.[17] With these

[14] G. Storms, *Anglo-Saxon Magic* (The Hague, 1948), p. 15.

[15] For a greater discussion of the contributions of Alexander of Tralles, see J. F. Payne, *English Medicine in Anglo-Saxon Times* (Oxford, 1904), pp. 102–8.

[16] Perhaps most grievously missed is ch. LX, which dealt with women's complaints, particularly those connected with childbirth. According to the table of contents, this chapter contained forty-one remedies, which scholars interested in Anglo-Saxon women particularly covet.

[17] Storms, *Anglo-Saxon Magic*, pp. 14–16.

three exceptions (Wright, Storms and the internal/external division), scholars have written little about the differences between the two books. Once we examine these two books, we find two primary writers. The first, whom we will call Writer A, wrote most of Book I and seems to have influenced Writer B, who wrote the greater part of Book II. Less significant writers doubtless contributed, but these writers are not assigned a designation because of the impossibility of differentiating among them.

Differences in vocabulary and phrasing occur in the two books because of the different stylistic features favoured by Writer A and Writer B. For example, in Book I, the preferred word to open a section is 'Wiþ', followed by the affliction, for example, 'Wiþ toþece' ('For tooth ache'),[18] or at times preceded by the word 'Læcedomas', as in 'Læcedomas wiþ eagna miste' ('Leechdoms for misty eyes').[19] The majority of chapters in Book I open this way. Of the eighty-eight chapters in Book I, fifty-nine begin with this formula (or a slight variation on it), and only twenty-nine do not. Although two-thirds is certainly a solid majority, the numbers become even more lopsided if we only include the first thirty chapters, which is the approximate demarcation line given by both Wright and Storms as the end of the head-to-toe organizational scheme and therefore likely the beginning of later additions. Of the first thirty chapters, only seven lack the 'Wiþ' opening and of those we find a second formula opening, 'Gif' ('If') followed by the symptoms or affliction, such as 'Gif mon blode hraece' ('If a man vomits blood').[20] Only two of the chapters do not open in this way, chapters I and XVIII. If we examine the entire book for these two opening phrases, only eleven lack the 'Wiþ' or 'Gif' opening, or some variation on the two, or only one-eighth. In the whole of Book I, seven-eighths of all chapters open with one of these two phrases and the vast majority of these chapters open with the 'Wiþ' phrase. Even taking into account the various sources from which these remedies may have been culled, this pattern is overwhelming enough to establish a particular writing and/or translation style for the writer of Book I, our Writer A, particularly of the first thirty chapters of the book.

In Book II, we still find these two formulae, but not to the same degree. Thirty-three of fifty-nine surviving chapters do not begin with either of these formulae. In other words, fewer than half of these chapters open in the way that seven-eighths of the previous book opened. Furthermore, we see in Book II the emergence of another formula that occurs only once in all of Book I, the 'Be' ('Of,' or 'About') formula. In this formula, the word 'Be' is followed by the subject pursued in that chapter, for example, 'Be wambe coþe' ('Of belly sickness', or 'About belly sickness').[21] The only occurrence of this formula in

[18] Royal 12. D. XVII, 113r.
[19] Royal 12. D. XVII, 9v.
[20] Royal 12. D. XVII, 19v.
[21] Royal 12. D. XVII, 66r.

Book I happens in ch. XXXV,[22] in the group of chapters at the end that Wright and Storms both identify as later additions.[23] In Book II, however, it is much more common, occurring ten times at the opening of chapters, or in about one-sixth of extant chapters.

These three different chapter openings – the 'Wiþ' formula, the 'Gif' formula and the 'Be' formula – are significant because semantically they all function in the same way in the text, not just because they are all transitional phrases. In the context of the *Leechbook*, it makes little difference whether a writer writes 'Against an eye ache', 'If a man has an eye ache', or 'About eye aches', The use of any one phrase was simply a matter of stylistic choice. As the text of Bald's *Leechbook* went through the various stages of compilation and writing, at least two different people seem to have had a hand in writing it and both left a mark through their stylistic predilections.

In fact, probably more people than solely Writers A and B worked on the writing of the two books, but any third or fourth member of the team of writers did not have as strong an influence on the text as the two main writers. Furthermore, beyond the primary writers, it frequently becomes impossible to say if an individual writer worked on the text during the initial writing, or perhaps during one of the stages of redaction that Bald's *Leechbook* underwent during its later decades of transmission before becoming attached to Book III. For example, one of the writers of Bald's *Leechbook* had a very conversational presentation, preferring fuller sentences to sentence fragments. Ch. XXI of Book II opens with 'Her sint tacn aheardodre lifre' ('Here are symptoms of hardened liver').[24] Just a few chapters earlier, however, ch. XVIIII begins 'Tacn be aswollenre *and* gepundadre lifre læcedomas wiþ þon, *and* be þære lifre aheardunge', ('Symptoms of swollen and wounded liver, leechdoms against that, and of the hardening of the liver').[25] The writer of ch. XVIIII was more than willing to open the chapter with a sentence fragment, which is then modified by two other fragments.

In this context, then, the 'Her sint' ('Here are')[26] opening of ch. XXI is unnecessary and much more conversational than we usually see in the *Leechbook*. The full sentence that opens this sections is 'Her sint tacn aheardodre lifre ge on þam læppum and heolocum and filmenum' ('Here are the symptoms of a hardened liver, whether on the lobes or the cavities or the membrane'). This entire chapter has a similarly conversational presentation. While some of the chapter is drawn from Alexander of Tralles, other parts of

[22] Royal 12. D. XVII, 30v.

[23] Wright, *Bald's Leechbook*, p. 14; Storms, *Anglo-Saxon Magic*, pp. 14–15.

[24] Royal 12. D. XVII, 76r. [25] Royal 12. D. XVII, 75r. [26] Royal 12. D. XVII, 76r.

it are not,[27] yet the presentation throughout the chapter, regardless of sources for individual passages, remains even, leading to the conclusion that the entire chapter was composed by a single person. Nevertheless, the use of Alexander of Tralles as a source here, as he is used in many other places throughout the book, suggests that the person who wrote this chapter was involved in the composition of the rest of the book as well.

Similarly conversational openings to chapters can be found in chs. XXIII, XXV, XXVIII, XXXII, XLVI and LI.[28] These chapters also tend to have more discussion of issues such as symptoms, prognosis, complications and characterization of the leechdom. My suspicion is that these and similar chapters are the ones that caused Wright to characterize Book II as more 'learned'. Indeed, the writers of Book II[29] often seem to be positioning themselves within a community of leeches, regardless of whether this community was a professional class or merely a part-time occupation for monks. References to leeches and their craft are relatively common in Book II, whereas while they occur in Book I, the writer(s) of Book I emphasize the community of leeches less. In fact, only two chapters in Book I have any mention of leeches other than the assumed practitioner of any charm. The first reference, which occurs twice in ch. XLVII, is to Oxa. The two references tell us nothing about Oxa, except 'Oxa lærde þisne læcedom' ('Oxa taught this leechdom'), a phrase which is repeated verbatim twice in the chapter, apparently in reference to two separate remedies.[30] The only other reference to other leeches and leechcraft is found in ch. LXXII, in a discussion of the times bloodletting is valuable and those times when bloodletting is harmful.

In ch. LXXII of *Leechbook* I, the writer goes to great lengths to validate his remedy through vague references to other leeches. For example, the writer claims that 'Læcas lærdon þa þe wisoste wæron *þæt* nan man on þam monþe ne drenc ne drunce no ahwær his lichoman wanige butan his nydþearf waere' ('The leeches that were wisest taught that in that month no man should drink a drink nor weaken his body anywhere unless he needs to').[31] The writer does not tell us exactly who these wisest leeches are, nor is it clear that he knows exactly who they are. The importance of the mention of the leeches in the chapter appears to be on using the authority of other leeches to lend confidence that the principles laid out are accurate. Two other times in this same

[27] T. O. Cockayne, *Leechdoms, Wortcunning and Startcraft of Early England, Being a Collection of Documents, for the Most Part Never Before Printed, Illustrating the History of Science in this Country Before the Norman Conquest.* 3 vols. Rolls Series (repr., London, 1961), p. 204.

[28] Royal 12. D. XVII, 78v, 81r, 83v, 87r, 96v and 99r, respectively.

[29] By 'writers' I mean Writer B, along with other minor writers.

[30] Royal 12. D. XVII, 45v.

[31] Royal 12. D. XVII, 55r.

chapter we again find the writer of the remedy appealing to other leeches for authority, writing, 'Eac secgeaþ læcas' ('Also leeches say. . .') and 'læcas læraþ eac' ('leeches teach also. . .').[32] Again, unlike the references to other leeches such as Oxa and Dun elsewhere, we do not get any sense that the writer is referring to a specific leech. Rather, he seems to be positioning himself within the community of leeches.

Both of these references to other leeches occur late in Book I, after the organizational format has broken down. Indeed, ch. LXXII is almost certainly a later addition, as whoever added it later also added the reference to it in the table of contents.[33] Therefore, we cannot be certain that these references to Oxa and Dun were added by the original team of compilers. Ch. LXXII was definitely not added by the original team. While we must note that these two references occur in Book I, we can see that they are the exception rather than the rule and were not likely part of the original compilation. Writer A of Book I did not resort to the rhetorical strategy of gaining legitimacy from other unnamed leeches, the strategy we see carried out here by the writers of these sections.

Book II, on the other hand, has many more such references. Interestingly, while these references do not appear frequently in the early chapters of the book, a small number can be found there and do not appear to be later additions as with Book I. The references found in Book II are not necessarily the rhetoric of reassurance as in Book I, though sometimes they may function this way. For example, ch. XV of Book II ends with the phrase, 'swa læcas cunnon' ('as leeches know').[34] This phrase may be to reassure the reader that the medical advice provided is not solely from the imagination of the compiler, but the presentation of it here sounds more as if it is intended to reaffirm that the writer is a leech, or at least is knowledgeable about them. In Chapter XXVIII, we read of a remedy that '*þæt* is suþerne læcedom' ('that is a southern leechdom'),[35] with the writer appearing to be simply giving the remedy a proper context.

We do see a value judgement in ch. XXXI, but instead of functioning as a way of borrowing legitimacy from other leeches as the writers do in the references in Book I, the rhetoric here is to put the writer among the ranks of leeches considered wise. In reference to a particular set of symptoms, the writer states that 'Wenaþ unwise læcas *þæt þæt* sie lenden adl oþþe milte wærc, ac hit ne biþ swa' ('Unwise leeches think that it is loin disease or spleen pain, but it is not so').[36] Besides showing a relatively sophisticated level of diagnosis (knowing where misdiagnosis is likely), the writer here appears to think of himself as a wise leech and also to know of other leeches who are less wise.

[32] Royal 12. D. XVII, 55r.
[33] Royal 12. D. XVII. See below, p. 65, for details.
[34] Royal 12. D. XVII, 72r.
[35] Royal 12. D. XVII, 84r.
[36] Royal 12. D. XVII, 86v–87r.

Regardless of whether or not the writer of Book II is more learned as Wright suggested, he certainly thinks so of himself.

Of course, these references are not the only ones relating to the origins of remedies found in Book II. Both the remedies that were sent by Elias of Jerusalem to King Alfred and the remedies attributed to Dun are found in Book II. The rhetorical functions and positioning within the manuscript of these references are all important in demonstrating that the stylistic features and the presentation of the manuscript change from Book I and Book II and that the changes in style cannot be attributed only to different sources for the compilers, or to the input of later redactors who altered the original compilation.

At this point, it would be tempting to argue for a separate genesis of the two texts. After all, they are organized under separate tables of contents and, as I have demonstrated here, were primarily composed by at least two different writers. Perhaps we might argue that the texts were entirely separate until Bald ordered Cild to copy them into the same book. Under scrutiny, however, this scenario is untenable. First, as we have discussed above, the two books have exactly the same structure. Secondly, despite occasional overlap in sources, the two books keep within their respective boundaries of external and internal medicine through the great bulk of chapters (with the exception of later alterations), anticipating that the other subject would be covered in the other book. Thirdly, unlike Book III, no remedies appear in both books, which is a remarkable coincidence if we consider the breadth and scope of these two books and the frequency of repeated remedies in other extant manuscripts and marginalia. Finally, the tables of contents for both of the books are set out in the same way and also appear to be in the same essential style as each other, suggesting that the Writer A of Book I was also in part the writer of the table of contents for Book II.

The tables of contents for these books have undergone some minor alteration in the course of their transmissions, but if we ignore these minor alterations, we see the essential stylistic features of Writer A. Naturally, as with a modern table of contents, the style is very bare-bones. The entry for each chapter begins with the roman numeral for that chapter, then is followed by a short description of the contents of the chapter. These descriptions can be either brief or detailed and occasionally list the number of remedies to be found within the chapter. At the beginning of these descriptions, the initial is larger and bolder, though not very elaborately executed. The end of each chapter listed in the table is followed by a punctuation marking. Each chapter-listing, therefore, has three redundant cues separating it from the previous and subsequent chapter listings, namely the roman numeral, the large initial and the final punctuation. Some chapter-headings are missing one of these elements, usually the roman numeral or the final punctuation, but as these two elements both occur very close to the edge of the leaf, in most cases they simply appear to have been cropped off. Therefore, the lack of one of these elements is probably insignificant. We have enough evidence from the other two markers that we can be very certain of where each chapter-listing begins in the table of contents and where each ends.

As was mentioned above, a single scribal hand copied the text of all three books in the extant manuscript (with the exception of some marginalia). This hand also wrote out the initials as he wrote out the text, before proofreading, as is evidenced by errors that he made in enumeration. For chs. XIV and XV, for example, he accidentally left off the roman numeral, then continued the numbering at ch. XVI, which he mislabelled 'XIIII', off by two because of the two previous unnumbered chapters. He apparently continued with his error up to ch. XVIIII, then noticed his error. Ch. XIX was originally listed as 'XVII'. The error was noticed and corrected with 'II' written in superscript over the line in the same hand. These two minims could not be placed next to the first two because they were already too close to the initial letter, indicating that the initial had already been placed there.

The medieval practice of writing roman numerals was slightly different from the modern practice. This difference is what allows us to see the sequence of error and correction by the scribe. The primary difference comes in the modern practice of writing four 'IV' and nine 'IX'. The medieval practice was to write four as 'IIII' and nine as 'VIIII'. Therefore, when the scribe reached ch. XX, he wrote it as we would, by this time picking up his previous error and returning to the correct numbering. If seventeen or nineteen had been written in the modern way, XVII and XIX respectively, the scribe would have had to make a far more drastic correction, eliminating the V somehow, probably resorting to erasure.[37] Under the medieval system, however, the scribe had only to add two minims to the end, changing 'XVII' to 'XVIIII'. As it was, he only emended the listing for ch. XVIIII and left chs. XIIII and XV unmarked, while XVI–XVIII were left unchanged. Regardless of the reason for this lack of emendation, through omission the scribe has left evidence that he wrote out the initials and descriptions of the contents before he wrote in the roman numerals, rather than by leaving a space and filling in the initials later, as was a common practice for manuscripts with more elaborate initials.

The attentions of the scribe, however, do not demonstrate that the tables of

[37] Another possible error is for a lazy 'v' to be improperly connected at the bottom, thereby appearing to the scribe as two minims, or 'ii'. In this particular case, however, that error is not in evidence. If the scribe had made this error for 'xviiii', then the result would have been the nonsensical 'xiiiiii'. If the scribe had misread his own handwriting and read his previous entry of 'xiiii' as 'xvii', then then following entry should have read 'xviii', rather than 'xv', as it does.

contents for the two books were actually composed in part by the same writer. They do demonstrate that the tables of contents were already established in the texts before our scribe ever took up pen. We do, however, see the signs of Writer A in the sparing and efficient descriptions of the contents. As with the main body of the text of Book I, the writer of the tables of contents prefers to open the description of the contents with the phrase 'Læcedomas wiþ' ('Leechdoms against') followed by the affliction. Again, occasionally the phrase 'Læcedomas gif' ('Leechdoms if') crops up. All of the contents listed in Book I contain one of these two formulae, or slight variations on them. Only four exceptions to this rule occur. All of these occur after the important ending of ch. XXX and so may have been emendations, though the differences are not so great as to make this conclusion very solid. Ch. LXXII, however, is certainly an emendation. As was discussed above, ch. LXXII is particularly odd and conversational. The entry for this chapter is no different, containing a long description that is so rambling that Cockayne felt compelled to give it two paragraphs in his edition, the only chapter in either Books I or II for which he did so. The table of contents for Book I also was written by the same person who wrote the main text of the book.

Book II is a little more complicated, for it contains strong evidence of Writer B in addition to Writer A. The earliest listings all show the very strong influence of Writer A, but eventually the stylistic features of Writer B begin to creep in. For example, the listing in the table of contents for ch. II begins, 'Læcedomas wiþ magan sare' ('Leechdomas against a sore stomach'),[38] which is the kind of listing we would expect from Writer A. The main text of the chapter opens with 'Wiþ sarum *and* aþundenu*m* magan' ('Against a sore and swollen stomach') and the contents of the chapter are sparse and efficiently laid out.[39] As the book progresses, however, we see this style established by Writer A fading out, replaced by these newer stylistic features. From the very beginning of the table of contents the influence of Writer A is strong, but not complete, as we find the 'Læcedomas be' construct occurring from the third chapter-listing in the table of contents for Book II, which while it is not a wide deviation from the stylistic features of Writer A, it is deviation.

The penchant of Writer B to use other, unnamed leeches as validation for his teachings begins to show in the entry for ch. XVIII. In the table of contents listing for this chapter, the entry is 'Læcas læraþ þisne læcedom wiþ lifre spyle *and* aþundenesse' ('Leeches teach this leechdom for the swelling and bloating of the liver').[40] This entry is especially significant because in the chapter itself no mention of other leeches occurs, demonstrating that while Writer A may have had a hand in compiling the table of contents for Book II,

[38] Royal 12. D. XVII, 58v. [39] Royal 12. D. XVII, 66v. [40] Royal 12. D. XVII, 59v.

at least some of the listings were composed by Writer B. The listings for the following two chapters, XIX and XX, both are short, but both also contain references to other leeches that are not found in their respective chapters. These chapter listings read 'Læceas secgeaþ þas tacn be aswollenre *and* gewundadre lifre' ('Leeches tell these symptoms of a swollen and wounded liver') and 'Læcas læraþ þis wiþ þære lifre wunde . . .' ('Leeches teach this for the liver wound. . .').[41] Certainly this section of the table of contents was written by Writer B.

We can therefore begin to discern a picture of these two main writers by examining their rhetorical styles. Of the two, Writer A influenced Writer B far more than the reverse. It may be that Writer B was simply trying to copy the style of Book I, or it may be that Writer A was also involved, to a lesser degree, in the writing of Book II. Since the two books were part of the same project, perhaps both writers were also on the team of compilers. More than two writers may have contributed to this project, but evidence of a third of fourth writer is so faint as to be lost in the background noise of the later alterations. We cannot possibly know for certain if these two main writers were members of a larger team of compilers, or if they were the only two compilers working on this project. Given the scope of the project, I suspect a greater number than two compilers, though likely only two wrote the original books. The greater influence of Writer A on Writer B implies a power relationship, suggesting that Writer B was somehow subordinate to Writer A. This relationship meshes nicely with what we know of the relationship between Cild and Bald. The colophon at the end clearly marks out a relationship in which Bald is the superior and Cild is the subordinate. We plausibly could identify Writer A as Bald and Writer B as Cild. While it would be nice to wrap this issue up into a neat little package and state firmly that we can identify the original compilers and writers of the *Leechbook*, such confidence would be misplaced. Given the murky transmission of the *Leechbook* to the scribe of Royal 12. D. XVII, Bald's and Cild's involvement with the *Leechbook* might have begun decades after the original compilation.

Many decades of transmission of these texts, which were intended to be used as reference works and so presumably found themselves in use whenever anyone was sick or injured, allowed for emendation. The emendation of the text is evident in two ways. The first way, which we have already discussed to some degree, is the difference in stylistic features between the primary writers[42] and the redactors. The second category of evidence is errors that crept into the tables of contents when people added or removed remedies to the main text of the books, whether intentionally or accidentally, but failed to adjust the table of contents accordingly.

[41] Royal 12. D. XVII, 59v.

[42] I.e., Writer A and Writer B.

Determining which differences are emendations based upon rhetorical style can be a complicated undertaking, since rhetorical style is subjective and one does not wish to detract from the work of the original compilers and writers of the text. Beyond looking at the transitional phrases at the beginnings and ends of chapters, the identification of a later emendation relies upon the redactor having had very poor editorial skills, or having been uninterested in editing a remedy to make it fit into the book. As often as not, the contents of a remedy, whether from the original compilation of Bald's *Leechbook* or from a later addition, come from a known source, such as Alexander of Tralles. Much of the rhetorical style may stem from the source text, not from the person who later added it to the *Leechbook*. Furthermore, the attempt to determine whether particular remedies were part of the original composition is even more difficult than determining that the original texts had two main writers. In determining the primary writers of the text, we were able to look for broad trends in rhetorical style and confirm our judgments based upon the frequency of use of particular rhetorical structures. When looking for emendations, we are looking for obvious exceptions to the broad stylistic trends.

We must therefore be careful of the conclusions we draw about emendations based upon rhetorical style. Except in a few cases in which the entry is wildly different from anything else found in the book, or in cases in which internal and external medicines were put into the wrong book, we cannot prove that a particular remedy was not part of the original compilation. We can demonstrate, however, through a preponderance of evidence that emendation of the *Leechbook* did occur during its transmission, even if we are often uncertain about the origins of a specific remedy. As is so common in medieval manuscripts, we find most of the suspected emendations near the end of their respective books.

As was mentioned above, one chapter of Book I is so radically different from the other chapters as to leave little doubt that it was a later addition. Ch. LXXII, regarding the times of month beneficial for bleeding, must have been added later. In the table of contents, the listing is so long that in Cockayne's edition he felt obligated to divide it into two paragraphs, the only table of contents entry in either book that he treated this way. The scribe of Royal 12. D. XVII also felt this way, having begun a new line without finishing the previous one, thus approximating the modern paragraph. The surrounding listings take up no more than two or three manuscript lines, while this listing takes up fifteen manuscript lines, the most to be found in Book I.

While other remedies may be additions, ch. LXXII is the only one that certainly is. Nevertheless, several strong suspects emerge. Chs. XXXVIII and XXXIX both open in the conversational style eschewed by the writer of Book I. Ch. XXXVIII opens with the words 'Her sindon dolh sealfa to eallu*m* wundum *and* drencas *and* clænsunga on gehwilce wisan ge utan ge on þa*m* innoþum' ('Here are wound salves for all wounds and drinks and cleansings (purgatives?) of all kinds, whether outward or inward').[43] Besides the words 'Her sindon', ('Here are'), which are unnecessary, the subject matter of this chapter seems to be rather inexplicably broad. Other chapters focus on a specific part of the body and, of course, the book as a whole deals with external medicine, rather than internal. Part of the peculiarity of this chapter may be that by focussing on 'ge utan ge on þa*m* innoþum' ('either outward or inward')[44] problems, it cannot be properly placed into the larger design of the *Leechbook*. Ch. XXXIX, while also opening in this conversational way with the words 'Her sint læcedomas' ('Here are leechdoms'),[45] focuses on a particular ailment at least, with an emphasis on the leg, suggesting perhaps that chs. XXXVIII and XXXIX were added by the same person, but not from the same source. Both chapters are quite long, indicating perhaps that each once existed independently of any of the other remedies.

Chs. LXII–LXV have very strong Christian mystical elements. The first half of ch. LXII is not unusual, but thereafter most of the remedies have Christian mystical symbols as components. The use of Latin becomes much more frequent here, as well as crosses and gibberish, perhaps the remains of some garbled Greek. Furthermore, two of the remedies found herein make reference to St Veronica, suggesting that the source materials had some sort of emphasis on St Veronica.[46] The content of this section tends to deal more with supernatural afflictions and remedies than in the rest of Book I. Ch. LXIII is for 'feond seocum men' ('fiend-sick men', that is, the demon-possessed)[47] and chapter LXIV is 'Læcedomas wiþ ælcre leodrunan *and* ælfsidenne' ('Leechdoms for any sorcery and elvish influence').[48] While the belief in such things is compatible with the rest of the *Leechbook* , their appearance here is singularly odd, as elsewhere in the text illness tends to be attributed to natural rather than supernatural influence. Most of the *Leechbook* does not enter into the supernatural causes of influence and works from the unstated assumption that the practitioner's role is to deal with the natural, leaving the supernatural to priests or monks. Even with the internal medicine of Book II such things are attributed to worms or imbalance in the humours.

Book II has no chapter that is so plainly an emendation as the bloodletting chapter in Book I. Nevertheless, certain remedies seem peculiarly placed and

[43] Royal 12. D. XVII, 34v. [44] Royal 12. D. XVII, 34v. [45] Royal 12. D. XVII, 37v.

[46] According to tradition, Veronica wiped the face of Jesus as he went to Calvary. The cloth that Veronica used is known as the 'Veil of Veronica', a relic that is still preserved in Rome. Although the Veil should be a unique item, it is possible that the use of Veronica's name was in part an attempt to create a personal relic. [47] Royal 12. D. XVII, 51v.

[48] Royal 12. D. XVII, 5r.

are suspicious. For example, ch. LXVI begins a section on 'sidan sare' ('sore sides') that continues for several chapters, ending with ch. L. Cockayne attributes much of this section to Alexander of Tralles. These four chapters stretch from 96v–99r. While they are not especially long, neither are they single paragraphs. Ch. L, the last in this sequence before Book II turns to lung disorders, reads in full, 'Eft wiþ sidan sare betonican leaf geseoþ on ele *and* gebryte alege on þa sidan' ('Again for sore sides, soak betony leaves in oil and crush *them*, lay on the side').[49] This very short remedy does not seem to merit its own chapter, suggesting that it was a later addition.

We also see the return of charms in ch. LXV. The placement of this chapter is important, because it comes immediately following the chapter which includes the remedies sent by Patriach Elias to Alfred, which itself immediately follows the large, multi-chapter lacuna. We have some indication of the contents of the missing chapters from the table of contents and they do not appear to have been remarkable in any way. Each appears to cover one part of the body and ailment in the same way earlier chapters do. Beginning with ch. LXV, however, we once again see the focus return to supernatural causes, involving the writing of 'Benedicite om*ni*a opera d*omi*ni d*omi*n*u*m' on a knife.[50] As with the suspect section in Book I, this chapter appears out of sorts with the whole of Book II, as if it were added later. Later in this same chapter is our reference to Dun, the only reference to an Anglo-Saxon physician in this book. In the next section of this chapter is a remedy that calls for making crosses on the head of someone with a 'færlice yfele pyrce' ('sudden evil pain'),[51] along with a drink that works 'wiþ feondes costungum yflum' ('against the devil's evil temptations').[52] The next section of this chapter contains a drink 'to þon ilcan' ('for the same') which involves singing masses over ground frankincense and myrrh around Christmas (likely a reference to the gifts of the magi) as well as during the feasts of SS Stephen and John.[53] This remedy is a remarkable bit of preventative medicine, in that the writer claims that it will protect against all dangerous illnesses for twelve months. The final section of this chapter also contains a remedy against an elf.

Ch. LXV of Book II is in content very different from the rest of Bald's *Leechbook*, reading more like something out of the *Lacnunga*, or perhaps *Leechbook III*. After it, only two chapters remain in the book. Ch. LXVI is about the properties of the agate stone. While the ability of stones to affect cures is testified in several places throughout Book II, this chapter is the only place in which a stone is given its very own chapter. The eight virtues listed here for the stone are not strictly medical either. They also include the ability to prevent

[49] Royal 12. D. XVII, 99r. [50] Royal 12. D. XVII, 106r. [51] Royal 12. D. XVII, 107r.
[52] Royal 12. D. XVII, 107v. [53] Royal 12. D. XVII, 107v.

being struck by lightning, to prevent fiends from entering your house, to reveal what is hidden and to prevent magical attacks. The final chapter of the book, ch. LXVII, is not about remedies or charms at all. It is essentially a conversion chart for weights and measures, which, while it may indirectly aid with assembling ingredients for cures, seems very out of place here.

Therefore, when we look at the evidence found in these final chapters of Book II, not one of them seems to fit here. In fact, the last chapter that seems to be in the proper place is the remainder of ch. LXIV – the remedies given to Alfred by Patriarch Elias. Most likely, then, the last chapter of the original composition was the Alfred the Great chapter and subsequent chapters were added later. The extant content of this Alfred the Great chapter appears to have much in common with the additional chapters, such as cures requiring putting crosses on the body and the use of stones to prevent lightning-strikes. When we examine the description in the table of contents, however, we see that the focus is on the medical remedies. Furthermore, the writer of the table of contents characterizes the use of the white stone[54] as being for 'eallu*m* uncuþu*m* brocu*m*' ('all strange afflictions'),[55] as if he too thought that what was contained in ch. LXIV was a little odd, but he felt compelled to include it nonetheless because of its provenance.

In addition to the rhetorical evidence for emendation, as well as the inclusion of odd remedies near the ends of both books, Book I and Book II each have remedies in them that belong to the other book. Occasionally internal afflictions appear in Book I and external afflictions in Book II. We must be careful, however, about what we consider as 'internal' and 'external' medicine. From the context of the *Leechbook* we find that anything with an externally visible symptom, such as vomiting, sometimes seems to have been considered the domain of external medicine. For example, Book I, ch. XIX, contains remedies against nausea, which is an obvious external symptom of what may perhaps be a less obvious internal ailment. Ch. X of Book II , however, also contains a remedy for nausea. At times the two categories seem to have been conflated.

Despite this confusion about what is internal and what is external, we do have a few cases in which the remedy is in the wrong book. Book I, ch. XLVIII, contains 'læcedomas wiþ þam wyrmu*m* þe innan eglaþ monnum, *and* wiþ þyrmum þe on cilda innoþe beoþ *and* wiþ cilda innoþ sare' ('leechdoms against the worms which inwardly trouble men, and against worms that are inwards in children, and against children's inner soreness').[56] The repetition of the words 'innan' and 'innoþe' drives home the point that these remedies are for internal

[54] Cockayne identifies the 'white stone' as *lapis Alabastrites.*

[55] Royal 12. D. XVII, 105v.

[56] Royal 12. D. XVII, 4v.

ailments. In fact, this word is the same as that used at the opening of Book II, which reads 'þas læcedomas belimpaþ to eallum *innoþa* mettrymnessum' ('These leechdoms concern all internal infirmities') (emphasis mine).[57] Clearly the writer of this particular entry in the table of contents realized that the remedy pertained to internal rather than external medicine, but included it in Book I anyway. This unselfconscious inclusion suggests that the remedy may have been a later addition, made either by someone who did not understand the different topics of the two books, or by someone who only had access to Book I. In either case, the person who made the additions was not likely involved in the initial compilation.

Book II also has a few questionable entries. One example is ch. LVII. This chapter contains 'Læcedomas wiþ þearmes utgange *and* gif men bilyhte sie ymb þone þearm *and* wiþ [bæc] þearmes utgange nigon wisan' ('Leechdoms against the guts going out and if boils are on a man around the guts, and against the guts going back. Nine methods').[58] Exactly what this disorder is supposed to be is unclear. The word 'þearm' can mean either 'guts' or 'entrails', not a very specific word. As this chapter is one of those lost in the lacuna, we must rely solely upon the description in the table of contents for information. Although we may not be certain exactly what affliction is in question, the evidence that it should have been considered an external ailment is strong. First, we have the repetition of the word 'utgange' ('outgoing') here, which certainly appears to refer to an external symptom. Secondly, we have the occurrence of boils or carbuncles around the guts. Again, boils or carbuncles are mainly external symptoms and should probably be included in Book I, along with other such ailments found in Book I as cysts.

These few entries are not the only ones that seem to have been placed incorrectly and may be the result of later additions, but they are representative of a larger group. This situation causes problems in trying to assess the transmission of these documents. Both books are certainly part of the same project. Moreover, we find the rhetorical fingerprints of the same men in both books. If we have a hypothetical team that compiled these books and we assume that the entire team understood the basic format of the project, then presumably all of the charms added by that team were placed in their proper context, whether they were part of the original compilation or not. Therefore, all these odds and ends uncharacteristic of the *Leechbook* would be found near the end of the book. Book I, however, seems to be more affected by later emendations than Book II (with the exception of the large lacuna missing from Book II). If the two books were originally compiled as part of the same codex, later additions would have to appear near the end of Book II, not Book I. These two

[57] Royal 12. D. XVII, 58v. [58] Royal 12. D. XVII, 63v.

books, while being part of the same project and originally produced by the same team, apparently have a different history of transmission down to their eventual conflation in Bald. At some point the two books were separated. People either without knowledge or access to the other book made changes, explaining why remedies seem improperly placed. Book I appears to have had a much more active life than Book II, given the number of uncharacteristic remedies found in the last chapters.

The likely reason for keeping the two books in separate codices is implied in the very organization of the project. Why separate external and internal afflictions, instead of simply organizing one comprehensive text in the top-down, outward–inward fashion? The *Leechbook* is intended to be a working reference book and might often have to be taken out to where a sick or injured person lay. Therefore, the book would have had to be portable. To make a larger codex, with one table of contents and the collected and conflated text of Books I and II, would have created an unwieldy codex. The manuscript Royal 12. D. XVII, which contains both books of Bald's *Leechbook* as well as *Leechbook III*, is quite large and would have been difficult to carry around. The manuscript that comes down to us today does not seem to have been intended to travel frequently. The original compilation, on the other hand, was intended to be portable. To this end, it was purposefully divided into two shorter books at the time of composition.

Even though we know that the *Leechbook* underwent emendation, we cannot simply search the end of each book for uncharacteristic remedies. Some of the emendations in the *Leechbook* were carefully intertwined with the original text, making them virtually impossible to extract. The redactor apparently saw that a new remedy could fit into an existing chapter, then tried to place it there. The most likely method for inclusion of new remedies would have been simply to write them in the margins of the leaf, then seamlessly include them in the main text when transcribing it later. In fact, we have an example of such marginalia on the upper-right hand side of 49r, where a later hand has included a remedy 'Wiþ þa blacan blegene' ('Against the black boils') at the end of ch. LVIII, Book I, which contains remedies for 'wen' ('tumors'), not an unreasonable place to include this remedy. Presumably, if a later scribe copied Royal 12. D. XVII, the subsequent version could have included this marginal remedy as part of the main text. In fact, in Cockayne's edition we have a modern example of this phenomenon, as Cockayne has added the remedy to the end of his chapter as if it were part of the main text of the original. On the Old English side of his parallel edition he puts the remedy between brackets and adds in a footnote "In the margin, in a different and later hand', while on the modern English side he leaves the brackets unexplained. In fact, Cockayne goes so far as to number the remedy '4', as if it were the fourth in a sequence in the section. If this treatment is what Cockayne, a modern scholar producing a diplomatic edition, provides, then we can imagine that no notation would have occurred in any manuscript copy produced by a medieval scribe.

Our evidence for these nearly seamless additions goes beyond simple supposition surrounding a single marginal entry in the extant manuscript. The evidence lies in errors found in the numbers of remedies listed both in the tables of contents and in the body of the chapters themselves. In some cases the errors are small and might be deemed simply the result of a less-than-perfect arithmetic prowess. In a few other cases, however, arguing for mathematical error stretches the numbers past plausibility. Some chapters have a discrepancy of as many as ten remedies different from the number listed in the table of contents and the actual number. Rather than suggesting that our team of compilers was composed of men with wildly poor skills in counting, the evidence points to alteration to the text after the table of contents had been completed. Later redactors were less careful about making certain that the number of remedies listed coincided with the new number after a marginal remedy was added, or one had been left out, either by accident or because it had been found useless.

The list of numbers of remedies given in the table of contents, numbers listed in the various chapters and actual numbers occurring can be found in Tables 1 and 2 (below), Table 1 covering Book I of the *Leechbook* and Table 2 covering Book 2. Many chapters have no number listed in either the table of contents or the opening of the chapter itself and therefore these chapters have been omitted for the sake of simplicity. Also omitted are chapters in which the number of remedies is implied by the use of the singular in the table of contents, because the compilers often appear to use the singular to describe a particular remedy in the chapter, rather than to give an accounting of the actual number of remedies. For example, the table of contents listing for Book I, ch. VII, reads, 'Læcedom gif mon blod hræce' ('Leechdom if a man vomits blood').[59] In fact ch. VII contains only one remedy. Ch. XII, however, demonstrates the unreliability of the singular as an indicator of actual number, in that it reads, 'Læcedom wiþ w[ouu]m muþ *and* wiþ ceolan swyle. Þry læcedomas' ('Leechdom against irritated mouth and against swollen throat. Three leechdoms').[60] This entry appears contradictory, in that the singular implies that only one remedy is to be found in this chapter, but then it clearly states that three remedies do in fact appear. When we examine the actual occurrence of remedies in the chapter, we find that three remedies do occur. The first is a single remedy for an irritated mouth and the second two are for a swollen throat. The implication of the table of contents is that the singular only applies to the one

[59] Royal 12. D. XVII, 1v. [60] Royal 12. D. XVII, 1v–2r.

remedy for an irritated mouth and does not imply a particular number for remedies for a swollen throat. The text is ambiguous, however, in that it could be read as meaning that only one remedy occurs and that this remedy cures both irritated mouth and swollen throat. Therefore, in order to avoid erring by assuming the count of one remedy when the singular is meant to be categorical rather than exhaustive, I have only included numbers in Table 1 and Table 2 for chapters that have an explicit statement of the number of remedies found therein.

Furthermore, the standards for counting remedies can be rather subjective. For example, at times a drink might be followed by a salve. Sometimes the writer is vague about whether the drink and salve are two different stages of the same cure, or are supposed to be completely independent of one another. While textual clues can exist, unambiguous textual clues are usually absent. I have therefore adopted a standard for counting remedies that assumes a very faithful and careful transmission of the text. Wherever it is possible to arrive at a figure in agreement with that found in either the table of contents or the beginning of the chapter, I have counted in a fashion to try to arrive as close to that figure as possible. In many cases this approach may be too conservative, but as a general principle we should assume the competence of the compilers. Other scholars counting remedies in the same chapters may come up with figures differing from mine. Nevertheless, despite this very conservative approach, enough evidence presents itself that we can safely conclude that the books, particularly Book I, underwent alterations during transmission which are impossible to distinguish from the original.

For example, Book I, ch. III, has no number listed in its entry in the table of contents, but the text of the chapter itself opens, 'Læcedomas wiþ eallu*m* earena sare *and* ece *and* wiþ earena adeafunge, *and* gif wyrmas on earan synd oþþe earwicga, *and* gif earan dynien, *and* earsealfa fiftyne cræftas' ('Leechdoms against all ear soreness and ache and against deafness of the ears, and if worms are earwigs are in the ears, and if the ears ring, and ear salves. Fifteen methods').[61] In this case, we do not have Writer A including the number in the table of contents, although in other instances the number occurs in both the table of contents and the openings of chapters.[62] When we count the actual number of remedies given in this particular chapter, however, the number is no smaller than twenty-five. At one time this chapter had at least ten fewer remedies in it than exist in our extant manuscript. We have no textual evidence to show from where these extra entries came. The most likely answer is that

[61] Royal 12. D. XVII, 14v.

[62] This marks another notable stylistic trait of Writer A. Book II has no references to the numbers of remedies in the body of a chapter itself. While Book I has some such references, they are mostly confined to the first thirty chapters and so are likely the product of Writer A.

the additional ten remedies were added later, after the initial composition of the chapter. The redactors were not careful to correct the number found at the beginning of the chapter. One other plausible answer is that in an earlier version of the text, the number was actually recorded as twenty-five, but one of the roman numeral tens was not copied and 'XXV' became 'XV'. This plausible solution is unlikely, however, for three reasons. First, the number twenty-five is the closest I could make the number of remedies match the number listed. I suspect the actual number was closer to twenty-eight. Second, in the extant manuscript, the number is written out as 'fiftyne' rather than in roman numerals, indicating that it was more likely written out in the exemplar of the manuscript as well. Finally, this gap between the number listed and the number actually occurring is part of a recurrent pattern, suggesting that whatever caused it, it was not a single incident of scribal error. From the evidence found here we can justifiably assume that the chapter has nearly doubled in length from its original form.

Book II also has similar errors likely resulting from later additions to the book, but two chapters in particular stand out. In these chapters, a number of remedies is listed in the table of contents, but in the actual chapter no remedies occur whatsoever. Chs. XXXI and XXXVI are both peculiar in this way. At the end of the entry in the table of contents for each is a statement of how many 'wisa' ('directions') and 'cræftas' ('methods'[63]), asserting that the chapters contain four and eight respectively.[64] In both cases, however, while the subject matter of the chapters is listed correctly, neither has any remedies found within. Rather, each deals with the symptoms and diagnosis of its designated ailment. The focus on symptoms is common in Book II and would not occasion remark if not for the mysterious phrases 'feower wisa' and 'eahta cræftas'. While possibly both chapters lost their endings during transmission, I think this scenario unlikely, since each chapter appears complete in its current state. More likely the original compilers decided to count methods of diagnosis in these chapters, but the way they used to discern one method from the next is unclear. Unlike the other chapters in which a discrepancy occurs, in these two chapters the reason is probably not error from transmission.

As the above discussion demonstrates, reconstructing what the original team of compilers did, in what context they did it, is not easy. Decades of transmission and redaction make it even more difficult. We can, however, discern some details through the murk. First, the contents of Bald's *Leechbook* are unusually authoritative. Rather than being the object of popular folklore, perhaps tacitly permitted by the church, these two books are the product of official efforts in

[63] This translation is mostly from context. Cræftas is a very general type of word, with a variety of meanings, such as talent, ability, might, courage, or trade.

[64] Royal 12. D. XVII, 60v–61r.

both church and state. The court of King Alfred the Great was involved either directly or indirectly in the compilation of the original text. Furthermore, some of the remedies in the end of Book I were transmitted to Wessex from the patriarch of Jerusalem. In a sense they have international approval. More than any other surviving charm text, Bald's *Leechbook* is an authorized, official text.

From the text we also see emerging a portrait of a body of professional leeches. While we only have two names for certain, Oxa and Dun, with one name in question, that of Bald, this text assures us that such people existed. If the contents of Bald's *Leechbook* are any indication, they were given to systematically cataloguing their knowledge for future use. These leeches were interested in the practical, in what works. Even in the more theoretical Book II we find mostly discussions of symptoms and how to vary treatments according to symptoms. Regardless of whether or not modern science deems these cures efficacious, the Anglo-Saxon leech believed that they were and organized them accordingly. The leeches gleaned their cures from any source that they could find, classical or contemporary. Rather than being secretive practitioners of hedge magic or herbal lore, trying to stay out of view of the church, these Anglo-Saxon leeches operated openly and with the collusion of the church. Very likely, some leeches may have been monks themselves. Bald's *Leechbook* is itself a practical book, each volume compact enough to be portable, with leeches feeling free to add and omit remedies as they saw fit throughout the transmission of the text.

In the broad scheme of 'charms', then, nothing comes as close to the modern usage of 'remedy' as the contents of Bald's *Leechbook* . The conclusions drawn by some scholars from sources such as marginal charms and the contents of the *Lacnunga* cannot be applied with validity to Bald's *Leechbook*. The remedies found within are organized and authorized. As we will see from the contents of Book III, also in Royal 12. D. XVII, not every extant text of Anglo-Saxon charms can make this same claim.

Chapter	Table of Contents	Body of Text	Actual Number
III	no listing	15	25
IV	no listing	14	18
V	3	no listing	3
VIII	4	no listing	5
IX	10	no listing	7
XII	3	no listing	3
XV	11	no listing	10
XVI	4	no listing	4
XVII	5	no listing	5
XIX	2	no listing	2
XX	3	no listing	3
XXI	6	no listing	6
XXII	4	no listing	4
XXIII	3	no listing	3
XXV	4	no listing	4
XXVI	4	no listing	4
XXVII	6	no listing	6
XXVIII	3	no listing	3
XXIX	3	no listing	3
XXXI	28	no listing	28
XXXII	15	15	15
XXXIII	8	no listing	8
XXXVII	14	no listing	15
XXXVIII	34	no listing	34
XXXIX	28	28	31
XL	6	no listing	6
XLI	3	no listing	5
XLIV	4	no listing	4
XLV	20	no listing	19
XLVI	5	no listing	6
XLVII	12	no listing	12
XLVIII	12	no listing	13
L	6	no listing	6
LII	2	no listing	2
LIII	2	no listing	2
LIX	3	no listing	3
LX	8	no listing	8
LXI	14	no listing	14
LXII	10	no listing	10
LXIII	6	no listing	4
LXIV	7	no listing	6
LXV	5	no listing	3
LXVII	3	no listing	3
LXVIII	6	no listing	6
LXIX	7	no listing	7

Fig. 1 Deviation in numbers of remedies listed in Book I

Chapter	Table of Contents	Body of Text	Actual Number
II	10	no listing	10
VI	4	no listing	4
VII	6	no listing	5
VIII	4	no listing	4
XXIV	13	no listing	14
XXX	16	no listing	22
XXXI	4	no listing	symptoms
XXXII	12	no listing	12
XXXIII	13	no listing	12
XXXIV	9	no listing	9
XXXVI	8	no listing	symptoms
XXXIX	10	no listing	10
XLI	3	no listing	5
LI	21	no listing	21
LII	20	no listing	17
LIII	8	no listing	7
LVI	75	lacuna	lacuna
LVII	9	lacuna	lacuna
LVIII	20	lacuna	lacuna
LIX	21	lacuna	lacuna
LX	41	lacuna	lacuna
LXI	3	lacuna	lacuna

Fig. 2 Deviation in numbers of remedies in Book II

Ælfric and late Old English verse

THOMAS A. BREDEHOFT

In his discussion of the formal structures characteristic of Ælfric's 'rhythmical prose' style, John C. Pope prints the following passage from Ælfric's homily on Cuthbert, calling attention especially to the pointing, given as it appears in Cambridge, University Library, Gg. 3. 28 (?Cerne, s. x/xi):

Ac an ðære fugela. eft fleogende com.
ymbe ðry dagas. þearle dreorig.
fleah to his foton. friðes biddende.
þæt he on ðam lande. lybban moste.
symle unscæððig. and his gefera samod.[1]

Although Pope's edition of the supplementary homilies was published in 1967, his comment on the remarkable nature of this passage's 'almost continuous half-line pointing' must call to more recent readers' minds the tradition of metrical pointing which Katherine O'Brien O'Keeffe has so ably described in Old English poetic texts.[2] O'Brien O'Keeffe's study concludes that eleventh-century scribal practice involved the pointing of both a-lines and b-lines of verse (as here), while tenth-century scribes frequently pointed only the b-line.[3] Her further comment that 'it is to the late tenth century that we should look for the development of new visual information in the writing of Old English

1 'But one of the birds came flying about three days after, utterly sad; it flew to his feet, asking for peace, that he and his companion might always live innocent together in that land' (*Homilies of Ælfric: a Supplementary Collection*, ed. J. C. Pope, 2 vols., EETS os 259–60 (London, 1967–8) I, 114; low points substituted for Pope's medial points). All translations from Old English are my own.

2 *Ibid.* I, 114. Cf. K. O'Brien O'Keeffe, *Visible Song: Transitional Literacy in Old English Verse*, CSASE 4 (Cambridge, 1990). Similar 'half-line' pointing occurs in other Ælfric manuscripts, as well as examples of b-line pointing. S. M. Kuhn, 'Was Ælfric a Poet?', *PQ* 52 (1973), 643–62, lists the following manuscripts as featuring full-line or half-line pointing with at least some regularity: London, British Library, Cotton Julius E. vii (s. xi^{in}; the base manuscript for *Ælfric's Lives of Saints*, ed. W. W. Skeat, 4 vols. in 2, EETS os 76, 82, 94 and 114 (London, 1881–1900, repr. 1966)); London, British Library, Cotton Vitellius C. v (s. x/xi); Cambridge, Trinity College B. 15. 34 (Canterbury CC, s. xi^{med}) and Cambridge, Corpus Christi College 178 (s. xi^{1}). The metrical effect of such pointing was recognized by Skeat: 'I have divided the matter into lines as well as I could, usually following the guidance of the points introduced into the MS. itself; these usually occur at the end of what is meant to be a line, and frequently also at the pause in the middle' (*Ælfric's Lives of Saints*, ed. Skeat, II, li).

3 O'Brien O'Keeffe, *Visible Song*, p. 137.

verse' seems especially relevant in the current context.[4] CUL Gg. 3. 28 dates from just around 1000, and if we could expand the relevant search to include Ælfric, we would seem to have precisely the manuscript evidence that O'Brien O'Keeffe suggests that we seek.

Of course, in modern times, Ælfric's characteristic style has often and insistently been identified as a prose style, emphatically not verse, even though at least eight of the ten 'half-lines' in the passage quoted above would scan perfectly well according to most theories of Old English metre.[5] It will be my contention in this article that the common designation of Ælfric's style as 'rhythmical prose' is, in fact, essentially incorrect, and that his compositions in this style are better identified as verse. The difference in how we describe such texts is an important one, I think, for if we conclude that Ælfric was writing verse, our understanding of the corpus of Old English verse would necessarily be transformed. While our aesthetic appreciation of Ælfric's works might not be much altered by the change in how we identify his form,[6] our understanding of the breadth, scope and extent of the Old English verse tradition would demand extensive reconsideration. What we call Ælfric's compositions, then, clearly makes a difference, and it is important to make every effort to get it right.[7]

In formulating the question of the generic identity of Ælfric's rhythmical works as a choice between 'prose' and 'verse', I realize that I am running against the tide of a recent critical trend that prefers to identify Ælfric's rhyth-

4 *Ibid.*

5 The final half-line is metrically acceptable, but it has problematic alliteration on the final stress, and the second half-line might be interpreted either as a Sieversian E-verse with anacrusis (and thus probably unmetrical for most descriptions of Old English metre) or as a B-verse, in which case it would be formally acceptable to most metricists, although involving a violation of Kuhn's first law. If the manuscript point were after 'eft' (rather than before) we could relineate to eliminate the breach of Kuhn's law, but it seems best to follow the pointing here. The rest of the verses in this brief passage offer no metrical difficulties.

6 That is, Ælfric's rhythmical prose is already appreciated for its rhythm (of course), and his use of alliteration in this style is widely recognized as contributory to the effect of these compositions. Since rhythm and alliteration are also commonly understood as the primary features of Old English verse, a change in how we identify the genre of Ælfric's works would not seem radically to alter the bases of our appreciation of his style. Nevertheless, I will suggest below that, at least on occasion, Ælfric uses secondary formal devices (such as cross alliteration) which seem to favour a reading of these texts as verse. Other formal features generally associated with Old English verse (such as diction, formulaic expression, and so on) will be further discussed below.

7 What we call Ælfric's compositions, of course, is significant, but I believe our taxonomies ought to at least attempt to reflect Anglo-Saxon understandings of form. If Anglo-Saxons (including Ælfric) may have understood the 'rhythmical prose' form as a verse form, it would be both anachronistic and misleading to label it as prose of any variety. The question of what we call these texts, then, is intimately dependent upon an assessment of how Anglo-Saxons might have understood them.

mical compositions as – quite literally – occupying some sort of middle ground between the two genres. 'Rhythmical prose', of course, is the most common term for this third entity, but Norman Blake's 'rhythmical alliteration' also has adherents, especially as it includes a somewhat broad spectrum of forms that seem to fall between unambiguous examples of verse and 'normal' prose. Faced with the problem of understanding the development of Layamon's verse form, in fact, a number of critics have found this middle ground to be a more plausible origin for Layamon's metre than 'classical' Old English verse.[8] The implied historical development – from classical Old English verse, to rhythmical prose or rhythmical alliteration, to rhyming and alliterating early Middle English verse – has nevertheless remained troublesome, both because of the suggested verse–prose–verse sequence and because of the difficulty of deriving Layamon's frequent use of rhyme from Ælfric's almost purely alliterative style.

By offering an argument for identifying Ælfric's rhythmical works as verse, however, I believe I can ameliorate both difficulties: a progression from classical Old English verse to late Old English verse (including Ælfric) to Layamon's form obviously allows us to see all of the relevant changes as evolutions in verse form. Further, if we see Ælfric as a late poet who happened to favour alliteration over rhyme (a stylistic choice that other late poets did not always make), we would be able to derive Layamon's use of rhyme from the practice of other late poets. Indeed, the possibility that Ælfric's vast preference for alliteration was idiosyncratic opens the door for a straightforward origin for Layamon's rhyme in the general use of rhyme in late Old English verse.[9]

[8] Perhaps the most cogent articulation of 'rhythmical alliteration' as the origin of Layamon's verse form is that of S. K. Brehe, '"Rhythmical Alliteration": Ælfric's Prose and the Origins of Laȝamon's Meter', *The Text and Traditions of Laȝamon's* Brut, ed. F. Le Saux, *Arthurian Studies* 33 (1994), 65–87. Brehe's detailed analysis of similarities between Ælfric and Layamon is telling; he suggests 'If we recognize Ælfric's rhythmical form as the source of the Middle English loose meter, we will find it easier to explain the enormous differences between the loose meter and Old English classical verse' (*ibid.* p. 78). Other scholars have also either noted such similarities or suggested the importance of Ælfric for understanding Layamon, notably T. Cable, *The English Alliterative Tradition* (Philadelphia, 1991) and A. McIntosh, 'Early Middle English Alliterative Verse', *Middle English Alliterative Poetry and its Literary Background*, ed. D. Lawton (Cambridge, 1992), pp. 20–33. Taking an opposing position, D. Moffat, 'The Intonational Basis of Layamon's Verse', *Prosody and Poetics in the Early Middle Ages: Essays in Honour of C. B. Hieatt*, ed. M. J. Toswell (Toronto, 1995), pp. 133–46, uses an argument based in intonation patterns, deciding 'I cannot agree with Norman Blake, who regards the *Brut* as a regularized, poeticized outgrowth of rhythmical prose of the Ælfrician sort' (*ibid.* p. 142).

[9] C. V. Friedlander, 'Early Middle English Accentual Verse', *MP* 76 (1979), 219–30, traces Layamon's use of rhyme to a tradition extending back at least to the *Chronicle*'s poetic entry in annal 1036CD, but appears to draw no clear distinction between the late Old English examples and the early Middle English texts. Nevertheless, Friedlander's essay finds some of the same vernacular sources for Layamon's rhyme as I propose here.

Traditionally, the single greatest obstacle to identifying Ælfric's rhythmical compositions as verse has been a scholarly inability to identify any clear metrical system that might describe them.[10] Other features (most frequently diction, syntax and tone) are sometimes invoked for distinguishing these works from classical Old English verse, but they seem to be subordinate to the metrical differences, in most accounts.[11] Certainly, however, despite the familiar feel of a passage such as that quoted above, it is quite clear that Ælfric's 'rhythmical prose' works in general cannot be accounted for within a Sieversian metrical system.[12] The conventional conclusion that Ælfric was not writing verse at all,

[10] One recent attempt at describing Ælfric's form concludes with the following descriptive comment: 'A half-line of rhythmical prose is a syntactic constituent containing at least five syllables and exactly two stresses' (Cable, *Alliterative Tradition*, p. 47). While there is an obvious degree of descriptive validity to such a formulation (if we accept in advance the limitation of two stresses in our scansions), it is equally obvious that such a formulation seems only poorly related to the operative principles behind Ælfric's forms. Yet Cable's formalism is perhaps the most precise description of Ælfric's 'rhythmical prose' yet offered, and it is easy to see how the lack of a clear metrical description has contributed to the continuing identification of Ælfric's style as a prose style.

[11] The comments of two scholars will have to serve as representative here. The first is S. K. Brehe, '"Rhythmical Alliteration"', p. 67: 'And what of other aspects of the classical Old English meter that vanished after the Conquest – strict alliterative patterning, enjambment, kennings, traditional themes like the beasts of battle, and others? Linguistic change cannot explain their disappearance'. Here, Brehe certainly begins with a consideration of meter (alliterative patterning), but the other poetic features he lists are not 'aspects of Old English meter' at all, having rather to do with style, diction, and content. While the classical Old English verse tradition did seem to share stylistic and other features, they are features of Old English poetics, not Old English metre; Brehe's line of reasoning here should be read as rhetorical, designed to discount the possibility of a direct metrical evolution by labelling all sorts of poetic differences as metrical differences. That is, by subsuming all sorts of poetic differences under the broader category of 'metrical differences' Brehe here attempts to strengthen his argument for metrical discontinuity. Likewise, Pope's comment about such other features is illuminating: the rhythmical style '[differs] markedly in the character and range of its rhythms as in strictness of alliterative practice, and [is] altogether distinct in diction, rhetoric, and tone' (*Homilies of Ælfric: a Supplementary Collection*, ed. J. C. Pope I, 105). Here, the 'metrical' differences of rhythm and alliteration are clearly foregrounded as the crucial differences, leaving the other differences as secondary; Pope's immediately following comment that 'It [that is, the rhythmical prose] is better regarded as a mildly ornamental, rhythmically ordered prose than as a debased, pedestrian poetry' (*ibid.* I, 105) certainly suggests that Pope's vision of the choice between labelling this style as poetry or prose is as deeply influenced by value judgements as by taxonomic precision. It seems likely that for Pope (as well as for others), the additional distinguishing criteria of diction, tone, rhetoric and so forth serve to support the conclusions drawn on the basis of metre, rather than standing as truly independent criteria; if the situation were reversed and Ælfric's metre were classical, I strongly doubt that these other criteria would be invoked to suggest that the works were prose.

[12] The 'Sieversian' perspective I have in mind is that which is based in the work of Eduard Sievers, especially as elaborated and refined in A. Bliss, *The Metre of Beowulf*, rev. ed. (Oxford, 1967). It might, therefore, be useful to describe it as a 'Sievers–Bliss' perspective, but I will use the simpler term here.

however, does not necessarily follow, as he may have been composing within a different metrical tradition, employing different metrical rules. The failure to have identified any such rules does not preclude their existence.[13]

The key to understanding the basic principles of Ælfric's form lies in a transformation in Old English metrical practice which can probably be dated to the mid-tenth century. As I have argued in the context of the non-canonical *Chronicle* poems (those not included in the ASPR), at least some poets in the second half of the tenth century began composing verse that made no use of resolution, an essential feature both of Sieversian analysis and of the poems on which that analysis is based.[14] As I will discuss in more detail below, the tenth-century changes also included relaxation (or alteration) of rules regarding metrical stress-levels and anacrusis; it seems likely that all of these changes were interrelated, and when taken together, they can be used to define a variety of Old English metrical practice quite different from the 'classical' Old English verse that we see in *Beowulf*, for example. This later type of poetry is the 'late Old English verse' of my article's title.

Beyond the non-canonical *Chronicle* poetry, however, the corpus of late Old English verse is more extensive than critics and metricists have apparently realized, including the whole of *The Metrical Psalms*, many of the Metrical Charms, *The Judgment Day II,* and a number of other poems.[15] The inclusion of the

13 P. Szarmach, 'Abbot Ælfric's Rhythmical Prose and the Computer Age', *New Approaches to Editing Old English Verse*, ed. S. L. Keefer and K. O'Brien O'Keeffe (Cambridge, 1998), pp. 95–108, has recently (and usefully) summarized the responses of textual editors and others to the problem of how to visually present Ælfric's texts in modern editions. He cites a telling opinion from Bruce Mitchell's *Old English Syntax* that may recall Pope's logic as quoted above in n. 11: 'To me, Ælfric's alliterative prose is good prose, not bad poetry . . . I do not agree with [Pope's] decision to print this prose in verse lines' (B. Mitchell, *Old English Syntax*, 2 vols. (Oxford, 1985) II, 998), quoted in Szarmach, 'Abbot Ælfric's Rhythmical Prose', p. 103, with Szarmach's ellipsis). Again, underlying the comments of Mitchell and Pope is the unstated assumption that, since Ælfric's works do not match up well to Sieverisan metrics, the choice in identifying their form is one between 'bad poetry' and 'good prose'. An alternative to a Sievers-based formalism will allow a third choice: 'non-Sieversian poetry'.

14 See my discussion of the *Chronicle* poems in T. A. Bredehoft, *Textual Histories: Readings in the Anglo-Saxon Chronicle* (Toronto, 2001), esp. pp. 91–9. There, I outline some of the distinguishing features of late Old English verse, although without attempting as complete an account as in the present essay.

15 Although it is not always easy to determine if a poem belongs to the late Old English verse system or not, I believe the following poems should be considered as late Old English verse: *The Metrical Psalms*; *Metrical Charms* 2, 4, 5, 6, 7, 9, 10, 11 and 12; the *Chronicle* poems in annals 959DE, 975DE, 975D, 979DE, 1011CDE, 1036CD, 1057D, 1067D, 1075D(1076E), 1086E and 1104E; *The Judgment Day II*; *The Battle of Maldon*; *Instructions for Christians*; *An Exhortation to Christian Living*; *A Summons to Prayer*; *Durham* and the Sutton Brooch inscription. Together, these poems total over 6,000 lines of verse; such a corpus is surely large enough to support the metrical analysis I undertake in this essay, especially since so much work on classical Old English metre uses a corpus of lines half this size: the poem of *Beowulf*. The general neglect

Psalms, Charms, and many of these other poems in the ASPR attests to a widespread (and widely-accepted) recognition of their generic identity as verse, and it is to these poems that I will turn in identifying the basic features of the late Old English verse form. In itself, such a metrical account has long been a *desideratum* of Old English studies. But I shall also suggest that Ælfric's rhythmical compositions can be described in precisely the same terms, and that an insistence that Ælfric was working exclusively in prose can hardly be sustained in the face of evidence that he shared a metrical system with the poets responsible for these other works.

THE METRE OF LATE OLD ENGLISH VERSE

Any account of Old English metre must make use of some descriptive formalism, and it is my suspicion that late Old English verse has not been well understood (at least in part) because of a too-heavy scholarly reliance upon the formalism of Sievers and his followers. In this and following sections, I will base my own descriptive practice on that of Geoffrey Russom.[16] Russom's

of these poems by metricists can be indicated by the fact that, of these poems, B. R. Hutcheson, *Old English Poetic Metre* (Cambridge, 1995), includes only *Maldon* and *Durham* in his analytical corpus, which is thus almost exclusively a corpus of classical Old English verse. Unless otherwise indicated, verses and poetic passages are cited by line numbers only from G. P. Krapp and E. V. K. Dobbie, *The Anglo-Saxon Poetic Records*, 6 vols. (New York, 1931–53); in citations of specific verses, abbreviated titles for poems will follow those set out in B. Mitchell, C. Ball and A. Cameron, 'Short Titles of Old English Texts', *ASE* 4 (1975), 207–22.

16 Cf. G. Russom, *Old English Meter and Linguistic Theory* (Cambridge, 1987). In brief, Russom argues that Old English verses were composed as combinations of two metrical feet, each of which followed the stress pattern of a single Old English word. Thus there were unstressed feet (symbolized as x, xx), singly-stressed feet (S, Sx, Sxx) and compound-stressed feet (Ss, Ssx, Sxs, Sxxs), which combined to form the following basic verse types:

Sieversian type and scansion		Corresponding Russom-type scansion
A3	xx/x	xx/Sx
A:	/x /x	Sx/Sx
B:	x/ x/	x/Sxs
C:	x/ /x	x/Ssx
D:	/ / \x	S/Ssx
D4:	/ / x \	S/Sxs
E:	/ \ x /	Ssx/S

For Russom, additional constraints apply, governing the placement of extrametrical (unstressed) words and elements (in general, allowed before either foot), allowing Russom's formalism to describe virtually all of the familiar specific verse-types of the classical Old English tradition, as well as accounting for much of what Bliss describes in his theory of the caesura. Russom's formalism thus offers a valuable insight into the underlying logic which results in the descriptive applicability of Sievers–Bliss formalism. In this respect, Russom's formalism seems more intuitively useful as a description of Old English metre than other formalisms.

formalism, I have found, is flexible enough to accommodate the changes necessary for describing late Old English verse; further, it can in some cases more accurately predict non-metrical types than Sieversian formalism can, even in *Beowulf* and other poems in the same metre. To take just one example, Russom's system can explain why, in *Beowulf*, verses of the form *Sxxx/Sx are not allowed when the Sxxx portion is filled by a single word: this formalism excludes Sxxx as a normal foot.[17] Neither Sievers nor Bliss offers any compelling argument for the non-occurrence of such forms in *Beowulf*, and in this matter at least, the newer system is distinctly superior. As will be seen, precisely such forms are crucial in identifying the features of late Old English verse, and the use of a descriptive system derived from Russom's has benefits outweighing its comparative unfamiliarity.

In the following paragraphs, I will discuss the major differences between what I will call 'classical' Old English verse (that is, verse which still makes use of resolution) and late Old English verse. Examples will generally be drawn from poems which are either clearly late in date (such as *Maldon*, the *Chronicle* poems and *Durham*) or from others which can clearly be shown to make use of late verse forms (such as *The Metrical Psalms*, the Metrical Charms and *The Judgment Day II*).

Lack of Resolution

Saying that resolution was not functional in late Old English verse is equivalent to saying that late verse made no meaningful distinctions between stressed syllables based on their length. Two types of evidence can immediately be brought forth to test the accuracy of a claim that resolution is non-functional in late verse: cases where short stressed syllables appear in positions where classical metre allowed only long syllables and (conversely) cases where long stressed syllables occur in positions previously open only to short syllables.

Examples of the first sort occur (although rarely) even in *Beowulf* (for example, line 262a: 'Wæs min fæder'), but with somewhat more frequency in late poems:

PPs 54.16 3a: and bodie
PPs 55.5 3a: and wiðer me
PPs 73.11 3b: efenmidre

Other, similar examples can also be found, but such verses might be explained (in classical terms) on the basis that resolution is blocked in them by a four-position rule. Such an explanation, however, cannot account for the following

[17] To be precise, 'Sxxx' words are excluded in *Beowulf*'s normal verses but four-position compounds like 'middangearde' are allowed, either as full-verse compounds or in hypermetric verses (but not, I believe, at the beginning of hypermetric verses; cf. *Beowulf* 2996a).

verses, in which long stressed syllables appear in positions where resolved sequences would be required in 'classical' verse:

PPs 72.5 1b: ungemete swyþe	Sxxx/Sx
Dur 17b: and he his lara wel genom	xx/(x)Sxxxs
JDay II 102b: ungerydre sæ	Sxsx/S

I have placed tentative 'late Old English verse' scansions to the right of each verse here for clarity's sake.[18] All three of these verses, of course, would be unmetrical in classical Old English poetry. In each verse it is the long (four- or five-position) foot which would cause difficulty in the classical system; each of the long feet in these verses corresponds to an acceptable classical foot (Sxx, Sxxs and Ssx) where the initial S-position (in classical verse, optionally filled by a resolved sequence) has been replaced by Sx. In other words, such verses are, in fact, precisely what we should expect to see in a system in which resolution does not apply. Further examples will be given below, but these verses should be sufficient to suggest the plausibility of the succeeding analysis.

Metrical Stress and Subordination

Late Old English verse seems to have made use of only two levels of metrically-significant stress, not three, as were employed in classical verse. That is, where classical verse had feet with two stressed positions with differing stress-levels (in Russom's account: Ss, Ssx, Sxs and Sxxs), late Old English verse made distinctions only between stressed and unstressed metrical positions. In practice, this change in metrical stress-assignment rules amounted to a virtually complete dissociation of acceptable verse-feet from the stress-patterns of existing words and compounds. Such a dissociation, of course, represents a radical change, since (in Russom's formulation), a link between word-stress patterns and metrical patterns was the very basis of classical metre. But the evidence for the use of only two metrically-significant stress levels in late verse is twofold. First, there is a clear tenth-century decline in the use of verse-types with three stress levels. But further, it seems clear that the late verse system allowed alliteration to fall in positions where it was excluded in classical verse, including on the second elements of compounds. Each type of evidence, and its relation to the issue of stress levels in late verse, demands at least a brief discussion.

The dissociation of word-level stress patterns and patterns of metrical stress

18 Below, I will offer more precise scansions for such verses, including there the probability that both 'ungemete' and 'ungerydre' should probably be scanned with two stressed positions; in both cases the relevant a-lines indicate vocalic alliteration, and thus I scan primary stress on the 'un-' prefix. Note, however, that regardless of how we scan these words, the four-position initial foot was disallowed by classical verse, as I indicated above.

appears to be directly related to the frequently observed decline in the numbers of Sieversian C, D and E types found in datable late poems.[19] C, D and E verses are precisely those that (in Russom's formalism) have feet with both primary and secondary stresses; such feet are paradigmatically filled by compound words. The use of compounds in classical verse, then, both authorized and (in a sense) generated these types, but compounds no longer played any definitive role in metrical verse structures once the conceptual equation between two-stress feet and compound words failed to hold. To put it another way, there was no longer any metrical impetus for poetic compounding in late Old English verse, since the principles of the verse form made no reference to compound-like stress structures.[20]

While the decline in types C, D and E can be understood as the result of a dissociation of word-stress and metrical stress patterns, the most direct evidence for the claim that late verse made use of only two stress levels rests on changes in alliteration patterns, which had formerly relied upon subordination of all rightward elements within the verse.[21] Such subordination, in Russom's account, explains why left-most elements of verses and compounds take alliteration. In late verse, however, the 'subordinated' elements of compounds may alliterate, if only occasionally:

Mald 242a: scyldburh tobrocen	alliteration on 'b'
DAlf 18a: to Eligbyrig	alliteration on 'b'
PPs 88.29 1a: Gif hi mine rihtwisnessa	alliteration on 'w'

Such examples certainly suggest a shift in the rules for where primary alliteration can occur, but the simplest account of such verses seems to be to interpret these compounds as having two stressed positions of equal metrical weight. We should, perhaps, scan such verses as follows:

19 Note Thomas Cable's comment on the decline in types C, D and E (all with secondary stress): 'After the mid-tenth century, there is a significant drop in the percentage of lines with three levels of ictus' (T. Cable, 'Metrical Style as Evidence for the Date of *Beowulf*', *The Dating of 'Beowulf'*, ed. C. Chase (Toronto1981), pp. 77–82, at 80). To this degree, Cable's analysis and my own are in complete agreement here, although I associate the decreased usage of 'compound-like' verse-types with the transition to 'late Old English verse'.

20 The signficance of this shift is played out most compellingly in the realm of diction: classical Old English verse used (and, indeed, needed) a complex and traditional compound-oriented poetic diction, resulting in the familiar poetic register shared by most classical compositions. The metrical use of poetic compounds, of course, kept otherwise archaic words and forms current (within poetry) long past the time when they were otherwise being used. Late Old English verse, by contrast, needed no such archaic compounding techniques, resulting in its simpler diction, which is frequently interpreted by modern commentators as comparatively prosaic. Once again, the interpretative choice between 'verselike' and 'prosaic' is a false dichotomy, one which has had crucial consequences for the proper identification and appreciation of late Old English verse.

21 See Russom, *Linguistic Theory*, esp. pp. 67–82.

Mald 242a: scyldburh tobrocen	SS/(x)Sx
DAlf 18a: to Eligbyrig	x/SxSx
PPs 88.29 1a: Gif hi mine rihtwisnessa	xx/(xx)SSxx

With such scansions, we can see that alliteration must still fall on a stressed syllable, but the position of that syllable is not determined by the rules of word- or compound-like subordination, which (in each case) would demand that the alliterating syllable should be the left-most S-position.

It is worth noting, of course, that alliteration is even more frequently delayed in verses without compounds; in the following examples the alliteration also fails to fall on the first stressed position:

PPs 118.71 3a: þin soðfæst weorc[22]	alliteration on 'w'
PPs 88.29b: fracoðe gewemmað	alliteration on 'w'
Mald 298a: Þurstanes sunu	alliteration on 's'
MCharm2 31a: Wyrm com snican	alliteration on 's'

Russom's argument that the alliteration rules in classical verse were derived from the rules of stress assignment (where alliteration, like word stress, was attracted to the leftmost element of a structure, while rightward elements were subordinated) cannot be used to explain these sorts of alliteration. Rather, it seems likely that simply the presence or absence of stress was the key criterion for whether an element could alliterate; once all the stresses in a verse became conceptually equal, alliteration was allowed to fall on any stress, even the last stressed element in a line.[23] What both types of evidence suggest, I believe, is that metrical subordination no longer worked in late verse as it had in classical verse; rather than having metrical verses be patterned on the juxtaposition of two word-stress patterns, late verses were defined by patterns of stressed and unstressed syllables. In short, secondary elements of compounds (which, linguistically, had secondary stress) were treated in the metre as either stressed or unstressed, since there was no longer an intermediate position.

Given the reduction to two metrically-signficant stress levels (and the use of unresolved forms) we can see that the four relevant classical feet would result in late feet of the following forms:

[22] Note that this verse, which has the second element of a compound in the 'dip' of a verse corresponding to a classical B-type, also supports the notion that relevant stress levels were reduced to two. The secondary element of the compound must be scanned with either full stress or no stress, and the placement of the compound in this position thus causes no problems in late Old English verse, although it was somewhat unusual in classical verse. See Russom's account of a similar verse, *Beowulf* 501b (Russom, *Linguistic Theory*, p. 35). Similar verses with the second elements of compounds in the 'dip' of B-type verses are quite common in *The Metrical Psalms*.

[23] Note in particular the innovative alliteration patterns described below, p. 92, n. 39 and p. 93, n. 41.

Classical foot	Corresponding late feet
Ss	SS, SxS, SSx, SxSx
Ssx	SSx, SxSx, SSxx, SxSxx
Sxs	SxS, SxxS, SxSx, SxxSx
Sxxs	SxxS, SxxxS, SxxSx, SxxxSx

As this chart indicates, the number of available metrical feet has greatly increased in the late verse; six new foot-forms appear in the right-hand column (SxSx, SSxx, SxSxx, SxxSx, SxxxS and SxxxSx), and a seventh (Sxxx) was also authorized as a descendant of the classical Sxx foot. It is this increase in available feet that gives late Old English verse such a different feel from most classical Old English poems.

Relaxed Constraints on Anacrusis

Classical B and C verses gave rise to late verses which formally mirrored classical A verses with anacrusis, as seen in the following comparisons:

Classical form	Corresponding late form
xx/Sxs	xx/SxSx
xx/Ssx	xx/SxSx

The difference between (xx)Sx/Sx and xx/SxSx may have been difficult for late poets and audiences to attend to, and since three, four, or even five unstressed syllables were not unusual at the start of classical B and C verses, the constraint on anacrusis to two syllables no longer seems to have had any force in the late verse tradition. Presumably as a result of this sort of metrical overlap, we find syllables in anacrusis in late Old English verse in a variety of contexts not allowed in the classical tradition.[24] A rule for extrametrical elements in late verse that would include so-called anacrusis might be articulated as follows: unstressed (extrametrical) syllables may precede any foot.

The Form of Late Old English Verses

Taken together, these three metrical changes (regarding resolution, stress-levels and anacrusis) obviously amounted to a radical and extensive revision to the classical Old English metrical system. We can schematize the resulting metrical system as follows, where metrical late verses are still (as in the classical verse

[24] The 'frequent use of anacrusis' (*The Battle of Maldon*, ed. E. V. Gordon (London, 1937), p. 29) is often cited as one of the late features of *Maldon*; see also R. D. Fulk's comments on the frequency and variety of this feature in *Maldon* (R. D. Fulk, *A History of Old English Meter* (Philadelphia, 1992), p. 259), *Judgment Day II* (*ibid.* p. 263), *Durham* (*ibid.* p. 260) and other poems in his chapter on 'Late Developments'. The 'BA' types used by Cable (Cable, *English Alliterative Tradition*) in the analysis of works from late in the Old English period capture this feature, and their increasing prevalence is precisely the point Cable calls our attention to.

described by Russom) made up of two juxtaposed metrical 'feet' and where (as noted above) extrametrical syllables can occur freely before either foot. Since inherited verses from the classical period allowed unstressed initial feet, there are two basic verse types in the late Old English verse tradition:

[x-foot]/[S-foot] and
[S-foot]/[S-foot].

Unstressed extrametrical elements are allowed before either foot, and the x-feet and S-feet are filled as follows:

x-feet	x, xx
S-feet (classically allowed)	S, Sx, Sxx, SxS, SxxS, SS, SSx
(newly authorized)	Sxxx, SxxxS, SxSx, SSxx, SxSxx, SxxSx, SxxxSx

Rules for stress assignment work generally as they do in classical verse: semantically important nouns, adjectives, adverbs and verbs are generally assigned to S positions, while prefixes, pronouns, prepositions and conjunctions are usually assigned to x-positions.[25] While the simplicity of this system obviously allows some verse types which cannot be directly derived from classically authorized ancestors, it has the dual advantages of ease of expression and great variety in the specific authorized types. While the number of possible feet has been greatly increased, the rules for combining feet into metrical verses have been correspondingly simplified, and the system itself remains useful in its flexibility and versatility.[26] Because late Old English verse evolved from classical verse, however, we ought to expect that the earliest examples of late verse should include the fewest numbers of such radically new types and that their numbers might well increase with time (see below).[27]

[25] In addition, there seems to be a rule (in both late verse and in classical Old English verse) that stresses the final word or element in any verse, regardless of its natural stress class. Note that the assignment of finite verbs to S-positions also stands as a simplification of the complex rules for stressing finite verbs in classical verse; it does continue to be the case that some finite verbs (especially those tending towards auxiliary function) may be scanned without stress even in late verse. Further, it seems likely that a general rule that a verse must have at least four syllables remained in effect (although it is important to note that some late poems may allow three-syllable verses; the status of such a rule perhaps ought to be treated as provisional until further work can be done).

[26] Although the system described here may seem to be so general that virtually any potential half-line can be accommodated within it, it is worth noting that no verse described by this system may have three stressed tri-syllabic words (since no single foot has two Sxx sequences). Although many verses have SxxSxx sequences, it appears that such sequences are always scanned in separate feet. In my reading of late Old English verse (and Ælfric) I have found no verses with three trisyllables or with three metrical Sxx sequences (three such sequences, of course, would demand that two of them be scanned in the same foot).

[27] In other words, we should expect that the consequences of these changes were evolutionary in nature. The verse system adapted slowly to these metrical changes, and (in general) poems

Note, of course, that this new descriptive system does little to support any notion that the late Old English verse system features two-stress verses. Since foot-forms are no longer closely associated with word-level stress patterns, any and all stressed positions within these verses are conceptualized as having full metrical stress. Verses, then, have from one to four full stresses, and while they continue to be made from two metrical feet, they cannot be said to feature two stresses with any truly descriptive validity.[28]

In the metrical transformation that led to late Old English verse, a number of verse-forms were authorized that had previously been excluded from the classical Old English verse tradition, and the most frequently-occurring sorts of these newly-authorized types can stand as diagnostic types for late Old English verse, in the sense that a cluster of diagnostic types occurring in a single poem provides strong evidence that that poem belongs to the late tradition. A sampling of such diagnostic types (by no means exhaustive) is given in fig. 3.

Clusters of these diagnostic verses in poems such as *The Metrical Psalms*, *The Judgment Day II*, *Durham* and *The Death of Alfred*, I believe, confirm that each of these poems belongs to the late Old English poetic tradition.[29] Further, such evidence also suggests that my analysis of this tradition as having descended from 'classical' Old English verse must be substantially correct. Such a conclusion, of course, is buttressed by the fact that each of these poems also includes numbers (sometimes large numbers) of verses which would be metrical in classical Old English metre as well. Of course, the continuing existence (and even composition) of classically metrical verses should be far from surprising: in a conservative verse tradition such as that of Anglo-Saxon England, the survival of older forms should always be expected.[30] In a poem like *The Battle of Maldon*,

early in the late period retained much more of the feel of classical poems than later, more innovative poems did.

[28] It seems worthwhile to note that the existence of three-stress verses in the late tradition accounts for the loss of hypermetric lines and clusters in late Old English verse. Classical Old English verse and its use of hypermetric verses depended upon a clear distinction between two-foot and three-foot verses, but in late verse, two-, three- and even four-stress verses could be derived from classical two-foot verses and the normal/hypermetric distinction could not be maintained. Note that four-stress verses have been identified in Layamon's *Brut*: cf. J. Noble, 'The Four-Stress Hemistich in Layamon's *Brut*', *NM* 87 (1986), 545–9. Once again, it seems likely that late Old English verse may stand as a clear antecedent of Layamon's verse.

[29] Examples from *The Battle of Maldon* are also included on the basis of this poem's date; its sporadic use of typical late verse-types, however, does serve to confirm the currency of these types even in an otherwise relatively classical poem.

[30] For a familiar example of Old English poetry's tolerance for the maintenance of metrically early forms alongside newer forms, compare the survival of uncontracted and non-parasited forms in the classical verse tradition; see the fine discussion of these issues in Fulk, *History of Old English Meter*, pp. 92–121.

Type	Classical Ancestors/Examples	Specific Scansions
xx/SxSx	xx/Ssx, xx/Sxs	
	PPs 61.9 4b: on þam ilcan fremmað	xx/SxSx
	Mald 75b: se wæs haten Wulfstan	xx/SxSx
	PPs 64.4 3a: and on his eardungstowum	xx/(x)SxSx
	MCharm2 10b: ofer þe fearras fnærdon	xx/(x)SxSx
	Dur 20a: ðær monia wundrum gewurðað	(x)xx/SxxSx[31]
xx/SSxx	xx/Ssx	
	PPs 71.4 1a: on his soðfæstnesse	xx/SSxx
	DAlf 25a: on þæm suðportice	xx/SSxx
Sx/SxSx	Sx/Ss, S/Ssx, S/Sxs	
	JDay II 81a: lifes læcedomas	Sx/SxSx
	PPs 66.1 1a: Miltsa us, mihtig drihten	Sx/(x)SxSx
	Dur 15a: and breoma bocera Beda	(x)Sx/SxxSx[32]
xx/SxxxS	xx/Sxxs	
	JDay II 18a: and synfulra gehwam	x/SxxxS
	PPs 57.7 3a: hi sunnan ne geseoð	x/SxxxS
	PPs 74.5 1a: Ne ahebbað ge to hea	xx/SxxxS
	DAlf 7a: and his geferan he todraf	xx/(x)SxxxS
	Dur 17b: and he his lara wel genom	xx/(x)SxxxS
SSx/Sx	Ssx/S, Ss/Sx	
	Mald 282a: Sibyrhtes broðor	SSx/Sx
	PPs 145.7 7a: soðfæste drihten	SSx/Sx
	Dur 4a: ea yðum stronge	SSx/Sx[33]
SSxx/S	Ssx/S	
	PPs 84.9 2a: mildheortnesse mod	SSxx/S
SxSx/Sx	SS/Sx, Ssx/S	
	PPs 98.1 2b: ungemete swiðe	SxSx/Sx
	JDay II 194b: ungemetum wepað	SxSx/Sx
SxSx/S	Ssx/S	
	PPs 67.1 1b: ungeleafe menn	SxSx/S
	JDay II 102b: ungerydre sæ	SxSx/S

Fig. 3 Diagnostic late Old English verse forms

[31] Note that all of the cited xx/SxSx verses would be unmetrical in classical verse, since anacrusis there is limited to two syllables in the a-verse and one syllable in the b-verse. The b-verse examples might be taken as hypermetric (if hypermetric verses were, in fact, acceptable in late verse), but in the context of the other items in the table, such an interpretation seems improbable.

[32] Sx/SxSx verses appear to be indistinguishable from one variety of classical hypermetric verse, but once again, such an explanation does not seem very compelling for these verses, which do not appear in hypermetric clusters. It is probable that hypermetric verses never appear in the late Old English verse under discussion; see above, p. 89, n. 28.

[33] This verse might better be scanned as S/SxSx, but it nevertheless stands as a diagnostic late type; note also that the *Chronicle*'s 1065 poem, *The Death of Edward*, contains a verse of the SSx/Sx type (28a: 'soþfæste sawle').

where classical forms greatly outnumber the late forms, we see such conservatism in its most powerful mode. Of the poems considered so far, only in *Durham* and *The Death of Alfred* do we really see late forms outnumbering classically metrical forms; the notably late date of these two poems offers strong evidence for the evolutionary development of late Old English verse away from classical norms.

What is most surprising (and most important) about my analysis so far, of course, is that all of the poems I have considered to this point are already included in the ASPR. Certainly, many of these late poems are labelled by Krapp and Dobbie as featuring metrical problems and difficulties, but to a very great degree these supposed metrical lapses are cleared up by interpreting these poems as having been composed in the late verse tradition, rather than the classical one. It is not the metre of these poems that is deficient, but rather our previous understandings of their metre.

Linking Late Old English Verses into Lines

Up to this point, my discussion of late Old English verse has been concerned primarily with changes in the forms of individual verses. It is clear, however, that there were also changes at the level of the full line. Further, the late poetic tradition itself evolved over time. The remainder of this section will examine three of the *Anglo-Saxon Chronicle*'s poems (those preserved in annals 975DE, 1036CD and 1086E), allowing us to explore how late Old English verse negotiated the necessary linkages between half-lines as well as other developments.

The brief poem from 975DE is one of the earliest datable pieces of late Old English verse, called *The Death of Edgar II* in Robinson and Stanley's facsimile volume.[34] The D version reads as follows:

Her Eadgar gefor,	Angla reccend,	x/SxxS[35]	Sx/Sx
Wesseaxena wine,	⁊ Myrcna mundbora.	SSxx/Sx	(x)Sx/SSx
Cuð wæs þæt wide	geond feola þeoda,	Sxx/Sx	x/SxSx
þæt afaren Eadmundes	ofer <ganetes> beð	(x)Sxx/SSx	xx/SxxS
cynegas hine wide	wurðodon swiðe,	Sxx/(xx)Sx	Sxx/Sx

[34] *Old English Verse Texts from Many Sources*, ed. F. C. Robinson and E. G. Stanley, EEMF 23 (Copenhagen, 1991).

[35] Note that I scan 'Her' as part of the poem here, although metricists have traditionally excluded this word from the *Chronicle* verse. The reasons for doing so, however, seem dubious to me, as they are either based on an assumption that the poems were not written for the *Chronicle* or based in Sieversian metrics. In my work on the *Chronicle*, I have argued that even *The Battle of Brunanburh* (the *Chronicle*'s first poem) was probably explicitly composed for the *Chronicle* (Bredehoft, *Textual Histories*, pp. 72–3 and 99–102). The argument from Sieversian metrics, of course, is not strictly relevant for this poem, which is in the late verse tradition, and it is possible that, even in *Brunanburh* 1a, we might see a mid-tenth-century example of a late Old English verse form.

bugon to þam cyninge	swa him wæs gecynde.	Sx/(xx)Sxx	xx/(xx)Sx
Næs <se> flota swa rang,	ne se here swa strang,	xx/SxxS	xx/SxxS
þæt on Angelcynne	æs him gefætte,	xx/SxSx	Sx/(x)Sx
þa hwile þe se æþela cyning	cynestol gerehte.[36]	xxx/(xx)SxxSx	SxS/(x)Sx

All of these verses, of course, can be derived quite straightforwardly from classical ancestors: a number are themselves classically acceptable (1a, 1b, 4b, 5a, 5b, 6a, 6b, 7a, 7b and 8b), although sometimes with alliteration or placement that would be unacceptable. Verse 2a (and possibly 9b as well) descends from a classical E verse and thus might be the most difficult to identify, but the remainder are fairly clear descendants of other classical forms.[37]

Note that the classical restriction against A3 verses in the b-line no longer seems to apply, as verse 6b indicates.[38] Alliteration, as noted above, can link any two stresses across the caesura, and rhyme is allowed as an occasional substitute for such linking alliteration (line 7, but also possibly line 3). Line 2 has AABB alliteration, and line 4 seems only to have AA alliteration: double alliteration in only one half-line does seem to be an acceptable, if somewhat unusual, practice of late poets.[39] Just as the forms of individual verses described above could serve as diagnostic types for late Old English verse, these innovative forms of linking and alliteration also characterize this variety of verse.

The Death of Alfred, from the *Chronicle*'s annal 1036 (manuscripts C and D), shows even more radical departures from the familiar forms of classical Old English verse. I quote the verse portions of annal 1036 as they appear in the ASPR (6–25):

Ac Godwine hine þa gelette	and hine on hæft sette,	(x)SSx/(xxxx)Sx	(xxx)x/SSx
and his geferan he todraf,	and sume mislice ofsloh,	(xx)x/SxxxS	(x)xx/SxxxS
sume hi man wið feo sealde,	sume hreowlice acwealde,	xx/(xxx)SSx	x/SxxxSx

36 'Her Eadgar passed forth, ruler of the Angles, friend of the West Saxons, and protector of the Mercians. It was widely known among many nations over the gannet's bath that kings widely and greatly honoured the offspring of Edmund, bowed to the king as was appropriate to him. There was no fleet so proud, nor an army so strong, that it fetched carrion to it amongst the English while the noble king ruled the throne' (*The Anglo-Saxon Chronicle MS D*, ed. G. P. Cubbin, The AS Chronicle: a Collaborative Edition 6 (Cambridge, 1996), 46; my lineation).

37 I have scanned 9b above as SxS/(x)Sx. That is, I scan it as a descendant of an A-type verse, such as Ss/(x)Sx. But it could just as likley be a descendant of an E-verse: SxSx/Sx. Such ambiguities of scansion are common in late Old English verse, but the metricality of such verses is not in doubt.

38 Classically, xx/Sxx verses are allowed in the b-line; when resolution no longer applied, both xx/Sx and xx/Sxx verses were seemingly allowed in that position.

39 Consider the following examples: *PPs* 54.8 2 (BB-alliteration); *JDay II* 28 (AA); *JDay II* 152 (BB); *MCharm2* 10 (AABB); *MCharm5* 3 (AABB); *MCharm7* 11 (BB); *MCharm10* 5 (BB).

sume hi man bende,	sume hi man blende,	xx/(xx)Sx	xx/(xx)Sx
sume hamelode,	sume hættode.	xx/Sxxx	xx/Sxx
Ne wearð dreorlicre dæd	gedon on þison earde,	xx/SxxS	x/SxxxSx
syþþan Dene comon	and her frið namon.	xx/SxSx	xx/SSx
Nu is to gelyfenne	to ðan leofan gode,	xx/(xx)Sxx	xx/SxSx
þæt hi blission	bliðe mid Criste	xx/Sxx	Sx/(x)Sx
þe wæron buton scylde	swa earmlice acwealde.	(x)xx/(xx)Sx	x/SxxxSx
Se æþeling lyfode þa gyt;	ælc yfel man him gehet,	(x)Sxx/SxxxS	SSx/SxxS
oðþæt man gerædde	þæt man hine lædde	xx/(xx)Sx	xx/(xx)Sx
to Eligbyrig	swa gebundenne.	x/SxSx	xx/Sxx
Sona swa he lende,	on scype man hine blende,	xx/(xx)Sx	(x)Sx/(xxx)Sx
and hine swa blindne	brohte to ðam munecon,	(x)xx/(x)Sx	Sx/(xx)Sxx
and he þar wunode	ða hwile þe he lyfode.	xx/(x)Sxx	(x)Sx/(xx)Sxx[40]
Syððan hine man byrigde,	swa him wel gebyrede,	xx/(xxx)Sxx	xx/SxSxx
ful wurðlice,	swa he wyrðe wæs,[41]	x/Sxx	xx/SxS
æt þam westende,	þam styple ful gehende,	xx/SSx	x/SxxxSx
on þam suðportice;	seo saul is mid Criste.[42]	xx/SSxx	x/SxxSx

Verse 16b here, for example, cannot readily be derived from a specific classical verse type (classically, Ss/Sxs is probably unmetrical, and certainly very rare at best). But 16b and the rest of the verses from this poem easily fit within the late Old English verse system described here.

The Death of Alfred, we should note, obviously relies upon rhyme to a much greater degree than most Old English poems, and rhyme and alliteration are both used on occasion (lines 9, 16, 19 and 22). It is also worth pointing out at least one other feature of the half-line linkages in *The Death of Alfred*: the degree to which this poet seems to intentionally balance paired verses. Verses

[40] I have scanned this verse with stress on 'hwile' and understand alliteration between 'w' and 'hw'; it may be possible that 'hwile' is unstressed and that the two verses in this line are linked only by inflexional rhyme; see the discussion of 1086E below.

[41] Notice the double alliteration in the b-line, here linked to an alliterating syllable in the a-line. Alliterating syllables on the fourth (or final) stress are fairly common in late verse; consider the following examples: *Maldon* 29, 75 and 288; *CEdg* 19; *JDay II* 169; *Pr* 18 and 41; *Seasons* 86 and *MCharm2* 34.

[42] 'But Godwine then hindered him and set him in captivity, and drove off his companions. Variously he slew some, some were given to people for money, some killed roughly, some bound, and some blinded, some hamstrung and some scalped. There was no more miserable deed done in this land since the Danes came and made peace here. It is now that we should believe in the dear God that they rejoice happily with Christ, who were, innocent, so horribly killed. The prince yet lived, each kind of wickedness promised to him, until they counselled that he be led to Ely, bound as he was. As soon as he arrived, they blinded him upon the ship, and brought him thus blind to the monks, and he dwelt there the time that he lived. Afterwards they buried him as was fitting, full honourably, as he was worthy, at the west end, right near the steeple, in the south porch; his soul is with Christ.'

with single S-positions are paired in lines 9, 10 and 17; those with two S-positions are paired in lines 7–8, 11–12 and 24–5. The two heaviest verses of the entire poem are paired with one another in line 16. With some frequency, a verse with one stress in the a-line is paired with a two-stress verse in the b-line, but this seems clearly preferable (7 examples) to having the single-stress verse in the b-line (1 example).[43] Note also that in lines 9 and 17, the parallelism and the balance involves b-verses which would have been disallowed in classical Old English verse. The implication of these observations, I believe, is that for this poet, at least, the proliferation of forms allowed in the late poetic tradition is brought under a degree of control by a general principle of balance within the full line. The formal innovations of the late tradition were accompanied by changes in the aesthetic values applied to Old English verse, and these values too have been little understood as a result of our failure to understand the basic principles of the late verse form.

Finally, it is worthwhile to turn our attention to the *Chronicle*'s poem for 1086, entitled *William the Conqueror*, preserved only in the twelfth-century Peterborough manuscript, although almost certainly composed before 1100:

castelas he let wyrcean.	7 earme men swiðe swencean.	Sxx/(x)SSx	(x)SxS/SxSx
Se cyng wæs swa swiðe stearc.	7 bena*m* of his underþeoddan man	(x)Sxx)SxS	(xx)S/(xx)SxxxS
manig marc goldes.	7 ma hundred punda seolfres.	Sx/SSx	(x)SSx/SxSx
Ðet he na*m* be wihte.	7 mid mycelan unrihte	(xx)Sx/Sx	(xx)Sxx/SSx
of his landleode, for litte[l]re neode.		xx/SSx	x/SxxSx
he wæs on gitsunge befeallan.	7 grædinesse he lufode mid ealle.	xx/(x)SxxxSx	(x)Sxxx/(x)SxxxSx
he sætte mycel deorfrið.	7 he lægde laga þær wið.	(x)SxSx/SS	(xx)SxSx/SS
þ*æt* swa hwa swa sloge heort oððe hinde.	þ*æt* hine man sceolde blendian.	(xxxx)Sx/SxxSx	(xxxx)Sx/Sxx
he forbead þa heortas.	swylce eac þa baras.	xx/SxSx	xx/(xx)Sx
swa swiðe \he/ lufode þa headeor.	swilce he wære heora fæder.[44]	(xxxx)Sxx/(x)Sx	(xxx)xx/(xx)Sx
Eac he sætte be þa*m* haran.	þ*æt* heo mosten freo faran.	(xx)Sx/(xx)Sx	(xx)Sx/SSx
his rice men hit mændon.	7 þa earme men hit beceorodan.	(x)SxS/(x)Sx	

[43] Recall, of course, the fact that single-stress A3 verses are allowed only in the a-line in classical verse, while b-lines generally have two stressed positions. *The Death of Alfred*'s use of single-stress a-lines (balanced with two-stress b-lines) may be inherited from this feature of the classical Old English verse system.

[44] The rhymes in this line and in line 7 are of particular importance. In line 7, *William the Conqueror* rhymes 'deorfrið' and 'þær wið', with the compound word necessarily scanned as SS. In line10, the 'headeor'/'fæder' rhyme indicates that the compound must be scanned as Sx. These rhymes, then, support the claim made above that there was no intermediate stress-level in late verse, and that compounds that would have been scanned Ss in classical verse were now scanned as either SS or Sx.

(xx)SxS/(xx)Sxx

Ac he [wæs] swa stið. *þæt* he ne rohte heora eallra nið. xx/(x)SS (xxx)Sx/(xx)SxS
ac hi moston mid ealle þes cynges wille folgian (xx)Sx/(x)Sx (x)SxSx/Sxx
gif hi woldon libban. oððe land habban. xx/SxSx xx/SSx
land oððe eahta. oððe wel his sehta. Sxx/Sx xx/SxSx
Wala wa. *þæt* ænig man sceolde modigan swa. SxS (xxxx)Sx/SxxS[45]
hine sylf upp ahebban. 7 ofer ealle men tellan. xx/SxxSx (x)xx/(xx)SSx[46]
Se ælmihtiga God cyþæ his saule mildheortnisse. (x)SSxx/S SxxSx/SxSx
7 do hi*m* his synna forgifenesse.[47] (x)Sx/(x)Sx SSx/Sx

In *William the Conqueror*, we see the ultimate reflexes of the changes brought about in the tenth century. Here, rhyme almost entirely supplants alliteration as the key linking device, although such extensive use of rhyme should probably be seen as idiosyncratic rather than typical.[48] Rhyme, it should be noted, sometimes appears to link full lines, rather than half-lines (19–20). Verses with three or even four stressed units are common (1b, 3b, 6b, 7a, 7b and so on). Likewise, verses that look like classical A-verses with anacrusis are also common. But, in

[45] The scansion of line 18 given here reflects manuscript pointing and rhyme; it might be possible to lineate the line as:

Wala wa. *þæt* ænig man sceolde modigan swa. SxS/(x)SxS Sx/SxxS

Such a relineation would give the line alliteration as the primary linkage, rather than rhyme, and it would also prevent the a-line from having only three syllables. As noted above, the status of three-syllable verses remains uncertain in late Old English verse, although the pointing of the present line suggests the possibility that three-syllable verses were acceptable.

[46] The scansion of this line is also somewhat uncertain; as I have scanned it, the verses have their primary linkage through inflexional rhyme (and, possibly, through assonance); it might, however, be the case that 'upp' and 'ealle' should be scanned on S positions to show vocalic alliteration.

[47] 'He ordered castles to be wrought and wretched men to work greatly. The king was very harsh, and demanded of his underlings many marks of gold and more hundreds of pounds of silver that he seized by weight and with great injustice from the people of the land – and for little need. He was fallen in avarice and loved greed above all; he established a great deer park and made a law for it that whoseoever should slay hart or hind would be blinded. He forbid the killing of harts and likewise boars; he loved the stags as greatly as if he were their father. And he ruled that the hares might roam freely. Powerful men complained and the poor lamented, but he was so rigid that he cared not for the enmity of them all; but they must entirely follow the king's will, if they would live, or have land, land or possessions, or even the king's favour. Alas – that any man should so proudly raise himself up and consider himself above all men. May the almighty God make mercy known to his soul and give him forgiveness of his sins' (*Two of the Saxon Chronicles Parallel*, ed. J. Earle and C. Plummer, 2 vols. (Oxford 1892–9) I, 220–1; my lineation). Note that I use '*þæt*' for Plummer's crossed thorn, the common manuscript abbreviation for 'þæt'.

[48] Note that the roughly contemporary *Durham* does not use rhyme so extensively, and that, when Layamon uses an early Middle English descendant of the late Old English verse form, rhyme and alliteration function as complementary systems of half-line linkage. The *William the Conqueror* poet's extensive use of rhyme therefore would have probably stood out as unusual even in the late eleventh century.

general, verses directly patterned on classically-authorized verse forms are comparatively rare: here the system described above has become almost entirely independent from the classical forms which gave rise to it, and the composition of verses relies only remotely upon the standards of classical verse. The large range of sizes for individual verses (from five to twelve syllables, if we exclude 17a) exemplifies the tendency in late verse towards larger verses; such a range would have been unusual at best in classical verse.[49]

In these three *Chronicle* poems, then, spanning from the late tenth to the late eleventh centuries, we can see a progression away from verses rooted closely in classical exemplars and towards a more general employment of those forms authorized in the late Old English verse system. Changes in metrical subordination that had formerly governed alliteration patterns seem to allow rhyme to begin functioning as a primary poetic link; the use of rhyme as such a link increases steadily in these three poems. The metrical differences in these poems can easily be accounted for in an evolutionary model, in which later poems use fewer classical verse-forms; the applicability of such an explanation (especially when coupled with the observation that these poems also conform to the metrical system described above) provides compelling evidence that Old English verse must have developed in just the ways under discussion in this article.

The changes involved in the shift from classical Old English verse to late Old English verse were radical indeed. The loss of secondary stress as a metrically signficant stress-level has been addressed above. But, simultaneously, the dissociation of metrical verse forms from the stress patterns of word pairs also necessitated (or at least accompanied) a break from the classical tradition of formulaic composition. That is, late Old English verses (especially those that would have been unmetrical in the classical tradition) would not (and perhaps could not) have been composed formulaically, and the transition to late Old English verse involved not only a loss of compound-based types, but the development of a composition method that was, at its heart, non-formulaic.

One hesitates to make too much of the connection, but it is difficult not to associate the development of late Old English verse with the increasing textualization (and decreasing 'orality') of classical verse in the manuscript record of the tenth century. We might recall O'Brien O'Keeffe's conclusion that 'the appearance, in the late tenth century, of a trend toward apparently metrical punctuation at the b-line coincides with the diminishing of "formulaic" reading in these records'.[50] It is at least possible that the development of met-

[49] Compare Cable's comments about Layamon's avoidance of four-syllable verses (Cable, *Alliterative Tradition* pp. 61–2); if *William the Conqueror* can be taken as typical of late Old English practice, the metrical impetus away from four-syllable verses was apparently already in force by the late eleventh century.

[50] O'Brien O'Keeffe, *Visible Song*, p. 192.

rical pointing in the latter tenth century might have arisen as a need to visually indicate verse boundaries after the metrical changes described in this essay had taken place. That is, new verse forms were less easily identifiable to readers (both because they were new and unfamiliar and because they were more varied and variable), and the pointing tradition may have developed as a way of marking such newly-confusing boundaries. Certainly the simultaneity of the metrical change and the change in pointing practice is striking, and the development of late Old English verse has important implications for our understanding of the process of textualization in this period. Certainly, it seems clear that late Old English verse was an essentially literary form, its basic forms descended from classical verse types, but otherwise radically separated from the formulaic, compound-filled, orally-derived standards of classical verse.[51] Late Old English verse differed from its classical ancestor not only in the specifics of verse forms, but in ways that are at the very heart of how we currently think about Old English poetry.

ÆLFRIC AND LATE OLD ENGLISH VERSE

At the beginning of the nineteenth homily of Ælfric's second series, we read the following passage, as it appears in Godden's edition:

Læwede menn behófiað. þæt him lareowas secgon. ða godspellican lare. ðe hí on bocum leornodon. þæt men for nytennysse misfaran ne sceolon; Ure drihten sæde. to sumum lareowe. ða ða he hine axode. be ðam hehstan bebode. Lufa ðinne drihten mid ealre ðinre heortan. and mid eallum móde. þis is þæt mæste bebod; Is eft oðer bebod. ðisum swiðe gelic. Lufa ðinne nextan. swa swa ðe sylfne. þæs twa bebodu. belucað ealle bec;[52]

As Godden notes, 'The punctuation and capitalization are those of the manuscript [CUL Gg. 3. 28]'[53] and, as in the passage from the homily on Cuthbert cited at the beginning of my essay, we see once again what might well be described as metrical pointing. We can relineate and scan the passage in order to clarify the metrical structure:

[51] It is worth pointing out that the changes were even more extensive than I have described here: virtually the whole machinery of oral-formulaic composition is no longer relevant during the late Old English verse period. Formulaic themes, kennings, and poetic compounding (things which have often been seen as basic to the distinction between Old English verse and prose) turn out to be relevant to only the classical verse tradition. Late Old English verse, it appears, was distinguished from prose primarily through formal criteria alone.

[52] 'It behooves unlearned men that teachers tell them the lore of the gospel that they have learned in books so that men shall not err on account of ignorance. Our Lord said to some teacher when he asked him about the highest command: "Love thy Lord with all thy heart and with all [thy] mind. That is the greatest command. There is afterwards a second command much like this one: Love thy neighbour just as thyself". All books embody these two commands' (*Ælfric's Catholic Homilies: the Second Series. Text*, ed. M. Godden, EETS ss 5 (London, 1979), 180).

[53] *Ibid.* p. xciv.

Læwede menn behófiað. þæt him lareowas secgon. SxxS/(x)Sxx xx/SxxSx
ða godspellican lare. ðe hí on bocum leornodon. (x)SSxx/Sx xx/(x)SxSxx
þæt men for nytennysse misfaran ne sceolon; (x)S/(x)Sxxx SSx/(x)Sx[54]
Ure drihten sæde. to sumum lareowe. xx/SxSx x/SxSxx
ða ða he hine axode. be ðam hehstan bebode. xx/(xxx)Sxx xx/SxxSx
Lufa ðinne drihten Sx/(xx)Sx
mid ealre ðinre heortan. and mid eallum móde. x/SxxxSx xx/SxSx
þis is þæt mæste bebod; Is eft oðer bebod. xx/(x)SxxS xx/SxxS
ðisum swiðe gelic. Lufa ðinne nextan. xx/SxxS Sx/(xx)Sx
swa swa ðe sylfne. xx/(x)Sx
þæs twa bebodu. belucað ealle bec; x/SxSx (x)Sx/SxS

As we can see, eighteen of twenty verses in this passage are pointed. As Godden notes, it is well recognized that such pointing constitutes 'a system clearly distinct from the normal punctuation'.[55] And although he does not say it explicitly, the implication seems to be that the punctuation seen in a passage such as this one marks out structural units, rather than syntactic ones. In this respect, it seems (again) most like the metrical pointing sometimes found in classical poetic texts.

Unlike the passage from the Cuthbert homily cited at the beginning of this essay, however, the verses here would not be mistaken for classical verses. They do, as the scansions I have provided suggest, fit well within the scheme of late Old English verse outlined above; from such a perspective all of these verses are perfectly well-formed. Likewise, the linking strategies used by Ælfric would often have been unacceptable in classical poems, but they certainly call to mind those used some forty years later by the poet of *The Death of Alfred*: Ælfric uses alliteration in ways not sanctioned in the classical tradition (lines 2, 4a, 8b, 9a and 11b), and he also may use rhyme as a primary linking device (lines 5–8; line 5 may alliterate as well, but this sequence of lines seems significant).[56] The use of single half-lines has precedents in other late poems, as well as in classical

[54] Note that I scan 'misfaran' with stress on the prefix, in order to provide alliteration for the line; cf. Brehe, '"Rhythmical Alliteration"', p. 70, who writes, 'Ælfric sometimes alliterated on "minor syllables", including . . . prefixes' (ellipsis mine).

[55] M. Godden, *Ælfric's Catholic Homilies: Introduction, Commentary and Glossary* EETS ss 18 (London, 2000), xxxvii.

[56] Line 5 might alliterate either if 'he' were scanned on an S position or if 'hehstan' were considered to alliterate with a vowel; such h/vowel alliteration might be possible in Ælfric. The 'drihten'/'heortan' rhyme may link the lines numbered here as 6 and 7a (the lineation given may not be the only lineation possible here); this rhyme is not particularly close, but it may well have been close enough to suit Old English conceptions of rhyme; recall that inflectional rhymes appear to serve in *The Death of Alfred* 21. For similar, though later, rhymes see also those in the *Chronicle*'s 1086E poem. Note that the rhyme in line 5 is also really an off-rhyme, as the syllables in question differ in stress.

poems.[57] It seems safe to say that if we had run into such a passage in the *Chronicle*, it would be implicitly accepted as verse, and my argument in this essay, of course, is that we should accept such compositions as verse.

In places, it seems clear, Ælfric moves beyond merely competent versifying into the realm of powerful and effective poetry, where the formal features of his compositions become a contributing factor to both their meaning and their effect. One such passage can be found at the end of Ælfric's *The Life of Oswald*:

Eft se halga Cuðberht,	þa þa he git cnapa wæs,	xx/SxSx	xx/(xx)SxS
geseah hu Godes ænglas	feredon Aidanes sawle,	(x)Sx/SxSx	Sxx/SxxSx[58]
þæs halgan bisceopes,	bliðe to heofenum	x/SxSxx	Sx/(x)Sxx
to þan ecan wuldre	þe he on worulde geearnode.	xx/SxSx	(xxx)Sxx/(x)Sxx
þæs halgan Oswoldes	wurdon eft gebroht	(x)Sx/SxxS	xx/SxS
æfter manegum gearum	to ban Myrcena lande	xx/SxxSx	x/SxxSx
into Gleawceastre,	and God þær geswutelode	xx/SSx	(x)Sx/(x)Sxxx
oft fela wundra	þurh þone halgan wer.	S/SxSx	x/(xx)SxS
Sy þæs wuldor þam Ælmihtigan	a to worulde.	(xx)Sx/(x)SSxx	Sx/Sxx

Amen.[59]

Of these nine lines, it is remarkable to note that no fewer than five feature 'cross alliteration' (lines 280–3 and 287), including a remarkable stretch of four consecutive lines.[60] Such a dense use of secondary alliteration is exceptional,

[57] Cf. A. J. Bliss, 'Single Half-Lines in Old English Poetry', *N&Q* ns 18 (1971), 442–9. But note also that the alliterative link which connects a lone half-line with a preceding line (as in lines 7–8 here) can also be found in the *Chronicle*'s 1011 poem, which provides a particularly close chronological and formal parallel.

[58] It may be more accurate to scan 'Aidanes sawle' as SxxxSx, if the two initial vowels are treated as separate syllables, rather than as a diphthong; in either case, the verse remains within the scope of late Old English verse forms.

[59] 'Afterwards, the holy Cuthbert, when he was still a youth, saw how God's angels carried the soul of Aidan, the holy bishop, happily to heaven, to the eternal glory that he earned in this world. The holy Oswald's bones were later brought after many years to the land of the Mercians, into Gloucester, and there God often made many wonders manifest through the holy man. May there be glory to the Almighty always and ever. Amen.' This relineated passage is cited from *Lives of Three English Saints*, ed. G. I. Needham (Exeter, 1976), p. 42, rather than *Ælfric's Lives of Saints*, ed. Skeat, as *Three English Saints*, ed. Needham, p. 42, indicates that a reviser has added five words in the last line. I use Skeat's line numbers for reference only, since Needham's edition uses a 'proselike' layout.

[60] The count of lines with cross alliteration might even be expanded here if 'h' alliterates with vowels (line 286; as I noted above, I believe there may be evidence for optional h/vowel alliteration in other Ælfrician texts), or if 'he' in 279b receives stress (which would be unusual in classical verse but is perhaps a possibility for Ælfric, who sometimes has functional alliteration on words which would be unstressed in classical verse). Here I consider ABBA alliteration as a variety of cross alliteration, rather than transverse alliteration, because this type of late Old English verse does not exhibit the metrical subordination which makes the distinction between the two types of secondary alliteration meaningful.

even in the classical verse tradition, although (as I have argued elsewhere) classical verse does sometimes make use of such ornamental effects. [61]

Godden, of course, has suggested that 'one of the functions of [Ælfric's alliterative] style was evidently to produce a concluding flourish'[62] citing the final paragraphs and doxologies from a handful of the *Catholic Homilies*. In *The Life of Oswald*, where the alliterative 'style' is used throughout, a similar concluding rhetorical flourish is here provided by the use of ornamental secondary alliteration. A comparable use of secondary poetic effects occurs, I believe, at the end of the classical poem *The Order of the World*: Ælfric's use of poetic effects here corresponds to that found within the classical tradition.[63] Here, then, we see Ælfric employing the possibilities of the form for literary effect, in a manner paralleled within the classical poetic tradition. It seems plausible to suggest, in fact, that Ælfric was drawing on that tradition.

Because Ælfric (and other late Old English verse) makes less use of poetic compounding than classical verse, the *Lives of Saints* feature fewer of the sorts of figurative and imaginative effects we associate with classical compounds. Of course, this should not be taken as evidence that Ælfric's works are comparatively prosaic: in the passage from the end of *The Life of Oswald* quoted above, the 'rhetorical flourish' resulting from the extensive use of cross alliteration does have a powerful poetic effect.[64] Not only does the density of the alliteration itself insist on a series of powerful imaginative links (epsecially in lines 281–2), but the 'interlace' effect of cross alliteration, which involves two alliterative links across the caesura, suggests a formal wholeness or completeness, a tidying up of loose ends, that is eminently appropriate for both concluding doxologies and for the final movement of a poem.

In other passages, Ælfric sometimes seems to use alliteration for a different kind of poetic effect, as in the following passage from the second homily in Pope's *Supplementary Collection*:

(God ge)sceop his gesceafta	on syx dagum ealle,	SxS/(xx)Sx	(x)SSx/Sx
and geswac (on þone) seofoþan,	swa þæt he syþþan ne gesceop	(xx)S/(xxx)Sxx	xx/(x)SxxxS
nane oþre gesceafta,	ac þa sylfan geedniwað	xx/SxxSx	(xx)Sx/(x)SSx
on mannum and on nytenum	mihtiglice oþ þis.	(x)Sx/(xx)Sxx	Sxxx/(x)S

[61] See T. A. Bredehoft, 'Estimating Probabilities and Alliteration Frequencies in Old English Verse', *OEN* 34.1 (2001), 19–23, for an argument that cross alliteration is sometimes used for effect in classical verse, including an example of four consecutive lines with cross alliteration.

[62] *Ælfric's Catholic Homiles: Introduction, Commentary and Glossary*, ed. Godden, p. xxxvi.

[63] Bredehoft, 'Estimating Probabilities', p. 22.

[64] Further evidence that Ælfric's works should not necessarily be considered prosaic can be found in the observation made in *Ælfric's Catholic Homiles: Introduction, Commentary and Glossary*, ed. Godden, p. xxxvii, where it is noted that Ælfric's rhythmical works are 'accompanied at times by a sprinkling of poetic vocabulary', including words such as 'metod', 'rodor' and 'folme'.

He gesceop þa twegen men,	and (ealle tida gesette,)	(xx)Sx/SxS	(x)xx/SxxSx
ac he ne gesceop na syþþan	seldcuþe (gesceafta,	xx/(xx)SxSx	SSx/(x)Sx
of þam ealdan) dihte	þe he æt fruman gesette;	xx/SxSx	xx/(x)SxxSx
ac he gescipð ælce dæge	edniwe sawla	(xxx)S/SxSx	SSx/Sx
and on lichaman geliffæst,	(swa swa we leorniað) on bocum,	(xx)SSx/(x)SS	xx/(x)SxxxSx
and þa sawla ne beoð	na(hwær gesceapene	xx/SxxS	Sx/(x)Sxx
æ)r þan þe God hi asent	to þam gesceape(nan lichama[n]	xx/(x)SxxS	(xxx)Sxx/SSx
on he)ora moddra innoþum,	and hi swa men (wurþað.)[65]	x/(xx)SxSxx	xx/(x)SSx

As this passage makes clear, Ælfric allows 's-' and 'sc-' to alliterate with one another, an alliterative peculiarity that is shared with the author of *The Metrical Psalms*.[66] But further, Ælfric shares with the *Psalms*-poet a tendency to use the same alliterating sound in a sequence of lines: eight of Ælfric's twelve lines in this passage have primary alliteration on the 's' sound.[67] In three lines (220, 221 and 225) there are four syllables alliterating on this sound, and three lines (222, 224 and 227) have cross alliteration. The only line in the passage without alliteration linking its verses (226) has 'gesette' on its final stressed position, and both the preceding and following lines have s-alliteration (the preceding with four 's-' words; the following with cross alliteration).

Such an extensive use of alliteration on a single sound, combined with 'quadruple' alliteration and cross alliteration is, from a purely statistical perspective, most probably intentional. Ælfric here uses alliteration to lend poetic and rhetorical power to this narrative of the Creation. The fact that similar extended passages using a single alliterating sound were used in *The Metrical Psalms* may suggest a source for Ælfric's alliterative usage here; once again, however, such a circumstance (as with the co-alliteration of 's-' and 'sc-') suggests that Ælfric does indeed use late Old English poetic models (as exemplified in *The Metrical Psalms*) for his own practice.[68]

[65] 'God shaped his creation all in six days, and ceased on the seventh so that afterwards he shaped no other creation, but mightily renews that selfsame one among men and beasts until today. He shaped then two humans, and established all the hours, but he has never since shaped novel creations from the old arrangement that he set at first. But he shapes each day new souls and fastens them in bodies (as we learn in books) and those souls are not created anywhere before God sends them to their appointed bodies in their mothers' insides, and so they become men' (*Homilies of Ælfric: A Supplementary Collection*, ed. Pope I, 240; spaces added to mark the caesura).

[66] Cf. *Homilies of Ælfric: A Supplementary Collection*, ed. Pope I, 128: 'Ælfric allows *sc*, *sp*, and *st* to alliterate with one another and with *s* followed by a vowel or any other consonant, though with *st* especially he seems to prefer exact correspondence.'

[67] For brief discussions of 'consecutive alliteration', see Bredehoft, 'Estimating Probabilities', pp. 19–20 and K. Grinda, 'Pigeonholing Old English Poetry: Some Criteria of Metrical Style', *Anglia* 102 (1984), 305–22.

[68] It should probably be noted, of course, that not all of Ælfric's lines seem to alliterate as clearly as most of my cited examples (although lingering uncertainties about what sorts of syllables Ælfric allows to alliterate make estimating the frequency of such lines difficult). A

It is worthwhile, finally, to consider two passages in which Ælfric shifts from prose to verse, after the introductory remarks preceding both the Cuthbert homily and *The Life of Edmund.* At the beginning of the Cuthbert homily (which seems to have been, we should recall, Ælfric's first extended composition in the rhythmical style), we read about Bede's treatment of the Cuthbert material in a passage of regular prose: 'Beda se snotera engla ðeoda lareow þises halgan lif. endebyrdlice mid wulderfullum herungum. ægðer ge æfter anfealdre gereccednysse. ge æfter leoðlicere gyddunge awrat.'[69] The distinction Ælfric draws here is an intriguing one: in Latin, at least, verse is contrasted to an 'anfealdre gereccednysse': a simple narrative. Of course, immediately after his comment that Bede wrote his second version of the *Life of Cuthbert* in the form of a song or poem, Ælfric shifts from the unornamented prose of this introductory matter to his rhythmical style. In this context, it seems difficult not to associate the conspicuous rhythmical and alliterative ornamentation of this style with verse; further, the fact that Bede's verse *Life* is more of a direct source for Ælfric than the prose *Life* may well suggest that Ælfric's first explorations in the rhythmical style were associated with Bede's own poem.[70]

The Life of Edmund, of course, also begins with a (non-rhythmical) prose account of the textual transmission of the Edmund material, first to Abbo of Fleury and thence to Ælfric, followed by the beginning of the 'rhythmical' remainder of the text. On folio 203r of London, British Library, Cotton Julius E. vii (Skeat's base manuscript), we see that the scribe has included a large (three-line) initial 'E' to mark the beginning of the rhythmical portion, which is also set off from the preceding 'plain' prose by nearly a full line of unused text-space.[71]

fuller consideration of Ælfric's practice is much needed to understand, for example, how he often seems to allow alliteration of prepositions (especially disyllabic ones). Likewise, it sometimes seems as if, in translations of scripture, Ælfric maintains his rhythm but does not employ alliteration, while in explanantory or narrative passages he does use alliteration. My purpose in this article is to address the formal identity of his works; but much remains to be done in exploring Ælfric's own ideas about the uses and purposes of his alliterative passages.

[69] 'Bede, the wise teacher of the English nation, wrote the life of this saint in order, with glorious praise, both in the manner of a simple narrative and in the manner of poetical singing' (*Ælfric's Catholic Homilies: the Second Series*, ed. Godden, p. 81).

[70] Cf. *Ælfric's Catholic Homilies: Introduction, Commentary and Glossary*, ed. Godden, p. xxxvii, who writes, 'The account of St Cuthbert, II.10, seems to be an early and experimental version of this [rhythmical] style, with very marked rhythms and a more extravagant use of poetic and colourful language; since one of its main sources was Bede's metrical life of the saint, and it is indeed the first and perhaps only work by Ælfric that used a poem as its main source, it seems likely that the inspiration and model for the use of this style *in extenso* was the use of Latin verse for hagiographical narrative.'

[71] In addition, the scribe writes the first line of the alliterative portion in capitals, as he does the very beginning of *The Life of Edmund* itself. The beginning of the alliterative passage, then, is visually marked almost as insistently as the beginning of the entire text.

As I have argued elsewhere, such blank space and *litterae notabiliores* often seem to mark boundary points between prose and verse.[72] While the shift from prologue to *vita* may be sufficient to result in such a heavily-marked textual boundary, the similarity of the treatment of the boundary point here to some prose-verse boundaries seems important as well.

But note also the particular form and effect of Ælfric's first alliterative paragraph from *The Life of Edmund:*

EADMUND SE EADIGA	EASTENGLA CYNINCG	SS/(x)Sxx	SSx/Sx
wæs snotor and wurðful.	and wurðode symble	x/SxxSx	x/SxxSx
mid æþelum þeawum	þone ælmihtigan god.	x/SxxSx	(xx)SSxx/S
He wæs ead-mod. and geþungen.	and swá an-ræde þurh-wunode	(xx)SS/(xx)Sx	(xx)SSx/(x)Sxx[73]
þæt he nolde abugan	to bysmorfullu*m* leahtrum.	xx/SxxSx	x/SxxxSx
ne on naþre healfe	he ne ahylde his þeawas.	xx/SxSx	xx/(x)SxxSx
ac wæs symble gemyndig	þære soþan lare	xx/SxxSx	xx/SxSx
[gif] þu eart to heafod-men ge-set.	ne ahefe þu ðe.	xx/(xx)SxxxS	xx/SxxS
ac beo betwux mannum	swa swa an man of him.	xx/(xx)Sx	xx/(x)SxS
He wæs cystig wædlum	and widewum swa swa fæder.	xx/SxSx	(x)Sxx/(xx)Sx
and mid wel-willendnysse	gewissode his folc	(xx)S/SxSx	x/SxxxS
symle to riht-wisnysse	and þam reþum styrde.	Sx/(x)SSxx	xx/SxSx
and gesæliglice leofode	on soþan geleafan.[74]	(xx)Sxxx/Sxx	x/SxxSx

[72] See T. A. Bredehoft, 'The Boundaries Between Verse and Prose in Old English Manuscripts', an essay written for the 1997 NEH Summer Seminar held at Corpus Christi College, Cambridge; this essay is forthcoming as part of a collection of papers from that seminar. For an especially close analogue to the treatment of the 'prose'/'rhythmical prose' boundary at this point in Julius E. vii, see the treatment of the Alfredian Boethius in London, British Library, Cotton Otho A. vi (s. $\mathrm{x}^{\mathrm{med.}}$), where heavy punctuation, blank space and display letters (or space left for such letters) generally mark the transitions between prose and verse portions of the text. Plate I of O'Brien O'Keeffe's *Visible Song* is a photograph of 87v of the Otho manuscript, perhaps the best-preserved relevant page of this manuscript.

[73] Note the manuscript point in the middle of 16a. This point may appear because points had become conventional before the Tironian '7', or it may be that this point signals a mistake on the scribe's part about the verse boundary (note that no point appears in the middle of 14a). It seems worth noting that this line is the heaviest line of the passage under consideration and thus perhaps the most likely to be mis-scanned by the scribe. Further study of mid-verse points may well offer additional insight into scribal perceptions of the structural units of late Old Engish verse.

[74] 'Edmund the blessed, king of the East Angles, was wise and worthy and contantly honoured the Almighty God with noble customs. He was blessed-minded and distinguished and remained so resolute that he would not stoop to shameful vices, nor on either side did he lay down his practices, but was always mindful of true learning. If you are made a chief-man, do not lift yourself up, but be among men just as a man of them. He was generous to the poor and to widows just as a father, and with benevolence he led his folk and steered the violent always to righteousness and happily lived in true belief' (*Ælfric's Lives of Saints*, ed. Skeat II, 314–16, lines 13–25; space added to mark caesura).

Here, an intense concentration of various sorts of wordplay and alliterative emphasis combine for a powerful rhetorical effect, precisely at the beginning of the alliterative passage. Twice (lines 13 and 16) Ælfric reuses the morpheme 'ead-' from Edmund's name, and three of the first four lines share vocalic alliteration, the first line having four alliterating syllables. The second line (the only one of the first four without vocalic alliteration) has cross alliteration, as do the two final lines of the paragraph (as 's-'/'st-' alliteration is probably functional here). Consecutive alliteration also appears twice in the final four lines, and three consecutive verses (23a–24a) may be linked by rhyme (on the syllables '-nysse', '-wissode' and '-nysse'). Paronomasia is probably to be understood in lines 14, 20 and 25; a further paronomastic linkage probably connects the words 'geþungen' and 'þeawas' in lines 15, 16 and 18.[75] The attention to formal features and wordplay here, I believe, powerfully suggests that we are in the realm of verse; when such a passage is also marked by the graphical means described above, it is clear that the scribe here perceived a major break in the contents of his text: to identify that break as a shift between prose and verse is not only plausible but attractive.

What I have tried to indicate in the preceding examples and discussion, of course, is that the evidence for considering Ælfric's rhythmical compositions as verse is too powerful to ignore. The taxonomic label we attach to these compositions is indeed meaningful, as it deeply affects our understanding of these works, their genres, and their literary effects; we should keep the conventional label 'rhythmical prose' only if it is truly the most accurate label we can find. As the direction of my argument should make clear, however, I believe that 'rhythmical prose' is not a sufficiently accurate label and that we should identify these works as verse. A brief summation of the arguments in favour of doing so may be of value here.

In the first place, I have shown here that we can identify a separate tradition of 'late Old English verse' that follows rules identifiably different from the rules encoded by Sieversian metrics. This late verse tradition is exemplified in *The Metrical Psalms*, many of the *Chronicle* poems, *The Judgment Day II*, *Durham* and a number of other works. The identification of the metrical principles behind these poems (and the relationship of those principles to those of Sieversian metrics) has two important consequences. On the one hand, we can now see late Old English verse developing in clear evolutionary ways from the earlier classical metrics described by Sievers and Bliss. But also, a useful metri-

[75] See R. Frank, 'Some Uses of Paronomasia in Old English Scriptural Verse', *Speculum* 47 (1972), 207–26; note that the *OED* entry for 'thew' cites passages from the Blickling Homilies and Layamon which feature collocations of 'þeawas' and 'geþeon', suggesting an enduring perception of a relationship between these words.

cal description of the late verse tradition removes a key obstacle to seeing Ælfric's rhythmical works as verse: readers can no longer simplistically suggest that since Ælfric's works do not agree with Sieversian metrics, they must be prose. To the contrary, as I have argued here, Ælfric's rhythmical works are, in fact, accurately described by the rules for late Old English verse.

Further, some aspects of Ælfric's practice seem to be modelled closely on the practices of at least some late Old English poets. Ælfric, for example, allows 'sc-' to alliterate with 's-', as does the poet of *The Metrical Psalms*. Likewise, Ælfric's occasional use of consecutive alliteration (where two or more lines in sequence alliterate on the same sound) is a feature also shared with the *Psalms*-poet. His use of cross alliteration, paronomasia, and other poetic effects (as at the end of *The Life of Oswald* or the beginning of *The Life of Edmund*) can be paralleled in acknowledged poems and should rightly be understood as representative of the elevated use of language and linguistic effects characteristic of poetry.

But the case does not rest on formal analysis alone. Anglo-Saxon scribes seem to have regularly treated Ælfric's rhythmical compositions in ways similar to how they treated Old English poems in general. Where normal prose abuts Ælfric's rhythmical compositions (as after the preface to *The Life of Edmund*), scribes at least sometimes used boundary-marking devices (such as blank space and *litterae notabiliores*) to indicate the shift, just as classical prose–verse boundaries were often marked (as in *The Metres of Boethius* from London, British Library, Cotton Otho A. vi). Further, the scribal habit of pointing the 'half-lines' of Ælfric's rhythmical works can be easily paralleled in the Old English verse tradition, but not in the tradition of Old English prose.[76] The simplest explanation for both practices lies in a conclusion that Anglo-Saxon scribes understood these rhythmical texts to be verse.

In some ways, it may be the case that Ælfric was even more conservative in his versifying than other late Old English poets, as in Ælfric's general avoidance of rhyme as a linking strategy. Even if that is not the case, the combination of metrical evidence, the evidence of poetic practice and the evidence of scribal habits makes the conclusion that these works were verse difficult to avoid. Our understanding of Ælfric and his place in Anglo-Saxon literary history may well change as a result of such an identification, but I believe the identification is secure. At the very least, any assessment of Ælfric and his works must attend to the powerful similarities those works share with poems from the late Old English verse tradition.

[76] Of course, CUL Gg. 3. 28 is often closely associated with Ælfric or his scriptorium: the points in this manuscript may even reflect an authorial habit, rather than scribal habit. Either way, the significant issue is the similarity of this pointing practice with the pointing practices encountered in the classical Old English verse tradition.

CONCLUSIONS

My purpose in this essay has been to describe the formal characteristics of late Old English verse, including the rhythmical and alliterating works of Ælfric. Signficantly, then, the description of the metre of late Old English verse offered here has implications not only for our understanding of the formal categories of Old English texts, but also for our broader understanding of Anglo-Saxon literature and culture. An extensive reassessment of a century and a half of Anglo-Saxon literary history is certainly a task too great for an essay such as this, but a few comments nevertheless deserve to be made.

First, so far as can be determined from relatively datable poems, the classical verse tradition (including the use of resolution) survived at least into the beginning of the tenth century: the extensive use of classical verse forms in *The Meters of Boethius* (and the lack of diagnostic late forms) is sufficient to show the survival of the old forms to the beginning of the tenth century, while *The Battle of Brunanburh* and *The Capture of the Five Boroughs* (the latter not written before 942) suggest the survival of classical forms into the middle of the century, despite these poems' brevity. But at the same time, note that Metrical Charm 7, *For the Water-Elf Disease* was written into London, British Library, Royal 12 D. xvii (?Winchester, s. x^{med}) by scribe 3 of the Parker Chronicle, the very scribe responsible for entering *Brunanburh* and *Capture* into that manuscript. Since the *Water-Elf* charm clearly has late forms (including a line of late verse printed as prose by Dobbie, in his lines 14–15), we ought to conclude that 'late Old English verse' was already being composed around the middle of the tenth century. The Sutton Brooch and the *Chronicle* poems in annals 975DE, 979DE and 1011CDE appear to confirm that the late verse tradition was widespread and current at just the time when Ælfric was writing.[77]

In all probability, then, the composition of *The Metrical Psalms* should be dated to the middle-to-late tenth century, and perhaps associated with the period of Benedictine reform in the second half of that century.[78] *The Metrical Psalms* feature many late verse forms, but they often seem fairly close to classical verse. This circumstance may be related to the date of their composition: *The Metrical Psalms* were probably composed relatively early in the late Old

[77] As I discuss elsewhere, Ælfric's contemporary and correspondent Wulfstan also wrote two verse passages for the *Chronicle*, s. a. 959DE and 975D (Bredehoft, *Textual Histories*, pp. 106–10). A. McIntosh, 'Wulfstan's Prose', *British Academy Papers on Anglo-Saxon England*, ed. E. G. Stanley (Oxford, 1990), pp. 111–44, at 117, also reminds his readers that these passages have been 'accepted implicitly' as poetry. For the Sutton Brooch, see E. Okasha, *Hand-List of Anglo-Saxon Non-Runic Inscriptions* (Cambridge, 1971), no. 114 (pp. 116–17).

[78] Cf. Fulk, *History of Old English Meter*, p. 414, who writes: 'The Psalms are probably rather late compositions . . . most of [their] metrical faults are like those of *Maldon* and other presumably late verse' (ellipsis mine).

English verse period, when contact with and influence from the classical tradition was high. Ælfric's homily on Cuthbert, which may have been his earliest attempt in the form, is the closest of all his works to classical verse; in many ways it is markedly reminiscent of *The Metrical Psalms*. Since Ælfric's own teachers were so prominent in the Benedictine reform, it seems probable that Ælfric (and his signature style) was heavily influence by the translation of *The Metrical Psalms*.

Nevertheless, Ælfric's mature rhythmical style did not remain so close to the style of *The Metrical Psalms*, but shared much more with the late Old English verse of the turn of the century as seen in the *Chronicle* poems. Ælfric, we might conclude, followed the metrical fashion of his time (possibly even innovating upon it), rather than attempting to produce more classical compositions, which, by then, would have seemed to be consciously (or at least conspicuously) archaizing, as *Maldon* is.

Notably, however, Ælfric remained fairly true to the alliterative origins of his verse form, making little use of rhyme as a substitute for alliteration. Nevertheless, such rhyme is prominent in *The Death of Alfred* (written sometime after 1036) and may be seen somewhat sporadically in the poems even of the late tenth century (as in *The Death of Edgar II* and the Sutton Brooch). The poet of *William the Conqueror*, working at the end of the eleventh century, used rhyme almost to the exclusion of alliteration, but it seems clear that alliteration was never entirely abandoned by late Old English poets, and a poem such as *Durham* suggests the continuity of alliteration as a structuring principle of late Old English verse. Layamon's use of a mixture of rhyme and alliteration a century or so later can surely be traced to the habits of late Old English poetry as seen in these latest examples of late Old English verse.

In short, then, the last two centuries of the Anglo-Saxon period witnessed a radical reorganization of the principles and practices of Old English verse. To understand the literary culture of those times, I believe, we must acknowledge the basic metrical innovations here identified as being typical of 'late Old English verse'. Crucially, verse continued to be composed throughout the period, and rather than characterizing late compositions according to a discourse of corruption and decay, we can appreciate the artistry of these late works in their own right: the greatest beneficiary of such a renewed look at the period is surely Ælfric, Anglo-Saxon England's most prolific poet.

Abbot Leofsige of Mettlach: an English monk in Flanders and Upper Lotharingia in the late tenth century

MICHAEL HARE

In a recent paper Michel Margue and Jean Schroeder have drawn a vivid picture of the intellectual life of the diocese of Trier in the time of Archbishop Egbert (977–93). They portray it as 'a colourful and busy world of small and greater personalities, who give the impression of being constantly under way: budding students, renowned teachers, talented copyists or recognised authors who do not cease moving from place to place for the purpose of education and knowledge and who do not keep to the rule of *stabilitas loci*'.[1] One of the greater personalities to whom Margue and Schroeder have drawn attention is an Englishman, Abbot Leofsige of Mettlach (*c.* 988–*c.* 993).[2]

The first scholar to pay detailed attention to Leofsige was Carl Nordenfalk, who published a paper about him in German in a Danish periodical in 1933.[3] Since then Leofsige has frequently been the subject of comment by German-language scholars, particularly those concerned with the abbeys of Mettlach and Echternach in the late tenth century.[4] However, Leofsige remains largely unknown to an English-speaking audience, a surprising omission for he was a man of considerable cultural accomplishments. Indeed one German scholar has gone so far as to describe him as 'this true Renaissance man' ('dieser wahre

[1] M. Margue and J. Schroeder, 'Zur geistigen Ausstrahlung Triers unter Erzbischof Egbert', *Egbert – Erzbischof von Trier 977–993. Gedenkschrift der Diözese Trier zum 1000. Todestag*, 2 vols, ed. F. J. Ronig, Trierer Zeitschrift für Geschichte und Kunst des Trierer Landes, Beiheft 18 (Trier, 1993) II, 111–21, at 120 (my translation from the German); Margue and Schroeder's paper is a translation and slight reworking of the second half of the same authors' work, 'Aspects du rayonnement intellectuel de Trèves dans la deuxième moitié du Xe siècle', *Échanges religieux et intellectuels du Xe au XIIIe siècles en Haute et en Basse Lotharingie. Actes des 5es Journées Lotharingiennes*, Publications de la Section Historique de l'Institut G.-D. de Luxembourg 106 (Luxembourg, 1991), 69–131.

[2] Margue and Schroeder, 'Zur geistigen Ausstrahlung', pp. 116–18; 'Aspects', pp. 103–6.

[3] C. Nordenfalk, 'Abbas Leofsinus. Ein Beispiel englischen Einflusses in der ottonischen Kunst', *Acta Archaeologica* 4 (Copenhagen, 1933), 49–83.

[4] The most important recent discussion is by S. Flesch, *Die monastische Schriftkultur der Saargegend im Mittelalter*, Veröffentlichungen der Kommission für Saarländische Landesgeschichte und Volksforschung 20 (Saarbrücken, 1991), 30–43.

Renaissancemensch').[5] While the evidence for such a claim is perhaps a little thin, Leofsige certainly deserves to be better known to Anglo-Saxonists.

LEOFSIGE'S CAREER

It is at Mettlach that Leofsige is best recorded. The monastery at Mettlach (Saarland) stood on the east bank of the river Saar, just north of the spectacular Saarschleife, which forms a large U-shaped bend in the course of the river. The monastery was established in the late seventh or very early eighth century by Liutwin, a Frankish noble who subsequently became bishop of Trier (*c.* 706 – *c.* 720). Liutwin was buried at Mettlach and was to become the principal saint of the monastery. Mettlach enjoyed a long and, for the most part, undistinguished history.[6] Its existence came to an end in 1794 when the monks fled in the aftermath of the French Revolution.

Little is known of the monastery during the first two and a half centuries of its existence. During this period Mettlach was first and foremost a proprietary monastery of the bishops (later archbishops) of Trier, who acted as abbots and appointed priors to lead the community. There is, however, sufficient evidence to show that other parties retained an active interest in Mettlach, including Liutwin's descendants, the Widonians (ancestors of the later Salian dynasty).[7] The monastery was reformed and acquired its own abbot in the 940s, soon after the reform in the 930s of the renowned Upper Lotharingian abbeys of Gorze, St Maximin at Trier and St Evre at Toul.[8] The history of Mettlach in the second half of the tenth century will be discussed further below.

5 *Ibid.* p. 41.

6 A useful summary of all aspects of Mettlach's history (with extensive bibliography) is provided by Dom Petrus Becker, 'Mettlach', in *Germania Benedictina*, IX, *Rheinland-Pfalz und Saarland*, ed. F. Jürgensmeier with R. E. Schwerdtfeger (St Ottilien, 1999), 517–45. See also T. Raach, *Kloster Mettlach/Saar und sein Grundbesitz. Untersuchungen zur Frühgeschichte und zur Grundherrschaft der ehemaligen Benediktinerabtei im Mittelalter*, Quellen und Abhandlungen zur mittelrheinischen Kirchengeschichte 19 (Mainz, 1974) and (for the tenth and eleventh centuries) Flesch, *Die monastische Schriftkultur*, pp. 12–71.

7 Becker, 'Mettlach', pp. 517–19; Raach, *Kloster Mettlach*, pp. 6–36. Two important episodes in Mettlach's history are discussed by M. Innes, *State and Society in the Early Middle Ages: the Middle Rhine Valley, 400–1000*, Cambridge Stud. in Med. Life and Thought, 4th ser. 47 (Cambridge, 2000), 183–5 and 211. A rather different view of Mettlach's early history has recently been taken by H. Schmal, *Die Gründung des Klosters Mettlach und der "Alte Turm"*, Veröffentlichungen der Abteilung Architekturgeschichte des Kunsthistorischen Instituts der Universtät zu Köln 73 (Cologne, 2000), 9–62; she rejects as spurious all sources purporting to give any information on Mettlach's history before the tenth century. It is certainly right that the sources (mainly hagiography from Mettlach and charter materials from Trier) need to be treated with great caution. The matter cannot be discussed fully here, but in my view Schmal's case is less than wholly convincing; in particular her discussion of the charter materials is not based on a sound understanding of the nature of diplomatic evidence.

8 For the wider context of reform in this period, see J. Nightingale, *Monasteries and Patrons in the Gorze Reform: Lotharingia c. 850–1000* (Oxford, 2001).

Unfortunately very little has survived from Mettlach's apparently respectable medieval library.[9] Much seems to have been destroyed during the Thirty Years' War and in the French invasions of the 1670s, while in the mid-eighteenth century the loss of the remaining manuscripts to the culinary predilections of the monks was noted despairingly by Bishop von Hontheim.[10] One source does, however, survive which gives much information about the history of Mettlach in the tenth and eleventh centuries, namely the *Miracula S. Liutwini.*

The *Miracula* was written in rhyming prose by an anonymous monk of Mettlach in the time of Abbot Nizo III, probably in the 1070s or 1080s and in any event before 1095. The earliest surviving manuscript dates from *c.* 1500.[11] Though large parts of the surviving text seem to be a reliable reproduction of the original eleventh-century version, Stefan Flesch has noted that, in addition to copying errors, the modern scholar must also bear in mind the possibility of 'editorial' alterations in the late medieval period.[12] The *Miracula* is divided into two parts. The first part (which is of especial relevance to this article) is not so much a hagiographical text as a *Gesta abbatum*, dealing with the history of the monastery down to the author's own day. The second part relates, in the traditional manner of *Miracula*, the miracles of healing performed at Liutwin's shrine.[13]

It is evident that the author of the *Miracula S. Liutwini* did not have any form of house chronicle in front of him, and the chronological details which he gives are often unreliable. Firm dates cannot indeed be given for any abbot of Mettlach of tenth or eleventh century date.[14] In putting together his account the author seems to have used a pot-pourri of sources such as charters, letters, epitaphs, book inscriptions and suchlike, perhaps with narrative accounts available for some individual episodes. The author was particularly interested in the

9 The exiguous remains are surveyed by P. Becker, 'Fragmente aus dem geistigen und geistlichen Leben der Abtei Mettlach', *Zeitschrift für die Geschichte der Saargegend* 21 (1973), pp. 7–17; see also Becker, 'Mettlach', pp. 536–7.

10 J. N. von Hontheim, *Prodromus historiae Trevirensis diplomaticae et pragmaticae*, 2 vols. (Augsburg, 1757) I, 331–2 (translation into German in Nordenfalk, 'Abbas Leofsinus', p. 66 n. 33, with the additional comment that von Hontheim's observation is a valuable 'Kulturdokument').

11 For the manuscripts of the *Miracula*, see E. Winheller, *Die Lebensbeschreibungen der vorkarolingischen Bischöfe von Trier*, Rheinisches Archiv 27 (Bonn, 1935), 95, n. 45.

12 Flesch, *Die monastische Schriftkultur*, pp. 12–13, 20, n. 56 and 62.

13 No edition of the whole text of the *Miracula* exists, and a modern edition is a desideratum. The part of the text which forms a *Gesta abbatum* was edited by H. V. Sauerland, *Miracula s. Liutwini auctore monacho Mediolacensi*, MGH SS 15/II (Hanover, 1888), pp. 1261–8, while the healing miracles were edited by J. Perier, *Acta Sanctorum*, Sept. VIII, pp. 176–9 (note that in references to the 'healing miracles', chapter numbers are based on the *incipits* listed in Sauerland's edition, with Perier's chapter numbers in brackets). Two previously unedited miracles at the end of the text have recently been published by Flesch, *Die monastische Schriftkultur*, pp. 25–7.

14 See the lists of abbots in Flesch, *Die monastische Schriftkultur*, pp. 13–14 and Becker, 'Mettlach', p. 538.

maintenance of regular discipline in the monastery and above all praised those abbots who fostered learning and the monastic school. He saw the late tenth century as a golden age in the cultural life of Mettlach, and enough can be teased from the surviving materials to show that the claim had some justification.[15]

This golden age was ushered in by the long abbacy of the first reform abbot, Ruotwich (*c.* 940/5–*post* 977).[16] Ruotwich had previously been a monk of Klingenmünster, but his original training seems to have been at St Maximin in Trier.[17] Ruotwich is credited with the acquisition of books and the establishment of a flourishing school, whose master was called Germanus. According to the *Miracula* two pupils of the school were sent towards the end of Ruotwich's abbacy for further study at Rheims with the renowned scholar, Gerbert of Aurillac. One of the two pupils was Ruotwich's successor, Abbot Nizo (Nithard) I (*c.* 980–*c.* 986).[18] The connection with Rheims is confirmed by the survival in Gerbert's letter-collection of two letters addressed to Nizo during his abbacy.[19] The author of the *Miracula* commends Nizo's holiness and wisdom, but has nothing further to report on his abbacy beyond the fact that he was much mourned when he died prematurely after six years in office.

The author of the *Miracula* had a very poor opinion of Nizo's immediate successor, Hezzel, whom he accuses of having led a dissolute lifestyle.[20] Hezzel is also reported to have pulled down the oratory dedicated to St Mary which had been built by St Liutwin, the founder of Mettlach. In its place he began a new oratory on the model of St Maximin in Trier (*ad exemplum monasterii Sancti Maximini*), but the structure was left unfinished when he was deposed from office. Hezzel's advisors were reportedly punished by an untimely death.

It is in the aftermath of Hezzel's deposition that Leofsige was appointed. The relevant passage deserves to be quoted in full:

Ecbertus autem, qui pro suis criminibus Heccelem deiecit, Lioffinum quendam Angligenam, artis medicine peritum, eius loco substituit. In cuius temporis spacio scolare exercitium in Mediolacu plurimum vigebat, et regularis discipline observatio inter monachos florebat. Precessorum eciam suorum sepulchra versibus adornavit. Necessaria quoque fratribus, quia rerum exuberantia sibi subpeditavit, copiose ministravit. Domunculam, quam Hezzel imperfectam reliquerat, ab imo eruit, et Aquisgrani palacium mittens et exinde similitudinem sumens, turrim, que adhuc superest, erexit. Sed postea accusatus, a prefato deponitur episcopo et exul moritur Efthernaco. Hezzel

15 Flesch, *Die monastische Schriftkultur*, pp. 12–71.

16 *Miracula S. Liutwini*, chs. 9–12, ed. Sauerland, pp. 1264–5.

17 Flesch, *Die monastische Schriftkultur*, pp. 14–15.

18 *Miracula S. Liutwini*, chs. 10 and 13, ed. Sauerland, pp. 1264–5.

19 *Die Briefsammlung Gerberts von Reims*, ed. F. Weigle, MGH, Die Briefe der deutschen Kaiserzeit 2 (Weimar, 1966), nos. 64 and 72; *The Letters of Gerbert with his Papal Privileges as Sylvester II*, trans. H. P. Lattin, Records of Civilization, Sources and Studies 60 (New York, 1961), nos. 71 and 79.

20 *Miracula S. Liutwini*, ch. 14, ed. Sauerland, p. 1265.

autem per quorundam suorum interventum prioris honoris iterum suscepit locum; sed priori crimine maculans vitam, pulsus et privatus meritis diem clausit ultimum.[21]

Good order was restored by the next abbot, Remigius (*c.* 995–998/1008), perhaps the most notable scholar among the abbots of Mettlach.[22]

The various accomplishments attributed to Leofsige will be discussed in the second half of this article. For the moment the dates of his abbacy are to be explored, and further evidence for his career is then considered. No documents associated with the abbacies of Hezzel and Leofsige survive, but there are some chronological indicators. Abbot Nizo I received a letter from Gerbert datable to 986;[23] he probably died later that year or in the early part of 987.[24] Egbert of Trier was archbishop from 977 until his death on 9 December 993.[25] Egbert's successor, Archbishop Liudolf (994–1008), was present when Countess Bertha made a donation of land to Mettlach on 25 February 995; the charter recording this gift makes no reference to an abbot of Mettlach.[26]

Since Leofsige seems to have achieved much in the course of his abbacy, not

21 *Ibid.* ch. 15, ed. Sauerland, p. 1265: 'Moreover Egbert, who deposed Hezzel on account of his evil deeds, substituted in his place Leofsige, a certain Englishman, experienced in the art of medicine. In his period of office, there was much vigorous scholarly activity in Mettlach, and the observance of regular discipline flourished among the monks. He also adorned the tombs of his predecessors with verses. In addition he copiously provided the necessities of life for the brothers, because everything was supplied in superabundance. He dug up from the foundations the little edifice which Hezzel had left unfinished, and upon sending for and obtaining thence a likeness of the palace of Aachen, he built the tower which still stands. But afterwards, upon accusation, he was deposed by the said bishop and died as an exile at Echternach. Indeed Hezzel, through the intervention of certain of his supporters, resumed his place of honour as before; but staining his life as before with misconduct, ended his days out of office and out of favour.' For confirmation that the name Lioffin does represent Old English Leofsige (rather than, say, Leofwine, which the form might suggest), see the book-inscriptions discussed in the second half of this article; see also below, p. 131, n. 122.

22 *Miracula S. Liutwini*, ch. 16, ed. Sauerland, p. 1266; Flesch, *Die monastische Schriftkultur*, pp. 44–71. There are five surviving letters from the years 988–90 written by Gerbert of Aurillac to Remigius, who was in all likelihood a monk of the monastery of St Eucharius in Trier before his appointment to Mettlach: *Die Briefsammlung Gerberts*, ed. Weigle, nos. 134, 148, 152, 162 and 169; *The Letters of Gerbert*, trans. Lattin, nos. 142, 156, 160, 170 and 178.

23 *Die Briefsammlung Gerberts*, ed. Weigle, no. 72; *The Letters of Gerbert*, trans. Lattin, no. 79.

24 There are three entries in the Echternach obituary corresponding to the three abbots of Mettlach called Nizo on 12 February, 18 October and 11 December: A. Steffen, 'Das älteste erhaltene Obituar der Abtei Echternach', *T'Hémecht. Zeitschrift für Luxemburger Geschichte* 14 (1961), Heft 3–4, 5–102, at 34, 85 and 96. The abbot who died on 11 December can be identified as Nizo III, but there is less certainty as regards Nizo I and Nizo II: see Flesch, *Die monastische Schriftkultur*, pp. 13–14, 16 and 20, n. 56; Becker, 'Mettlach', pp. 520–1, 525 and 527.

25 F. J. Ronig, 'Einige Anmerkungen zu Egberts Leben und Werk', *Egbert*, ed. Ronig I, 11–15.

26 H. Beyer, *Urkundenbuch zur Geschichte der, jetzt die preussischen Regierungsbezirke Coblenz und Trier bildenden, mittelrheinischen Territorien*, 3 vols. (Koblenz, 1860–74) I, 326 (no. 270). For the family of Countess Bertha and their patronage, see Nightingale, *Monasteries and Patrons*, pp. 89–90, 160–2, 242–5 and 278.

least the construction of a substantial building which still exists, an abbacy of several years' duration must be assumed. It is usually considered that his deposition must have happened towards the end of Archbishop Egbert's life in 993 – or even after it if there has been an error in transmission, as has recently been suggested.[27] Tentative dates for Leofsige's abbacy of *c.* 988/9–*c.* 993/4 can therefore be advanced, with Hezzel's two periods in office belonging to the years *c.* 987–9 and *c.* 994–5.[28]

There is an early modern source which perhaps gives a little further information about Leofsige's abbacy, namely Benoît Picart's history of the town and diocese of Toul, published in 1707. In 996 a monk of Mettlach called Robert was chosen to succeed Bishop Stephen (994–6) of Toul, who had himself been consecrated at Mettlach. It seems that Robert did not live to take up the appointment.[29] Picart writes:

> Robert étoit religieux de Meteloc abbaie de l'ordre de S. Benoit au diocese de Tréves. On en parle comme d'un homme de piété et d'érudition. Quelques manuscrits raportent qu'étant simple religieux, il entreprit Hezzel son abbé dont la conduite étoit peu exemplaire, et qu'il le fit déposer, nonobstant ses intrigues et son credit, par Egbert archévêque de Tréves, qui mit en sa place un Anglois de nation nommé Liofin.
>
> Ce nouvel abbé parut trop regulier pour des religieux qui n'aimoient point ces grandes austeritez qu'il leur vouloit faire pratiquer; ainsi ils rapélérent Hezzel qui étoit plus à leur gout. Mais l'archévêque de Tréves toûjours attentif à son devoir, déposa deréchef Hezzel et lui substitua un nommé Remi. Ces mêmes manuscrits de l'abbaie de Meteloc ajoutent que . . .[30]

This account does not seem to be derived from the *Miracula* (which makes no mention of Robert's role), and it would seem likely that Picart had access to Mettlach sources which have since been destroyed. Just possibly Picart saw the same materials which the author of the *Miracula* had used at the end of the eleventh century, or at any rate something derived from the same source.

27 For the suggestion that Leofsige was deposed by Archbishop Liudolf, see Becker, 'Mettlach', pp. 521–2.

28 The absence of an abbot in Countess Bertha's charter of February 995 may perhaps be connected with the difficulties in the abbatial succession at this time.

29 Flesch, *Die monastische Schriftkultur*, pp. 29–31.

30 B. Picart, *Histoire ecclésiastique et politique de la ville et du diocèse de Toul* (Toul, 1707), p. 341: 'Robert was a monk of Mettlach, an abbey of the order of St Benedict in the diocese of Trier. He is spoken of as a man of piety and of erudition. Several manuscripts relate that, as a simple monk, he mounted a challenge against Hezzel his abbot, whose conduct was far from exemplary, and that he had him deposed, despite Hezzel's intrigues and his influence, by Archbishop Egbert of Trier, who appointed in his place an Englishman called Leofsige. This new abbot seemed too regular for some monks, who much disliked the great austerities which he wished to make them practise; thus they recalled Hezzel who was more to their taste. But the archbishop of Trier, always attentive to his duty, deposed Hezzel a second time and replaced him with a monk called Remigius. These same manuscripts of the abbey of Mettlach add that . . .'

It is evident both from the *Miracula* and from Picart that there were competing factions within the monastery of Mettlach in Leofsige's time. Picart's evidence would suggest that some of the tensions revolved around the particular brand of reformed monasticism which Leofsige represented, but sadly any further information seems irrecoverable. It is also possible that Leofsige suffered from the fact that he is unlikely to have enjoyed any links of kinship or other ties to the local aristocracy. The active role of Archbishop Egbert in the affairs of Mettlach requires comment. Although Mettlach had in principle acquired the right of free election of its abbots, in practice the archbishops of Trier seem to have intervened with some regularity.[31] Mettlach was by no means unique in this respect in the diocese of Trier, and the archbishops were frequently involved in similar fashion in the affairs of other monasteries in the diocese at this time. Similar circumstances can also be seen at this period in other dioceses, for instance Cologne.[32]

There is no evidence to indicate how long Leofsige lived at Echternach until his death. Moreover, there is no entry for Leofsige in the surviving Echternach obituary.[33] This has led Stefan Flesch to hint at the possibility of a *damnatio memoriae*, but he also points out that, since the obituary is defective, no firm conclusion can be drawn.[34] Leofsige's connection with Echternach is, however, confirmed by a book inscription, to be discussed below.

It is also possible to learn a little of Leofsige's earlier career, and this in turn sheds light on how he came to be appointed to Mettlach. The late tenth-century Canterbury letterbook contains a letter from Abbot Wido (980/1–6) of St Peter's, Ghent (Blandinium) to Archbishop Dunstan of Canterbury (959–88).[35] In this letter Wido states that he hesitates to write so soon after the embassy undertaken by Leofsige, a monk of Blandinium whom Wido calls *nonnus*. However, Wido now wishes to ask for help as the crops have failed. He

[31] Becker, 'Mettlach', pp. 527–8; Raach, *Kloster Mettlach*, p. 48. In a hagiographical work written at Mettlach for Archbishop Egbert, he is described as the monastery's *serenissimus dominus*: *De Vita Sancti Adalberti Confessoris*, ch. 28, ed. G. N. M. Vis, in *Egmond en Berne. Twee verhalende historische bronnen uit de middeleeuwen*, Nederlandse Historische Bronnen 7 (The Hague, 1987), p. 70 (see also below, pp. 137–8, on the authorship and context of this work).

[32] E. Wisplinghoff, 'Die lotharingische Klosterreform in der Erzdiözese Trier', *Landeskundliche Vierteljahrsblätter* 10 (1964), 145–59, at 151–5; Raach, *Kloster Mettlach*, pp. 48–9.

[33] Steffen, 'Das älteste erhaltene Obituar'. Steffen's edition is of limited value, as it does not distinguish between the different tiers of entry.

[34] Flesch, *Die monastische Schriftkultur*, p. 41. Material has been lost from the beginning and end of the obituary, so that there are no entries for the period from 27 December to 23 January, while some early entries have been erased to make way for later entries. Flesch estimates that about a twelfth of the material has been lost in total.

[35] *Memorials of Saint Dunstan*, ed. W. Stubbs, RS (London, 1874), pp. 380–1. For St Peter's, Ghent, see U. Berlière *et al.*, *Monasticon Belge*, VII.1, *Province de Flandre Orientale* (Liège, 1988), 69–154, esp. 102–3 for Abbot Wido; see also *Ganda & Blandinium. De Gentse abdijen van Sint-Pieters en Sint-Baafs*, ed. G. Declercq (Ghent, 1997).

also requests that the bearers of the letter should act in concert with Leofsige, if he is still with Dunstan. The letter cannot be more precisely dated than to the years 981–6.[36]

It was tentatively suggested by Petrus Becker in 1981 that the Leofsige of this letter might be the later Abbot Leofsige of Mettlach. The proposal was taken up and elaborated by Stefan Flesch, who has put forward convincing arguments in favour of the identification.[37] What follows is based largely on Flesch's discussion.

Leofsige is not an uncommon Old English name,[38] but it is certainly improbable that there were many English monks of this name on the Continent in the 980s and 990s! In Abbot Wido's letter Leofsige is described as *nonnus*, that is to say an experienced, senior monk. Exactly what role Leofsige played at St Peter's, Ghent is uncertain; he was certainly not the prior.[39] He may well have had some responsibility for the abbey's English possessions; Abbot Wido's reference to the possibility that Leofsige might no longer be with Dunstan may mean that he envisaged that Leofsige might have travelled on to visit these possessions.[40] In any event Leofsige's senior status indicates the likelihood that he was ripe for further promotion.

36 It has been suggested by Flesch that the letter should be dated 983 on the basis of the drought recorded under that year for the Trier region: see S. Flesch, 'Egbert, Trier, Gent und Egmond', *In het spoor van Egbert: Aartsbisschop Egbert van Trier, de bibliotheek en geschiedschrijving van het klooster Egmond*, ed. G. N. M. Vis, Egmondse Studiën 3 (Hilversum, 1997), pp. 13–24, at 20, based on C. Brower and J. Masen, *Antiquitatum et Annalium Trevirensium libri XXV*, 2 vols. (Liège, 1670) I, 486. However, Trier is about 250 km south-east of Ghent, and disasters such as crop-failures were frequent and often very localized. The brief Corvey annals, written at a centre some 400 km east of Ghent, record a similar drought in 981: *Annales Corbeienses*, ed. G. H. Pertz, MGH SS 3 (Hanover, 1839), p. 5.

37 P. Becker, 'Eine liturgische Handschrift aus Trier nach der Jahrtausendwende', *Abteistadt Echternach. Cité abbatiale. Festschrift Georges Kiesel*, ed. P. Schritz and A. Hoffmann (Luxembourg, 1981), pp. 151–5, at 155; Flesch, *Die monastische Schriftkultur*, pp. 36–41; Flesch, 'Egbert, Trier, Gent'.

38 W. G. Searle, *Onomasticon Anglo-Saxonicum: a list of Anglo-Saxon proper names from the time of Beda to that of King John* (Cambridge, 1897), pp. 331–2. Among the 725 masculine names recorded in the *Liber Vitae* of the New Minster at Winchester, Leofsige occurs seven times: J. Gerchow, *Die Gedenküberlieferung der Angelsachsen. Mit einem Katalog der* libri vitae *und Necrologien*, Arbeiten zur Frühmittelalterforschung 20 (Berlin, 1988), 320–6 and 400.

39 Flesch, *Die monastische Schriftkultur*, p. 38, n. 156.

40 *Ibid.* pp. 38–9. However, this suggestion is based on the assumption that the monastery of Blandinium had acquired its English lands by the 980s, something which cannot be demonstrated unequivocally. The lands belonging to the abbey were at Lewisham, Greenwich, Woolwich and elsewhere in Kent, but none of the documentation of pre-1066 date is without problems. The material has recently been discussed by S. Keynes, 'The Æthelings in Normandy', *ANS* 13 (1991), 173–205, at 177–81. A. Verhulst, 'Bezittingen en inkomsten van de Gentse abdijen', *Ganda & Blandinium*, ed. Declercq, pp. 103–14, at 109–10, considers the gift of these estates to have been made by King Edgar in 964, and the period of Edgar's reign (959–75) would seem to provide the most likely context for their acquisition.

Not only does the chronology fit, but close links can be established at this time between Ghent and Trier. First we may note a point to which Flesch has drawn attention. In a marginal note the early modern Jesuit historian Christopher Brower described Leofsige as 'Lioffinus Britannus vel Hollandus Abbas Mediolacensis'.[41] Brower, who died in 1617, certainly visited Mettlach and thus had access to materials now lost. What led him to make this particular remark is unclear. It could be that Leofsige was himself of mixed ancestry. Another possibility is that Leofsige had ties with the abbey of Egmond, a matter discussed further in the second half of this paper. However, the family of the counts of Holland was closely associated with Ghent at precisely this period. After the long and successful rule of Count Arnulf I of Flanders (918–65), he was succeeded by his grandson Arnulf II (965–88), a minor at the time of his grandfather's death. Count Dietrich II of Holland took the opportunity to acquire control of part of the county of Ghent, a position which he maintained until shortly before his death in 988. Dietrich became advocate of the monastery of St Peter at Ghent and probably also of the monastery of St Bavo in the same city.[42]

Count Dietrich was the father of Egbert of Trier, whom we have already encountered as the archbishop who hired and fired Leofsige. Egbert himself had close ties to the abbey of St Peter's, Ghent. In 976 Emperor Otto II (973–83) issued two charters in favour of St Bavo's abbey in Ghent, and in 977 (shortly before Egbert became archbishop) he issued two further charters in favour of St Peter's abbey. Egbert was Otto's chancellor at this period and performed the *recognitio* in all four charters; it is likely that they were issued on his intervention.[43] Soon after becoming archbishop of Trier, Egbert appointed Gother, a monk of St Peter's, Ghent, as abbot of the newly-reformed monastery of St Eucharius in Trier.[44] In 979 Egbert performed the consecration of the west tower of the abbey church of St Peter's, Ghent, and the annals of the abbey also record his death.[45]

Egbert's links to Ghent thus provide a context which is sufficient to explain

41 Brower and Masen, *Antiquitatum* I, p. 490 (a convenient facsimile of pp. 480–93, covering the period of Archbishop Egbert's tenure of the see of Trier, will be found in *Egbert*, ed. Ronig II, pp. 245–59.); Flesch, *Die monastische Schriftkultur*, pp. 37–8.

42 Margue and Schroeder, 'Zur geistigen Ausstrahlung', pp. 112–14; A. C. F. Koch, 'De betrekkingen van de eerste graven van Holland met het vorstendom Vlaanderen', *Tijdschrift voor Geschiedenis* 61 (1948), 31–8.

43 *Diplomata Belgica ante annum millesimum centesimum scripta*, 2 vols., ed. M. Gysseling and A. C. F. Koch (Brussels, 1950) I, nos. 136, 137, 65 and 66.

44 P. Becker, *Die Benediktinerabtei St. Eucharius-St. Matthias vor Trier*, Germania Sacra, neue Folge 34, Die Bistümer der Kirchenprovinz Trier, Das Erzbistum Trier 8 (Berlin, 1996), 246–7 and 583–4.

45 *Les annales de Saint-Pierre de Gand et de Saint-Amand*, ed. P. Grierson, Commission Royale d'Histoire, Receuil de textes pour servir à l'étude de l'Histoire de Belgique (Brussels, 1937), *s.a.* 979 and 994 (*recte* 993), at pp. 21–2.

Leofsige's arrival in Mettlach.[46] However, Flesch prefers an alternative explanation, and is inclined to see the influence of Gerbert of Aurillac behind Leofsige's move from Ghent to the diocese of Trier.[47] Gerbert's links to Mettlach have already been noted, and he was also in touch with the community of St Peter's, Ghent. In 984 he wrote to Abbot Wido about a scholarly exchange, while in 986 he wrote to the community expressing his condolences over Wido's death and requesting the return of certain manuscripts; in the following year he sent another letter, castigating the monks because the manuscripts had not yet been returned.[48] Gerbert and Egbert were in regular communication with one another, and in two letters written in the course of 988, Gerbert comments on Egbert's health. In the first he expresses concern and holds out the possibility of medical advice; in the second he expresses his pleasure at Egbert's recovery from his long illness.[49] Flesch has concluded that Leofsige arrived in the diocese of Trier on Gerbert's recommendation, and that his principal role was to act as physician to Egbert, whom he characterizes as 'sickly'; Flesch suggests that he was made abbot of Mettlach primarily to provide him with maintenance.[50] This is a perfectly plausible hypothesis, though it should be emphasized that there is no concrete evidence for a link between Gerbert and Leofsige (a point which we shall have occasion to consider again in the second half of this article in relation to the Echternach scriptorium). One could also consider a slightly different hypothesis, namely that Leofsige did indeed arrive in the diocese of Trier as Egbert's physician (whether or not on Gerbert's recommendation) and that his appointment to Mettlach was his reward for Egbert's recovery.

In the first part of this article, it remains to be considered whether anything

[46] There were continuing contacts between Ghent and Mettlach. According to the *Miracula*, Abbot Remigius of Mettlach composed a *cantus* in honour of St Bavo for two visiting monks (probably pupils) from Blandinium: *Miracula S. Liutwini*, ch. 16, ed. Sauerland, p. 1266. As it stands the story is most improbable for there was great rivalry between the two Ghent abbeys over their relics; the visiting monks probably came from St Bavo's abbey. On these and later links, see Flesch, *Die monastische Schriftkultur*, pp. 23–5 and 55–6; Flesch, 'Egbert, Trier, Gent', pp. 23–4.

[47] Flesch, *Die monastische Schriftkultur*, pp. 40–1.

[48] *Die Briefsammlung Gerberts*, ed. Weigle, nos. 36, 96 and 105; *The Letters of Gerbert*, trans. Lattin, nos. 44, 98 and 111.

[49] *Die Briefsammlung Gerberts*, ed. Weigle, nos. 114 and 126; *The Letters of Gerbert*, trans. Lattin, nos. 122 and 127. There are twenty-five surviving letters to Egbert from the Gerbert letter-collections: see the list of addressees in *Die Briefsammlung Gerberts*, ed. Weigle, p. 283.

[50] Flesch, *Die monastische Schriftkultur*, pp. 40–1; Flesch, 'Egbert, Gent, Trier', p. 20. The evidence that Egbert was sickly is not entirely convincing. Only one other illness seems to be known, namely a fever which he suffered as a young sub-deacon; this illness is mentioned in the *Vita S. Adalberti*, a work commissioned by Egbert, in which his recovery is attributed to the intercession of St Adalbert: *Vita S. Adalberti*, ch. 19, ed. Vis, pp. 60–2. The evidence is hardly sufficient to conclude that Egbert suffered from ill-health. He survived the gruelling life of an archbishop of the *Reichskirche* for sixteen years and made at least two visits to Italy, the graveyard of so many from north of the Alps at this period.

can be learned of Leofsige's career before his arrival in Ghent. It is possible that some or even all of Leofsige's earlier career may have been on the Continent; this could possibly have involved a period at Rheims with Gerbert. However, it is certainly unsurprising to find an English monk at the monastery of St Peter's, Ghent, for it is quite clear that there were regular and sustained contacts between reformed English and Flemish monastic houses in the second half of the tenth century, and that St Peter's, Ghent was in the forefront of these exchanges.[51] When Dunstan (then abbot of Glastonbury) was exiled by King Eadwig in 956, it was at St Peter's, Ghent that he spent his exile of more than a year; our knowledge of this episode is derived from the *Vita* written at Blandinium by the monk Adelard for Archbishop Ælfheah of Canterbury (1006–12).[52] Monks from Ghent as well as from Fleury were present at the Council of Winchester in *c.* 973 when the customary known as *Regularis concordia* was drawn up.[53] Whether Abbot Womar (953–80) of St Peter's, Ghent was present at the council is not known, but he was certainly remembered with favour in England, for his death was recorded in the 'C' text of the *Anglo-Saxon Chronicle*, and his name was entered in the *Liber Vitae* of the New Minster at Winchester; it would seem from the entry that Womar had commended himself to the prayers of the community of the Old Minster.[54] Abbot Wido's letter to Dunstan has already been mentioned.

If Leofsige is to be located in England, it is no doubt at one of the reformed Benedictine monasteries of the period that he should be sought, perhaps at one of the foundations connected either with Archbishop Dunstan of Canterbury or with Bishop Æthelwold of Winchester (963–84). Unfortunately a search of the sources has so far failed to find any clear leads.[55] First of all it should be noted that an Abbot Leofsige attests two charters, one dated 986 from the archive of the Winchester Old Minster, the other dated 16 April 988

[51] On exchanges between England and Flanders, see P. Grierson, 'The Relations between England and Flanders before the Norman Conquest', *TRHS* 4th ser. 23 (1941), 71–112; V. Ortenberg, *The English Church and the Continent in the Tenth and Eleventh Centuries: Cultural, Spiritual and Artistic Exchanges* (Oxford, 1992), pp. 21–40.

[52] *Memorials of Saint Dunstan*, ed. Stubbs, pp. 53–68, at pp. 59–60.

[53] *Regularis Concordia Anglicae Nationis Monachorum Sanctimonialiumque: the Monastic Agreement of the Monks and Nuns of the English Nation*, ed. and trans. T. Symons (London, 1953), ch. 5 (p. 3).

[54] On Womar, see Berlière *et al.*, *Monasticon Belge* VII.1 (see above, p. 115, n. 35), pp. 101–2; *Anglo-Saxon Chronicle* 981 C: *The Anglo-Saxon Chronicle MS C*, ed. K. O'Brien O'Keeffe, The AS Chronicle: a Collaborative Edition, ed. D. Dumville and S. Keynes 5 (Cambridge, 2001), 84 (text); *The Anglo-Saxon Chronicle: a Revised Translation*, ed. D. Whitelock, with D. C. Douglas and S. I. Tucker (London, 1961; rev. 1965), p. 80 (translation). For Womar's commemoration at Winchester, see Gerchow, *Gedenküberlieferung*, p. 323, and *The Liber Vitae of the New Minster and Hyde Abbey, Winchester*, ed. S. Keynes, EEMF 26 (Copenhagen, 1996), 88 (see also 18r for facsimile of the entry).

[55] Final judgement on this point must await completion of the Prosopography of Anglo-Saxon England project currently in hand.

from the archive of the New Minster in the same city.[56] It seems unlikely that either or both of these could be Leofsige of Mettlach on a return visit to England. The first was issued before Leofsige became abbot, and it is simplest to assume that both attestations are by an abbot of one of the many English houses whose abbatial succession is poorly recorded.[57]

There is, however, one possibility which has been noted briefly by Flesch and which is worth further consideration.[58] The Ely source known as the *Libellus quorundam insignium operum beati Æthelwoldi episcopi* preserves an account of a dispute over land at Bluntisham in Huntingdonshire (now Cambridgeshire), which Wulfnoth had sold to Bishop Æthelwold of Winchester for the endowment of the monastery of Ely.[59] After the death of King Edgar in 975 and before the death of Æthelwold in 984, it was alleged by the sons of Boga that Wulfnoth had not been entitled to sell the land. The matter was decided in favour of Wulfnoth and of the abbey of Ely at a meeting of the shire court, at which the abbey was represented by a monk called Leofsige, who brought to the court a *cirographum*, probably in this context a royal charter.[60]

There is a little to be said in favour of Leofsige of Ely. He was evidently of sufficient standing to represent Ely at the shire court in a complex matter, and he was a member of a monastery which had been refounded *c.* 970 by Bishop Æthelwold, whose foundations at Winchester commemorated Abbot Womar of St Peter's, Ghent. It is, however, also possible that the monk of Ely who represented the abbey in the Bluntisham affair was one and the same as the Ely monk called Leofsige found acting in conjunction with Abbot Ælfsige (996 × 9–1012 × 19)[61] and/or one of the three monks of Ely called Leofsige commemorated in the twelfth-century Ely calendar.[62] He could also just as well have become the abbot named Leofsige, who attests charters of 986 and 988.

[56] P. H. Sawyer, *Anglo-Saxon Charters: an Annotated List and Bibliography*, R. Hist. Soc. Guides and Handbooks 8 (London, 1968), no. 861 (J. M. Kemble, *Codex Diplomaticus Aevi Saxonici*, 6 vols. (London, 1839–48), no. 655) and no. 869 (*Charters of the New Minster, Winchester*, ed. S. Miller, AS Charters 9 (Oxford, 2001), no. 30).

[57] D. Knowles, C. N. L. Brooke and V. C. M. London, *The Heads of Religious Houses: England and Wales* I, *940–1216*, 2nd ed. (Cambridge, 2001), pp. 23–84, 225–7, 240–59 and 298–9.

[58] Flesch, *Die monastische Schriftkultur*, p. 39.

[59] The *Libellus* is an early twelfth-century translation into Latin of Old English material composed *c.* 990. For the Bluntisham dispute, see *Liber Eliensis*, ed. E. O. Blake, Camden 3rd ser. 92 (London, 1962), 98–9 (bk II, ch. 25) and S. Keynes and A. Kennedy, *Anglo-Saxon Ely: Records of Ely Abbey and its Benefactors in the Tenth and Eleventh Centuries* (Woodbridge, forthcoming).

[60] See A. Kennedy, 'Law and Litigation in the *Libellus Æthelwoldi episcopi*', *ASE* 24 (1995), 131–83, at 162.

[61] *Liber Eliensis*, ed. Blake, pp. 130–1 (bk II, ch. 59).

[62] Gerchow, *Gedenküberlieferung*, pp. 343–50 (21 March, 25 July and 10 October). It is also worthy of note that at the end of the account in the *Libellus*, it is mentioned that Wulfnoth was about to cross the sea in the service of his lord. As Wulfnoth and Leofsige clearly worked in harness at the shire court, it is just possible that Leofsige travelled overseas with him or that Wulfnoth's journey could in some way have led to his – entirely hypothetical – move to the Continent.

LEOFSIGE'S CULTURAL ACTIVITIES

In the second part of this article, the various achievements ascribed to Leofsige by the *Miracula S. Liutwini* are discussed. In addition the evidence of two book-inscriptions is considered. Since Leofsige was evidently a man of wide-ranging accomplishments, scholars have not unnaturally been tempted to ascribe other achievements to him. Some of these suggestions have been very speculative. In what follows, an attempt is made to distinguish between what is established with reasonable certainty on the one hand and what is speculation on the other hand.

A cautionary tale is provided by the monastic customary known as the *Virdunenses*. In 1951 Dom Kassius Hallinger suggested that Leofsige was probably the author of the *Virdunenses*, basing this suggestion on the medical knowledge displayed in the text.[63] Although doubts were soon expressed,[64] the theme was enthusiastically elaborated by Theo Raach, who pointed to some similarities in points of detail with *Regularis Concordia*, the tenth-century English customary.[65] However, when Hallinger himself came to edit the *Virdunenses*, he was able to demonstrate that it was compiled after 1060.[66]

The 'Alter Turm' at Mettlach

The *turris* built by Leofsige still stands and is the only remaining medieval building to survive at Mettlach. It is indeed considered to be the oldest standing building in the modern Saarland. The 'Alter Turm' (old tower), as it is universally known, was a church of octagonal plan dedicated to St Mary (pl. I). The principal church at Mettlach, dedicated to St Peter, was pulled down in 1819, but its plan is known in outline; it was a substantial structure with a west tower, an aisled nave, transepts and a polygonal choir. The church of St Mary stood to the east of the south transept of St Peter's and projected eastwards beyond its choir. The monastic buildings still stand to the north of the site of St Peter's; they were completely rebuilt in Baroque style in the eighteenth century and now serve as the headquarters of the well-known firm of ceramic

[63] K. Hallinger, *Gorze-Kluny. Studien zu den monastischen Lebensformen und Gegensätzen im Mittelalter*, 2 vols., Studia Anselmiana 22–5 (Rome, 1950–1) II, 884.

[64] H. Dauphin, 'Le renouveau monastique en Angleterre au Xe siècle et ses rapports avec la réforme de Saint Gérard de Brogne', *RB* 70 (1960), 177–96, at 193, n. 5.

[65] T. Raach, 'Klosterleben in Mettlach gegen Ende des 10. Jahrhunderts', *Libellus ad magistram. Frau Professor Dr Edith Ennen zum 60. Geburtstag* (Saarbrücken, 1967), pp. 27–42; Raach, *Kloster Mettlach*, p. 46, n. 58.

[66] K. Hallinger, 'Redactio Virdunensis' and 'Appendix: *Virdunenses*', *Consuetudinum saeculi X/XI/XII monumenta. Introductiones*, ed. K. Hallinger, Corpus Consuetudinum Monasticarum [CoCM] 7.1 (Siegburg, 1984), 196–205 and 436–55 (comment); 'Redactio Virdunensis', ed. M. Wegener and K. Hallinger, *Consuetudinum saeculi X/XI/XII monumenta non-Cluniacensia*, ed. K. Hallinger, CoCM 7.3 (Siegburg, 1984), 375–426 (text).

manufacturers, Villeroy and Boch. St Mary's is preserved as a monument in parkland.[67]

There were extensive excavations on the site of St Peter's church and inside the 'Alter Turm' in 1954–5 and 1959–60. Unfortunately the results of the excavations have not yet been published and are known only from very brief accounts by the excavator.[68] The excavations within the 'Alter Turm' are stated by the excavator to have been of especial complexity; he reports that the present structure was the fifth church built on the site. Apparently all the earlier buildings were of axial plan and the 'Alter Turm' was the first church built on a central plan. As to the unfinished *domuncula* begun by Abbot Hezzel on the model of St Maximin in Trier, the excavator mentions only that the apse of this building was seen.

The octagonal church built by Leofsige was substantially remodelled *c.* 1300. By the middle of the nineteenth century, the building was in a state of some dilapidation, and there was a major restoration in 1851.[69] A further programme of conservation was carried out between 1989 and 1997. The internal elevation of the octagon consists of three storeys, and, by contrast with Aachen, there are no aisles. The internal width of the building is 10.80 m, and the walls of the ground storey are of considerable strength, measuring 2.70 m in thickness. The western face of the octagon is occupied by a tall round-headed arch belonging to the original structure. The remaining seven sides now contain lofty niches of sub-rectangular plan belonging to the remodelling of *c.* 1300; the niches have pointed arches internally and traceried windows externally. To the east there was originally a short projecting square-ended choir of two storeys, the plan of which is known from excavation. It is generally assumed that the remaining six sides of the original octagon all contained tall round-headed niches of semicircular plan. In the *Miracula S. Liutwini*, it is related that an insane woman from nearby Tholey was allowed to spend the night *in una fornicum turris*;[70] it is probable that one of these niches is meant.

[67] For a general introduction to the buildings at Mettlach, see M. Klewitz, *Mettlach an der Saarschleife*, 3rd ed., Rheinische Kunststätten 164 (Cologne, 1994). For a plan of the buildings before the demolition of the main church in 1819, see (K.) A. von Cohausen, *Der alte Thurm zu Mettlach. Eine Polygonalkirche nach dem Vorbilde des Aachener Münsters aus dem Ende des X. Jahrhunderts* (Berlin, 1871), fig. 1.

[68] Klewitz, *Mettlach*, pp. 3–9; M. Klewitz, 'Zur Baugeschichte der Benediktinerabtei Mettlach', *1300 Jahre Mettlach* (Mettlach, 1976), pp. 81–93.

[69] The fullest description is by the architect responsible for the 1851 restoration: von Cohausen, *Der Alte Thurm*, a work still of great value. See also H. E. Kubach and A. Verbeek, *Romanische Baukunst an Rhein und Maas*, 4 vols. (Berlin, 1976–89) II, 776–9. The most important art-historical assessment is A. Verbeek, 'Der Alte Turm in Mettlach. Seine Stellung in der ottonischen Baukunst des Rheinlandes', *Trierer Zeitschrift* 12 (1937), 65–80. Also valuable is M. Untermann, *Der Zentralbau im Mittelalter. Form – Funktion – Verbreitung* (Darmstadt, 1989), pp. 128–9.

[70] *Miracula S. Liutwini*, ch. 27 (7), ed. Perier, p. 178.

In the middle storey, the thick wall of the ground stage is divided into inner and outer skins, with a continuous passageway (originally vaulted) right round the building.[71] All eight faces open towards the central space above a continuous string-course through round-arched triple openings; these openings are supported on columns with bases and sculptured capitals, all recessed on both faces beneath an enclosing arch.[72] The outer skin of the wall has now disappeared on six sides, so that the triple openings stand open to the elements; on the remaining two sides the outer wall is now largely of late medieval date. Externally the original arrangement is obscured by the alterations of *c.* 1300, when substantial buttresses were added to the corners and most of the walling was refaced. However, it seems clear that the two internal storeys were not reflected in a similar division externally. To either side of the arch in the west wall, the remains can be seen of broad angle-pilasters, cut in two planes at the same angle as the wall faces; the angle-pilasters carried blind arches in the now vanished upper zone of the wall, probably two to each face supported on a central corbel.[73] The remaining angle-pilasters disappeared in the course of subsequent alterations.

The third storey is carried on the inner wall of the middle stage (there must have been a narrow roof above the vault of the passageway). There are large round-headed windows in each face of the upper stage, and broad angle-pilasters can be detected behind later buttresses at six of the angles. There is

[71] The wall-passage is unparalleled in surviving tenth-century architecture, and Mettlach has been seen as a precursor of the form of construction known as 'thick wall' or 'double-shell': P. Héliot, 'Les antécédents et les débuts des coursières anglo-normandes et rhénanes', *CCM* 2 (1959), 429–43, at 431.

[72] The bases, columns, capitals and imposts have attracted much attention, particularly as regards the delicately carved foliate ornament of some of the capitals and imposts. This sculpture has proved difficult to classify, and widely differing views have been put forward. There are recent discussions by R. Meyer, *Frühmittelalterliche Kapitelle und Kämpfer in Deutschland: Typus – Technik – Stil*, 2 vols. (Berlin, 1997) I, 256–90 (text and drawings) and II, 718–37 (plates); G. Skalecki, 'Der sogenannte "Alte Turm" in Mettlach, eine ottonische Marienkirche – Kunstgeschichte und Denkmalplflege', *Die Denkmalpflege* 56 (1998), 26–40, at 32–4; Schmal, *Die Gründung des Klosters Mettlach*, pp. 85–140. Meyer considers that much of the sculpture consists of Carolingian *spolia* reused at the time of construction *c.* 990, Skalecki maintains that the sculpture is contemporary with the tower and shows Byzantine influence, while Schmal dates the sculpture to the late twelfth or early thirteenth century (see also below, p. 124, n. 76). Also useful is the detailed description and discussion in P. Volkelt, *Die Bauskulptur und Ausstattungsbildnerei des frühen und hohen Mittelalters im Saarland*, Veröffentlichungen des Instituts für Landeskunde des Saarlandes 16 (Saarbrücken, 1969), 21–37, 377–81 and pls. 3–18; Volkelt rejects the suggestions of English influence in the sculpture which have sometimes been made. Further work is desirable, but great clarity of thought will be needed!

[73] Rather more can be seen (from within the later stair-turret) of the blind arch on the south side than of the blind arch on the north side.

now a Gothic rib-vault of *c.* 1300, but the thin walls of the top stage must originally have carried a wooden roof, a point which is corroborated by one of the stories in the *Miracula*.[74] There is a stair-turret to the south of the entrance archway on the west side; the present turret was built in 1851, an earlier turret having collapsed in 1841.[75] On the west side of the 'Alter Turm', there are remains of thirteenth-century vaulting belonging to the vestibule which linked the octagon to the south transept of the main church; an earlier structure probably stood in the same position.

Archaeological observation during the recent conservation work has produced confirmation of the traditional view that the early work in the ground, middle and upper stages all belongs to the same building campaign. It has been observed that 'the high degree of uniformity in the building stone, the tooling and the mortar implies a rapid and unbroken construction of the main fabric'.[76]

The main function of St Mary's church, the 'Alter Turm', was to house the remains of the saintly founder of the monastery, Liutwin.[77] The exact position of the tomb was not located by the archaeological investigations inside the structure; his remains seem to have been housed in a freestanding shrine around which it was possible to walk.[78] At a later date, perhaps in the mid-thirteenth century, Liutwin's remains were translated from St Mary's church into St Peter's church.[79] The dedication of the 'Alter Turm' to St Mary has long antecedents among rotundas and other buildings on a central plan, going back ultimately to the church built over the tomb of the Virgin in the valley of Josaphat outside Jerusalem.[80] In the late-eleventh-century *Miracula*, the octagon

[74] The account in the *Miracula* says that a possessed woman named Waldrada was allowed to spend the night at Liutwin's shrine; her watchers were disturbed by the devil who tried to frighten them by making a fearful noise in the ceiling timbers (*in laqueari turris*): *Miracula S. Liutwini*, ch. 29 (10), ed. Perier, p. 178.

[75] The lower courses of the turret survived the collapse of 1841; the turret was of later date than the original construction.

[76] Skalecki, 'Der sogenannte "Alte Turm"', p. 36 (my translation from the German). Despite these observations, a highly complex sequence of development, involving the insertion of the triple arcades into an earlier building in the late twelfth or early thirteenth century, has been proposed by Schmal, *Die Gründung des Klosters Mettlach*, pp. 63–178. Schmal's suggestions present more problems than they solve; it is possible that some of the sculpture is of the late Romanesque date which she proposes, but, if so, then it is most likely that it was inserted in the course of a programme of repair.

[77] This point is clear from the various healing miracles related in the *Miracula S. Liutwini*, chs. 24–32 (1–15), ed. Perier, pp. 176–9,

[78] *Miracula S. Liutwini*, ch. 27 (8), ed. Perier, p. 178.

[79] J. C. Lager, *Urkundliche Geschichte der Abtei Mettlach* (Trier, 1875), p. 219.

[80] R. Krautheimer, 'Sancta Maria Rotunda', *Arte del primo millennio (Atti dell IIº convegno per lo studio dell' arte dell' alto medioevo, Pavia, 1950)* (Turin, 1953), pp. 23–7, repr. in his *Studies in Early Christian, Medieval and Renaissance Art* (New York, 1969), at pp. 107–114.

is designated as *turris* on a number of occasions, a name which has survived until today in the form 'Alter Turm'.[81] The word *turris* is in fact not uncommonly used for churches built on a central plan.[82] An English parallel is provided by the mid-twelfth-century writer, Richard of Hexham, in his account of the church of St Mary built at Hexham by St Wilfrid in the early eighth century; according to Richard, Wilfrid's church was *in modum turris erecta, et fere rotunda* ('built in the form of a tower and nearly round').[83]

In his discussion of Abbot Leofsige, Nordenfalk argued that in building a church on a central plan at Mettlach, Leofsige was introducing a form of structure which derived from the traditions of his English homeland.[84] He based this thesis partly on the parallel with Hexham and partly on the architectural detail. There was indeed a tradition of buildings of central plan in England, probably including the church dedicated *c.* 963 at the reformed monastery of Abingdon.[85] However, Nordenfalk's thesis attracted little support and was quickly refuted by Albert Verbeek.[86] Verbeek was able to demonstrate convincingly that the 'Alter Turm' stood firmly in the context of architectural developments in the Rhineland and in Lotharingia, both as regards its form and its architectural detailing.

The derivation from Aachen indicated by the *Miracula S. Liutwini* should not lightly be discarded. It is naturally uncertain whether Leofsige himself knew Aachen. However, as a senior monk of St Peter's, Ghent, he will in all likelihood have been familiar with the church of St Donatian at Bruges, a copy of Aachen built within the principal residence of the counts of Flanders. Ghent and Bruges are less than 40 km apart, and in the tenth century St Peter's, Ghent stood high in the favour of the counts; it was indeed their normal place of burial.[87] The church of St Donatian was extensively rebuilt in later centuries before being pulled down in 1799–1800; excavations took place on the site of the church in 1955 and 1987–9.[88] Even before the excavations the written sources (principally the accounts of the murder of Count Charles the Good in the church in 1127) had led to suggestions that St Donatian was built in

[81] *Miracula S. Liutwini*, ch. 15, ed. Sauerland, p. 1265 and chs. 27 (7, 8) and 29 (10), ed. Perier, p. 178. [82] Untermann, *Zentralbau*, p. 40.

[83] Richard of Hexham, *History of the Church of Hexham*, ch. 4, ed. J. Raine, *The Priory of Hexham*, 2 vols., Surtees Soc. 44, 46 (Durham, 1864–5) I, 14–15.

[84] Nordenfalk, 'Abbas Leofsinus', pp. 61–5.

[85] R. Gem, 'Towards an Iconography of Anglo-Saxon Architecture', *Jnl of the Warburg and Courtauld Institutes* 46 (1983), 1–18, at 7–12. [86] Verbeek, 'Der Alte Turm'.

[87] G. Declercq, 'Heiligen, lekenabten en hervormers. De Gentse abdijen van Sint-Pieters en Sint-Baafs tijdens de Eerste Middeleeuwen (7de-12de eeuw)', *Ganda & Blandinium*, ed. Declercq, pp. 13–40, at 29–30.

[88] Both excavations were published in *De Brugse Burg. Van grafelijke versterking tot moderne stadskern*, ed. H. De Witte, Archeo-Brugge 2 (Bruges, 1991).

imitation of Aachen; the excavations have confirmed that St Donatian was a very exact copy of Charlemagne's chapel at Aachen, albeit on a slightly smaller scale.[89] Recent dendrochronological analysis suggests that St Donatian was begun in or very soon after the year 950.[90] It would thus seem to have been built in the later years of Count Arnulf I (918–65), who was himself evidently proud of his descent from the Carolingians.[91] In the early 980s, when Leofsige was at Ghent, St Donatian would therefore have been a new and no doubt impressive structure. In this connection one might note that the building of such a close copy of Aachen at Bruges will in all likelihood have involved the use of some form of likeness or *similitudo* of Aachen. If, as the *Miracula S. Liutwini* suggests, Leofsige obtained a *similitudo* of Aachen, then it could very well be that he acquired it from Flemish contacts at Bruges rather than direct from Aachen. The *similitudo* could still have been at Mettlach in the second half of the eleventh century, and might itself have been one of the sources used by the author of the *Miracula*.

Unlike Bruges, Mettlach is far from an exact copy of the palace chapel at Aachen. Mettlach has in common with Aachen the octagonal plan and the elevation of the central space, but at Mettlach, Aachen's ground-floor aisle is replaced by niches, while its spacious gallery with tall openings has become a narrow passageway with much lower openings. Verbeek has observed that, 'This arrangement, which brings the adjoining elements into the surrounding wall of the central space, is the architectural essence of the structure.'[92] The niches in the ground storey can moreover be related to an earlier tradition of centrally-planned buildings, that of the sepulchral church. Indeed Matthias Untermann has neatly linked these different elements, pointing out that by the late tenth century, the reasons for building a church in citation of Aachen had changed. By this time Aachen could be cited not as the palace chapel built by

89 L. Devliegher, 'De voorromaanse, romaanse en gotische Sint-Donaaskerk. Evolutie en invloeden', *De Brugse Burg*, ed. De Witte, pp. 118–36, at 118–25; see also Untermann, *Zentralbau*, pp. 115–17. The original dedication of the church was jointly to St Mary and St Donatian.

90 The evidence comes from a palisade of oak posts considered likely to be associated with the start of construction work: see H. De Witte *et al.*, 'Sint-Donaas en de Brugse Burg: Dendrochronologisch onderzoek en radiokoolstofdateringen', *Jaarboek 1997–99. Brugge Stedelijke Musea* (Bruges, 2000), pp. 178–87.

91 Arnulf was descended from the Carolingians through the third marriage of Charles the Bald's daughter, Judith, to Count Baldwin I (862–79), Arnulf's grandfather. Arnulf is known to have been a benefactor of the palatine church of St Mary at Compiègne, built by Charles the Bald in the 870s as his Aachen-substitute. See G. Derclercq, 'Oorsprong en vroegste ontwikkeling van de burcht van Brugge (9de-12de eeuw)', *De Brugse Burg*, ed. De Witte, pp. 15–45, at 24–5 and 45.

92 Verbeek, 'Der Alte Turm', p. 71 (my translation from the German). On the derivation from Aachen, see also Untermann, *Zentralbau*, pp. 128–9.

Charlemagne *pro statu regni*, but as Charlemagne's place of burial; it was soon after the building of Mettlach that Otto III had Charlemagne's grave opened in May 1000, while in 1003 Otto was buried there.[93]

Untermann has compared Mettlach to two other centrally-planned churches of the same period, the church of St John the Baptist at Liège begun around 980 by Bishop Notker (972–1008) and the slightly later abbey church of Deutz built by Archbishop Heribert of Cologne (999–1021).[94] Both Liège and Deutz were built as episcopal burial places. The church of St John in Liège was pulled down and rebuilt in the eighteenth century; it is known only from drawings and from its Baroque successor of broadly similar plan. Notker's church seems to have been of similar design to Mettlach though on a grander scale. It could well have been Notker's church which was Leofsige's most immediate model. Whether or not that is the case, many of the most important structures built in imitation of Aachen were in Lower Lotharingia,[95] and it is most probably in that region and in adjacent Flanders that the models for Mettlach were located.

Verse epitaphs

According to the *Miracula*, Abbot Leofsige decorated the tombs of his predecessors with verses.[96] It is not improbable that Leofsige's predecessors were buried close to the tomb of St Liutwin, and the verse epitaphs may well have been produced in connection with the rebuilding of the 'Alter Turm'. Nordenfalk characterized Leofsige as a poet, and other scholars, most recently Flesch, have followed him.[97] While it is perfectly possible, perhaps even likely, that Leofsige composed the epitaphs in question, the text would also permit another interpretation, namely that Leofsige did no more than commission the verses. There may well have been other monks at Mettlach capable of producing verses, for the *Miracula* comments expressly on the flourishing state of

93 Untermann, *Zentralbau*, p. 130. In a recent paper Untermann has also suggested that Leofsige was attempting to demonstrate that Liutwin's status was equivalent to that of Charlemagne; alternatively (and less satisfactorily) he has suggested that the author of the late-eleventh-century *Miracula* decided to explain the unusual form of the building by reference to the best-known prototype: see M. Untermann, 'Karolingische Architektur als Vorbild', *Kunst und Kultur der Karolingerzeit. Karl der Große und Papst Leo III. in Paderborn*, ed. C. Stiegemann and M. Wemhoff, 3 vols. (Mainz, 1999) III, 165–73, at 167.

94 Untermann, *Zentralbau*, pp. 126–30. On the date of St John in Liège, see J. Deckers, 'Notger et la fondation de la collégiale Saint-Jean l'Evangéliste à Liège', *La Collégiale Saint-Jean de Liège. Mille ans d'art et d'histoire*, ed. J. Deckers (Liège, 1981), pp. 13–19; L. F. Génicot, 'L'octogone de Notger et son avant-corps', *ibid.* pp. 47–56.

95 A. Verbeek, 'Zentralbauten in der Nachfolge der Aachener Pfalzkapelle', *Das erste Jahrtausend. Kultur und Kunst im werdenden Abendland an Rhein und Ruhr*, ed. V. H. Elbern, 3 vols. (Düsseldorf, 1962–4) II, 898–947, at 940–2.

96 *Miracula S. Liutwini*, ch. 15, ed. Sauerland, p. 1265 (see also above, p. 112).

97 Nordenfalk, 'Abbas Leofsinus', p. 57; Flesch, *Die monastische Schriftkultur*, pp. 41–2.

scholarly activity during Leofsige's abbacy. One monk is known to have been engaged in literary activity at around this time, namely Ruopert who was commissioned by Archbishop Egbert to write a *Vita S. Adalberti* (to be discussed in more detail below). Alternatively it is not impossible that Leofsige could have turned to Trier for a poet to compose the epitaphs.

A little can be said of the epitaphs commissioned or composed by Leofsige. Since the community had acquired abbots in the reform of the 940s, only two had died in office, Ruotwich and Nizo I. Their epitaphs have not survived, though as Flesch has noted, traces of them may be preserved in the accounts of Ruotwich and Nizo in the *Miracula*.[98] It is also worth considering the inscription from the tomb of St Liutwin himself; this inscription was recorded by Brower, who saw Liutwin's tomb.[99] Karl Strecker included the piece in the MGH edition of Ottonian poetry on the basis of its overall impression.[100] As Leofsige rebuilt the 'Alter Turm' which housed Liutwin's tomb, and as Liutwin could in some sense be described as his predecessor, the possibility that Leofsige was responsible for the Liutwin epitaph should certainly be entertained. Flesch considers it more probable that the epitaph for Liutwin belongs to the period of the Bursfeld Reform abbot, Tilmann von Prüm (1480–1505).[101] However, Flesch's objections to an early date are based solely on the poem's use of the word *archimandrita*. He points out that this word was used in an epigram about Liutwin by Tilmann's contemporary, Prior Eberhard von Kamp of Tholey. However, it is also possible that Eberhard himself derived the word directly or indirectly from Liutwin's epitaph. In addition it is worth making the point that grecisms such as *archimandrita* were common currency in the late tenth and early eleventh centuries, both in England and Germany.[102] Two examples of the use of the word will suffice. In the late tenth-century Canterbury letterbook, there is a letter from an anonymous bishop, almost certainly Æthelwold of Winchester (963–84), to a Count Arnulf, either Arnulf I (918–65) or Arnulf II (965–88) of Flanders; the bishop styles himself *archimandrita*.[103] Archbishop Egbert of Trier is himself described

[98] Flesch, *Die monastische Schriftkultur*, p. 41. He draws particular attention to the passage on Nizo reading . . . *sanctitate et sapientie flore preditus, . . . nimis matura morte preventus* (*Miracula s. Liutwini*, ch. 13, ed. Sauerland, p. 1265).

[99] Brower and Masen, *Antiquitatum* I, p. 363.

[100] MGH, *Poetae Latini Medii Aevi* V.2, ed. K. Strecker (Berlin, 1939), p. 313.

[101] Flesch, *Die monastische Schriftkultur*, pp. 42 and 155. The verses are described by Brower (see above, n. 99) as ancient (*antiqui*); on Flesch's dating they would have been little more than a hundred years old when Brower saw the epitaph.

[102] In general on the context, see (for Germany) W. Berschin (trans. J. C. Frakes), *Greek Letters and the Latin Middle Ages: From Jerome to Nicholas of Cusa* (Washington DC, 1988), pp. 172–200 and 327–33, and (for England) M. Lapidge, 'The Hermeneutic Style in Tenth-Century Anglo-Latin Literature', *ASE* 4 (1975), 67–111.

[103] *Memorials of St Dunstan*, ed. Stubbs, pp. 361–2.

as *archimandrita* in the *Translatio s. Celsi*, a work composed between 1010 and 1023 by Theoderich, a monk of St Eucharius in Trier.[104] Leofsige's responsibility for the Liutwin epitaph thus remains possible, but is far from established.

Flesch has also drawn attention to two epitaphs from St Peter's, Ghent, one for Abbot Womar (d. 980), the other for Abbot Wido (d. 986).[105] Their epitaphs survive in a substantial collection from St Peter's, Ghent preserved in a fourteenth-century manuscript; Strecker considered that only a handful of these epitaphs were of Ottonian date, among them the epitaphs for Womar and Wido.[106] Both epitaphs seem to be by the same author, who borrows from Venantius Fortunatus.[107] As Leofsige was at St Peter's, Ghent in the 980s and as he is known to have been involved in the production of epitaphs elsewhere, Leofsige certainly has a strong claim to be considered as the author of these two epitaphs. Flesch considers the case to be established 'with apparent certainty', but that may be overstating the case a little for, as at Mettlach, there may well have been other monks at St Peter's, Ghent capable of producing Latin poetry.

Unfortunately little survives from St Peter's, Ghent of late-tenth-century date, but the correspondence with Gerbert suggests that it is likely to have been intellectually active.[108] Of especial interest is the reference to a scribe called Claudian in the first of Gerbert's letters, addressed to Abbot Wido. This classical name could well have been a nick-name bestowed by a master (perhaps Gerbert himself) on a pupil. The best-known Claudian is the late antique pagan poet,[109] and it is possible that Claudian of Blandinium acquired this nick-name because he had aspirations in the art of poetry.[110] Abbot Wido's

104 Theoderich, *Translatio s. Celsi*, ch. 2, ed. G. Waitz, MGH SS 8 (1848), p. 205. On Theoderich, see Becker, *Die Benediktiner Abtei St. Eucharius*, pp. 681–2.

105 Flesch, *Die monastische Schriftkultur*, pp. 41–2.

106 *Poetae Latini Medii Aevi* V.2, ed. Strecker, pp. 297–301.

107 See Strecker's footnotes (as previous note). If Leofsige was the poet, then it is possible that he could have become acquainted with the work of Venantius in England: see R. W. Hunt, with an appendix by M. Lapidge, 'Manuscript Evidence for Knowledge of the Poems of Venantius Fortunatus in Late Anglo-Saxon England', *ASE* 8 (1979), 279–95.

108 See above, p. 118, n. 48. For the intellectual life of St Peter's, Ghent, see also Declercq, 'Heiligen, lekenabten en hervormers', pp. 32–6, and A. Derolez, 'Scriptorium en bibliotheek tijdens de middeleeuwen', *Ganda & Blandinium*, ed. Declercq, pp. 147–60, at 147–50.

109 The works of Claudian were not part of Gerbert's syllabus at Rheims, but there are grounds for thinking that he could have been familiar with Claudian. The ninth-century library catalogue of Bobbio (where Gerbert was resident as abbot in 982–3) lists four (unspecified) books of Claudian: A. Cameron, *Claudian: Poetry and Propaganda at the Court of Honorius* (Oxford, 1970), p. 422. In addition one of Gerbert's letters begins with a quotation which derives from Claudian: *Die Briefsammlung Gerberts*, ed. Weigle, no. 70; *The Letters of Gerbert*, trans. Lattin, no. 77.

110 If Claudian is indeed a nickname, then one could not exclude the possibility that it was Leofsige who was so called.

own letter to Dunstan (in which Leofsige is mentioned) is couched in elaborate Latin, full of fancy phrases; it was not necessarily composed by Wido himself. A little later the monk Adelard of St Peter's, Ghent composed a *Vita Dunstani* in the form of a series of lections at the request of Archbishop Ælfheah of Canterbury (1006–12).[111] Some caution does therefore need to be exercised in assessing Leofsige's claim to be considered as the author of the Ghent epitaphs.

As already noted, it is not known how long Leofsige lived after his move to the monastery of Echternach. It is possible (though perhaps unlikely) that he survived until 1007; if so, he could conceivably be associated with the epitaph for Abbot Ravanger (973–1007).[112]

Inscriptions in manuscripts of Paschasius Radbertus

Two surviving inscriptions attest to Leofsige as a donor of books. In both cases the manuscripts given by Leofsige seem to have contained only the treatise *De corpore et sanguine Domini*, written by Paschasius Radbertus in the second quarter of the ninth century.[113] The two inscriptions are couched in almost identical terms, but were written by two different hands.

The first of the two manuscripts of Paschasius Radbertus to be considered is Trier, Stadtbibliothek, 588/1543 (?Mettlach, s. x^{med}; provenance St Eucharius/ St Matthias, Trier), fols. 1–49.[114] The manuscript was written at an unknown scriptorium towards the middle of the tenth century. Mettlach has often been considered as a strong contender, though it should be noted that the ascription is based on no more certain ground than the later association of the manuscript with Leofsige.[115] The inscription on 1r is in a later hand and reads, 'Dedit Liofsinus abba indignus et peccator hunc librum pro remedio animae sue sancto Euchario illique servientibus. Si quis illum abstulerit et fratres in hoc conturbaverit, anathematis iaculo in adventu domini perpetualiter feriatur.'[116] Hartmut Hoffmann has characterized the hand of the inscrip-

[111] For Adelard's *Vita*, see above, p. 119, n. 52.

[112] *Poetae Latini Medii Aevi* V.2, ed. Strecker, pp. 315–16.

[113] Paschasius Radbertus, *De corpore et sanguine Domini*, ed. B. Paulus, CCCM 16 (Turnhout, 1969); the two manuscripts discussed below are considered at pp. xix–xxi.

[114] Becker, *Die Benediktiner Abtei St. Eucharius*, p. 108.

[115] Nordenfalk, 'Abbas Leofsinus', pp. 65–7; Flesch, *Die monastische Schriftkultur*, p. 37. The manuscript has decorated initials, the three most elaborate of which have been published, one by Nordenfalk, 'Abbas Leofsinus', pl. 10 (p. 65) and two by A. Weiner, 'Katalog der Kunstwerke um Erzbischof Egbert', *Egbert*, ed. Ronig I, 17–242, at 187 (pl. 137).

[116] H. Hoffmann, *Buchkunst und Königtum im ottonischen und frühsalischen Reich*, 2 vols., Schriften der MGH 30 (Stuttgart, 1986) I, 508 (text) and II, pl. 299b (facsimile): 'The unworthy sinner, Abbot Leofsige, gave this book for the benefit of his soul to St Eucharius and to the brothers serving him. If anyone steals it and troubles the brothers thereby, may he be smitten for ever by the dart of anathema at the coming of the Lord.' The inscription is followed on 1r–1v by

tion as not English, but 'trierisch'; he has drawn attention to work, perhaps by the same hand or at any rate by a school companion, in another manuscript, probably written and certainly preserved at St Eucharius, Trier (Trier, Priesterseminar 100 (s. x^{ex}), fols. 17–46).[117]

The second manuscript of Paschasius Radbertus is Paris, Bibliothèque Nationale, lat. 8915 (Echternach, s. x^{ex}); it was copied using Trier 588/1543 as its exemplar.[118] In this case the inscription on 1r was written by the principal scribe of the manuscript.[119] It has been badly damaged by erasures, but in the early 1930s Nordenfalk was able to read the name of the donor after arranging for chemical treatment.[120] The text has been read as follows, 'Dedit Leofsinus abba indignus et peccator hunc librum pro remedio anime sue sancto Uuillibrordo illique servientibus. Si quis illum abstulerit et fratres in hoc conturbaverit anathematis jaculo in adventu domini perpetualiter feriatur. Fiat. Fiat.'[121] The discovery of the name Leofsinus enabled Nordenfalk to identify the donor with the abbot of Mettlach who had retired to Echternach.[122]

BN lat. 8915 was the main focus of Nordenfalk's study. It is a quite exceptionally luxurious volume for what was a library text, spaciously laid out and ornamented with a number of attractive decorated initials. The manuscript has two scribes, Hand A being responsible for fols. 1–109 (including the *ex-dono*), Hand B for the remainder (fols. 110–24).[123] Hand A wrote a stately minuscule with letters of such substantial size that Nordenfalk commented that he had

a hymn in honour of Pope Gregory the Great and there is other material in honour of Gregory on 50r–50v. The possibility that the hymn may be linked to Leofsige has been suggested: Paschasius Radbertus, *De corpore*, ed. Paulus, p. xx.

117 Hoffmann, *Buchkunst* I, 507–8.

118 Nordenfalk, 'Abbas Leofsinus', p. 66; Paschasius Radbertus, *De corpore*, ed. Paulus, p. xx; J. Schroeder, *Bibliothek und Schule der Abtei Echternach um die Jahrtausendwende* (Luxembourg, 1978), pp. 37–8 (originally printed in Publications de la Section Historique de l'Institut G.-D. de Luxembourg 91 (1977), 201–378). All references are to the separate publication.

119 Nordenfalk, 'Abbas Leofsinus', p. 52.

120 *Ibid.* p. 49.

121 M.-P. Laffitte, J. Sclafer, F. Bléchet *et al.*, *Catalogue général des manuscrits latins nᵒˢ 8823 à 8921*, Bibliothèque nationale de France (Paris, 1997), p. 163: 'The unworthy sinner, Abbot Leofsige, gave this book for the benefit of his soul to St Willibrord and to the brothers serving him. If anyone steals it and troubles the brothers thereby, may he be smitten for ever by the dart of anathema at the coming of the Lord. So be it. So be it.' I have had the opportunity of making only a brief examination of the inscription. Even under ultra-violet light the text of the inscription is extremely difficult to read after the word *abstulerit*, and it would seem likely that some of the reading quoted is a reconstruction based on Trier 588/1543.

122 It has been suggested that at Echternach, with its long history of connections with Anglo-Saxon England, Leofsige felt able to use the Latin form (Leofsinus) normal for his Old English name, but for Mettlach and St Eucharius he used forms of his name which were easier for continental tongues: Flesch, *Die monastische Schriftkultur*, p. 37. The form Lioffinus occurs only at Mettlach and in sources deriving from Mettlach; it is not attested in any tenth-century source, and it may be based on a careless reading of the name Liofsinus at a later date.

123 Nordenfalk, 'Abbas Leofsinus', pp. 49–54.

never seen anything equivalent from this period except in *de luxe* liturgical volumes; Hand A averaged no more than ninety words to a page measuring 387 × 273 mm (pl. II). Hand B (who occurs in other Echternach manuscripts and who will be discussed further in the next section) followed the same format, but wrote in a slightly more compressed script, averaging 150 words to the page. The result is that Paschasius Radbertus's treatise, which is not a long text, occupies an entire manuscript of 124 (originally 128) folios.

The decorated initials in BN lat. 8915 can only be considered briefly here. There are twenty surviving decorated initials with finely drawn foliate ornament; there were originally three more on leaves now lost.[124] The first nine initials between fols. 2–38 have rich background painting and are in an expressionistic style derived from Alemannic models. The next eight initials between fols. 53–100 have no background painting and correspond more closely to other decorated initials from Echternach at this period. The last three initials between fols. 107–19 are in a more linear style with ornament which is less rich. Despite the change in manner between fols. 38 and 53, Nordenfalk was of the view that a single artist was responsible for all the initials down to fol. 100. More recent observers have been less certain that there were only two artists, but all agree that the last three initials are by a different artist.[125]

The work of a new artist beginning on 107r corresponds closely though not exactly to the change in hand after 109v. Nordenfalk pointed out that the initial drawn on 107r did not correspond exactly to the space which Hand A had left for it. He deduced that Hand A was one and the same as the artist responsible for the first seventeen initials, while Hand B was likewise the second artist. Nordenfalk had no doubt about the conclusion to be reached; Hand A was to be identified with Leofsige himself. He toyed with the idea that the initials down to fol. 38 were produced at Mettlach, while the remainder were drawn after Leofsige's move to Echternach, but recognized that this point could not be pursued in the absence of material of this date from Mettlach.[126] Nordenfalk also thought that he could detect the influence of pre-Viking English art in two initials with animals enmeshed in the foliage, but Reichenau models have subsequently been suggested as a more likely source.[127]

[124] What follows is based on Nordenfalk, 'Abbas Leofsinus', pp. 54–6 and 65–76. See also F. Avril and C. Rabel, *Manuscrits enluminés d'origine germanique*, I, *X^{e}–XIVe siècle* (Paris, 1995), pp. 8–9 and Weiner, 'Katalog', no. 30 (pp. 33–4) and pls. 133–6 (pp. 183–6). Although the exemplar for Paris BN lat. 8915 was Trier 588/1543, the decoration of its initials owes nothing to the initials in the Trier manuscript (on which see above, p. 130, n. 115).

[125] See for instance Avril and Rabel, *Manuscrits enluminés*, p. 9 and Weiner, 'Katalog', p. 33.

[126] Nordenfalk, 'Abbas Leofsinus', pp. 67–9.

[127] *Ibid.* pp. 69–74; J. M. Plotzek, 'Zur Initialmalerei des 10. Jahrhunderts in Trier und Köln', *Aachener Kunstblätter* 44 (1973), 101–28, at 120. See also the reservations expressed by R. Deshman, '*Christus rex et magi reges*: Kingship and Christology in Ottonian and Anglo-Saxon Art', *FS* 10 (1976), 367–405, at 393.

Subsequent commentators have been rather more cautious than Nordenfalk. It has been pointed out that Leofsige could have commissioned BN lat. 8915 without being involved as a scribe or artist in its production.[128] It does seem likely that the manuscript was prepared, or at least completed, after Leofsige's arrival in Echternach *c.* 993/4; it was presumably given by him to the community as a token of thanks for his reception.[129] As Trier 588/1543 served as the exemplar for BN lat. 8915, it was in all likelihood given to the monastery of St Eucharius at around the same time. It may be noted that Leofsige's connections with St Eucharius could go back to his days in Ghent. As already noted, Abbot Gother (977–980/1) was a monk of St Peter's, Ghent before his appointment to St Eucharius by Archbishop Egbert; Gother may well have brought monks from Ghent to Trier, who might still have been members of the community in the later 980s and 990s.

One speculative point may be made in conclusion. There may well have been a number of similar inscriptions with Leofsige's name in books in the library of Mettlach. Conceivably it was inscriptions of this sort which led the late eleventh-century author of the *Miracula sancti Liutwini* to write in such glowing terms about the flourishing state of the Mettlach school in Leofsige's time.

The scriptorium of Echternach in the late tenth century

Hand B of Paris BN lat. 8915 was also the principal scribe of a group of manuscripts produced at Echternach towards the end of the tenth century. The last part of Nordenfalk's study of Leofsige was devoted to the decorated initials of these manuscripts, and Jean Schroeder has subsequently published a detailed survey of the group.[130] Schroeder demonstrated that there is a very close correspondence between the manuscripts produced at Echternach at this time and the curriculum of Gerbert of Aurillac at Rheims, as described by Gerbert's pupil Richer.[131] Gerbert's teaching of the liberal arts was based first and foremost on Greek philosophy, as transmitted by the commentaries and translations of Boethius, together with an unprecedented collection of Latin authors including Plautus, Terence, Vergil, Juvenal, Persius, Horace and Lucan.[132] The

128 Weiner, 'Katalog', p. 33; M. C. Ferrari, *Sancti Willibrordi venerantes memoriam. Echternacher Schreiber und Schriftsteller von den Angelsachsen bis Johann Bertels. Ein Überblick*, Publications du Centre Luxembourgeois de documentation et d'études médiévales 6 (Luxembourg, 1994), 25, n. 115.

129 It has been suggested that Leofsige died while still working on the manuscript and that Hand B (conceivably a companion in exile from Mettlach) took over to complete the work: Schroeder, *Bibliothek und Schule*, p. 38.

130 Nordenfalk, 'Abbas Leofsinus', pp. 76–83; Schroeder, *Bibliothek und Schule*.

131 Richer, *Historiae* III.46–50, ed. H. Hoffmann, MGH SS 38 (Hanover, 2000), 193–6.

132 For Gerbert's teaching, see R. W. Southern, *The Making of the Middle Ages* (London, 1953), pp. 175–9 and C. E. Lutz, *Schoolmasters of the Tenth Century* (Hamden, CT, 1977), pp. 127–47.

works used by Gerbert are listed by Richer, and it is precisely the texts listed by Richer that were produced at Echternach in the late tenth century.[133]

Hoffmann has subsequently challenged some of Schroeder's detailed palaeographical conclusions; certain of the works attributed to Hand B are now thought to be the work of other scribes.[134] However, Schroeder's portrayal of the intellectual interests of the Echternach scriptorium remains unaffected by these details.[135] It is evident that a determined effort to produce the works in Gerbert's curriculum was both planned and executed. As Gerbert's library from Rheims does not survive and as there is no other library of the period which contains his curriculum in its entirety, the Echternach volumes are an especially significant survival. The books in this group were written as library texts; although a number of them (especially the works of Latin poetry) are handsomely produced in large format, they do not have the same luxurious character as BN lat. 8915.[136]

After establishing the nature of book-production at Echternach in the late tenth century, Schroeder then attempted to determine the channels through which Gerbert's curriculum was introduced to Echternach.[137] He could find no evidence for direct contact between Echternach and Rheims. Echternach is not mentioned in Gerbert's correspondence, while the obituaries of Echternach and Rheims reveal no evidence of links between the two establishments.[138] A major influence on Echternach in the late tenth century was the monastery of St Maximin in Trier. The first abbot of Echternach after the reform of 973 was Ravanger (973–1007), who had been a monk of St Maximin. Ravanger evidently brought colleagues with him who had been trained in the school of St Maximin, for Echternach script is often difficult to distinguish from that of St Maximin at this period.[139] However, Schroeder was able to rule out St Maximin, for the works of the Gerbert curriculum are not represented there; in the St Maximin library catalogue of *c.* 1100, there is not a single work of Boethius nor of any author of pagan antiquity.[140]

[133] Schroeder, *Bibliothek und Schule*, pp. 67–76.

[134] Hoffmann, *Buchkunst* I, 509–16.

[135] See the comments of Ferrari, *Sancti Willibrordi venerantes memoriam*, p. 25, nn. 113 and 116.

[136] The manuscripts of this group show little sign of use for higher education in the liberal arts, and Schroeder has concluded that the Gerbert curriculum was not in practice taught at Echternach: Schroeder, *Bibliothek und Schule*, pp. 129–32. Something of an exception is provided in the field of music, a subject in which Echternach excelled: see F. Lochner, 'Die *Ars Musica* im Willibrorduskloster zu Echternach', *Willibrord, Apostel der Niederlände, Gründer der Abtei Echternach. Gedenkausgabe zum 1250. Todestag des angelsächsischen Missionars*, ed. G. Kiesel and J. Schroeder (Luxembourg, 1989), pp. 150–65.

[137] Schroeder, *Bibliothek und Schule*, pp. 76–88.

[138] *Ibid.* p. 77.

[139] Hoffmann, *Buchkunst* I, 510–11. The script of St Eucharius at Trier is likewise not easy to distinguish from that of St Maximin (*ibid.* I, 504–9); although nothing of Mettlach origin is known to survive from the late tenth century, it would not be surprising if Mettlach script also derived from the St Maximin school.

[140] Schroeder, *Bibliothek und Schule*, pp. 81–2.

Schroeder considered it probable that it was from the nearby abbey of Mettlach that the Gerbert curriculum was introduced to Echternach; Mettlach's connections with Gerbert of Rheims are well documented.[141] Schroeder thought that the immediate stimulus was likely to have been provided by the arrival of Leofsige *c.* 993, perhaps with companions from Mettlach. The thesis is attractive, but is certainly not established beyond doubt. Indeed Schroeder thought he had found a chronological peg for the work of Hand B in a charter of 997, but Hoffmann has now argued against Hand B as the scribe of this charter.[142] Hoffmann has also drawn attention to another manuscript partly written by Hand B, Trier, Stadtbibliothek, 1093/1694 (Echternach, s. x^{ex}); one of the other scribes of this manuscript also wrote a charter in favour of Echternach dated 973.[143] This evidence might suggest that work on the group began rather earlier than the 990s.

Schroeder thought it likely that the manuscripts were copied from exemplars provided by Mettlach, but was unable to pursue the point further in the absence of surviving Mettlach manuscripts. He also brought to notice the commentary of Remigius of Auxerre which forms a contemporary marginal gloss to the text of Boethius's *De consolatione Philosophiae* in Trier 1093/1694; the evidence of this gloss suggested the possibility of a Cologne exemplar.[144] It should, however, be pointed out that there are other possible sources for the exemplars. Schroeder himself noted how little was known of the libraries of the monasteries of Prüm, Stablo, Gorze and St Arnulf, Metz, which all had ties of confraternity with Echternach.[145] In a later paper he has also emphasized the possible role of Count Siegfried of Luxembourg.[146] It was through

141 See above, p. 112; Schroeder, *Bibliothek und Schule*, pp. 76–81 (it should, however, be noted that Remigius, who was in correspondence with Gerbert in the 980s, was almost certainly a monk of St Eucharius in Trier until *c.* 995: see Becker, *Die Benediktiner Abtei St. Eucharius*, p. 681).

142 Schroeder, *Bibliothek und Schule*, pp. 64–6; Hoffmann, *Buchkunst* I, 509.

143 *Ibid.* I, 510–11.

144 Schroeder, *Bibliothek und Schule*, pp. 85–8. If the Cologne derivation is right, the exemplar may have derived from the cathedral library (where the Gerbert curriculum was in use) rather than the library of St Pantaleon: see Ferrari, *Sancti Willibrordi venerantes memoriam*, p. 26, n. 117, and I. Jeffré, 'Handschriftliche Zeugnisse zur Geschichte der Kölner Domschule im 10. und 11. Jahrhundert', *Kaiserin Theophanu. Begegnung des Ostens und Westens um die Wende des ersten Jahrtausends*, ed. A. von Euw and P. Schreiner, 2 vols. (Cologne, 1991) I, 165–71. On the other hand, it has been suggested that the evidence of Old High German glosses may point in the direction of St Pantaleon: E. Glaser and C. Moulin-Fankhänel, 'Die althochdeutsche Überlieferung in Echternacher Handschriften', *Die Abtei Echternach 698–1998*, ed. M. C. Ferrari, J. Schroeder and H. Trauffler, Publications du Centre Luxembourgeois de documentation et d'études médiévales 15 (Luxembourg, 1999), 103–22, at 110–17.

145 Schroeder, *Bibliothek und Schule*, pp. 83–4.

146 J. Schroeder, 'Le comte Sigefroid de Luxembourg et la réforme de l'abbaye d'Echternach (973)', *La Maison d'Ardenne, X^{e}–XIe siècles. Actes des Journées Lotharingiennes*, Publications de la Section Historique de l'Institut G.-D. de Luxembourg 95 (1981), 283–98, at 295–6.

Siegfried's agency that Echternach was reformed in 973, and he was the patron and lord of the monastery. Siegfried is mentioned in favourable terms in five letters, all dating from 985, written by Gerbert, one of them addressed to Siegfried's son.[147] A recent study has drawn attention to the exceptional interest of the musical manuscripts of Echternach in the late tenth and early eleventh centuries.[148] For present purposes the evidence of a manuscript of Boethius' treatise *De institutione musica* is of especial interest (Paris, Bibliothèque Nationale, lat. 10275 (Echternach, s. x^{ex}), fols. 1–77). The exemplar for this work seems likely to have been provided by Fleury; two scholia deriving from Gerbert added to the manuscript after its completion indicate contact either with Rheims or with another centre in touch with Rheims.[149]

The last word on what Nordenfalk termed the 'classics group' (Klassikergruppe) of manuscripts from Echternach has certainly not been said; the need for further codicological and palaeographical study has recently been emphasized.[150] The hypothesis of Mettlach involvement in the production at Echternach of the works of the Gerbert curriculum is entirely reasonable, but the connection between Leofsige and the 'classics group' is rather more tenuous than is often believed. Further work may well establish a more complex picture of the influences underlying the work of the Echternach scriptorium. The one manuscript with which Leofsige is associated is far from typical of Echternach book production at this period, both as regards its *de luxe* format and its contents, a treatise by a Carolingian author.[151] It certainly seems a little perverse to call the Echternach manuscripts of this period the 'Leofsige group' (Leofsinus-Gruppe), as some scholars have recently done.[152]

It would be intriguing if an Anglo-Saxon monk did indeed play a major role in the introduction of Gerbert's curriculum to the abbey founded by St Willibrord some 300 years earlier. In contrast to his rival, Abbo of Fleury, Gerbert's teaching seems to have had little immediate impact on England.[153]

147 *Die Briefsammlung Gerberts*, ed. Weigle, nos. 41, 51, 52, 58 and 59; *The Letters of Gerbert*, trans. Lattin, nos. 53, 58, 59, 65 and 67.

148 Lochner, 'Die *Ars Musica* im Willibrorduskloster'.

149 *Ibid.* pp. 157–8.

150 Glaser and Moulin-Fankhänel, 'Die althochdeutsche Überlieferung', p. 110; Hoffmann, *Buchkunst* I, 509.

151 The only other substantial texts of Carolingian date known to have been copied at Echternach at this period are Amalarius of Metz, *Liber officialis* and Haimo of Auxerre, *In Isaiam*; see Ferrari, *Sancti Willibrordi venerantes memoriam*, p. 26.

152 For instance *ibid.* pp. 26–9.

153 An instructive comparison between Gerbert and Abbo is provided by M. Mostert, 'Gerbert d'Aurillac, Abbon de Fleury et la culture de l'an mil: étude comparative de leurs oeuvres et de leur influence', *Gerberto d'Aurillac da Abate di Bobbio a Papa dell'Anno 1000*, ed. F. G. Nuvolone, Archivum Bobiense Studia 4 (Bobbio, 2001), 397–431; see also Lutz, *Schoolmasters*, pp. 41–52 and 127–47.

England is not so much as mentioned in Gerbert's correspondence,[154] and there seems to be no evidence that any of his (fairly small) corpus of work was known in Anglo-Saxon England.[155]

The abbey of Egmond

The abbey of Egmond (on the Dutch coast 20 km north of Haarlem) was established by Count Dietrich II of Holland and his wife Hildegard, the parents of Archbishop Egbert of Trier. The date of foundation is usually thought to be *c.* 950, though a date in the 970s has recently been proposed.[156] The founding monks are normally considered likely to have come from one or other of the two Ghent abbeys.[157]

Archbishop Egbert and his parents are recorded to have given both books and precious ornaments to Egmond. In addition Egbert commissioned a life of Egmond's patron saint, St Adalbert; the final chapter of the *Vita S. Adalberti* relates that the commission was given to unnamed monks (in the plural) of Mettlach.[158] Further information is provided by the *Miracula S. Liutwini*, which names the author as Ruopert and says that he was a fellow-pupil (*ex eorum condiscipulatu*) of the two Mettlach monks who studied under Gerbert at Rheims.[159]

154 There is one apparent reference to the Insular world in Gerbert's correspondence. Two letters refer to a monk of Corbie called Meingaud, who had travelled to Rouen and who was subsequently induced to return from overseas: *Die Briefsammlung Gerberts*, ed. Weigle, nos. 61 and 67; *The Letters of Gerbert*, trans. Lattin, nos. 68 and 74. The phraseology (*transmarina mutare*) could reflect Gerbert's attitude to the Insular world, but it should be recognized that the surviving letters are a selection and that the guiding principles behind the selection are not entirely clear.

155 No works by Gerbert are listed by H. Gneuss, *Handlist of Anglo-Saxon Manuscripts: a list of Manuscripts and Manuscript Fragments Written or Owned in England up to 1100*, Med. and Renaissance Texts and Stud. 241 (Tempe, AZ, 2001) or by M. Lapidge, 'Surviving Booklists from Anglo-Saxon England', *Learning and Literature in Anglo-Saxon England: Studies Presented to Peter Clemoes on the Occasion of his sixty-fifth birthday*, ed. M. Lapidge and H. Gneuss (Cambridge, 1985), pp. 33–89. Some post-Conquest material is noted by M. Mostert, 'Les traditions manuscrites des oeuvres de Gerbert', *Gerbert l'Européen*, ed. N. Charbonnel and J.-E. Iung, Société des lettres, sciences et arts 'La Haute-Auvergne', Mémoires 3 (Aurillac, 1997), 307–24. The Gerbertian material in the mathematical anthology in Oxford, St John's College 17 (Thorney, *c.* 1110), fols. 41–56, is likely to have reached England much later than the Abbonian material in the same manuscript: see F. E. Wallis, 'MS Oxford St John's College 17: a Mediaeval Manuscript in its Context' (unpubl. PhD dissertation, Univ. of Toronto, 1985), pp. 461–501, 652–3 and 691–3.

156 For the earlier date, see M. Embach, 'Die Adalbert-Vita des Benediktinermönchs Ruopert von Mettlach – eine hagiographische Auftragsarbeit Erzbischof Egberts von Trier', *Egbert*, ed. Ronig II, pp. 15–36, at 19; for the later date, see J. P. Gumbert, 'Egberts geschenken aan Egmond', *In het spoor van Egbert*, ed. Vis, pp. 25–43, at 35–6.

157 Declercq, 'Heiligen, lekenabten en hervormers', p. 32.

158 *Vita S. Adalberti*, ch. 28, ed. Vis, pp. 70–2.

159 *Miracula S. Liutwini*, ch. 10, ed. Sauerland, p. 1264. Since the *Miracula* specifies that two Mettlach monks studied under Gerbert, the sense is presumably that Ruopert was a fellow-pupil at Mettlach: see *Vita S. Adalberti*, ed. Vis, pp. 13–15.

On stylistic grounds most of the *Vita S. Adalberti* (chapters 1–25 and 28) seems to have been written in rhyming prose by a single author, presumably Ruopert. However, the double-chapter 26–7 is written in a quite different style; Vis has concluded that the anonymous author of this double-chapter was another monk of Mettlach.[160] Flesch has subsequently suggested that the anonymous author was Leofsige.[161] This hypothesis is based on two points. First Flesch suggests that Ruopert is likely to be one and the same as the Robert, monk of Mettlach, who was elected bishop of Toul in 996; according to Picart, it was Robert's actions which led to the dismissal of Abbot Hezzel of Mettlach and to Leofsige's appointment in his place. Hence Flesch points out that Robert and Leofsige are likely to have been of similar orientation within the Mettlach community and that they could well have collaborated together. Secondly, Flesch draws attention to the fact that chapters 26–7 concern two brothers who were condemned to wear iron chains as a penance for the murder of an uncle; the first brother was miraculously freed from his chains at Nivelles, the second at Egmond.[162] Flesch notes that, as a former monk of Ghent, Leofsige may well have been familiar with Nivelles, which is some 60 km distant.

There is nothing particularly implausible in the hypothesis that Leofsige was the author of chapters 26–7 of the *Vita S. Adalberti*, but the arguments are far from compelling. In the time of Archbishop Egbert, there are likely to have been a number of monks of Mettlach who could have produced this double-chapter. It is also far from certain that Ruopert was one and the same as Robert, bishop-elect of Toul.[163] It should be borne in mind that Robert was a very popular name among the Upper Lotharingian aristocracy in the tenth century; John Nightingale has pointed out that there were no fewer than four Roberts in the reform community of St Maximin at Trier under Abbot Ogo (934–45).[164]

Flesch has also tentatively proposed that Leofsige might be the artist responsible for the donor miniatures with short verse inscriptions, which were added to the ninth-century West Frankish gospelbook known as the Egmond Gospels (The Hague, Koninklijke Bibliotheek, 76 F 1 (Rheims, s. ix^3; provenance Egmond), 214v and 215r); these miniatures both portray Dietrich and

[160] On the style, see *Vita S. Adalberti*, ed. Vis, pp. 15–17 (for the principal author) and pp. 23–6 (for chs. 26–7). [161] Flesch, *Die monastische Schriftkultur*, pp. 27–36.

[162] *Vita S. Adalberti*, chs. 26–7, ed. Vis, pp. 66–70.

[163] Much more contentious is the suggestion revived by Flesch that Ruopert was also the monk Ruodpreht who appears in the famous donor-portrait in the Egbert Psalter (Cividale, Museo Archeologico Nazionale 136 (Reichenau, 977–93), 16v and 17r): see Flesch, *Die monastische Schriftkultur*, pp. 28–9 and Weiner, 'Katalog', no. 3 (p. 20) and pls. 8–9 (pp. 58–9).

[164] Nightingale, *Monasteries and Patrons*, p. 215.

Hildegard, who gave the book to Egmond.[165] One scholar has indeed seen parallels to English manuscripts of late tenth-century date (in particular the Benedictional of St Æthelwold).[166] Flesch bases his suggestion on the belief that Leofsige was himself the artist responsible for the initials in BN lat. 8915, a proposition which is (as already noted) by no means established; there are in any event no evident stylistic links between the miniatures of the Egmond Gospels and the initials of the Paris manuscript.[167]

Both Ghent and Mettlach seem to have played a role in the early history of Egmond. Thus it is not in itself improbable that Leofsige came into contact with Egmond, and, as already noted, it is possible that Brower's marginal note describing Leofsige as 'Britannus vel Hollandus' might indicate links with Egmond. However, solid evidence for ties is lacking, and the suggestions made by Flesch should be treated with great caution.[168]

Leofsige the physician

According to the *Miracula S. Liutwini*, Leofsige was experienced in the art of medicine (*artis medicine peritum*). There is not a great deal that can be said about this aspect of Leofsige's career, but the text would seem to imply that he was a practising physician. Leofsige can thus be added to the small handful of physicians known by name from Anglo-Saxon England.[169] It should not, however, necessarily be assumed that he acquired his medical skills in England. The possibility that Leofsige moved to the diocese of Trier to serve as Egbert's physician, perhaps on the recommendation of Gerbert, has already been noted.[170]

165 Flesch, *Die monastische Schriftkultur*, pp. 33–4. For the two miniatures, see Weiner, 'Katalog', no. 28 (pp. 32–3) and pls. 125–6 (pp. 175–6). For the inscriptions, see K. Ciggaar, 'The Dedication Miniatures in the Egmond Gospels: a Byzantinizing Iconography?', *Quaerendo* 16 (1986), 30–62, at 35. See also K. G. Beuckers, 'Das ottonische Stifterbild. Bildtypen, Handlungsmotive und Stifterstatus in ottonischen und frühsalischen Stifterdarstellungen', *Die Ottonen. Kunst – Architektur – Geschichte*, ed. K. G. Beuckers, J. Cramer and M. Imhof (Petersberg, 2001), pp. 63–102, at pp. 77, n. 73 and 93.

166 B. Brenninkmeyer-de Rooy, 'The Miniatures of the Egmond Gospels', *Simiolus* 5 (1971), 150–71, at 161–8.

167 I am grateful to Dr Klaus Gereon Beuckers for useful comments on the miniatures in the Egmond Gospels.

168 Note for instance the doubts expressed by Gumbert, 'Egberts geschenken', p. 25, n. 4.

169 M. L. Cameron, *Anglo-Saxon Medicine*, CSASE 7 (Cambridge, 1993), 20–1.

170 See above, p. 118. It may be noted that an important ninth-century medical manuscript, Paris, Bibliothèque Nationale, lat. 11219 (St Denis, s. ix; provenance Echternach) reached Echternach at an early date. It is not known how the manuscript reached Echternach; the possibility that Leofsige, as a known physician and the donor of another book to Echternach, played a role in its transmission might at least be considered. On the manuscript, see M. E. Vazquez Bujan, 'Codicologie et Histoire des Textes Medicaux. A propos du Codex Paris, Bibliothèque Nationale, latin 11219', *I testi di medicina latini antichi. Problemi filologici e storici*, ed. I. Mazzini and F. Fusco (Rome, 1985), pp. 75–88.

DISCUSSION AND CONCLUSION

As a monk of St Peter's, Ghent, Leofsige was at one of a number of centres in Flanders which were in regular and sustained contact with England.[171] In Upper Lotharingia contacts were more occasional; even the old insular foundation at Echternach seems to have lost touch with England after the early ninth century.[172] Nevertheless there is a fair amount of evidence for contact between England and Trier in the tenth century. The Breton scholar Israel the Grammarian spent a number of years in England at the court of King Æthelstan (924–39); soon after Æthelstan's death he entered the service of Archbishop Ruotbert of Trier (931–56) and later became a monk of St Maximin in Trier where he died, perhaps *c.* 970.[173]

Much attention has been paid to the role of Benna, a canon of the collegiate church of St Paulinus at Trier, as recounted by Goscelin in his *Vita S. Edithae* written *c.* 1080.[174] According to Goscelin, Benna was first summoned to England to act as tutor to Edith, the natural daughter of King Edgar (959–75), at the nunnery of Wilton; Benna is also credited with having decorated the walls of the chapel of St Denis at Wilton with a passion cycle and with the production of metalwork ornaments. On a return visit to Trier, Benna negotiated the purchase of a fragment of the Trier relic of the holy nail. After Edith's death he seems to have returned to Trier, but subsequently visited Wilton again on a pilgrimage to Edith's shrine. The exact chronology of Benna's travels is hard to recover, but his initial departure from Trier would seem to have taken place before Edgar's death in 975, while the chapel of St Denis is stated by Goscelin to have been dedicated by Archbishop Dunstan in the year of Edith's death, which can be dated to the years 984–7.[175]

171 Grierson, 'Relations between England and Flanders'; Ortenberg, *The English Church and the Continent*, pp. 21–40; see also above, p. 119.

172 J. Schroeder, 'Zu den Beziehungen zwischen Echternach und England/Irland im Frühmittelalter', *T'Hémecht. Zeitschrift für Luxemburger Geschichte* 31 (1979), 363–89, at 383.

173 M. Lapidge, 'Israel the Grammarian in Anglo-Saxon England', *From Athens to Chartres: Neoplatonism and Medieval Thought*, ed. H. J. Westra (Leiden, 1992), pp. 97–114.

174 A. Wilmart, 'La légende de Ste Édith en prose et vers par le moine Goscelin', *AB* 56 (1938), 5–101 and 265–307, at 50–1, 73–4, 86–7 and 271–2. See the discussions by T. E. Kempf, 'Benna Treverensis, Canonicus de Sancti Paulini patrocinio', *Mainz und der Mittelrhein in der europäischen Kunstgeschichte. Studien für Wolfgang Fritz Volbach*, ed. F. Gerke, Forschungen zur Kunstgeschichte und christlichen Archäologie 6 (Mainz, 1966), 179–96; Deshman, '*Christus rex*', pp. 393–5; R. Gem, 'Documentary References to Anglo-Saxon Painted Architecture', *Early Medieval Wall Painting and Painted Sculpture in England*, ed. S. Cather, D. Park and P. Williamson, BAR British ser. 216 (Oxford, 1990), 1–16, at 6–10; Hoffmann, *Buchkunst* I, 122–6.

175 For the date of Edith's death, see B. Yorke, 'The Legitimacy of St Edith', *Haskins. Soc. Jnl* 11 (2003 for 1998), 97–113, at 111.

No works attributable to Benna survive, but there is evidence for artistic exchanges between England and Trier in the time of Archbishop Egbert (977–93). Robert Deshman has drawn attention to parallel developments in royal iconography (specifically the crowned Christ and the crowned Magi) in English and Trier manuscripts at this period.[176] In addition English *spolia* have been detected in the portable altar commissioned by Archbishop Egbert as a reliquary shrine for the sandal of St Andrew.[177]

There are moreover grounds for thinking that Egbert is likely to have been well disposed towards England and the English, for he bore a distinctively English name in which he evidently took some pride. He was of ultimately English descent through his mother, Hildegard, a daughter of Count Arnulf I of Flanders (918–65);[178] Arnulf was the son of Count Baldwin II (879–918), who had married Ælfthryth, a daughter of King Alfred (871–99).[179] Through Alfred Egbert could thus trace his ancestry back ultimately to his namesake, King Ecgberht of Wessex (802–39), Alfred's grandfather. Several English names are found in the comital family of Flanders in the generations succeeding Ælfthryth's marriage to Baldwin II.[180] Arnulf I's second son (a brother of Hildegard and thus an uncle of Egbert of Trier) was likewise called Egbert.[181]

Archbishop Egbert's pride in his English name is demonstrated by the *Vita S. Adalberti*, the work which he commissioned from Ruopert of Mettlach for the abbey of Egmond. According to the *Vita*, Adalbert was one of the eleven

[176] Deshman, '*Christus rex*'.

[177] H. Westermann-Angerhausen, 'Spolie und Umfeld in Egberts Trier. Hanns Swarzenski zum Andenken', *Zeitschrift für Kunstgeschichte* 50 (1987), 305–36, at 310–11 and 330–1; Weiner, 'Katalog', nos. 41–2 (pp. 36–8) and pls. 146–59 (pp. 196–209).

[178] The common error that Egbert's mother was herself English goes back to E. A. Freeman, *The History of the Norman Conquest of England, its causes and its results*, 6 vols. (Oxford, 1867–79) I, 634. The error doubtless derives ultimately from the somewhat exaggerated account of Egbert's Insular origins contained in the B recension of the *Gesta Treverorum*, written after 1132. This account begins, 'Ekebertus episcopus. Hic de Brittannia ortus, patre Theoderico comite et matre Hildegarda nomine, divitiis et nobilitate Anglorum primoribus, divinitus, ut credimus, huic sedi est praedestinatus . . .' ('Bishop Egbert. He was a scion of Britain, his father Count Dietrich and his mother Hildegard by name, foremost in wealth and nobility among the English; he was predestined, as we believe, by divine providence for this see . . .'): *Gesta Treverorum*, ed. G. Waitz, MGH SS 8 (Hanover, 1848), 111–200, at 169.

[179] For Egbert's ancestry, see R. Laufner, 'Die Vorfahren des Trierer Erzbischofs Egbert und ihre Herkunft. Ein Beitrag zur Sozial- und Familiengeschichte des 9. und 10. Jahrhunderts', *Egbert*, ed. Ronig II, pp. 103–9.

[180] Grierson, 'Relations between England and Flanders', pp. 85–6. For a useful genealogical table showing Archbishop Egbert's descent from King Ecgberht, see J. L. Nelson, 'Alfred's Carolingian contemporaries', *Alfred the Great: Papers from the Eleventh-Centenary Conferences*, ed. T. Reuter (Aldershot, 2003), pp. 293–321, at 295.

[181] It has reasonably been suggested that this Egbert (who died in 953) is likely to have been the godfather of Egbert of Trier: Laufner, 'Die Vorfahren', p. 106.

companions of St Willibrord in his missionary journey from Ireland to the continent. Adalbert is said, like Willibrord, to have studied under the saintly monk Ecgberht at the English community of Rath Melsigi in Ireland. Ruopert evidently knew the glowing accounts given by Bede of Ecgberht (d. 729) in his *Historia ecclesiastica*,[182] and it is with Ecgberht of Rath Melsigi that the *Vita S. Adalberti* begins.[183]

Leofsige thus arrived in the diocese of Trier at a time when an Englishman was likely to receive a favourable reception. The glowing account of him in the *Miracula S. Liutwini* has led modern scholars to make wide-ranging claims for him. In one recent account he has been described as a 'many-sided Englishman . . . who was eminent among other things as architect, scribe of *de luxe* manuscripts, poet of short verse inscriptions as well as a man of notable theological and medical knowledge'; another similar account calls him 'this great scholar'.[184] There is very little solid evidence for such statements. There is nothing which can be adduced to indicate the level of Leofsige's own theological and scholarly attainments. While St Peter's, Ghent, Mettlach and Echternach all had links (direct or indirect) with the world of Gerbert of Rheims, any direct association between Gerbert and Leofsige remains unproven. The *de luxe* manuscript bearing Leofsige's name (BN lat. 8915) may well have been commissioned rather than written and decorated by him, and the same applies to the verse epitaphs. At best it may be said that the account in the *Miracula* indicates that he played an active role in the design of the 'Alter Turm' at Mettlach.

A sideways glance at Archbishop Egbert is illuminating; he has been described as 'perhaps the greatest episcopal patron of art in the whole Ottonian period'.[185] No contemporary source describes Egbert as participating with his own hands in the processes of making the manuscripts, metalwork and ivories associated with him; it is in the role of patron and commissioner of works of art that he is perceived by modern scholarship.[186] Perhaps Leofsige should be considered in similar terms. There are possible indications that Leofsige may have disposed of considerable means, specifically the reference in the *Miracula* to his provision of *rerum exuberantia* and the lavish use of parchment in BN lat. 8915; the source of such means remains unknown. It is the

182 Bede, *Historia ecclesiastica* III.4, 27, IV.3, 26, V.9, 10, 22 (*Bede's Ecclesiastical History of the English People*, ed. B. Colgrave and R. A. B. Mynors (Oxford, 1969), pp. 224, 312–14, 344, 428, 474–80, 552–4).

183 *Vita S. Adalberti*, chs. 1–3, ed. Vis, pp. 40–4 (see also pp. 17–18 for comment on Ruopert's use of Bede and his even more extensive use of Alcuin's *Vita Willibrordi*).

184 Embach, 'Die Adalbert-Vita', p. 28; Margue and Schroeder, 'Zur geistigen Ausstrahlung', p. 117 (my translation from the German in both cases).

185 H. Mayr-Harting, *Ottonian Book Illumination: an Historical Study*, 2 vols. (London, 1991) II, 61.

186 See the various contributions in *Egbert*, ed. Ronig.

contention of this article that there is as yet no evidence for seeing Leofsige as anything more than a patron of arts such as the production of fine manuscripts and verse epitaphs. His career is no less interesting for that.

Perhaps it is no coincidence that the English influence which the young Nordenfalk was so keen to detect in Leofsige's career has receded. Subsequent studies of the architecture of the 'Alter Turm' at Mettlach and of manuscripts associated with Leofsige have failed to detect English influence and have placed much greater emphasis on the Lotharingian context. Nordenfalk's preoccupation was betrayed by his sub-title, 'an example of English influence', but in a happier turn of phrase he also called Leofsige an 'Ottonian Englishman'.[187] As such Leofsige would be no different to another contemporary English abbot in the imperial church, Gregory of Einsiedeln in Suabia. Gregory had a long and successful career at Einsiedeln, entering the community in 949 and becoming abbot from 964 to 996, a period when Einsiedeln was high in the favour of the Ottonian emperors.[188] At Einsiedeln English influences are similarly hard to detect, and Gregory and Leofsige are perhaps both best described as 'Ottonian Englishmen'.

APPENDIX

ENGLISH PILGRIMS AT METTLACH AND EGMOND

Both the hagiographical works discussed in this paper, the *Miracula S. Liutwini* and the *Vita S. Adalberti*, contain evidence for English pilgrims visiting their respective shrines. The *Miracula S. Liutwini* gives an account of eleven miracles worked by the merits of St Liutwin.[189] One of these recounts the story of an

[187] Nordenfalk, 'Abbas Leofsinus', pp. 72–3.

[188] D. Rees, 'Abt Gregor von Einsiedeln. Ein Bindeglied zwischen der Schweiz und England', *Studien und Mitteilungen zur Geschichte des Benediktinerordens* 107 (1996), 13–27; J. Salzgeber, 'Einsiedeln', in *Helvetia Sacra* III.1, *Frühe Klöster, Die Benediktiner und Benediktinerinnen in der Schweiz*, 3 vols., ed. E. Gilomen-Schenkel (Berne, 1986) I, 517–94, at 550–1. There were close connections in the second half of the tenth century between Trier and the Suabian monasteries of Reichenau, St Gallen and Einsiedeln, typified by the career of St Wolfgang. Wolfgang first studied at Reichenau and subsequently became master of the cathedral school at Trier under Archbishop Henry (956–64); on Henry's death he moved to Einsiedeln as master of the school under Gregory before becoming bishop of Regensburg (972–94): see E. Boshof, *Das Erzstift Trier und seine Stellung zu Königtum und Papsttum im ausgehenden 10. Jahrhundert. Der Pontifikat des Theoderich*, Studien und Vorarbeiten zur Germania Pontificia 4 (Cologne, 1972), 2–5. According to Einsiedeln sources, Gregory was a member of the English royal house (Rees, 'Abt Gregor', 15–18); the Einsiedeln stories of Gregory's royal origins are problematic and perhaps fictitious, but if they have some basis in fact, he would presumably have been a distant kinsman of Archbishop Egbert of Trier.

[189] *Miracula S. Liutwini*, chs. 24–32 (1–15), ed. Perier, pp. 176–9; Flesch, *Die monastische Schriftkultur*, p. 26.

unnamed Englishman possessed by an evil spirit.[190] He is reported to have exclaimed on his arrival at Mettlach that on account of Liutwin's repute, he had travelled long distances to visit his shrine. When the monks of Mettlach learned from his companions of the homeland and of the suffering of the Englishman, they decided to do everything in their power to help. The evil spirit was eventually driven out while the prior was reciting the litany by the power of the name of Liutwin. The grateful Englishman is reported to have proclaimed the name and merits of Liutwin on his return home.

The date of the anonymous Englishman's visit to Mettlach is uncertain. The *Miracula* was written in the 1070s or 1080s, and it seems likely that many, perhaps all, of the healing miracles belong to the late tenth and eleventh centuries. The first of the eleven miracles mentions Abbot Remigius and must therefore be dated close to the year 1000; two others refer to the *turris*, the 'Alter Turm' built by Leofsige.[191] If the Englishman did proclaim Liutwin's merits on his return to England, then there is no trace in the surviving sources; Liutwin is not mentioned in any extant litany or calendar of the late Saxon period.[192]

Ruopert of Mettlach's *Vita S. Adalberti* tells of an English priest called Volmarus, who had been blind for twenty years. Volmarus visited many holy places in the course of a pilgrimage to Rome, but when he reached Rome it was revealed to him that he should visit the shrine of St Adalbert. When Volmarus eventually arrived at Egmond, he washed his eyes three times in the spring beneath the tomb of the saint; his sight was then restored.[193] Ruopert's *Vita* was written between 977 and 993, and this miracle is one of a number which Ruopert notes as having occurred in the recent past, with little doubt after the establishment of monks at Egmond by Count Dietrich II towards the middle of the tenth century.[194] Although Adalbert was purportedly an Englishman, there seems to be no evidence for his cult in pre-Conquest England.[195]

[190] *Miracula S. Liutwini*, ch. 26 (6), ed. Perier, pp. 177–8.

[191] *Miracula S. Liutwini*, chs. 24, 27 and 29 (3, 7–8 and 10), ed. Perier, pp. 177–8.

[192] *Anglo-Saxon Litanies of the Saints*, ed. M. Lapidge, HBS 106 (London, 1991); R. Rushforth, *An Atlas of Saints in Anglo-Saxon Calendars*, ASNC Guides, Texts and Studies 6 (Cambridge, 2002).

[193] *Vita S. Adalberti*, ch. 21, ed. Vis, p. 62 (see also p. 78 for an *abbreviatio* of the *Vita*). None of the manuscripts is of earlier than fourteenth-century date, and the name of the priest is variously given as Volmarus, Wolmarus, Vulmarus and Fulmarius; the forms most probably represent Old English Wulfmær.

[194] Ruopert refers to some miracles as having occurred in the time of Count Dietrich II and says of the miracle immediately after the restoration of Volmarus's sight that it occurred *Moderno quoque tempore*: *Vita S. Adalberti*, chs. 18 and 22, ed. Vis, pp. 60 and 62.

[195] I am grateful to Joy Jenkyns and to Klaus Gereon Beuckers for helpful observations on a first draft of this paper. John Rhodes notably improved the elegance of my Latin translations. The staff of Villeroy and Boch (particularly Frau Fischer and Herr Ritter) provided valuable help on the occasion of visits to the 'Alter Turm' in Mettlach.

The Taunton Fragment: a new text from Anglo-Saxon England

MECHTHILD GRETSCH

The Taunton Fragment (now Taunton, Somerset, Somerset County Record Office, DD/SAS C/1193/77) consists of four leaves containing portions of brief expositions or homilies on the pericopes[1] for four successive Sundays after Pentecost. In the Fragment, brief passages in Latin regularly alternate with the Old English translations of these passages.[2] The manuscript to which the four leaves once belonged was written probably at some point around or after the middle of the eleventh century in an unknown (presumably minor) centre in Anglo-Saxon England. Until recently, the existence of the Taunton leaves had escaped the notice of Anglo-Saxonists; the texts which they contain are printed here for the first time. It will be obvious that eight pages, half of which are in Old English prose, add in no negligible way to the corpus of Old English. Through analysis of the texts in the second part of this article, I hope to show that their contribution to our knowledge of various kinds of literary activity in Anglo-Saxon England is significant indeed, and that the linguistic evidence they present has no parallel elsewhere in the corpus of Old English.

The story of the recent discovery of the Taunton Fragment by Anglo-Saxonists almost reads as if the texts themselves had decided that, at last, the time had come for a professional interest to be taken in them, about nine and a half centuries after they were written down. As far as can be established now, the first mention of the leaves was made in 1883 in *A Guide to the Museum of the Somerset Archaeological and Natural History Society in Taunton Castle*, compiled by William Bidgood, curator of the Museum.[3] In this catalogue, the Taunton Fragment is described (not entirely inappropriately) as 'Four leaves of a Saxon homily, written probably in the eighth or ninth centuries'.[4] It seems no longer to be known when and under what circumstances the Fragment was acquired by the Somerset Archaeological and Natural History Society; in any case, this must have occurred at some point after the foundation of the Society in 1849. The history of the four leaves before they came into the Society's possession

[1] Pericopes are passages from the gospels assigned for reading at mass during Sundays and certain weekdays: see below, pp. 183–4.

[2] The nature of the text and its intention will be discussed below, pp. 183–90.

[3] This is the second edition; a search for the first edition has, so far, been unsuccessful.

[4] *Guide*, p. 10.

presently remains in the dark. They are not recorded in Neil Ker's *Catalogue* or in its *Supplement*, nor in Helmut Gneuss's *Handlist*.[5] It is interesting to note that the Taunton Fragment (DD/SAS C/1193/77) is not mentioned in the relevant volume of *Medieval Manuscripts in British Libraries*, although four manuscripts from the Taunton archive having adjacent shelfnumbers are recorded there,[6] and although, in 1951, Neil Ker had published an article on these four manuscripts.[7] This gives rise to the suspicion that, at the time Ker examined the medieval manuscripts in the Taunton Castle Museum, the Taunton Fragment was not on its shelf. In 1995 Dr Nigel Ramsay came across the entry in Bidgood's *Catalogue*, but, at that time, the Fragment was definitely not on its shelf, nor could it be traced in the Taunton archive. A year later, Ramsay happened upon the Fragment under its present shelfmark in one of the Somerset Record Office's calendars, where it is described as '4 mm. of an Anglo-Saxon commentary on the New Testament, ?tenth century'.[8] In the summer of 2002 there was a small exhibition at the Somerset County Museum at Taunton, bringing together items connected with Athelney Abbey and of related interest. In this exhibition the Taunton leaves, with the caption 'Part of an Anglo-Saxon Commentary on the New Testament' were on public display all summer, but apparently the only Anglo-Saxonist who made his way to Taunton during that summer was Simon Keynes. A few weeks later, by a strange coincidence, Nigel Ramsay mentioned to Simon Keynes an Anglo-Saxon manuscript at Taunton, to which he had found references but which he had not seen. Keynes, as he said, 'put two and two together' and had photocopies made of the leaves. He gave these photocopies to Helmut Gneuss in Munich, in November 2002, at a party on the occasion of his 75th birthday. So, finally, the Taunton leaves had succeeded in attracting the almost simultaneous attention of two historians and Anglo-Saxonists, Nigel Ramsay and Simon Keynes, and it was obvious that they now called for an edition, a task which fell to me.[9]

[5] The Fragment is, however, recorded in H. Gneuss, 'Addenda and Corrigenda to the *Handlist of Anglo-Saxon Manuscripts*', *ASE* 32 (2003), 293–305, no. *756.8 (p. 303).

[6] See N. R. Ker and A. J. Piper, *Medieval Manuscripts in British Libraries* (Oxford, 1992) IV, 487–94, recording DD/SAS C/1193/66, 68, 70 and 74.

[7] See N. R. Ker, 'Four Medieval Manuscripts in the Taunton Castle Museum', *Proc. of the Somersetshire Archaeol. Soc.* 96 (1951), 224–8.

[8] I owe this information to Simon Keynes.

[9] Here I should like to thank those who have generously given help and advice at various points: Helmut Gneuss, who took an active and abiding interest in his 'birthday present', extending from his initial transcription of the text to a final critical reading of the present article, with many helpful discussions in between; Michael Lapidge, who, with characteristic generosity and expertise, advised me on the script and date of the manuscript and searched the electronic databases for possible sources of the text; Ursula Lenker, who inspected the manuscript before I had an opportunity to see it (on this occasion she was kindly instructed by Mervyn Richens, Senior Conservator in the Somerset Record Office, on the various kinds of repair executed on the leaves); Christy Hosefelder and Janna Riedinger, without whose

THE MANUSCRIPT

It is not known when the manuscript to which the leaves belonged was dismembered. The leaves may at one time have served as flyleaves to a printed book, but nothing further is known about their post-medieval history. The parchment was repaired in various and not always very competent ways, probably in the 1950s or 1960s; three pages (pp. 5–7) are now overlaid with silk. The pages have been trimmed, measuring now *c.* 24.5 × 18.5 cm; the written space is *c.* 20.5 × 13.5 cm; there are invariably twenty lines of text to a page. The leaves may have formed part of the same quire, as is suggested by the text portions preserved on them. This would have been a quire of eight or ten folios; a tentative arrangement of its folios and the position of the Taunton leaves within the quire is shown in fig. 4: the page numbers of the leaves are given in arabic numerals; the roman numerals refer to the Sundays after Pentecost to which the texts pertain; the broken lines signal two bifolia that have certainly been lost, the dotted line indicates a third bifolium that may have been lost as well. For a discussion of the arrangement of the folios and a calculation of the missing text portions for the individual Sundays, see below, pp. 184–5.

Script and Date

The four leaves were written by one hand; the script for the Latin and Old English text is Anglo-Saxon minuscule of an unpretentious kind (pls. III and IV).[10]

Anglo-Saxon minuscule, or English vernacular minuscule, was characteristically used in the eleventh century for writing the vernacular and represents a fusion and development of Anglo-Saxon Square minuscule (used in the later tenth century for writing the vernacular) and Anglo-Caroline script. It is remarkable that (with the exception of **f**, **g**, **r** and **s**) the scribe of the Taunton Fragment allows himself only occasionally to use Caroline letter-forms and ligatures: there are a few examples of the **ct**-ligature (e.g. lu**ct**us, 1.19; dile**ct**issimi, 3.11; resurræ**ct**ionem, 7.17),[11] and one of the final **nt**-ligature (su**nt**, 1.18); and, with one exception (**a**it, 8.13), he avoids using the Caroline form of

expert and speedy word-processing of my difficult handwritten exemplar, the text could not have seen light so soon after it had been discovered; Rebecca Rushforth, who kindly provided the digital images reproduced here; and Clare Orchard for carefully copyediting the typescript. Finally, I am grateful to Simon Keynes, who, by haunting once again the Somerset marshes, made it all possible.

[10] For this script see D. N. Dumville, '*Beowulf* Come Lately. Some Notes on the Palaeography of the Nowell Codex', *Archiv für das Studium der neueren Sprachen und Literaturen* 225 (1988), 49–63, esp. 53–4; *idem*, *English Caroline Script and Monastic History* (Woodbridge, 1993), p. 154; and *idem*, 'Specimina Codicum Palaeoanglicorum', *Kansai University Collection of Essays in Commemoration of the 50th Anniversary of the Institute of Oriental and Occidental Studies* (Osaka, 2001), pp. 1–24, at 10–12.

[11] Page references are always to the present pagination of the Taunton Fragment.

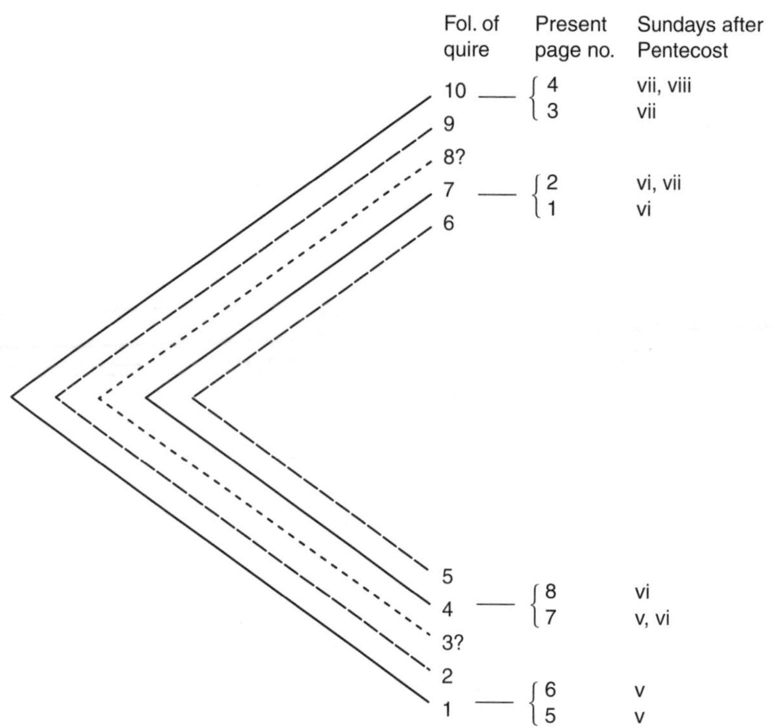

Fig. 4 The reconstructed quire

the letter **a**. By the same token, the scribe has rigorously suppressed the use of the ligatures characteristic of tenth-century (Square minuscule) script, most of them involving **e** (**ec**, **en**, **er**, **et** and others), as also the use of the curved vernacular form of **y**, which is replaced throughout with the straight-limbed, two-stroke form of the letter (usually with a dot). The fact that such ligatures are wholly avoided, even when the scribe is copying Old English, suggests that the specimen dates from a time when the script had developed to the point where such ligatures were eliminated. To judge from dated examples, the elimination took place during the earlier eleventh century.[12] The fact that the process is complete by the time the Taunton Fragment was written suggests that it does not date from the early eleventh century, when the canons of Anglo-Saxon vernacular minuscule were being worked out. A date later than the early eleventh century may further be suggested by a number of individual letter forms: on the one occasion when the scribe slips and uses Caroline **a** (**a**it,

[12] See, for example, N. R. Ker, *Catalogue of Manuscripts containing Anglo-Saxon* (Oxford, 1957), p. xxxiii.

8.13), he uses a 'tall-backed' **a**, where the final stroke assumes an exaggerated height. Such tall-backed **a**'s are a feature of the second quarter of the eleventh century but rarely occur earlier.[13] To a similar date point the mannered finials of the ascenders of **h**, **l**, **b** and **þ** ('split-top' finials), e.g. ha**bb**ene (1.1), **h**odium **h**abeat (3.13), **þ**o**l**odon (4.14), as does the Caroline ligature **ct**, which is written in a mannered way, so that the two letters are exaggeratedly separated from each other, e.g. dile**ct**issimi (3.11). This mannered way of writing the **ct**-ligature does not occur habitually before the second quarter of the eleventh century. Also distinctive is the form of Insular **g** with rounded, nearly circular, bowl. Close parallels to these and other letter forms in the Taunton Fragment are found in a document dated *c.* 1045 and preserved in contemporary form in London, British Library, Cotton Augustus ii. 70.[14] However, to confirm the dating 'around the middle of the eleventh century', tentatively suggested here, an exhaustive search through securely datable documents (i.e. charters) would have to be made. This is a task for an expert palaeographer.

EDITION

In the following edition the pages have been rearranged according to their original order, and they are numbered consecutively 1 to 8. In addition, for each page I give in brackets its present numbering as found in the four Taunton leaves. Note that in the discussion of the text, in the second part of this article, page references are always to the actual (not the reconstructed) page numbering of the leaves. In order to give as authentic an impression of the Fragment as possible, the edition is almost diplomatic: lineation, punctuation, spelling and capitalization are reproduced as in the manuscript, but word-division is modern (a hyphen is added to the first part of a word whenever it is separated from its second part by the end of a line). Abbreviations are normally expanded, with the expanded letters in italics. I have, however, not expanded *ƀ* for the reason that <æ> is used very sparingly by the scribe and that no substitute for it is employed with any regularity: <e> and <a> (occasionally <ea>) occur indiscriminately (see below, pp. 172–4). Expanding *ƀ* to *þæt* would there-

[13] This form of **a** is used, for example, by the second scribe of BL, Cotton Titus D. xxvi + xxvii, written 1023 × 1031; for an illustration, see T. A. M. Bishop, *English Caroline Minuscule* (Oxford, 1971), pl. XXIII (lower half of right-hand plate); for the date of the manuscript, see *Ælfwine's Prayerbook*, ed. B. Günzel, HBS 108 (London, 1993), 2, and *The Liber Vitae of the New Minster and Hyde Abbey Winchester: British Library Stowe 944*, ed. S. Keynes, EEMF 26 (Copenhagen, 1996), 111.

[14] The document in question is P. H. Sawyer, *Anglo-Saxon Charters: an Annotated List and Bibliography* (London, 1968), no. 1471; for a facsimile, see *Facsimiles of Ancient Charters in the British Museum*, ed. E. A. Bond, 4 vols. (London, 1873–8) IV, no. 27. For the distinctive form of **g** and the split-top finials, see also BL, Cotton Cleopatra B. xiii, dated by Ker (*Catalogue*, no. 144, p. 182) to the third quarter of the eleventh century, and illustrated (fol. 38r) *ibid.* as pl. V.

fore have altered the picture presented by the edited text in favour of *æ*-spellings in a way that is not warranted by the original text.

The text is crawling with errors of all sorts, especially in its English but also in its Latin parts. Correcting all these errors in the edition and recording them in an apparatus criticus would have altered the text almost beyond recognition and would have produced an enormously inflated apparatus, cumbersome to consult, without yielding a clear and coherent picture of the original state of the text. To provide such a picture, I have therefore preferred to discuss the most important and recurrent types of error in a systematic fashion in the section on language (pp. 160–82). The very few emendations to the text, all made for the sake of clarity, are in square brackets and are explained in the textual notes. Also in square brackets I have indicated the Sundays for which the individual texts were intended. No such indications are given in the manuscript, where a new homily simply starts on a fresh line, introduced by the formulaic phrase *In illo tempore* (on this, see below, p. 185). I have identified in the text the quotations from the gospel pericopes; for a discussion of further sources on which the Taunton Commentator may have drawn, see below, pp. 186–90.

The translation into Modern English is provided for the sole reason of facilitating access to the original texts. Obviously, it cannot be a text in its own right, since it translates into Modern English first, a Latin passage and subsequently, the Old English rendering of this passage, both languages alternating throughout the Taunton Fragment; duplication of wording is therefore inevitable. For easy reference the originally Latin passages are printed in italics and the originally Old English passages are printed in roman type. In each case a colon separates the Modern English translation of a Latin passage from the Modern English translation of the following Old English passage. Latin quotations from the gospels are given in the translation of the Douai-Rheims version, now conveniently available on the Web, and are identified in the text.

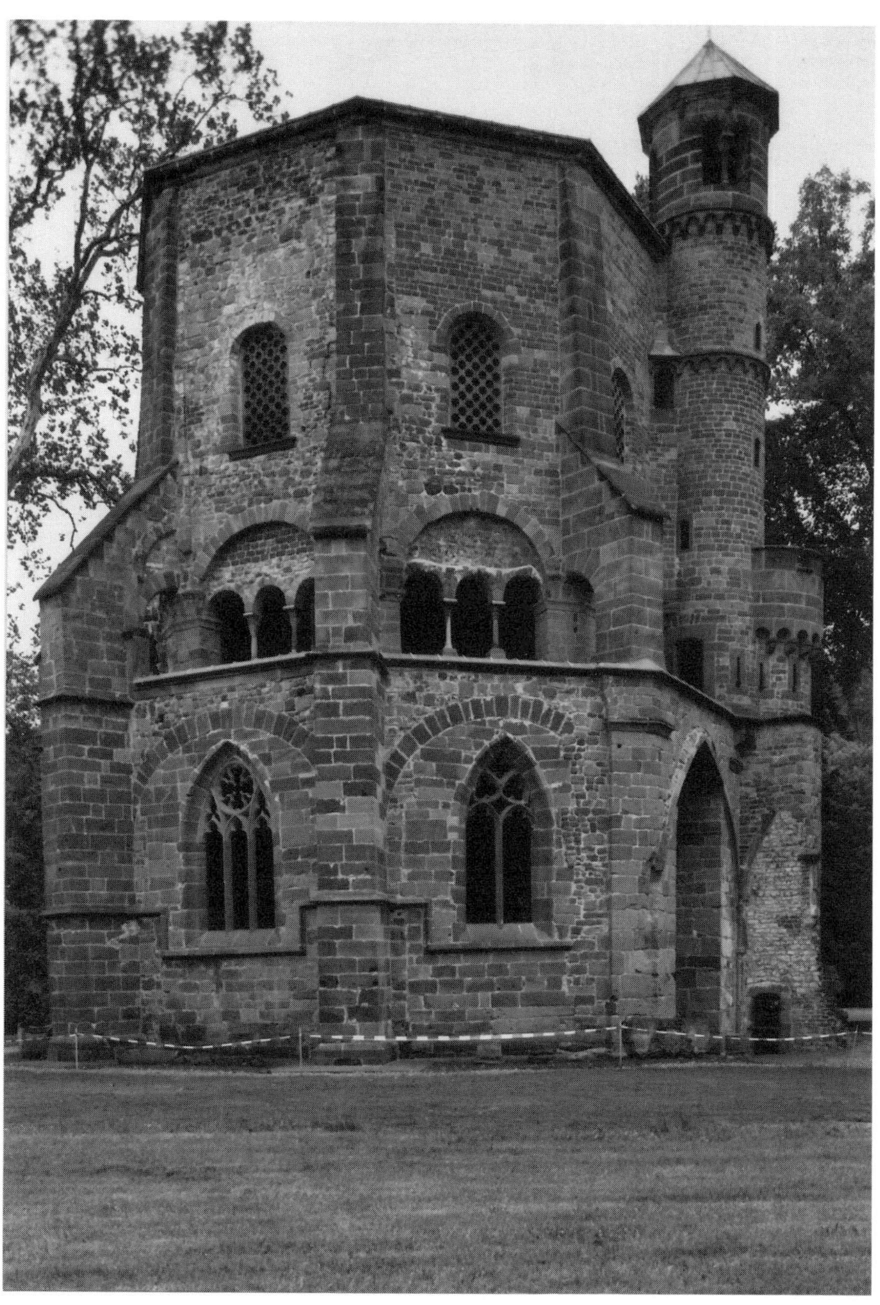

I The 'Alter Turm' at Mettlach from the north-west

menta · & ipse penitus ignore-
tur a dño ;· Quid sint sacra- III
menta · uel quare dicantur ;·
SACRAMENTUM IGITUR
est · quic quid in aliqua
celebratione diuina nobis
quasi pignus salutis traditur ·
cum res gesta uisibilis · longe a-
liud inuisibile intus operatur ·
quod sancte accipiendum sit · Vn-
de & sacramenta dicuntur · aut
a secreto · eo quod in re uisibili diui-
nitas intus aliquid ultro secreti-
us efficiat per speciem corporalem ·
aut a consecratione sanctificationis ·
quia sps scs manens in corpore xpi ·
latenter haec omnia sacramento-
rum mysteria · sub tegimento

II Paris, Bibliothèque Nationale de France. lat. 8915, 20r

-1-

cniet to habbene clenesse · 7 swiðe swang
lice, to wiðstandene ðem deofle; Iohannis
gratia dei interpretatur: debet ecclesia gratia
dei agere laudare dominum et benedicere;
Iohannis godes gyfe ys gereaht byreð on cyrice
god to ðeonenne · 7 to herienne · 7 to blet
sienne; Illa retia intellegitur sanctarum
scripturarum: per quae homines capiuntur
et ueniunt ad litus id est ad finem mundi
· Ða net getacnað þa halgan gewritu ðurh
þa men man nimeð 7 cumað to þam sæ ofre:
þæt is to þyssere middaneardes endunge; Re
linquamus in quantum possumus mundum:
ne perdamus uitam perpetuam; Forletan we
swa mycel swa we æt læst mugon ðisne mid
dangeardes ydelnesse · þæt we þæt ece lyf ne for
leosan; Ubi non est famis; Ðær nis nan hun
gor · Non est sitis · Nis þær þurst · Non sunt
tenebras · Nis þær þeostru; Non est luctus;
Nis þær wop; Non est timor · Nis þær ege ·

III Taunton Fragment, Somerset Record Office, p. 1

IV Taunton Fragment, Somerset Record Office, p. 6

TEXT

1 (=p. 5 fragment)
[The Fifth Sunday after Pentecost]

misericordes ⹎ quomodo sicut *et* pat*er* u*este*r ⹎
misericors e*st* (Luke VI.36); Ernnostlice wese ge mildheorte
3 hu gemete. swá swá eowre heofonlic fedur mildheorte is; Nos fra*tre*s cotidie peccauimus c*on*tra
d*omi*n*u*m ⹎ in multis modis; Leofe breoðre deg-
6 hwamlice we synigað ongean ure drihtin on
felæ wisan; Ille nos non occidat ⹎ non sper-
nit non condempn*et*; Hæ ne ofsléþ us. ne
9 he us ne tostrégdeð ne us ne niðrað; S*et* se*m*p*er*
nos exspect*et* ut nos em*en*dem*us* in meliu*s et* q*ui*d*em*
p[e]ius[1] est si frat*er* n*oste*r peccat contra nos nullam
12 mis*ericor*dia*m* uolum*us* habere contra illu*m*; Æac
efre he us onbydeð ꝥ we gebetæð þa yfela cystas
ðe we don[2] habbað. ⁊ ꝥ is eallra forcuðest. gif enig
15 ure broðor gegiltað hefð ongean us nan mildheorte ne willan we habban ongean heom; Aliquando ⹎ uolunt occidere; Eac sume[3] we
18 willað ofslean; Aliquando condempnare;
Sume nyðrian; Aliquando in pena*m* mitte[re];[4]
Sume willað heom on mycel pine ðrowian;

[*be*] *merciful, as your Father is also merciful* (Luke VI.36): Therefore be merciful to the same degree as your Father in heaven is merciful. *Brethren, daily we sin against the Lord in many ways*: Dear brethren, daily we sin against our Lord in many ways. *He does not kill us*; *He does not reject us*; *He does not condemn us*: He does not kill us; nor does He destroy us; nor does He condemn us. *But He is always waiting for us to mend our ways*; *and certainly*, *it is worse*, *if our brother offends us, and we refuse to show mercy to him*: Also, He is always waiting for us to repair the wicked deeds that we perpetrated; and, if any of our brethren committed an offence against us, it is most shameful that we should refuse to show mercy to him. *On occasion they will kill* [*them*]: rather, some we will kill; *on occasion* [*they will*] *condemn* [*them*]: some [we will] condemn; *on occasion* [*they will*] *punish* [*them*]: some desire them to suffer great pain.

TEXT

2 (=p. 6 fragment)
[Fifth Sunday after Pentecost: Continuation]

Considerem*us* fr*atre*s k*arissi*mi ⁊ agite mis*eri*co*r*dia*m* contra
fr*atre*s u*est*ros sicut piu*s* pat*er* celestis hab*et* mis*eri*co*r*dia*m*
contra nos; Gesceawian we leofe breoðre. hab-
ban ge mycell myldheortnesse ongean eow-
re breoðre. swa se arfesta heofo[n]lic[5] fedur hefð
mildheortnesse ongean us; Nolite iudica-
re ⁊ et non iudicabimini (Luke VI.37); Nille ge deman
þ ge ne worðen fordemde; Id e*st* iudicare a p*er*-
ditione mortis ⁊ ne uos ipsum iudicium a
beatis ante tribunal cristi iudicitis; Ðæt is
þonne ðu demest mon to deade oððe on oðer wise buton gewrihta. Gewarnian ge gu þ
ge þ ilce dom ne habbað toforen drihtnes
ðrymsetle; Nolite condempnare ⁊ *et* non
condempnabimini (Luke VI.37); Nille ge nyðran. þ ge
ne[6] beon genyðrad; Timete fr*atre*s k*arissi*mi ⁊ in ma-
lum iudicium ⁊ ne forte ueniat sup*er* nos ⁊
ipsum iudicium ⁊ *et* ipsum condemnatio;
Ondredan ge gu leofe breoðre ongean þa yfela domas ðe ge oðrum deman. ðyles cumað

Dearest brethren, let us be considerate; be merciful towards your brethren as the holy Father in heaven is merciful towards us: Dear brethren, let us be provident; you should be abundantly merciful towards your brethren, as the holy Father in heaven is merciful towards us. *Judge not: and you shall not be judged* (Luke VI.37): You should not judge so that you will not be condemned. *That is, do not sentence* [*anyone*] *to death, lest you are meted out the same judgement by the Blessed before Christ's tribunal*: This means: if you sentence anyone to death, undeservedly, or to any other punishment, beware that you are not meted out the same judgement before the Lord's throne. *Condemn not: and you shall not be condemned* (Luke VI.37): Do not condemn lest you should be condemned. *Dearest brethren, dread evil judgement so that the same judgement and the same condemnation may not come upon us*: Dear brethren, dread evil judgement which you mete out to others, lest [ ] come

TEXT

3 (= p. 7 fragment)

[Fifth Sunday after Pentecost: Conclusion after a Lacuna]

ure sinne for[gif]nesse[7]. ꝥ we moton to þam æcan wuldor becumon; Qui cum patre *et* sp*irit*u s*anct*o uiuit *et* regnat in s*ae*c*u*la s*ae*c*u*lor*um*; Ðe mid fedur ⁊ mid halig gast lyfoð. ⁊ rixað on weorulde[8] weoruld. am*en*. seo hit swa.

[The Sixth Sunday after Pentecost]

[I]n illo t*em*p*ore* ⁛ Cum turba inruerent ad i*esu*m ut audirent uerbu*m* dei ⁛ *et* ipse stabat secus stagnu*m* genesareth (Luke V.1); *et* rel*i*qua; On ðam tide mid ði ꝥ folc geðrungon to ðem helende. ꝥ he geherdon godes word. ⁊ he seolf stód wið ꝥ ses deopnesse; Ista turba *et* ista piscatio s*ecun*d*u*m istoriam fuit ⁛ tribus uicibus iussit d*omin*u*s* re*ti*a mittere in mare; þisne [gefylce][9]. ⁊ þisne fiscunge æfter ðisne redunge. hit wes ðrym siðum. ꝥ se helend hǽt here nét leggen on se; Duas ante passionem *et* tertia post resurræctionem[10] .,. Twywwa ær his ðrowunge. ⁊ se ðredde syðe æfter is upriste; Ante passionem rumpebatur rete[11] *et* post passionem [non][12] rumpeba-

[Fifth Sunday after Pentecost: Conclusion after a Lacuna]

forgiveness of our sins that we may attain eternal glory. *Who with the Father and the Holy Ghost lives and reigns in eternity*: Who with the Father and with the Holy Ghost lives and reigns in eternity. Amen. So be it.

[The Sixth Sunday after Pentecost]

At this time, when the multitudes pressed upon [*Christ*] *to hear the word of God, he stood by the lake of Genesareth* (Luke V.1); *and so on*: At this time, when the people crowded upon Christ to hear the word of God; and he stood beside the deep lake. *This multitude and this fishing were attested in the* [*biblical*] *story*; *three times the Lord commanded to throw out the nets into the lake*: These people and this fishing [were] according to this reading; it was three times that Christ commanded that they lay out their nets in the lake. *Two before the Passion and the third after His Resurrection*: Twice before His Passion and the third time after His Resurrection. *Before the Passion the net was torn, and after the Passion*

TEXT

4 (= p. 8 fragment)
[Sixth Sunday after Pentecost: Continuation]

tur[13] rete; Ær his ðrowunge ða net toslyton. ⁊ æfter his ðrowunga ne toslyton
þa net nan ðing; In ista piscatione prima
ascendit d*omin*us in illa nauicula ubi erat ⁒
simon pe*t*rus ibi cepit docere (cf. Luke V.3) ⁒ ibi fuit beatus confessus ad d*omin*u*m* quando dixit; On
ðisne fiscinge ærest astah se helend on
ðem scype ðer simon pe*t*rus wes on. ðer
he ongean to tecen ꝥ folc; Đer wes se eadiga petrus begihti[14] to drihtne ða he cwæð;
Exi a me d*omi*ne quia homo peccator sum (Luke V.8) .,.
Gewit fro*m* me laford leof forþon ic eam sinfull mon; Ait ei i*esu*s Noli timere[15] ex hóc
iam ominis eris capiens (Luke V.10); Đa cweð se helend
ne ondred þu þe petrus ofer ðissum þu be-
ost men fangande; Erat autem beatus
pe*t*rus piscator pisces maris aquaticos
et postmodum fecit illum d*omin*us piscato-
res hominum (cf. Mark I.17). Wes soðlice se eadiga pe*t*rus
sefiscere[16] ⁊ efter ðissum him dydæ se he[lend][17]

the net was not torn: Before His Passion the nets burst and after His Passion they did not burst at all. *During the first of these fishings the Lord entered the boat in which Simon Petrus was, and there He began to teach. There the blessed man made his confession to the Lord when he said*: During this fishing Christ first entered the ship in which Simon Petrus was; there He began teaching the people. There the blessed Peter was anxious before the Lord when he said: '*Depart from me, for I am a sinful man, O Lord*' (Luke V.8): 'Go away from me, dear Lord, because I am a sinful man'. *Jesus said to him*: '*Fear not: from henceforth thou shalt catch men*' (Luke V.10): Thereupon Christ said: 'Peter do not be afraid, hereafter you shall catch men'. *Now the blessed Peter was a fisher of fish living in the sea, and afterwards the Lord made him a fisher of men*: Indeed, the blessed Peter was a fisher of fish, and afterwards the Lord made him

The Taunton Fragment

TEXT

5 (= p. 1 fragment)

[Sixth Sunday after Pentecost: Continuation after a Lacuna]

circe to habbene clenesse. ⁊ swiðe strángTlice to wiðstandene ðem deofle; Iohan*ne*s gr*ati*a dei interpretatur ;̇ deb*et* eccl*esi*a gr*ati*a dei agere laudare d*eu*m *et* benædicere[18] .,. Ioh*anne*s godes gyfe ys geraht byreð on cyrce god to ðeonene. ⁊ to herienne. ⁊ to blitsienne; Illa retia intellegitur s*anct*aru*m* scripturarum ;̇ p*er* que*m* homines capiunt[19] *et* ueniunt ad litus id e*st* ad finem mundi Ða net getacnað þa halige writu ðurh ꝥ men nimen ⁊ cumon to þem ses ofre. ꝥ is to þisne middaneardes endunge; Relinquamus in quantum posum*us* mundi ;̇ ne p*er*damus uitam p*er*petuam; Forletan we swa mycel swa we mast[20] mugon ðisne middangeardes ydolnesse. ꝥ we ꝥ ece lyf ne forleosan; Ubi non e*st* famis; ðer nis nan hungor. Non e*st* sitis. Nis þer þirst. Non sunt tenebras. Nis þer þeoster; N*on* e*st* luctus; Nis þer wóp; Non e*st* timor. Nis þer ege.

[in] church to have purity and to oppose the devil very resolutely. *'Iohannes' signifies 'God's favour'. The Church ought to thank God, to extol God and to praise him*: 'Iohannes' is explained as 'God's gift'. It is fitting in church to serve God, and to praise Him, and give thanks to Him. *Those nets signify the Holy Scriptures, by which men arrive and come to the shore, that is, to the end of the world*: The nets signify the Holy Scriptures, by which men seize and arrive at the shore of the sea, that is, at the end of this world. *Let us abandon the world as much as is possible, so that we may not lose eternal life*: Let us abandon as much as we ever may the vanity of this world, so that we may not lose eternal life. *Where there is no hunger*: there is no hunger; *there is no thirst*: there is no thirst; *there is no darkness*: there is no darkness; *there is no grief*: there is no lamentation; *there is no fear*: there is no fear;

TEXT

6 (=p. 2 fragment)

[Sixth Sunday after Pentecost: Continuation and Conclusion]

Non e*st* tristitia; Nis þer unrotnesse; Non e*st* discordia. Nis ðer unðwernesse. Non e*st* inuidia; Ne sint ðar nyðas; S*et*[21] semper[22] gaudium *et* letitiam ⁝ cu*m* angelis. *et* archangelis. cu*m* thronis *et* dominationibus ⁝ laudantes d*eu*m ⁝ *et* benedicentes d*omi*n*u*m in s*ae*c*u*la s*ae*c*u*lor*um*. am*en*. Eac efre ðer ys blysse 7 gladscype mid englum. and mid hæahenglum. 7 mid ða ðe ða reoduras wealdan heriende gode. 7 drihtin blitsiende on weorolde weruld seo hit efre swa ⁝ buton eghwilcum ende. am*en*[23].

[The Seventh Sunday after Pentecost]

[I]N illo t*em*p*or*e ⁝ Dixit i*esu*s discipulis suis; On ðam tyde se helend cwæð to his lernunge cnihtas; Am*en* dico uobis ⁝ nisi abundauerit iustitia u*est*ra plus quam scribarum ⁝ *et* fariseorum (Matthew V.20). *et* rel*i*q*ua*; Soð Soð ic eow secce buton geni[h]tsumian[24] geowre rihtwisnesse ma ðanna ða writras. 7 þa sundorhalegan ne cumon ge on heofona rice; Timeam*us*

[Sixth Sunday after Pentecost: Continuation and Conclusion]

there is no sadness: there is no sadness; *there is no discord*: there is no discord; *there is no envy*: there is no hatred. *But ever gladness and joyfulness with angels and archangels, with thrones and dominations, praising God and extolling the Lord in eternity. Amen*: But there is always happiness and gladness with angels and archangels, and with those who rule the heavens, praising God and extolling the Lord in eternity; let it ever be so, without end. Amen.

[The Seventh Sunday after Pentecost]

At this time Jesus said to his disciples: At this time Christ said to his disciples '*For I tell you, that unless your justice abound more than that of the scribes and Pharisees*' (Matthew V.20); *and so on*: Verily, I tell you, unless your righteousness is more abundant than [that of] the scribes and Pharisees, you may not enter the kingdom of heaven. *Let us dread*

TEXT

7 (= p. 3 fragment)

[Seventh Sunday after Pentecost: Continuation after a Lacuna]

et proicis iam foras quia ante ea non pr*ae*uale-
at oratio tua aput d*omi*n*u*m; Ðisne lác ꝥ is sun-
3 nandeges bene.[25] ꝥ byþ pat*er* n*oste*r. ⁊ credo in d*eu*m.
ða ðu hafost on þin heorte ꝥ eorre forlet
ðer þin bene. ⁊ cleope þin broðor út þe þu
6 hefst yrre wið. ⁊ bid hine forgifnesse. forþon ær þu þis gedost ne helpeð þin bene toforen gode; et postea uade offers mun*us*
9 tuum ·'[26] id e*st* horatio tua coram deo; And
siððan ga þu and beod þin lac. ꝥ is þin halgan
bene teforen gode; Nullas ex uobis di-
12 lectissimi ·' fr*atre*s k*arissi*mi. hoc teneat in corde suo ·' neq*ue* ullum hodium habeat contra
fratrem suum s*et* puro corde orate ·' ut
15 horatio u*est*ra sit exaudita a deo; Nan
iure leofe breoðre ne geheal[de][27] ðisne erscipe on his heorte ongen his broðor.
18 eác luttor heorte bidde ge to drihtne
ꝥ drihtin iure bene gehere; Ipse uos ex-
audire dignetur ·' qui cu*m* patre *et* sp*irit*u s*anct*o

and you throw out instantaneously because otherwise your prayer may not avail with the Lord: This offering is the Lord's Prayer, that is the *pater noster*, and the Creed. If any anger resides in your heart, desist from your prayer and call out your brother with whom you are angry and ask for forgiveness, because, unless you do this, your prayer will not avail with God. *And afterwards go and you offer your gift*; *that is your prayer before God*: And afterwards go and offer your gift, that is, your holy prayer before God. *Dearest and most beloved brethren*, *none of you should keep in his heart such* [*anger*], *nor should anyone feel any hatred against his brother*, *but pray with pure hearts*, *so that your prayer may be heard by God*: None of your dear brethren should keep in his heart such anger against his brother, but pray to the Lord with a pure heart, so that the Lord may hear your prayer. *May He deign to listen to you*, *Who with the Father and the Holy Ghost*

TEXT

8 (=p. 4 fragment)

[Seventh Sunday after Pentecost: Continuation and Conclusion]

uiuit *et* regnat in s*ae*c*u*la s*ae*c*u*lor*um* am*en*; He self drihtin werðige iu to geheranne iure bene. þe mid fedur 7 mid halig gast lyfo[ð][28]. 7 rixað on weorulde werold seo hit swa buton eghwilcum ende am*en*.

[The Eighth Sunday after Pentecost]

[I]N illo t*em*p*ore* ∴ Cum turba multa e*ss*et cu*m* ie*s*u (Mark VIII.1) ∴ *et* rel*i*q*u*a. On ðam tyde mycel folc wes mid þem helende. 7 he ne hafdon hwet he aton; Pius d*omi*n*u*s *et* misericors se miserebitur[29] ∴ illa turba erat de longe *et* sustinuerunt; [tr]es[30] dies p*ro*pt*er* d*omi*n*u*m ∴ *et* deficit panes eor*um*;[31] Se arfesta drihtin 7 se mildheorte æfre he wes miltsiende. 7 his ꝥ folc com from feorran. 7 he geþolodon þreo dagas for drihtne. 7 here laf hem geteorode; Inde dixit d*omi*n*u*s; Si dimisero eos geiunos in domu*m* suam deficient in uia (Mark VIII.3); Be þon cwað se helend. Gif ic forlete heom festende faren on here husas þonn*e* teorgon he on wege; Quidam enim ex eis

[Seventh Sunday after Pentecost: Continuation and Conclusion]

lives and reigns in eternity. Amen.: The Lord Himself may honour you by listening to your prayer, Who with the Father and with the Holy Ghost lives and reigns in eternity. Be it so without end. Amen.

[The Eighth Sunday after Pentecost]

At this time, when there was a great multitude with Jesus (Mark VIII.1); *and so on*: At this time a great multitude was with Christ and they had nothing to eat. *The holy and merciful Lord felt compassion*; *that crowd had gathered from afar and they had held out for three days because of the Lord, and they were running out of bread*: The gracious and merciful Lord always felt compassion, and the crowd had come from afar and they held out for three days because of the Lord, and they were running out of bread. *Thereupon the Lord said*: '*If I shall send them away fasting to their home, they will faint in the way*'. (Mark VIII.3): Then Christ said: 'If I let them return to their houses fasting, they will be exhausted on their way'. *Indeed a certain one of these*

The Taunton Fragment

Textual Notes

[1] *pius*, MS.
[2] *doð*, MS; *ð* expuncted and *n* written above it.
[3] For *aliquando* being translated by *eac sume*, see below, pp. 178 and 182.
[4] *mitte[re]*: *mitte*, end of line; beginning of next line: space for two letters, followed by *punctus uersus*.
[5] *heofolic*, MS.
[6] *ne* added in left margin, probably by the original scribe; *genyðrad*: *d* corrected from *ð*.
[7] *fornesse*, MS.
[8] *weoruld | de*, MS.
[9] [*gefylce*]: perhaps, the original reading was *folce*; the reading is now *fylc*[ ]*e*; the letter between *c* and *e* is probably *k*, and *o* has been altered to *y* with an additional small *y* written above it (all in the same ink). Perhaps, the intention was to alter *folce* into *gefylce* 'band of men, army, host' to provide a close translation for *turba*.
[10] *resurræctionem* has a superfluous suspension mark above the second *e*.
[11] *recte*, MS, *c* expuncted.
[12] [*non*]: not in MS.
[13] *rumpeba | batur*, MS.
[14] Perhaps *begihti*, unattested elsewhere, is a garbled form of *behȳdig*, *behygdig* 'anxious'.
[15] Corrected from *temere*, *i* above first *e*.
[16] The manuscript reading *sefiscere* is probably not to be understood as definite article + noun, 'the fisherman'; rather, it is a compound (unattested elsewhere): *sǣfiscere* 'sea-fisher'.
[17] The line ends with *he*.
[18] *benædicere*: *n* above line.
[19] On *capiunt* and its OE translation *nimen*, see below, p. 182.
[20] Above *mast*: *.æfre.*, probably by the same scribe.
[21] For *sed* translated by *eac*, see below, p. 178.
[22] *semper*: *p* above line.
[23] In the left margin of line 12: *ath*, probably by the same hand; presumably an abbreviation for *Matthew* (*M* lost by clipping), since the pericope for the exposition beginning in line 13 is taken from this gospel.
[24] *genitsumian*, MS.
[25] On *sunnandeges bene* for the Lord's Prayer, see below, p. 179.
[26] Lines 8 and 9 are an elliptic and hence somewhat garbled quotation from Matthew V.24: *uade prius reconciliare fratri tuo et tunc ueniens offers munus tuum*: 'go first to be reconciled to thy brother, and then coming thou shalt offer thy gift'.
[27] *geheal*, MS.
[28] *lyfo*[*ð*]: *ð* only partially legible.
[29] *miserebitur* for *miserebatur*.
[30] *c.* five letters have been erased before *es*.
[31] The passage 8.9–12 has verbal echoes from Mark VIII.2 and VIII.3; the present tense in *deficit* may be due either to the present tense prevailing in the gospel text or to a confusion with *fecit*.

THE LANGUAGE

The language is one of the most interesting but also one of the most baffling aspects of the Taunton Fragment (hereafter TF) – baffling because, as we shall see, its evidence is extremely difficult to evaluate. In the following discussion of the linguistic features of TF I do not aim to represent an exhaustive inventory of all morphological and phonological forms. Rather, I shall adopt a structural approach whereby I attempt to analyse in what ways the language of the Taunton Commentator is different from 'normal' Old English and whether, in spite of such differences, it still would have served him as a means of effective communication. Needless to say, perhaps, that in the compass of the present article it is impossible to discuss all aspects of the Commentator's linguistic usage which would merit attention. In an attempt to assess his unorthodox written form of Old English we have to address three primary questions: first, are the many deviations from correct Old English usage just mindless blunders of a person who had not been trained to put Old English into writing, or are they, rather, indications of the Commentator's endeavour to represent contemporary speech in a written form? If so, the numerous violations of correct Old English usage would no doubt signal an advanced stage in the eventual breakdown of the Old English inflexional system and of the received norm of representing Old English sounds in writing. Secondly, is it possible to detect any patterns in the deviations from correct Old English usage? And thirdly, if such patterns can be detected, is it possible to connect one or several of them to developments leading up to Middle English? There is yet a fourth question which needs consideration and to which we will have to turn in due course, but let us first try to establish what answers the evidence may yield to the three just mentioned.

A further preliminary remark is necessary here. When discussing the language of an Old English text it is axiomatic to observe that this is, *prima facie*, the language of the scribe who wrote the manuscript, and that, more often than not, it is difficult to establish how faithfully this scribe reproduced the forms and spellings of his exemplar, let alone to establish the precise linguistic forms in which the text was originally couched. To some extent this axiom holds true in the case of TF as well. Errors such as the occasional omissions of words or the doubling of syllables[15] could be laid at the door of either a scribe or the author himself. However, in light of the numerous reasonably normalized late-eleventh-century copies of earlier texts such as Ælfric's, it may not seem very plausible to assume that any intervening scribe(s) garbled a text originally composed in Standard Old English in the way it has been preserved in TF. On the other hand, it is certain that, if one or several scribes intervened

[15] See above, p. 159, nn. 12 and 13.

between the Taunton Commentator and the transmitted text, such scribe(s) made no serious effort to remedy the unorthodox form of Old English which the text presents. Furthermore, judging by the content and linguistic appearance of TF, we may perhaps be permitted to suspect that this text never enjoyed a wide circulation and that, therefore, the surviving leaves represent fairly accurately what the Commentator originally wrote.

Inflexional Morphology

Let us begin our synopsis with inflexional morphology. I take this as our starting point for two reasons: firstly, in the course of a small project on the forms and dissemination of Standard Old English, conducted at the University of Göttingen, it has emerged with some probability that linguistic standardization in Late Old English was more effective with regard to inflexional endings than with regard to the orthography of stressed vowels, where some amount of variation seems to have been permissible.[16] Secondly, in Early Middle English the representation of stressed vowels in writing is notoriously chaotic, whereas some fairly clear patterns with regard to morphology can be discerned already in the incipient stages of Middle English.

The Noun Phrase

In this section we shall consider the declensions of nouns, adjectives and pronouns. Some simple statistics for correct and erroneous use of nouns and adjectives are as follows: on a count by token (that is, counting every occurrence of a given noun), approximately seventy nouns occur in their correct Old English form, whereas about fifty-three exhibit an error of some sort. For adjectives the respective figures are as follows: about nine occur with a correct ending and about seventeen are wrong in one way or another. These figures embrace strong and weak adjectives; there is scarcely any difference in the ratio between correct and erroneous forms in the strong and weak declensions respectively. However, matters are somewhat more complex than these statistics suggest, and the simple and apparently obvious deduction which they seem to invite, namely that the declension of nouns is better preserved than the declension of adjectives, is misleading, as we shall see presently.

Dative and Accusative Forms

One of the most important Middle English developments in the declension of nouns is the breakdown of the distinction between dative and accusative,

[16] For this project and some of its preliminary results, see M. Gretsch, 'In Search of Standard Old English', *Bookmarks from the Past. Studies in Early English Language and Literature in Honour of Helmut Gneuss*, ed. L. Kornexl and U. Lenker (Munich, 2003), pp. 33–67, esp. 59–60.

followed by the emergence of an 'objective case' in the form of the original accusative. Apparently, this merger of dative and accusative occurred during the transitional period between Old and Middle English, since it is found already in the earliest Middle English texts such as the First and Second Continuation of the Peterborough Chronicle (written 1122–31 and 1155 respectively).[17] The ways in which the dative and accusative are used by the Taunton Commentator offer, therefore, an obvious avenue to be explored in our attempt to structure the amorphous linguistic evidence. In the entire text we meet with seven instances each of correct use of dative and accusative.[18] These twice seven correct forms comprise only those instances where (a) the dative and accusative of a noun are distinguished by different endings, and (b) in case of a noun accompanied by modifiers (pronouns, adjectives), these modifiers also exhibit correct forms.[19] Correct forms of a noun, but wrong forms in accompanying modifiers occur once in the dative and four times in the accusative.[20] Wrong forms for dative and accusative of nouns, often aggravated by wrong forms in an accompanying modifier, occur seven times for the dative and five times for the accusative.[21]

It is important to note that all instances of wrong forms for dative and accusative are confusions between these two, and only these two, case endings; that is, the ending for the dative is found in the accusative and vice versa, and no

[17] For the merger of dative and accusative in the Peterborough Chronicle, see *The Peterborough Chronicle 1070–1154*, ed. C. Clark, 2nd ed. (Oxford, 1970), pp. liii–liv; for the date of the two continuations, see *ibid.* pp. xxiv–xxvi. For a recent general treatment of Middle English developments in the Noun Phrase, see R. Lass, 'Phonology and Morphology', *The Cambridge History of the English Language* II, *1066–1476*, ed. N. Blake (Cambridge, 1992), pp. 23–155, at 103–22. There is a still valuable account, specifically of the merger between dative and accusative, by K. Brunner, *Die englische Sprache. Ihre geschichtliche Entwicklung*, 2 vols., 2nd ed. (Tübingen, 1960–2) II, 42–5.

[18] Examples of correct use of dative: *ðem deofle* (1.2) and *mid englum and mid hæahenglum* (2.8–9); examples of correct use of accusative: *þæt ece lyf* (1.16) and *ða reoduras* (2.9). Recall that all page references are to the present page numbering of TF, which is given in brackets in the edition above.

[19] For a discussion of the frequently attested nouns *dryhten*, *Hælend*, *fæder* and *broðor*, see below, p. 164.

[20] Dative: *on mycel* (for *mycelre*) *pine* (5.20); accusative: *þa halige* (for *halgan*) *writu* (1.10).

[21] Examples for the dative: *God* (for *Gode*, 1.6), *mid halig gast* (for *halgum* or *ðam halgan gaste*, 4.3 and 7.4); examples for the accusative: *Gode* (for *God*, 2.10), *on ðem scype* for *on ðæt scyp*, 8.7–8), and *on weorulde weoruld* (2.10–11 and 7.4–5). The latter is a calque on *in saecula saeculorum* 'in eternity', and probably *weorulde* (for *worolda*) is meant to translate the accusative *saecula*. In any case, both forms are wrong, either as accusative or as genitive. For a brief discussion of this very common phrase (also occurring in the singular, *in saeculum saeculi*), see M. Gretsch, *The Intellectual Foundations of the English Benedictine Reform*, CSASE 25 (Cambridge, 1999), 392–3. It is curious that the author or, possibly, the scribe should have got confused twice about this common liturgical expression, but see below, pp. 179–80. Note that in the adjectives *luttor* (3.18), *mycell* (6.4), *oðer* (6.11), as well as in *mycel* (5.20, see above, n. 20), there is also confusion of gender in addition to confusion of case.

other inflexional ending is ever used unambiguously for one of these two cases. For the language of the Taunton Commentator this evidence suggests that, on the one hand, the distinction between dative and accusative had become seriously impaired but that, on the other hand, no substitutional pattern to replace this distinction can as yet be discerned, and therefore no pattern which would point to the Middle English survival of only the accusative form, now carrying the functions of both the original accusative and the original dative. The one pattern which seems to emerge, however, is that errors are more likely to occur when a noun phrase consists of several constituents than when it is made up of a noun only. Almost all the noun phrases showing correct usage of dative and accusative consist of a noun, either occurring alone or preceded by just the definite article. The same pattern can also be observed in noun phrases other than those containing a dative or an accusative. This may, perhaps, suggest that the Early Middle English breakdown of the Old English system of nominal and pronominal declension began with a loss of congruence in complex noun phrases: a suggestion which will not come as a great surprise to speakers and learners of a modern inflected language, but also a suggestion which has not always been given due consideration in discussions of Early Middle English inflexional morphology. In any case, this marked difference between simple and complex noun phrases helps to explain why the statistical survey yielded a greater percentage of correct forms for nouns than for adjectives, adjectives usually being part of a complex noun phrase.

Further Signs of Disintegration in the Noun Phrase

Confusion of dative and accusative is the only class of grammatical errors which can be ascribed with some certainty to a diminishing notion of what would be the correct usage of the two cases. In numerous other instances it is impossible to decide whether erroneous endings in nouns are due either to a similar uncertainty about the correct case, or to the transfer of a noun to another declension, or to a generalization of certain case endings within the paradigm such as is recorded for some declensions, or merely to a reduction of unstressed syllables in Late Old English. Examples are: *on cyrce* (dat. sg. for *cyrcan*, 1.5); OE *cyrce* is a feminine noun of the n-declension. Do we have here confusion of nominative and dative (unlikely, perhaps, in light of what we have observed above), or is *cyrce* inflected according to the ō-declension, or are we simply confronted with a reduction of its unstressed syllable? By the same token, *heorte* (feminine, n-declension) occurs three times as a dative (instead of correct *heortan*, which never occurs);[22] and *wise* (also feminine, n-declension) occurs once (6.12) as a dative but also once (5.7) in the correct dative form *wisan*. The feminine i-declension noun *bēn* occurs consistently as *bene* in the

[22] See 3.4, 3.17, 3.18.

accusative singular (instead of *ben*).[23] This could be taken to indicate an assimilation to the ō-declension (which is well attested for the long-stem feminine nouns of the i-declension).[24] However, the occurrence of *bene* also in the nominative singular (3.3) makes one hesitate to suggest this explanation, since the long-stem feminines of the ō-declension do not normally take *-e* in the nominative singular. Similarly, *blisse* (2.7) occurs in the nominative singular instead of *blis(s)*, whereas long-stem nouns of the jō-declension do not normally end in *-e* in the nominative singular. Also, one wonders whether *gyfe* (nominative singular, feminine ō-declension, 1.5), instead of correct *gyfu*, is to be explained by a transfer of the *-e* from inflected forms (apparently not attested for short-stem ō-declension nouns),[25] or whether it is not just a further instance of confusion of inflexional endings without any recognizable pattern.

When we take a look at the nouns which occur frequently in the text, namely *Hælend*, *dryhten*, *fæder*, and *broðor*, it turns out that the first three are always used with their correct inflexional ending,[26] whereas *broðor* occurs correctly as accusative singular once (3.5), but instead of *broðra* in the genitive plural we get the forms *breoðre* (3.16) and *broðor* (5.15), and in the nominative plural occurs *breoðre* (5.5, 6.3 and 6.19) instead of correct *broðor* (*-ru*, *-ra*). Note also the variation in the spelling of the stressed vowel in this word, whereas the other three words offer remarkably consistent (if not Standard Old English) spellings: *helend*, *fedur* and *drihtin*.[27] However, in spite of the correct inflexion of *Hælend*, *dryhten* and *fæder*, blunders do occur in the noun phrases in which they are embedded; for example, *se arfesta heofolic* (instead of *heofonlica*) *fedur* (6.5).

In addition to this rather advanced breakdown of the nominal inflexion, there are signs of an incipient breakdown of gender: *tīd*, a long-stem noun of the feminine i-declension, is consistently coupled with the masculine or neuter article in the phrase *on ðam tide* (2. 13–14, 4.7, and 7.9); and instead of *hus* in the accusative plural of this noun of the neuter a-declension, we find *husas*, the ending of the masculine a-declension (4.19).[28]

With two pronouns we find a complete elimination of gender combined with

23 See 3.5, 3.7, 3.11, 3.19 and 4.3.

24 Cf. K. Brunner, *Altenglische Grammatik. Nach der angelsächsischen Grammatik von E. Sievers*, 3rd ed. (Tübingen, 1965) [hereafter SB], § 269, n. 1, and A. Campbell, *Old English Grammar* (Oxford, 1959) [hereafter Campbell], § 604.

25 Cf. SB, § 252, n. 4 and Campbell p. 586, attesting a transfer only of the *-u* of the nom. sg. to the oblique cases of the singular. Note that for reasons of clarity I have occasionally normalized idiosyncratic spellings when they are irrelevant to the discussion.

26 For *Hælend*, see 2.14, 4.18, 7.10 etc.; for *dryhten*, see 2.10, 3.18, 4.2 etc.: for *fæder*, see 4.3, 5.3, 7.3 etc.

27 In inflected forms the unstressed *i* in *drihtin* is syncopated, e. g. *to drihtne* (3.18). On the spellings in the Taunton Fragment in general, see below, pp. 172–5.

28 With regard to adjectives we have already noted (above, p. 162, n. 21) some amount of gender confusion.

an equally complete loss of inflexion: *þisne* and *þis*. OE *þisne* is the form of the accusative singular masculine of the demonstrative pronoun *þes*. However, in the Taunton Fragment it is used indiscriminately with nouns of all genders and in all cases as, for example, *þisne lac* (3.2, in the nominative singular with a noun of either neuter or feminine gender), *þisne middaneardes* (1.12, genitive singular, with a masculine noun) and *þisne redunge* (7.14–15, dative singular, with a feminine noun). In view of this evidence, the one correct usage of *ðisne* in the entire text, in the phrase *ðisne erscipe* (3.16–17, accusative singular, with a masculine noun), is probably no more than an inadvertent hit at grammatical correctness. OE *þin*, the second person possessive pronoun, presents us with the same disregard for case and gender (normally, possessives are inflected as strong adjectives). We invariably get *þin*, as in *þin broðor* (3.5, for *þinne broðor*, accusative singular masculine), *on þin heorte* (3.4, for *þinre heortan*, dative singular feminine) and *þin bene* (3.5, for *þine ben*, accusative singular feminine).[29] Such tendencies to neglect gender may be seen as preliminary to the Middle English loss of gender; in the case of the two pronouns, *þisne* and *þin*, used in an invariable form, we may also be confronted with an incipient stage of Middle English developments, where for demonstratives and adjectives only one form prevails for singular and plural respectively. However, even if seen in this context, the choice of the accusative singular masculine, *þisne*, as the sole representative of the singular demonstrative (there are no plural forms in the text) is curious indeed.

A further pronoun which by its orthography points towards the Old English pronunciation gradually giving way to the Middle English one is *eow* 'you' (dative and accusative of the second person plural pronoun) and *eower* 'your' (possessive pronoun of the second person plural). The normal Old English spelling <eow> is retained in 2.17, but the spellings <gu> (6.12, 6.19) and <iu> (4.2) probably indicate that in the language of the Taunton Commentator the pronunciation of this pronoun had almost reached its Middle English form /ju:/. The possessive, OE *eower*, occurs as <eowre> (5.3), <geowre> (2.18), and <iure> (3.19, 4.2), which may also indicate a development towards ME /ju:r(ə)/. Note that this pronoun, again, invariably occurs with the same inflexional ending <e>, regardless of gender and case.[30]

29 To the complete and consistent levelling of the forms of the singular demonstrative and the second person singular possessive pronouns should be added occasional confusions with regard to case and gender in the use of the definite article, as *wið þæt ses deopnesse* (7.11, *þæt*, nominative or accusative neuter, for *þæs* or *þære*; *sæ* being a masculine or feminine noun, here used in the genitive); or *to þem ses ofre* (1.11, *þæm*, dative, again for *þæs* or *þære*).

30 Note also that for *eower* forms such as *iuer*, *iurre* are attested in the mid-tenth-century Northumbrian gloss to the Lindisfarne gospels, a gloss which is well known for its morphology anticipating Middle English developments. And note that palatal <g> = /j/ is spelled <i> before /u/ also in West Saxon manuscripts of a fairly early date such as BL, Cotton Julius E.vii (s. xi[in]), the only relatively complete manuscript of Ælfric's *Lives of Saints*: cf. *Ælfric. Lives of Three English Saints*, ed. G. I. Needham (London, 1966), p. 8.

Verb Inflexion

When turning to the conjugation of verbs, our first impression is that, on the whole, it is better preserved than the inflexion in the noun phrases. As we shall see, this impression bears scrutiny. Strong verbs are used with their correct forms of vowel gradation, and the distinction between the first and second weak conjugation is almost always preserved. Although there are clear signs of the Late Old English merger of unaccented vowels, especially in inflexional endings in *-en*, *-an* and *-on*, it is important to note that final *-n* has been lost on no occasion. In what follows I give a brief synopsis of all the verb forms occurring in the text (unless otherwise stated, examples only are quoted for each of the attested variants of a specific form). For easy reference I also give the received Late West Saxon endings for each of the verb forms in accordance with the standard Old English grammars.[31]

Infinitive

The correct ending would be *-an* (*-ian* in weak II conjugation). Examples are: *ðrowian* (5.20), *deman* (6.7), *becumon* (7.2), *leggen* (7.16), *tecen* (8.9). There is no clear predominance of one particular vowel.

Inflected infinitive

Presumably, the ending was originally *-enne*, but variation in the vowel and elimination of one *-n-* occurs throughout the Old English period.[32] In accordance with the Old English rules, in TF the inflected infinitive is always used after the preposition *to*, and the preposition is never used with the uninflected infinitive. Examples are: *to herienne* (1.6), *to wiðstandene* (1.2), *to habbene* (1.1).

First and second person present indicative

They occur twice each, and with the correct forms; e. g. *ic forlete* (4.18) and *ðu demest* (6.11).

Third person present indicative

The correct ending is *-eð* (*-að* in weak II conjugation). Examples are: *helpeð* (3.7), *tostregdeð* (5.9), *rixað* (4.4); rarely with confusion of the inflexional vowel, e. g. *lyfoð* (7.4). Note that *hefð* (5.15 and 6.5) and *hefst* (3.6) are the only forms of the second and third person singular showing syncopation of the inflexional

[31] Obvious errors such as lack of concord in *genihtsumian* (plural) and *rihtwisnesse* (singular) have been omitted here; on some such errors, see below, p. 178.

[32] See SB, § 363.2 and Campbell, §§ 731(f) and 736(i).

vowel. This general lack of syncopation may be a clue to a non-West Saxon dialect colouring.[33]

Plural present indicative

The correct ending is *-að* (*-iað* in weak II conjugation). Examples are: *willað* (5.18), *synigað* (for *synigiað* 5.6); once with confusion of inflexional vowel: *gebetæð* (5.13, for *gebetað*).[34]

Singular present subjunctive

The correct ending is *-e* (*-ige* in weak II conjugation). There are two occurrences of the third person singular, both with the correct ending: *gehere* (3.19) and *werðige* (4.2).

Plural present subjunctive

The correct ending is *-en* (*-igen* in weak II conjugation). There is one occurrence of the correct ending: *worðen* (6.8); two further occurrences show confusion of the inflexional vowel: *forleosan* (1.16) and *cumon* (2.20).[35]

Second person singular imperative

The correct forms are: no ending in strong verbs and originally long-stem verbs of weak I conjugation; *-e* in originally short-stem verbs of weak I conjugation; *-a* in weak II conjugation. Examples for the correct forms are: *forlet* and *beod* (3.4 and 3.10, both strong verbs); there is one occurrence with confusion of the inflexional vowel: *cleope* (3.5, for *cleopa*, weak II), and one occurrence also, where the ending is erroneously omitted: *bid* (3.6, for *bide*, a strong verb but in the present inflected according to weak I).

Second person plural imperative

The correct ending is *-að* (*-iað* in weak II conjugation); especially in negative clauses this is often substituted by the ending of the plural present subjunctive *-en* (later *-an*, *-on*, with confusion of inflexional vowel).[36] If followed by the personal pronoun (*ge*), the inflexional ending may be reduced to *-e*.[37] In TF all occurrences of the second person plural imperative are followed by the pronoun, three of them in the shortened form, ending in *-e*: *bidde ge* (3.18), *wese ge* (5.2), *nille ge* (6.7); also three with the full inflexional ending, always in *-an*:

[33] For dialectal features in TF, see below, p. 170; *hefst* and *hefð* are the original weak III conjugation forms of *habban* which show syncopation in *all* dialects: SB, § 417.

[34] For further information on the plural present indicative forms, see below, pp. 170–2.

[35] See SB, § 361, n. 1. [36] *Ibid.*, §§ 360, n. 5. and 362.3.

[37] *Ibid.*, § 360.2 and Campbell, § 730, and note that both grammars refer to this development as occurring mainly in West Saxon texts.

gewarnian ge (6.12), *ondredan ge* (6.19) and *habban ge* (6.3–4). Six occurrences are not many, but a pattern is clearly discernible, and this pattern is in broad accordance with received Old English usage.

First person plural imperative

The correct ending in this adhortative form is *-an*, or the ending of the plural present subjunctive *-en*, acting as a substitute.[38] In TF there are two attestations of this form and they are identical with the full inflexional ending of the second person plural imperative in TF: *forletan we* (1.14) and *gesceawian we* (6.3).[39]

Present participle

The correct ending is *-ende* (*-iende* in weak II conjugation). This form is used correctly four times, for example, *festende* (4.19) and *miltsiende* (4.13), and once with confusion of inflexional vowel: *fangande* (8.16).

Third person singular preterite indicative

The correct forms are, for strong verbs: no ending but specific gradation vowel for first and third person (or distinctive preterite vowel for originally reduplicative verbs); *-(e)de* for weak I conjugation, and *-ode*, *-ade* for weak II conjugation. In TF the form is attested frequently (some twenty times), though, with one exception (*geteorode*, 4.15), for strong verbs only. They always present the correct Old English forms, e. g. *com* (4.14) or *astah* (8.7).[40]

Plural preterite indicative

The correct forms are, for strong verbs: *-on* plus specific gradation vowel (or preterite vowel for reduplicative verbs); *-(e)don* for weak I conjugation and *-odon*, *-adon* for weak II conjugation. All of Taunton's forms (five occurrences) are correct, e. g., *geðrungon* (7.9), *geherdon* (7.10) and *geþolodon* (4.14). Note that all forms present the correct inflexional vowel *-on*; no confusion with *-en* or *-an* occurs.

38 See SB, § 362.2.

39 It is impossible to say whether *-an* is here a retention of the original adhortative form or a substitution of the plural present subjunctive showing confusion of the inflexional vowel. But this would apply to all late texts with variation in the inflexional vowel of the plural present subjunctive. It is probable, however, that a distinction between the original adhortative ending and the substitute subjunctive ending can only be made in a historical retrospective. Once *-en*, *-an* and *-on* had become accepted endings for the subjunctive, it must have appeared to contemporary speakers that the first and second plural imperative could have an identical ending, and that this ending was identical also with the ending of the plural present subjunctive.

40 For the vowels in *cwæð* (2.14), *cwað* (4.18), *cweð* (8.14), *wes* (4.7 etc), *ongean* (8.9), and *hæt* (7.15) we have to take into account the various forms in which original OE *æ* and *a* are attested in TF; for discussion, see below, pp. 172–4.

Plural preterite subjunctive

The correct forms are, for strong verbs: *-en* plus specific gradation vowel (or preterite vowel for reduplicative verbs); *-(e)den* for weak I conjugation, and *-oden, -aden* for weak II conjugation. Only one form is attested: *aton* (4.9), showing confusion of the inflexional vowel.[41]

Past participle

The correct forms are, for strong verbs: *-en*, plus specific gradation vowel (or present tense vowel for reduplicative verbs); *-ed* for weak I conjugation, and *-od*, *-ad* for weak II conjugation. Two of the four occurrences in TF show orthodox forms: *fordemde* (6.8, weak I, with correct inflexion as nominative plural and syncopation of the intermediate vowel) and *geraht* (1.5, past part. of *gereccan* 'explain', weak I, irregular). The other two are noteworthy: *genyðrad* (6.16, weak II); in weak II verbs the intermediate vowel *-a-* generally points to the Anglian or Kentish dialect, whereas *-o-* is the West Saxon form.[42] However, since the vowel is *-o-* in the two preterite forms which occur of weak II verbs (*geteorode*, 4.15 and *geþolodon* 4.14), *genyðrad* could indicate, not a non-West Saxon dialect, but rather the confusion of unstressed vowels. This suspicion may be confirmed by the second noteworthy participle: *gegiltað* (5.15). This form not only shows a confusion of *d* and *ð* in the inflexional consonant, which is not accounted for in the standard grammars of Old English,[43] more importantly, the participle belongs to *gyltan* 'to sin', a weak I verb, and should therefore be *gegilted.*

To summarize our results thus far: an inspection of all attested forms has confirmed our intial impression that verb inflexion is much better preserved than nominal and pronominal inflexions. Irregularities such as the indiscriminate use of *-en*, *-on* and *-an* in verbal endings can be found even in the best manuscripts of Ælfric's *Catholic Homilies*, and to a much larger extent in manuscripts of these texts which were written in the course of the eleventh century.[44] In light of this situation, Taunton's consistent preservation of the correct ending *-on* in the plural preterite indicative seems remarkable indeed. As a rule, verb inflexion offers more dialectally relevant features than the inflexion of nouns,

[41] For the gradation vowel, not attested elsewhere in Old English, see below, p. 176.

[42] Cf. SB, § 413 and 414, and Campbell § 757.

[43] The confusion may be due to the verb phrase in which the participle occurs: *gegiltað hefð*.

[44] For this variation in the best manuscripts of the *Catholic Homilies*, see M. Godden, *Ælfric's Catholic Homilies. Introduction, Commentary and Glossary*, EETS ss 18 (Oxford, 2000), 672; the much greater variation in this respect occurring in later manuscripts of the *Catholic Homilies* is currently being established in the course of the Göttingen project on Standard Old English mentioned above, p. 161, n. 16.

and we have already noted in passing that in TF, too, verb inflexion may, perhaps, provide us with some tentative clues to the dialectal colouring of the text.[45] Thus, it is by no means impossible that the variation between *o* and *a* in the suffix of the preterite and past participle of weak II verbs points to a non-West Saxon dialect and not (as I tentatively suggested) to a confusion between unstressed vowels. More tellingly, perhaps, *helpeð* (3.7), *tostregdeð* (5.9), and *onbydeð* (5.13) present unsyncopated endings (and, in the case of *helpeð*, *e* as the stem-vowel, instead of *i* which normally goes with the syncopated ending). Syncopated forms do not appear in the text.[46] This may, as we have noted (above, p. 167 and n. 33), again point to a non-West Saxon colouring (that is, Anglian or Kentish). It may also be relevant to observe that TF reads *tostregdeð* (5.9) and not *tostredeð* with loss of /j/ in front of /d/, typical of Late West Saxon, and that therefore this form may also point to a non-West Saxon dialect area.[47] But, again, we cannot be sure since there is much fluctuation in West Saxon texts showing this sound change. In contradistinction to such rather elusive evidence pointing to the non-West Saxon area is the also slender evidence of the reduced forms of the second person plural imperative pointing to precisely this area.[48] So the picture so far is not clear, and before leaving verb inflexion we have to consider briefly one further complication.

Plural Present Indicative in -an, -on, -en

On at least five, perhaps six, occasions we find the endings *-an*, *-on*, *-en*, which would be correct or acceptable for the subjunctive, in forms which would most naturally be identified as plural present indicative: *nimen*, *cumon* (1.11), *wealdan* (2.9), *willan* (5.16), *deman* (6.20) and perhaps *teorgon* (4.19). If these forms are indeed indicatives, they would by far outnumber the regular ending of the plural present indicative which occurs only three times (*willað*, 5.18 and 5.20, and *cumað*, 6.20). Even with Bruce Mitchell's authoritative guidance, the rules governing the use of indicative and subjunctive remain the most ferociously difficult aspect of Old English syntax.[49] When I stated above that the forms in question would 'most naturally' pass as plural present indicative, I meant to imply that an interpretation of these forms as subjunctives might be conceivable but that their syntactic contexts would rather require indicatives. Thus,

45 For surveys of dialectal features in verb inflexion, see the standard grammars of Old English: conveniently in Campbell, §§ 735, 752 and 757, and more detailed in SB, §§ 360–3, 368–78, 400–6 and 409–14.

46 For *hefst* and *hefð*, see above, p. 167, n. 33.

47 For this development, see SB, § 214.3 and n. 9, and Campbell § 242.

48 See above, p. 167 and n. 37.

49 Bruce Mitchell's discussion of the subjunctive is found in his *Old English Syntax*, 2 vols. (Oxford, 1985) I, §§ 874–913 (general discussion and simple sentences), and II, ch. vii, *passim* (in his treatment of the various types of subordinate clauses: see list of contents for vol. II). There is a convenient first introduction to the subject in R. Quirk and C. L. Wrenn, *An Old English Grammar*, 2nd ed. (London, 1958), pp. 81–5.

nimen and *cumon* (1.11) might be taken to express a possibility, but they translate Latin indicatives; *wealdan* (2.9) and *deman* (6.20) occur in relative clauses, which normally take the indicative; *willan* (5.16) might, by a very considerable stretch of imagination, be taken as an adhortative imperative (and hence as a subjunctive form, see above, p. 168); and *teorgon* (4.19) occurs in a conditional construction, but of the type which normally takes the indicative. Furthermore, it is clear on at least two occasions that the Taunton Commentator was unusually progressive in employing the indicative in types of subordinate clauses where the subjunctive is almost invariably found throughout the Old English – and even the Middle English – period: *ær þu þis gedost* (3.7),[50] and *ðyles cumað* (6.20) are the clauses in question.[51] It is therefore most unlikely that he should have meant the six verbs under discussion here to be read as subjunctives.

But how are we then to explain this situation? The ending *-en* (*-on*, *-an*) of the subjunctive and the ending *-aþ* of the indicative never coalesced through the reduction of unstressed syllables, and we have seen that otherwise the Commentator kept formally distinct verbal endings distinct also in his text. In light of the development of these two endings in Middle English a possible solution easily comes to mind. In the Midland dialects of Middle English the original ending of the plural present indicative (OE *-að* > ME *-eth*) was replaced by the ending of the plural present subjunctive (OE *-en* etc. > ME *-e(n)*). Conceivably, such replacement might have occurred already in the case of our six verbs. If so, this would also give us a definite clue to the dialect origin of TF: ME *-e(n)* in the plural present indicative occurs only in the Midland area, beginning in the East Midlands. The one serious problem with this solution is, however, the chronology. Standard treatments of Middle English morphology agree that *-e(n)* is the Midland indicative form by about 1300 at the latest.[52] But how much earlier did this replacement begin? To my knowledge, the earliest text showing a recognizable tendency to use *-en* in the indicative is the Peterborough Chronicle in its original sections, written from the 1120s onwards.[53] Note, however, that in the Peterborough Chronicle the

[50] For the subjunctive in temporal clauses beginning with *ær* 'before', see Mitchell, *Old English Syntax* II §§ 2731–42, and Quirk and Wrenn, *Old English Grammar*, p. 84 (g).

[51] For the subjunctive in clauses of purpose introduced by *ðy læs* 'lest', see Mitchell, *Old English Syntax* II, §§ 2928–36, esp. 2933, and Quirk and Wrenn, *Old English Grammar*, p. 84 (e).

[52] See, for example, Lass, 'Phonology and Morphology', pp. 136–7, and, with some useful information on texts, Brunner, *Englische Sprache* II, 189–90.

[53] For these forms, see *Peterborough Chronicle*, ed. Clark, pp. xlvii–xlviii. For a more detailed treatment of the *-en*-indicatives in the Peterborough Chronicle, see W. F. Bryan, 'The Midland Present Plural Indicative Ending *-e(n)*', *MP* 18 (1921), 121–37, at 121–4. For a convincing refutation of the claim made by E. M. Brown (*The Language of the Rushworth Gloss to the Gospel of St. Matthew and the Mercian Dialect* (Göttingen, 1892)) to have detected *-en*-forms for the indicative already in the late-tenth-century Mercian gloss to the Rushworth gospels, see Bryan, pp. 124–6 and, briefly, *Peterborough Chronicle*, ed. Clark, p. xlviii, n. 1.

plural present indicative is attested extremely rarely and that a few *-eth*-forms still occur. In any case, the relevant sections in the Peterborough Chronicle were composed about seventy years after the manuscript of TF was written. It is the frequent occurrence of the *-en*-forms for the plural present indicative at such an early date which makes one hesitate to embrace wholeheartedly the attractive solution of seeing the Taunton Commentator as the harbinger of Middle English developments. So this explanation can be no more than a hypothesis. It may be possible, nevertheless, to broach the problem which these forms present from an altogether different angle, but this will have to wait until we have considered the phonology and orthography of the stressed vowels.

The Phonology and Orthography of Stressed Vowels

In order to complement the survey of inflexional endings, in this section I shall concentrate on the vowels in stressed syllables. Again, no complete inventory of the Old English phonemes and their representation in TF will be given. Rather, I shall aim to draw attention to some peculiarities in the orthography of stressed vowels and attempt to assess them in the context of Late Old English spellings.

Old English ǣ̆ (and ēă)

One of the most recurrent features of Taunton's orthography are the inconsistent spellings of OE long and short *æ*.[54] For short *æ* TF clearly prefers the spelling <e>, e.g. *sunnandeges* (3.2), *deghwamlice* (5.5), *wes* (7.15 etc.), *hwet* (4.8), *efter* (8.20), and always *fedur* (see above, p. 164). The spelling <a> occurs only sporadically, e.g. *gladscype* (2.8) and *cwað* (4.18), as does the correct spelling <æ>, e.g. *æfter* (8.2) and *cwæð* (8.10).

Long *ǣ* is represented by <e> even more frequently, e.g. *forletan* (1.14), *þer* (1.17 etc.), *unðwernesse* (2.2), *eghwilcum* (2.11), *efre* (2.11), *ses* (7.11), *ondred* (8.15), all from West Germanic *ā*; and *clennesse* (1.1), *enig* (5.14), *tecen* (8.9), and always *Helend* (see above, p. 164), from Germanic *ai*. The spelling <a> occurs only sporadically for *ǣ* of both origins, e.g. *mast* (1.15) and *ðar* (2.3), as does the correct spelling <æ>, e.g. *æfre* (4.13), *ær* (3.7) and *æcan* (7.1). Very occasionally we find <æ> for original long *ē* by way of an inverted spelling: *hæ* (5.8) and *hæt* (7.15).

The spelling <æ> for *e* also occurs sporadically in the diphthong *ēă*: *hæahenglum* (2.8) and *æac* (5.12). Otherwise the diphthong preserves its normal Late West Saxon spelling, e. g. *middaneardes* (1.12), *wealdan* (2.9), *gehealde* (3.16), *ongean*

[54] For the origin of OE *æ* (mainly from Germanic *a*) and *ǣ* (mainly from West Germanic *ā* and Germanic *ai* under conditions of *i*-mutation), see SB, §§ 14–17, and Campbell, §§ 126–34 and 197.

(5.6), all for short *ea*; and *ofslean* (5.18), *gesceawian* (6.3), *eadiga* (8.9) for long *ēa*. Sporadically the spelling <e> occurs for *ea*, as in *ofsleþ* (5.8) and *ongen* (3.17).[55] On one occasion we find the idiosyncratic spelling <ea> for *a* (in *ongean* for *ongan* 'began', 8.9), which – if any significance is to be attributed to it at all – may confirm the impression of a prevalent confusion between the spellings <e>, <æ>, <a> and <ea>.

How are we to interpret the sum of this evidence? First, it is important to note that confusion in writing between *æ* and *e* occurs frequently at a rather early date and in manuscripts which otherwise preserve Standard Old English spellings, at least to some extent, such as Cotton Julius E. vii, the manuscript of the *Lives of Saints*, already referred to above (p. 165, n. 30), which was written at the beginning of the eleventh century in an unknown centre in the South of England.[56] However, in contradistinction to the scribe of Julius E. vii (and the scribal practice in other manuscripts) it is evident that the Taunton scribe clearly preferred the spelling <e>, and only sporadically used <æ>. While the avoidance of the grapheme <æ> may point to the transitional period between Old and Middle English, when <æ> became obsolete, the preference of <e>, at least for short *æ*, does not point in the same direction: OE *æ* was lowered to *a* in Early Middle English, which was soon represented universally by <a>. On the other hand, the frequent <e>-spellings for short *æ* may be of dialectal relevance and may point either to the Kentish or to a not clearly defined part of the Mercian dialect, where by the so-called 'second fronting' *æ* was raised to *e* at some point during the Old English period.[57] By the same token, the preference of the spelling <e> for long *ǣ* from West Germanic *ā* may point to the Anglian and Kentish dialect area,[58] whereas the spelling <e> for long *ǣ*, ultimately from Germanic *ai*, if taken as a dialect marker, would point exclusively to the Kentish area.[59] However, the spelling <e> for *ǣ* of whatever origin might equally be interpreted as pointing towards developments

55 Note that *ongen* for *ongēan* 'towards' could be due to Late West Saxon smoothing; see SB, § 123 and Campbell § 312.

56 For the confusion between *æ* and *e* in Julius E. vii, see *Lives of Three English Saints*, ed. Needham, p. 7, and apparatus criticus, *passim*. For the confusion in later manuscripts (where also <ea> spellings for *æ* are attested), see W. Schlemilch, *Beiträge zur Sprache und Orthographie spätaltenglischer Sprachdenkmäler der Übergangszeit (1000–1150)* (Halle, 1914), pp. 5–8, 18–21 and 24–8.

57 See SB, § 52 and Cambell, §§ 164–9. There is a recent synopsis and reassessment of the Kentish dialect features which conveniently summarizes previous literature on the subject: U. Kalbhen, *Kentische Glossen und kentischer Dialekt im Altenglischen*, Texte und Untersuchungen zur Englischen Philologie 28 (Frankfurt, 2003), 241–71; for Kentish *e* for *æ* and the 'second fronting', see pp. 262 and 267.

58 See SB, § 62, Campbell, § 128 and Kalbhen, *Kentischer Dialekt*, pp. 259–60.

59 See SB, § 97, n. 1, Campbell, §§ 288–90, and Kalbhen, *Kentischer Dialekt*, p. 267. Cf., however, Campbell, § 292, for *ē* from Germanic *ai* also in some forms in Mercian texts.

in Middle English, where OE *ǣ* and *ē* are represented by <e>. This complication apart, the evidence which might, conceivably, be of dialectal relevance is not consistent. Thus, forms such as *hæahenglum* (2.8), *gehealde* (3.16) and *wealdan* (2.9) show West Saxon and Kentish breaking or retention of *ēa* which in these words would not be found in the Anglian dialects.[60]

Old English i *and* y

In TF, words with original OE (WS) long and short *i* are frequently spelled <y>, for example *gyfe* (1.5), *ys* (1.5), *lyf* (1.16), *onbydeð* (5.13), *scype* (8.8); vice versa, if much less frequently, words with original OE (WS) long and short *y* are spelled <i>, for example, *þirst* (1.18), *gegiltað* (5.15), *sinfull* (8.12), and consistently in *drihtin* (see above, p. 164). This feature, again, is not infrequently found in eleventh-century manuscripts, and again, as early as Julius E. vii.[61] In view of the <e>-spellings discussed above and possibly pointing to the Kentish dialect, it is relevant to note here that *i*-mutation of *u* regularly occurs in the West Saxon and Anglian form *y*, spelled <y> or <i>, and never as *e*, the normal form in Kentish; for example, *þirst* (1.18), *gegiltað* (5.15), *synigað* (5.6), *cystas* (5.13).[62]

The Spellings <eo>, <e>, <o>

Here three points deserve mention:

1. The diphthong *eo* occurs frequently in words where it is etymologically correct; it never occurs in its typically Kentish form *io*.[63] Examples are: *forleosan* (1.16), *mildheorte* (5.3), and *deopnesse* (7.11).

2. There is, however, a considerable amount of confusion between the spellings <eo> and <e>, and occasionally <eo> represents original *o*, an idiosyncrasy which is difficult to explain. Cf., for example, *lernunge* (2.14), *weruld* (2.11), *werðige* (4.2), *breoðre* (6.3), and *reoduras* (2.9, for *roderas*).[64]

3. It is unlikely that such confusion is indicative of the Middle English monophthongization of *eo* to *e*, which probably did not occur before the

[60] For the Anglian forms, see SB, §§ 85 and 119, and Campbell, §§ 143 and 222. For evidence pointing away from a Kentish dialect origin, see below, on *i/y* and *<eo> etc.*

[61] See *Lives of Three English Saints*, ed. Needham, p. 8, and apparatus criticus, *passim*, and Schlemilch, *Zur Sprache und Orthographie*, pp. 9–13 and 22–3.

[62] For the dialectal distribution of *y* and *e*, see SB, §§ 31, n.1, 102–3, Campbell, § 190 and Kalbhen, *Kentischer Dialekt*, pp. 268–9. Confusingly, however, *i*-mutation of *ēa* in the verb 'to hear' always occurs in TF in the Anglian and Kentish form *gehēran* (three times); WS *gehȳran* is never used.

[63] For this Kentish dialect feature, see SB, §§ 36 and 77, n. 3, Campbell, § 297, and Kalbhen, *Kentischer Dialekt*, p. 266.

[64] Note that 'anger' occurs in the Anglian form *eorre* (3.4), as *erscipe* (3.16, with <e> for <eo>), *and* in the West Saxon form *yrre* (3.6).

twelfth century.[65] Rather, such variant forms seem to reveal an uncertainty (for whatever reasons) concerning the correct use of the grapheme <eo>.

In sum, it is abundantly clear, even from this brief glance at a few outstanding peculiarities in the orthography of stressed vowels, that the evidence is confusing indeed. Some of the peculiarities seem to point to the Kentish dialect, others to the Kentish and Anglian dialects, others again to the West Saxon and Anglian dialects, or to the West Saxon and Kentish dialects, or even only to the West Saxon dialect. Some may indicate phonological developments *en route* towards Middle English, while others may simply be explained as confusion about what the correct spelling should be. If anything, these results fill in the outline sketch drawn by our examination of the inflexional morphology, in particular of the chaotic nominal inflexion. In other words, TF allows us to glimpse an author, who was not trained in writing Standard Old English, whose inflexional system had broken down in a rather dramatic way at an unusually early date, whose dialect seems to have been an amalgam of almost all Old English dialects (excluding only typically Northern features), and who does not seem to have made any serious attempt to record contemporary spoken English. It is possible that this is how the evidence should be read. Even the curious mixture of dialects could, conceivably, be explained as standard (i. e. Late West Saxon) forms impinging on an original southeastern dialect of the author.

A Different Explanation

It is time now to broach the linguistic evidence from the different angle I alluded to earlier. What if the Taunton Commentator was not a native speaker of Old English but a foreigner coming from the Old Saxon or Old High German territory? On this hypothesis a considerable number of the text's peculiarities could be explained plausibly and at a stroke. On the phonological level this hypothesis could explain the confusion in the writing of <eo> and <æ>: both phonemes and, accordingly, graphemes do not occur in any of the German dialects.[66] Even today the pronunciation of Modern English /æ/ as /e/ is a shibboleth for recognizing native speakers of German, and Taunton's clear preference of the spelling <e> for OE /æ/ squares with this modern linguistic evidence. Germanic short and long *a* are normally retained in the German dialects,[67] which could explain spellings such as *gladscype* or *cwað* (for short *a*) and

65 See K. Luick, *Historische Grammatik der englischen Sprache* (Leipzig, 1914–40; repr. with an index by R. F. S. Hamer, Oxford, 1964), § 357.

66 There is limited occurrence of *eo* in Old Saxon, but the same diphthong may also occur as *io*, *ia*, *ea* or *ie*; see J. H. Gallée, *Altsächsische Grammatik*, 3rd ed. (Tübingen, 1993), §§ 102–5; so this was certainly not a clearly defined phoneme with one widely accepted spelling.

67 See W. Braune, *Althochdeutsche Grammatik*, 14th ed. rev. H. Eggers (Tübingen, 1987), §§ 25 and 34, and Gallée, *Altsächsische Grammatik*, §§ 45 and 81.

aton (for long *ā*). For the last example it may be relevant to note that this preterite form of the verb *etan* 'to eat' (instead of normal *ǣton* or *ēton*) is attested only here and that it corresponds almost precisely to OS *ātun* or OHG *āzzum*.[68]

In light of a possible German author, the frequent spelling <e> for Germanic *ai* plus *i*-mutation (used, for example, consistently in *Helend* 'Saviour') need no longer be interpreted as an exclusively Kentish dialect feature. The spelling might equally point to interference from German, where, in Old Saxon, *ai* regularly developed to *ē*, as is well known from the (modern) title of the Old Saxon *Heliand*.[69] It is important to note that, as a consequence of this observation, the one seemingly clear pointer to the Kentish dialect (and to the Kentish dialect only) has become ambiguous.[70] Similarly, we are no longer on firm ground with the phonological features mentioned above, which could point to the Kentish *and* Anglian dialects; features such as <e> for short *æ*, or <e> for WS *ǣ* from West Germanic *ā*. Even the three occurrences of seemingly Anglian and Kentish *e* in *gehēran* (instead of WS *gehȳran*) may lose their dialectal relevance, since *gehēran* would be much closer to the contemporary Old Saxon and Old High German pronunciation of the word 'to hear' than WS *gehyran*.[71]

Evidence of inflexional morphology may further consolidate the 'German hypothesis', in particular the curious forms of the plural present indicative with the ending *-on*, *-an*, or *-en* (see above, pp. 170–2). Perhaps these forms, so baffling by their frequency at such an early date, are not at all the earliest occurrences of the Middle English plural present indicative in the Midlands, but are rather due to interference by one of the German dialects. In Old Saxon, as well as in the Old High German dialects, an intrusion of the endings of the plural present subjunctive (*-en*, *-an*) into the forms of the plural present indicative can be observed from the ninth century onwards;[72] and such intrusion is precisely what we find in TF (and more than a century later in the Middle English Midlands). Furthermore, our observation that verbal inflexions are better preserved than nominal and pronominal inflexions would be consonant with the

[68] There is one attestation of a preterite *aten* in the First Continuation of the Peterborough Chronicle (ed. Clark, p. 44.30, *s.a.* 1124), but as we have seen (above p. 162 and n. 17) the two continuations to this chronicle can no longer pass as Old English texts.

[69] See Gallée, *Altsächsische Grammatik*, § 89; in Old High German *ai* is often retained as a diphthong but also frequently monophthongized to *ē*; see Braune-Eggers, *Althochdeutsche Grammatik*, § 43.

[70] Cf. also above, pp. 173–4, where I already entered the caveat that <e> in the words in question might, possibly, be indicative of Middle English developments.

[71] See Braune-Eggers, *Althochdeutsche Grammatik*, § 51, and Gallée, *Altsächsische Grammatik*, § 87. For *geheran* in TF, see above, p. 174, n. 62.

[72] See Braune-Eggers, *Althochdeutsche Grammatik*, §§ 307, n. 6 and 309, n. 4, and Gallée, *Altsächsische Grammatik*, § 379, n. 4.

notion of a non-native author. In languages such as Old English, Old Saxon, Old High German (or, to some extent, Modern German) the inflexion of pronouns, adjectives and nouns with their numerous classes of declension is, as a rule, more difficult to control than verb inflexion, where more or less the same endings apply to all conjugations. Similarly, our observation that the breakdown of the inflexional system is more advanced in complex noun phrases than with simple nouns could be explained by the circumstance, widely known in language teaching and learning, that the intricacies of concord in noun phrases of a language, where demonstratives, adjectives and nouns are inflected according to case, number and gender, set up one of the most dangerous traps for learners of that language.

In a word, it has emerged from our consideration of the morphology and phonology of TF that the sum of their evidence can be read in various ways and that, in a surprisingly large number of instances, the same piece of evidence admits various interpretations: either as pointing to a certain dialect area – though the overall picture is not clearly defined; or as pointing towards developments in Middle English – but here again, the picture is not clearly focused; or as pointing to the author's pervasive linguistic incompetence – for philologists only the last straw; or, finally, as pointing to a non-native author – a suspicion which will probably always fall short of incontestable proof. Where is the line to be drawn between the sloppiness of an extremely careless, even illiterate English author and the linguistic struggles of a continental cleric trying to express himself in a foreign language? Moreover, to my knowledge, in discussions of authorship to date no need has ever arisen for assuming a non-native author for an Old English text, so there is no precedent to be guided by.

However, we emerge from our exploration of TF's morphology and phonology with at least one reasonably safe result: this text can never have existed in a form of Standard Old English; it must have left its author's desk more or less in the form it has survived. What I suggested at the outset has been confirmed by the linguistic details: it is scarcely conceivable that around the middle of the eleventh century, a scribe would have garbled a standardized text in the way we have it here.[73] On the other hand, there are no insuperable

[73] For a few eleventh- and twelfth-century scribes, not all of them competent but, nevertheless, faithfully copying standardized texts and, in one case, even bringing an idiosyncratic exemplar into conformity with the standard, see M. Gretsch, 'Winchester Vocabulary and Standard Old English: the Vernacular in Late Anglo-Saxon England', The Toller Memorial Lecture 2000, *Bull. of the John Rylands Univ. Lib. of Manchester* 83 (2001), 41–87, at 72–4. For mid-eleventh-century readers of Ælfric's homilies correcting even the occasional error of concord in noun phrases, or of mood in verbs, in the manuscript they were perusing, see M. Godden, 'Ælfric as Grammarian: the Evidence of his *Catholic Homilies*', *Early Medieval English: Texts and Interpretations. Studies Presented to Donald G. Scragg*, ed. E. Treharne and S. Rosser (Tempe, AZ, 2002), pp. 13–29, at 19 and 23–4.

difficulties in imagining an eleventh-century scribe, trained and prepared to copy faithfully (for whatever reasons) any exemplar set before him, without giving much thought to its linguistic form.

The Lexical and Syntactical Evidence

We may next turn to the vocabulary and the syntax of TF as a class of evidence which may be expected to yield further information on the possibility of a non-native author. When attempting to assess unusual or incorrect word usage or awkward phrasing, and to detect possible 'Germanisms' in TF, we have to bear in mind the deficient nature of our knowledge of Old English vocabulary and idiomatic usage. In the case of suspected 'Germanisms' this problem is compounded by the fact that considerably fewer texts in Old High German or Old Saxon have survived than in Old English, and that therefore our knowledge of the vocabulary and word usage of these languages is even more deficient.[74] In what follows I discuss only examples of words and phrases which, for one reason or another, are clearly unusual or awkward. There are numerous other instances where one suspects unidiomatic usage, but for the reasons given above I shall concentrate on a few clear examples.

Thus, the Taunton Commentator often uses *eac* 'also, and, likewise, moreover' in an adversative function, often translating Lat. *sed.*[75] On one occasion he has *be þon* (4.18) to translate *inde* 'thereupon, then', when one would have expected, for example, *þonne*; *be þon* (= *be þæm*) meaning 'thereon, with regard to this matter'. *On here husas* (4.19) translates Latin *in domum*. Apart from *hus* being erroneously inflected as a masculine noun instead of a neuter, the Latin phrase is an adverbial here and simply means 'home', and, for example, *ham* or *to heora eðel* would have been idiomatic translations; buildings are not in question. The syntax in 2.17–20 is definitely awkward: there is lack of concord between *genihtsumian* (pl.) and *rihtwisnesse* (sg.); and, in order to make sense, in line 19 one would need a wording such as *ðe ma ðe ða ðæra writera*, instead of what we get there (*ma ðanna ða writras*). The sentence in 5.14–16 is awkward, too, without the conjunction *þæt* which one would expect between *us* and *nan* in line 15.

The verb *toslitan* occurs frequently in Old English and is always used as a

[74] The Old High German vocabulary is controlled by means of R. Schützeichel, *Althochdeutsches Wörterbuch*, 4th ed. (Tübingen, 1989) and G. Köbler, *Wörterbuch des althochdeutschen Sprachschatzes* (Paderborn, 1993). Work on the definitive dictionary of Old High German is still in progress: *Althochdeutsches Wörterbuch* (begründet von E. Karg-Gasterstädt and T. Frings), ed. R. Grosse (Berlin, 1968– ; vol. IV, G-J was publ. in 2002). For the Old Saxon vocabulary (of which our knowledge is even more restricted than in the case of Old High German), see E. H. Sehrt, *Vollständiges Wörterbuch zum Heliand und zur altsächsischen Genesis*, 2nd ed. (Göttingen, 1966) and F. Holthausen, *Altsächsisches Wörterbuch* (Münster, 1954).

[75] See, for example, 2.7, 3.18, 5.12 and 5.17.

transitive verb 'to tear asunder, rend' etc.[76] In TF *toslitan* is used twice (8.2) as an intransitive verb ('the nets burst'). Alternatively, the author could have meant the verb to be understood in a passive sense ('the nets were torn'; *toslyton* translates *rumpebatur* on both occasions),[77] in which case the author would have been incapable of forming a correct passive for an Old English transitive verb. In any event, *toslitan* is a common Old English verb, the construction of which was not clear to the Taunton Commentator. In this connection it may be relevant to note that etymologically corresponding OS *toslitan* and OHG *zeslizan* can be used intransitively.[78]

A most egregious error is *sunnandeges bene þæt byþ pater noster* (3.2–3). The Latin text (which has not been preserved) must have read *oratio dominica*, a common Latin term for the *pater noster*, 'the Lord's prayer'. Obviously, the Taunton Commentator confused the identical adjective ('of *or* belonging to the Lord') in *oratio dominica* and in (*dies*) *dominica* 'Sunday', hence his *sunnandeges bene* 'Sunday's prayer'. An established Old English rendering for *oratio dominica* is *drihtenlic gebed*.[79] Even if this loan translation should not have been of general currency in Old English, an English cleric might reasonably be expected to have been familiar with it; and, even more tellingly, it is difficult to see how any cleric, of whatever nationality, could have mistaken the meaning of *oratio dominica*. Therefore, the nonsensical Old English calque *sunnandeges bene* on *oratio dominica* strongly suggests a translator not much at home in Old English liturgical terminology.

Another example pointing in the same direction is *uprist* (7.19) for *resurrectio* (*domini*). This word is otherwise attested only in one of the twelfth-century homilies in Oxford, Bodleian Library, Bodley 343.[80] The usual Old English

76 Bosworth–Toller have one attestation for intransitive use 'to be different', a meaning which does not apply here: J. Bosworth and T. N. Toller, *An Anglo-Saxon Dictionary* (Oxford, 1882–98); T. N. Toller, *An Anglo-Saxon Dictionary; Supplement* (Oxford, 1908–21) [hereafter BT and BTS respectively]. The intransitive use of *toslitan* is listed in BT.

77 Note that the Latin singular *rete* is erroneously translated as plural: *þa net.*

78 See W. Pfeifer, *Etymologisches Wörterbuch des Deutschen*, 2nd ed. (Berlin, 1993), *s. v.* 'verschleissen', and F. Kluge, *Etymologisches Wörterbuch der deutschen Sprache*, 24th ed. by E. Seebold (Berlin, 2002), *s.v.* 'schleissen' and 'verschleissen' (more detailed information in the earlier editions of this dictionary, rev. by W. Mitzka; the 20th ed., 1967 is the last which was rev. by Mitzka).

79 It occurs twelve times in the electronic Old English Corpus; add to this one further occurrence, not attested there, but found in its predecessor, the Microfiche Concordance: BR 38.15 (in the notation of the OEC).

80 Originally ptd by A. O. Belfour, *Twelfth-Century Homilies in MS. Bodley 343. Part I, Text and Translation*, EETS os 137 (London, 1909); see now the edition of some of these homilies by S. Irvine, *Old English Homilies from MS Bodley 343*, EETS os 302 (Oxford, 1993). The homily in question is Belfour, no. XII and Irvine, no. VI; for the four occurrences there of *uprist*, see Irvine, p. 178, notes to lines 152 and 155. The word is listed only in the second supplement to BT(S): A. Campbell, *An Anglo-Saxon Dictionary. Enlarged Addenda and Corrigenda* (Oxford, 1972).

word for this key term of Christianity is *ærist*, a very common word, attested some 400 times.[81] Note that in Old High German *urristi*, *urresti* is used among other synonyms with the prefix *ur-*, such as *urstand* or *urstendi*, for *resurrectio* (*domini*). Should the Taunton Commentator have been familiar with such German prefix formations, and should he have known *ærist* at all, he was certainly unaware that OHG *ur-* and OE *ǣ-* derive from the same root.[82] But he would no doubt have noticed the phonological similarity between the prefixes *ur-* and *up-* and the identity of the simplex in *urristi* and *uprist*. In any case, it is curious that he should have employed such an exceedingly rare word for 'resurrection', ignoring the established and universally current synonym *ærist*.

Our next example, *leorningcniht*, is also well established in the Christian terminology of Old English. The word is attested frequently, especially in the West Saxon gospels and in Ælfric, where it translates *discipulus* in the sense 'one of Christ's disciples'. It is clear that the Taunton Commentator had heard this Old English word but he employs it in a highly idiosyncratic form: *se helend cwæð to his lernunge cnihtas* (2.14–15; note the wrong inflexional ending *cnihtas* instead of *cnihtum*). Here *lernunge* is formed with the suffix *-ung* which otherwise never occurs in *leorningcniht*. Furthermore, if the Commentator had in mind the compound noun, the final *-e* in *lernunge* would be wrong in terms of word-formation; if he intended a genitive construction, 'young man of learning', this would make little sense, especially after the compound *leorningcniht* had become current. It seems clear, therefore, that the Commentator simply garbled a well-established Old English word. It is noteworthy that, again in Old High German, the suffix he employs in *lernunge* is more frequent than the sister suffix *-ing*.[83] The Taunton Commentator has this suffix in two further deverbal nouns: *fiscung* (7.14; in 8.7 *fiscing*, for *piscatio*) and *redung* (7.14 for *historia*). Neither *fiscung* nor *fiscing* is attested in Old English: *fisc(n)oþ* is the usual Old English term for 'fishing'.[84] OE *rædung* is attested only twice in the Old English Corpus (besides frequent *ræding*).[85]

We may conclude this brief survey with three final examples where some interference from German dialects is possible. On one occasion the adjective

81 For *ærist* as a rendering for Christ's resurrection, see J. Roberts *et al.*, *A Thesaurus of Old English*, 2 vols. (London, 1995) I, 651 (16. 01. 02. 09). According to the *Dictionary of Old English* [hereafter DOE], ed. A. Cameron *et al.* (Toronto, 1986–), most of the *c.* 400 occurrences of *ærist* denote Christ's resurrection. There are 112 attestations of *ærist* in Ælfric's two series of *Catholic Homilies* (see Godden, *Ælfric's Catholic Homilies*, *Glossary*) but the word is not restricted with regard to time or dialect.

82 See [H. Krahe and] W. Meid, *Germanische Sprachwissenschaft. III: Wortbildung* (Berlin, 1967), § 44 (p. 39), and OED, *s. v. arist.*

83 See Kluge-Seebold, *Etymologisches Wörterbuch*, *s. v. -ung*.

84 See Roberts *et al.*, *Thesaurus of Old English* I, 221 (04. 03. 05).

85 I have not counted the two attestations in the Winteney Version of the Benedictine Rule because this is a thirteenth-century adaptation of the Old English Rule, which itself has invariably *ræding*. *Redung*, with *-e-* as the stressed vowel is not attested outside TF.

dead 'dead' occurs as a noun (*ðu demest mon to deade*, 6.11). In Old English, the adjective *dead* and the noun *deað* are not interchangeable; they are, however, interchangeable in Old High German, where both *tot* and *tod* can either be an adjective or a noun.[86] Also, on one occasion (5.15), the adjective *mildheort* 'merciful' is used as a noun, translating *misericordia* (and occurring in a wrong form: *mildheorte*). While, again, noun (*mildheortness*) and adjective (*mildheort*) consistently present distinct forms in Old English texts, they are almost identical in Old High German, where *armherz* is the adjective and *armherzi, armherzin* the noun. Note that the curious form *-heorte* in TF looks suspiciously like a calque on *armherzi*, but is of course impossible in terms of Old English word-formation. On two further occasions (6.4 and 6.6) the correct form of the noun, *mildheortness*, is used in TF, so the Commentator knew this form but apparently he was unaware that it is the only form in which the noun can occur. Taunton's *þæt we gebetæð þa yfela cystas ðe we don habbað* (5.13–14; note the wrong form of the adjective: *yfela* instead of *yfelan*) translates somewhat freely *ut nos emendemus in melius*. The meaning of *cyst* must here be 'deed, action' or possibly (if we take *don* in a wider sense 'to show, reveal' etc.) 'attitude, demeanour, habits'. None of these meanings is attested in Old English, where (according to the DOE) the noun denotes (a) 'an excellent or precious thing' or (b) 'excellence, goodness, virtue, merit, worth'.[87] In Old High German, however, the etymologically corresponding *kust*, in addition to meaning 'virtue, excellence', can be used in a neutral sense 'state, attitude'.[88] Again, German influence cannot, ultimately, be proved, but it is clear that, given the attested meanings of *cyst* in Old English, the Commentator produced nonsense when asking his audience to improve their 'depraved excellence'.

To sum up: the consistently erroneous use of *eac*, the phrases *be þon* and *on here husas*, unidiomatic in their context (to say the least), the awkward syntax of 2.17–20 and 5.14–16, the intransitive use of *toslitan* – all these examples point to an author who had no great familiarity with the composition of Old English prose. The grotesque rendering of *oratio dominica*, *uprist* for 'resurrection', *lernunge cniht* for 'disciple', *redung* for 'reading', *dead* and *mildheort* used as nouns, and *cyst* employed in a neutral sense – these examples reveal an author who has no knowledge of some of the most important and most recurrent terms in

86 Note that the form *tot* is originally that of the adjective and *tod* that of the noun (see Kluge-Seebold, *Etymologisches Wörterbuch*, *s. v. Tod* and *tot*), but the distinction between final *t* and *d* became blurred at an early stage, and in Modern German is preserved in writing only: <Tod> (n.) vs. <tot> (adj.).

87 Two further senses given by the DOE, 'choice' and 'a band of chosen men', are not pertinent here.

88 Note that, in spite of the spelling, the vowel in OHG *kust* must already have shown influence of *i*-mutation (see Braune-Eggers, *Althochdeutsche Grammatik*, § 51), and that hence *kust* and *cyst* will have been pronounced almost identically.

Old English homiletic prose. We have seen that a substantial number of these blunders could be explained on the hypothesis of an author of German extraction. No doubt further examples could be found in the text to feed this suspicion; examples such as *nið* (2.3) for *inuidia* 'envy', which is not its primary meaning in English, but *is* in German; or *behygdig* 'anxious' (8.10), not frequently attested in Old English, garbled by the scribe, and, perhaps, employed after German *pihuctik*. In other words, examples which, judged by themselves, may not carry much weight, but when judged cumulatively, and together with more blatant examples, gain in conviction. By the same token, some further erroneous or peculiar translation equivalents may be due, not to the translator's shaky Latin, but to his shaky English. Examples would be: *aliquando* 'sometimes' translated three times by *sume* 'some' (5.16–20), or the feminine adjective *prima* translated by the adverb *ærest* (8.7). Similarly, when *capiunt* 'they arrive' is translated by *nimen* 'they take' (1.11), and *consideremus* 'let us consider' by *gesceawian we* 'let us behold' (6.3), the English words cover part of the semantic range of *capere* and *considerare* but do not have the meanings of the Latin words which are in question here.

To whatever conclusion we may eventually come with regard to the possible foreign extraction of our author, it has become abundantly clear from a brief survey of some of his syntactical and lexical blunders that almost all of these must unequivocally be laid at his own door. A mindless scribe may occasionally have garbled a syntactical construction, but it is inconceivable that he should have committed the lexical and idiomatic solecisms that pervade the text. This evidence, in turn, corroborates our earlier assumption that most of the blunders concerning inflexional morphology and Old English orthography should be traced back to the author's original copy.

In our attempt to assemble from the text a picture of its author as complete as possible, we must next turn briefly to his competence in Latin.

THE LATIN TEXT

The Commentator's performance in Latin is rather poor. Again, the following list of errors is not exhaustive but aims to give a synopsis of the most recurrent types of mistakes; only unambiguous cases are listed.[89] Errors involving case are the most frequent type. Thus, we get *gratia* (1.3) instead of *gratiam* or *gratias*; *dei* (1.4) for *deo*; *tenebras* (1.19) for *tenebrae*; *letitiam* (2.4) for *laetitia*; *laudantes . . . benedicentes* (2.6) for *laudantibus . . . benedicentibus*; *duas* (7.16) for *duo*; *in illa nauicula* (8.4) for *in illam nauiculam*. Errors in gender occur in *per quem* (1.8) for *per quas*, and *ipsum condemnatio* (6.18) for *ipsa condemnatio*. Errors in the mood

[89] For unidiomatic or erroneous translations from Latin into English which may have been occasioned rather by the Commentator's difficulties with English than with Latin, see above, pp. 178 and 182.

of verbs occur in *occidat*, *condempnet* (5.7–8), and *exspectet* (5.10), all subjunctive forms where the indicative would be required. An incorrect tense form is *deficit* (4.11), where the present is used instead of the past or perfect. Rather frequently lack of concord occurs in a sentence: *retia* (pl.) is coupled with *intelleg-itur* (sg., 1.7), as are *deficit* (sg.) and *panes* (pl., 4.11–12), *turba* (sg.) and *inruerent* (pl., 7.6), and *illum* (sg.) and *piscatores* (pl., 8.18–19); cf. also *habeat . . . orate* (3.13–14), where the syntax is incoherent.

In addition to such grammatical blunders there are clear signs of carelessness: thus, it should be *in ecclesia* (1.3); at least this is what the Old English translates. In the phrase *Relinquamus in quantum posumus mundi* (1.12–13) apparently a noun such as *otiositatem* or *uanitatem* has been left out (cf. *ydolnesse* (1.16) in the English text); in *erat de longe* (4.10) a past participle seems to have fallen out (cf. again the OE *com*, 4.14). The correct reading for *pius est* (5.11) appears to be *peius est*; *rumpebatur* (7.20) is nonsense without a preceding *non*; *Petrus* is probably omitted after *beatus* (8.6; cf. 8.16–17: *beatus Petrus*); in 4.10–11 the punctuation is erroneous. Similarly, a number of incorrect spellings occur, most prominent among these is the confusion about initial <h>: *horatio* (3.9 and 3.15) for *oratio*, *hodium* (3.13) for *odium*, *ominis* (8.14) for *homines*, and *istoriam* (7.12) for *historiam*.[90]

Such errors, which are due to carelessness, may or may not go back to the author's autograph but, again, it is unlikely that the frequent grammatical solecisms should all, or even in their majority, be laid at the scribe's door. It seems rather that the Latin text lets us glimpse an author who cannot be reckoned among the outstanding Latin scholars of his age – regardless of whether he was of foreign or English extraction. This being said, it is obvious, nevertheless, that his blunders in Latin are less pervasive than is his maltreatment of the vernacular.

THE NATURE OF THE TEXT

The Pericopes

As has been noted above (p. 145), the four leaves of the Taunton Fragment contain expositions or homilies on gospel pericopes. Parts of four homilies are preserved, which expound the pericopes of four successive Sundays after Whitsun. The leaves on which the homilies are preserved were perhaps part of one quire (see above, fig. 4, p. 148). Pericopes are those portions of the gospels which are read during mass on Sundays and feast days (and, at certain times of

[90] This feature, however, is rather frequently found in medieval, and even late classical, Latin texts of all provenances: see P. Stotz, *Handbuch zur lateinischen Sprache des Mittelalters* III, *Lautlehre* (Munich, 1966), §§ 118–19 (pp. 156–60).

the year, also on Wednesdays and Fridays). In the early Middle Ages several systems of selecting and arranging the pericopes can be distinguished; these various systems have been authoritatively classified by Antoine Chavasse.[91] Ursula Lenker in her comprehensive study of the systems of pericopes in the early English church has adopted Chavasse's classification and has traced the various systems throughout the liturgy of Anglo-Saxon England.[92]

The pericopes of the Taunton homilies for the four Sundays in question represent Chavasse's type 3B, the system which was in universal use in the English church in the eleventh century; it is also the system that was used by Ælfric in his exegetical homilies.[93] The four homilies which are preserved in fragmentary form in the Taunton manuscript pertain to the fifth to eighth Sundays after Pentecost. In each case the pericope they expound can be clearly identified. The following pericopes are in question:

Fifth Sunday: Luke VI.36–42; Lenker #167[94]
Sixth Sunday: Luke V.1–11; Lenker #170
Seventh Sunday: Matthew V.20–4; Lenker #173
Eighth Sunday: Mark VIII.1–9; Lenker #177

The Texts: Present State and Losses

In what follows I give a synopsis of the lines of text that have been preserved for each homily, and on which pages they occur according to the present numbering of the leaves. (Recall that the present numbering of the leaves does not agree with their original order: see fig. 4, above, p. 148.) I have indicated in each case where a lacuna through the loss of one or more folios occurs in the text. In addition to the number of lines preserved for each homily, I also give the number of lines to which a homily would amount, if either one or two folios would have been preserved in each lacuna. Since in the surviving text there are invariably twenty lines to a page, the calculation is fairly safe.

Fifth Sunday: pp. 5 + 6; lacuna; + p. 7, lines 1–5 (end of homily). Preserved: 45 lines; total number of lines if one folio is missing: 85; if two folios are missing: 125.

Sixth Sunday: p. 7, lines 6–20 (beginning of homily) + p. 8; lacuna; + pp. 1–2, line 12

[91] See A. Chavasse, 'Les plus anciens types du lectionnaire et de l'antiphonaire romains de la messe. Rapports et date', *RB* 62 (1952), 1–91.

[92] U. Lenker, *Die westsächsische Evangelienversion und die Perikopenordnungen im angelsächsischen England*, Texte und Untersuchungen zur Englischen Philologie 20 (Munich, 1997); for a summary of Chavasse's three types of pericope systems and their continental dissemination, see *ibid.* pp. 154–60.

[93] For the characteristics of type 3, see Lenker, *Perikopenordnungen*, pp. 163–74; for the Sundays after Pentecost in England, see *ibid.* pp. 189–90; for Ælfric's system of pericopes, see *ibid.* pp. 498–500.

[94] The reference to Lenker is to her table identifying the pericopes of the *temporale* throughout the liturgical year: *Perikopenordnungen*, pp. 298–343.

(end of homily). Preserved: 66 lines; total number of lines if two folios are missing: 146. It is probable that the lacuna in this homily comprises at least two folios, which would have been the inner bifolium of the gathering.

Seventh Sunday: p. 2, lines 13–20 (beginning of homily); lacuna; + pp. 3–4, line 5 (end of homily). Preserved: 32 lines; total number of lines if one folio is missing: 72; if two folios are missing: 112.

Eighth Sunday: p. 4, lines 6–20 (beginning of homily). Preserved: 14 lines; no calculation of the lost lines is possible, since this homily begins on what presumably was the verso of the final leaf of the quire.

Comparing the figures for the best preserved homily (sixth Sunday), for which we can also be reasonably sure about the number of missing lines, it would seem that the length of the homilies for the fifth and seventh Sunday would be more consonant with that for the homily for the sixth Sunday, if we assume the loss of two folios for their lacunae. No calculation can be made for the homily for the eighth Sunday (see above): it was probably continued on a new quire. It is not very likely that the original outer bifolium of the reconstructed quire has been lost: only one or two sentences can be missing at the beginning of the homily for the fifth Sunday, which occupies what was presumably the left-hand folio (pp. 5 + 6) of the same bifolium which, on the verso of its right-hand folio (p. 4), has the beginning of the homily for the eighth Sunday. Hence, the beginning of the homily for the fifth Sunday was probably written (similar to the beginning of the homily for the eighth Sunday) on the lower part of the verso of the final leaf of the preceding quire. Assuming an additional bifolium as the lost outer bifolium of the Taunton Fragment would, for reasons of space, still leave us with fragmentary homilies at the beginning and end of the quire (presumably for the fourth and the ninth Sunday), and would result in an unusual total of twelve folios to the quire.

Opening and Doxology

From the above list it will be seen that the beginnings of three of the four homilies are preserved (for the sixth, seventh and eighth Sunday), as are also the conclusions of three homilies (for the fifth, sixth and seventh Sunday). Both opening and conclusion are formulaic. The homilies are introduced by the phrase *In illo tempore*, which habitually introduces the reading of the pericope during mass, and signals their *incipits* in liturgical books.[95] The homilies conclude with a similarly formulaic doxology: *Qui cum patre et spiritu sancto uiuit et regnat in saecula saculorum*, which is slightly varied in the homily for the sixth Sunday. Both the introductory formula and doxology are given in Latin and Old English.

[95] See Lenker, *Perikopenordnungen*, p. 85. This formula may be expanded by the addition of *dixit Iesus discipulis suis*, as it is at the beginning of the homily for the seventh Sunday.

Synopsis of Contents (as Preserved)

For reasons of quick reference in the following discussion I here give a brief summary of the contents of the fragments.

Fifth Sunday; pp. 5–6: the first verse of the pericope, Luke VI.36, in Latin and Old English; the following one and a half pages elaborate on this (Latin and Old English alternating sentence by sentence, here as everywhere in the homilies): day after day we sin against the Lord, but he does not kill us; rather, he is waiting patiently for us to mend our ways. We ought to show the same patience towards our fellow-Christians. Subsequently, the next gospel verse is quoted, translated and elaborated in a similar way. After the lacuna we get only the doxology (p. 7).

Sixth Sunday; pp. 7–8: Luke V.1 quoted and translated. Reference to three hauls of fish: two before Christ's passion and one after it. Biblical narrative continued: Luke V.3, 8 and 11 quoted or alluded to, and, very briefly, explained, especially with regard to St Peter as first fisher of fish and subsequently of men. After the lacuna, on pp. 1–2: etymological explanation of the name *Iohannes* (occurring in Luke V.10); allegorical interpretation of the fishing nets as the Holy Scriptures; description of Paradise (with vague reminiscences of Revelation XXI); doxology.

Seventh Sunday; p. 2: Matthew V.20 quoted in part and translated wholly. After the lacuna, pp. 3–4.5: explanation of the gist of Matthew V.23–4 to the effect that we need to be reconciled with our fellow-Christians before offering a gift on God's altar; the gift is explained as our prayers, especially the *Pater noster* and the Creed; doxology.

Eighth Sunday; p. 4.6–20: Mark VIII.1 quoted in part, translated wholly; followed by botched versions of Mark VIII.2, and a verbatim quotation and translation of Mark VIII.3. End of the text.

The Sources and the Exegesis

The brief summary of the contents and even a cursory glance at the texts themselves strongly suggest that, apart from the gospels, no significant verbal parallels are likely to crop up when searching the electronic databases for possible sources.[96] The surviving texts are basic and commonplace throughout, consisting of quotations and translations of verses of the relevant pericopes, and of moralizing and exhortatory comments in Latin and Old English on a most unpretentious level. With one or two exceptions there is no attempt at biblical exegesis on an allegorical level.[97] We do not know if further attempts at allegorical exegesis in the four homilies have been lost, but from what has survived we may be almost sure that, if so, these were few and brief.

[96] The databases that have been consulted are the Patrologia Latina database and the CETEDOC database, CLCLT-4.

[97] The exceptions are: 1.6–12 (the fishing nets signifying the Scriptures) and, very brief and basic, 3.9–10 (prayers as offerings to God).

Predictably then, the isolated parallels in patristic literature that can be traced through the databases are of such general character that they would not seem to allow us to postulate the Commentator's knowledge of the works in question. Thus, the phrase *ne perdamus uitam perpetuam* (1.14) is found in the *Dialogus confessionalis* by Rather of Verona;[98] the phrase *hoc teneat in corde suo* (3.12–13) occurs in the *Verba seniorum*;[99] or *retia mittere* (7.13) is in one of Augustine's sermons.[100] It would seem hazardous to assume on the basis of such slender evidence that the Commentator had done some patristic reading and was recycling it in his exposition. The one passage where we are on firmer ground is the etymological explanation of the name *Iohannes* (1.2–5) which derives from Isidore's *Etymologiae.*[101]

The four Sundays after Pentecost which are covered by the Taunton Fragment are also provided with exegetical homilies by Ælfric (but by no other text from the extant corpus of Old English homilies). The following homilies by Ælfric are in question: Pope, no. xiii (for the fifth Sunday), no. xiv (for the sixth Sunday), no. xv (for the seventh Sunday),[102] and *Catholic Homilies* II.xxv (for the eighth Sunday).[103] It would be unfair (and consequently no attempt is made here) to compare our unpretentious little fragments with Ælfric's professional exegesis, controlling and combining a wide variety of identifiable and authoritative patristic sources;[104] and there is indeed no indication whatsoever that the Commentator had knowledge of Ælfric's homilies. Nevertheless, the longest surviving fragment, that for the sixth Sunday after Pentecost,[105] when set against the foil of Ælfric's homily for the same Sunday (Pope, no. xiv), lets us glimpse some interesting details concerning the working of the Commentator's mind.

98 Cf. Ratherius Veronensis, *Praeloquiorum libri VI. Phrenensis. Dialogus confessionalis . . .*, ed. P. L. D. Reid *et al.*, CCCM 46A (Turnhout, 1984), pp. 221–65, at 241.

99 Cf. PL 73, col. 864.

100 Cf. Augustine, *Sermo de tempore,* PL 38, col. 1159. The phrase *exaudire dignetur* (3.20) occurs several times in Augustine's *Sermones* and his *Enarrationes in psalmos.*

101 See *Isidori Hispalensis Episcopi Etymologiarum siue Originum Libri XX*, ed. W. M. Lindsay, 2 vols. (Oxford, 1911) VII, ix.12. Isidore's source is Jerome's explanation of Hebrew names, and it is possible that the Commentator refers to this text: Sanctus Hieronymus, *Liber interpretationis hebraicorum nominorum*, ed. P. de Lagarde, in *S. Hieronymi Presbyteri Opera I: Opera exegetica*, CCSL 72 (Turnhout, 1959), 57–161, at 69 and 76 (the edition is rptd from de Lagarde, *Onomastica sacra*; 2nd ed., Göttingen 1887).

102 All ed. by J. C. Pope, *Homilies of Ælfric. A Supplementary Collection*, 2 vols. EETS os 259–60 (Oxford, 1967–8) II, 493–543.

103 Ed. M. Godden, *Ælfric's Catholic Homilies. The Second Series. Text*, EETS ss 5 (Oxford, 1979), pp. 230–40.

104 For Ælfric's sources for the homilies in question, see Pope's introductions to the individual homilies (cf. above, n. 102) and his list of sources I, 163–71; and M. Godden, *Ælfric's Catholic Homilies. Introduction, Commentary and Glossary*, EETS ss 18 (Oxford, 2000), pp. 564–70. Godden's identification of the sources for the homilies in question are also available on the website of *Fontes Anglo-Saxonici* <http://fontes.english.ox.ac.uk>.

105 The fragment is on pp. 7.6–8.20 + 1.1–2.12, some 66 lines in all.

The pericope for the sixth Sunday after Pentecost is Luke V.1–11, and Ælfric's principal sources for his homily[106] are: Bede's exegesis of the gospel passage in his commentary *In Lucae euangelium expositio* (Bede's comments were incorporated in Paul the Deacon's homiliary); Haymo of Auxerre's homily no. 117, assigned to the sixth Sunday after Pentecost and, for the most part, simply a re-writing of Bede; Pope Gregory's homily no. 24 from his *Homiliae .xl. in euangelia* (also incorporated in Paul the Deacon's homiliary); and (Pseudo)-Augustine's *Sermo* no. 248, *De duabus piscationibus*, which had been the principal source for Gregory.[107] The pericope Luke V.1–11 relates how Christ, having preached to the people on the Sea of Galilee from a boat which belonged to the fisherman Simon Peter, commanded Peter and his colleagues to row out on the lake and cast out their nets. They caught an enormous haul of fish but, when trying to heave the nets into the boat, the nets burst. The important point is that Ælfric and all his sources for Pope xiv (and Smaragdus, see p. 188, n. 107) connect this incident with a second catch of fish, related in John XXI.1–14,[108] when, after his resurrection, Christ appeared to his disciples at the Sea of Galilee, again commanding them to cast out their nets. They duly caught another huge haul, and this time the nets did not burst. Ælfric, in accordance with his sources, then goes on to elaborate on the allegorical significance of the two hauls, one before, the other after the Resurrection. The Taunton Commentator also mentions several hauls occurring before and after the Resurrection, and for this passage he provides one of his rare allegorical explanations. But he is alone (and without biblical authority) in assuming three hauls, two before and one after the Resurrection; and with the results of the electronic search in mind, it scarcely needs saying that his equation of the fishing nets with the Holy Scriptures has no base in patristic (and in Ælfric's) exegesis. Does the Commentator's allusion to more than one haul and his assignment of some allegorical significance to the incidents in question permit us, nevertheless, to assume that he remembered, if in a rather muddle-headed way, some previous reading on the pericope for the sixth Sunday after Pentecost? We cannot be sure. The pericope for the Wednesday after Easter is

[106] For the sources of Pope xiv, see Pope, *Homilies* II, 511–14, and (with bibliographical references to the standard editions), *ibid.* I, 163–71.

[107] Ælfric had drawn already on the relevant passages in Gregory's homily 24 for a piece in his *Catholic Homilies* (*CH* II.xvi, second part); for this he possibly drew in addition on Smaragdus's *Collectiones in euangelia et epistolas* (Smaragdus himself had recycled Gregory). For *CH* II.xvi and its sources, see Godden, *Commentary*, pp. 501 and 505–7; Smaragdus as a source is suggested by J. Hill, 'Ælfric and Smaragdus', *ASE* 21 (1992), 203–37, at 228–32. For the relation of *CH* II.xvi to Pope xiv, see Pope, *Homilies* II, 512.

[108] For Gregory's homily 24, John XXI.1–14 is the principal passage; cf. also the title of Pseudo-Augustine's *Sermo* 248 (*De duabus piscationibus*).

John XXI.1–14, the very same passage that relates the haul after the Resurrection,[109] and a priest may be assumed to remember at least those parts of the gospels that were read, year after year, during mass. So combining the two pericopes may have come naturally to the Commentator. On the other hand, we have seen that allegorical exposition is extremely rare in the surviving fragments, and one wonders whether the Commentator's 'Illa retia intellegitur sanctarum scripturarum per quem homines capiunt et ueniunt ad litus id est ad finem mundi' (1.7–9) may not be, after all, a very remote and muddled reflex of Bede's exposition 'Piscatores sunt ecclesiae doctores, qui nos rete fidei comprehensos, et de profundo ad lumen elatos, quasi pisces litori, sic terrae uiuentium aduehunt.'[110] Certainty is not attainable.

In sum, judging from what has survived, the conclusion is inevitable that, even in its original complete state, the Taunton text held little intellectual interest. Rather, its interest lies in what it attempted to do. The gathering of which the four leaves have been preserved demonstrably contained homilies for four successive Sundays after Pentecost. This, in combination with the probability that the beginning of the homily for the fifth Sunday was written on the preceding quire and that the homily for the eighth Sunday was continued on the next quire (see above, p. 185), may permit us to assume that the surviving leaves formed part of a book which provided homilies for a considerably larger series of successive Sundays, perhaps even for all the Sundays and major feast days during the church year. This is, however, an achievement with which, so far, only Ælfric has been credited, and the uniqueness of his achievement in an Anglo-Saxon and European perspective has duly been stressed.[111] While Ælfric's intellectual and stylistic achievement in providing a vernacular homiliary for the *temporale* throughout the year remains unchallenged, the evidence of the Taunton Fragment permits us to think that at least one further attempt was

[109] Cf. Lenker, *Perikopenordnungen*, p. 319, #112.

[110] See Bede, *In Lucae euangelium expositio*, in *Bedae Venerabilis Opera, Pars II, Opera Exegetica*, ed. D. Hurst, CCSL 120 (Turnhout, 1960), 113–14. 'The fishermen are the doctors of the church, who bring us (caught in the net of faith and drawn from the depths [of the sea] to the light) to the land of the living like fish are brought to the shore.' Pope, *Homilies* II, 518, adduces this passage as a source for Ælfric (Pope xiv. 66–71).

[111] See, for example, P. Clemoes, 'The Chronology of Ælfric's Works', *The Anglo-Saxons. Studies in some Aspects of their History and Culture presented to Bruce Dickins*, ed. P. Clemoes (London, 1959), pp. 212–47, esp. 227 and 232; Pope, *Homilies* I, 137; M. McC. Gatch, 'The Achievement of Ælfric and his Colleagues in European Perspective', *The Old English Homily and its Backgrounds*, ed. P. E. Szarmach and B. Huppé (Albany, NY, 1978), pp. 43–73; and S. B. Greenfield and D. G. Calder, *A New Critical History of Old English Literature*, 2nd ed. (New York, 1986), pp. 75–6. For the few pericopes of the *temporale* (that is the Sundays and movable feasts) which are expounded in the non-Ælfrician corpus of homilies, see Lenker, *Perikopenordnungen*, pp. 469–70.

made in Anglo-Saxon England to provide a comprehensive vernacular homiliary for the Proper of the Season.[112]

CONCLUSION

We may now draw together the various strands of evidence from our exploration of the language and of the nature of the fragments and see what final picture may be assembled of the author and the audience he had in mind. We have seen that there is serious linguistic evidence pointing towards a non-English author, but we have also seen that this evidence does not amount to absolute proof. Regardless of what his extraction was, the author's performance in Latin is mediocre to poor. If he was English after all, he must pass as rather illiterate: he had no experience in putting Old English discourse into a written form; he had an inexplicable deficiency in the Old English core vocabulary of Christianity; some of his mistranslations are apparently due to a deficiency in the Old English lexicon in general; his grammar reveals a breakdown of the Old English inflexional system which is difficult to explain by the middle of the eleventh century. But if he *was* English, this might at least give us a reliable clue as to the date of the text, which in this case must have immediately preceded the date of the manuscript. The texts themselves, with their simple translations of the pericopes, followed by general Christian exhortations, at first glance seem to square with this picture of a rustic, rather illiterate English author, as would his apparent deficiency in patristic reading. But what, then, about his ambitious undertaking to provide a full vernacular homiliary (if that is what the manuscript once contained)?

If we assume that the author was a non-native speaker of English this would solve all the problems of vocabulary, inflexional endings and erratic spellings convincingly and at a stroke. He would still remain a rather poor Latinist, but the rustic simplicity of his homilies might be more convincingly attributed to the needs of his audience – though the blunder he made of the fishing episodes and the unorthodox allegorical explanation he gives for them would remain. Assuming a non-native author would leave us with a less secure base for dating the texts since, presumably, a foreigner around the year 900 would have made the same types of mistakes in English that would have been made by a foreigner around the year 1000. However, if the texts had originated as early as during the reign of Æthelstan, or even that of Alfred, it is probable that several copies would have intervened between the original and the extant fragments, and it is perhaps reasonable to assume that at least

[112] In his *Catholic Homilies* and *Lives of Saints* Ælfric also provided preaching and reading materials for the *sanctorale* of the liturgical year (i.e. the feast days of the saints). There is no way of saying whether saints' feasts were also part of the Taunton homiliary.

some attempt at correcting the abominable English would have been made in the course of such copying. Also, there are no signs of an Early Old English precursor of the fragments such as remaining *ie* for *i* or *y*, or vacillation between *a* and *o*. On the hypothesis of a foreign author, the Taunton fragments rather present themselves as the remnants of a homiliary which was composed by some continental cleric (perhaps in the middle or even the higher ranks of the ecclesiastical hierarchy), and then copied by an English scribe (the script is unequivocally English), perhaps his secretary, who did not see fit to alter the linguistic peculiarities of his exemplar. On this assumption, the homiliary would probably have had a very limited circulation, restricted perhaps to just one copy – the fragments of which have survived – and the text would have been composed more or less contemporaneously with the surviving fragments, that is, at some point around the middle of the eleventh century.

It is futile to speculate about the clerical community to which our hypothetical foreign author belonged, let alone about his identity: too numerous are the contacts between England and the Continent in the eleventh century, contacts which often occasioned the temporary or permanent sojourn of continental clerics in England.[113] Given the author's lack of erudition, we may, perhaps, suspect that he was not active in one of the mainstream intellectual centres such as Winchester, Canterbury or Worcester. (This is not tantamount to saying that these centres housed only first-class patristic scholars; the suggestion is merely that here, presumably, some scholar could have been found who would have been better equipped to the ambitious task at hand.) We have seen that some of the linguistic evidence seems to point to a native from the German territory where Old High German or Old Saxon was spoken, but again, these are indications, not indisputable facts.[114] There were numerous contacts with Flanders in the period which seems to be in question,[115] but no texts in the West-Frankish dialect spoken in that area have survived; it is therefore impossible to gauge any native linguistic interference in the English of a West-Frankish speaker. Or what kind of errors in English would have been made by

113 For a survey of such contacts involving the English church, see V. Ortenberg, *The English Church and the Continent in the Tenth and Eleventh Centuries* (Oxford, 1992), esp. chs. 2 ('Flanders'), 3 ('The Empire') and 7 ('France'). When going through the records of continental clerics in eleventh-century England, we will have to bear in mind that most of the higher ecclesiastics of whom we have records will have had in their train numerous unnamed clerics, some of whom may have ended up as priests in utterly undistinguished minsters.

114 On English contacts with Germany, see, in addition to Ortenberg, *English Church*, ch. 3, the collection of articles by K. J. Leyser, *Medieval Germany and its Neighbours 900–1250* (London, 1982), and esp. *idem*, 'Die Ottonen und Wessex', *FS* 17 (1983), 73–97.

115 On these, see, in addition to Ortenberg, *English Church*, ch. 2, P. Grierson, 'Relations between England and Flanders before the Norman Conquest', *TRHS* 4th ser. 23 (1941), 71–112.

a speaker of French in its incipient stages, again a region from which there was some influx of clerics into England?[116]

Nevertheless, in the midst of all these uncertainties, the pointers towards the German dialects are something to go by, as is, perhaps, the regular alternation between Latin and Old English sentences in the Taunton Fragment: unlike in Old English, Latin alternating with the vernacular had some tradition in Old High German translations, Notker III of St Gallen (*c.* 950–1022) being the most conspicuous example.[117]

Whoever the author was, there can be little doubt that he embarked on his project for the purpose of administering the parish. He may have had in mind also the young or unlearned members of a monastic or clerical community, but we must not be misled by his frequent use of the address 'brothers'. This address includes all fellow-Christians, as Ælfric's homilies will reveal at a glance.[118] If, as seems reasonable, we assume that the Taunton Commentator set about composing his homiliary by the time that Ælfric's *Catholic Homilies* were already in circulation,[119] why did he at all undertake such an arduous task? Ælfric had written his *Catholic Homilies* (and his later homilies) for a non-clerical audience, as he himself remarked on several occasions, and in particular his homilies on the gospel pericopes he had devoted explicitly 'simplicibus ad animarum emendationem', 'to simple folk for the improvement of their souls'.[120] Was it simply because they could not get hold of a copy of the *Catholic Homilies* at the centre where the Commentator was active? Or was it rather because the Commentator – more of a preacher and less of a scholar than Ælfric – was more realistic about what the 'simple folk' really needed for their Sunday sermons? Again, we do not know, but the intellectual gap between Ælfric's homily for the sixth Sunday after Pentecost and the Taunton fragment for the same occasion could not be wider.

In spite of its unpretentious character, the Taunton Fragment is remarkable

[116] Conceivably perhaps, the Taunton Commentator even came to England in the wake of the Norman Conquest.

[117] On Notker's method of translation, see H. de Boor, *Die deutsche Literatur von Karl dem Grossen bis zum Beginn der höfischen Dichtung, 770–1170*, Geschichte der deutschen Literatur von den Anfängen bis zur Gegenwart I, 9th ed., rev. by H. Kolb (Munich, 1979), 110–18; and W. Haubrichs, *Die Anfänge: Versuche volkssprachlicher Schriftlichkeit im frühen Mittelalter (ca. 700–1050/60)*, Geschichte der deutschen Literatur von den Anfängen bis zum Beginn der Neuzeit I.1, 2nd ed. (Tübingen, 1995), 209–11. While the bulk of Notker's translations belongs in the category of the more demanding school texts, he also explains elementary Christian texts such as the psalter and the *Pater noster* by the same method.

[118] See, conveniently, the glossary in Godden, *Commentary*, *s. v. broþor* and *gebroþra.*

[119] By their dedication to Archbishop Sigeric, the issue of both series of the *Catholic Homilies* must fall within Sigeric's archiepiscopate, 990–4.

[120] See Latin Preface to *CH* I, ed. P. Clemoes, *Ælfric's Catholic Homilies. The First Series. Text*, EETS ss 17 (Oxford, 1997), 173.

in various respects: it is the one Old English text which was arguably composed by a foreign cleric, living and preaching in late Anglo-Saxon England. Apart from Ælfric's great achievement, it is arguably the only other attempt in Anglo-Saxon England to provide a comprehensive vernacular homiliary for the *temporale*. And it is a text which, in its complete form, would have taken care of the needs of the unlearned parish in an unparalleled way. But, tantalizingly, for us it will probably remain for ever a text without a context.[121]

[121] After the present article was completed, I had an opportunity to consult Michael Gullick on the script of TF. His opinion (personal communication, for which I am very grateful) is that the leaves are 's. xi^2 and post-Conquest'. Interestingly, the ductus of the script suggests to him 'a scribe who was self-taught and not quite sure of "proper" writing'; he tentatively assigns the leaves to 'a rustic' (?small) centre', perhaps in the west country. This view squares strikingly with what the analysis of the text and its language suggest about the origin of the fragments.

Pre-Conquest manuscripts from Malmesbury Abbey and John Leland's letter to Beatus Rhenanus concerning a lost copy of Tertullian's works

JAMES P. CARLEY AND PIERRE PETITMENGIN

According to the treatise which he presented as a New Year's Gift to King Henry VIII in January 1546, the English antiquary John Leland (*c.* 1503–52) received 'a moste gracyouse commyssion' from the monarch in 1533 'to peruse and dylygentlye to searche all the lybraryes of Monasteryes and collegies of thys your noble realme'.[1] As he travelled from monastery to monastery he compiled lists of books, some brief, some considerably more thorough.[2] Leland had a strong interest in pre-Conquest writings and his lists testify both to lost exemplars of known texts and to otherwise unattested writings from the early period.[3] His principles of selection were not always consistent, however, and on occasion he omitted manuscripts of historical or literary interest which he must have seen: in no sense was he setting out to be a cataloguer as such. Ultimately his enterprise was a bibliographical one and he envisaged a volume in four books, *De uiris illustribus siue de scriptoribus Britannicis*, of which 'the seconde is from the tyme of Augustyne, unto the aduente of the Normanes'.[4] The original draft of the *De uiris illustribus* was composed around 1535/6 – it

[1] Quoted from John Bale's annotated edition of the text, *The laboryouse journey & serche of Johan Leylande, for Englandes antiquitees geuen of hym as a Newe Yeares gyfte to Kynge Henry the VIII. in the XXXVII. yeare of his reygne, with declaracyons enlarged by Johan Bale* (London, 1549; repr. Amsterdam, 1975), sig. B.viii[r]. In his Latin writings Leland described the commission as a 'diploma'.

[2] Recorded in the private notebooks which were meant to form the groundwork for the many learned volumes he never lived to complete, they were edited by the eighteenth-century scholar Thomas Hearne in his *Joannis Lelandi Antiquarii De rebus Britannicis collectanea* (Oxford, 1715; London, 1774). Leland's lists represent one of the principal sources for the Corpus of British Medieval Library Catalogues being published under the general editorship of Richard Sharpe.

[3] He attempted to teach himself Old English, moreover, and took extracts from a lost manuscript of Ælfric's *Glossary*: see R. E. Buckalew, 'Leland's Transcript of Ælfric's *Glossary*', *ASE* 7 (1978), 149–64.

[4] He outlined the structure of this intended work in *The laboryouse journey*, sig. C.vii[v]–Di[r].

was in part a response to Polydore Vergil's *Anglica Historia* published in Basel by John Bebel in 1534 – but after this burst of activity there was a gap of almost ten years before Leland's next major phase of composition.[5]

The year in which Leland received his commission is significant both in terms of his own career and of political events in England. After having completed his studies – first at Cambridge (where he was a student at Christ's College and admitted BA in 1522), and then at Oxford (where he may have been associated with All Souls College) – he travelled to France around 1527. By 1528 he was in receipt of a royal exhibition and seems to have led a kind of 'freelance' student life, cultivating the great humanist scholars in Paris: he specifically named Guillaume Budé, Jacques Lefèvre d'Etaples, Paolo Emilio and Jean Ruel in his encomiastic verse.[6] Particularly influential was François Du Bois (Silvius), professor of rhetoric and principal of the Collège de Tournai, who introduced him to the study of ancient texts. On one occasion Du Bois showed him an incomplete manuscript of Joseph of Exeter's writings, the corpus of whose works Leland would subsequently spend many years attempting to track down.[7] His developing fascination with textual studies is described in the verse epistles he composed in Paris and he observed to his Cambridge friend Robert Severus that he was making it his task: 'ueterum multa exemplaria quaero, / Exploro, crassis eruo de tenebris' ('I seek for, investigate and dig out from the deep shadows many manuscripts of the ancients').[8]

There is some evidence that Cardinal Thomas Wolsey was Leland's chief patron during these years and he returned to England shortly before Wolsey's death in 1530. After Wolsey's downfall Leland cultivated Thomas Cromwell, with some success: he soon became a royal chaplain, and was appointed rector of Pepeling in the marches of Calais on 17 June 1530. On 12 July 1533 he was granted a papal dispensation to hold up to four benefices, the income from which was not to exceed 1000 ducats, provided that he take subdeacon's orders within two years and priest's orders within seven years. In 1535 he was made a prebendary of Wilton Abbey and benefices continued to accrue over the next decade.

[5] *De uiris illustribus* survives in Leland's autograph copy, now Oxford, Bodleian Library, Top. gen. C.IV. When Leland revised the text in the 1540s he regularly changed 'nunc' to 'nuper' in his description of monastic houses. There were many deletions as well as revisions and Anthony Hall's edition as *Commentarii de scriptoribus Britannicis* (Oxford, 1709) does not accurately reflect the complex layering of the manuscript. In our citations we have provided page references to Hall, but the transcription is our own. For more detailed arguments on the dating of the various portions, see the introduction to the forthcoming edition by Caroline Brett and James P. Carley for Oxford Medieval Texts.

[6] On this topic, see Carley, 'John Leland in Paris: the Evidence of his Poetry', *SP* 83 (1986), 1–50.

[7] For this episode, see *Commentarii de scriptoribus Britannicis*, ed. Hall, pp. 236–7.

[8] See 'John Leland in Paris', p. 35.

During the early 1530s Cromwell took on an increasingly pivotal role in the attempt to resolve the king's 'Great Matter'. After the failure of the legatine commission of 1529 to rule in Henry's favour and declare his marriage to Catherine of Aragon invalid, Henry's advisers canvassed foreign universities for their opinions; they also began examining English monastic collections for historical documents which might support their position on the limits of papal authority (especially in matters relating to 'divine' law). As a result, a significant number of manuscripts were brought from the monasteries to the royal library, especially in 1530 and 1531.[9] Although the original impetus for the researches had been the divorce itself, the related question of the pope's jurisdiction in England was soon raised and this led to the Act in Restraint of Appeals in April 1533. As its opening clause emphasized, this Act was firmly grounded on the testimony of ancient documents: 'Where by divers sundry old authentic histories and chronicles it is manifestly declared and expressed that this realm of England is an empire, and so hath been accepted in the world, governed by one supreme head and king having the dignity and royal estate of the imperial crown of the same.'[10] By the time the Act was promulgated Henry had already married the pregnant Anne Boleyn and her coronation took place soon afterwards, on 31 May 1533. Catherine continued to enjoy popular support, nevertheless, and the festivities connected with the coronation, masterminded to a great extent by Cromwell, had a strong propaganda element. As a part of an attempt to win the sympathy of the Londoners, Leland and Nicholas Udall, dramatist and schoolmaster, were commissioned to write verses for the pageants celebrating Anne's royal entry into London, and these drew attention in particular to her fecundity and imperial status.[11]

In 1533, then, Leland showed himself extremely useful to Cromwell and no doubt the commission was linked to his services, those already rendered and those yet to come. It is likely too that he began his first journey immediately after the coronation, in the best season for travel. Both Leland and Cromwell had good reason to be enthusiastic about what might be uncovered. Leland had a strong sense that the monasteries contained rare texts that, once discovered, would bring glory to Henry's England. For his part, Cromwell had already realized that, 'sundry old authentic histories and chronicles' could be employed effectively in the campaign against Rome, a campaign which was

[9] See Carley, *The Libraries of King Henry VIII* (London, 2000), pp. xxxiii–xxxix.

[10] *The Tudor Constitution: Documents and Commentary*, ed. G. R. Elton, 2nd ed. (Cambridge 1982), p. 353.

[11] On these 'Verses and dities made at the coronation of Quene Anne', which are being re-edited by Ágnes Juhasz Ormsby from the autograph manuscript, see E. Ives, *The Life and Death of Anne Boleyn* (Oxford, 2004), pp. 218–30.

quickly intensifying. The Act of Supremacy, which released England from papal control on all matters not relating to divine law, was passed in 1534 and soon afterwards, on 21 January 1535, Cromwell was appointed vicegerent for the purpose of undertaking a general ecclesiastical visitation.[12] Basing himself on the evidence of the 1535 visitations, Cromwell then presented a bill for the suppression of all religious houses having an annual income of less than £200 and this became law in March 1536.[13] Further suppressions occurred over the next years, culminating in a second Act of Dissolution in 1539, which effectively signalled the end of the monastic orders in England. The decade in which Leland exercised his commission was a crucial one, then, and our sense of the English Middle Ages would be very different without his testimony.

One letter of introduction, intended to supplement the official 'diploma', still survives:

> And where as Master Leylande at this praesente tyme cummith to Byri to see what bookes be lefte yn the library there, or translatid thens ynto any other corner of the late monastery, I shaul desier yow upon just consideration right redily to forder his cause, and to permitte hym to have the use of such as may forder hym yn setting forth such matiers as he writith for the King's Majeste.[14]

Written from Barnwell almost immediately after the fall of Bury St Edmunds on 4 November 1539, this letter makes clear that Leland's primary remit towards the end of the decade was as an agent of Henry's propaganda team – in 1539 he was no doubt gathering materials for the antipapal treatise, the *Antiphilarchia,* which he would present to Henry several years later. Nevertheless, his researches also involved ferreting books out of the 'deadly darkness' of the monastic libraries, dissolved or otherwise, where they had putatively been gathering dust for centuries, and bringing them to light through the medium of print (as he intended) to promote the greater glory of king and

[12] One of the primary functions of the visitation was to ensure acceptance of the Supremacy by the religious, but Cromwell's agents also sent him manuscripts: see *The Libraries of King Henry VIII*, ed. Carley, pp. xli–xlii. See below, p. 204.

[13] According to Anthony Wood, Leland responded quickly to this law and wrote to Cromwell on 16 July 1536, requesting assistance in preserving books which were fast being dispersed: 'whereas now the Germanes perceiving our desidiousness and negligence, do send dayly young Scholars hither, that spoileth them, and cutteth them out of Libraries, returning home and putting them abroad as Monuments of their own Country' (*Athenae Oxonienses*, ed. P. Bliss, 4 vols. (London, 1813–20; repr. 1969), I, 198). Chief among the Germans to whom reference was being made was, no doubt, Simon Grynaeus, on whom see below.

[14] Quoted in *The Itinerary of John Leland*, ed. L. Toulmin Smith, 5 vols. (London 1906–10) II, 148. Several years earlier he had noted copies of works by pre-Conquest writers at Bury: Abbo of Fleury's *Vita S. Edmundi* and Alcuin's *Epistolae*, Aldhelm's *Carmen de uirginitate* and his *Aenigmata*. (See *English Benedictine Libraries: the Shorter Catalogues*, ed. R. Sharpe, J. P. Carley, R. M. Thomson and A. G. Watson (London, 1996), B16.)

country. 'Have the use of' is thus an ambiguous phrase and no doubt Leland interpreted it broadly.[15]

In his enterprise Leland was no doubt inspired by developments in France and there are remarkable parallels, down to details of language, with the career of Jean de Gagny (d. 25 November 1549), whose acquaintance he may have made when he was in Paris in the 1520s. Gagny, rector of the University of Paris in 1531, published his *Epitome paraphrastica in epistolam ad Romanos* in 1533 and was made almoner to Francis I in 1536.[16] In the preface to his edition of the commentary on the Pauline Epistles misattributed to Primasius (Lyons, 1537), Gagny described to Francis I the genesis of his antiquarian project:

Memini enim, cum Primasii Uticensis in Africa episcopi commentarios ut antiquissimos, ita doctissimos, e tenebris illis (ubi apud diuum Theudericum Viennensis archipiscopi coloniam annos supra mille latuerant) assertos tuae semel maiestati inter prandendum explicarem . . . memini, inquam, quanta tum illos, Deus bone, gratia, quamque gratabunda fronte exceperis, simul et admirabunda, hactenus delituisse tanta regni litterarii iactura, thesauros tam raros atque pretiosos. Hic ego sanctissimum tuum institutum, ac plane regiam uoluntatem qualicunque mea opera adiuturus, cum dicerem eiusdem te materiei siluas habere in regno tuo quamplurimas, sed barbararum aliquot nationum custodia inaccessas, obstinate librarias suas occludentibus coenobitis aliquot, illarumque ingressum sibi ac caeteris tanquam Vestae adytis interdicentibus: te statim mihi uiam facturum pollicitus es . . . Huius ego tam egregiae sponsionis tuae accepto in pignus diplomate publico, quo uniuersas mihi patere regni tui librarias iuberes, atque inde quotquot e re philologiae uiderentur monimenta, describendi potestatem faceres, coepi omnium coenobiorum quae iter in comitatu tuo facienti occurrerunt, librarias uerrere: unde cum centum prope non inferioris notae uolumina e tenebris uindicassem, ni tua tandem auctoritas intercessisset, perpetuis illis, facinus concepisti nulla unquam hominum memoria delebile, uereque regio atque humano principe dignissimum . . . Non enim nescius quo in statu res sint mortalium, porro etiam compertum habens, quam praeclara aedificia quam subitus ignis euerterit, in animum induxisti non prius ueterum librorum bibliothecam struere, quam in commune philologiae bonum e prelo illi exirent in exemplaria quam castigatissimi. Cuius ego rei per te mihi demandata prouincia, cum multos haberem hominum conuentu ac conspectu litteratorum dignissimos libros, ab eo auspicandum duxi, quem ego tibi dudum probari censura sciebam

[15] His comments in the New Year's Gift make clear that he did gather as well as examine: 'Fyrst I haue conserued many good authors, the whych otherwyse had ben lyke to haue peryshed, to no small incommodyte of good letters. Of the which parte remayne in the most magnificent libraryes of your royall palaces. Part also remayne in my custodie, wherby I trust right shortly, so to describe your moste noble realme, and to publyshe the maiestie of the excellente actes of youre progenytours, hytherto sore obscured, bothe for lacke of empryntynge of such workes as laye secretely in corners' (*The laboryouse journey*, sig.C.ii^{r}).

[16] On Gagny, see A. Jammes, 'Un bibliophile à découvrir, Jean de Gagny', *Bulletin du bibliophile* 1996 (1), 35–81; also R. W. Hunt, 'The Need for a Guide to the Editors of Patristic Texts in the 16th Century', *Studia Patristica* 17.1 (1982), 365–71, at 367.

non iniqua, ac docti omnes rerum amantes diuinarum amplexuri sint lubentissime. Is est Primasii Uticensis in Africa episcopi commentarius (si quo possum esse hac in re iudicio) omnium quos hactenus uidi doctissimus, Graecorum iuxta ac Latinorum.[17]

Both the Frenchman and the Englishman had the support of their monarch, then, in their endeavours and both received a royal *diploma* of some sort (in French Gagny refers to 'letres patentes'), which permitted them access to otherwise impenetrable monastic libraries.[18] Sometimes they were provided with

[17] Repr. PL 68, cols. 410–11. For an edition of the expanded French version, printed in 1540, and found in the manuscript copies owned by Gagny and Francis, see Jammes, 'Un bibliophile', pp. 78–9: 'Certes il me souvient comme quelque jour à ton disner . . . je leusse ces commentaires de Primasius racheptez des perpétuelles ténèbres, où des ans plus de mille avoient esté cachez et ensepveliz à Sainct-Chef en Daulphiné, colonie et membre de l'archevesché de Vienne, de quant bonne grâce et accueil ta majesté receut la lecture d'iceulx: s'esmerveillant entre aultres choses comme si longuement au grand détriment du royaulme de Philologie avoient esté célez trésors si rares et précieulx. Lors, je désirant tousjours stimuler, et de ma peine et industrie telle quelle ayder ton sainct propos et volunté plainement royalle, me advançay te dire comme en ton royaulme estoient plusieurs forestz de pareil boys et matière: mais jusques ici non fréquentées pour la superstitieuse garde d'aulcunes nations barbares: qui d'icelles spatieuses et fructueuses forestz défendent l'entrée non seullement aux estrangiers, mais aussi à ceulx mesmes plus religieusement que jadis aux prophanes le temple de la déesse Vesta ses prebstres. Telle nation consiste en aulcuns moynes claustriers qui leurs librairies jadis par leurs antiens doctes religieulx plantées de beaux et singuliers livres obstinément gardent et ferment, myeulx aymants en froict et nuyct d'ignorance se morfondre que du boys d'icelles se chauffer. A ce propos entendu incontinent me respondit ta majesté que facile et patente entrée m'y donneroit . . . De laquelle tienne promesse incontinent ordonnas me estre despeschées letres patentes, par lesquelles commandoys me estre par toutes librairies publicques faicte ouverture, pour d'icelles transcripre quels livres verroye estre au profict de la républicque litéraire et accession de l'empire de Philologie. Parquoy exécutant ton royal vouloir commençay à fouiller et fueilleter toutes les librairies des monastères et chapitres, lesquelz suyvant ta compaignye se sont offerts en chemin. Dont après avoir vendicqué des ténèbres perpétuelles (sans l'intervention de ta majesté) plusieurs antiens livres de marcque non petite, entreprint ta majesté un affaire véritablement digne de prince royal et très-humain qui à jamais demourra en la mémoire des hommes . . . Car bien entendant de quant fragile et caducque condition sont ces choses inférieures, cognoissant aussy tant de beaulx et sumptueulx édifices avoir esté par subit accident de feu démoliz, as délibéré de ne assembler ni congérer librarie que premier au bien commun et profict de la républicque de Philologie ne fussent les bons et antiens livres, par stampe et impression en tres correctz exemplaires transfférez. Duquel tien vouloir exécuter ayant charge comme je eusse plusieurs excellents livres dignes de la congregation et veue des gens doctes, m'a semblé bon de commencer à celluy que de longtemps je scavoie estre de toy (par un jugement bien fondé) approuvé: et que toutes gens letrez et aymants choses divines très voluntiers recepvront. C'est le commentaire de Primasius sur les épistres saint Paul, de tous les aultres que jusques cy ay veu (si je suys en telles matières de quelque jugement) le plus docte et utile, grecz ou latins.'

[18] Both also dismiss contemptuously the 'tenebrae' of the monastic libraries. Around 1525 Johann Sichard obtained a similar diploma from the archduke Ferdinand authorizing him to visit monastic and cathedral libraries and to remove manuscripts he wished to publish: see P. Lehmann, *Johannes Sichardus und die von ihm benutzten Handschriften und Bibliotheken* (Munich, 1911), p. 20.

copies of rare texts by monastic officials and sometimes they removed the manuscripts themselves and brought them back to the royal collection.[19] Some manuscripts they retained for themselves.[20] Some, as in the case of their newly discovered manuscripts of Tertullian (*c.* 160–*c.*225), the first Christian Latin father to write in Latin, they hoped to see in print.[21]

LELAND'S JOURNEY OF 1533

Long famous for its antiquity and for the richness of its manuscript collections, Glastonbury Abbey would have been a natural focus for Leland's first tour[22]

19 His vaunted accomplishments notwithstanding, it is not altogether clear precisely what role Leland played in the formation of the royal library: see *The Libraries of King Henry VIII*, ed. Carley, pp. xliii–xlvi. The same is true of Gagny: 'Même si le nom de l'aumônier n'apparaît pas dans les textes retrouvés à ce jour, il est probable qu'il collabora d'une manière directe ou indirecte à l'édification des bibliothèques royales' (Jammes, 'Un bibliophile', p. 41).

20 As Jammes observed, Gagny 'a pu se constituer une bibliothèque privée sans doute importante' ('Un bibliophile', p. 42). Some fifty manuscripts in Latin, identifiable by bindings containing the arms of Henry II and sometimes by a note of provenance in Gagny's hand as well, must have entered the royal collections when the latter died: see M.-P. Laffitte and F. Le Bars, *Reliures royales de la Renaissance: la librairie de Fontainebleau* (Paris, 1999), pp. 21–2.

21 Gagny's ancient manuscript of Tertullian's works was the source for the added treatises in the 1545 Paris edition, printed by Charlotte Guillard. The question of its precise relationship to the printed text is, however, a complex one and the '*uetustissimus codex* . . . cache sans doute une pluralité de sources': see Petitmengin, 'John Leland, Beatus Rhenanus et le Tertullien de Malmesbury', *Studia Patristica* 18.2 (1989), 53–60, at 54 and 57. By rendering manuscripts widely accessible through publication Gagny wished to serve the *commune philologiae bonum*; Leland, for his part, saw printing as a means whereby 'the monumentes of auncyent wryters, as well of other nacyons as of your owne prouynce, myghte be brought out of deadly darkenesse to lyuelye lyght, and to receyue lyke thankes of their posteryte, as they hoped for at suche tyme, as they employed their longe and great studyes to the publyque wealthe' (*The laboryouse journey,* sig. B.viii[r]).

22 In 1421, the Italian humanist Poggio Bracciolini – not necessarily a reliable witness – had reported: 'In hac mea peregrinatione uisitaui antiquius monasterium omnibus aliis, que sunt in insula, et magnificentius. Diligenter inspexi bibliothecam: libri sunt multi, sed nihil pro nobis' ('In my travels I visited the oldest and most magnificent monastery in the island. I diligently inspected the library where there are many books but nothing for my purposes') (Quoted by Carley in *English Benedictine Libraries,* ed. Sharpe *et al.*, p. 159). A century later Leland's description was highly enthusiastic: 'Itaque statim me contuli ad bibliothecam, non omnibus peruiam, ut sacrosanctae uetustatis reliquias, quarum tantus ibi numerus quantus nullo alio facile Britanniae loco, diligentissime euoluerem. Vix certe limen intraueram, cum antiquissimorum librorum uel solus conspectus religionem, nescio an stuporem animo incuteret meo; eaque de caussa pedem paululum sistebam' ('And so I straightway went to the library, which is not open to all, in order to examine diligently all the relics of most sacred antiquity, of which there is so great a number that it is not easily paralleled anywhere else in Britain. Scarcely had I crossed the threshold when the mere sight of the ancient books struck my mind with an awe or stupor of some kind, and for that reason I stopped in my tracks for a while') (*Commentarii de scriptoribus Britannicis*, ed. Hall, p. 41). In both cases, of course, one needs to consider the audience to whom the account was directed.

and there are other indications, apart from the intrinsic fascination of the place, that this was one of a cluster of houses he visited in 1533. In the hand characteristic of the *c.* 1536 draft of *De uiris illustribus* Leland stated: 'Cum aliquot abhinc annis essem Glessoburgi Somurotrigum, Fontanetum diuertebam, ut aliquid penitioris antiquitatis eruerem' ('When I was at Glastonbury in Somerset a few years ago, I made a detour to Wells, hoping I might discover something of remote antiquity').[23] From Glastonbury and Wells he went on to Bath – 'Paucis abhinc annis fui in Badunensi bibliotheca' ('A few years ago I saw the library at Bath')[24] – where, as we shall see, he abstracted books. After he left Bath he turned northeast, and inspected the collections at Malmesbury, Cirencester and elsewhere before making his way to Oxford.[25]

Some years later, after the last dissolutions of 1539/40, Leland set out on another series of travels, but this time the focus was topographical rather than bibliographical. Once again he took notes, but these were primarily in English rather than in Latin.[26] This second phase continued for some six years, as he proudly vaunted, and by the end he had covered the length and breadth of the kingdom, so that:

> there is almost neyther cape nor baye, hauen, creke or pere, ryuer or confluence of ryuers, breches, washes, lakes, meres, fenny waters, mountaynes, valleys, mores, hethes, forestes, woodes, cyties, burges, castels, pryncypall manor places, monasteryes and colleges, but I haue seane them and noted in so doynge a whole worlde of thynges verye memorable.[27]

One of these trips was begun, as a heading in Leland's own hand indicates, on 5 May 1542. Setting out from London he returned to the West Country, reversing the sequence of his earlier itinerary: from Cirencester he went to Malmesbury, and next to Bath, then to Wells via Paulton and Chewton Mendip, followed by Glastonbury. At Bath he was quite specific about dates, mentioning *inter alia* an image of the Norman bishop John of Tours (d. 1122) he had seen 'an 9. yere sins'.[28] Nine is a very specific number, not a vague approximation, and it takes us back to 1533, the year he received his commission.[29]

[23] *Commentarii de scriptoribus Britannicis*, ed. Hall, p. 387. He found several pre-Conquest manuscripts at Wells, including two in Old English: Waerferth of Worcester's translation of Gregory's *Dialogues* and Ælfric of Eynsham's Catholic Homilies. [24] *Ibid.* p. 160

[25] The sequence of this particular group of booklists reflects his movements: see *Collectanea*, ed. Hearne IV, 153–9. Before he got to Glastonbury he travelled through Hampshire and then down to houses in Dorset and Devon.

[26] Ed. Toulmin Smith as *The Itinerary of John Leland.* [27] *The Laboryouse Journey*, sig. D.iiii^{v}.

[28] See *The Itinerary of John Leland,* ed. Toulmin Smith I, 143.

[29] The next year he made a northern circuit: on 5 June 1534 Sir George Lawson wrote to Cromwell describing his disfigurement of a *tabula* at York Minster which contained a reference to the pope's authority in England. (See *The Itinerary of John Leland,* ed. Toulmin Smith I,x.)

As we have seen, Leland requisitioned manuscripts as well as examining them, but the precise relationship between his booklists and his acquisitions is a difficult one to determine. His technique, as one might expect, varied from house to house. When he found a copy of Henry of Huntingdon's *Historia Anglorum* at the Augustinian Priory of Southwick in Hampshire he borrowed it.[30] It was still in his possession when John Bale examined his library soon after 1547.[31] At the Augustinian house in Christchurch, Hampshire, he saw a now lost manuscript of Alfred the Great's law-code in Old English.[32] From Bath Priory he removed a copy of the Acts of the Council of Constantinople, now BL, Cotton Claudius B. v, for the royal library: he gathered it up because it had been presented to the monks by King Æthelstan himself.[33] At Glastonbury he was on good terms with the abbot, Richard Whiting, whom he described (in a phrase which would be deleted after Whiting's execution) as 'homine sane candidissimo, ac amico singulari meo';[34] Whiting provided him with a copy of Stephen of Ripon's Life of Wilfred.[35]

LELAND'S APPROPRIATION OF PRE-CONQUEST BOOKS FROM MALMESBURY ABBEY

Unlike Glastonbury, where there was a welcoming abbot and a stable community, Malmesbury Abbey was in a state of flux in 1533. Shortly before 13 May the old abbot, Richard Camme, died and Thomas Cromwell, who had recently been appointed Secretary of State, was determined that his candidate for the

[30] See *Collectanea*, ed. Hearne III, 306: 'quod ego mutuo sumpsi a canonicis Sudouicanis, non longe a Portcestre' ('which I borrowed from the canons of Southwick not far from Portchester'). The manuscript survives, with annotations in Leland's hand, as London, British Library, Arundel 48. It is one of the three items Leland listed at Southwick; the other two are Anglo-Saxon texts: Bede's *Versus de die iudicii* and Bede's *Historia ecclesiastica* in Old English translation. (See *The Libraries of the Augustinian Canons*, ed. T. Webber and A. G. Watson (London, 1998), A31.)

[31] See *Index Britanniae Scriptorum: John Bale's Index of British and Other Writers*, ed. R. L. Poole and M. Bateson, intr. C. Brett and J. P. Carley (Cambridge 1990) p. 166.

[32] *The Libraries of the Augustinian Canons*, ed. Webber and Watson, A8.1. The copy of Bede from Southwick also contained Anglo-Saxon laws.

[33] See Carley, 'John Leland at Somerset Libraries', *Somerset Archaeol. and Natural Hist.* 129 (1985), 141–54, at 143–4; also S. Keynes, 'King Athelstan's books', *Learning and Literature in Anglo-Saxon England*, ed. M. Lapidge and H. Gneuss (Cambridge, 1985), pp. 143–201, at 159–65. Leland maintained that Bath had been presented several books by Æthelstan, but he did not include them in his booklist.

[34] Top. gen. C.IV, p. 35: not printed in Hall's edition.

[35] *Commentarii de scriptoribus Britannicis*, ed. Hall, p. 107: 'cuius nuper copiam mihi fecit' ('a copy of which [Richard Whiting] recently had made for me'). Presumably this means that Whiting had a copy of the original text (which was found in the 1247/48 catalogue) made for Leland, but this seems an unexpected thing for him to have done since Leland's normal practice was to take away the original text with him. In this chapter Whiting was originally called 'noster summus amicus' (Top. gen. C.IV, p. 82).

position, Robert Frampton, be elected.[36] There was resistance within the community, however, and another monk, Walter Jay, had strong local support. Cromwell sent Leland's acquaintance and fellow royal chaplain, Dr Rowland Lee (who may have officiated at the marriage of Henry and Anne Boleyn earlier in the year), to the monastery in mid-June. Once arrived, Lee assessed the situation and had the election postponed until mid-July; he also used the *comperta* drawn up after the 1527 visitation by the abbot of Gloucester to discredit Jay. He then departed, but returned in July, and Frampton was duly elected on the twenty-second of that month. It is likely that Leland visited the monastery during the period of the interregnum and he showed himself unsympathetic to the demoralized community, observing that 'cum ego nuper Melduni essem et locum eius sepulturae [William of Malmesbury's] quererem, tam obscurus suis monachis fuit ut unus aut alter tantum nomen in memoria retinuerit' ('Yet when I was at Malmesbury recently and inquired for his burial-place, such was his obscurity among his own monks that only one or two of them even remembered his name').[37] As the subsequent history of the Tertullian manuscript proves, he felt entitled to take full advantage of the powers implicit in his commission in this unsettled environment.[38] His intimacy with Cromwell, too, must have carried considerable weight: certainly, Cromwell's own requests for books had the force of commands and on 25 September 1535, for example, the prior of Bath wrote to him stating: 'I have send your maistershipp hereyn an old boke *Opera Anselmi* which one William Tildysleye [the royal librarian] after scrutinye made here in my libarye willed me to send unto youe by the kynge ys grace and commawndment.'[39]

Leland examined several other Malmesbury manuscripts and perhaps even carried them off at the same time as the Tertullian. In his list of books at Malmesbury, for example, he included a copy of 'Epistolae Albini' [that is, Alcuin].[40] The *Collectanea* contains extracts (some later incorporated into the *De uiris illustribus*) from an Alcuin letterbook: Leland described it as a 'uetus codex' and variants indicate that it must have been BL, Cotton Tiberius A. xv, fols. 1–173 (hereafter T) or a twin.[41] Written around 1100, T was badly

[36] On this episode, see the excellent account by A. Watkin in the *Victoria Country History of Wiltshire* 3 (1956), 225–6. [37] *Commentarii de Scriptoribus Britannicis*, ed. Hall, p. 196.

[38] After his election, the new abbot complained about conditions during the recent vacancy when, as he observed, part of the plate and cattle had been stolen, the abbey 'sore decayed'.

[39] See *The Libraries of King Henry VIII*, ed. Carley, pp. xli–xlii.

[40] For an edition of the list, see *English Benedictine Libraries,* ed. Sharpe *et al.*, B54. More generally, see R. M. S. Thomson, *William of Malmesbury* (Woodbridge, 1987), pp. 100–11. (This volume is made up primarily of revised versions of previously published essays and I cite it rather than the earlier publications.)

[41] See *Collectanea*, ed. Hearne II, 392–404. For a discussion of the relationship between Leland's extracts and T, see Thomson, *William of Malmesbury*, pp. 163–4. Thomson argues that T itself 'was doubtless made and kept' at Christ Church Canterbury (*ibid.* p. 130). See more recently

damaged in the fire at the Cotton Library in 1731, but much of the text can still be deciphered.[42] In the twelfth century William of Malmesbury incorporated letters from the same manuscript tradition into his *Gesta regum Anglorum* and his *Gesta pontificum Anglorum*. Although closely similar to T in their readings, letters copied both by Leland and William do share a certain number of variants not found in T and Thomson has therefore argued that 'Leland's "uetus codex" is identical with the manuscript of "epistolae Albini" which he found at Malmesbury. This was a transcript of A1 [our T] and the exemplar of its last section made by William, probably at Canterbury, into which he had already worked some textual modifications.'[43] In fact, it is not necessary to postulate a lost transcript. Even if T were written at Canterbury, it is quite possible that it had already got to Malmesbury before William's time or that William acquired it when he was at Canterbury.[44] More significantly, it can be shown that Leland handled T itself – the manuscript contains many marginalia in his hand – and this would suggest that T is the manuscript from which he made extracts.[45] Otherwise we have to assume that he saw two manuscripts, read and annotated one (T), but copied from the other (the putative apograph). Nevertheless, the readings shared by William and Leland against T, and this is crucial to Thomson's arguments, remain to be explained. One of these is particularly significant. Acording to the text in T of a letter from Pope Sergius I to Abbot Ceolfrid of Wearmouth–Jarrow, the pope invited the abbot to send a 'religiosum Dei famulum N. uenerabilis monasterii tui' to Rome. Both William and Leland have emended to 'religiosum Dei famulum *Bedam*, uenerabilis monasterii tui *presbyterum*'.[46] Leland, as he himself points out, was aware that William had quoted from this letter:

C. Brett, 'A Breton Pilgrim in England in the Reign of King Æthelstan', *France and the British Isles in the Middle Ages and Renaissance: Essays by Members of Girton College, Cambridge, in Memory of Ruth Morgan*, ed. G. Jondorf and D. N. Dumville (Woodbridge, 1991), pp. 43–70. Brett (pp. 53–4, 55 and 57) raises the slight possibility that T was written at Glastonbury. For a precise description of the contents of T, see 'A Breton Pilgrim', pp. 50–2.

42 Cambridge, Trinity College, O. 10. 16 (1468) contains a transcription by Thomas Gale (d. 1702); this was used by E. Dümmler to supplement illegible readings from T (his A1) in his edition of Alcuin's letter.

43 *William of Malmesbury*, pp. 163–4. See also p. 104: 'The . . . "Epistolae Albini", from which Leland quotes elsewhere in the *Collectanea*, refers to the apograph of BL Cott. Tib. A. xv and the exemplar of its last section, made by William of Malmesbury, now lost.'

44 Patrick Sims-Williams has maintained that William probably brought another ancient manuscript back with him from elsewhere ('say, Worcester or Canterbury'): see 'Milred of Worcester's Collection of Latin Epigrams and Its Continental Counterparts', *ASE* 10 (1982), 21–38, at 23–4; also his *Religion and Literature in Western England, 600–800*, CSASE 3 (Cambridge, 1990), 339 and 345.

45 Brett ('A Breton Pilgrim', p. 55) makes this point but does not pursue the implications: 'Thomson did not take into account the appearance of Leland's handwriting in Cotton Tiberius A.xv, which, if correctly identified, must undermine his argument.'

46 *William of Malmesbury*, pp. 172–3. See *Collectanea*, ed. Hearne II, 397.

Hoc certe constat, nihil enim studiosum celare uolo, Bedam olim a Sergio Pontifice Romam accitum, missis ad Ceolfridum, abbatem Girouicanum, eadem de caussa literis, quas ego etiam aliquando legi, et Gulielmus a Meildulphi curia libro historiae regum primo annexuit.

It is certainly evident – I wish to hide nothing from the studious reader – that Bede was once summoned to Rome by Pope Sergius, who sent letters to Abbot Ceolfrid at Jarrow concerning this matter, which I once read, and which William of Malmesbury appended to the first book of his history of the kings.[47]

In other instances, Leland combined readings from different sources, not always signalling where he emended one version from the other.[48] No doubt this is precisely what happened here: the 'N' in T cried out for an identification and William provided one.[49] In the margin of the manuscript itself (52r), Leland has written 'Beda' along with some other now indecipherable words. In his extracts from several other letters in the collection, moreover, Leland has corrected his original readings from the *uetus codex* after having consulted William's text. For example, he has emended 'quia' of T to William's 'quam'.[50] One of these emendations is especially revealing. In his rendition of a letter of Alcuin to Eanbald, archbishop of York, William transformed the *Aelberthus* of T into *Egbertus*. Leland originally wrote *Aelberthus*, but later corrected above the line to *Eg-* based on William.[51] Beside his extracts from a letter addressed by the community of Sainte-Geneviève in Paris to King Edgar, Leland has observed: 'Vetus codex sic habuit. Eadgarum', and this is precisely what is found on T, 167r.[52] Leland must, then, have seen T rather than a lost jumelle at Malmesbury and T should thus be added to N. R. Ker's list of medieval manuscripts whose provenance, if not actual origin, is a Malmesbury one.[53] Leland's marginalia are prolific, and they are the sort that

47 *Commentarii de scriptoribus Britannicis*, ed. Hall, p. 119.

48 In his extracts from William's *Gesta pontificum,* for example, Leland quoted verses which were also found in the *codex epigrammaton* he had seen at Malmesbury: 'Hos uersus, sed corruptos, alias legi in uetustissimo codice sacrorum carmini Melduni sed sine autoris nomine' ('On another occasion I read these verses in a very ancient volume of sacred poetry at Malmesbury, but they were corrupt and did not contain the name of the author') (*Collectanea*, ed. Hearne III, 265). For some readings he emended William silently from the *codex epigrammaton* and for others he listed variant readings: see Sims-Williams, 'Milred of Worcester's Collection of Latin Epigrams', p. 23; also *Religion and Literature,* p. 340, n. 50.

49 On the reasons behind William's emendation, see Thomson, *William of Malmesbury*, pp. 169–70.

50 See *Collectanea*, ed. Hearne II, 395. He has made the same correction in T itself, 35r.

51 The passage is found on 53v of T, but is too badly damaged to be deciphered.

52 *Collectanea*, ed. Hearne II, 404.

53 *Medieval Libraries of Great Britain*, 2nd ed. (London, 1964), pp. 128–9 ; *Supplement to the Second Edition*, ed. A. G. Watson (London, 1987), p. 48. See also Brett, 'A Breton Pilgrim', p. 55, who suggests tentatively that T might be the manuscript seen by Leland at Malmesbury.

would have been useful for him as *aide mémoire* for future writings: they would have quickly led him to significant points for his proposed histories of England.[54] It is almost certain, therefore, that he appropriated the manuscript for his own collection rather than just reading it at Malmesbury.[55]

In his account of Aldhelm, abbot of Malmesbury and bishop of Sherborne (d. 709 or 710), Leland referred to five other Malmesbury manuscripts he considered to be particular treasures:

Vidi etiam atque adeo ibidem inueni his multo praestantiora: Tertulliani librum de spectaculis, de ieiunio, Fortunati omnia opera, Grosolanum, episcopum Mediolanensem, de spiritu sancto, fragmenta Iunilii et Primasii, aliquid etiam Apuleii a Bebelio nuper imperfectissime aeditum.

I also saw and discovered there something much more noteworthy than these [the relics of Aldhelm pointed out by the monks]: namely, Tertullian's book *On the Spectacles* and *On Fasting*; all the works of Fortunatus; Grossolanus, bishop of Milan, *On the Holy Spirit*; fragments of Junilius and Primasius; and also something by Apuleius which was very imperfectly edited not long ago by Bebel.[56]

Thomson has suggested that the fragment of Junilius's *Instituta regularia diuinae legis*, dedicated to Primasius, must almost certainly be that found in Tiberius A. xv, fols. 175–80, and the identification of fols. 1–173 as the copy of Alcuin's letterbook which Leland saw at Malmesbury adds strong support to this hypothesis.[57] Tiberius A. xv is a composite manuscript, made up of four

[54] On marginalia and their uses in this period, see Carley, 'Religious Controversy and Marginalia: Pierfrancesco di Piero Bardi, Thomas Wakefield, and their Books', *Trans. of the Cambridge Bibliographical Soc.* 12 (2002), 206–45, esp. 228–33.

[55] On this likelihood, see also R. Flower, 'Laurence Nowell and the Discovery of England in Tudor Times', *PBA* 21 (1935), 47–73, at 52: '[t]his was probably one of the books reserved by Leland for himself after his laborious search'. Flower believed that it was subsequently owned by Laurence Nowell (c. 1510/20–c. 1569/74), who lent it to John Joscelyn (1529–1603). (Joscelyn describes it as 'in manibus Magistri Nowell'.) From Nowell, by Flower's reckoning, it passed to William Lambarde (1536–1601), and thence to Sir Robert Cotton (1571–1631). In fact, as one of Cotton's loans lists dating to c. 1616 informs us, it came to Cotton from Joscelyn: see C. G. C. Tite, *The Early Records of Sir Robert Cotton's Library* (London, 2003), no. 49.10.

[56] *Commentarii de scriptoribus Britannicis*, ed. Hall, pp. 100–1. For identifications, see *English Benedictine Libraries*, ed. Sharpe *et al.*, B54.23, 2, 19, 20, 21. The reference to these two works make it clear that the Tertullian derived from the Corpus Corbeiense tradition, on which see Thomson, *William of Malmesbury*, p. 108. On the Apuleius, see below, p. 217, n. 94.

[57] See *William of Malmesbury*, pp. 105–7. Written in early eighth-century Anglo-Saxon minuscule, the Junilius was incomplete even before the 1731 fire at Ashburnham house: in Thomas Smith's Catalogue of 1696 (ed. C. G. C. Tite (Cambridge, 1984), p. 21) it is described as 'Fragmentum Theologicum, characteribus uetustis, et a festinante scriba exaratis' ('a theological fragment in ancient letters, written by a hasty scribe'). As Sir Frederic Madden (1801–73) noted (*ibid.* appendix), it now lacks a leaf from its pre-fire state; this is also apparent from the Cottonian numeration of the subsequent articles. (The missing leaf would have contained bk

distinct sections. It begins with the Alcuin letterbook and this is followed by a single leaf containing on the recto the final verses of the last chapter of the gospel of St John (s. x), written in a continental hand in Square Minuscule. On the verso is part of a charter by William II, duke of Normandy, for the chapel of Notre Dame, Cherbourg (1063 × 1066).[58] Next comes the Junilius. The final booklet, on fols. 181–94, contains three works by Richard Rolle of Hampole: these were previously part of a more extensive manuscript seen by Leland at St Mary's York (although there is no evidence he acquired it).[59] After the dissolution, the York manuscript came into the hands of Henry Savile of Banke (d. 1617).[60] It was then dismembered, possibly after Cotton acquired it, and part went to Corpus Christi College, Oxford, where it survives as OCCC 193. When Tiberius A. xv was lent to Patrick Young around 1616, it did not contain the Rolle texts; nor did they appear in the original version of a catalogue of Cotton's library begun in 1621.[61] After he obtained the York material and incorporated it into the manuscript, Cotton updated the entry; he also inserted a reference to the Junilius fragment, which was no doubt already there but unrecorded.[62] It seems highly unlikely that Cotton would have combined by chance two Malmesbury manuscripts, both admired by Leland and one at least almost certainly owned by him. Even though his marginalia are not found in the Junilius as it now survives, one can assume that he did acquire this manuscript and that it was he, not Cotton, who combined the two previously discrete units into one composite.[63] If this is the case, Leland must have removed both when he visited Malmesbury in 1533 and bound them together as the composite which eventually passed to Cotton.

Cotton Tiberius A. xv, fols. 1–173, is not the only Malmesbury manuscript

2, ch. 18–ch.22 [beg.].) It is also misbound: fol. 175 = bk 2, chs. 13–17; fol. 176 = bk 2, chs. 5–13; fol. 177 = bk 1, chs. 9–18 (beg.); fol. 178 = bk 2, ch. 22 (end)–24; fol. 179 = bk 1, ch. 18 (end)–bk 2, ch. 2; fol. 180 = bk 2, chs. 2–4. It is included with a query in Watson's *Supplement* to the second edition of Ker's *Medieval Libraries*, p. 48.

[58] See D. N. Dumville, *Liturgy and the Ecclesiastical History of late Anglo-Saxon England* (Woodbridge, 1992), pp. 121 and 146. In the present state of the manuscript it is impossible to know the relationship of this leaf to the letterbook, that is whether it formed part of that booklet as a flyleaf or something similar when it was at Malmesbury, or whether it was inserted later.

[59] See *The Shorter Catalogues*, ed. Sharpe *et al.*, B.121.7–15.

[60] See A. G. Watson, *The Manuscripts of Henry Savile of Banke* (London, 1969), no. 56.

[61] BL, Harley 6018, no. 150: see Tite, *The Early Records*, p. 106; also Watson, *The Manuscripts*, no. 56.

[62] Cotton was unaware of the authorship and described it as 'Fragmentum Theologicum literis antiquissimis et peregrinis'.

[63] Originally the Junilius must have been written on leaves of larger dimensions than the Alcuin. Presumably these were trimmed when the booklets were combined and putative marginalia would have disappeared. There is one interlinear gloss in a much later hand ('suo' on 177v), but it is impossible to say whether or not it is Leland.

annotated by Leland. In his chapter on Cuthbert, archbishop of Canterbury, he described an ancient book of epigrams he had found there:

Ornamenta uero ecclesiae multa, quae moriens Valstodus imperfecta reliquit, ipse perfecit, inter quae uexillum crucis erat, ut his testatur carminibus, quae ego non modo in quarto libro Gulielmi Meldunensis de pontificibus Anglorum offendi, uerum cum nuper Meldunum inuiserem, monasterium Seuerianae siue (ut nunc appellant) Vilugianae prouinciae, in uetustissimo libro sacrorum epigrammaton repperi.

For the church he completed many furnishings which had been left unfinished by Wealhstod at the time of his death; among them was a processional banner bearing a cross, as indicated in these verses, which I found not only in the fourth book of William of Malmesbury's *On the English Bishops*, but also in a most ancient book of sacred epigrams when I recently visited Malmesbury, a monastery in the county of Salisbury, or, as it is now called, Wiltshire.[64]

The *Collectanea* contains a set of extracts from this codex, a tenth-century copy of a *Sylloge Inscriptionum Latinarum Christianarum* put together *c.* 760 by Milred of Worcester.[65] A bifolium survives as Urbana, Univ. of Illinois Library, 128.[66] Although the bifolium contains marginal annotations in Leland's hand, nothing is known of its subsequent history until it surfaced in Berlin around 1934.[67] As its present state shows, the fragment served as a pastedown in a printed book, but it cannot be determined if the manuscript as a whole was dismembered at Malmesbury itself at some point after the dissolution or elsewhere after 'Leland or some other carried it off'.[68] If it had been used locally as a binding fragment, however, it is surprising that it would turn up in Berlin, and the place of its reappearance does suggest that like the Tertullian (as we shall see below) it was sent off by Leland to the German printers.[69]

64 *Commentarii de scriptoribus Britannicis*, ed. Hall, p. 134. He also referred to the book of epigrams in his entry on Milred: *ibid.* p. 113.

65 *Collectanea*, ed. Hearne III, 114–18; ed. M. Lapidge, 'Some Remnants of Bede's lost *Liber Epigrammatum*', *EHR* 90 (1975), 798–820 (repr. in his *Anglo-Latin Literature 600–899* (London, 1996), pp. 357–79). See A. Orchard, *The Poetic Art of Aldhelm*, CSASE 7 (Cambridge, 1994), 203–12, for a discussion of a possible link between Aldhelm and an earlier version of such a collection of sylloges: 'there are good reasons to believe that Aldhelm was both interested in and indebted to a wide range of epigraphical verses reflected in a fairly limited group of sylloges which can for other reasons be considered to be related; it seems possible that he was in Rome at precisely the time such a collection of verse can be deduced to have been made' (p. 212).

66 See Lapidge, *Anglo-Latin Literature*, pp. 510–11, and the references cited therein.

67 On the annotations, see in particular D. J. Sheerin, 'John Leland and Milred of Worcester', *Manuscripta* 21 (1977), 172–8.

68 Sims-Williams, 'Milred of Worcester's Collection of Latin Epigrams', p. 25.

69 Whatever else, there is a good chance that other leaves still survive undetected in binding structures.

LELAND'S LETTER TO BEATUS RHENANUS

A recently discovered letter written by Leland to Beatus Rhenanus (1485–1547) and dated to 1 June [1539] concerning the manuscript of Tertullian to which he makes reference in his account of Aldhelm, with whom he associates it, sheds further light on his activities at Malmesbury Abbey in 1533. Surviving as Sélestat, Bibl. humaniste, Corr. B.Rh 223, it is one in a series of letters, the others of which are no longer extant, but a sequence of events can be reconstructed from internal allusions.

As far as can be ascertained, copies of Tertullian were rare in England in the early period: none turns up in pre-Conquest booklists and direct citations (of the *Apologeticus aduersus gentes*) occur only in Bede's *Historia ecclesiastica gentis Anglorum*.[70] There are, however, several English survivors of the *Apologeticus* dating from the twelfth century, indicative, so it seems, of a manuscript tradition deriving from Normandy.[71] In 1521, however, Johann Froben published Rhenanus's *editio princeps* based on texts contained in what is known as the Corpus Cluniacense; a second edition was issued by Froben's heirs Hieronymus Froben and Nicolaus Episcopius in 1528.[72] As Rhenanus

[70] Tertullian is also quoted in Paulus Orosius's *Historia aduersus Paganos*, and thus appears in the Old English translation. (On these citations see Fontes Anglo-Saxonici Project, ed., Fontes Anglo-Saxonici: World Wide Web Register, http://fontes.english.ox.ac.uk.) For other references, see J. D. A. Ogilvy, *Books known to the English, 597–1066* (Cambridge, MA, 1967), p. 250. On booklists, see M. Lapidge, 'Surviving Booklists from Anglo-Saxon England', *Learning and Literature in Anglo-Saxon England*, ed. Lapidge and Gneuss, pp. 33–89.

[71] At the beginning of the second book of his *Polyhistor* (ed. H. T. Ouellette (Binghamton, NY, 1982)), William of Malmesbury quotes from the *Apologeticus*: on the manuscript tradition, see the review by Petitmengin in *Revue des études augustiniennes* 30 (1984), 321. In his *Catalogus scriptorum ecclesiae*, Henry of Kirkestede (*c.* 1314–after 1378), subprior and librarian of Bury St Edmunds, has an entry for Tertullian based primarily on Jerome, apart from the eighth title, 'Apolegeticum lib. 1', whose source is probably a manuscript: see Henry of Kirkestede, *Catalogus de libris autenticis et apocrifis*, ed. R. H. Rouse and M. A. Rouse, (London, 2003), K578. 8.

[72] On Rhenanus, see J. F. D'Amico, 'Beatus Rhenanus and Italian Humanism' *Jnl of Med. and Renaissance Stud.* 9 (1979), 237–60; 'Beatus Rhenanus, Tertullian and the Reformation: a Humanist's Critique of Scholasticism', *Archiv für Reformationsgeschichte* 71 (1980), 37–62; 'Ulrich von Hutten and Beatus Rhenanus as Medieval Historians and Religious Propagandists in the Early Reformation', in his *Roman and German Humanism, 1450–1550*, ed. P. F. Grendler (Aldershot, 1993), pp. 1–33. The first two articles are reprinted in the same volume. See also *Beatus Rhenanus (1485–1547), lecteur et éditeur des textes anciens*, ed. J. Hirstein (Turnhout, 2000). Rhenanus was closely involved with the Froben family and lived in Hieronymus's household for a time. In 1527 he left Basel for good, returning permanently to his native Sélestat. On the Rhenanus editions of Tertullian, see Hunt, 'The Need for a Guide'; Petitmengin, 'John Leland, Beatus Rhenanus et le Tertullien de Malmesbury', and the references cited therein.

observed, Tertullian could be interpreted as denying the absolute authority of the Roman pontiff, and in the early 1530s, when papal jurisdiction in England was being questioned, Leland would have been keenly interested in his arguments on this topic.[73] Almost certainly he would have been familiar with one of the Froben editions when he arrived at Malmesbury and discovered the ancient (and more complete) codex of Tertullian's works in the monastic library. Realizing that this manuscript of a particularly rare and important author contained hitherto unknown texts, Leland carried it off into his own 'custodie' for future consultation.[74]

Rhenanus's third edition of Tertullian, seen through the press by Sigismond Gelen (1497–1554), was published by the *officina Frobeniana* some five years later,

[73] See D'Amico, 'Ulrich von Hutten and Beatus Rhenanus', p. 27: 'In these annotations [to the 1521 edition] Beatus maintained that Tertullian had denied the primacy of the Roman bishops. Tertullian, Beatus explained, held that the Roman Church enjoyed no absolute dominion over other churches; rather it was merely one of the *summae ecclesiae*, one of the chief churches established by the apostles.' Leland would take up this same point in his *Antiphilarchia* originally drafted towards the end of the 1530s (now CUL. Ee. 5. 14, 118v): 'Tertullianus in libro *de praescriptionibus hereticorum* sic loquitur. "Necesse est itaque quia tot ac tantae ecclesiae, unam esse, illam ab apostolis primam, ex qua omnes. Sic omnes primae et omnes apostolicae, dum omnes unam probent unitatem [20.7–8]." Audis quae sit Tertulliani sententia. At non audis illum disertis uerbis adfigentem hanc primam Romanae sedi ecclesiam. Quin potius Romanam apostolicis annumerat ecclesiis [cf. 32.2]: sed hoc non est adfirmare Romanam solam apostolicam esse: quemadmodum neque summam, sed summatem facere. Et idem libro [36.3] eodem Romanam ecclesiam foelicem, non primam appellat.' (In his book *The Prescriptions Against Heretics* Tertullian states the following: 'Because there are so many and such great churches, it is thus necessary that there be one unique, the one founded at the beginning by the apostles, from which they all derive. Thus all are primitive and all are apostolic, as long as all demonstrate one unity [20.7–8].' You hear Tertullian's judgement. But you do not hear him adding to these eloquent words that this primitive church was in the Roman seat. Rather he includes the Roman among the apostolic churches [cf. 32.2], but this is not to affirm that the Roman is the only apostolic church, just as he did not make it the highest, but a noble one. And likewise in the same book [36.3] he calls the Roman church 'happy, but not the first'.) Leland has followed, with slight variations, the text proposed by Rhenanus in his second edition of 1528, p. 101, rather than the reading of the 'Masburensis'.

[74] Like Gagny, Leland was on the lookout for manuscripts which would provide better witnesses to materials already in print. As a coda to his chapter on Joseph of Exeter, for example, he contemptuously observed: 'Haec cum scripsissem, prodiit Iosephi opus interpretis de *bello Troiano* typis excusum Germanicis, sed tam corrupte ut si pater ipse in prolem rediuiuus oculos conuerteret tam informem, cognosceret plane nunquam. Vtque fucus aedito praefigeretur libro, Cornelii Nepotis Romani nomine inscriptus est' ('After I had written the above, Joseph's translation of *The Trojan War* appeared, printed in German type, but it was so corruptly done that if the father had come back to life and set eyes on his child in such a deformed state, he would scarcely have recognized it. To apply a cosmetic improvement to the book, it is inscribed with the name of "Cornelius Nepos of Rome"') (*Commentarii de scriptoribus Britannicis*, ed. Hall, p. 239). Leland's reference is to the edition by Alban Thorer (Basel (Jacobus Parcus), 1541.

in March 1539.[75] Like the earlier editions it was based on the Corpus Cluniacense and its appearance galvanized Leland – ever slow to follow through with projects – into action. Not personally acquainted with Rhenanus, Leland must have written to his friends at the *officina Frobeniana*, announcing his more authorative witness ('longe auctiori') to Tertullian.[76] Leland's subsequent concern about the safety of the manuscript – 'tantus et tam rarus thesaurus' – presumably indicates that he was not keen, however, to send it to the Basel printers. Gelen, who no doubt conveyed the information about Leland's codex to Rhenanus on behalf of the press, must also have concocted a strategy whereby it might be winkled out of Leland's hands. What was needed, of course, was somebody of influence who would intercede with the English antiquary.

Among his acquaintances Gelen included the Portugese nobleman and humanist Damião de Góis (1502–74), whom he may have first met in the

[75] On Gelen's role in this enterprise, see Rhenanus's preface, dated at Sélestat to 1 March 1539: 'Non licuit adesse Basileae dum editur opus. Verum Sigismundus Gelenius, homo magni in literis iudicii et eruditione summa praeditus, in recognoscendo opere uicariam operam in officina praestitit, qui merita laude sua non est fraudandus' ('I was not able to be present at Basel while the work was being edited. However, Sigismond Gelen, a man of great judgement in letters and possessed with the highest learning, acted as my substitute in the workshop, and he must not be deprived of his deserved praise') (sig. a*2r).

[76] The context of our letter – i.e. Rhenanus's need for intermediaries in the transaction—indicates that the men did not know one another personally. Leland did, however, admire the writings of the German scholar, citing the *Rerum germanicarum libri tres* (Basel: Hieronymus Froben, 1531) in the early version of the *De uiris illustribus* (ch. 92). He would later construe himself as the British Rhenanus and would compose verses to this effect:

Instauratio Britannicae antiquitatis
Quantum Rhenano debet Germania docto,
Tantum debebit terra Britanna mihi.
Ille suae gentis ritus & nomina prisca
Aestiuo fecit lucidiora die.
Ipse antiquarum rerum quoque magnus amator,
Ornabo patriae lumina clara meae.
Quae quum prodierint niueis inscripta tabellis,
Testes tum nostrae sedulitatis erunt.

On the Renewal of British Antiquity
As much as Germany owes to the learned Rhenanus
So much will the land of Britain owe me.
He elucidated the rites and ancient names of his country
With the brightness of the summer sun.
I, who am also a great lover of things from the past,
Will extol the luminaries of my native land.
When they appear inscribed on snowy-white tablets
They will be witnesses to my zeal.

(Ptd in *Collectanea*, ed. Hearne V, 120; also John Bale, *Scriptorum illustrium maioris Brytanniae . . . catalogus*, 2 vols. (Basel, 1557–9) I, 672–3.)

spring of 1533 when Góis visited Basel.[77] In 1535 Gelen dedicated his *Annotationes in Plinium* to Góis and in a letter to Góis written from Basel in 1539 he commended the methodology of the *Siege of Diu*.[78] Góis, who had been appointed secretary of the India House in Antwerp in 1523, had a number of English contacts and had visited England in 1528. In 1531 he enrolled as a student at the University of Louvain and in 1534 he moved to Padua to continue his studies. There he made the acquaintance of Henry VIII's cousin, Reginald Pole.[79] In 1538 he was back at Louvain, where he remained until 1545 when he was recalled to Portugal.

It was at Gelen's prompting, no doubt, that Rhenanus wrote to Góis in Louvain requesting assistance in this delicate matter. As Leland's phrasing makes clear ('quodam Damiano Agoe Hispano'), Góis had not had previous dealings with Leland, but in Padua Góis had come across another Englishman, Sir Richard Morison (1514?–56), who moved in the same academic and ecclesiastical circles as Leland.[80] Like Leland, Morison had originally been a client of Wolsey, and like Leland he later turned to Cranmer.[81] After studying in Oxford and Cambridge he was at the University of Padua from 1532 to 1536. Devoting himself primarily to *bonae litterae* he lived for some time in the home of Reginald Pole and then joined the service of Thomas Cromwell, who made him a member of his household when he returned to England in 1536. Distancing himself from 'Mr Traitor Pole' once back in England, he soon became the principal agent of Cromwell's propaganda programme and in 1539 he was appointed gentleman of the privy chamber and elected MP.[82] Recognizing that Morison would be a powerful advocate in his case, Góis

[77] On this trip, see E. F. Hirsch, *Damião de Gois: The Life and Thought of a Portuguese Humanist, 1502–1574* (The Hague, 1967), p. 67. Góis travelled to Basel from Freiburg, where he had been provided with an introduction to Erasmus. After Erasmus's death in 1536, Boniface Amerbach suggested that Góis approach Froben about the publication of a collected edition of Erasmus's works, but Góis withdrew from the project later in the year. Froben then passed the commission to Rhenanus and the edition appeared in 1540: *ibid.* pp. 86–8.

[78] See Hirsch, *Damião de Gois*, pp. 78 and 142.

[79] *Ibid.* p. 107; also M. Bataillon, *Études sur le Portugal au temps de l'humanisme* (Paris, 1974), p. 115.

[80] According to Pole, Góis showed himself generous to Morison during the Padua years.

[81] On Morison, see Jonathan Woolfson's forthcoming entry in the *Oxford Dictionary of National Biography*; also J. Liedl, 'Richard Morison (1514?–20 March 1556)', in *Sixteenth-Century British Nondramatic Writers: Second Series*, ed. D. A. Richardson, Dictionary of Literary Biography 136 (Detroit, 1994), 255–8.

[82] In the *Antiphilarchia*, Leland singled out for praise Morison's role in the commission which drafted Henry's response to the papal call for a General Council of the Church at Mantua in May 1537, observing that 'Multa praeterea huc pertinentia sunt, quae partim a Coruino, partim a Richardo Morysino, iuuene cum eleganti, tum docto, et inprimis ingenioso cognoscere potes' ('There are, moreover, many things pertinent to this matter, which you can learn, partly from Corvinus and partly from Richard Morison, a young man both judicious and learned, and above all talented') (184v).

wrote immediately to him ('summa cum diligentia') rather than approaching Leland himself. Leland in turn realized that he could not refuse the request of one of Cromwell's agents, one who also enjoyed the favour of the king; as he observed in his letter: 'Is quod a me rogauit tuo nomine facile impetrauit.'[83]

Once Morison obtained the precious manuscript, he passed it on to a certain 'Pintous', a Portugese merchant active in Flanders, for delivery to Góis in Louvain. Pintous can be identified as Sebastian Roderigo Pinto, to whom Henry had granted arms for his services, and who had numerous dealings with Arthur Plantagenet, Viscount Lisle, Lord Deputy of Calais.[84] Pinto fulfilled his mission with despatch and Góis wrote to Morison, stating that he had received the manuscript and that he was about to transmit it to Rhenanus ('breui ad te transmissurum esse'). Having seen Góis's letter to Morison, but not having heard directly from Rhenanus himself, Leland wrote the surviving letter, in which he expressed his concerns about the safety of the manuscript. He provided a brief history of Malmesbury Abbey, and his theory concerning the origins of the codex.[85] Aldhelm was the most famous of the early scholar

[83] Although Góis was reformist in many of his beliefs, he remained orthodox. After his sojourn in Padua he retained a strong sympathy for Pole and was no doubt appalled by the purge of the latter's family after the so-called Exeter conspiracy of 1538/9. On the other hand, Morison's *An invective agenste the great and detestable vice, treason* (1539) was written in justification of execution of the rebels, and was vehement in its condemnation of the 'archetraytour' Pole. Clearly, Góis had a bad conscience about having been in touch with Morison, and on 12 October 1540 he wrote to Pole from Louvain, enclosing a copy of *Faith of the Ethiopians*. In his letter he expressed distress at the way his former intimate 'Ricardus Moryzinus' had repaid Pole's generosity. Ultimately, he predicted, Pole would emerge triumphant as king of England. In his reply Pole deftly sidestepped Góis's flattering – although treasonous – prophecy, but he did point out that Góis was correct to detest Morison, whose disloyalty to Pole was matched by his disloyalty to God. The letters are ptd in Bataillon, *Études sur le Portugal au temps de l'humanisme,* pp. 117–19; see also T. F. Mayer, *The Correspondence of Reginald Pole*, I: *A Calendar, 1518–1546: Beginnings to Legate of Viterbo* (Aldershot, 2002), nos 309–10.

[84] See *Letters and Papers, Foreign and Domestic, of the Reign of Henry VIII . . .*, catalogued by J. S. Brewer *et al.*, 21 vols. in 33 and addenda (London 1862–1932), 5 (1531–2), 1344 (a letter dated to 24 September 1532, by Henry to 'Lewis Infant of Portugal' confirming the grant); *The Lisle Letters,* ed. M. St Clare Byrne, 6 vols. (Chicago, 1981), nos. 132, 269, 825, 829–30 and 1020. On 27 September 1537, John Husee, the Lisles' London agent, wrote to Lady Lisle on behalf of Pinto, reminding her that 'the said Pynto is a knight' (no. 1020).

[85] The same series of names and etymologies for Malmesbury appears in the chapter on Aldhelm in *De uiris illustribus* (ed. Hall, p. 98), where Leland gives as his source a book of uncertain authorship, possibly by William of Malmesbury (who does give the derivation from Meildulf in the *Gesta regum Anglorum* bk I, c. 29 and in the *Gesta Pontificum* c. 189). See also *The Itinerary of John Leland,* ed. Toulmin Smith I, 131 and the commentary to the *Cygnea cantio*. He also knew the version found in the *Eulogium historiarum*, which he quoted in *Collectanea*, ed. Hearne II, 302–3; III, 395. In our letter, he cites Bede's *Historia ecclesiastica gentis Anglorum*, where all that is stated (V.18) is that the monastery over which Aldhelm presided was called 'Maildufi urbem'. On the accepted modern derivation of the name from OIr Maeldub or Maildub, meaning 'black prince or chief', see J. E. B. Gover, A. Mawer and F. M. Stenton, *The*

abbots of Malmesbury and he had travelled to Rome: Leland assumed – as he also explained to Gelen and Froben – that it must have been he who brought back such a treasure from Italy.[86]

As a subsequent letter from Góis to Rhenanus reveals, Góis used Froben as an intermediary and sent the Tertullian to him to pass on to Rhenanus.[87] On 23 June Gelen wrote to Góis: calling him his 'excellent patron', he thanked him for his greetings and for the excellent news about the Tertullian:

Mirifice me nuper exhilarauit Frobenius, patrone eximie. Non solum enim salute tuis uerbis renuntiata memorem te amiculi intellexi, sed etiam ex eiusdem sermone percepi te ueterem erga officinam hanc feruorem retinere, quandoquidem et Tertulianicum thesaurum benigne communicas, et insuper alia ultro polliceris omnibus rerum mirandarum studiosis uel ambitiose expetenda.

Froben recently cheered me wonderfully, O excellent patron. Not only did I learn that you were mindful of your little friend through the greeting you sent back, but I also discovered from his conversation that you have retained your ardour for your old workshop, since you kindly share your treasured Tertullian, and in addition you spontaneously promise other discoveries which all researchers of marvellous things would ambitiously covet.[88]

From Froben the manuscript went to Rhenanus, but the latter showed himself as dilatory in his dealings with Góis as he had been in communicating with Leland, and on 24 October 1540 Góis wrote to him from Louvain complaining about his silence:

Anno superiore literas et Tertullianum et oppugnationem Diensem a nobis in lucem editam ad te misimus, amantissime Rennane, sed tu nobis respondere minime dignatus es. Nihilo minus, etsi tam negligenter nobiscum agas, non desinam epistolis meis te impetere, donec rescribas. Quamobrem ad te iam mittimus libellum, quem de fide et moribus Aethiopum circuncisa narratione modo composuimus.

Place-Names of Wiltshire, EPNS 16 (Cambridge, 1939), 47–8; also *Venerabilis Baedae Historiam Ecclesiasticam . . . Historia Abbatum Auctore Anonymo*, ed. C. Plummer, 2 vols. (Oxford, 1896) II, 310–11.

[86] According to *De uiris illustribus*, Aldhelm studied with Hadrian and Theodore at Canterbury, and was summoned by Pope Sergius I to Rome. When he left he received gifts from the pope, and Leland presumably assumed that the Tertullian was among the gifts. Given that the other examples of this Tertullian tradition derived from Corbie and Cologne, Leland's hypothesis is unlikely. Nevertheless, the possibility that Aldhelm might have carried manuscripts back with him from Italy has been suggested by modern scholars in other contexts – see, for example, above, p. 209, n. 65. Elsewhere in *De uiris illustribus* Leland referred to manuscripts he believed to have been brought back from Italy: in the chapter on Benedict Biscop he stated that Biscop stocked the monastery at Wearmouth–Jarrow with books in Greek and Latin acquired from various places in Italy and he maintained that Augustine of Canterbury procured Greek and Latin codices for Canterbury.

[87] See below, p. 216, n. 91.

[88] Ptd in Góis's *Aliquot opuscula* (Louvain, 1544), sig. *2v–3r.

Last year, my dear Rhenanus, I sent you a letter with the Tertullian and a copy of my recently published *Siege of Diu*, but you did not deign to respond. Even though you treat me so negligently, however, I shall not desist from importuning you with my letters until you respond. I am, therefore, now sending you the treatise I have just written containing a brief narration of the faith and customs of the Ethiopians)[89]

It was not until 21 March 1542 that Rhenanus wrote back and thanked him for the Tertullian and his for own writings:

Pro Tertuliani quibusdam commodato [*recte* commodatis], proque commentariis rerum in Indis per Lusitanos tuos gestarum dono ad me missis maximas tibi habeo gratias.

I am most grateful to you for the loan of certain works by Tertullian, and for the commentary on deeds of your Lusitanians in India sent to me as a gift.[90]

Rhenanus's excuse for the delay was that he had not been not sure of Góis's whereabouts, and therefore did not know where to direct correspondence. Góis took the response as a positive one and answered the letter on 1 June, addressing Rhenanus as 'nobili et erudito uiro . . . amico non uulgari' ('a noble and learned man . . . a special friend'), and sending a copy of his *Hispania* (Louvain 1541 *etc*). Concerning the Tertullian he stated:

Quod Tertulliani librum a me tibi missum acceperis, maximopere laetor. Eram huius rei anxius, cum nihil literarum a te nec a Frobenio, cui eum tibi tradendum commiseram, a multis diebus accepissem. Eundem Tertullianum propediem a te repurgatum multi uiri docti auidissime expectant. Quare fac, uti tantorum uirorum spem ne fallas.

I am very pleased that you have received the volume of Tertullian which I sent you. I was very worried about this business, since I had not received letters from you for months, nor from Froben, whom I had commissioned to deliver it to you. Many learned men most eagerly await at an early date an edition, corrected by you, of this Tertullian. Therefore I do hope you will do it, and not disappoint the hopes of such great individuals.[91]

Presumably by the 'multi uiri docti' Góis meant Leland, Gelen and Froben in particular. Although Rhenanus did in due course collate the Malmesbury codex

[89] *Briefwechsel des Beatus Rhenanus*, ed. A. Horawitz and K. Hartfelder (Leipzig, 1886), no. 341. Horawitz and Hartfelder have inserted an extraneous 'mi' before 'amantissime'.

[90] Ptd in *Aliquot opuscula,* sig. * k. 2rv. *On Portuguese Matters* ('commentarii rerum in Indis per Lusitanos tuos gestarum') was appended to the *Siege of Diu* (*Oppugnatio Diensis*) published in 1539: see Hirsch, *Damião de Gois*, p. 226.

[91] *Briefwechsel*, ed. Horawitz and Hartfelder, no. 359 (we have silently corrected the transcription). Unaware of the context, Hirsch misconstrued the Tertullian reference: 'Having prepared a commentary to some writing of Tertullian, Gois asked Froben, who was to publish it, to send it to Beatus, apparently for corrections. (Strangely, however, no trace of this writing has come down to us)' (Hirsch, *Damião de Gois,* p. 88). See also the comments of A. Torres, in *As cartas latinas de Damião de Góis* (Paris, 1982), pp. 343–5.

with his copy of the 1539 edition for the three texts which were found in it (*De resurrectione carnis*, *De praescriptionibus aduersus haereticos* and *De monogamia*), there is no evidence that he made a transcription of the four others (*De trinitate*, *De spectaculis*, *De pudicitia* and *De ieiunio*), and he never brought out a fourth edition.[92]

SUBSEQUENT FATE OF THE MANUSCRIPT

What happened to the manuscript after 1542? In the New Year's Gift of 1546 Leland observed: 'part of the exemplaries, curyously sought by me, and fortunately found in sondry places of this youre dominion, hath bene emprynted in Germany, and now be in the presses chefely of Frobenius'.[93] As Bale pointed out in his commentary to this passage, Leland was no doubt thinking principally of Joseph of Exeter when he stated that some of the works he had discovered had already been printed in Germany.[94] Concerning those which had gone to Froben and were awaiting publication Bale professed himself baffled:

> Of the bokes which shoulde be in the handes of Hieronymus Frobenius, can I nothyng heare. Yet haue I made thydre most instaunt sute and labour by diuerse honeste men, at the least to haue had but theyre tytles; but I neuer coulde obtayne them. Whiche maketh me to thinke, that eyther they haue peryshed by the waye, or els that they are throwne a syde in some corner, and so forgotten.[95]

In fact, Leland must have been alluding, *inter alia*, to the Tertullian, of which a new edition, as far as he knew, was imminent.[96]

[92] See Petitmengin, 'John Leland, Beatus Rhenanus et le Tertullien de Malmesbury', p. 56; also P. Petitmengin and J. P. Carley, 'Malmesbury – Sélestat – Malines. Les tribulations d'un manuscrit de Tertullien au milieu du XVIe siècle', *Annuaire des amis de la Bibliothèque humaniste de Sélestat* (2003), pp. 63–74. Rhenanus called the codex 'Anglicanum exemplar' (p. 68) or 'Anglicum' (p. 668), and he did refer to *De spectaculis* and *De ieiuniis* in his collation. During the 1540s Rhenanus's health deteriorated and his main energy was devoted to writing a sequel to the *Res germanicae*.

[93] *The laboryouse journey*, sig. C.iiii[r].

[94] Leland dismissed this edition with contempt: see above, p. 211, n. 74. He described the edition of Pseudo-Apuleius (Basel: Henricus Petri, 1533), and inaccurately attributed by him to Johannes Bebel's press, as 'imperfectissime aeditum' (above, p. 207) in comparison to the Malmesbury manuscript containing the *Liber peri hermeneias* (see *The Shorter Catalogues*, ed. Sharpe *et al.*, B54.21).

[95] *Ibid.* sig. C.iiii[v].

[96] Leland, as Bale noted, claimed that Froben and his associates had manuscripts in the plural ('boke*s*'). It may be possible to identify one of the others. In the 1520s Rhenanus and Froben obtained a copy of the unique manuscript, now almost entirely destroyed, of the illustrated *Notitia Dignitatum* preserved at Speyer. (On the history of this text, see M. D. Reeve in *Texts and Transmissions: a Survey of the Latin Classics,* ed. L. D. Reynolds (Oxford, 1983), pp. 253–7.) Gelen's *editio princeps* of the illustrated collection (Basel: Hieronymus Froben & Nicolaus Episcopius, 1552) is based on this copy, but in his preface Gelen alleged other sources as well: 'haec NOTITIA . . . cum caeteris spoliis in barbarorum manus delata, nunc demum ex ultimis Britannis studiis antiquariorum repetita' ('this Register . . . carried off with other spoils into

In the spring of 1547 Rhenanus's health worsened and he died at Strasbourg on 20 July, en route home from the spa of Wildbad. On 19 January 1549 the Bürgermeister of Basel wrote to the Bürgermeister of Sélestat concerning the return of manuscripts lent to Rhenanus by Froben and Episcopius, amongst which the Malmesbury Tertullian would have been numbered.[97] This latter must have come back to Basel soon afterwards and thus would have been available to Gelen, whose new edition (Basel: Hieronymus Froben and Nicolaus Episcopius, 1550) was based primarily on its text:[98]

Tandem ex ultima Britannia Ioannes Lelandus, uir antiquarius & feliciori dignus ualetudine, communicauit exemplar in Masburensi coenobio gentis eius uetustissimo repertum, in quo nihil desiderare posses amplius. Tanta erat integritas, nisi quod aliquot libri deerant. Continebat autem et omnia illa quae accesserunt ad postremam editionem Lutetiae; quae si quis cum hac praesenti contulerit, uidebit non uanum esse Gelenium. Vtinam habuisset codex is etiam reliqua, nihil in hoc scriptore requireretur in posterum.

the hands of the barbarians, and now at last brought back from furthest Britain by the efforts of antiquaries'). There have been various explanations of the meaning of 'ex ultimis Britannis' (the term derives ultimately from Catullus and is also found in Horace), but none of them are entirely satisfactory – Reeve, for example, suggests that Gelen's comment arose from the fact that the Spirensis was written in insular script. In 'The *Notitia Dignitatum* in England' (*Aspects of the Notitia Dignitatum*, ed. R. Goodburn and P. Bartholomew (Oxford, 1976), pp. 211–24), C. E. Stevens has argued that Giraldus Cambrensis (1146–1226) had consulted a copy sent over the Channel to England by Alcuin. He maintained, moreover, that this was the manuscript used by Gelen, although, as Reeve observed, he gives no indication about how he thought Gelen obtained it. In the 1550 edition of Tertullian, Gelen used a version of the same phrase, 'ex ultima Britannia', to describe Leland's manuscript, and he also called Leland 'uir antiquarius', which would seem to be echoed in the term 'studiis antiquariorum repetita'. In the concluding section of a letter written in 1540 and addressed to Boniface Amerbach, Gelen, Froben and Episcopius, Rhenanus stated: 'Si Ioannes Lelandus aliquid miserit [he had just mentioned a Greek manuscript he had received from elsewhere], curate diligenter ut ad me perferatur. Nam in quibusdam Notitiae Occidentis locis eius mihi auxilio opus' ('If John Leland has sent me anything, be sure that it is brought to me, for his work has been of assistance to me in certain places of the Western Register'). (See F. Hieronymus, 'Ein vergessener Brief des Rhenanus und andere vergessene Briefe an Nicolaus Episcopius', *Annuaire des amis de la Bibliothèque humaniste de Sélestat*, 1987, p. 159; also B. R. Jenny, *Die Amerbachkorrespondenz* X.1 (Basel, 1991), LXXII–LXXVII.) There is a slight possibility, then, that a copy of the *Notitia Dignitatum* did circulate in England, that Leland did send it to Rhenanus, that Gelen later retrieved it from Rhenanus's possessions along with the Tertullian (see below) and then consulted it in his edition.

97 The letter is printed by B. R. Jenny, 'Zwei Basler Quellentexte zu Beat Rhenans Lebensende und Nachlass', *Annuaire des amis de la Bibliothèque humaniste de Sélestat*, 36 (1985), 286.

98 Between the time Rhenanus acquired the Malmesbury codex and his death, the 1545 Paris edition had appeared, which also made use of the Corbie Corpus: see Petitmengin, 'John Leland, Beatus Rhenanus et le Tertullien de Malmesbury', pp. 55 and 57.

At last John Leland, an antiquary who deserves better health, provided an exemplar from furthest Britain, found in the most ancient monastery of Malmesbury, in which you could wish for nothing more. It was so complete that it was lacking only a few books. It contained, moreover, all the works that were added to the most recent Paris edition and if anyone compares it with the present edition, he will see that I do not speak in vain. If only this codex also had the remnants, posterity would lack nothing by this author.[99]

In 1583/4 Jacques de Joigny De Pamèle (1536–87) brought out another edition, for which he consulted a manuscript owned and greatly treasured by the Englishman John Clement.[100] The *Notarum Explicatio* makes it apparent that the manuscript derived from the Corpus Corbeiense tradition – 'Anglicus codex antiquissimus Ioannis Clementis Angli, e quo VII castigati sunt libri' ('a very ancient English manuscript belonging to the Englishman John Clement, from which seven books were corrected') – and variants confirm that it was the Malmesbury manuscript.[101] Pamèle's working copy of the 1566 Paris reprint of Gelen's version survives and the note prefacing the *De resurrectione carnis* states that the collation is taken from an ancient manuscript from Malmesbury, now owned by the Englishman John Clement.[102] John Clement (d. 1572) was a

[99] Quoted in *Novatiani Opera*, ed. G. F. Diercks, CCSL 4 (Turnhout, 1972), 3. Leland became insane in 1547. In the *Index Britanniae Scriptorum*, ed. Poole and Bateson, p. 408, Bale made the following entry: 'Sigismundus Gelenius, a Ioanne Lelando, feliciori ualetudine digno, xiiii Tartuliani opera cum aliis antiquitatibus, adiutore Frobenio suscepit' ('Through the agency of Froben, Sigismond Gelen received fourteen of Tertullian's works as well as other antiquities from John Leland, worthy of better health'). He gave the library of Thomas Wentworth, first Baron Wentworth of Nettlestead (1501–51), as his source.

[100] This is taken from Pamèle's letter of dedication to Gregory XIII (14 September 1579): 'Nec parum ad hanc rem contulerunt MS. libri Monasteriorum S. Amandi ac Bauonis, & Anglicus quidam, quem thesauri loco penes se adseruabat quondam Ioan. Clemens Anglus. Quibus accesserunt coniecturae doctissimorum uirorum, Latini Latinii Itali, et Ioan. Harrisii Angli [John Harris, formerly secretary to Thomas More], ab ipsis mecum communicatae . . .' ('Manuscripts of the monasteries of St Amand and St Bavo were compared in this undertaking with an English one, which the Englishman John Clement formerly kept in his house in the place of treasure. To these were added conjectures communicated to me by the most learned individuals, John Harris, an Englishman, and Latino Latini, an Italian') (*Opera omnia* (Paris, 1583/4), p. 8).

[101] See Petitmengin, 'John Leland, Beatus Rhenanus et le Tertullien de Malmesbury', p. 57.

[102] 'Collatio huius libri facta est ad ueterem MS. codicem bibliothecae [cenobii?] Maliuesburiensis (*sic*) nunc Ioannis Clementis Angli' ('A collation of this book was made with an old manuscript from the library of Malmesbury now owned by the Englishman John Clement') (I, 78). See P. Petitmengin 'Une nouvelle édition et un ancien manuscrit de Novatien', *Revue des études augustiniennes* 21 (1975), 256–72; also Petitmengin and Carley, 'Malmesbury – Sélestat – Malines'. From the collation we learn that in the Malmesbury manuscript the *De resurrectione* was mutilated (it began at 2.9 [*depreciantur*]) and lacked 8.5 (*fide*) to 13.3 (*documentum*).

humanist scholar and physician, an old friend of Leland's.[103] Both men were collectors of manuscripts and they shared an interest in Latin and Greek literature.[104] Clement received a degree in medicine from the University of Siena by 1528 and in 1544 he was elected president of the Royal College of Physicians. Two years before Leland received his commission in 1533, Simon Grynaeus made a trip to England and met Clement, whose collection of manuscripts, 'kept like a rich treasure', he greatly praised. Later in the same year Grynaeus dedicated his edition of Proclus's *De motu* (Basel: Johannes Bebel and Michael Isingrinius, 1531) to the Englishman.[105] It is likely that Clement knew about the Tertullian through Leland himself – whose religious views were more conservative than scholars have generally realized and who would not have been out of sympathy with Clement's stance during the last years of Henry's reign – and he may have considered it his duty to retrieve it for his incapacitated friend, who presumably had done no more than lend it to Rhenanus. After Edward VI came to the throne Clement went into exile in the Low Countries – he fled from England in July 1549 and returned on 19 March 1554. During this same period Gelen completed his edition and this would provide the logical moment for the return of the codex to Clement. By the time Clement got back to England in 1554 Leland was already dead and he must therefore have held on to the manuscript. In Elizabeth's reign Clement left England again, taking his considerable

103 Both men were students at St Paul's School and both later enjoyed the patronage of Cardinal Wolsey. Leland wrote verses for Clement's marriage in 1526 to Margaret Giggs, the foster daughter of Thomas More. On Clement, see A. B. Emden, *A Biographical Register of the University of Oxford: AD 1501 to 1540* (Oxford, 1974), pp. 121–2; also *Contemporaries of Erasmus: a Biographical Register of the Renaissance and Reformation*, ed. P. G. Bietenholz, and T. B. Beutscher, 3 vols. (Toronto, 1985–7) I, 311–12.

104 On Clement's books, see A. W. Reed, 'John Clement and his Books', *The Library*, 4th ser. 6 (1926), 329–39; also G. Mercati, 'Sopra Giovanni Clement e i suoi manoscritti', *La Bibliofilia* 28 (1926), 81–99; repr. in Mercati's '*Opere Minori*' IV, Studi e Testi 79 (Vatican City, 1937), 292–315.

105 See Hunt, 'The Need for a Guide', p. 369. The description of Clement's collection is found in the preface to the edition, pp. 3–4: 'Huc enim tu, tuopte sponte non monumenta solum, quae plurima ueterum apud te habes, mira diligentia peruestigata, mox ingenti cum labore et sumptu conquisita, ac diuitis demum thesauri instar conseruata destinasti, sed studium praeterea omne tuum eodem conferre libenter soles' ('You have on your own both gathered together monuments here, of which you possess very many ancient examples, sought out with wonderful diligence, acquired with much labour and at great cost, and kept like a rich treasure, and you are also accustomed gladly to bestow your own learning in that same place'). Grynaeus was accompanied by Bebel and borrowed manuscripts from John Claymond: see J. Woolfson, 'John Claymond, Pliny the Elder, and the Early History of Corpus Christi College, Oxford', *EHR* 112 (1997), 882–903, at 893–4: 'During this period Claymond helped Grynaeus to consult manuscripts in Oxford colleges, and permitted him to borrow a Corpus manuscript of Proclus's commentary on Euclid, which was used for the Basel edition of Euclid of 1533. Grynaeus returned the work to Claymond and it is still extant – marked up for printing – in the Corpus library (OCCC 97).'

collection of books with him.[106] Between 1568 and 1571 Pamèle was dean of chrétienté at Bruges. For his edition of Cyprian in 1568 Clement had sent him readings from a manuscript in his possession, although he did not consult the manuscript itself: 'Codex anglicus MS. Io. Clementis, qui ad me quasdam inde castigationes misit' ('The English manuscript of John Clement, who sent me some corrections from it').[107] As we have seen, Pamèle did manage to obtain a collation of Clement's manuscript of Tertullian, although the manuscript itself remained with Clement. The first sack of Mechelen by Spanish troups occurred a matter of months after Clement's death on 1 July 1572. Soon afterwards his son sent a list of the Greek manuscripts to Cardinal Guglielmo Sirleto. The second sack of Mechelen in 1580 by the followers of William of Orange brought about the destruction of what remained, including (probably) the precious Tertullian: when Caesar Clement presented a friend with one of his grandfather's Greek manuscripts in 1607, he stated that it was the sole remaining manuscript, Greek or Latin, from the collection.[108] It seems ironic, then, that our manuscript, which escaped the pillages engendered by the destruction of the English monasteries – Bale lamenting the fact 'that in turnynge ouer of the superstycyouse monasteryes, so lytle respecte was had to theyr lybraryes for the sauegarde of those notble and precyouse monumentes'[109] – fell victim to similar forces on the Continent. As both Leland and Bale had predicted, nevertheless, it was thanks to the invention of the printing press that the evidence of such a rare and precious treasure would be passed down to posterity, brought out of deadly darkness to lively light.[110]

[106] There is some evidence that Clement was reduced to selling books during his final years: 'In Christopher Plantin's journal for 1561 there is an entry of purchase from Dr. Clemens Anglus "cent livres pesant de parchemin" for 16 gulden' (see Hunt, 'The Need for a Guide', p. 370). [107] Quoted in *ibid.* p. 370.

[108] 'Admodum R*euerend*o D*omino* D*omino* Petro Pantino, linguae graecae peritiss*i*mo, hunc unicum ex multis libris m*anuscriptis* gr*aecis* atque latinis foelic*is* record*ationis* D*omini* Iohannis Clementis aui mei in his tumultubus Belgii infoeliciter amissis, fortuito reseruatum, Caesar Clemens nepos amico optimo d*ono* d*edit* d*edicauit* 1607' (1607. Caesar Clement has presented to his dearest friend, the Right Reverend Master Pierre Pantin, most skilled in the Greek language, the single chance survivor of the many Greek and Latin manuscripts of my grandfather of blessed memory Master John Clement, but sadly lost in these Belgian upheavals'). See Mercati, 'Sopra Giovanni Clement', p. 296, n. 19.

[109] *The laboryouse journey*, sig. A.vii^{v}.

[110] While undertaking research for this article James Carley was a Visiting Fellow at Oriel College, Oxford, and he acknowledges the generous support of the college. We both thank Andy Orchard, Simon Keynes, Colin Tite, James Willoughby and Jonathan Woolfson for their assistance on individual points. Roger Pearse read the article carefully and has been a great support all through the project. We are particularly indebted to the work of two previous scholars, the late Richard W. Hunt and Rodney Thomson: Leland's letter to Rhenanus confirms the findings of their pioneering studies. We have published our analysis of the printing history of the Tertullian manuscript in 'Malmesbury – Sélestat – Malines'.

APPENDIX

Joannes[111] Lelandus Antiquarius Beato Rhenano S.P.D.

Aegisti cum quodam Damiano Agoe Hispano ut tuo, immo publico literatorum nomine, mecum ageret de transmittendo ad uos Tertulliani exemplari, impresso nuper a Frobenio longe auctiori. Ille mecum nihil egit: scripsit tamen summa cum diligentia ad Richardum Morysinum, uirum ingenio, literis et fauore nostri principis insignem. Is quod a me rogauit tuo nomine facile impetrauit, et mature ad Pintoum, mercatorem Lusitanum in Flandria agentem, transmittendum curauit. Pintous suam liberauit fidem, reddito exemplari Damiano. Nam ipse uidi literas Damiani, quibus fatetur se codicem accepisse, et breui ad te transmissurum esse. Si iam accepisti bene habet: si non, cura modis omnibus ne orbi dispereat tantus et tam rarus thesaurus.

Quod si praeterea cognoscere cupias quo loco exemplar inuentum sit, accipe. Est locus in Seueria prouincia Britanniae primae propter ripas Auonae fluminis antiquitus Bladunum dictum, cuius urbis moenia, quanuis semilacera, adhuc cernuntur. Saxones hanc, ut Beda in ecclesiastica testatur historia, *Ingelburne* postea uocabant. Sed postquam Maildulphus Scotus ludum bonarum literarum ibi aperuerat, monasteriumque, fauente Ina, Visisaxonum regem, et Agilberto, Ventano episcopo, construxerat, incepit dici *Maildulphsbyri*, id est Maildulphi curia: quod nomen hodie, quanuis corruptum, seruat. Hic ego inter alia uenerandae uetustatis monimenta inueni Tertulliani exemplar nunc ad te missum, quod, ut ego quibusdam coniecturis colligo, Aldelmus, proximus a Maildulpho abbas et deinde Shiroburnae Dutrotrigum episcopus, ex Italia in Britanniam ante annos octingentos traduxit. Haec habui, quae in praesentia ad te scriberem. Gelenius tuus atque Frobenius de eadem re literas a me acceperunt, et nisi uestris negotiis maxime seriis molestum sit, hoc idem repeterem. Vale.
Londini Trenouantum. Cal. Iun.

Verso: Beato Rhenano Selestadiensi, uiro undecunque eruditissimo

John Leland, Antiquary, sends his greetings to Beatus Rhenanus.

You asked one Damião de Góis, a Spaniard, to negotiate with me about sending you for your sake, or rather for the sake of the republic of letters, a manuscript of Tertullian which is much more complete than the one recently published by Froben. He did not contact me, but he did write with the greatest assiduity to Richard Morison, a man who is distinguished for his abilities, his culture and for the favour of our prince. Morison easily obtained what he asked from me in your name, and he promptly organized for the manuscript to be delivered to Pinto, a Portugese merchant active in Flanders. Pinto acquitted his mission faithfully and gave the manuscript to Damião. I myself have seen a letter from Damião, in which he affirms that he received the codex,

111 Jo*an*nnes *MS*

and that he will deliver it to you before long. If you have already received it, all is well; if not, do take all care to prevent the world from being deprived of such a grand and such a rare treasure.

If you wish, moreover, to know where this treasure was found, let me tell you. In Wiltshire, a province of *Britannia prima*, there is a place situated by the banks of the river Avon, which was called *Bladunum* in ancient times, and the ruins of the city's walls can still be seen. As Bede relates in his *Ecclesiastical History*, the Saxons later called it *Ingelburne*. After the Irishman Maildulphus opened a school for good letters there, however, and built a monastery with the help of Ine, king of the West Saxons, and Agilbert, bishop of Winchester, it began to be called Maildulphsbury, that is the city of Maildulph; this name is still preserved today, although it has been corrupted. Here I found among other monuments of venerable antiquity the exemplar of Tertullian which has now been sent to you. As a result of various conjectures I suspect it was brought from Italy to Britain some eight hundred years ago by Aldhelm, who succeeded Maildulph as abbot and then became bishop of Sherborne of the *Durotriges*. This is what I had to write to you at this time. Both your friend Gelen and Froben have received a letter from me on the same subject, and hoping that it might not be a nuisance to your most important affairs, I have repeated it to you. Farewell.
London of the *Trinovantes*, the first of June.

Verso: To Beatus Rhenanus of Selestat, an exceptionally learned man in all subjects.

A third supplement to *Hand-List of Anglo-Saxon Non-Runic Inscriptions*

ELISABETH OKASHA

This supplement brings up to date my *Hand-List of Anglo-Saxon Non-Runic Inscriptions* (Cambridge, 1971), and the two supplements which appeared in *Anglo-Saxon England* 11 (1983) and 21 (1992). It contains twenty-nine entries and includes all the Anglo-Saxon non-runic inscriptions that have come to my notice since the publication of the second supplement. I have personally examined all the existing inscriptions included in this third supplement, with the exception of 233 Sleaford and 240 'in deo' ring, both of which are in private possession.

There is, however, one important omission to the inscriptions included here: a group of eleven coin-brooches. Six coin-brooches were included in the original *Hand-List*: 19 Canterbury I; 104 Rome II; 113 Sulgrave; 139 Winchester II; 141 Winchester IV; 154 'eadward' brooch. However, from now onwards, pieces of coin jewellery are excluded as being more properly the concern of numismatists. The publication of new pieces of coin jewellery is being undertaken by Marion Archibald and Gareth Williams. The eleven new coin-brooches known to me are listed in Index III below.

This supplement follows the same pattern as the two previous ones. First are given the Entries, the system and layout of which are explained below. The Entries are followed by the Bibliography. This gives in full the references quoted in abbreviated form throughout this third supplement, unless they have already appeared in the General Bibliography of the *Hand-List* or the two earlier supplements. This is followed by Addenda to the *Hand-List* and supplements, where additional information about several inscriptions is given, and then by Corrigenda to the *Hand-List* and supplements. Finally there is given a list of Addenda to the bibliographies of the individual inscriptions from the *Hand-List* and supplements, to bring these up to date.

The Entries in this supplement follow the same layout as before. The following paragraphs explain the system adopted in the Entries. This information is adapted from the introduction to the *Hand-List* and is repeated here for the convenience of the reader.

Each inscription is entered in alphabetical order according to its place of finding in modern times and is given a running number, starting at 212, where the second supplement stopped. This is followed by a more detailed account of its place of finding and present locality, including where known the town, the county, and the country where this is other than England. The present locality is stated in general if the object is merely housed there, but is particularized if it forms part of the fabric of a building. In this context, where an object is said to be set into a wall, this indicates an exterior wall unless the contrary is stated. The dedications of the parish churches are given only where there is more than one parish church in the town.

Each entry then continues with a paragraph containing the factual information known about the object. If any fact is uncertain, this is stated. The information is given in abbreviated form in the following order:

(i) Find-place and date, where known, with brief details of the find. Unless the contrary is stated, objects are not assumed to have been found *in situ*, nor in their present *situs*, nor during excavation.

(ii) Maximum measurements in centimetres, in the order height × width × thickness, unless different measurements are stated.

(iii) Description of the object, including its material and function and the type of stone, where known. Unless the contrary is stated, it should be assumed that objects are: complete; uncarved and undecorated; containing neither original nor modern paint; and that stones are rectangular or of rectangular section.

(iv) Description of the text, including its position on the object. This position is described as on 'one face' if only the text distinguishes the faces, as on 'visible face' if only one face of the object is discernible, and otherwise as on 'face'. Unless the contrary is stated, texts are assumed to be: complete; primary; incised (except in the case of metalwork objects where the lettering is described); set horizontally; and set within framing lines but not within panels. (Framing lines divide lines of text while panels enclose the text). Legibility is described in one of five ways:

legible: the reading of the text is certain
slightly deteriorated: the text is a little damaged but the reading is virtually certain
rather deteriorated: the text is significantly damaged but the reading can be made out
highly deteriorated: the text consists largely of editorial reconstruction
illegible: no meaningful text can be made out.

(v) Language and formula of the text. All the legible texts are in Old English and/or Latin and employ one or more of the following formulae:

descriptive formula type a (referring to the object itself)
descriptive formula type b (referring to carving or decoration on the object)
descriptive formula type c (referring outside the object)
maker and owner formulae (X made me; Y owns me)
memorial formulae, as on grave-stones
personal name(s).

(vi) Script of the text. The script is described either as 'AS capitals' or, where a manuscript script is used, following the terminology of Lowe (1972). For epigraphic dating, see Okasha (1968), 321–38.

(vii) Approximate date of the object. Where possible the objects are dated on both direct and indirect evidence. Indirect evidence includes formulaic comparison of the text with other similar ones, and the architectural or historical dating of an associated building where the object does not form part of its fabric. Direct evidence comprises: linguistic dating of the text where it is in Old English; epigraphic dating of the text; artistic dating of the carving or decoration of the object; archaeological dating of the object when found during controlled excavation; historical dating of the object; architectural dating of the fabric of which the object forms part. The date is given in one of five forms, as illustrated below by the eighth century, and, where necessary, a discussion of the date is given in the commentary at the end of the entry.

AD 750–7: a certain date, based on direct evidence

Eighth century: a certain, but unspecifiable, date, based on direct evidence

Probably eighth century: a date suggested by direct evidence, but where this is insufficient to make it certain

Possibly eighth century: a date suggested by indirect evidence, or by one piece of inconclusive direct evidence

Date uncertain: insufficient evidence for dating.

Each entry then continues with a comprehensive bibliography of the object, abbreviated and in chronological order. This is followed by the text, which is transliterated according to the following system: non-runic letters are shown as capitals, with the letters Ð, þ, V and ƿ retained as in the text. Ligatures, but not the Old English monophthongs 'æ' and 'œ', appear as 'A/B'. Abbreviation and punctuation marks of any sort are shown as '⁻' and ':' respectively, except where ':' is an abbreviation mark, in which case it remains. Deliberate spaces between letters in the text are indicated by spaces. Ends of lines of text, and ends of complete texts, are shown by '|'. The following signs are also used:

'*A*': a letter damaged but legible

'[*A*]': a damaged letter where the restoration is fairly certain

'[A]': a legible and undamaged letter of unusual form, probably A

'. . .': three letters lost, the number varying according to the number of dots

'…': an indefinite number of letters lost in a text

'—': a complete loss of text at beginning or end.

The text is then transliterated again, into small capitals, with the insertion of word division and of obvious contextual letters, but with no editorial punctuation and with bracketed letters remaining so. This is followed by a translation;

with the exceptions of 'a' and 'the', words added to make a fluent translation appear in brackets. In the translations, Latin names are normalized but vernacular names appear as in the texts.

Each entry ends with an interpretative commentary, restricted to that which is essential for an understanding of the text. Where possible, each object is illustrated by a photograph.

The inscribed objects in this third supplement, where they are not in private ownership, are in parish churches, cathedrals, museums (permanently or temporarily) or in the care of archaeological units. I should like to record my thanks to the owners of inscriptions, the incumbents of the churches and cathedrals, and the directors and staffs of the museums and archaeological units concerned, for enabling me to examine the objects in their care. I am grateful for the financial support that I have received from the Research Fund of the Faculty of Arts, University College Cork. Help with individual inscriptions is acknowledged in the appropriate entry, but here I should like to record my particular thanks to Leslie Webster of the British Museum for her continued interest in, and help with, this project.

ENTRIES

212 Bawburgh

Plate V*a*

Currently in the care of Norfolk Museums and Archaeology Service, Norwich.

Found October 2002 in Bawburgh, Norfolk, by Damien Alger, using metal-detector. 3.5 × 5 × 0.1 cm. Lead plate, decorated but incomplete. Text i on one face, text ii on other, set upside down with respect to each other. Both texts slightly deteriorated. Text i probably complete, set within incised cross-arms but without framing-lines; text ii incomplete but set within double framing-lines. Text i probably OE personal name; text ii probably Latin descriptive formula, type c. AS capitals. Date uncertain.

Unpublished

i: [*F* R]/C*A* | [*T*] SA | WAR[O] | *D* |
ii: [... *RC.DR.*] | [...]*N*[*E*]S:SCIEH+ | +[... .]+DWERH
+ | ++S[*I*]/*N*[*FO*]NDIA*B*+ |

Part of text i reads: SAWARD. These letters are all of a similar large size, are deeply incised, and the first five are all in one line although divided between the two cross-arms. The other marks on these cross-arms, which might be interpreted as letters as above, are smaller and fainter and are set amongst various small crosses. It may be better to interpret these 'letters' as incised decorative elements rather than as text. SAWARD is a form of the recorded OE masculine name *Sæweard*.

In text ii, line 1, about five letters are lost from the initial lacuna and the letter read as [D] could instead be [E]; this line is too deteriorated to be interpreted. In line 2, about two letters are lost from the initial lacuna and the letter read as [E] could instead be a cross. In line 3, about three letters are lost from the lacuna. In line 4 the letters read as [FO] could instead be [ER]. Text ii contains a large number of crosses, placed at beginning and end of the lines, with at least one in the middle of a line (line 3). Such a layout with crosses is unparalleled amongst AS inscriptions, although the use of crosses as a decorative feature seems quite appropriate to a funerary object.

With the crosses omitted, text ii might have read: – N[E]S : SCIE H[...]DWERH S [I]N [FO]NDI AB . A possible interpretation of this could be *[iohan]n[e]s scie h[ear]dwerh s [i]n [fo]ndi ab* '– of St John, abbot *H[ear]dwerh, in the ground'. If, as seems likely, texts i and ii read together, they could suggest that the burial of Saward took place, perhaps in a foundation dedicated to St John, at a time when the abbot was named *H[ear]dwerh. There are, however, several problems associated with such an interpretation. Although *ab* is a recorded abbreviation for *abbas* 'abbot', *scie* is very odd for *sancti*. The *s* before *[in]* is hard to explain unless it is an abbreviation for *sed* 'but'. Latin *fundus* can appear in Medieval Latin as *fondus*, but *[i]n [fo]ndi* would then be an error for *in fundo* 'in the ground'. The name is extremely problematic: *heard-* (if this is the correct interpretation) is recorded, but neither *-wer* nor *-werh*, *-werg* is recorded as a second name-element.

There are three other AS inscribed lead plates known: 193 Flixborough II, 225 Kirkdale II and 234 Weasenham. On the evidence of the script and of the personal name Saward, the Bawburgh plate appears to be AS but cannot be more closely dated.

213 Bury St Edmunds II

Plate V*b*

Now in Moyse's Hall Museum, Bury St Edmunds, Suffolk, no. BSEMS 1976.276 (OS).

Found in Abbey Cemetery, Bury St Edmunds. First mentioned 1903, probably referred to 1855 (see below). 13.2 × 9.8 × 0.3 cm. Lead cross with faint and slightly deteriorated texts set without framing lines on face. Text i set as print across cross-arms, text ii set vertically downwards, texts sharing intersecting letter in middle of cross. Latin descriptive formula, type c. Insular minuscule. Date uncertain, possibly eleventh or twelfth century.

(—) (1903a), 24 (no. 37); Okasha (1996b), 68

i: CRVX X P̄ *I*T/RIV̄*PHA*T |
ii: CRVX X P/I PELLITH+OS/T[.]M |

Text i reads: CRVX XP̄I TRIV̄PHAT 'the cross of Christ triumphs' with XP̄I for CHRISTI and TRIV̄PHAT for TRIUMPHAT. Text ii reads: CRVX XPI PELLIT H+OST[E]M, although the cross in the middle of HOST[E]M might alternatively be accidental markings. XPI, for CHRISTI, shares the P with text i; however the horizontal stroke, indicating a ligatured I, is part only of text ii. Text ii can be translated, 'the cross of Christ drives away (the) enemy'.

The first mention made of the five inscribed lead crosses from Bury St Edmunds was in 1855 when Tymms exhibited two of them, 214 Bury St Edmunds IV and 216 Bury St Edmunds VI, to the Society of Antiquaries. They were then in the Museum of the Suffolk Institute of Archaeology, along with 'several specimens of a larger size than those now sent' on which 'the Inscription in every case appears the same'.[1] In 1903, the five crosses included here were published in the Moyses's Hall Museum catalogue, and again the texts were said to be the same on each cross. Two of the crosses in the 1903 catalogue certainly appear to be the two illustrated by Tymms and it seems likely that these five were ones, possibly the ones, known to Tymms.

The comments made by Tymms and in the 1903 catalogue about the texts being the same seems to be an over-simplification. The texts are certainly similar but are not identical. For example, Bury St Edmunds II, text ii has the letters set vertically downwards; nos III, IV and VI have or had text ii set downwards but with the letters facing the viewer's left. Bury St Edmunds VI, text i consists of the form of words that on nos. II, III, IV and VI constitutes text ii. The number of small crosses inscribed as part of the texts, and the abbreviations used, both differ slightly from one lead cross to another.

It seems likely that all five lead crosses are or were funerary crosses. Apart from the examples recorded from Bury St Edmunds, seven other inscribed lead crosses of the period are known. They are: 7 Bath; 21 Canterbury III; 180 Wells I; 219 Chichester; 220 Cumberworth; 226 Lincoln II; 239 Worcester. All the Bury St Edmunds crosses are tentatively dated by comparison with these and on the evidence of the script used.

214 Bury St Edmunds III

Plate V*c*

Now in Moyse's Hall Museum, Bury St Edmunds, Suffolk, no. BSEMS 1976.280.

[1] Tymms (1855), 167.

Found in Abbey Cemetery, Bury St Edmunds. First mentioned 1903, probably referred to 1855 (see 213 Bury St Edmunds II above). 10.4 × 8 × 0.3 cm. Lead cross with faint and rather deteriorated texts set without framing lines on face. Text i set as print across cross-arms, text ii set downwards, with letters facing left. Latin descriptive formula, type c. Insular minuscule. Date uncertain, possibly eleventh or twelfth century.

(—) (1903a), 24 (no. 39); Okasha (1996b), 68

i: *CR*[*V*]*X*[...]*T*/*R*/*I*ŪPH/A/T |
ii: *C*R*V*X *X*[. ... ...]T/E[.] |

Text i reads: CR[V]X [...] TRIŪPHAT, where TRIŪPHAT is for TRIUMPHAT. There is space for three or four letters in the lacuna: by comparison with 213 Bury St Edmunds II, text i, it seems reasonable to reconstruct these as [XPI] for [CHRISTI], and to translate 'the cross of Christ triumphs'. Text ii probably begins: CRVX X[P]—, presumably for CRVX X[PI]—, 'the cross of Christ —'. There is space for around four letters in the lacuna, followed by three which could read [R], followed by [A] or [S], followed by a letter ligatured to the T, probably [L] or a long [S]. Only part of the final letter of this text remains and its reading is uncertain. Although it is possible to reconstruct the final word as [HOS]TE[M], this is by no means a certain reading. It is only considered since Tymms and the Moyses's Hall Museum catalogue describe all the crosses as having the same texts as each other (see under 213 Bury St Edmunds II). In the case of this cross, there certainly seems insufficient room for the word [PELLIT] to have been lost from the lacuna unless it were heavily ligatured or abbreviated. For general discussion of the Bury St Edmunds lead crosses, see 213 Bury St Edmunds II above.

215 Bury St Edmunds IV

Plate VI*a*

Bury St Edmunds, Suffolk. Lost.

Found 'on the breast' of skeleton in Abbey Cemetery, Bury St Edmunds. First mentioned 1855. *c.* 15 × *c.* 13.8 cm. Lead cross with legible texts set without framing lines on face.[2] Text i set as print across cross-arms, text ii set downwards, with letters facing left. Latin descriptive formula, type c. Insular minuscule. Date uncertain, possibly eleventh or twelfth century.

Tymms (1855), 165–7 & fig.; Tymms (1856), 215–17 & fig.; (—) (1903a), 24 (no.32); Radford (1940), 508; Rodwell *et al.* (1979), 409–10[3]

[2] The description, text etc. are taken from Tymms (1855), 165–7 & fig. and from (—) (1903), 24. [3] Alternatively, this may be a reference to 217 Bury St Edmunds VI.

i: +C*R*UXXP̄I TRIŪPH[..+] |
ii: +CRUXXPI P/ELLITHO[Ʃ]T/EM+ |

From the context, the two lost letters are likely to have been AT; the drawing suggests that they may have been ligatured to each other and also perhaps to the final cross. Text i probably then read: + CRUX XP̄I TRIŪPH[AT] [+], 'the cross of Christ triumphs', with XP̄I for CHRISTI and TRIŪPH[AT] for TRIUMPHAT. Text ii read: + CRUX XPI PELLIT HO[S]TEM +, 'the cross of Christ drives away (the) enemy', with XPI for CHRISTI. For general discussion of the Bury St Edmunds lead crosses, see 213 Bury St Edmunds II above.

216 Bury St Edmunds V

No illustration exists

Bury St Edmunds, Suffolk. Lost.

Found in Abbey Cemetery, Bury St Edmunds. First mentioned 1903, probably referred to 1855 (see 213 Bury St Edmunds II above). *c.* 15.3 × *c.* 12 cm.[4] Lead cross, apparently with legible texts set on cross-arms of face. Latin descriptive formula, type c. Probably insular minuscule. Date uncertain, possibly eleventh or twelfth century.

(—) (1903a), 24 (no. 36)

The texts may be reconstructed:

+ CRUX XPI TRIUMPHAT
+ CRUX XPI PELLIT HOSTEM

Since the texts on all the Bury St Edmunds lead crosses were described as being the same as each other (see 213 Bury St Edmunds II above), it is probable that these texts were of the form: + CRUX XPI TRIUMPHAT, 'the cross of Christ triumphs', and + CRUX XPI PELLIT HOSTEM, 'the cross of Christ drives away (the) enemy'. For general discussion of the Bury St Edmunds lead crosses, see 213 Bury St Edmunds II above.

217 Bury St Edmunds VI

Plate VI*b*

Bury St Edmunds, Suffolk. Lost.

Found 'on the breast' of skeleton in Abbey Cemetery, Bury St Edmunds. First mentioned 1855. *c.* 11.5 × *c.* 8.8 cm. Lead cross with legible texts set without

[4] The description and text are taken from (—) (1903), 24.

framing lines on face.[5] Text i set as print across cross-arms, text ii set downwards, with letters facing left, with incised cross at the intersection of texts. Latin descriptive formula, type c. Insular minuscule. Date uncertain, possibly eleventh or twelfth century.

Tymms (1855), 165–7 & fig.; Tymms (1856), 215–17 & fig.; (—) (1903a), 24 (no. 38); Radford (1940), 508; Rodwell *et al.* (1979), 409–10[6]

i: +CRVXXP̄I PELLI[*T*]*H*O*S*TĒ*:+* |
ii: +CRUX XPI TRIUMPHAT+ |

Text i read: + CRVX XP̄I PELLI[T] HOSTĒ, 'the cross of Christ drives away (the) enemy', where XP̄I is for CHRISTI and HOSTĒ for HOSTEM. Text ii read: + CRUX XPI TRIUMPHAT, 'the cross of Christ triumphs', with XPI for CHRISTI. For general discussion of the Bury St Edmunds lead crosses, see 213 Bury St Edmunds II above.

218 Castlesteads

Plate VI*c*

Castlesteads, Cumbria. Lost.

Found before 1921, possibly in 1791, at Castlesteads; still in existence 1941. *c.* 122 × *c.* 41 cm. Red sandstone shaft, probably complete, with highly deteriorated text set without framing lines on visible face; text was probably primary but incomplete.[7] Language and formula uncertain. Probably AS capitals. Date uncertain.

Collingwood, R. G. (1922), no. 17, p. 212; Collingwood, R. G. and Wright, R. P. (1965), no. 2389*, p. 748 & fig.

*PA*S | *I*[*S* .] | [....] | *T*[....] | [....] | *P*[.*N*] | [....] | *TR*[.] | *PO*[.] —

The text apparently read: PASI[S...]T[...]P[.N...]TR[.]PO[.] — but is not now interpretable. When he drew the text in 1941, Wright noted that the interpretation of the text was 'not clear' and added 'Nothing in the existing form of the stone suggests a Roman origin.'[8] It is possible that the stone was Anglo-Saxon but, since it is now lost, this is unverifiable.

[5] The description, text etc. are taken from Tymms (1855), 165–7 & fig. and from (—) (1903), 24.
[6] Alternatively, this may be a reference to 215 Bury St Edmunds IV.
[7] The description etc. is taken from Collingwood, R. G. and Wright, R. P. (1965), 748.
[8] Collingwood, R. G. and Wright, R. P. (1965), 748.

219 Chichester

PlateVII*a*

Chichester Cathedral, West Sussex, in the Cathedral Library.

Found between September and November 1830, beneath ground in medieval burial ground within cathedral cloisters. 19.1 × 12.6 × 0.05 cm. Lead funerary cross, with legible text incised on visible face. Latin descriptive formulae, type c. Insular minuscule (lines 1–9) and insular majuscule (lines 10–16). AD 1088.

Cartwright (1830), 447; Cartwright (1831), 419–20; Dally (1831), 55–6, 65; Crocker (1849), 23–4, 36–7; (—) (1853), 76–7; Wylie (1854), 299 & fig.; Walcott (1878), 15; Page, W. *et al.* (1935), 126; Barker (1944–5), 163–4; Peckham (1944–5), 112–17, 164; Mayr-Harting (1963), 1–2; Steer (1963), 21 & fig.; Okasha (1996b), 63–9 & figs; Rodwell *et al.* (2001), 148; Meier (2002), 194 & fig.

ABSOLUIMUS [.*E*]GO*DE*|FRIDEEP̄E UICE SCĪ|PETR/ IPRINCIPIS[*E*]|APL̄*M* CUIDN̄SDED̄|LIGANDIA*T*Q[:]SOLUĒ*D*[*I*]| POT/EST/ATĒ UTQUĀTŪ T/UAEXP*E*[*TIT*]|*A*CCUSAT/IO [*&*] *A*DNŌSPT̄INA/E/TR/E/MISĪO|SITTIBIDS̄REDĒPT/O/*R* OM̄PS SALUS OM/*N*Ū|PECCATOR̄TUO[.] PIUSIND*U*LTO/R AMEN|VII KL̄ OCTOBRIS INFESTIVITATE|SC̄I FIRMINI EP̄I & *M̄*[*R*]|OBII*T* GODE|FRIDVSEP̄S̄|CICESTREN|SIS: IPSODIE|V LVNA/T FVIT|

The text reads: ABSOLUIMUS [TE] GODEFRIDE EP̄E UICE SCĪ PETRI PRINCIPIS[E] APL̄M CUI DN̄S DED̄ LIGANDI ATQ[:] SOLUĒD[I] POTESTATĒ UT QUĀTŪ TUA EXPE[TIT] ACCUSATIO [&] AD NŌS PT̄INAET REMISĪO SIT TIBI DS̄ REDĒPTOR OM̄PS SALUS OMNŪ PECCATOR̄ TUO[.] PIUS INDULTOR AMEN VII KL̄ OCTOBRIS IN FESTIVITATE SC̄I FIRMINI EP̄I & M̄[R] OBIIT GODEFRIDVS EP̄S̄ CICESTRENSIS : IPSO DIE V LVNAT FVIT. The text is heavily abbreviated, mostly by the use of macrons, but TIBI has the BI in small letters above the line, and some manuscript abbreviations are used, for example in ATQ[:] and TUO[.].The abbreviations are, in order of occurrence: EP̄E = EPISCOPE; SCĪ = SANCTI; APL̄M = APOSTOLORUM; DN̄S = DOMINUS; DED̄ = DEDIT; ATQ[:] = ATQUE; SOLUĒD[I] = SOLUEND[I]; POTESTATĒ = POTESTATEM; QUĀTŪ = QUANTUM; [&] = [ET]; PT̄INAET = PERTINEAT; REMISĪO = REMISSIO; DS̄ = DEUS; REDĒPTOR = REDEMPTOR; OM̄PS = OMNIPOTENS; OMNŪ = OMNIUM; PECCATOR̄ = PECCATORUM; TUO[.] = TUO[RUM]; KL̄ = KALENDIS; SC̄I = SANCTI; EP̄I = EPISCOPI; & = ET; M̄[R] = M[ARTYRIS]; EP̄S̄ = EPISCOPUS. There are also four errors: PRINCIPIS[E] is for PRINCIPIS; NŌS is incorrectly shown as an abbreviation; PT̄INAET is for PT̄INEAT; and LVNAT is for LVNAE.

With the errors corrected and the abbreviations expanded, the text reads: ABSOLUIMUS [TE] GODEFRIDE EPISCOPE UICE SANCTI PETRI PRINCIPIS APOSTOLORUM CUI DOMINUS DEDIT LIGANDI ATQUE SOLUEND[I] POTESTATEM UT QUANTUM

TUA EXPE[TIT] ACCUSATIO [ET] AD NOS PERTINEAT REMISSIO SIT TIBI DEUS REDEMPTOR OMNIPOTENS SALUS OMNIUM PECCATORUM TUO[RUM] PIUS INDULTOR AMEN VII KALENDIS OCTOBRIS IN FESTIVITATE SANCTI FIRMINI EPISCOPI ET M[ARTYRIS] OBIIT GODEFRIDVS EPISCOPUS CICESTRENSIS : IPSO DIE V LVNAE FVIT. This can be translated: 'We absolve you, O Bishop Godfrey, in place of St Peter, prince of the apostles, to whom the Lord gave the power of binding and releasing, so that in so far as your accusation warrants and the remission pertains to us, God the omnipotent redeemer, the kind forgiver, may be to you the healing of all your sins. Amen. On the 25th of September, on the feast of St Firmin bishop and martyr, Bishop Godfrey of Chichester died. On the same day it was five days after the (new) moon.' The first part of the text is a papal absolution relating to Bishop Godfrey; the second part of the text gives the date of his death although, in fact, 25 September 1088 was the sixth, not the fifth, day after the new moon.[9] There is nothing in the text to suggest that it is not contemporary with Bishop Godfrey's death. Other inscribed lead crosses of the period are known and are listed above under 213 Bury St Edmunds II. All may be funerary but none contains an absolution text.

220 Cumberworth

Plate VII*b*

Cumberworth parish church, Lincolnshire. Now in private possession.

Found July 1992 by owner during excavation in St Helen's church. 10.6 × 5.7 × 0.1 cm. Lead cross, decorated and with rather deteriorated text set above and below incised cross on face. Latin descriptive formula, type b or c. Insular minuscule. Possibly tenth to eleventh century.

Okasha (1996b), 68; Sawyer (1998), 156–7 & fig.

+ XP̄I EX HOCSIGNO | [. .]*O*[... .*C*]*TAS*[*T*] | [*TEX*. .]O[. ...]*EX*PIATUM | [*P*. .]COREXIGUUMSQUALO | REM M[. .*T*.]OLU*T*UMQU[.] | INUIRT [*UT*. .*R*]UCISMUNDUM | DEMORT*E*RED[*EM*]IT TA[*R*] | TARA DISRUPIT AUTCELES | TIA PAN DIT |

The text reads: + XP̄I EX HOC SIGNO [–] EXPIATUM [P..]COR EXIGUUM SQUALOREM M[..T] [U]OLUTUM QU[I] IN UIRT[UTE] [CR]UCIS MUNDUM DE MORTE RED[EM]IT TA[R]TARA DISRUPIT AUT CELESTIA PANDIT. The text begins, '+ through this sign of Christ', with XP̄I for CHRISTI. A considerable amount of text is then lost, approximately fifteen letters altogether between SIGNO and EXPIATUM. The last lost word might have been [EST], to accompany EXPIATUM, hence 'was purified,

[9] For a full discussion of the text, see Okasha (1996b), 63–9.

atoned for'. The following word could have been [PRE]COR 'I pray for, beg' and the phrase EXIGUUM SQUALOREM might mean 'small foulness' in the accusative. [U]OLUTUM could be the past participle of VOLVO, hence '[was] turned round', less likely the noun meaning 'circular motion'. However the precise interpretation of this part of the text remains uncertain.

From the end of line five, the text is much clearer and can be translated, 'he who by the power of the cross redeemed the world from death, shattered hell and threw open heaven'. Although the sentiments expressed are not unusual, the exact wording is hard to parallel. Similar, but not identical, phrasing occurs in some sacramentaries, for example *deus qui tartara fregisti resurgens, aperuisti caelos ascendens*, 'God, you who rising again have broken up hell, ascending have opened heaven';[10] *qui per passionem crucis mundum redemit*, 'he who redeemed the world through the passion of the cross'.[11]

Other inscribed lead crosses are listed under 213 Bury St Edmunds II. The lead cross with the most similar text was apparently 7 Bath. However the text in question on the Bath cross is now illegible and its similarity to this text is dependent on the reading given by Smith.[12] The Cumberworth cross is dated on the resemblance of the script to manuscript hands.

221 Deer Park Farms

Plate VII*c*

Deer Park Farms, Glenarm, Co. Antrim, N. Ireland. Property of the Department of the Environment for Northern Ireland, find no. 2083, now in the Ulster Museum, Belfast.[13]

Found 1986 in midden layer, context no. 1286, during excavation at Deer Park Farms. 0.54 × 1.31 × 0.96 cm. Stone hone with convex face and flat back, decorated but incomplete; stone is fine-grained shale. Text, legible but probably not primary, is set on back, upside down with respect to decoration, inside panel open at end. Language and formula uncertain. Insular minuscule. Seventh to eighth century.

Lynn and McDowell (forthcoming)

DNISIST |

The text probably reads DNISIST, although the second letter could alternatively be R and the fourth G. It is probably to be interpreted as practice letters, beginning with the sequence DNI, perhaps the abbreviation for DOMINI. 182 Winchester VII, a piece of lead spillage, also contains practice letters, the first

[10] (—) (1983), no. 1219. [11] (—) (1983), no. 3992. [12] Smith, R. A. (1906a), 380–1.

[13] I am most grateful for permission to include the hone in advance of the forthcoming publication of the site.

three being DNE, probably for DOMINE. On archaeological grounds the hone is dated to the period AD 660–780, a date which is in accordance with the animal-head decoration incised adjacent to the text.

222 Dublin VI

Plate VIII*a*

Now in the National Museum of Ireland, Dublin, no. E 122:14490.[14]

Found 1974 during excavation at Christchurch Place, Dublin, in square 1. Fragment i: 3.5 × 4.8 × 0.1 cm; ii: 5 × 4 × 0.1 cm. Leather sheath, decorated but incomplete: in at least eight pieces, two being inscribed. Both inscribed fragments contain incomplete, rather deteriorated texts on face, set within double margins which probably form panels. Language and formula uncertain. AS capitals. Probably tenth to eleventh century.

Unpublished

i: — [...]*E*[.] —
ii: — [.]*M*IN[.] —

The texts read: — E[.] — and — [.]MIN[.]. The final letter of text i could have been R or S; the final letter of text ii was probably S or Q. The two inscribed fragments do not fit together, and it is uncertain how much text has been lost. Too little text remains for it to be interpreted. On archaeological grounds, the sheath is likely to date from the tenth to eleventh century. Another inscribed leather sheath, but more nearly complete, 163 Dublin II, was also found at the same site.

223 Egginton

Plate VIII*b*

Egginton, Derbyshire. Now in private possession.

Found February 1987 by owner using metal-detector, to south of church. Diam. *c.* 0.13 cm. Circular silver stud, decorated and originally mounted on larger object. Legible text set right round face, with letters in relief and facing inwards. OE descriptive formula, type c. AS capitals. Probably mid-ninth to mid-tenth century.

Okasha and Langley (1999), 203–5 & fig.

LAED*E*L[V]FIE |

[14] I am most grateful for permission from Eamonn P. Kelly, Keeper of Irish Antiquities, National Museum of Ireland, and from the excavator, Breandán O Riordáin, to include this unpublished sheath.

The text probably reads: LAEDE L[V]FIE, although the second word could alternatively be L[Y]FIE. The most likely translation is, 'may (you) love (me); may (you) take (me)', which might suggest that the stud is a secular love-token. Alternative interpretations include 'may (you) take (me) in love' and 'may (you) lead (me) to life', texts which could be either religious or secular.[15] The stud is dated on artistic grounds.

224 Kirby Hill[16]

Plate VIII*c*

Built in sideways at the base of the south-west corner of the tower of Kirby Hill parish church, North Yorkshire.

First mentioned 1922, in present *situs*: church tower rebuilt 1870. 100 × 60 × 52 cm. Stone, probably complete, with incomplete and illegible text on visible face. Text is set within panel but probably without framing lines. Language and formula uncertain. Possibly AS capitals. Date uncertain.

(—) (1922), 365; Hassall and Tomlin (1978), no. 6, p. 474

— [*ANR* .] | [— . *CR* .] | [—] | [—] | [—] | [—] | [—] | [—] | [—] | [—] | [— *R*] | [—] | [—] |

The text is now too deteriorated for any part to be legible. Enough remains to show that the panel originally contained thirteen inscribed lines, but only a few letters towards the ends of lines 1, 2 and 11 can now be attempted. Too little remains to be certain what language or script was used. In 1978, however, Hassall and Tomlin reconstructed lines 1, 2, 3, 6, 7 and 8 as: *Divo Antonino [Ma]gn[o] Firmin- ob hon[orem] dd*, where *dd* was expanded to *domus divinae*. This they describe as 'a posthumous dedication to either Antoninus Pius or Caracella, the first such recorded from Roman Britain'.[17] In my view it is not possible to tell whether the text is Anglo-Saxon or Roman. Equally, the size and shape of the stone could belong to either period.

225 Kirkdale II

Plate IX*a*

Kirkdale, North Yorkshire. Now in the Yorkshire Museum, York.

Found July 1996 during excavation at Kirkdale, in Trench II, Context AA, just north of north churchyard wall. Fragments i and ii together, 4.7 × 6.2 × 0.1

[15] See further Okasha and Langley (1999), 203–5.
[16] I am most grateful to Richard Morris for drawing my attention to this stone.
[17] Hassall and Tomlin (1978), 474.

cm. Lead plate, undecorated and incomplete: plate in six fragments, of which fragments i and ii are inscribed and fit together. Incomplete but legible text on face. OE: probably descriptive formula, type a, and maker formula. Insular majuscule. Probably eighth to ninth century.

Rahtz and Watts (1997), 421 & fig.; Watts *et al.* (1997), 52–75, 89 & figs; Rahtz and Watts (1998), 5–6 & figs; Higgitt (1999c) 139; Rahtz (2000), 7 & fig.; Rahtz and Watts (2003), 291, 300, 305

— [.]*E*R[+ ...] | [...]+BA*N*C[...] | [...]*I*S*BR*EFDE*R* —

The text probably reads: —[T]ER [+ ...] + BANC[Y...] [.]IS BREFDE R — and could be expanded to — [T]ER [+ ...] + BANC[YST ...] [þ]IS BREFDE R — , '— coffin. R[—] wrote this —'. The first part of the text appears to refer to a *ban-cyst*, perhaps a form of an unrecorded **ban-cest* meaning 'bone-chest' or 'coffin'; compounds beginning *ban-* and ending *-cest* are quite common. The lost text may have contained the name(s) of one or more people buried, or deposited, in the coffin. The third line of text appears to be the final one since the space below is blank. The letters of this line are smaller than those above, fitting the interpretation of this part of the text as a maker formula. The OE verb *brefan* 'to write' is rare but is recorded.[18] The most comparable AS object is the inscribed lead plate from Flixborough, 193 Flixborough II, which contains a list of personal names. Detailed argument for the dating of Kirkdale II is given in Watts *et al.* (1997), 52–75.

226 Lincoln II[19]

Plate IX*b*

Lost.

Found 1847, in or on stone coffin, in Cathedral Close, either near entrance to Precentor's House or in south-east of Close; kept in Cathedral Library at least until 1965, but lost by 2002. 11 × 11.8 × 0.01 cm. Lead cross with text i on one face, texts ii and iii on other: texts i and iii set along width of cross, upside down with respect to each other; text iii set on either side of, and at right angles to, text ii. Text i legible and set without framing lines; texts ii and iii highly deteriorated, set within panels, text ii in three lines with blank line below, text iii in three lines with two blank lines below. Text i Latin memorial formula; text ii

[18] A full discussion, including a variety of possible interpretations, is given in Watts *et al.* (1997), 52–75.

[19] This text was excluded from the *Hand-List* proper, but was listed in Index III, Index of inscriptions excluded from the *Hand-List*, pp. 149–50. I now accept it as falling within the chronological limits of the *Hand-List*. Unfortunately, since I examined the cross in 1965, it has disappeared and the Cathedral authorities have been unable to locate it.

probably Latin, formula uncertain; text iii Latin, possibly descriptive formula, type c. Text i AS capitals; texts ii and iii insular minuscule. Possibly eleventh or twelfth century.

(—) (1850), xliv & fig.; Wylie (1854), 299–300 & fig.; Hill, J. W. F. (1948), 142–3; Okasha (1971), 149; Hinton and Cunliffe (1979), 139; Jones, S. *et al.* (1987), 4; Okasha (1996b), 68

i: CORPVS:SIFORDI:PRESBITE | RI:SC̄EELENE:7SC̄EM/AR/GARETE | *TI*T*V*LA*T*VS HICIACET |
ii: *CR*[*U*]*NL*[...]*DOMA* | [...] | [...*A* .. ...*TIT*] | [.. *N*] *IT TAI TA*[.] |
[. ...*D* ...] | [*IC.*]*IT NI*[.] *THE*[..] |
iii: *HOC* [.*ON*] *O CUNABULA* [*IT*...] | [...*EC.X*]*PIAT*[...*P*]*R*[.]*CORE*[...] |
[.*OR*...*O.TI*...*HTU.*]

Text i read: CORPVS : SIFORDI : PRESBITERI : SC̄E ELENE : 7 SC̄E MARGARETE TITVLATVS HIC IACET, 'here lies named the body of Siford, priest of St Helen and St Margaret'. SC̄E in both cases is for SANCTAE. SIFORDI might be a form of one of the recorded male names SIGEFRIÐ or SIGEWEARD. DB forms of SIGEFRIÐ include SIUERD and of SIGEWEARD include SIUUARD.[20] DB contains a number of references to one or more people named Siward in Lincoln, including Siward a priest and Siward a lawman and priest.[21] Several spellings of the name are used, including *Seuard*, *Seuuard*, *Siuard* and *Siuuard*, although the forms with *i* are more frequent. It is possible, but by no means certain, that Siford the priest is to be identified with one of these men.

Text ii, when examined in 1965, was too illegible for a meaningful text to be reconstructed. About nine letters were lost from the first lacuna, twelve from the second, four from the third, eleven from the fourth and eight each from the fifth and sixth. Text iii, although also highly deteriorated, appeared to contain parts that could be reconstructed. The first word was probably HOC 'this' and the third CUNABULA 'from childhood'. About eight letters are lost from each of the first two lacunas, after which [EX]PIAT 'atones for' seems likely. The next lacuna contained about four letters after which there might have been a form of PRECOR 'I pray'. The last three lacunas contained about three, eight and four letters and too little remains from this part for any reconstruction. In 1850 this side was described as 'now illegible'.[22]

The cross was found inside the Cathedral Close, in association with a stone coffin. The earliest reference states that it was found 'in a stone coffin, on the S.E. side of the Minster Close'.[23] However the notice which was attached to the cross in 1965 stated that it was found on the lid of a stone coffin near the

[20] Feilitzen (1937), 360–3.
[21] See, for example, Morgan and Thorn (1986), C2, folio 336a; and 68: 38, 42, 46, all folio 371b.
[22] (—) (1850), xliv. [23] (—) (1850), xliv.

entrance to Precentor's House: the Precentor's House is on the south-west side of the Close. Inside the Close, to the south-east of the Cathedral, there was, until its demolition *c* 1780, a church dedicated to St Margaret.[24] This church, known as St Margaret in Pottergate or St Margaret in the Close, apparently contained a tower of Norman date.[25] There is no evidence that the church had a dual dedication, to St Helen as well as to St Margaret, but nevertheless it seems likely that Siford the priest is to be associated with this church. What can be read or reconstructed of the texts on the cross is perfectly in accordance with its identification as a coffin cross. For other lead crosses, see the list above under 213 Bury St Edmunds II. The Lincoln cross is tentatively dated by comparison with these and on the evidence of the script used.

227 London V

Plate IX*c*

Now in the care of Pre-Construct Archaeology Ltd, Brockley, London.

Found 1995 in rubbish pit, during excavation at 33–7 Exeter Street, London. Diam. of base 2.3 cm. Fossilized echinoid (sea-urchin), probably amulet. Rather deteriorated text, probably primary and complete, set without framing lines but within panels formed by fossilization marks, on outside of echinoid. Language and formula uncertain. AS capitals. Eighth century.

Farid and Brown (1997), 150, 152; Holder (1999), 85–6, 92–3; Brown *et al.* (2001), 204, 206–10 & figs; Notton (2002), 107–10

E | EB | [..] |

The first of the two uncertain letters could be N or U, followed by A or R; these two letters are set one above the other and ligatured. The text could then read EEB[UR] or one of the other alternatives. EEB[UR] could possibly be a spelling of OE EOFOR 'boar', as in *eburðring* for *eofor-þring* 'Orion' in the Corpus Glossary.[26] Such a word might be appropriate for a magical text, if the echinoid were indeed an amulet. Alternatively, the text could consist of a meaningless sequence, either as a magical text or as practice letters.[27] The echinoid is dated on archaeological evidence. An alternative suggestion, that the marks interpreted as letters are not such but are naturally formed grooves, is put forward by Notton.[28]

24 Jones, S. *et al.* (1987), 4–5.

25 See the reproduction of a painting of the church prior to its demolition in Hill, J. W. F. (1948), plate 11, opp. p. 161. I am most grateful to David Stocker for providing me with this and other references to Lincoln churches.

26 Sweet (1885), p. 83, line 1464.

27 For further discussion see Brown *et al.* (2001), 206–10.

28 Notton (2002), 107–10.

228 Marcham

No illustration exists

Marcham, Berkshire. Lost.[29]

Found 1837, built into wall of old church at its rebuilding. Dimensions unknown.[30] Stone, probably incomplete, with incomplete but legible text set on face. Uncertain whether or not text: was incised; contained framing lines; was primary. Probably OE, possibly personal name. Probably AS capitals. Date uncertain.

Ingram (1838), 18–21

The text may be reconstructed:
+ÆLEGY[...] | +ÆLEGY[...] | —

The stone apparently contained two lines of text and might have been broken; Ingram suggested that a third line might have been broken off by workmen. The text was probably incomplete and read: + ÆLEGY[...] + ÆLEGY[...] —. Ingram suggested that the initial cross represented the letter H and that the text was to be translated as 'Holy, Holy; or Saints, Saints';[31] this suggests that he took ÆLEGY as a form of OE HALIG or HALGAN. It is more likely, however, that the text represented an incomplete personal name. The first element ÆLE- could be a late spelling of OE ÆÞEL- or ÆLF-; Ingram could indeed have misread ÆLF- as ÆLE- . The second element could be an incomplete form of the element -GYÞ; both ÆÞELGYÞ and ÆLFGYÞ are recorded OE feminine names. The repetition of a personal name occurs elsewhere; see, for example, 118 Wallingford II and 198 London IV.

229 Nassington

Plate X*a*

Nassington, Northamptonshire. Now in private possession.

Found 1992 in residual context, in late AS pit, during excavation at Prebendal Manor, Nassington. 0.9 × 2.7 × 0.2 cm. Comb of pig-bone, fragmentary, with incomplete text set without framing lines on one face; text may be primary but is highly deteriorated. Possibly OE text, formula uncertain. Insular minuscule. Possibly ninth or tenth century.

[29] I am most grateful to Nicholas Rogers, Sydney Sussex College, Cambridge, for bringing this stone to my attention.

[30] The description etc., is taken from Ingram (1838), 18–21.

[31] Ingram (1838), 18.

Okasha (1999b), 203–5 & fig.

— [. . .]EHIR/[.] —

The text reads: — [...]EHIR[.] —. The first fragmentary letter cannot be recovered, although it appears to have been ligatured to the second, which could have been D or E. The third letter might have been H, and the last was possibly E, ligatured to the preceding R. The letter H, since it appears between vowels, is likely to be the beginning of a word. The text might then read: — [.E H]E HIR[E] — or — [. DN]E HIR[E]. The first alternative could contain OE [H]E 'he', and HIR[E] 'her' or HIR[E-] as a spelling of the common name-element HERE-. The second alternative could contain [DN]E, a common abbreviation for DOMINE 'O Lord'. Such a text could have commended a maker or owner of the comb to God. However, it is also possible that the text simply consists of practice letters, perhaps incised after the comb was broken.[32] The comb must pre-date the late-tenth-century context in which it was found, but such combs were used in both the middle and late AS periods.

230 North Petherton

Plate X*b*

Combe St Nicholas, North Petherton, Somerset. Now in private possession.

Found 2000, in parish of Combe St Nicholas, near North Petherton, by metal-detector.[33] 0.9 × 74 × 0.3 cm. Copper alloy strip, decorated but in two pieces and broken at wide end; function uncertain. Text i on one face, text ii on other, both reading from broken to complete end, thus upside down with respect to each other; both texts legible but incomplete. OE, probably descriptive formulae, type a. AS capitals. Late eleventh or early twelfth century.

Unpublished

i: — [*E*]AHAHEHI*N*E |
ii: — [*T*]ENNABBE S*E*ME |

Text i reads: — [E] AH A HE HINE, '— he will always possess it', with HINE referring to an object that is grammatically masculine. Text ii reads: — [T]EN NABBE SE ME, '— he who may not own me', where NABBE is a late spelling of NAEBBE, present subjunctive singular of the negative form of HABBAN 'to have, own, look after' etc. The ending —[T]EN could be the inflexion of a strong past

32 For a full discussion, see Okasha (1999b), 203–5.

33 This find was reported to the Finds Liaison Officer for Somerset and Dorset under the Portable Antiquities Scheme.

participle or a late spelling of an adjectival or adverbial ending -AN. It is not clear how much text is lost and the whole cannot therefore be reconstructed. It could have been of the form: '[This belongs to X and] he will always possess it. [May God curse the loser], he who may not look after me, *or* [May God curse the taker], he who may not own me.' Such putative curses occur in some Anglo-Saxon wills and charters and on 114 Sutton. The strip is dated on artistic grounds.

231 Oxted

Plate X*c*

Oxted, Surrey. Now in the British Museum, no. MLA 1993.10–1.1.

Found March 1992 by metal-detector, isolated find from field at Limpsfield Grange, near Oxted. Diam. 0.89 cm. Gold disc, decorated and with legible text set without framing lines beside decoration on face; letters gold on niello. Latin descriptive formula, type b. One capital and one Insular letter. Ninth century.

Hunt (1993), 42 & fig.; Okasha and Youngs (1996), 63–8 & figs; Holder (1999), 84

AQ̄

The text reads: AQ̄. This is presumably an abbreviation for the Latin AQUILA 'eagle', describing the bird depicted alongside, the eagle being the symbol of the evangelist St John. The disc is likely to have been one of a set of evangelists' symbols on discs which would have originally been fastened on to some larger piece of decorative work. The disc is dated on artistic grounds.

232 Postwick

Plate XI*a*

Postwick, Norfolk. Now in Norwich Castle Museum, no. NWCHM:2000.42.

Found March 1998 by metal-detector, in field at Postwick, 6 km east of Norwich. Diam. 0.16 cm. Swivelling bezel from seal-ring, ring not found; bezel of gold and decorated. Circular text set right round face, surrounding human bust; text legible and set clockwise without framing lines, letters laterally displaced and facing outwards. Personal name. Capitals. Seventh century.

Geake *et al.* (2000), 509–10 & fig.

+BALDE HILDIS |

The text reads: + BALDEHILDIS, with the first D and the S reversed. The text consists of a female personal name, possibly in a Latinized genitive singular form, thus meaning 'of Baldhild'. A Latinized genitive singular name form ending in *-is* would be unusual in an AS text: vernacular personal names in AS texts, whether OE or Latin, are invariably latinized as first- or second-declension nouns, not third-declension nouns. If the Postwick name is Merovingian, the *-is* ending may not be genitive, since Merovingian female names can end in *-is* or *-a* in the nominative, or have no ending.[34] Both name-elements are recorded in OE, although *bald-*, *beald-* is rare and is not otherwise recorded in the form **balde-*. The name itself is recorded by Bede as that of a seventh-century Frankish queen.[35]

The text resembles most other AS seal texts in being circular and retrograde.[36] However, all the other circular texts are set anti-clockwise, with the letters facing inwards, and the majority utilize a formula including the word *sigillum* 'seal'. In these ways, the Postwick text is clearly different. These differences, along with the *-is* ending on the name, might suggest that the Postwick seal-ring was of Merovingian manufacture. Alternatively, if it was made in Anglo-Saxon England, the differences might be explicable in terms of Merovingian influence on the name and of chronological difference. The Postwick ring is dated to the seventh century on the evidence of its decoration and gold content, while all the other AS seal-dies date from the eighth century onwards, the majority from the tenth century onwards.

233 Sleaford

Plate XI*b*

Near Sleaford, Lincolnshire. Location unknown, probably in private possession.

Found May 1992 by metal-detector near Sleaford. Diam. *c.* 2.2 cm. Ring of gilded silver, with legible text incised in two lines right round exterior of hoop.[37] Latin descriptive formula, type a, and OE personal name. AS capitals. Date uncertain.

Ulmschneider (2000b), 61, 131

+ANULUMFIDEI | +EADBERHT |

The text reads: + ANULUM FIDEI + EADBERHT, '+ ring of faith + Eadberht'. ANULUM is an error for ANULUS, perhaps because the composer of the text

[34] See, for example, Förstemann (1966), cols. 693–4, 818–20.
[35] *Historia ecclesiastica* V.19: Bede (1969), 520–1.
[36] They are: 38 Eye; 103 Rome I; 117 Wallingford I; 119 Weeke; 176 Sittingbourne II; 177 Totnes; 184 York IX; 187 Chester; 191 Evesham; 197 Lincoln III; 238 Witney.
[37] I have not examined the ring. The description and text are taken from a drawing made by Jim Patterson in Scunthorpe Museums in June 1992.

knew the phrase in a context demanding ANULUM in the accusative. The phrase *anulum fidei* occurs occasionally in this form, for example in the context of spiritual marriage. The word ANULUM presumably refers to the actual ring although no other AS inscribed ring uses this word. FIDEI might refer to religious faith or to secular faith; in the latter case the ring could have been a pledge of faith between two people. EADBERHT is a form of the recorded masculine name EADBEORHT.

234 Weasenham

Plate XI*c*

Weasenham, Norfolk. Now in Norwich Castle Museum, no. NWCHM 2000.3.

Found 1998, isolated metal-detector find from near Weasenham All Saints. 2.3 × 1.5 × 0.1 cm. Lead pendant, surfaces covered with modern sealant; sub-rectangular in shape with projecting tab for suspension; decorated. Rather deteriorated text set inside panel on back; text reads horizontally from narrow to wide end of pendant, i.e. at right-angles to suspension tab. Latin descriptive formula, probably type b. Insular majuscule. Probably tenth to twelfth century.

Okasha and Youngs (2003), 225–30 & figs.

+*N*OMEN | DEI*I*ST*I*[*N*] | *E*/B*R*AICE*E* | [...]*NE*/[.][*T.*] | *E*/*T*[*.T..NO.*] |

The last two lines of text are not now legible but the first three read: + NOMEN DEI IST I[N] EBRAICE E —. This is probably to be translated, '+ this name of God in Hebrew —', where IST is an abbreviated form of ISTUD, 'this, that'. The face of the pendant contains a roughly executed crucifixion scene formed of incised lines. The pendant may have been a protective amulet worn by a member of the religious, or a funerary object. It is dated on the grounds of iconography and script.

235 West Kirby I

Plate XI*d*

West Kirby, Merseyside (Cheshire). Lost.

First mentioned 1888, in 'hearse house' near West Kirby church.[38] 30 × 18 cm. Stone; incomplete, white sandstone, with incomplete, rather deteriorated text on face; text possibly within panel but without framing-lines. Language and formula uncertain. Capitals. Date uncertain.

[38] Watkin, W. T. (1888), 182, from which the description etc. is also taken.

V*a* 212 Bawburgh

V*b* 213 Bury St Edmunds II

V*c* 214 Bury St Edmunds III

VI*a* 215 Bury St Edmunds IV

VI*b* 217 Bury St Edmunds VI

VI*c* 218 Castlesteads

VII*b* 220 Cumberworth

VII*a* 219 Chichester

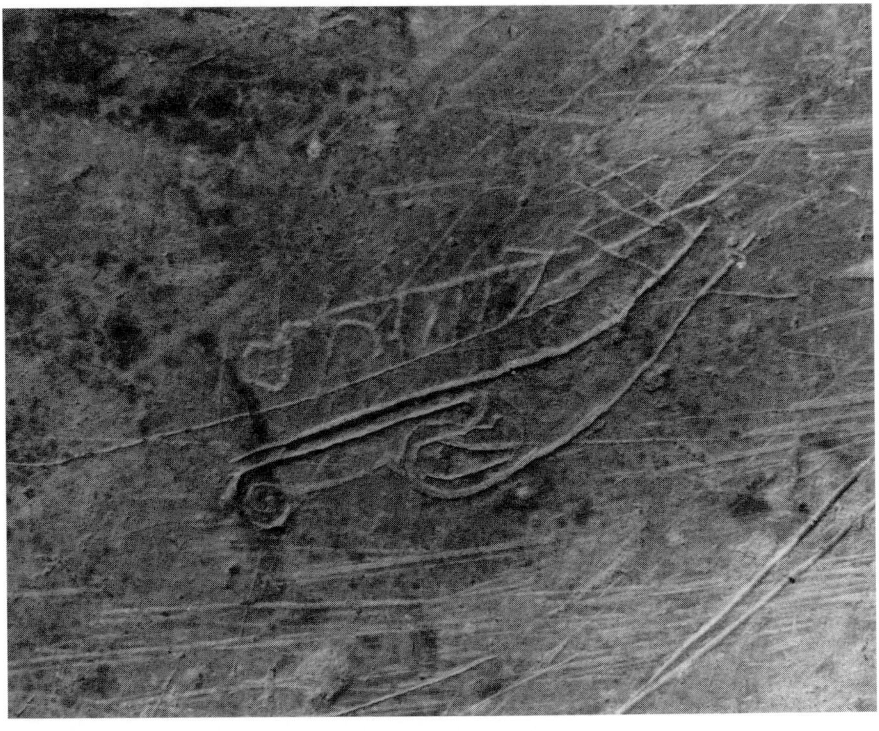

VII*c* 221 Deer Park Farms

VIII*a* 222 Dublin VI

VIII*b* 223 Egginton

VIII*c* 224 Kirby Hill

IX*a* 225 Kirkdale II

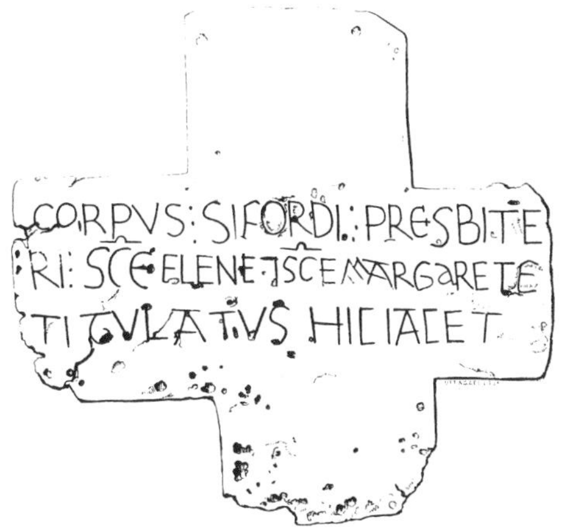

IX*b* 226 Lincoln II

IX*c* 227 London V

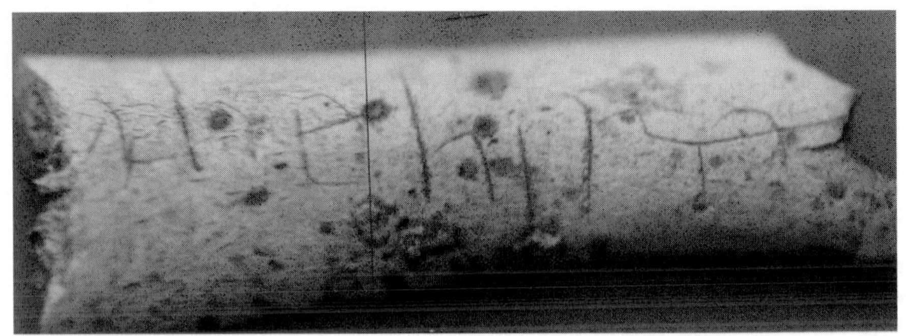

X*a* 229 Nassington

X*b* 230 North Petherton

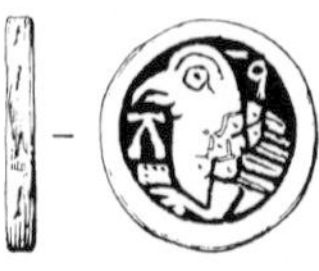

0 1cm.

X*c* 231 Oxted

XI*a* 232 Postwick

XI*b* 233 Sleaford

XI*c* 234 Weasenham

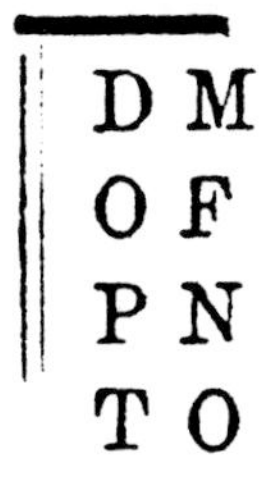

XI*d* 235 West Kirby I

XII*a* 237 Whitby XV

XII*b* 238 Witney

XII*c* 239 Worcester

XII*d* 240 'in deo' ring

Watkin, W. T. (1888), 182 & fig.; Haverfield (1892), no. 915*a*, p. 296; Haverfield (1913), 554; Collingwood, R. G. and Wright, R. P. (1965), no. 2369*, p. 743 & fig.

DM[...] | *OF*[...] | *P*[*N*...] | *TO* —

The text may have read: DM[...]OF[...]P[N...]TO — ; it cannot now be interpreted. Watkin, who took the stone to be Roman and the text in rustic capitals, suggested that DM was the usual RB abbreviation for *diis manibus*. However, Haverfield, who examined the stone before it was lost, considered it to be post-Roman.

236 West Kirby II

No illustration exists

West Kirby, Merseyside (Cheshire). Lost.

First mentioned 1888, in 'hearse house' near West Kirby church.[39] 24 × 30 cm. Stone; incomplete, red sandstone, with incomplete, highly deteriorated text on face; uncertain whether text was primary and had framing lines or panels. Language and formula uncertain. Capitals. Date uncertain.

Watkin, W. T. (1888), 182; Haverfield (1892), no. 915*b*, p. 296; Haverfield (1913), 554; Collingwood, R. G. and Wright, R. P. (1965), no. 2386*, p. 747

[*LEG*] —

The text may have read [LEG] —, although Watkin suggested as an alternative [GIO] —. The text cannot now be interpreted. Watkin considered the stone to be Roman, describing the first letter as 'rustically formed'. However, Haverfield, who examined the stone before it was lost, considered it to be post-Roman.

237 Whitby XV

Plate XII*a*

Whitby, North Yorkshire. Owned by Scarborough Borough Council, now kept in Cholmley House Interpretation Centre, Whitby Abbey.

Found July 2001 during excavation on Whitby headland, site code 490, trench Q31, context 30790. 7.6 × 7 × 5.8 cm. Stone; incomplete carved sandstone forming top arm of cross, with incomplete text on face. Text is legible and is set within panel but without framing-lines. Latin memorial formula. AS capitals. Eighth to ninth century.

[39] Watkin, W. T. (1888), 182, from which the description etc. is also taken.

Cramp (2001), 302–3 & figs; Higgitt (2001b), 302–3; Higgitt (2001c) 51n; Allfrey (2002), 5 & fig.

*O*R | ATE | P*R*[*O*] —

The text reads: ORATE PR[O] —, 'pray for —' and no doubt was originally followed by the personal name of the deceased. The most similar inscribed cross-arm is 24 Carlisle II, although it is on a less dainty scale. It too lacks an initial cross in the text, which is otherwise usual in such texts. The Whitby stone is dated on artistic evidence.

238 Witney

Plate XII*b*

Witney, Oxfordshire. Now in the Ashmolean Museum, Oxford, no. 1939.463.

Found 1939 in drainage trench in High Street, *c.* 45 cm beneath ground. 4.5 × 4.2 × 0.6 cm. Seal-die of walrus ivory, decorated and with rather deteriorated text set without framing lines right round face of die; letters are laterally displaced, face inwards and read anti-clockwise. Latin descriptive formula, type a. AS capitals. Probably late eleventh or twelfth century.

(—) (1939a), 18 & fig.; MacGregor (1985), 127 & figs

+[*S*]IGILL*V*M *ROB*[*ER .I*]:DE*FO*[. *AN*]ETO |

The text reads: +[S]IGILLVM ROB[ERTI] : DE FO[..AN]ETO. The missing letters have been read as [NT], a reading which fits the remaining traces. The text can then be interpreted, '+ the seal of Rob[ert] of Fo[ntan]et'. *Fontanet* is a modern French surname and as a place-name was the site of the battle of Fontanet in AD 871, probably the modern Fontenoy near Auxerre. Similar place-names are the modern Fontenay, north of La Rochelle, and Fontenoy, near Tournai, Belgium. ROBERT is a common name in the eleventh and twelfth centuries and this Robert cannot be identified. The figure in the centre of the die has been identified as Sagittarius.[40]

239 Worcester[41]

Plate XII*c*

Worcester. At present in the care of Worcestershire Archaeological Service, ref. no. HWCM 3899.

[40] MacGregor (1985), 127.

[41] I am most grateful for permission to include the cross in advance of the forthcoming publication of the site.

Found 1988, residual find in medieval context, found during excavation at Deansway, Worcester; site code 3899, context 12011. 5.2 × 2.8 × 0.05 cm. Lead cross, virtually complete, with highly deteriorated text incised without framing lines on one face; text reads clockwise from bottom, one line per cross-arm, with letters facing centre of cross. Latin, probably descriptive formula, type c. AS capitals with insular forms. Date uncertain, possibly eleventh or twelfth century.

Okasha (1996b), 68

*S*E/NTIO | *A*/EL/F[.*INE*] | [*A*]R[*T*...] | FVID[:] |

The text probably reads: SENTIO AELF[ƿINE] [A]R[T —] FVID. This might be interpreted as, 'I perceive (*or* think of) Aelf[ƿine] (who) was a [craftsman]', where FVID is for FUIT and a connective, possibly QVI 'who', is supplied; [A]R[TIFEX] 'craftsman' is a possibility for the word beginning [A]R[T —], a word used on 85 Little Billing, a stone font. AELFWINE is a well-recorded OE masculine name. An alternative reading of the second line is AELF [DNI], possibly followed by an abbreviation symbol for QVI. The whole could then be, 'I perceive (*or* think of) Aelf [who] was a [craftsman] of God', with DNI the common abbreviation for DOMINI. However, although recorded, the name AELF is rare and this alternative is less likely. For other lead crosses, see the list under 213 Bury St Edmunds II. All of these are probably funerary crosses; none, however, is exactly the same shape as the Worcester cross, and all are considerably larger.

240 'in deo' ring

Plate XII*d*

Provenance unknown. Now in private possession.

Found pre 1991, location and circumstances unknown; sold at Christies 12 April 2000 to private buyer. Diam. 1.6 cm. Octagonal ring of gold, with legible text incised without framing lines right round outside of hoop.[42] Latin, descriptive formula, type c. AS capitals with insular forms. Probably late eleventh to early twelfth century.

Eisenberg (2000), 33 & fig.

IND | ŌBT̄ | D̄SI | NAI | *T̄*UM*L̄* | M̄INĪ | DĒLI | LIOS̄: |

The text, which is heavily abbreviated, reads: IN DŌ BT̄ D̄S IN AIT̄UM L̄M̄IN Ī DĒ LILIOS̄ :. The abbreviations appear to be: DŌ = DEO; BT̄ = BEATUS; D̄S = DEUS;

[42] I have not examined the ring. The description and text are taken from photographs.

AITUM = AITERNUM (for AETERNUM); LMIN = LUMINE; I = IN; DE = DEI; and LILIOS = LILIOSUS. This could perhaps be translated: 'in God, O God blessed eternally, pure in the light of God', although there are some peculiarities of syntax and the meaning is less than transparent. The ring is dated on artistic grounds, a dating supported by the script and the large quantity of abbreviation used.

BIBLIOGRAPHY

This Bibliography gives in full the references quoted in abbreviated form in this Supplement, unless they were included in the General Bibliography of the *Hand-List* or of the first two supplements.

J. S. Alexander, 'The Use of Masons' Marks and Construction Instructions in Medieval Buildings', *Roman, Runes and Ogham: Medieval Inscriptions in the Insular World and on the Continent*, ed. J. Higgitt *et al.* (Donington, 2001), pp. 211–22

M. Allfrey, 'Archaeological Finds at Whitby Abbey', in J. Goodall, *Whitby Abbey* (London, 2002), p. 5

J. R. Allen, in *Proc. Soc. Ant. London*, 2nd ser. 19 (1902–3), 87–95

T. Allen *et al.*, *The History of the County of Lincoln, from the Earliest Period to the Present Time*, 2 vols. (London and Lincoln, 1834)

T. Astle, 'Observations on Stone Pillars, Crosses, and Crucifixes', *Archaeologia* 13 (1800), 208–22

R. N. Bailey, 'The Ruthwell Cross: a Non-Problem', *AntJ* 73 (1993), 141–8

R. N. Bailey, '"What Mean These Stones?" Some Aspects of pre-Norman Sculpture in Cheshire and Lancashire', *Bull. of the John Rylands Univ. Lib. of Manchester* 78(i) (1996a), 21–46

R. N. Bailey, *Ambiguous Birds and Beasts: Three Sculptural Puzzles in South-West Scotland.* Fourth Whithorn Lecture (Whithorn, 1996b)

R. N. Bailey, *England's Earliest Sculptors* (Toronto, 1996c)

E. E. Barker, 'The Successors of Bishop Stigand', *Sussex N & Q* 10 (1944–5), 163–4

M. P. Barnes, 'Aspects of the Scandinavian Runes of the British Isles', *Roman, Runes and Ogham: Medieval Inscriptions in the Insular World and on the Continent*, ed. J. Higgitt *et al.* (Donington, 2001), pp. 103–11

P. S. Barnwell *et al.*, 'The Confusion of Conversion: *Streanæshalch*, Strensall and Whitby and the Northumbrian Church', *The Cross Goes North. Processes of Conversion in Northern Europe, AD 300–1300*, ed. M. O. H. Carver (York, 2003), pp. 311–26

J. Bayley *et al.*, 'A Tenth-Century Bell-Pit and Bell-Mould from St Oswald's Priory, Gloucester', *MA* 37 (1993), 224–36

G. Benson, *York from its Origin to the End of the Eleventh Century* (York, 1911)

M. Biddle *et al.*, *Object and Economy in Medieval Winchester.* Winchester Stud. 7 (ii) (Oxford, 1990)

P. B. G. Binnall, *Caistor Lincolnshire,* rev. ed. (Gloucester, 1960)

J. Blair, 'Anglo-Saxon Minsters: a Topographical Review', *Pastoral Care Before the Parish*, ed. J. Blair and R. Sharpe (Leicester, 1992), pp. 226–66

R. M. Bradfield, *The Newent Carved Stones Unravell'd* (Newent, 1999)

S. A. J. Bradley, *Orm Gamalson's Sundial. The Lily's Blossom and the Roses' Fragrance*. The 1997 Kirkdale Lecture (Kirkdale, 2002)

R. R. Brash, 'The Camp, or Glenfais, Ogham-inscribed Stone', *Jnl. R. Soc. Ant. of Ireland* 13 (1874–5), 320–2

T. A. Bredehoft, 'A New Reading of the Lancashire Ring', *ELN* 32.4 (1995), 1–8

T. A. Bredehoft, 'First-Person Inscriptions and Literacy in Anglo-Saxon England', *ASSAH* 9 (1996), 103–10

J. Britton, 'An Essay towards a History and Description of Ancient Stone Crosses', in J. Britton, *The Architectural Antiquities of Great Britain* I (London, 1807)

E. P. L. Brock, 'Christianity in Britain in Roman Times', *AC* 15 (1883), 38–58

C. N. L. Brooke and G. Keir, *London 800–1216: the Shaping of a City* (London, 1975)

G. Brown *et al.*, 'A Middle-Saxon Runic Inscriptions [*sic*] from the National Portrait Gallery and an Inscribed Fossilised Echinoid from Exeter Street, London', *MA* 45 (2001), 203–10

G. B. Brown, 'The Statistics of Saxon Churches', *Builder* (20 Oct. 1900), 335–8

M. P. Brown, in *The Making of England: Anglo-Saxon Art and Culture AD 600–900*, ed. L. E. Webster and J. Backhouse (London, 1991)

G. F. Browne, '"Scandinavian" or "Danish" Sculptured Stones found in London …', *ArchJ* 42 (1885), 251–9

G. Butterworth, 'A Saxon House at Deerhurst', *Walford's Antiquarian* 9 [49] (1886), 46–8

M. Campbell, 'Gold, Silver and Precious Stones', *English Medieval Industries: Craftsmen, Techniques, Products*, ed. J. Blair and N. Ramsay (London, 1991), pp. 107–66

R. Cant, 'The Minster', *The Noble City of York*, ed. A. Stacpoole *et al.* (York, 1972), pp. 23–66

R. D. Carr *et al.*, 'The Middle-Saxon settlement at Staunch Meadow, Brandon', *Antiquity* 62 (1988), 371–7

E. Cartwright, in 'Antiquarian Researches', *Gents. Mag.* 100 (1830), 447

E. Cartwright, 'Discovery of a Plate commemorating Geoffrey Bishop of Chichester, A. D. 1088', in 'Appendix', *Archaeologia* 23 (1831), 419–20

M. O. H. Carver, 'Exploring, Explaining, Imagining: Anglo-Saxon Archaeology 1998', *The Archaeology of Anglo-Saxon England: Basic Readings*, ed. C. E. Karkov (New York, 1999), pp. 25–52

B. Cassidy, 'The Later Life of the Ruthwell Cross: from the Seventeenth Century to the Present', *The Ruthwell Cross*, ed. B. Cassidy, Index of Christian Art Occasional Papers 1 (Princeton, 1992), 3–34

B. Cassidy and D. Howlett, 'Some Eighteenth-Century Drawings of the Ruthwell Cross', *AntJ* 72 (1992), 102–17

B. Cassidy and K. Kiefer, 'A Bibliography of the Ruthwell Cross', *The Ruthwell Cross*, ed. B. Cassidy, Index of Christian Art Occasional Papers 1 (Princeton, 1992), 167–99

S. Cather *et al.*, 'Introduction', *Early Medieval Wall Painting and Painted Sculpture in England*, ed. S. Cather *et al.*, BAR Brit. Ser. 216 (Oxford, 1990), iii–xxii

T. O. Clancy, 'The Drosten Stone: a New Reading', *Proc. Soc. Ant. Scotland* 123 (1993), 345–53

A. W. Clapham, in 'Proceedings at Meetings [19/7/1929]', *ArchJ* 86 (1929), 279–80

J. Clark, 'London's King Alfred', *Minerva* 10.6 (1999), 18–21

E. Coatsworth, 'The "Robed Christ" in pre-Conquest Sculptures of the Crucifixion', *ASE* 29 (2000), 153–76

G. Cobb, *London City Churches*, rev. N. Redman (London, 1989)

R. G. Collingwood, 'Castlesteads', *TCWAAS* n.s. 22 (1922), 198–233

M. Covert, 'An Exciting Find', *Friends of Rochester Cathedral: Report for 1988* (Rochester, 1989), pp. 10–11

J. C. Cox, rev. A. H. Thompson, *Lincolnshire*, 2nd ed. (London, 1924)

J. C. Cox, *The Little Guides: Hampshire*, rev. R. L. P. Jowitt (London, 1949)

D. J. Craig, in *Corpus of Anglo-Saxon Stone Sculpture*, VI. *Northern Yorkshire,* ed. J. T. Lang *et al.* (Oxford, 2001)

R. J. Cramp, 'A Reconsideration of the Monastic Site of Whitby', *The Age of Migrating Ideas. Early Medieval Art in Northern Britain and Ireland,* ed. R. M. Spearman and J. Higgitt (Edinburgh, 1993), pp. 64–73

R. J. Cramp, 'The Northumbrian Identity', *Northumbria's Golden Age*, ed. J. Hawkes and S. Mills (Stroud, 1999), pp. 1–11

R. J. Cramp, in *Corpus of Anglo-Saxon Stone Sculpture*, VI. *Northern Yorkshire,* ed. J. T. Lang *et al.* (Oxford, 2001)

C. Crocker, *A Visit to Chichester Cathedral,* 2nd ed. (Chichester, 1849)

J. Crowley, 'Sundials in North Devon', *Report & Trans. Devon Assoc.* 89 (1956), 175–91

R. Dally, *The Chichester Guide* (Chichester, 1831)

R. Daniels, 'The Anglo-Saxon Monastery at Hartlepool, England', *Northumbria's Golden Age*, ed. J. Hawkes and S. Mills (Stroud, 1999), pp. 105–12

R. M. Davies and P. J. Ovenden, 'Bell-Founding in Winchester in the Tenth to Thirteenth Centuries', in M. Biddle *et al.*, *Object and Economy in Medieval Winchester.* Winchester Stud. 7 (ii) (Oxford, 1990), 100–22

W. Davies, *Wales in the Early Middle Ages* (Leicester, 1982)

M. Dockray-Miller, *Motherhood and Mothering in Anglo-Saxon England* (Basingstoke and London 2000)

M. Dolley and M. Mays, 'Nummular Brooches', in M. Biddle *et al.*, *Object and Economy in Medieval Winchester*, Winchester Stud. 7 (ii) (Oxford, 1990), 632–5

T. Eaton, *Plundering the Past. Roman Stonework in Medieval Britain* (Stroud, 2000)

N. Edwards, 'Monuments in a Landscape: the Early Medieval Sculpture of St David's', *Image and Power in the Archaeology of Early Medieval Britain. Essays in honour of Rosemary Cramp*, ed. H. Hamerow and A. MacGregor (Oxford, 2001), pp. 78–130

W. Edwards, *The Early History of the North Riding* (London, 1924)

H. Eichner, 'Zu Franks Casket/RuneAuzon (Vortragskurzfassung)', *Old English Runes and their Continental Background,* ed. A. Bammesberger (Heidelberg, 1991), pp. 603–28

J. M. Eisenberg, 'Spring 2000 Antiquities Sales: 21st Biannual Report', *Minerva* 11.5 (2000), 28–37

P. Everson and D. Stocker, *Corpus of Anglo-Saxon Stone Sculpture*, V. *Lincolnshire* (London and Oxford, 1999)

S. Farid and G. Brown, 'A Butchery Site in *Lundenwic*', *London Archaeologist* 8 (1997), 147–52

C. Farr, 'Questioning the Monuments: Approaches to Anglo-Saxon Sculpture through Gender Studies', *The Archaeology of Anglo-Saxon England: Basic Readings*, ed. C. E. Karkov (New York, 1999), pp. 375–402

R. T. Farrell and C. E. Karkov, 'The Construction, Deconstruction, and Reconstruction of the Ruthwell Cross: Some Caveats', *The Ruthwell Cross*, ed. B. Cassidy, Index of Christian Art Occasional Papers 1 (Princetown, 1992), 35–47

C. E. Fell *et al.*, *Women in Anglo-Saxon England and the Impact of 1066* (Oxford, 1984)

C. E. Fell, 'Runes and Semantics', *Old English Runes and their Continental Background*, ed. A. Bammesberger (Heidelberg, 1991), pp. 195–229

C. E. Fell, 'Anglo-Saxon England: a Three-Script Community?', *Proceedings of the Third International Symposium on Runes and Runic Inscriptions, Grindaheim, Norway, 8–12 August 1990*, ed. J. E. Knirk (Uppsala, 1994), pp. 119–37

C. E. Fell, 'Runes and Riddles in Anglo-Saxon England', *'Lastworda betst': Essays in Memory of Christine E. Fell with her Unpublished Writings*, ed. C. Hough and K. A. Lowe (Donington, 2002), pp. 264–77

G. Fellows Jensen, *Scandinavian Personal Names in Lincolnshire and Yorkshire* (Copenhagen, 1968)

G. Fellows Jensen, 'Of Danes – and Thanes – and Domesday Book', *People and Places in Northern Europe 500–1600*, ed. I. Wood and N. Lund (Woodbridge, 1991), pp. 107–21

E. Fernie, *The Architecture of the Anglo-Saxons* (London, 1982)

S. Foot, '"By Water in the Spirit": the Administration of Baptism in early Anglo-Saxon England', *Pastoral Care Before the Parish*, ed. J. Blair and R. Sharpe (Leicester, 1992), pp. 171–92

E. W. Förstemann, *Altdeutsches Namenbuch* I. *Personennamen* (Bonn, 1900; repr. 1966)

R. Gameson and F. Gameson, 'The Anglo-Saxon Inscription at St Mary's Church, Breamore, Hampshire', *ASSAH* 6 (1993), 1–10

M. Gardiner, 'The Excavation of a late Anglo-Saxon Settlement at Market Field, Steyning, 1988–89', *Sussex Archaeol. Collections* 131 (1998), 21–67

A. Gardner, *English Medieval Sculpture* (Cambridge, 1951)

H. Geake *et al.*, 'Medieval Seal Matrices from Norfolk, 1999', *Norfolk Archaeol.* 43 (2000), 508–12

E. A. Gee, 'The Architecture of York', *The Noble City of York*, ed. A. Stacpoole *et al.* (York, 1972), pp. 337–408

J. Goodall, *Whitby Abbey* (London, 2002)

K. Gosling, 'Recent Finds from London', *Old English Runes and their Continental Background*, ed. A. Bammesberger (Heidelberg, 1991), pp. 191–4

K. Gosling, 'Runic Finds from London', *Nytt om Runer* 4 (1989), 12–13

C. Haith, in *The Golden Age of Anglo-Saxon Art 966–1066*, ed. J. Backhouse *et al.* (London, 1984)

R. A. Hall, 'St Mary's Church, Castlegate: Observations and Discoveries', *St Mary Bishophill Junior and St Mary Castlegate. Anglo-Scandinavian York*, ed. L. P. Wenham *et al.*, The Archaeol. of York 8 (ii) (York, 1987), 147–54

W. Hamper, *Observations on Certain Ancient Pillars of Memorial, called Hoar-Stones; to which is added, A Conjecture on the Croyland Inscription* (Birmingham, 1820)

P. Harbison, *The High Crosses of Ireland: an Iconographical and Photographic Survey*. Römisch-Germanisches Zentralmuseum Forschunginstitut für Vor- und Frühgeschichte: Monographien 17 (Dublin and Bonn, 1992)

P. Harbison, *Ancient Irish Monuments* (Dublin, 1997)

M. Hare, 'Cnut and Lotharingia: Two Notes', *ASE* 29 (2000), 261–78

P. D. A. Harvey and A. McGuinness, *A Guide to British Medieval Seals* (London, 1996)

M. W. C. Hassall and R. S. O. Tomlin, 'Roman Britain in 1977. II. Inscriptions', *Britannia* 9 (1978), 473–85

F. J. Haverfield, 'Additamenta quarta ad corporis vol. VII', *Ephemeris Epigraphica* 7 (1892), 273–354

F. J. Haverfield, 'Additamenta quinta ad corporis vol. VII', *Ephemeris Epigraphica* 9 (1913), 509–690

J. Hawkes, 'Statements in Stone: Anglo-Saxon Sculpture, Whitby and the Christianization of the North', *The Archaeology of Anglo-Saxon England: Basic Readings*, ed. C. E. Karkov (New York, 1999), pp. 403–21

J. Hawkes, 'Sacraments in Stone: the Mysteries of Christ in Anglo-Saxon Sculpture', *The Cross Goes North. Processes of Conversion in Northern Europe, AD 300–1300*, ed. M. O. H. Carver (York, 2003), pp. 351–70

J. Hawkes *et al.*, 'John the Baptist and the *Agnus Dei*: Ruthwell (and Bewcastle) Revisited', *AntJ.* 81 (2001), 131–53

P. Head, 'Voices of Stone: the Multifaceted Speech of *The Dream of the Rood* and the Ruthwell Cross', *Assays: Critical Approaches to Med. and Renaissance Texts* 9 (1996), 57–77

C. M. Heighway, *Deerhurst St. Mary and Gloucester St. Oswald: Two Anglo-Saxon Minsters*. Sixth Deerhurst Lecture (Deerhurst, 2001)

C. M. Heighway and R. Bryant, *The Golden Minster. The Anglo-Saxon Minster and Later Medieval Priory of St Oswald at Gloucester*. CBA Research Reports 117 (York, 1999)

I. Henderson, 'The Shape and Decoration of the Cross on Pictish Cross-Slabs Carved in Relief', in *The Age of Migrating Ideas. Early Medieval Art in Northern Britain and Ireland*, ed. R. M. Spearman and J. Higgitt (Edinburgh, 1993), pp. 209–18

I. Henderson and E. Okasha, 'The Early Christian Inscribed and Carved Stones of Tullylease, Co. Cork', *CMCS* 24 (Winter 1992), 1–36

I. Henderson and E. Okasha, 'The Early Christian Inscribed and Carved Stones of Tullylease, Co. Cork: Addendum', *CMCS* 33 (Summer 1997), 9–17

M. Herity, 'The Forms of the Tomb-Shrine of the Founder Saint in Ireland', *The Age of Migrating Ideas. Early Medieval Art in Northern Britain and Ireland*, ed. R. M. Spearman and J. Higgitt (Edinburgh, 1993), pp. 188–95

J. Higgitt, 'The Roman Background to Medieval England', *JBAA* 3rd ser. 36 (1973), 1–15

J. Higgitt, 'Anglo-Saxon Painted Lettering at St Patrick's Chapel, Heysham', *Early Medieval Wall Painting and Painted Sculpture in England*, ed. S. Cather *et al.*, BAR Brit. ser. 216 (Oxford, 1990), 31–40

J. Higgitt, in *Corpus of Anglo-Saxon Stone Sculpture*, III. *York and Eastern Yorkshire*, ed. J. Lang *et al.* (Oxford, 1991)

J. Higgitt, 'The Wall Plaster: Decoration and Lettering', pp. 118–20 in T. W. Potter and R. D. Andrews, 'Excavation and Survey at St Patrick's Chapel and St Peter's Church, Heysham', *AntJ* 74 (1994), 55–134

J. Higgitt, 'The Inscriptions in Latin Lettering', *Corpus of Anglo-Saxon Stone Sculpture*, IV. *South-east England*, ed. D. Tweddle *et al.* (Oxford, 1995a), 108–113

J. Higgitt, in *Corpus of Anglo-Saxon Stone Sculpture*, IV. *South-east England*, ed. D. Tweddle *et al.* (Oxford, 1995b)

J. Higgitt, 'Monasteries and Inscriptions in Early Northumbria, the Evidence of Whitby', *From the Isles of the North. Early Medieval Art in Ireland and Britain*, ed. C. Bourke (Belfast, 1995c), pp. 229–36

J. Higgitt, 'The Wall Plaster: Decoration and Lettering', pp. 62–3 in T. W. Potter *et al.*, 'Excavation and Survey at Heysham, Lancashire, 1977–8', *Contrebis* 21 (1996), 28–73

J. Higgitt, 'Early Medieval Inscriptions in Britain and Ireland and Their Audiences', *The Worm, the Germ and the Thorn: Pictish and Related Studies presented to Isabel Henderson*, ed. D. Henry (Balgavies, 1997), pp. 67–78

J. Higgitt, 'The Non-Runic Inscriptions', *Corpus of Anglo-Saxon Stone Sculpture*, V. *Lincolnshire*, ed. P. Everson and D. Stocker (London, 1999a), 67–8

J. Higgitt, in *Corpus of Anglo-Saxon Stone Sculpture*, V. *Lincolnshire*, ed. P. Everson and D. Stocker (London, 1999b)

J. Higgitt, 'Epigraphic Lettering and Book Script in the British Isles', *Inschrift und Material, Inschrift und Buchschrift*, ed. W. Koch and C. Steininger (Munich, 1999c), pp. 137–49

J. Higgitt, 'Form and Focus in the Deerhurst Dedication Inscription', in *Roman, Runes and Ogham: Medieval Inscriptions in the Insular World and on the Continent*, ed. J. Higgitt *et al.* (Donington, 2001a), pp. 89–93

J. Higgitt, in *Corpus of Anglo-Saxon Stone Sculpture*, VI. *Northern Yorkshire*, ed. J. T. Lang *et al.* (Oxford, 2001b)

J. Higgitt, 'The Inscriptions', *Corpus of Anglo-Saxon Stone Sculpture*, VI. *Northern Yorkshire*, ed. J. T. Lang *et al.* (Oxford, 2001c), 51–4

J. Higgitt, 'Design and Meaning in Early Medieval Inscriptions in Britain and Ireland', *The Cross Goes North. Processes of Conversion in Northern Europe, AD 300–1300*, ed. M. O. H. Carver (York, 2003), pp. 327–38

D. A. Hinton, *Alfred's Kingdom: Wessex and the South 800–1500* (London, 1977)

D. A. Hinton and B. Cunliffe, 'Saxon Finds', *Excavations in Bath 1970–1975*, ed. B. Cunliffe, Committee for Rescue Archaeol. in Avon, Gloucestershire and Somerset, Excavation Report no. 1 (Bristol, 1979), 138–40

D. A. Hinton, *Archaeology, Economy and Society: England from the Fifth to the Fifteenth Century* (London, 1990)

N. Holder, 'Inscriptions, Writing and Literacy in Saxon London', *Trans. London Middlesex Archaeol. Soc.* 49 (1999), 81–97

B. Holdich, *The History of Crowland Abbey* . . . (Stamford, 1816)

D. R. Howlett, 'Inscriptions and Design of the Ruthwell Cross', *The Ruthwell Cross*, ed. B. Cassidy, Index of Christian Art Occasional Papers 1 (Princeton, 1992), 71–93

M. Hughes, *The Small Towns of Hampshire: the Archaeological and Historical Implications of Development*, Hampshire Archaeol. Committee (Southampton, 1976)

D. Hunt, 'The Story of a Little Gold Disc', *The Searcher* (June 1993), 42

J. Ingram [on 15 June 1838], in *The Fourth Annual Report of the Proceedings of the Oxford University Archæological and Heraldic Society* (Oxford, 1838), pp. 18–21

H. L. Jessep, *Notes on Pre-Conquest Church Architecture in Hampshire and Surrey* (Winchester, 1913)

H. L. Jessep, *Anglo-Saxon Church Architecture in Sussex* (Winchester, 1914)

P. M. Johnston, 'Some Curiosities and Interesting Features of Surrey Ecclesiology', *Surrey Archaeol. Collections* 15 (1900), 51–79

P. M. Johnston, 'Stoke D'Abernon Church', *Surrey Archaeol. Collections* 20 (1907), 1–89

S. Jones *et al.*, *The Survey of Ancient Houses in Lincoln*, II. *Houses to the South and West of the Minster* (Lincoln, 1987)

C. E. Karkov, 'The Chalice and Cross in Insular Art', *The Age of Migrating Ideas. Early Medieval Art in Northern Britain and Ireland*, ed. R. M. Spearman and J. Higgitt (Edinburgh, 1993), pp. 237–44

C. E. Karkov, 'Whitby, Jarrow and the Commemoration of Death in Northumbria', *Northumbria's Golden Age*, ed. J. Hawkes and S. Mills (Stroud, 1999), pp. 126–35

S. Kelly, 'The Bishopric of Selsey', *Chichester Cathedral. An Historical Survey*, ed. M. Hobbs (Chichester, 1994), pp. 1–10 and 297–9

S. Keynes, 'Royal Government and the Written Word in late Anglo-Saxon England', *The Uses of Literacy in Early Medieval Europe*, ed. R. McKitterick (Cambridge, 1990), pp. 226–57

S. Keynes, 'The Discovery and First Publication of the Alfred Jewel', *Proc. of the Somerset Archaeol. Nat. Hist. Soc.* 136 (1992), 1–8

S. Keynes, 'Giso, Bishop of Wells', *ANS* 19 (1997), 203–71

S. Keynes, 'The Cult of King Alfred', *ASE* 28 (1999), 225–356

Lord Killanin and M. V. Duignan, *The Shell Guide to Ireland* 3rd ed., rev. P. Harbison (Dublin, 1989)

D. P. Kirby, 'The Church in Saxon Sussex', *The South Saxons*, ed. P. Brandon (London, 1978), pp. 160–73

E. Kitzinger, 'Interlace and Icons: Form and Function in Early Insular Art', *The Age of Migrating Ideas. Early Medieval Art in Northern Britain and Ireland*, ed. R. M. Spearman and J. Higgitt (Edinburgh, 1993), pp. 3–15

W. Koch, 'Insular Influences in Inscriptions on the Continent', *Roman, Runes and Ogham: Medieval Inscriptions in the Insular World and on the Continent*, ed. J. Higgitt *et al.* (Donington, 2001), pp. 148–57

J. T. Lang, 'Pre-Conquest Sculpture in Eastern Yorkshire', *Medieval Art and Architecture in the East Riding of Yorkshire*, ed. C. Wilson, Brit. Archaeol. Assoc. Conference Trans. 9 [for 1983] (London, 1989), 1–8

J. T. Lang, 'The Imagery of the Franks Casket: Another Approach', *Northumbria's Golden Age*, ed. J. Hawkes and S. Mills (Stroud, 1999), pp. 247–55

J. T. Lang, in *Corpus of Anglo-Saxon Stone Sculpture*, VI. *Northern Yorkshire*, ed. J. T. Lang *et al.* (Oxford, 2001)

J. T. Lang *et al.*, *Corpus of Anglo-Saxon Stone Sculpture*, III. *York and Eastern Yorkshire* (Oxford, 1991)

K. Leahy, in *The Making of England: Anglo-Saxon Art and Culture AD 600–900*, ed. L. E. Webster and J. Backhouse (London, 1991)

K. Leahy, 'The Middle Saxon Site at Flixborough, North Lincolnshire', *Northumbria's Golden Age*, ed. J. Hawkes and S. Mills (Stroud, 1999), pp. 87–94

C. Loveluck, 'The Development of the Anglo-Saxon Landscape: Economy and Society "On Driffield", East Yorkshire, 400–750 AD', *ASSAH* 9 (1996), 25–48

C. Loveluck, 'A High-Status Anglo-Saxon Settlement at Flixborough, Lincolnshire', *Antiquity* 72 (1998), 146–61

C. Loveluck, 'Wealth, Waste and Conspicuous Consumption. Flixborough and its Importance for Mid and Late Saxon Settlement Studies', *Image and Power in the Archeaology of Early Medieval Britain. Essays in honour of Rosemary Cramp* (Oxford, 2001), pp. 78–130

K. A. Lowe, '*Swutelung/swutelian* and the Dating of an Old English Charter (Sawyer 1524)', *N & Q* 236 (1991), 450–2

M. A. Lower, *A Compendious History of Sussex* . . . I (Lewes and London, 1870)

C. J. Lynn and J. A. McDowell, ed., *The Excavation of an Early Christian Settlement Site at Deer Park Farms, Glenarm, Co. Antrim* (forthcoming)

A. MacGregor, 'Antler, Bone and Horn', *English Medieval Industries: Craftsmen, Techniques, Products*, ed. J. Blair and N. Ramsay (London, 1991), pp. 355–78

D. Mac Lean, 'The Date of the Ruthwell Cross', *The Ruthwell Cross*, ed. B. Cassidy, Index of Christian Art Occasional Papers 1 (Princeton, 1992), 49–70

D. Mac Lean, 'The Northumbrian Perspective', *The St Andrews Sarcophagus*, ed. S. M. Foster (Dublin, 1998), pp. 179–201

D. McManus, *A Guide to Ogam* (Maynooth, 1991)

C. Manning, *Early Irish Monasteries* (Dublin, 1995)

H. M. R. E. Mayr-Harting, 'The Bishops of Chichester 1075–1207: Biographical Notes and Problems', *Chichester Papers* 40 (1963), 1–19

A. Mee, rev. C. L. S. Linnell, *The King's England: Sussex* (London, 1964)

T. Meier, *Die Archäologie des mittelalterlichen Königsgrabes im christlichen Europa* (Stuttgart, 2002)

P. Meyvaert, 'A New Perspective on the Ruthwell Cross: Ecclesia and Vita Monastica', *The Ruthwell Cross*, ed. B. Cassidy, Index of Christian Art Occasional Papers 1 (Princeton, 1992), 95–166

J. T. Micklethwaite, 'Some Further Notes on Saxon Churches ', *ArchJ* 55 (1898), 340–9

A. Middleton, 'Analysis of the Plaster', pp. 63–4 in T. W. Potter *et al.*, 'Excavation and Survey at Heysham, Lancashire, 1977–8', *Contrebis* 21 (1996), 28–73

S. H. Miller and S. B. J. Skertchly, *The Fenland Past and Present* (Wisbech and London, 1878)

J. Mitchell, 'Script about the Cross: the Tombstones of San Vincenzo al Volturno',

Roman, Runes and Ogham: Medieval Inscriptions in the Insular World and on the Continent, ed. J. Higgitt *et al.* (Donington, 2001a), pp. 158–74

J. Mitchell, 'The High Cross and Monastic Strategies in Eighth-Century Northumbria', *New Offerings, Ancient Treasures*, ed. P. Binski and W. Noel (Stroud, 2001b), pp. 88–114

P. Morgan and C. Thorn, ed., *Domesday Book*, XXXI. *Lincolnshire* (Chichester, 1986)

B. S. Nenk *et al.*, 'Medieval Britain and Ireland in 1990', *MA* 35 (1991), 126–238

D. Notton, 'An Anglo-Saxon Inscribed Fossil Echinoid from Exeter Street, London? An Alternative Interpretation', *MA* 46 (2002), 107–10

E. O'Brien, 'Contacts Between Ireland and Anglo-Saxon England in the Seventh Century', *ASSAH* 6 (1993), 93–102

E. Ó Carragáin, 'The Necessary Distance: *Imitatio Romae* and the Ruthwell Cross', *Northumbria's Golden Age*, ed. J. Hawkes and S. Mills (Stroud, 1999), pp. 191–203

B. Odenstedt, 'The Gilton Runic Inscription', *ASSAH* 2 [BAR Brit. Ser. 92] (Oxford, 1981), 37–47

E. Okasha, 'The Inscriptions on the Bell-Moulds', in M. Biddle *et al.*, *Object and Economy in Medieval Winchester*. Winchester Stud. 7 (ii) (Oxford, 1990a), 122–4

E. Okasha, 'Inscription on a Lead Sheet', in M. Biddle *et al.*, *Object and Economy in Medieval Winchester*. Winchester Stud. 7 (ii) (Oxford, 1990b), 758–9

E. Okasha, 'The English Language in the Eleventh Century: the Evidence from Inscriptions', *England in the Eleventh Century*, ed. C. Hicks (Stamford, 1992a), pp. 333–45

E. Okasha, 'Anglo-Saxon Inscribed Sheaths from Aachen, Dublin and Trondheim', *MA* 36 (1992b), 59–66

E. Okasha, 'The Inscriptions', in D. Tweddle, *The Anglian Helmet from 16–22 Coppergate*, The Archaeology of York 17.8 (York, 1992c), 1012–15

E. Okasha, 'Old English *hring* in Riddles 48 and 59', *MÆ* 62 (1993), 61–9

E. Okasha, 'The Commissioners, Makers and Owners of Anglo-Saxon Inscriptions', *ASSAH* 7 (1994), 71–7

E. Okasha, 'Literacy in Anglo-Saxon England: the Evidence from Inscriptions', *ASSAH* 8 (1995), 69–74

E. Okasha, 'The Early Christian Carved and Inscribed Stones of South-West Britain', *Scotland in Dark Age Britain*, ed. B. E. Crawford (Aberdeen, 1996a), pp. 21–35

E. Okasha, 'The Lead Cross of Bishop Godfrey of Chichester', *Sussex Archaeol. Collections* 134 (1996b), 63–9

E. Okasha, 'Anglo-Saxon Architectural Inscriptions', *The Worm, the Germ and the Thorn: Pictish and related studies presented to Isabel Henderson*, ed. D. Henry (Balgavies, 1997), pp. 79–84

E. Okasha, 'The Inscribed Stones from Hartlepool', *Northumbria's Golden Age*, ed. J. Hawkes and S. Mills (Stroud, 1999a), pp. 113–25

E. Okasha, 'An Inscribed Bone Fragment from Nassington', *MA* 43 (1999b), 203–5

E. Okasha, 'Anglo-Saxon Women: the Evidence from the Inscriptions', *Roman, Runes and Ogham: Medieval Inscriptions in the Insular World and on the Continent*, ed. J. Higgitt *et al.* (Donington, 2001), pp. 79–88

E. Okasha, 'Inscribed Lead Cross', *Deansway, Worcester: Excavations by Charles Mundy 1988–89*, ed. H. Dalwood and E. Edwards (forthcoming) [draft held in Worcester: *Worcestershire Archaeological Service Report* no. 290, vol. 4, pp. 34–5]

E. Okasha, 'Name-Stones', *Reallexikon der Germanischen Altertumskunde begründet von Johannes Hoops*, ed. R. Müller (Berlin, 2002), cols. 544–50

E. Okasha, 'Spaces Between Words: Word Separation in Anglo-Saxon Inscriptions', *The Cross Goes North. Processes of Conversion in Northern Europe, AD 300–1300*, ed. M. O. H. Carver (York, 2003), pp. 339–49

E. Okasha and K. Forsyth, *Early Christian Inscriptions of Munster: a Corpus of the Inscribed Stones* (Cork, 2001)

E. Okasha and R. Langley, 'An Inscribed Stud found at Egginton, Derbyshire: an Anglo-Saxon Love-Token?', *Derbyshire Archaeol. Jnl* 119 (1999), 203–5

E. Okasha and S. Youngs, 'The Limpsfield Grange Disc', *ASE* 25 (1996), 63–8

E. Okasha and S. Youngs, 'A Late Saxon Inscribed Pendant from Norfolk', *ASE* 32 (2003), 225–30

F. Orton, 'Rethinking the Ruthwell Monument: Fragments and Critique; Tradition and History; Tongues and Sockets', *Art Hist.* 21 (1998), 65–106

F. Orton, 'Northumbrian Sculpture (the Ruthwell and Bewcastle Monuments): Questions of Difference', *Northumbria's Golden Age*, ed. J. Hawkes and S. Mills (Stroud, 1999), pp. 216–26

M. Osborn, 'The Lid as Conclusion of the Syncretic Theme of the Franks Casket', *Old English Runes and their Continental Background*, ed. A. Bammesberger (Heidelberg, 1991), pp. 249–68

R. I. Page, 'Anglo-Saxon Runes and Magic', *JBAA* 3rd ser. 27 (1964), 14–31

R. I. Page, 'Dating Old English Inscriptions: the Limits of Inference', *Papers from the 5th International Conference on English Historical Linguistics*, ed. S. Adamson *et al.*, *Current Issues in Linguistic Theory* 65 (1990), 357–77

R. I. Page, in *Corpus of Anglo-Saxon Stone Sculpture*, III. *York and Eastern Yorkshire*, ed. J. Lang *et al.* (Oxford, 1991a)

R. I. Page, in *The Making of England: Anglo-Saxon Art and Culture AD 600–900*, ed. L. E. Webster and J. Backhouse (London, 1991b)

R. I. Page, 'Runes in East Anglia', *Proceedings of the Third International Symposium on Runes and Runic Inscriptions, Grindaheim, Norway, 8–12 August 1990*, ed. J. E. Knirk (Uppsala, 1994), pp. 105–17

R. I. Page, *Runes and Runic Inscriptions: Collected Essays on Anglo-Saxon and Viking Runes*, ed. D. N. Parsons (Woodbridge, 1995)

R. I. Page, 'Runic Writing, Roman Script and the Scriptorium', in S. Nyström, *Runor och ABC* (Stockholm, 1997), pp. 119–36

R. I. Page, *An Introduction to English Runes*, 2nd ed. (Woodbridge, 1999)

R. I. Page, 'The Provenance of the Lancashire Runic Ring', *N & Q* 246 (2001a), 217–9

R. I. Page, 'Inscriptions and Archives', *Roman, Runes and Ogham: Medieval Inscriptions in the Insular World and on the Continent*, ed. J. Higgitt *et al.* (Donington, 2001b), pp. 94–102

W. Page *et al.*, *VCH Sussex* III (London, 1935)

D. Parsons, 'Stone', in *English Medieval Industries: Craftsmen, Techniques, Products*, ed. J. Blair and N. Ramsay (London, 1991), pp. 1–27

D. Parsons, 'Odda's Chapel, Deerhurst: Place of Worship or Royal Hall?', *MA* 44 (2000), 225–8

D. N. Parsons, *Recasting the Runes: the Reform of the Anglo-Saxon 'Futhorc'* (Uppsala, 1999)

D. N. Parsons, in *Corpus of Anglo-Saxon Stone Sculpture*, VI. *Northern Yorkshire*, ed. J. T. Lang *et al.* (Oxford, 2001)

J. Parsons, 'Orpington Historical Records and Natural History Society Archæological Report', *AC* 72 (1958), 209–11

N. Paul, 'English Fonts and Font Covers: Developments in Styles and Designs', *The Local Historian* 23 (1993), 130–45

W. D. Peckham, 'The Successors of Bishop Stigand', *Sussex N & Q* 10 (1944–5), 112–17, 164

S. J. Plunkett, 'The Mercian Perspective', *The St Andrews Sarcophagus*, ed. S. M. Foster (Dublin, 1998a), pp. 202–26

S. J. Plunkett, 'Anglo-Saxon Stone Sculpture and Architecture', in S. West, *A Corpus of Anglo-Saxon Material from Suffolk*, East Anglian Archaeology. Report no. 84 (Ipswich, 1998b), 323–57

T. W. Potter and R. D. Andrews, 'Excavation and Survey at St Patrick's Chapel and St Peter's Church, Heysham', *AntJ* 74 (1994), 55–134

T. W. Potter and R. D. Andrews, 'Excavation and Survey at St Patrick's Chapel and St Peter's Church, Heysham, Lancashire, 1977–8', pp. 29–46 in T. W. Potter *et al.*, 'Excavation and Survey at Heysham, Lancashire, 1977–8', *Contrebis* 21 (1996), 28–73

A. Preston-Jones, 'Decoding Cornish Churchyards', *The Early Church in Wales and the West*, ed. N. Edwards and A. Lane (Oxford, 1992), pp. 104–24

H. Pryce, 'Ecclesiastical Wealth in early Medieval Wales', *The Early Church in Wales and the West*, ed. N. Edwards and A. Lane (Oxford, 1992), pp. 22–32

C. A. R. Radford, 'A Medieval Leaden Cross from Whitby', *AntJ* 20 (1940), 508–9

P. Rahtz, 'Anglo-Saxon Yorkshire: Current Research Problems', *Early Deira: Archaeological Studies of the East Riding in the Fourth to Ninth Centuries AD*, ed. H. Geake and J. Kenny (Oxford, 2000), pp. 1–9

P. Rahtz and L. Watts, 'Kirkdale Anglo-Saxon Minster', *CA* 155 (1997), 419–22

P. Rahtz and L. Watts, 'Kirkdale Archaeology 1996–1997', Supplement to *The Ryedale Historian* no. 19 (1998–1999) (Helmsley, 1998)

P. Rahtz and L. Watts, 'Three Ages of Conversion at Kirkdale, North Yorkshire', *The Cross Goes North. Processes of Conversion in Northern Europe, AD 300–1300*, ed. M. O. H. Carver (York, 2003), pp. 289–309

A. Raine, *Medieval York* (London, 1955)

H. G. Ramm, 'The Site of St. Leonard's Hospital, York, before the Norman Conquest', *Yorkshire Philosophical Soc. Ann. Report for 1970* (1971), 43–5

H. G. Ramm, 'The Growth and Development of the City to the Norman Conquest', *The Noble City of York*, ed. A. Stacpoole *et al.* (York, 1972), pp. 225–54

I. A. Richmond, 'The Roman City of Lincoln', *Arch J* 103 (1946), 26–56

F. C. Robinson and E. G. Stanley, *Old English Verse Texts from Many Sources: a Comprehensive Collection*, EEMF 23 (Copenhagen, 1991)

W. J. Rodwell, 'Anglo-Saxon Painted Sculpture at Wells, Breamore and Barton-upon-Humber', *Early Medieval Wall Painting and Painted Sculpture in England*, ed. S. Cather *et al.*, BAR Brit. Ser. 216 (Oxford, 1990), 161–75

W. J. Rodwell and E. C. Rouse, 'The Anglo-Saxon Rood and other Features in the South Porch of St. Mary's Church, Breamore, Hampshire', *AntJ* 64 (1984), 298–325

W. J. Rodwell *et al.*, *Wells Cathedral. Excavations and Structural Studies, 1978–93* (London, 2001)

D. W. Rollason *et al.*, *Sources for York History to AD 1100* (York, 1998)

P. Saunders, 'Anglo-Saxon Jewel Found in Wiltshire', *Minerva* 11.2 (2000), 6

P. H. Sawyer, *Anglo-Saxon Lincolnshire*, History of Lincolnshire III (Lincoln, 1998)

M. Seidler, *Der Schatz von St. Heribert in Köln-Deutz*, Rheinische Kunststätten 423 (Cologne, 1997)

R. Sermon, 'The Hackness Cross Cryptic Inscriptions', *Yorkshire Archaeol. Jnl* 68 (1996), 101–11

J. J. Sheahan and T. Whellan, *History and Topography of the City of York* II (Beverley, 1856)

W. H. Smyth, 'Description of an Astrological Clock, belonging to the Society of Antiquaries of London . . .', *Archaeologia* 33 (1849), 8–35

P. Stafford, *The East Midlands in the Early Middle Ages* (Leicester, 1985)

E. G. Stanley, 'Owen Manning (1.) on Old English *æstel* and (2.) on the Aldbrough Inscription', *N & Q* 240 (1995), 10–13

F. W. Steer, 'A Note on the Illustrations', *Chichester Papers* 40 (1963), 20–21

D. Stocker, '"Also a Soldier . . .". Evidence for a Mithraeum in Lincoln?', *Lincolnshire Hist. and Archaeol.* 32 (1997), 21–4

D. Stocker, 'A Hitherto Unidentified Image of the Mithraic God Arimanius at Lincoln?', *Britannia* 29 (1998), 359–63

D. Stocker, 'Monuments and Merchants: Irregularities in the Distribution of Stone Sculpture in Lincolnshire and Yorkshire in the Tenth Century', *Cultures in Contact. Scandinavian Settlement in England in the Ninth and Tenth Centuries*, ed. D. M. Hadley and J. D. Richards (Turnhout, 2000), pp. 179–212

D. Stocker and P. Everson, 'Rubbish Recycled: a Study of the Re-Use of Stone in Lincolnshire', *Stone. Quarrying and Building in England AD 32–1525*, ed. D. Parsons (Chichester, 1990), pp. 83–101

T. W. T. Tatton-Brown, 'Building Stone in Canterbury, *c.* 1070–1525', *Stone. Quarrying and Building in England AD 32–1525*, ed. D. Parsons (Chichester, 1990), pp. 70–82

T. W. T. Tatton-Brown, 'Kent Churches – Some New Architectural Notes (contd.)', *AC* 114 (1995), 189–235

J. Tavenor-Perry, 'Saxon Architecture', *Memorials of Old Sussex*, ed. P. C. D. Mundy (London 1909), pp. 54–71

A. Taylor, *Burial Practice in Early England* (Stroud, 2001)

H. M. Taylor, 'St Mary-le-Wigford, Lincoln', *ArchJ* 131 (1974), 348

H. M. Taylor, 'Characteristics and Dating of Anglo-Saxon Churches', *The Fourth Viking Congress*, ed. A. Small (London, 1965a), pp. 41–55

H. M. Taylor, 'Anglo-Saxon Churches in Yorkshire', *The Fourth Viking Congress*, ed. A. Small (London, 1965b), pp. 56–66

E. C. Teviotdale, 'Latin Verse Inscriptions in Anglo-Saxon Art', *Gesta* 35 (1996), 99–110

A. C. Thomas, 'The Early Christian Inscriptions of Southern Scotland', *Glasgow Archaeol. Jnl* 17 (1991–2), 1–10

A. C. Thomas, 'Form and Function', *The St Andrews Sarcophagus*, ed. S. M. Foster (Dublin, 1998a), pp. 84–96

A. C. Thomas, *Christian Celts. Messages and Images* (Dublin, 1998b)

M. Townend, 'Viking Age England as a Bilingual Society', *Cultures in Contact. Scandinavian Settlement in England in the Ninth and Tenth Centuries*, ed. D. M. Hadley and J. D. Richards (Turnhout, 2000), pp. 89–105

M. Townend, 'Contextualizing the *Knútsdrápur*: Skaldic Praise-Poetry at the Court of Cnut', *ASE* 30 (2001), 145–79

M. Townend, *Language and History in Viking Age England. Linguistic Relations between Speakers of Old Norse and Old English* (Turnhout, 2002)

F. Tupper, 'Anglo-Saxon Dæg-Mæl', *PMLA* 10 (1895), 111–241

D. Tweddle, 'Anglo-Saxon Sculpture in South-East England before *c.* 950', *Studies in Medieval Sculpture*, ed. F. H. Thompson (London, 1983), pp. 18–40

D. Tweddle, 'Sculptured Fragments', *St Mary Bishophill Junior and St Mary Castlegate. Anglo-Scandinavian York*, ed. L. P. Wenham *et al.*, The Archaeology of York 8.2 (York, 1987), 155–65

D. Tweddle, 'Paint on pre-Conquest Sculpture in South-East England', *Early Medieval Wall Painting and Painted Sculpture in England*, ed. S. Cather *et al.*, BAR Brit. Ser. 216 (Oxford, 1990), 147–59

D. Tweddle, in *The Making of England: Anglo-Saxon Art and Culture AD 600–900*, ed. L. E. Webster and J. Backhouse (London, 1991)

D. Tweddle, *The Anglian Helmet from 16–22 Coppergate*, The Archaeol. of York 17.8 (York, 1992)

D. Tweddle *et al.*, *Corpus of Anglo-Saxon Stone Sculpture*, IV. *South-East England* (Oxford, 1995)

D. Tweddle *et al.*, *Anglian York: a Survey of the Evidence*. The Archaeol. of York 7.2 (York, 1999)

S. Tymms, in 'Proceedings' [15 March 1855], *Proc. Soc. Ant. London* 3 (1855), 165–73

S. Tymms, in 'Quarterly Meetings' [10 January 1856], *Proc. of the Suffolk Inst. Archaeol.* 2 (1856), 215–19

K. Ulmschneider, 'Settlement, Economy and the "Productive" Site: Middle Anglo-Saxon Lincolnshire A.D. 650–780', *MA* 44 (2000a), 53–79

K. Ulmschneider, *Markets, Minsters, and Metal-detectors: the Archaeology of Middle Saxon Lincolnshire and Hampshire Compared*, BAR Brit. Ser. 307 (Oxford, 2000b)

A. Vince, 'Where *is* Lincoln's Oldest Church?', *Lincoln Archaeol.* 3 (1990–1), 31–44

M. E. C. Walcott, 'The Bishops of Chichester, from Stigand to Sherborne', *Sussex Archaeol. Collections* 28 (1878), 11–58

W. T. Watkin, 'Roman Inscriptions found in Britain in 1887', *ArchJ* 45 (1888), 167–86

L. Watts *et al.*, 'Archaeology at Kirkdale', Supplement to *The Ryedale Historian* no. 18 (1996–7) (Helmsley, 1996)

L. Watts *et al.*, 'Kirkdale: the Inscriptions', *MA* 41 (1997), 51–99

R. Weatherhead, 'The +ABBAE+ Stone Found at Whitby Abbey in the Anglo-Saxon Layer', *Hist. of the Berwickshire Naturalists' Club* 48, pt 2 (2000), 175–6

L. E. Webster, in *The Golden Age of Anglo-Saxon Art 966–1066*, ed. L. E. Webster and J. Backhouse (London, 1984)

L. E. Webster, in *The Making of England: Anglo-Saxon Art and Culture AD 600–900*, ed. L. E. Webster and J. Backhouse (London, 1991)

L. E. Webster, 'The Iconographic Programme of the Franks Casket', *Northumbria's Golden Age*, ed. J. Hawkes and S. Mills (Stroud, 1999), pp. 227–46

L. E. Webster, 'Metalwork of the Mercian Supremacy', *Mercia. An Anglo-Saxon Kingdom in Europe*, ed. M. P. Brown and C. A. Farr (London, 2001), pp. 263–78

S. West, *A Corpus of Anglo-Saxon Material from Suffolk,* East Anglian Archaeol., Report no. 84 (Ipswich, 1998)

J. O. Westwood, *Lapidarium Walliæ: the Early Inscribed and Sculptured Stones of Wales* (Oxford, 1876–9)

J. B. Whitwell, 'Flixborough', *CA* 126 (1991), 244–7

A. Williams, *Land, Power and Politics: the Family and Career of Odda of Deerhurst.* Deerhurst Lecture 1996 (Deerhurst, 1997)

P. Williamson and L. E. Webster, 'The Coloured Decoration of Anglo-Saxon Ivory Carvings', *Early Medieval Wall Painting and Painted Sculpture in England*, ed. S. Cather *et al.*, BAR Brit. Ser. 216 (Oxford, 1990), 177–94

B. C. Withers, 'Unfulfilled Promise: the Rubrics of the Old English Prose Genesis', *ASE* 28 (1999), 111–39

M. A. Woodward and G. A. C. Binnie, 'Anglo-Saxon Carved Stones in Norham Church', *Hist. of the Berwickshire Naturalists' Club* 48, pt 2 (2000), 161–70

R. P. Wright and R. S. O. Tomlin, 'Roman Inscribed Stones', in D. Phillips and B. Heywood, *Excavations at York Minster*, I. *From Roman Fortress to Norman Cathedral,* ed. M. O. H. Carver (London, 1995), pp. 246–7

W. M. Wylie, 'Observations on certain Sepulchral Usages of Early Times', *Archaeologia* 35 (1854), 298–304

S. Youngs, 'A Northumbrian Plaque from Asby Winderwath, Cumbria', *Northumbria's Golden Age*, ed. J. Hawkes and S. Mills (Stroud, 1999), pp. 281–95

(—) (1827), 'Jarrow Church and Monastery. – Durham', *Catholic Miscellany* 8 (68) (1827), 73–8

(—) (1853), Dean and Chapter of Chichester, in *Report of the Transactions at the Annual Meeting of the Archaeological Institute of Great Britain and Ireland, held at Chichester July 12th to 19th 1853* (London, 1853), pp. 75–7

(—) (1903a), *Moyses' Hall Museum Bury St. Edmund's. Catalogue of the Specimens in the Anglo-Saxon and Mediæval Sections* (Bury St Edmunds, 1903)

(—) (1922), 'Proceedings at Meetings of the Royal Archaeological Society. The Summer Meeting at Ripon 19th to 26th July, 1922', *ArchJ* 79 (1922), 361–91

(—) (1928), 'The Missing Hartlepool Gravestone', *AntJ* 8 (1928), 524

(—) (1939a), *University of Oxford, Ashmolean Museum, Report of the Visitors 1939* (Oxford, 1939)

(—) (1975), *An Inventory of the Historical Monuments in the City of York*, IV. R. Commission on Hist. Monuments, England (London, 1975)

(—) (1981), *An Inventory of the Historical Monuments in the City of York*, V. R. Commission on Hist. Monuments, England (London, 1981)

(—) (1983), *Concordances et tableaux pour l'étude des grand sacramentaires* (Fribourg, 1983)

ADDENDA TO THE *HAND-LIST*, THE FIRST SUPPLEMENT AND THE SECOND SUPPLEMENT

1 Aldbrough	The stone is identified as fine-grained sandstone.[43]
12 Bishopstone	The stone is identified as fine-grained limestone.[44]
15 Breamore I	The stone is identified as fine- to medium-grained sandstone.[45]
22 Canterbury IV	The stone is identified as medium- to coarse-grained limestone.[46]
26 Crowland	The stone is identified as shelly oolitic limestone.[47]
41 Great Edstone	The stone is identified as medium-grained sandstone.[48]
42 Hackness	The stone is identified as medium-grained sandstone.[49]
51 Hauxwell	The stone is identified as medium-grained deltaic sandstone.[50]
64 Kirkdale I	The stone is identified as fine-grained sandstone.[51]
66 Lancashire	Page suggests that this ring may not after all be from Manchester (see *Second Supplement* p. 73).[52]
71 Leake I	The stone is identified as medium-grained sandstone.[53]
72 Leake II	The stone is identified as medium-grained sandstone.[54]
73 Lincoln I	The stone is identified as shelly oolitic limestone.[55]
87 London I	The stone is identified as fine-grained sandstone.[56]
88 London II	The stone is identified as medium- to coarse-grained limestone.[57]
94 Newent	This stone was moved in February 1990 to Gloucester City Museum and Art Gallery, no. L535.
98 Old Byland	The stone is identified as medium-grained sandstone.[58]
99 Orpington	The stone is identified as fine-grained sandstone.[59]
110 Skelton	The stone is identified as medium-grained deltaic sandstone.[60]

[43] Lang *et al.* (1991), 123. [44] Tweddle *et al.* (1995), 124. [45] Tweddle *et al.* (1995), 253.
[46] Tweddle *et al.* (1995), 136. [47] Everson and Stocker (1999), 323.
[48] Lang *et al.* (1991), 133. [49] Lang *et al.* (1991), 135. [50] Lang (2001), 120.
[51] Lang *et al.* (1991), 164. [52] Page, R. I. (2001a), 217–19. [53] Higgitt (2001b), 301.
[54] Higgitt (2001b), 301. [55] Everson and Stocker (1999), 214.
[56] Tweddle *et al.* (1995), 221. [57] Tweddle *et al.* (1995), 218.
[58] Lang *et al.* (1991), 195. [59] Tweddle *et al.* (1995), 147. [60] Craig (2001), 195.

111 Stratfield Mortimer	The stone is identified as medium limestone.[61]
120 Wensley I	The stone is identified as medium-grained micaceous Millstone Grit.[62]
121 Wensley II	The stone is identified as medium-grained micaceous Millstone Grit.[63]
122–134 Whitby	The Whitby stones have now been re-identified geologically. In addition, several of them have been moved.[64]
122 Whitby 0	Now in the care of English Heritage and is kept in the English Heritage North Region store, Helmsley, North Yorkshire, accession no. EH 88092805. The stone is identified as medium-grained micaceous sandstone.[65]
123 Whitby II	Now owned by Whitby Literary and Philosophical Society and is kept in Whitby Town Museum. The stone is identified as medium-grained micaceous sandstone.[66]
124 Whitby III	Now owned by Whitby Literary and Philosophical Society and is kept in Whitby Town Museum. The stone is identified as medium-grained deltaic sandstone.[67]
125 Whitby IV	Now owned by Whitby Literary and Philosophical Society and is on loan to the Yorkshire Museum, York. The stone is identified as fine-grained micaceous sandstone.[68]
126 Whitby V	Now owned by Whitby Literary and Philosophical Society and is on loan to the British Museum. The stone is identified as medium-grained deltaic sandstone.[69]
127 Whitby VI	Now owned by Whitby Literary and Philosophical Society and on loan to the British Museum. The stone is identified as fine-grained micaceous deltaic sandstone.[70]
128 Whitby VII	Now owned by Whitby Literary and Philosophical Society and on loan to the British Museum. The stone is identified as medium-grained deltaic sandstone.[71]
129 Whitby VIII	Now owned by Whitby Literary and Philosophical Society and on loan to the British Museum. The stone is identified as fine-grained micaceous deltaic sandstone.[72]
130 Whitby XI	Now owned by Whitby Literary and Philosophical Society. It is on loan to English Heritage and is on display in Cholmley House Interpretation Centre,

[61] Tweddle *et al.* (1995), 335. [62] Lang (2001), 224. [63] Lang (2001), 226.
[64] I am most grateful to Derek Craig, University of Durham, for his information about the Whitby stones. [65] Cramp (2001), 238. [66] Lang (2001), 248. [67] Cramp (2001), 241.
[68] Cramp (2001), 242. [69] Cramp (2001), 245. [70] Cramp (2001), 244.
[71] Lang (2001), 253. [72] Lang (2001), 251.

	Whitby Abbey. The stone is identified as fine-grained micaceous deltaic sandstone.[73]
131 Whitby XII	Now owned by Whitby Literary and Philosophical Society and on loan to the British Museum. The stone is identified as fine-grained micaceous deltaic sandstone.[74]
132 Whitby XIV	Now owned by Whitby Literary and Philosophical Society and kept in Whitby Town Museum. The stone is identified as medium-grained deltaic sandstone.[75]
133 Whitby DCCXXXII	Now owned by Whitby Literary and Philosophical Society. It is on loan to English Heritage and is on display in Cholmley House Interpretation Centre, Whitby Abbey. The stone is identified as medium-grained deltaic sandstone.[76]
134 Whitby DCCXXXIII	Now owned by Whitby Literary and Philosophical Society and kept in Whitby Town Museum. The stone is identified as fine-grained micaceous deltaic sandstone.[77]
135 Whitchurch	The stone is identified as fine-grained sandstone.[78]
138 Winchester I	The stone is identified as fine-grained limestone.[79]
140 Winchester III	The stone is identified as medium- to coarse-grained limestone.[80]
144 Wycliffe	The stone is identified as fine-grained dolomitic limestone.[81]
145 Yarm	The stone is identified as medium-grained sandstone.[82]
146 York I	The stone is identified as medium-grained grit.[83]
147 York II	The stone is identified as coarse-grained Millstone Grit.[84]
148 York III	The stone is identified as fine-grained dolomitic limestone.[85]
150 York V	The stone is identified as fine-grained dolomitic limestone.[86]
151 York VI	The stone is identified as fine-grained dolomitic limestone.[87]
152 York VII	The stone is identified as medium-grained Millstone Grit.[88]

[73] Cramp (2001), 246. [74] Craig (2001), 247. [75] Craig (2001), 261.
[76] Craig (2001), 258. [77] Craig (2001), 260. [78] Tweddle *et al.* (1995), 271.
[79] Tweddle *et al.* (1995), 278.
[80] Tweddle *et al.* (1995), 273. [81] Cramp (2001), 266. [82] Lang (2001), 274.
[83] Lang *et al.* (1991), 99. [84] Lang *et al.* (1991), 108. [85] Lang *et al.* (1991), 86.
[86] Lang *et al.* (1991), 53, 64. [87] Lang *et al.* (1991), 63. [88] Lang *et al.* (1991), 54, 75.

153 York VIII	The stone is identified as fine-grained dolomitic limestone.[89]
160 Breamore III	The stone is identified as medium- to coarse-grained limestone.[90]
161 Canterbury VII	The stone is identified as fine-grained sandstone.[91]
183 Winchester VIII	The stone is identified as medium- to coarse-grained limestone.[92]
189 Cologne	The crozier head was moved in 1996 from the Cathedral Treasury, Cologne, to the sacrarium of the parish church of Neu-St Heribert, Deutz.[93]
201 Rochester	The stone is identified as fine-grained sandstone.[94]
205 Stow	The stone is limestone.[95]

89 Lang *et al.* (1991), 53, 64. 90 Tweddle *et al.* (1995), 256. 91 Tweddle *et al.* (1995), 128.
92 Tweddle *et al.* (1995), 331. 93 Hare (2000), 276. 94 Tweddle *et al.* (1995), 166.
95 Everson and Stocker (1999), 258.

INDEXES

Index III Index of inscriptions excluded from the Hand-List

As explained above, in the Introduction, coin-jewellery is now excluded from the *Hand-List* proper. The eleven new coin-brooches known to me are from: Alfriston, Sussex; Avebury, Wiltshire; Bicester, Oxfordshire; Burbage, Wiltshire; Caldecote, Norfolk; Chichester, Sussex; Edington, Wiltshire; Hose, Leicestershire; London (Billingsgate); London (Vintry); Trowbridge, Wiltshire.

The following is excluded on the grounds that it probably dates from after A.D. 1100:

Lincoln IV: lead plate in the Cathedral Library, Lincoln, found *c.* 1670, near the tomb of Bishop Remigius. The text commemorates William, son of Walter de Aincourt. (—) (1850), xliv & fig.

Index V Index of vernacular personal names used in the texts[96]

Old English names

Ælfgȳþ *fem.*: *possibly* ælegy[-] (*twice*) *Marcham*, or Æþelgyþ *q.v.*
Æþelgȳþ *fem.*: *possibly* ælegy[-] (*twice*) *Marcham*, or Ælfgyþ *q.v.*
Ælfwine *masc.*: *probably* aelf[ƿine] *Worcester*
*Bealdhild *fem.*: *possibly* baldehildis *Postwick*
Ēadbeorht *masc.*: eadberht *Sleaford*
Godfrið *masc.*: godefride, godefridvs *Chichester*
Robert *masc.*: *probably* rob[erti] *Witney*
Sǣweard *masc.*: saward *Bawburgh*
Sigefrið *masc.*: *possibly* sifordi *Lincoln II*, or Sigeweard *q.v.*
Sigeweard *masc.*: *possibly* sifordi *Lincoln II*, or Sigefrið *q.v.*

Index VI Index of abbreviations used in the texts[97]

Latin

abbas: *possibly* ab *Bawburgh*
aeternus: aitūm = aeternum *'in deo' ring*
apostolus: apl̄m = apostolorum *Chichester*
aquila: aq̄ *Oxted*
atque: atq[:] *Chichester*
beatus: bt̄ *'in deo' ring*
christus: xpi = christi *Bury St Edmunds II*; *Bury St Edmunds IV*; *Bury St Edmunds VI*; *probably* [xpi] *and* x[pi] = christi *Bury St Edmunds III*; *possibly (twice)* xpi = christi *Bury St Edmunds V*; xp̄i = christi *Bury St Edmunds II*; *Bury St Edmunds IV*; *Bury St Edmunds VI*; *Cumberworth*
dedicare: ded̄ = dedit *Chichester*

[96] The same layout is used here as was used in the *Hand-List* and in the other supplements.
[97] The same layout is used here as was used in the *Hand-List* and in the other supplements.

deus: d̄s *Chichester*; d̄s *'in deo' ring*; dē = dei *'in deo' ring*; dō = deo *'in deo' ring*
dominus: dn̄s *Chichester*; *possibly* dni = domini *Deer Park Farms*
episcopus: ep̄s̄ *Chichester*; ep̄e = episcope *Chichester*; epī = episcopi *Chichester*
et: &, [&] *Chichester*
hostis: hostē = hostem *Bury St Edmunds VI*
in: ī *'in deo' ring*
iste: *probably* ist = istud *Weasenham*
kalendae: kl̄ = kalendis *Chichester*
liliosus: lilios̄ *'in deo' ring*
lumen: l̄m̄in = lumine *'in deo' ring*
martyr: *probably* m̄[r] = m[artyris] *Chichester*
omnipotens: om̄ps *Chichester*
omnis: omnū = omnium *Chichester*
peccatum: peccator̄ = peccatorum *Chichester*
pertinere: p̄tinaet = pertineat *Chichester*
potestas: potestatē = potestatem *Chichester*
quantum: quātū *Chichester*
redemptor: redēptor *Chichester*
remissio: remis īo *Chichester*
sanctus: sc̄e = sanctae (*twice*) *Lincoln II*; scī, sc̄i = sancti *Chichester*; *possibly* scie = sancti *Bawburgh*
solvere: soluēd[i] = soluend[i] *Chichester*
triumphare: triūphat *Bury St Edmunds III, IV*; triv̄phat *Bury St Edmunds II*
tuus: tuo[.] = tuo[rum] *Chichester*

Elisabeth Okasha

CORRIGENDA TO THE *HAND-LIST*, THE FIRST SUPPLEMENT AND THE SECOND SUPPLEMENT

Hand-List

Page	*Line*	*For*	*Read*
21	15	*A Grammatical Miscellany* . . .	in N. Bøgholm *et al.* ed., *A Grammatical Miscellany* . . .
29	31	104–9	104–8
38	9	XY	X.Y.
115	21	1911	1903, in Moyse's Hall Museum
137	28	Mitchell	Mitchell, H. P.
150	21	Bury St Edmunds	Bury St Edmunds I
154	23	London II	London I

First supplement

95	2	*T* . . . *þ*	T . . . þ
96	6	Mitchell	Mitchell, H. P.
107	22	K. Hughes	K. W. Hughes
118	2	Willett (1955–7)	Willett (1956–7)

Second supplement

65	3	LXIII	LIII
plate VIII*c*		24 Carlisle	24 Carlisle II

ADDENDA TO THE BIBLIOGRAPHIES OF THE ENTRIES IN THE *HAND-LIST* AND IN THE FIRST AND SECOND SUPPLEMENTS

Aachen: Okasha (1992b), 59–66 & fig.; Okasha (1994), 71–7; Bredehoft (1996), 105–6, 109; Okasha (2001), 82.

Aldbrough: Sheahan and Whellan (1856), 356; Allen, J. R. (1902–3), 93, 95; Fellows Jensen (1968), 118, 321; Fell *et al.* (1984), 135, 147; Lang (1989), 5 & fig.; Fellows Jensen (1991), 110–11; Higgitt (1991), 46–7, 124; Lang *et al.* (1991), 123–4 & fig.; Okasha (1992a), 333–45; Fell (1994), 134; Okasha (1994), 71–7; Higgitt (1995b), 148–9, 223; Okasha (1995), 71; Stanley (1995), 11–13; Everson and Stocker (1999), 258–9; Townend (2000), 95; Higgitt (2001b), 196–7, 248–9; Higgitt (2001c), 53; Okasha (2001), 82, 85, 88; Bradley, S. A. J. (2002), 35n, 40n; Townend (2002), 189–92

Alnmouth: Clancy (1993), 349, 351; Okasha (1994), 71–7; Higgitt (1995b), 222; Bailey, R. N. (1996c), 105; Bredehoft (1996), 105; Higgitt (1999c), 138–9; Page, R. I. (1999), 219–20; Higgitt (2001b), 252; Higgitt (2001c), 53–4.

Ardwall: Thomas, A. C. (1991–2), 10n.

Athelney: Hinton (1977), 49–51 & figs; Hinton (1990), 80–1 & fig.; Page, R. I. (1990),

358; Webster (1991), no. 260, pp. 282–3 & fig.; Keynes (1992), 1–8; Gameson, R. and Gameson, F. (1993), 1; Okasha (1994), 71–7; Bailey, R. N. (1996c), 97; Bredehoft (1996), 103, 105, 107; Head (1996), 62; Bradfield (1999), 27–8; Clark (1999), 21 & fig.; Keynes (1999), 269; Saunders (2000), 6; Okasha (2001), 82; Fell (2002), 267; Okasha (2003), 341, 348 & figs.

Auzon: Page, R. I. (1964), 26; Haith (1984), no. 13, pp. 33–4 & figs; Page, R. I. (1990), 360, 372; Eichner (1991), 603–28 & figs; Osborn (1991), 249–68; Robinson and Stanley (1991), no. 46, p. 29 & figs; Webster (1991), no. 70, pp. 101–3 & figs; Fell (1994), 130; Page, R. I. (1995), 310–12; Bailey, R. N. (1996c), 62, 71; Head (1996), 62; Page, R. I. (1997), 131; Cramp (1999), 11; Lang (1999), 247–55; Page, R. I. (1999), 219; Parsons, D. N. (1999), 24–5, 77, 94, 98–100, 110, 123; Webster (1999), 227–46 & figs; Brown, G. *et al.* (2001), 210; Koch (2001), 155; Fell (2002), 270–2, 274–5.

Barton St David: Okasha (1992a), 333–45; Bredehoft (1996), 105, 110n; Parsons, D. (1999), 116; Brown, G. *et al.* (2001), 208; Okasha (2001), 80–1.

Bath: Hinton (1979), 138–9; Okasha (1996b), 68.

Beckermet: Everson and Stocker (1999), 124, 215.

Billingham: Karkov (1993), 241–2; Bailey, R. N. (1996c), 40; Bradfield (1999), 61; Higgitt (1999c), 139; Higgitt (2001b), 303.

Birtley: Bailey, R. N. (1996c), 40; Watts *et al.* (1997), 69; Okasha (2002), 546.

Bishop Auckland: Higgitt (1995b), 220–1; Okasha (1997), 81; Higgitt (1999b), 123; Coatsworth (2000), 159–62 & fig.

Bishopstone: Lower (1870), 55; Tupper (1895), 130; Brown, G. B. (1900), 336; Johnston (1900), 75–6; Johnston (1907), 17; Tavenor-Perry (1909), 62; Jessep (1914), 26–7; Mee (1964), 21 & fig.; Kirby (1978), 164; Okasha (1992a), 333–45; Higgitt (1995a), 108–13; Higgitt (1995b), 124–5, 222; Tweddle *et al.* (1995), 28, 45, 124–5 & figs; Watts *et al.* (1997), 57; Higgitt (2001b), 195; Bradley, S. A. J. (2002), 32n.

Bodsham: Okasha (1993), 66; Okasha (1994), 71–7; Okasha (1995), 69–70 & figs; Bredehoft (1996), 105; Gardiner (1998), 47, 49.

Bossington: Hinton (1977), 27 & fig.; Hinton (1979), 139; Okasha (1993), 67; Kelly (1994), 297n; Ulmschneider (2000b), 61, 154.

Brandon: Carr *et al.* (1988), 375–6 & fig.; Page, R. I. (1990), 363; Brown, M. P. (1991), no. 66 (a), pp. 81–2 & fig.; Foot (1992), 262; Page, R. I. (1994), 112; Page, R. I. (1995), 324; Okasha and Youngs (1996), 65, 67; Plunkett (1998b), 355; West (1998), 12 & fig. on cover; Page, R. I. (1999), 217; Parsons, D. (1999), 118–19; Ulmschneider (2000a), 65; Koch (2001), 155–6n & fig.

Breamore I: Micklethwaite (1898), 345–6; Brown, G. B. (1900), 338 & fig.; Jessep (1913), 16 & fig.; Cox, J. C. (1949), 56–7 & fig.; Fernie (1982), 112–14; Rodwell (1990), 165; Tweddle (1990), 147, 150; Lowe (1991), 451n; Okasha (1992a), 333–45; Gameson, R. and Gameson, F. (1993), 1–10 & figs; Higgitt (1995a), 108–13; Higgitt (1995b), 253–5; Okasha (1995), 71; Tweddle *et al.* (1995), 27, 64, 253–5 & figs; Bailey, R. N. (1996a), 33n; Higgitt (1997), 74; Okasha (1997), 80, 82–3; Higgitt (1999c), 141–2; Withers (1999), 120–4; Koch (2001), 155–6n.

Breamore II: Gameson, R. and Gameson, F. (1993), 2; Higgitt (1995a), 108–13; Higgitt (1995b), 255; Tweddle *et al.* (1995), 27, 64, 255 & fig.; Okasha (1997), 82–3; Withers (1999), 124n.

Breamore III: Rodwell and Rouse (1984), 317; Higgitt (1995a), 108–13; Higgitt (1995b), 256; Tweddle *et al.* (1995), 27, 64, 256 & fig.; Okasha (1997), 82–3.

Brussels I: Webster (1984), no. 75, pp. 90–2 & fig.; Page, R. I. (1990), 363, 365, 368; Campbell, M. (1991), 152; Graham Campbell and Okasha (1991), 227; Robinson and Stanley (1991), no. 45, p. 29 and figs; Okasha (1992a), 333–45; Gameson, R. and Gameson, F. (1993), 1; Karkov (1993), 239, 243; Okasha (1994), 71–7; Bredehoft (1996), 104–5, 107–9; Head (1996), 62; Okasha (2001), 82, 85; Fell (2002), 264, 268.

Caistor: Allen, T. *et al.* (1834), 225–6; Binnall (1960), 6–7; Everson and Stocker (1999), 121–5, 215 & figs; Higgitt (1999a), 67–8; Higgitt (1999b), 122–3, 215.

Canterbury I: Okasha (1993), 66; Okasha (1994), 71–7; Bredehoft (1996), 106; Okasha (2001), 82–3.

Canterbury II: Haith (1984), no. 77, p. 94 & fig.; Okasha (1994), 71–7; Bradley, S. A. J. (2002), 35n.

Canterbury III: Hinton (1979), 139; Rodwell *et al.* (1979), 409; Okasha (1996b), 68; Watts *et al.* (1997), 74; Okasha (2001), 83, 88; Rodwell *et al.* (2001), 148.

Canterbury IV: Brock (1883), 52–3; (—) (1886), 480; Clapham (1929), 280; Tweddle (1983), 30; Tatton-Brown (1990), 59–61; Higgitt (1995a), 108–13; Higgitt (1995b), 136–7; Tatton-Brown (1995), 216; Tweddle *et al.* (1995), 31, 34, 136–7 & fig.; Everson and Stocker (1999), 124.

Canterbury VII: Okasha (1994), 71–7; Higgitt (1995a), 108–13; Higgitt (1995b), 128–30, 272; Tweddle *et al.* (1995), 23, 82, 84–5, 128–31 & figs; Bredehoft (1996), 105; Okasha (2001), 82.

Carlisle I: Okasha (1994), 71–7; Higgitt (2001b), 303.

Carlisle II: Higgitt (2001b), 303.

Chester: Okasha (1994), 71–7.

Chester-le-Street: Page, R. I. (1990), 359–60; Higgitt (1995b), 220–1; Page, R. I. (1995), 308n; Page, R. I. (1997), 130, 134; Higgitt (2001b), 252; Higgitt (2001c), 53–4.

Cologne: Seidler (1997), 14 & figs; Hare (2000), 273–4, 276–7.

Crowland: Astle (1800), 214; Britton (1807), [O] 6[98]; Holdich (1816), 52–3; Hamper (1820), 25–7 & fig.; Allen, T. *et al.,* (1834), 298; Miller and Skertchly (1878), 76–7 & fig.; Cox, J. C. (1924), 107; Pevsner and Harris (1964), 26, 501; Everson and Stocker (1999), 89, 323–5 & figs.

Cuxton: Okasha (1993), 66; Okasha (1994), 71–7; Bredehoft (1996), 105, 107; Okasha (2001), 84, 87.

Deerhurst I: Butterworth (1886), 47–8; Allen, J. R. (1888a), 171; Allen, J. R. (1902–3), 94–5; Taylor, H. M. (1978), 738–9; Fernie (1982), 159; Haith (1984), no. 138, pp. 131–2 & fig.; Page, R. I. (1990), 358; Clancy (1993), 348; Gameson, R. and

[98] '[O]' refers to the printer's letter and '6' to the page in that part. This is the system used in the index to the volume, since the pages are not numbered consecutively.

Gameson, F. (1993), 1–2; Okasha (1994), 71–7; Williams (1997), *passim*; Everson and Stocker (1999), 215–16; Higgitt (1999c), 142; Parsons, D. (2000), 225–8 & fig.; Heighway (2001), 4, 7; Higgitt (2001a), 89–93 & figs; Okasha (2001), 83; Higgitt (2003), 332–4, 336; Okasha (2003), 342, 348 & fig.

Deerhurst II: Butterworth (1886), 47; Routledge (1891), 143–4n; Allen, J. R. (1902–3), 94; Higgitt (1999c), 142; Parsons, D. (2000), 225–8; Higgitt (2001a), 89–90.

Dewsbury I: Page, R. I. (1964), 26; Robinson and Stanley (1991), no. 37, p. 28 and fig.; Fell (1994), 128–9; Okasha (1995), 70–1; Page, R. I. (1995), 298; Watts *et al.* (1997), 59–60, 64–5, 70–1, 75; Cramp (1999), 9 & fig.; Higgitt (1999c), 139; Parsons, D. N. (1999), 23; Koch (2001), 154–5 & fig.

Dewsbury II: Cramp (1999), 9 & fig.

Dewsbury III: Harbison (1992), 253, 257, 322–3 & fig.; Cramp (1999), 9 & fig.; Hawkes (2003), 359–65 & fig.

Driffield: Okasha (1993), 66–7; Loveluck (1996), 45; Okasha and Youngs (1996), 66.

Dublin I: Okasha (1999b), 205.

Dublin II: Okasha (1992b), 59–66 & figs; Okasha (1994), 71–7; Bredehoft (1996), 105; Fell (2002), 267.

Dublin IV: Webster (1984), no. 272, p. 207 & fig.

Dublin V: Parsons, D. N. (1999), 116.

Durham I: Page, R. I. (1964), 26–7; Page, R. I. (1990), 357; Mac Lean (1992), 51–4 & fig.; Page, R. I. (1994), 112–15; Page, R. I. (1995), 3, 5–6, 9–10, 299, 324–5; Higgitt (1997), 67, 69; Page, R. I. (1997), 129–30, 134; Hawkes (1999), 416–17; Page, R. I. (1999), 219, 223; Parsons, D. N. (1999), 41, 77, 90–2, 110, 121.

Durham II: Page, R. I. (1990), 358; Webster (1991), no. 99, pp. 134–5 & fig.; Thomas, A. C. (1998a), 86; Everson and Stocker (1999), 124; Higgitt (2001b), 225; Koch (2001), 155–6n.

Exeter: Okasha (1994), 71–7; Bredehoft (1996), 105.

Eye: Hinton (1990), 81, 127; Webster (1991), no. 205, p. 238 & fig.; Okasha (1994), 71–7; Harvey and McGuinness (1996), 3 & figs; West (1998), 36 & fig.

Falstone: Page, R. I. (1964), 26–7; Robinson and Stanley (1991), no. 38, p. 28 & fig.; Fell (1994), 128–9; Okasha (1994), 71–7; Okasha (1995), 70–1; Page, R. I. (1995), 3, 11, 273, 298; Bailey, R. N. (1996c), 120 & fig.; Higgitt (1997), 69; Page, R. I. (1997), 130; Everson and Stocker (1999), 123–4, 215; Page, R. I. (1999), 219; Parsons, D. N. (1999), 23, 110, 113; Page, R. I. (2001b), 99–100.

Fletton: Gardner (1951), 38 & fig.; Okasha (1997), 80–1, 83; Plunkett (1998b), 357n.

Flixborough I: Brown, M. P. (1991), no. 69 (b), pp. 95–6 and fig.; Leahy (1991), 94–5; Nenk *et al.* (1991), 168–9 and fig.; Whitwell (1991), 246–7 & figs; Page, R. I. (1994), 112; Loveluck (1998), 154–5, 158–9 & figs; Leahy (1999), 92 & fig.; Parsons, D. N. (1999), 116; Sawyer (1998), 68 & fig.; Ulmschneider (2000a), 65; Ulmschneider (2000b), 61, 70–1, 136 & fig.

Flixborough II: Brown, M. P. (1991), no. 69 (a), p. 95 and fig.; Leahy (1991), 94–5, 96; Whitwell (1991), 245–6 & figs.; Fell (1994), 126–7 & figs; Watts *et al.* (1997), 70–1, 73–4; Loveluck (1998), 154–5, 158–9 & fig.; Sawyer (1998), 66, 68 and fig.; Everson and Stocker (1999), 124; Higgitt (1999b), 123; Higgitt (1999c), 139; Leahy (1999), 92–3 & fig.; Ulmschneider (2000a), 65; Ulmschneider (2000b), 61, 70–1, 136 & fig.; Loveluck (2001), 100, 113, 116 & fig; Okasha (2001), 85, 88.

Gainford: Okasha (1994), 71–7.

Gloucester: Haith (1984), no. 145, p. 138 & fig.; Bayley, J. *et al.* (1993), 224–36 & fig.; Heighway and Bryant (1999), 61; Heighway (2001), 5.

Great Edstone: Smyth (1849), 21n; Johnston (1900), 75–6; Johnston (1907), 17; Edwards, W. (1924), 60; Lang (1989), 5; Page, R. I. (1990), 361; Higgitt (1991), 46–7, 134–5; Lang *et al.* (1991), 133–5 & figs; Okasha (1992a), 333–45; Fell (1994), 134; Okasha (1994), 71–7; Higgitt (1995a), 109–10; Higgitt (1995b), 124–5, 149; Bredehoft (1996), 105; Okasha (1997), 79; Watts *et al.* (1997), 64; Everson and Stocker (1999), 215, 258; Higgitt (1999c), 142; Higgitt (2001b), 196–7; Higgitt (2001c), 53; Okasha (2001), 82; Bradley, S. A. J. (2002), 11, 29, 32n, 34–35n.

Hackness: Allen, J. R. (1888a), 166; Edwards, W. (1924), 41 & fig.; Fell *et al.* (1984), 114, 121; Lang (1989), 1–2 & figs; Higgitt (1991), 46–7, 136–7, 138–9; Lang *et al.* (1991), 135–41 and figs; McManus (1991), 132; Page, R. I. (1991a), 136–7, 139; Fell (1994), 127–8; Sermon (1996), 101–11 & figs; Higgitt (1997), 71, 76; Everson and Stocker (1999), 124; Farr (1999), 380–92 & fig.; Hawkes (1999), 415–16; Karkov (1999), 133–4; Tweddle *et al.*(1999), 136; Higgitt (2001b), 303; Koch (2001), 155–6n & fig.; Barnwell *et al.* (2003), 322.

Haddenham: Higgitt (1995b), 167; Okasha (1995), 71; Plunkett (1998a), 206.

Hartlepool stones: (—) (1928), 524 [I]; Page, R. I. (1964), 26 [general]; Fell *et al.* (1984), 121 [general]; Page, R. I. (1990), 358 [general]; Cramp (1993), 68–9 [general]; Karkov (1993), 241–2 [general]; Fell (1994), 125–6 & figs [I, VI]; Page, R. I. (1995), 11, 298–9, 307–8 [general]; Bailey, R. N. (1996c), 40 [general]; Higgitt (1997), 69, 74 [general]; Bradfield (1999), 16–19, 61–2 & figs [general; figs of I, VI]; Daniels (1999), 110–12 [general]; Higgitt (1999b), 123 [III, IV]; Karkov (1999), 134 [general]; Okasha (1999a), 113–25 [general]; Parsons, D. N. (1999), 41n, 92 [general]; Higgitt (2001b), 303 [IV, V]; Mitchell, J. (2001a), 170–1 & fig. [general; fig. of I]; Okasha (2001), 80, 85, 88 [III, IV, V, VI, VIII]; Fell (2002), 277 [general]; Okasha (2002), 544–50 [general; fig. of VI].

Hauxwell: Higgitt (2001b), 121–2; Higgitt (2001c), 51, 53; Lang (2001), 120–2 & figs.

Hexham III: Gardner (1951), 29 & fig.; Mac Lean (1992), 50 & fig.; Bailey, R. N. (1996c), 44–5, 121–2 & figs; Everson and Stocker (1999), 124.

Heysham: Higgitt (1990), 31–40 & figs; Higgitt (1994), 118–20 & figs; Potter and Andrews, R. D. (1994), 62, 117 & figs; Higgitt (1996), 62–3 & fig.; Middleton (1996), 63–4; Potter and Andrews, R. D. (1996), 30–1, 33, 61, 67–8 & figs; Higgitt (1997), 72; Higgitt (1999c), 140.

Hornby II: Harbison (1992), 256–7, 323, 325, 343 & fig.; Bailey, R. N. (1996c), 59–61 & fig.; Hawkes (2003), 359–61 & fig.

Inglesham: Okasha (1997), 80–1, 83.

Ipswich I: Gardner (1951), 48 & fig.; Okasha (1992a), 333–45; Higgitt (1995b), 220–1; Okasha (1995), 71 & fig.; Okasha (1997), 80–1, 83; Plunkett (1998b), 329, 352–5 & fig.; Higgitt (1999c), 143; Okasha (2003), 342, 346, 348 & fig.

Ipswich II: Allen, J. R. (1902–3), 94; Gardner (1951), 48; Okasha (1997), 79–81, 83; Plunkett (1998b), 328–9, 352–5 & fig.

Ipswich III: Okasha (1997), 80–1, 83; Plunkett (1998b), 328, 352, 355–6 & figs; Bradley, S. A. J. (2002), 35n.

Jarrow I: (—) (1827), 77; Allen, J. R. (1888a), 166; Allen, J. R. (1902–3), 93; Fernie (1982), 50; Page, R. I. (1990), 358; Clancy (1993), 348; Gameson, R. and Gameson, F. (1993), 1; Fell (1994), 123–4, 126, 133 & fig.; Okasha (1995), 71; Bailey, R. N. (1996c), 49; Higgitt (1997), 74–5; Okasha (1997), 79; Karkov (1999), 127; Okasha (2001), 83; Bradley, S. A. J. (2002), 2, 8; Higgitt (2003), 331, 335; Okasha (2003), 341, 347 & fig.

Jarrow II: Fell (1994), 124–5; Everson and Stocker (1999), 123–4; Mitchell, J. (2001a), 170.

Jarrow III: Parsons, D. (1991), 15; Mac Lean (1992), 68; Henderson, I. (1993), 210, 213; Fell (1994), 124–5; Bailey, R. N. (1996c), 49–50; Teviotdale (1996), 99–101, 110 & fig.; Mac Lean (1998), 180–1; Mitchell, J. (2001a), 170; Bradley, S. A. J. (2002), 2.

Jarrow IV: Mac Lean (1998), 180.

Jarrow VI: Okasha (2001), 88.

Kirkdale I: Smyth (1849), 21n; Allen, J. R. (1888a), 166; Tupper (1895), 129–30; Johnston (1900), 75–6; Allen, J. R. (1902–3), 93, 95; Johnston (1907), 17; Edwards, W. (1924), 58, 60 & fig.; Gardner (1951), 23; Crowley (1956), 176; Taylor, H. M. (1965b), 61–2, 66; Fellows Jensen (1968), 63, 91, 136, 205, 291; Gee (1972), 339–40; Fernie (1982), 159–60; Jones, S. *et al.* (1987), 4; Lang (1989), 2–3, 5–6; Page, R. I. (1990), 358, 361–2, 365, 368, 372–3, 375; Fellows Jensen (1991), 111; Higgitt (1991), 46–7, 164–6; Lang *et al.* (1991), 163–6 and figs; Okasha (1992a), 333–45; Clancy (1993), 348–9, 351; Gameson, R. and Gameson, F. (1993), 1–2; Fell (1994), 133–4; Okasha (1994), 71–7; Higgitt (1995a), 109–10; Higgitt (1995b), 124–5, 149; Okasha (1995), 71, 73; Page, R. I. (1995), 309–10; Bredehoft (1996), 105, 108; Watts *et al.* (1996), 7–8; Higgitt (1997), 75–6; Okasha (1997), 79; Rahtz and Watts (1997), 419 & fig.; Watts *et al.* (1997), 51, 64, 75–92 & figs; Williams (1997), 13, 30n; Everson and Stocker (1999), 124, 215, 258; Higgitt (1999c), 142–3; Okasha (1999b), 204; Rahtz (2000), 7; Townend (2000), 95; Higgitt (2001b), 196–7; Higgitt (2001c), 53; Okasha (2001), 82–3; Bradley, S. A. J. (2002), 1–31, 32–36n, 39–41n & fig.; Townend (2002), 189–91; Higgitt (2003), 331–2, 336; Rahtz and Watts (2003), 289, 299, 301, 306–8 & fig.

Knells: Higgitt (2001b), 225.

Lancashire: Page, R. I. (1964), 26; Odenstedt (1981), 44; Robinson and Stanley (1991), no. 42, p. 28 & fig.; Okasha (1993), 66; Okasha (1994), 71–7; Bredehoft (1995), 1–8 & fig.; Okasha (1995), 70; Page, R. I. (1995), 305; Bredehoft (1996), 105, 107; Gardiner (1998), 49; Bradfield (1999), 27–8; Page, R. I. (1999), 219; Parsons, D. N. (1999), 24; Okasha (2001), 84; Page, R. I. (2001a), 217–19; Page, R. I. (2001b), 98; Fell (2002), 269.

Lancaster I: Higgitt (2001b), 303.

Lancaster II: Bailey, R. N. (1996a), 33; Watts *et al.* (1997), 59; Higgitt (2001b), 303.

Lanteglos: Okasha (1992a), 333–45; Preston-Jones (1992), 123; Okasha (1994), 71–7; Okasha (1996a), 27, 34.

Laverstock: Hinton (1977), 52; Haith (1984), no. 9, p. 30 & fig.; Page, R. I. (1990), 358; Webster (1991), no. 243, pp. 268–9 & fig.; Okasha and Youngs (1996), 64, 66; Gardiner (1998), 49; Dockray-Miller (2000), 48–9; Okasha (2001), 83; Webster (2001), 275 & fig.

Leake I: Higgitt (2001b), 301 & fig.; Higgitt (2001c), 51; Bradley, S. A. J. (2002), 32n.

Leake II: Higgitt (1995b), 125, 149; Higgitt (2001b), 301 & fig.; Higgitt (2001c), 51, 53; Bradley, S. A. J. (2002), 32n.

Lincoln I: Haddan and Stubbs (1869), 39; Allen, J. R. (1902–3), 93, 95; Richmond (1946), 49; Taylor, H. M. (1965a), 46; Taylor, H. M. (1974), 348 & fig.; Stafford (1985), 186 & figs; Stocker and Everson (1990), 93–4, 97; Vince (1990–91), 31; Okasha (1992a), 333–45; Stocker (1997), 22–3; Stocker (1998), 362; Everson and Stocker (1999), 64, 89, 124, 214–16, 258 & figs; Higgitt (1999a), 67–8; Eaton (2000), 63, 82–3, 92 & figs; Stocker (2000), 189; Higgitt (2003), 332, 336.

Lincoln III: Keynes (1990), 247n.

Lindisfarne stones: Page, R. I. (1964), 26–7 [general]; Page, R. I. (1990), 358 [general]; Fell (1991), 215 [II]; Tweddle (1991), no. 71, pp. 103–4 & fig. [II]; Cramp (1993), 68–9 [general]; Karkov (1993), 241–2 [general]; Fell (1994), 125–6, 128, 130, 132–3 [general]; Higgitt (1995c), 229 [general]; Page, R. I. (1995), 3, 11 [general]; Bailey, R. N. (1996c), 40 & fig. [general; fig. of II]; Higgitt (1997), 69, 72 [general]; Page, R. I. (1997), 130 [II]; Watts *et al.* (1997), 59 [II]; Bradfield (1999), 61–2 [general]; Everson and Stocker (1999), 123–4 [I]; Holder (1999), 93 [general]; Karkov (1999), 134 [general]; Parsons, D. N. (1999), 23, 41n, 92 [general]; Mitchell, J. (2001a), 170 [general]; Okasha (2001), 80, 88 [II, VII]; Okasha (2002), 544–50 [general; fig. of II].

Little Billing: Blair (1992), 182; Gameson, R. and Gameson, F. (1993), 1; Okasha (1994), 71–7; Alexander, J. S. (2001), 222; Koch (2001), 155–6n.

Llysfaen: Page, R. I. (1964), 26; Davies, W. (1982), 48; Pryce (1992), 31n; Page, R. I. (1995), 305; Okasha and Youngs (1996), 64–6; Page, R. I. (1997), 130; Page, R. I. (1999), 219; Parsons, D. N. (1999), 24; Brown, G. *et al.* (2001), 210.

London I: Cobb (1989), 141; Tweddle (1990), 147, 150–1; Okasha (1992a), 333–45; Okasha (1994), 71–7; Higgitt (1995a), 108–13; Higgitt (1995b), 221–3; Tweddle *et al.* (1995), 24, 93–4, 221–3 & figs; Bailey, R. N. (1996a), 33n; Bailey, R. N. (1996c), 7; Watts *et al.* (1997), 57; Holder (1999), 83–4, 92–3.

London II: Brooke and Keir (1975), 137 & figs; Cobb (1989), 141; Tweddle (1990), 147, 151; Okasha (1992a), 333–45; Higgitt (1995a), 108–13; Higgitt (1995b), 219–21, 272; Tweddle *et al.* (1995), 23, 88–90, 218–21 & figs; Bailey, R. N. (1996a), 33n; Holder (1999), 83–4, 92–3.

London IV: Gosling (1989), 12–13 & figs; Gosling (1991), 193–4; Okasha (1992a), 333–45; Okasha (1995), 70; Holder (1999), 86, 92–3; Okasha (2001), 81.

Lund: Bredehoft (1996), 105.

Manchester: Okasha (1997), 80–1, 83; Okasha (1999b), 204.

Monkwearmouth I: Page, R. I. (1990), 358; Fell (1994), 125; Bailey, R. N. (1996c), 40; Parsons, D. N. (1999), 41n, 92; Mitchell, J. (2001a), 170.

Monkwearmouth II: Page, R. I. (1990), 358; Tweddle (1991), no. 72, pp. 104–5 & fig.; Mac Lean (1992), 68–9 & fig.; Henderson, I. (1993), 210, 213; Fell (1994), 126;

Higgitt (1995b), 272, 279; Mac Lean (1998), 180–2; Everson and Stocker (1999), 123–4; Higgitt (2001b), 242, 244; Mitchell, J. (2001a), 170 & fig.; Higgitt (2003), 329.

Mortain: Brown, M. P. (1991), 176; Page, R. I. (1991b), 176; Webster (1991), no. 137, pp. 175–6 & figs.; Page, R. I. (1995), 312; Page, R. I. (1997), 130–1; Page, R. I. (1999), 219; Parsons, D. N. (1999), 24, 77; Youngs (1999), 290, 293–4; Higgitt (2001b), 225.

Newent: Higgitt (1995b), 220–1; Bailey, R. N. (1996c), 122 & fig.; Watts *et al.* (1997), 64; Bradfield (1999), 16–32, 61–5 & figs; Higgitt (2001b), 225; Okasha (2002), 547, 549 & fig.

Norham I: Woodward and Binnie (2000), 162 & fig.

Norham II: Higgitt (2001b), 303.

Old Byland: Edwards, W. (1924), 60; Lang (1989), 5; Higgitt (1991), 46–7, 195; Lang *et al.* (1991), 195 and figs; Higgitt (1995a), 110; Higgitt (1995b), 125; Higgitt (2001b), 196–7; Higgitt (2001c), 53; Bradley, S. A. J. (2002), 32n.

Orpington: Parsons, J. (1958), 211; Higgitt (1995a), 108–13; Higgitt (1995b), 147–9, 223; Tweddle *et al.* (1995), 28, 72, 147–9 & figs; Everson and Stocker (1999), 258; Holder (1999), 84, 89, 92 & fig.; Higgitt (1999c), 141–2; Page, R. I. (1999), 223–4 & fig.; Higgitt (2001b), 197; Bradley, S. A. J. (2002), 32n.

Paris: Webster (1984), no. 76, p. 92 & fig.; Campbell, M. (1991), 152; Okasha and Youngs (1996), 64; Teviotdale (1996), 102–3, 110 & fig; Higgitt (1999c), 141; Okasha (2003), 345, 348.

Pershore: Page, R. I. (1964), 26; Haith (1984), no. 74, p. 90 & fig.; Page, R. I. (1990), 360–1; Okasha (1992a), 333–45; Gameson, R. and Gameson, F. (1993), 1; Okasha (1994), 71–7; Bredehoft (1996), 105, 107; Okasha (2001), 82.

Potterne: Blair (1992), 182; Gameson, R. and Gameson, F. (1993), 9n; Paul (1993), 132; Higgitt (1995b), 167.

Putney: Okasha (1992a), 333–45; Holder (1999), 84–5, 93; Okasha (2001), 84.

Ripon: Cramp (1993), 69; Cramp (1999), 7–8.

Rochester: Covert (1989), 10–11 & figs; Cather *et al.* (1990), v & figs; Higgitt (1995a), 108–13; Higgitt (1995b), 166–7, 273; Tweddle *et al.*, (1995), 22, 87, 166–7 & figs.

Ruthwell: Gardner (1951), 22, 28 & figs; Robinson and Stanley (1991), no. 44, pp. 28–9 & figs; Cassidy (1992), 3–34 and figs; Cassidy and Howlett (1992), 102–17 & figs; Cassidy and Kiefer (1992), 167–99; Farrell and Karkov (1992), 35–47; Howlett (1992), 71–93 & figs; Mac Lean (1992), 149–70; Meyvaert (1992), 95–166 & figs; Bailey, R. N. (1993), 141–8 & figs; Kitzinger (1993), 8–10 & fig.; Fell (1994), 130; Okasha (1995), 72–3; Bailey, R. N. (1996b), *passim* [99]; Bailey, R. N. (1996c), 42–4, 52–3, 61–5, 110 & figs; Bredehoft (1996), 104–5, 107–9; Head (1996), 62–71, 74–7 & figs; Higgitt (1997), 67, 69, 75–6; Orton (1998), 65–106 & figs; Carver (1999), 38 & fig.; Cramp (1999), 8–9; Ó Carragáin (1999), 191–203 & figs; Orton (1999), 216–26; Page, R. I. (1999), 219 & fig.; Parsons, D. N. (1999), 24, 113n, 123; Hawkes *et al.* (2001), 131–53 & figs; Koch (2001), 155–6n; Mitchell, J. (2001b), 88–114; Fell (2002), 264, 270, 274; Hawkes (2003), 353–5 & fig.; Higgitt (2003), 330–1, 334–5.

[99] This work has no page numbering.

Sandford: Haith (1984), no. 268, pp. 203–4 & fig.; Higgitt (1995b), 222; Okasha (1995), 70; Watts *et al.* (1997), 57.

Shaftesbury: Higgitt (1995b), 332–3; Higgitt (1997), 73; Higgitt (1999b), 122.

Sherburn: Hinton (1977), 52; Fell *et al.* (1984), 93–4, 102 & fig.; Haith (1984), no. 10, p. 30 & fig.; Page, R. I. (1990), 358; Webster (1991), no. 244, p. 269 & fig.; Okasha (1993), 67; Okasha and Youngs (1996), 64, 66; Okasha and Langley (1999), 203; Dockray-Miller (2000), 48–9; Okasha (2001), 83, 87; Webster (2001), 275 & fig.

Sinnington: Bradley, S. A. J. (2002), 32n.

Sittingbourne I: Page, R. I. (1964), 28; Odenstedt (1981), 44; Haith (1984), no. 95, pp. 102–3 & fig.; Okasha (1994), 71–7; Bailey, R. N. (1996c), 105–6; Bredehoft (1996), 105, 107–9; Okasha (2001), 82.

Sittingbourne II: Webster (1984), no. 113, p. 114 & fig.; Keynes (1990), 246–7; Okasha (1994), 71–7.

Skelton: Fell (1994), 134–5; Everson and Stocker (1999), 124, 215; Barnes (2001), 111; Craig (2001), 195–7 & fig.; Higgitt (2001b), 195–7; Higgitt (2001c), 53–4; Parsons, D. N. (2001), 195–7; Bradley, S. A. J. (2002), 32n, 40-41n; Townend (2002), 192.

Steyning: Okasha (1993), 66–7; Okasha (1994), 71–7; Bredehoft (1996), 105; Gardiner (1998), 38–9, 47–50 & fig.

Stow: Okasha (1992a), 333–45; Higgitt (1995b), 149; Everson and Stocker (1999), 89, 124, 215, 258–9 & fig.; Higgitt (1999a), 67–8; Higgitt (2001b), 197, 248–9.

Stratfield Mortimer: Higgitt (1995a), 108–13; Higgitt (1995b), 335–7; Okasha (1995), 70 & fig.; Tweddle *et al.* (1995), 82, 84, 335–7 & figs; Bredehoft (1996), 105, 107; Watts *et al.* (1997), 69; Higgitt (2001b), 248–9; Okasha (2001), 83.

Suffolk: (—) (1903a), 21.

Sutton: Fell *et al.* (1984), 102 & fig.; Haith (1984), no. 105, pp. 109–11 & figs; Page, R. I. (1990), 368; Robinson and Stanley (1991), no. 39, p. 28 and fig.; Okasha (1992a), 333–45; Okasha (1993), 66; Okasha (1994), 71–7; Tweddle *et al.* (1995), 167; Bredehoft (1996), 105, 107–8; Watts *et al.* (1997), 59; Okasha (1999b), 204; Okasha and Langley (1999), 205; Okasha (2001), 84, 87; Okasha (2003), 342, 345, 348.

Swindon: Okasha (1993), 67; Gardiner (1998), 47, 49; Dockray-Miller (2000), 49; Okasha (2001), 87.

Thornhill: Fell (1994), 128–9; Page, R. I. (1995), 298; Everson and Stocker (1999), 124; Parsons, D. N. (1999), 23; Koch (2001), 155–6n.

Thornton-le-Moors: Okasha (1992a), 333–45; Higgitt (1995b), 222; Watts *et al.* (1997), 57.

Totnes: Okasha (1994), 71–7.

Trondheim: Okasha (1992b), 59–66 & figs; Okasha (1994), 71–7; Bredehoft (1996), 105.

Tullylease: Brash (1874–5), 321–2; Westwood (1876–9), 145; Killanin and Duignan (1989), 136 & fig.; Henderson, I. and Okasha (1992), no. 1, pp. 1–36 & figs; Henderson, I. (1993), 210; Herity (1993), 191; Karkov (1993), 241; O'Brien (1993), 94–5; Manning (1995), 36 & fig.; Harbison (1997), 37–8; Henderson, I. and Okasha (1997), 9; Higgitt (1997), 69, 72 and fig.; Thomas, A. C. (1998b), 191n; Edwards, N.

(2001), 66–7; Mitchell, J. (2001a), 171; Okasha and Forsyth (2001), 119–23 & figs; Higgitt (2003), 329–30; Okasha (2003), 345, 349.

Wallingford I: Allen, J. R. (1888a), 167; Hinton (1977), 94; Fell *et al.* (1984), 122; Webster (1984), no. 112, pp. 113–4 & figs; Hinton (1990), 127; Keynes (1990), 246–7; Williamson and Webster (1990), 185; Okasha (1994), 71–7; Watts *et al.* (1997), 59; Okasha (2001), 84, 87.

Wallingford II: MacGregor (1991), 361 & fig.; Okasha (1992a), 333–45; Okasha (1994), 71–7; Bredehoft (1996), 104–5; Okasha (2001), 84, 87.

Waltham Abbey: Okasha (1995), 70; Okasha and Youngs (1996), 64; Holder (1999), 86, 92–3; Parsons, D. N. (1999), 116; Brown, G. *et al.* (2001), 208.

Wareham: Okasha (1994), 71–7; Bredehoft (1996), 105.

Weeke: Haith (1984), no. 111, p. 113 & figs; Keynes (1990), 246–7; Okasha (1994), 71–7.

Wells I: Okasha (1996b), 68; Keynes (1997), 205, 216n & fig.; Watts *et al.* (1997), 74; Rodwell *et al.* (2001), 147–9, 495 & figs.

Wells II: Rodwell *et al.* (2001), 49–50 & figs.

Wensley I: Edwards, W. (1924), 41; Page, R. I. (1964), 26; Higgitt (1999b), 122–3; Higgitt (2001b), 224–5, 227; Higgitt (2001c), 52–4; Lang (2001), 224–6 & figs.

Wensley II: Page, R. I. (1964), 26; Fell (1994), 126; Everson and Stocker (1999), 123–4; Higgitt (1999b), 122; Higgitt (2001b), 225–7; Higgitt (2001c), 52–4; Lang (2001), 226–7 & figs.

Whitby stones: Fell *et al.* (1984), 122 [general]; Cramp (1993), 64–73 [general]; Fell (1994), 125, 127 [general]; Higgitt (1995c), 229–36 & figs [general; figs of III, IV, V, VI, VII, VIII, XI, XIV, DCCXXXII, DCCXXXIII]; Watts *et al.* (1997), 64 [IV]; Everson and Stocker (1999), 124, 215–6 [DCCXXXII, DCCXXXIII]; Hawkes (1999), 415–7 [general]; Karkov (1999), 133–4 [general]; Tweddle *et al.* (1999), 136 [DCCXXXII]; Dockray-Miller (2000), 17 [DCCXXXII]; Weatherhead (2000), 175–6 & fig. [IV]; Craig (2001), 247–8, 258–62 & figs [XII, XIV, DCCXXXII, DCCXXXIII]; Cramp (2001), 238, 241–7 & figs [0, III, IV, V, VI, XI]; Higgitt (2001b), 227, 238, 241–9, 251–2, 254–5, 258–62, 303 [general]; Higgitt (2001c), 51–3 [general]; Lang (2001), 248–9, 251–5 & figs [II, VII, VIII]; Okasha (2001), 81, 88 [IV, XIV]; Cramp (2001), 303 & figs [general]; Goodall (2002), 4, 19 & fig. [DCCXXXII]; Barnwell *et al.* (2003), 313, 315 [IV, DCCXXXII].

Whitchurch: Browne (1885), 255; Allen, J. R. (1888a), 166–7; Jessep (1913), 21; Cox, J. C. (1949), 182; Gardner (1951), 42; Higgitt (1973), 13; Hughes, M. (1976), 138; Hinton (1977), 100–1; Tweddle (1983), 21–2 & figs; Higgitt (1995a), 108–13; Higgitt (1995b), 167, 271–3, 279; Tweddle *et al.* (1995), 22, 40–1, 167, 271–3 & figs; Higgitt (1999c), 140; Ulmschneider (2000b), 15, 63, 68–70, 168; Okasha (2001), 85, 88.

Wimbourne I-II: Brown, G. *et al.* (2001), 209.

Winchester I: Hinton (1977), 101; Okasha (1992a), 333–45; Higgitt (1995a), 108–13; Higgitt (1995b), 278–80; Tweddle *et al.* (1995), 23, 82, 86–7, 278–80 & figs; Bailey, R. N. (1996c), 96–7; Higgitt (2001b), 248–9; Okasha (2001), 85; Townend (2001), 170–1.

Winchester II: Dolley and Mays (1990), 633 & figs; Taylor, A. (2001), 177 & fig.

Winchester III: Higgitt (1995a), 108–13; Higgitt (1995b), 274; Tweddle *et al.* (1995), 273–4 & figs; Higgitt (1999c), 140; Ulmschneider (2000b), 68–9, 169.

Winchester IV: Dolley and Mays (1990), 635 & figs.

Winchester V: Haith (1984), no. 146, p. 138 & fig.; Biddle *et al.* (1990), 168 & figs; Davies, R. M. and Olvenden (1990), 106; Okasha (1990a), 122–4.

Winchester VII: Okasha (1990b), 758–9 & figs; Okasha (1995), 70; Okasha (1999b), 205; Brown, G. *et al.* (2001), 208.

Winchester VIII: Higgitt (1995a), 108–13; Higgitt (1995b), 332–3; Tweddle *et al.* (1995), 331–3 & figs; Higgitt (1999b), 122.

Wycliffe: Okasha (1994), 71–7; Everson and Stocker (1999), 123–4; Cramp (2001), 266–9 & figs; Higgitt (2001b), 227–9; Higgitt (2001c), 53–4; Higgitt (2003), 330.

Yarm: Clancy (1993), 349, 351; Okasha (1994), 71–7; Higgitt (1995b), 167; Okasha (1997), 81; Watts *et al.* (1997), 59, 64–5, 70–1, 75; Everson and Stocker (1999), 123–4; Higgitt (1999c), 139; Stocker (2000), 202; Higgitt (2001b), 268–9, 274–6; Higgitt (2001c), 53–4; Lang (2001), 274–6 & figs; Okasha (2003), 341–2, 348 & fig.

York I: Allen, J. R. (1902–3), 93, 95; Benson (1911), 64 & fig.; Raine, A. (1955), 194; Fellows Jensen (1968), 24, 106; Gee (1972), 339; (—) (1981), 33 & fig.; Hall, R. A. (1987), 147; Tweddle (1987), 165 & fig.; Higgitt (1991), 46–7, 100–1; Lang *et al.* (1991), 99–101 & figs; Okasha (1992a), 333–45; Fell (1994), 134 & fig.; Okasha (1994), 71–7; Higgitt (1997), 75; Rollason *et al.* (1998), 176–7; Everson and Stocker (1999), 124, 215–16; Tweddle *et al.* (1999), 186; Townend (2000), 95; Okasha (2001), 82; Townend (2002), 189–90.

York II: Benson (1911), 35; Raine, A. (1955), 113; Ramm (1971), 43, 45; (—) (1981), 95 & fig.; Higgitt (1991), 45–7, 109; Lang *et al.* (1991), 108–9 & figs; Rollason *et al.* (1998), 162; Tweddle *et al.* (1999), 186, 243.

York III: Benson (1911), 35; (—) (1975), xliv, xlvi & fig.; Higgitt (1991), 45–7, 86; Lang *et al.* (1991), 85–7 & figs; Watts *et al.* (1997), 71, 86; Rollason *et al.* (1998), 157; Tweddle *et al.* (1999), 245; Higgitt (2001b), 121, 303.

York IV: Gardner (1951), 46 & fig.; Cant (1972), 36–7 & fig.; Okasha (1997), 80–3; Rollason *et al.* (1998), 148.

York V: Ramm (1972), 247 & fig. Higgitt (1991), 44–7, 64; Lang *et al.* (1991), 63–4 & figs; Rollason *et al.* (1998), 148; Tweddle *et al.* (1999), 245; Higgitt (2001b), 303; Mitchell, J. (2001a), 171.

York VI: Higgitt (1991), 44–7, 63; Lang *et al.* (1991), 62–3 & figs; Page, R. I. (1995), 308; Bailey, R. N. (1996c), 36 & fig.; Rollason *et al.* (1998), 149; Tweddle *et al.* (1999), 245; Higgitt (2001b), 303; Mitchell, J. (2001a), 171 & fig.

York VII: Higgitt (1991), 46–7, 75–6; Lang *et al.* (1991), 75–6 & figs; Wright and Tomlin (1995), 246 & fig.; Rollason *et al.* (1998), 149; Tweddle *et al.* (1999), 246; Eaton (2000), 76–7, 92 & fig; Higgitt (2001b), 303.

York VIII: Higgitt (1991), 44–7, 64–6; Lang *et al.* (1991), 64–6 & figs; Karkov (1993), 241–2; Rollason *et al.* (1998), 149; Tweddle *et al.* (1999), 245–6; Mitchell, J. (2001a), 171.

York IX: Okasha (1994), 71–7; Page, R. I. (1995), 196.

York X: Hinton (1990), 61; Brown, M. P. (1991), no. 47, pp. 60–2 & figs; Higgitt

(1991), 45–7; Okasha (1992c), 1012–15; Tweddle (1992), *passim* & figs; Kitzinger (1993), 4 & fig.; Okasha (1995), 73 & fig.; Bredehoft (1996), 110n; Rollason *et al.* (1998), 160–1; Tweddle *et al.* (1999), 137, 262 & figs; Higgitt (2001b), 225; Okasha (2001), 80–1.

'eadward' brooch: Okasha (2001), 83.

'eawen' ring: Fell *et al.* (1984), 93–4 & fig.; Okasha (1993), 67; Okasha (1994), 71–7; Bredehoft (1996), 105; Okasha (2001), 84, 87.

'sigerie' ring: Okasha (1994), 71–7; Bredehoft (1996), 105.

V&A crucifix: Webster (1984), no. 118, pp. 117–18 & fig.

Bibliography for 2003

DEBBY BANHAM, CAROLE P. BIGGAM, MARK BLACKBURN, CAROLE HOUGH, SIMON KEYNES, PAUL G. REMLEY and REBECCA RUSHFORTH

This bibliography is meant to include all books, articles and signicant reviews published in any branch of Anglo-Saxon studies during 2003. It excludes reprints unless they contain new material. It will be continued annually. The year of publication of a book or article is 2003 unless otherwise stated. The arrangement and the pages on which the sections begin are as follows:

Paul Remley has been responsible mainly for sections 2, 3 and 4, Rebecca Rushforth for section 5, Debby Banham for section 6, Mark Blackburn for section 7, Carole Hough for section 8 and Carole Biggam for section 9. Additional entries have been supplied throughout by Simon Keynes. References to publications issued in Japan, and elsewhere in eastern Asia, have been contributed mainly by Professor Yoshio Terasawa. Paul Remley has been responsible for co-ordination of the contributions and has prepared the bibliography for publication.

The following abbreviations occur where relevant (not only in the bibliography but also throughout the volume):

AAe	*Archaeologia Aeliana*
AB	*Analecta Bollandiana*
AC	*Archaeologia Cantiana*
AHR	*American Historical Review*
ANQ	*American Notes and Queries*
ANS	*Anglo-Norman Studies*
AntJ	*Antiquaries Journal*
ArchJ	*Archaeological Journal*
ASE	*Anglo-Saxon England*
ASNSL	*Archiv für das Studium der neueren Sprachen und Literaturen*
ASPR	Anglo-Saxon Poetic Records
ASSAH	*Anglo-Saxon Studies in Archaeology and History*
AST	Anglo-Saxon Texts
AUON	*Annali, Sezione germanica* ns (Università degli studi di Napoli 'L'Orientale')
BAR	British Archaeological Reports
BGDSL	*Beiträge zur Geschichte der deutschen Sprache und Literatur*
BIAL	*Bulletin of the Institute of Archaeology* (London)
BN	*Beiträge zur Namenforschung*
BNJ	*British Numismatic Journal*
CA	*Current Archaeology*
CBA	Council for British Archaeology
CCM	*Cahiers de civilisation médiévale*
CCSL	Corpus Christianorum, Series Latina
CMCS	*Cambrian Medieval Celtic Studies*
CSASE	Cambridge Studies in Anglo-Saxon England
CSEL	Corpus Scriptorum Ecclesiasticorum Latinorum
DAEM	*Deutsches Archiv für Erforschung des Mittelalters*
EA	*Études anglaises*
EconHR	*Economic History Review*
EEMF	Early English Manuscripts in Facsimile
EETS	Early English Text Society
EHR	*English Historical Review*
ELN	*English Language Notes*
EME	*Early Medieval Europe*
EPNS	English Place-Name Society
ES	*English Studies*
FS	*Frühmittelalterliche Studien*
HBS	Henry Bradshaw Society Publications
HS	*Historische Sprachforschung*
HZ	*Historische Zeitschrift*
IF	*Indogermanische Forschungen*
JBAA	*Journal of the British Archaeological Association*
JEGP	*Journal of English and Germanic Philology*
JEH	*Journal of Ecclesiastical History*

JEPNS	*Journal of the English Place-Name Society*
JMH	*Journal of Medieval History*
JTS	*Journal of Theological Studies* ns
LH	*The Local Historian*
MA	*Medieval Archaeology*
MÆ	*Medium Ævum*
MGH	Monumenta Germaniae Historica
MLR	*Modern Language Review*
MP	*Modern Philology*
MS	*Mediaeval Studies*
N&Q	*Notes and Queries* ns
NChron	*Numismatic Chronicle*
NCirc	*Numismatic Circular*
NH	*Northern History*
NM	*Neuphilologische Mitteilungen*
OEN	*Old English Newsletter*
PA	*Popular Archaeology*
PBA	*Proceedings of the British Academy*
PL	Patrologia Latina
PMLA	*Publications of the Modern Language Association of America*
PQ	*Philological Quarterly*
RB	*Revue bénédictine*
RES	*Review of English Studies* ns
RGA	*Reallexikon der germanischen Altertumskunde*, 2nd ed. (Berlin)
RS	Rolls Series
SBVS	*Saga-Book* (London, Viking Society for Northern Research)
SCBI	Sylloge of Coins of the British Isles
SettSpol	*Settimane di studio del Centro italiano di studi sull'alto Medioevo* (Spoleto)
SM	*Studi medievali*, 3rd ser.
SN	*Studia Neophilologica*
SP	*Studies in Philology*
TLS	*Times Literary Supplement*
TPS	*Transactions of the Philological Society*
TRHS	*Transactions of the Royal Historical Society*
YES	*Yearbook of English Studies*
ZAA	*Zeitschrift für Anglistik und Amerikanistik*
ZDA	*Zeitschrift für deutsches Altertum und deutsche Literatur*
ZVS	*Zeitschrift für vergleichende Sprachforschung*

Online journals cited in the bibliography are currently located at the following addresses on the Internet:

Antiquity antiquity.ac.uk	University of York

Archaeol. Rev. [*Archaeology Review*] www.eng-h.gov.uk/ArchRev/	English Heritage (London)
Cotswold Archaeol. Ann. Rev. www.cotswoldarch.org.uk/	Cotswold Archaeology (Cirencester)
Heroic Age www.mun.ca/mst/heroicage/issues/	Belleville, IL
Histos www.dur.ac.uk/Classics/histos/	University of Durham
Internet Archaeol. [*Internet Archaeology*] intarch.ac.uk/journal/	University of York
Med. Rev. [*The Medieval Review*] www.hti.umich.edu/t/tmr/	Western Michigan University (Kalamazoo, MI)
Ohio State Univ. Working Papers in Ling. www.ling.ohio-state.edu/publications/osu_wpl/	Ohio State University (Columbus, OH)

1. GENERAL AND MISCELLANEOUS

Altman, Cristina, 'Meeting Vivien Law, Oxford, September 1996', *Historiographia Linguistica* 29 (2002), 17–18

[Anon.], 'List of Publications by Manfred Görlach (1972–2002)', *Of dyuersitie*, ed. Lenz and Möhlig, pp. xix–xxvii

'The Writings of Helmut Gneuss', *Bookmarks from the Past*, ed. Kornexl and Lenker, pp. xvii–xxxiii

'The Medieval Libraries of Britain', *Book Collector* 52, 151–70 [on Corpus of British Medieval Library Catalogues]

Baker, Peter, 'Toller at School: Joseph Bosworth, T. Northcote Toller and the Progress of Old English Lexicography in the Nineteenth Century', *Textual and Material Culture*, ed. Scragg, pp. 283–300

Bankert, Dabney Anderson, 'T. Northcote Toller and the Making of the *Supplement* to the *Anglo-Saxon Dictionary*', *Textual and Material Culture*, ed. Scragg, pp. 301–21

Beck, Heinrich, Dieter Geuenich and Heiko Steuer, ed., *RGA* XV–XVI (2000) and XXII–XXV [cited below by vol. and pp.]

Benediktson, D. Thomas, 'Cambridge University Library Ll 1 14, f. 46^{r-v}: a Late Medieval Natural Scientist at Work', *Neophilologus* 86 (2002), 171–7 [Aldhelm-derived animal lore]

Biggam, C. P., ed., *From Earth to Art: the Many Aspects of the Plant-World in Anglo-Saxon England – Proceedings of the First ASPNS Symposium, University of Glasgow, 5–7 April 2000*, Costerus ns 148 (Amsterdam)

Bodleian Library, *Sir Thomas Bodley and His Library: an Exhibition to mark the Quatercentenary of the Bodleian, February to May 2002* (Oxford, 2002)

Brady, Niall, and James Schryver, 'Obituary: Robert T. Farrell 1939–2003', *Antiquity* 77, 878–9

Breeze, David J., 'Gerard Baldwin Brown (1849–1932): the Recording and Preservation of Monuments', *Proc. of the Soc. of Antiquaries of Scotland* 131 (2001), 41–55

Breuker, P. H., 'Junius, Franciscus', *RGA* XVI, 129–32

Brooks, Nicholas, 'Henry Royston Loyn, 1922–2000', *PBA* 120, 303–24

Brown, Keith, and Vivien Law, ed., *Linguistics in Britain: Personal Histories*, Publ. of the Philol. Soc. 36 (Oxford, 2002) [R. Quirk *et al.*]

Chevallier, Raymond, 'La bibliothèque de Des Esseintes ou le latin "décadent": une question toujours d'actualité', *Latomus* 61 (2002), 163–77 [use of Aldhelm and Boniface]

Clancy, Thomas Owen, 'Magpie Hagiography in Twelfth-Centry Scotland: the Case of *Libellus de nativitate Sancti Cuthberti*', *Celtic Hagiography and Saints' Cults*, ed. Jane Cartwright (Cardiff), pp. 216–31

Clarke, Howard B., '1066, 1169 and All That: the Tyranny of Historical Turning Points', *European Encounters: Essays in memory of Albert Lovett*, ed. Judith Devlin and Howard B. Clarke (Dublin), pp. 11–36

Donoghue, Daniel, *Lady Godiva: a Literary History of a Legend* (Oxford) [ch. 1]

Donoghue, Daniel, R. D. Fulk and R. M. Liuzza, ed., 'The Year's Work in Old English Studies 2000', *OEN* 35.2, 3–166

Gain, Benoît, 'Répertoire des traductions françaises des pères de l'église. Un travail en cours à partir des dépouillements effectués par le Frère Jacques Marcotte (Saint-Wandrille)', *Revue Mabillon* ns 14, 262–6 [Bede *et al.*]

Godden, Malcolm R., 'The Alfredian *Boethius* Project', *OEN* 37.1, 26–34

Godden, Malcolm R., and Rohini Jayatilaka, 'The *Fontes Anglo-Saxonici* Database: the Stand-Alone Version', *OEN* 36.1 (2003 for 2002), 17–23

Görlach, Manfred, *An Annotated Bibliography of Nineteenth-Century Grammars of English*, Amsterdam Stud. in the Theory and Hist. of Ling. Science, ser. 5: Lib. and Information Sources in Ling. 26 (Amsterdam, 1998) ['Books on Anglo-Saxon and Language History', appendix 1]

Gorrie, Bruce, '"The Wanderer", from the Old English', *Agenda* (London) 35.1 (1997), 54–7 [parody in Scots dialect]

Haft, Adele J., 'Earle Birney's "Mappemounde": Visualizing Poetry without Maps', *Cartographic Perspectives* 43 (2002), 4–24 and 65–75 [debt to OE verse]

Haines, Dorothy, 'The *Dictionary of Old English*', *Florilegium* 20, 95–6

Hall, Thomas N., with Melinda Menzer, 'Old English Bibliography 2002', *OEN* 36.4, 3–37

Hamilton, Donna B., 'Catholic Use of Anglo-Saxon Precedents, 1565–1625', *Recusant Hist.* 26 (2002–3), 537–55

Hardie, Caroline, 'Bede's World: the Museum of Early Medieval Northumbria at Jarrow', *Archaeol. North* 11 (1996), 13–17

Healey, Antonette diPaolo, 'The *Dictionary of Old English*: from Manuscripts to Megabytes', *Dictionaries* 23 (2002), 156–79

Herde, Peter, 'Die Äbtissin Cuthsuuith, Anton Chroust und der Sturz des bayerischen Kultusminsters Robert von Landmann (1901/02)', *Universität Würzburg und*

Wissenschaft in der Neuzeit, ed. Herde and Anton Schindling (Würzburg, 1998), pp. 231–72

Herren, Michael, 'Vivien Anne Law', *Peritia* 16 (2002), 524–5

Hough, Carole, 'Victor Watts (1938–2002)', *Nomina* 26, 129–30

Howe, Nicholas, 'What We Talk about When We Talk about Style', *Anglo-Saxon Styles*, ed. Karkov and Brown, pp. 169–78

Huntington, Joanna, 'Edward the Celibate, Edward the Saint: Virginity in the Construction of Edward the Confessor', *Medieval Virginities*, ed. Anke Bernau, Ruth Evans and Sarah Salih (Cardiff), pp. 119–39

Insley, John, 'Victor Ernest Watts (1938–2002)', *JEPNS* 35 (2002–3), 59–60

Ireland, Colin, 'Aldfrith of Northumbria and the Learning of a *sapiens*', *A Celtic Florilegium*, ed. Kathryn A. Klar, Eve E. Sweetser and Claire Thomas (Lawrence, MA, 1996), pp. 63–77

Jankowsky, Kurt R., 'Sound Physiology in the Making: on the Role of Henry Sweet (1845–1912) and Eduard Sievers (1850–1932) in the Development of Linguistic Science', *The Emergence of the Modern Language Sciences*, ed. Sheila Embleton, John E. Joseph and Hans-Josef Niederehe, 2 vols. (Philadelphia, 1999) I, 77–91

Joseph, John E., 'Obituary, Vivien Anne Law, Lady Shackleton', *Beiträge zur Geschichte der Sprachwissenschaft* 13, 9–10

Karkov, Catherine E., '*In memoriam*: Robert T. Farrell, November 16, 1938–July 31, 2003', *OEN* 37.1, 6

Karkov, Catherine E., and George Hardin Brown, ed., *Anglo-Saxon Styles*, SUNY Ser. in Med. Stud. (Albany, NY)

Kerecuk, Nadia, 'Eulogy for Vivien Law', *Beiträge zur Geschichte der Sprachwissenschaft* 13, 3–8

Keynes, Simon, 'A Tribute to Helmut Gneuss from Cambridge', *Bookmarks from the Past*, ed. Kornexl and Lenker, pp. xi–xv

Kipper, Rainer, *Der Germanenmythos im deutschen Kaiserreich. Formen und Funktionen historischer Selbstthematisierung*, Formen der Erinnerung 11 (Göttingen, 2002) [esp. on Boniface, sects. *b–c*]

Klein, Stacy S., and Mary Swan, 'Old English Literature', *Year's Work in Eng. Stud.* 82, 115–36 [for 2001]

Kleinman, Scott, 'The Legend of Havelok the Dane and the Historiography of East Anglia', *SP* 100, 245–77 [figures of Æthelberht *et al.*]

Koerner, E. F. K., 'Bibliography of Vivien A. Law, 1975–2002', *Historiographia Linguistica* 29 (2002), 7–13

Kornexl, Lucia, and Ursula Lenker, ed., see sect. 3*a*

Kries, Susanne, '"Westward I came across the sea": Anglo-Scandinavian History through Scandinavian Eyes', *Leeds Stud. in Eng.* ns 33, 47–76 [Egill Skallagrímsson, *Aðalsteinsdrápa*]

Leasure, T. Ross, 'The Genesis of *Paradise Lost*: what Milton may have seen in the Junius Manuscript', *Cithara* 41.2 (2002), 3–17

Lenz, Katja, and Ruth Möhlig, ed., see sect. 2*b*

Lerer, Seth, *Error and the Academic Self: the Scholarly Imagination, Medieval to Modern* (New York, 2002) ['Sublime Philology: an Elegy for Anglo-Saxon Studies', ch. 2]

Lewis, Katherine J., 'Becoming a Virgin King: Richard II and Edward the Confessor', *Gender and Holiness*, ed. Samantha J. E. Riches and Sarah Salih (London, 2002), pp. 86–100

Lucas, Peter J., 'John Minsheu, Polymath and Poseur: Old English in an Early Seventeenth-Century Dictionary', *Of dyuersitie*, ed. Lenz and Möhlig, pp. 144–56

'From Politics to Practicalities: Printing Anglo-Saxon in the Context of Seventeenth-Century Scholarship', *The Library* 7th ser. 4, 28–48

McInerney, Maud Burnett, *Eloquent Virgins from Thecla to Joan of Arc*, New Middle Ages (Basingstoke) [Aldhelm, esp. in ch. 3]

McLean, Janet, Richard Pelter and Rupert Shepherd, '"Gazing, but not copying": the Creation of G. F. Watts's "Alfred inciting the Saxons to prevent the landing of the Danes"', *Apollo* 158.500 [*recte* 158.501], 35–8 [painting, from 1847, now in Palace of Westminster]

Mattingly, Joanna, 'Pre-Reformation Saints' Cults in Cornwall, with Particular Reference to the St Neot Windows', *Celtic Hagiography and Saints' Cults*, ed. Jane Cartwright (Cardiff), pp. 249–70 [Alfred, Asser *et al.*]

Mitchell, Emily, 'Patrons and Politics at Twelfth-Century Barking Abbey', *RB* 113, 347–64 [hagiography of Edward the Confessor]

Mittman, Asa Simon, 'The Other Close at Hand: Gerald of Wales and the "Marvels of the West"', *The Monstrous Middle Ages*, ed. Bettina Bildhauer and Robert Mills (Toronto), pp. 97–112 [esp. on *Liber monstrorum* and *Marvels of the East*]

Nelson, Janet L., David A. E. Pelteret and Harold Short, 'Medieval Prosopographies and the Prosopography of Anglo-Saxon England', *PBA* 118, 155–67

Nerlich, Brigitte, 'Vivien Law: Some Memories', *Historiographia Linguistica* 29 (2002), 15–16

Page, R. I., 'The Transcription of Old English Texts in the Sixteenth Century', *Care and Conservation of Manuscripts 7*, ed. Gillian Fellows-Jensen and Peter Springborg (Copenhagen), pp. 179–90

Parish, Helen L., '"Impudent and Abhominable Fictions": Rewriting Saints' Lives in the English Reformation', *Sixteenth Century Jnl* 32 (2001), 45–65 [esp. on Dunstan]

Petitmengin, Pierre, 'Les éditions patristiques de la contre-réforme romaine', *I Padri sotto il torchio*, ed. Mariarosa Cortesi (Florence, 2002), pp. 3–31 [Bede]

Proud, Joana, 'Collections of Saints' Lives in the Thirteenth and Fourteenth Centuries: Interpreting the Manuscript Evidence', *Lives in Print*, ed. Robin Myers, Michael Harris and Giles Mandelbrote (London, 2002), pp. 1–21 [fortunes of AS works]

'Thomas Northcote Toller: "This Fearless and Self-Sacrificing Knight of Scholarship"', *Textual and Material Culture*, ed. Scragg, pp. 333–45

Read, Allen Walker, 'The Beginnings of English Lexicography', *Dictionaries* 24, 187–226 [esp. on Somner, Junius *et al.*; posthumous publ.]

Reames, Sherry L., ed., *Middle English Legends of Women Saints* (Kalamazoo, MI) ['The Legend of Frideswide of Oxford, an Anglo-Saxon Royal Abbess', pt. i]

Reuter, Timothy, ed., see sect. 6

Roelcke, Thorsten, 'Die englische Sprache im deutschen Sprachdenken des 17. und 18. Jahrhunderts', *Beiträge zur Geschichte der Sprachwissenschaft* 13, 85–113

Rollason, David, 'Durham *Liber vitae* Project', *OEN* 37.1, 23–4

Römer, Christine, 'Eduard Sievers als Erneuerer der Lautlehre', *Gesprochene Sprache*, ed. Margret Bräunlich, Baldur Neuber and Beate Rues (Frankfurt am Main, 2001), pp. 119–25

Royal Commission on Historical Manuscripts, *Papers of British Antiquaries and Historians*, Guides to Sources for Brit. Hist. 12 (London)

Rumble, Alexander R., 'Items of Lexicographical Interest in the Toller Collection, John Rylands University Library of Manchester', *Textual and Material Culture*, ed. Scragg, pp. 323–32

Ryan, John S., 'J. R. R. Tolkien's Formal Lecturing and Teaching at the University of Oxford, 1925–1959', *VII: an Anglo-Amer. Lit. Rev.* (Wheaton, IL) 19 (2002), 45–62

Scahill, John, 'Trilingualism in Early Middle English Miscellanies: Languages and Literature', *YES* 33, 18–32 [esp. on med. lists of AS letters]

Schipper, William, 'Vivien A. Law (1954–2002)', *Historiographia Linguistica* 29 (2002), 1–5

Scragg, Donald, ed., see sect. 3*a*

Shepherd, Colin, *A Study of the Relationship between Style I Art and Socio-Political Change in Early Mediaeval Europe*, BAR International Ser. 745 (Oxford, 1998) [includes Eng. material]

Shippey, Tom, 'Bilingualism and Betrayal in Chaucer's *Summoner's Tale*', *Speaking in the Medieval World*, ed. Jean E. Godsall-Myers (Leiden), pp. 125–44 [Chaucerian mimicry of OE]

Smith, Nicola, *The Royal Image and the English People* (Aldershot, 2001) [figures of Alfred, Athelstan *et al.*, esp. in chs. 2 and 5–6]

Smith, Robin D., 'Investigating Older Germanic Languages in England', *History of the Language Sciences* II, ed. Sylvain Auroux, E. F. K. Koerner, Hans-Josef Niederehe and Kees Versteegh, Handbücher zur Sprach- und Kommunikationswissenschaft 18.2 (Berlin, 2001), pp. 1129–36

Teresì, Loredana, 'L'analisi testuale con TACT: un'esperienza nel campo dell'inglese antico', *Poetry of the Early Medieval Europe*, ed. Edoardo D'Angelo and Francesco Stella (Florence), pp. 217–33

Thompson, Anne B., *Everyday Saints and the Art of Narrative in the 'South English Legendary'* (Aldershot) [reception of OE prose; figures of Frithuswith, Edmund *et al.*]

Tompkins, J. Case, '"The Homecoming of Beorhtnoth Beorhthelm's Son": Tolkien as a Modern Anglo-Saxon', *Mythlore* 23.4 (2002), 67–74

Townend, Matthew, 'Norse Poets and English Kings: Skaldic Performance in Anglo-Saxon England', *Offa* 58 (2003 for 2001), 269–75

'Whatever Happened to York Viking Poetry? Memory, Tradition and the Transmission of Skaldic Verse', *SBVS* 27, 48–90

Wallach, Rick, 'From *Beowulf* to *Blood Meridian*: Cormac McCarthy's Demystification of the Martial Code', *Cormac McCarthy: New Directions* (Albuquerque, NM, 2002), pp. 199–214

Ward, Charlotte, 'Pound's Humanistic Paradigm for the Rejuvenation of Modern

Poetics', *Medieval and Renaissance Humanism*, ed. Stephen Gersh and Bert Roest (Leiden), pp. 243–77

Yorke, Barbara, 'Alfredism: the Use and Abuse of King Alfred's Reputation in Later Centuries', *Alfred the Great*, ed. Reuter, pp. 361–80

2. OLD ENGLISH LANGUAGE

a. Lexicon and glosses

Amodio, Mark C., and Katherine O'B. O'Keeffe, ed., see sect. 3*a*

Bammesberger, Alfred, 'The Entry *henna* in Dictionaries of Old English', *N&Q* 50, 258

'The Provenance of the Old English Suffix *-stre*', *North-Western European Lang. Evolution* 43, 53–63

Beck, Heinrich, and Karl Hauck, 'Zur philologischen und historischen Auswertung eines neuen Drei-Götter–Brakteaten aus Sorte Muld, Bornholm, Dänemark. (Zur Ikonologie der Goldbrakteaten, LXIII)', *FS* 36 (2002), 51–94 [*salu*, sect. I.3, by Beck]

Bierbaumer, Peter, 'Real and Not-So-Real Plant-Names in Old English Glosses', *From Earth to Art*, ed. Biggam, pp. 153–60

Biggam, C. P., 'The *æspe* Tree in Anglo-Saxon England', *From Earth to Art*, ed. Biggam, pp. 195–230

Biggam, C. P., ed., see sect. 1

Blažek, Václav, 'The "Beech"-Argument: State-of-the-Art', *HS* 115 (2002), 190–217 [*bōc* and *bēce*]

Boutkan, Dirk, 'On Gothic *magaþs* ~ Old Frisian *megith* and the Form of Some North European Substratum Words in Germanic', *Amsterdamer Beiträge zur älteren Germanistik* 58, 11–27 [esp. on *mægden* and *mægð*, 'virgin']

Brogyanyi, Bela, ed., with Thomas Krömmelbein, *Germanisches Altertum und christliches Mittelalter. Festschrift für Heinz Klingenberg zum 65. Geburtstag*, Schriften zur Mediävistik 1 (Hamburg, 2002)

Brosman, Paul W., Jr, 'The Cognates of the Latin *ti-* Abstracts', *Jnl of Indo-European Stud.* 31, 1–19 [esp. on *cynd* and *tyht*]

Cameron, Angus, Ashley Crandell Amos and Antonette diPaolo Healey, ed., *Dictionary of Old English A–F* (Toronto) [CD-ROM]

Ciszek, Ewa, 'ME *-lich(e)/-ly*', *Studia Anglica Posnaniensia* 38 (2002), 105–29

Cooke, William, '"Aluen swiðe sceone": How Long did OE *ælfen/elfen* Survive in ME?', *ELN* 41.1, 1–7

Dance, Richard, *Words Derived from Old Norse in Early Middle English: Studies in the Vocabulary of the South-West Midland Texts*, Med. and Renaissance Texts and Stud. 246 (Tempe, AZ)

Eichner, Heiner, and Robert Nedoma, 'Die *Merseburger Zaubersprüche*: philologische und sprachwissenschaftliche Probleme aus heutiger Sicht', *Die Sprache* 42 (2000–1), 1–195 [OE *comparanda*, sect. 3]

Esposito, Anthony, 'Medieval Plant-Names in the *Oxford English Dictionary*', *From Earth to Art*, ed. Biggam, pp. 231–48

Falileyev, Alexander, and G. R. Isaac, 'Leeks and Garlic: the Germanic Ethnonym *cannenefates*, Celtic **kasn-* and Slavic **kesn-*', *North-Western European Lang. Evolution* 42, 3–12 [*clufu*]

Fell, Christine, 'Old English Semantic Studies and Their Bearing on Rune-Names', *Runor och runinskrifter*, ed. Kungl. vitterhets, historie och antikvitets akademien, pp. 99–109

Filppula, Markku, 'The Quest for the Most "Parsimonious" Explanations: Endogeny vs. Contact Revisited', *Motives for Language Change*, ed. Raymond Hickey (Cambridge), pp. 161–73 [*dēor* and *gōp* as Celtic loanwords, sect. 4]

Fischer, Andreas, 'Notes on Kinship Terminology in the History of English', *Of dyuersitie*, ed. Lenz and Möhlig, pp. 115–28

Frank, Roberta, 'Sex in the *Dictionary of Old English*', *Unlocking the 'wordhord'*, ed. Amodio and O'Keeffe, pp. 302–12

González Orta, Marta María, 'Lexical Templates and Syntactic Variation: the Syntax–Semantics Interface of the Old English Verb *secgan*', *New Perspectives on Argument Structure in Functional Grammar*, ed. Ricardo Mairal Usón and María Jesús Pérez Quintero (Berlin, 2002), pp. 281–302

Greenberg, Joseph H., *Indo-European and its Closest Relatives: the Eurasiatic Language Family*, 2 vols. (Stanford, CA, 2000–2) [OE lexis, esp. in sect. II.2]

Harm, Volker, 'Zur semantischen Vorgeschichte von dt. *verstehen*, e. *understand* und agr. 'ἐπίσταμαι', *HS* 116, 108–27 [*forstandan*, *onfindan*, *onfōn*, *onginnan*, *ongietan* and *understandan*]

Healey, Antonette diPaolo, 'Questions of Fairness: Fair, not Fair and Foul', *Unlocking the 'wordhord'*, ed. Amodio and O'Keeffe, pp. 252–73 [*fæger*]

Heizmann, Wilhelm, and Astrid van Nahl, ed., see sect. 3*a*

Hogg, Richard, 'Regular Suppletion', *Motives for Language Change*, ed. Raymond Hickey (Cambridge), pp. 71–81 ['*Syndon*', sect. 4; note also proposal of adj. **bæd*, 'bad', sect. 2]

Hough, Carole, 'The Surname Purrock', *N&Q* 50, 375–7 [esp. on *āc*, *pūr* and OE diminutives]

see also sect. 8 [*hwīt* and similar]

Iglesias-Rábade, Luis, 'The Middle English Preposition *in*: a Semantic Analysis', *Studia Anglica Posnaniensia* 39, 57–76

Iyeiri, Yoko, 'A Historical Study of the Verb *forbid* in Different Versions of the English Bible', *Jnl of Eng. Ling.* 31, 149–62

Kalbhen, Ursula, *Kentische Glossen und kentischer Dialekt im Altenglischen, mit einer kommentierten Edition. Der altenglischen Glossen in der Handschrift London, British Library, Cotton Vespasian D. vi*, Münchener Universitätsschriften, Texte und Untersuchungen zur englischen Philologie 28 (Frankfurt am Main)

Karasawa, Kazutomo, 'Christian Influence on OE *dream*: Pre-Christian and Christian Meanings', *Neophilologus* 87, 307–22

Kitson, Peter, 'Old English Literacy and the Provenance of Welsh *y*', *Yr hen iaith: Studies in Early Welsh*, ed. Paul Russell (Aberystwyth), pp. 49–65

'Topography, Dialect, and the Relation of Old English Psalter-Glosses (II)', *ES* 84, 9–32

Kleparski, Grzegorz A., '"Churls", "Harlots" and "Sires": the Semantics of Middle English Synonyms of "Man"', *Studia Anglica Posnaniensia* 39, 47–55

Kornexl, Lucia, 'Die etymologischen Erklärungsansätze für die Bildungen auf ae. *-estre*: eine kritische analyse', *North-Western European Lang. Evolution* 42, 69–98

Kornexl, Lucia, and Ursula Lenker, ed., see sect. 3*a*

Krotz, Elke, *Auf den Spuren des althochdeutschen Isidor. Studien zur Pariser Handschrift, den Monseer Fragmenten und zum Codex Junius 25, mit einer Neuedition des Glossars Jc*, Beiträge zur älteren Literaturgeschichte (Heidelberg, 2002) [esp. on Leiden-family glossaries and on related metrological treatises, sect. 2.6]

Kungl. vitterhets, historie och antikvitets akademien, ed., see sect. 9*l*

Lehmann, Winfred P., 'Version in Active Languages', *General Ling.* 40 (2003 for 2000), 57–70 [esp. on *beran*, *īecan* and *secgan*]

Lendinara, Patrizia, 'Was the Glossator a Teacher?', *Quaestio* (Cambridge) 3 (2002), 1–27

Lenker, Ursula, '*Forsooth*, a Source: Metalinguistic Thought in Early English', *Bookmarks from the Past*, ed. Kornexl and Lenker, pp. 261–88 [*sōð*, *sōðlic* and similar]

Lenz, Katja, and Ruth Möhlig, ed., see sect. 2*b*

Lewickij, Viktor, 'Zur germanischen Etymologie', *HS* 116, 100–7 [*āc*, *bān* and *snell*]

Liberman, Anatoly, '*Bird* and *toad*', *Runica – Germanica – Mediaevalia*, ed. Heizmann and van Nahl, pp. 375–88 [*brid(d)*, *tāde* and *tādi(g)e*]

'Gothic *þrutsfill*, Old English *þrustfell*, "Leprosy", and the Names of Some Other Skin Diseases in Germanic', *Germanisches Altertum und christliches Mittelalter*, ed. Brogyanyi, pp. 197–211

'The Etymology of the Word *slang*', *North-Western European Lang. Evolution* 42, 99–113 [comparison with *slingan*]

Lindeman, Fredrik Otto, 'Indo-European *H_3ek^w, "to see; eye": a Speculative "Laryngeal" Note', *IF* 108, 47–57 [esp. for *oð-ēawan* and *scēawian*]

'On the Origin of the Germanic Verb **neman-*', *HS* 116, 302–7 [*niman*]

Lockwood, W. B., 'Etymological Notes on *bergander* and *Eligug*', *TPS* 101, 1–5 [proposes OE **beorggandra*, sect. 1]

McConvell, Patrick, and Michael A. Smith, 'Millers and Mullers: the Archaeo-Linguistic Stratigraphy of Technological Change in Holocene Australia', *Language Contacts in Prehistory*, ed. Henning Andersen (Amsterdam), pp. 177–200 [*hænep*, sect. 1.4]

McGowan, Joseph P., '*Praefanda Anglosaxonica*', *SN* 75, 3–10 [*drisne*, *feorting*, *fisting* and *goldhordhūs*; compounds in *ears-*, and *gang-*]

Manzelli, Gianguido, 'Parallelismi semantici indoeuropei e uralici', *Fare etimologia*, ed. Marina Benedetti (Rome, 2001), pp. 475–93 [*nasu* and *næs(s)*, sect. 6.4]

Martín Díaz, María Auxiliadora, 'Old English *ēa* in Middle Kentish Place-Names', *Studia Anglica Posnaniensia* 38 (2002), 331–51

Mees, Bernard, 'Runic *erilaR*', *North-Western European Lang. Evolution* 42, 41–68 [OE analogues]

Meier, Hans Heinrich, 'Their *burh* was their Homestead: or, an Old Sense Overlooked', *Of dyuersitie*, ed. Lenz and Möhlig, pp. 129–43

Méndez-Naya, Belén, 'On Intensifiers and Grammaticalization: the Case of *swīþe*', *ES* 84, 372–91

Molencki, Rafał, 'The Status of *dearr* and *þearf* in Old English', *Studia Anglica Posnaniensia* 38 (2002), 363–80

Naumann, H.-P., and R. Schmidt-Wiegand, 'Rechtssprache', *RGA* XXIV, 268–76

Nedoma, R., 'Runennamen', *RGA* XXV, 556–62

Ó Cróinín, Dáibhí, 'The Old Irish and Old English Glosses in Echternach Manuscripts (with an Appendix on Old Breton Glosses)', *Die Abtei Echternach*, ed. Michele Camillo Ferrari, Jean Schroeder and Henri Traffler (Echternach, 1999), pp. 85–101

Ogura, Michiko, 'Verbs of Motion in Laȝamon's *Brut*', *Laȝamon: Contexts, Language and Interpretation*, ed. Rosamund Allen, Lucy Perry and Jane Roberts (London, 2002), pp. 211–25

'The Variety and Conformity of Old English Psalter Glosses', *ES* 84, 1–8

'Words of Emotion in Old and Middle English Psalms and Alliterative Poems', *Jnl of Humanities* (Chiba) 32, 393–427

Paraschkewow, Boris, 'Nhd. *kitzeln*: ein Germanismus oder ein Indogermanismus?', *Zeitschrift für germanistische Linguistik* 31, 105–8 [*citelian*]

Pierce, Marc, 'Zur Etymologie von germ. *rûna*', *Amsterdamer Beiträge zur älteren Germanistik* 58, 29–37 [*rūn*]

Pons Sanz, Sara María, 'Datos para la reconstrucción léxica del inglés antiguo: de las glosas de Aldred a los Evangelios de Lindisfarne', *De lenguas y lenguajes*, ed. Alexandre Veiga, Miguel González Pereira and Montserrat Souto Gómez (Noia, 2001), pp. 271–9

'Aldred's Glosses to Numismatic Terms in the Lindisfarne Gospels', *The Grove: Stud. on Med. Eng. Lang. and Lit.* (Jaén) 8 (2001), 111–20

Roberts, Jane, see sect. 3*a* [*wealhstod*]

Rübekeil, Ludwig, 'Einige Bemerkungen zur Wortfamilie um germ. **hatis-*', *Germanisches Altertum und christliches Mittelalter*, ed. Brogyanyi, pp. 239–94 [esp. on *hātan* and *hettan*]

Rusche, Philip G., 'Dioscorides' *De materia medica* and Late Old English Herbal Glossaries', *From Earth to Art*, ed. Biggam, pp. 181–94

Sauer, Hans, 'The Morphology of the Old English Plant-Names', *From Earth to Art*, ed. Biggam, pp. 161–79

Schleburg, Florian, *Altenglisch 'swa'. Syntax und Semantik einer polyfunktionalen Partikel*, Sprachwissenschaftliche Studienbücher (Heidelberg, 2002)

Skaffari, Janne, '"Touched by an alien tongue": Studying Lexical Borrowings in the Earliest Middle English', *A Changing World of Words*, ed. Javier E. Díaz Vera (Amsterdam, 2001), pp. 500–21

Stacey, Robin Chapman, 'King, Queen and *edling* in the Laws of Court', *The Welsh King and His Court*, ed. T. M. Charles-Edwards, Morfydd E. Owen and Paul Russell (Cardiff, 2000), pp. 29–62 [*æðeling*]

Staiti, Chiara, 'Dal cielo all'inferno. Osservazioni su un campo semantico tra antico sassone e antico inglese', *Circolazione di uomini, di idee e di testi nel Medioevo germanico*, ed. Franco De Vivo (Cassino, 2002), pp. 131–56

Stanley, E. G., 'Middle English *neotsum*', *N&Q* 50, 276–7 [*nēat*]

Stifter, David, 'Study in Red', *Die Sprache* 40 (1998), 202–23

Thier, Katrin, 'Sails in the North – New Perspectives on an Old Problem', *International Jnl of Nautical Archaeol.* 32, 182–90 [hist. of term *sail*, with discussion of cognates]

Toorians, Lauran, 'Magusanus and the "Old Lad": a Case of Germanicised Celtic', *North-Western European Lang. Evolution* 42, 13–28 [*mago*]

Trotter, David, '*Oceano vox*: You Never Know where a Ship Comes From – on Multilingualism and Language-Mixing in Medieval Britain', *Aspects of Multilingualism in European Language History*, ed. Kurt Braunmüller and Gisella Ferraresi (Amsterdam), pp. 15–33 [nautical and marine terminology]

Van Herreweghe, Mieke, '*Motan in the Anglo-Saxon Poetic Records', *Belgian Jnl of Ling.* 14 (2000), 207–39

Vennemann, Theo, 'Etymologische Beziehungen im Alten Europa', Vennemann, *Europa Vasconica*, pp. 203–97 [OE treated *ad indicem*; reissue of stud. publ. in 1995]

'Some West Indo-European Words of Uncertain Origin', Vennemann, *Europa Vasconica*, pp. 343–70 [OE treated *ad indicem*; reissue of stud. publ. in 1997]

Europa Vasconica – Europa Semitica, ed. Patrizia Noel Aziz Hanna, Trends in Ling., Stud. and Monographs 138 (Berlin) [OE lexical indices at pp. 946 and 954–5; reissued and newly ptd papers]

'Germania Semitica: **sibjō*', *Runica – Germanica – Mediaevalia*, ed. Heizmann and van Nahl, pp. 871–91 [*sib(b)*]

'Zur Frage der vorindogermanischen Substrate in Mittel- und Westeuropa', Vennemann, *Europa Vasconica*, pp. 517–90 [esp. for *beallucas*; also on *īsearn* and late OE *knīf*]

Wagner, Norbert, 'Vulgärlateinisches in germanischen Namen bei klassischen Autoren', *HS* 116, 132–41 [*faroð* and *waroð*]

Weinstock, Horst, 'Historical and Comparative Aspects of English Numerals between Twenty-One and Ninety-Nine', Weinstock, *Kleine Schriften*, pp. 137–49 [reissue of essay publ. in 1999]

'Französisches im Englischen', Weinstock, *Kleine Schriften*, pp. 151–61 ['Altfranzösisches im Altenglischen?', sect. 3; reissue of essay publ. in 2002]

see also sect. 2*b*

York, Michael, 'In Defense of Indo-European Studies: Ethical and Theological Implications from a Sociological Analysis of Terms for "God", "Worship" and "Awe"', *General Ling.* 40 (2003 for 2000), 183–97

Zavaroni, Adolfo, 'Etr. *ana*, lat. *ānus*, *annus*, got. *aþn*, germ. **ansi-*', *IF* 108, 223–47 [esp. on *seono*, with many OE *comparanda*]

b. Syntax, phonology and other aspects

Adamczyk, Elżbieta, 'Reduplication and the Old English Strong Verbs, Class VII', *Studia Anglica Posnaniensia* 38 (2002), 23–34

Allen, Cynthia L., 'Case and Middle English Genitive Noun Phrases', *Syntactic Effects*, ed. Lightfoot (Oxford, 2002), pp. 57–80

'Deflexion and the Development of the Genitive in English', *Eng. Lang. and Ling.* 7, 1–28

Antonsen, Elmer H., '"Weil die Schrift immer strebt . . .": on Phonological Reconstruction', *North-Western European Lang. Evolution* 43, 3–20

Baker, Peter S., *Introduction to Old English* (Oxford)

Bald, Wolf-Dietrich, 'Speculation about *wife* and *wives*', *Of dyuersitie*, ed. Lenz and Möhlig, pp. 1–5

Bauer, Laurie, *Morphological Productivity*, Cambridge Stud. in Ling. 95 (Cambridge, 2001) [esp. in ch. 6, on *-dōm* and *-ter*]

Bejar, Susana, 'Movement, Morphology and Learnability', *Syntactic Effects*, ed. Lightfoot, pp. 307–25

Bondaruk, Anna, and Magdalena Charzyńska-Wójcik, 'Expletive *pro* in Impersonal Passives in Irish, Polish and Old English', *Linguistische Berichte* 193–6, 325–62

Boškovič, Željko, 'Split Constituents within NP in the History of English: Commentary on Allen', *Syntactic Effects*, ed. Lightfoot, pp. 81–7

Burnley, David, 'The T/V Pronouns in Later Middle English Literature', *Diachronic Perspectives on Address Term Systems*, ed. Irma Taavitsainen and Andreas H. Jucker (Amsterdam), pp. 27–45 [in sects. 1–2]

Bybee, Joan, 'Mechanisms of Change in Grammaticization: the Role of Frequency', *The Handbook of Historical Linguistics*, ed. Brian D. Joseph and Richard D. Janda (Oxford), pp. 602–23 ['From Noun Phrase Complement to Verb Phrase Complement (Old English)', on *cunnan*, sect. 4.2]

Čermák, Jan, 'A Diachronic Perspective on Old English Deadjectival Nouns Ending in *-þ(u)/-t(u)*', *Brno Stud. in Eng.* 28 (2002), 19–25

Choi, Byung Jung, 'Productive Word-Formation Pattern in Old English', *Hist. of Eng.* (Seoul) 14 (2002), 41–61 [in Korean]

Christensen, Ken Ramshøf, 'On the Synchronic and Diachronic Status of the Negative Adverbial *ikke/not*', *Working Papers in Scandinavian Syntax* (Lund) 72, 1–53 [*ne* and *nō*, sect. 4]

Chudy, Wiesław, and Piotr P. Chruszczewski, 'Dynamizm kontekstualny gramatyki komunikacyjnej dyskursu militarnego na przykładzie tekstów roty przysięgi wojskowej w Polsce w latach 1918–1999', *Anglica Wratislaviensia* 40, 123–51 [discussion of OE grammar, sect. 2]

Cortés Rodríguez, Francisco José, and Dolores Torres Medina, 'Old English Verbs-of-Running: Linking Semantic Representation and Morphosyntactic Structure', *Folia Linguistica Historica* 24, 153–74

Croft, William, *Radical Construction Grammar: Syntactic Theory in Typological Perspective* (Oxford, 2001) [clauses with *þe* and *þȳ*, sects. 1.3.1 and 9.1.2]

Curzan, Anne, *Gender Shifts in the History of English*, Stud. in Eng. Lang. (Cambridge)

Dawson, Hope C., 'Defining the Outcome of Language Contact: Old English and Old Norse', *Ohio State Univ. Working Papers in Ling.* 57, 40–57 [online]

Denton, Jeannette Marshall, 'Reconstructing the Articulation of Early Germanic **r*', *Diachronica* 20, 11–43

Drinka, Bridget, 'The Development of the Perfect in Indo-European: Stratigraphic Evidence of Prehistoric Areal Influence', *Language Contacts in Prehistory*, ed. Henning Andersen (Amsterdam), pp. 77–105 [modal auxiliaries, sect. 2.1.1]

Erickson, Jon L., 'Historical *that* and Indirect Questions in Modern English', *Of dyuersitie*, ed. Lenz and Möhlig, pp. 55–65

Fikkert, Paula, 'The Prosodic Structure of Prefixed Words in the History of West Germanic', *Development in Prosodic Systems*, ed. Paula Fikkert and Haike Jacobs (Berlin), pp. 315–48

Filppula, Markku, 'A Tale of Two English Perfects: a Case of Competition between Grammars', *Of dyuersitie*, ed. Lenz and Möhlig, pp. 66–76

'More on the English Progressive and the Celtic Connection', *The Celtic Englishes III*, ed. Hildegard L. C. Tristram (Heidelberg), pp. 150–68

Fischer, Olga C. M., 'Principles of Grammaticalization and Linguistic Reality', *Determinants of Grammatical Variation in English*, ed. Günther Rohdenburg and Britta Mondorf (Berlin), pp. 445–78 [esp. on *to* with (inflected) infinitives, sect. 3]

Fischer, Roswitha, *Tracing the History of English: a Textbook for Students*, with an overview of Eng. lit. up to 1790 by Daniela Schwepper (Darmstadt) ['Old English', ch. 3]

Frank, Roberta, 'The Discreet Charm of the Old English Weak Adjective', *Anglo-Saxon Styles*, ed. Karkov and Brown, pp. 239–52

Fraser, Tom, 'Remarques sur le passage du préverbe au postverbe en vieil-anglais tardif', *Les préverbes dans les langues d'Europe*, ed. André Rousseau (Villeneuve d'Ascq, 1995), pp. 95–104

Fukushima, Osamu, 'A Note on the Perfective Aspect in *Beowulf*, *Daito Bunka Rev.* 34, 1–10

Fulk, R. D., 'On Argumentation in Old English Philology, with Particular Reference to the Editing and Dating of *Beowulf*, *ASE* 32, 1–26

Fuss, Eric, 'On the Historical Core of V2 in Germanic', *Nordic Jnl of Ling.* 26, 195–231

Giurgea, Ion, 'Sur l'origine de la 3[e] classe des verbes faibles germaniques', *Revue roumaine de linguistique* 44 (2003 for 1999), 65–70

Goblirsch, Kurt Gustav, 'The Voicing of Fricatives in West Germanic and the Partial Consonant Shift', *Folia Linguistica Historica* 24, 111–52

González Orta, Marta María, 'Sobre la interficie semántica–sintaxis de los verbos de habla en inglés antiguo: los verbos que designan manera de hablar', *Revista española de lingüística* 32 (2002), 507–28

Görlach, Manfred, *Still More Englishes*, Varieties of Eng. around the World, General Ser. G28 (Amsterdam, 2002) ['Old English', sect. 2.2.1, on standardization]

Gotti, Maurizio, Marina Dossena, Richard Dury, Roberta Facchinetti, and Maria Lima, *Variation in Central Modals: a Repertoire of Forms and Types of Usage in Middle English and Early Modern English*, Ling. Insights 4 (Bern, 2002) ['Old English', in sect. I.3]

Green, Eugene, 'On *habban* + Second Participle in Old English Poetry', *Interdisciplinary Jnl for Germanic Ling. and Semiotic Analysis* 8, 191–242

Gretsch, Mechthild, 'In Search of Standard Old English', *Bookmarks from the Past*, ed. Kornexl and Lenker, pp. 33–67

Haeberli, Eric, *Features, Categories and the Syntax of A-Positions: Cross-Linguistic Variation in the Germanic Languages*, Stud. in Natural Lang. and Ling. Theory 54 (Dordrecht, 2002) [esp. in ch. 4]

'Inflectional Morphology and the Loss of Verb-Second in English', *Syntactic Effects*, ed. Lightfoot, pp. 88–106

Haumann, Dagmar, 'The Postnominal "and Adjective" Construction in Old English', *Eng. Lang. and Ling.* 7, 57–83

Heizmann, Wilhelm, and Astrid van Nahl, ed., see sect. 3*a*

Hickey, Raymond, 'Language Change in Early Britain: the Convergence Account', *Sounds and Systems*, ed. Restle and Zaefferer, pp. 185–203

Hiltunen, Risto, and Janne Skaffari, ed., *Discourse Perspectives on English: Medieval to Modern*, Pragmatics and Beyond ns 119 (Amsterdam)

Hiyama, Susumu, 'Impersonals in the *Vercelli Homilies*: Postscript', *Jnl of the Faculty of Foreign Languages* (Komazawa Univ.) 30 (2001), 127–88, and 31 (2002), 111–32 [in Japanese]

Hogg, Richard, 'Regular Suppletion', *Motives for Language Change*, ed. Raymond Hickey (Cambridge), pp. 71–81

Hopper, Paul, 'Hendiadys and Auxiliation in English', *Complex Sentences in Grammar and Discourse*, ed. Joan L. Bybee and Michael Noonan (Amsterdam, 2002), pp. 145–73 [sect. 1]

Hreinn Benediktsson, *Linguistic Studies, Historical and Comparative*, ed. Guðrún Þórhallsdóttir, Höskuldur Þráinsson, Jón G. Friðjónsson and Kjartan Ottosson (Reykjavik, 2002) [reissued papers; 'Old English', *ad indicem*, p. 571]

Hudson, Richard, 'Gerunds without Phrase Structure', *Natural Lang. and Ling. Theory* 21, 579–615 [sects. 1 and 7–8]

Iglesias-Rábade, Luis, 'A Semantic Study of *on*-phrases in Middle English', *SN* 75, 104–18

Ingham, Richard, 'The Development of Middle English Expletive Negative Sentences', *TPS* 101, 411–52 [esp. in sect. 2]

Isakson, Bo, 'How Primary was the OHG Primary Umlaut?', *North-Western European Lang. Evolution* 41 (2002), 99–104

Iwata, Ryoji, 'On the Ellipsis of the Object in Coordinate Constructions in Old English', *Tenri Univ. Jnl* 55.2 (2002), 17–30 [in Japanese]

'On the Syntactic Forms of Coordinate Constructions in Old English', *Tenri Univ. Jnl* 55.1, 1–28 [in Japanese]

Iyeiri, Yoko, *Negative Constructions in Middle English* (Fukuoka, 2001) [esp. in chs. 1, 3 and 7]

Jakubowski, Piotr, 'West Midland and Southwestern Adjectival Systems in Early Middle English: a Reanalysis', *Studia Anglica Posnaniensia* 38 (2002), 271–8

Jasanoff, Jay, 'Acute vs. Circumflex: Some Notes on PIE and Post-PIE Prosodic Phonology', *Harvard Working Papers in Ling.* 8, 19–31 [esp. on OE morphology]

Karkov, Catherine E., and George Hardin Brown, ed., see sect. 1

Kastovsky, Dieter, 'The "Haves" and the "Have-Nots" in Germanic and English: from *bahuvrihi* Compounds to Affixal Derivation', *Of dyuersitie*, ed. Lenz and Möhlig, pp. 33–46

Kishida, Takayuki, 'On the Prepositional Case in *Peri didaxeon*', *Ann. Collection of Essays and Stud.* (Gakushuin Univ., Faculty of Letters) 49, 109–48

Kleiner, Yuri, 'Compensatory Variation', *New Insights in Germanic Linguistics II*, ed.

Irmengard Rauch and Gerald F. Carr (New York, 2001), pp. 57–78 [esp. in lengthening before *f*, *s* and *þ*]

König, Ekkehard, and Peter Siemund, 'Intensifiers and Reflexives: a Typological Perspective', *Reflexives: Forms and Functions*, ed. Zygmunt Frajzyngier and Traci S. Curl (Amsterdam, 2000), pp. 41–74

Kornexl, Lucia, and Ursula Lenker, ed., see sect. 3*a*

Kortlandt, Frederik, 'Early Runic Consonants and the Origins of the Younger Futhark', *North-Western European Lang. Evolution* 43, 71–6

'Glottalization, Preaspiration and Gemination in English and Scandinavian', *Amsterdamer Beiträge zur älteren Germanistik* 58, 5–10

Krug, Manfred G., *Emerging English Modals: a Corpus-Based Study of Grammaticalization*, Topics in Eng. Ling. 32 (Berlin, 2000) [esp. in chs. 2–4]

'Frequency as a Determinant in Grammatical Variation and Change', *Determinants of Grammatical Variation in English*, ed. Günther Rohdenburg and Britta Mondorf (Berlin), pp. 7–67 [esp. on third person singular, in sect. 2.2.2]

Krygier, Marcin, 'A Re-Classification of Old English Nouns', *Studia Anglica Posnaniensia* 38 (2002), 311–19

Kwon, Young-Kook, 'The Role of /x, *r*, *l*/ in Sound Change: Old English Breaking and Other Processes', *Eng. Lang. and Ling.* (Seoul) 16, 243–70

Lenz, Katja, and Ruth Möhlig, ed., *Of dyuersitie and chaunge of langage: Essays presented to Manfred Görlach on the Occasion of His Sixty-Fifth Birthday*, Anglistische Forschungen 308 (Heidelberg, 2002)

Lightfoot, David W., ed., *Syntactic Effects of Morphological Change* (Oxford, 2002)

Los, Bettelou, *Infinitival Complementation in Old and Middle English*, LOT International Ser. 31 (The Hague, 1999)

Los, Bettelou, and Ans van Kemenade, 'Particles and Prefixes in Dutch and English', *Yearbook of Morphology*, 79–117 ['Old English', sect. 5.2; also in sect. 4]

McCully, Chris, 'Left-Hand Word-Stress in the History of English', *Development in Prosodic Systems*, ed. Paula Fikkert and Haike Jacobs (Berlin), pp. 349–93

McFadden, Thomas, 'Rise of the *to*-dative in Middle English', *Syntactic Effects*, ed. Lightfoot, pp. 108–23

Machan, Tim William, *English in the Middle Ages* (Oxford) [esp. in chs. 2–3]

Mańczak, Witold, 'The Method of Comparing the Vocabulary in Parallel Texts', *Jnl of Quantative Ling.* 10, 93–103 [Verner's Law]

Martín, María Auxiliadora, 'Old English *eo* in Middle Kentish Place-Names', *SELIM: Jnl of the Spanish Soc. for Med. Eng. Lang. and Lit.* 10 (2002 for 2000), 55–75

Miller, D. Gary, 'The Origin and Diffusion of English 3sg -*s*', *Studia Anglica Posnaniensia* 38 (2002), 353–61

Minkova, Donka, see sect. 3*bi* [alliteration and sound change]

Mitchell, Bruce, and Susan Irvine, 'A Critical Bibliography of Old English Syntax: Supplement 1993–1996, Part I', *NM* 104, 3–32

Murray, Robert W., 'Accents and Medieval English Phonologists', *Sounds and Systems*, ed. Restle and Zaefferer, pp. 91–120

Nagucka, Ruta, 'Agency and Passive in Old English', *Studia lingwistyczne ofiarowane*

Profesorowi Kazimierzowi Polańskiemu na 70-lecie Jego urodzin, ed. Wiesław Banys, Leszek Bednarczuk and Stanisław Karolak (Katowice, 1999), pp. 164–71

'Determination and Interpretation of Semantic Lexical Underspecification in Old English Homilies', *Studia Anglica Posnaniensia* 38 (2002), 381–92

Nevalainen, Terttu, 'English', *Germanic Standardizations: Past to Present*, ed. Ana Deumert and Wim Vandenbussche (Amsterdam), pp. 127–56 [sect. i]

Nielsen, Hans Frede, 'On the Demise of Old English', *Runica – Germanica – Mediaevalia*, ed. Heizmann and van Nahl, pp. 496–508

Nunes, Jairo, 'VO or OV? That's the Underlying Question: Commentary on Pintzuk', *Syntactic Effects*, ed. Lightfoot, pp. 300–6

Ogura, Michiko, '"Reflexive" and "Impersonal" Constructions in Medieval English', *Anglia* 121, 535–56

Osawa, Fuyo, 'The Rise of IPs in the History of English', *Historical Linguistics 2001*, ed. Barry J. Blake and Kate Burridge (Amsterdam), pp. 321–37

Park, Sae-Gon, 'A Study of English Infinitives Used as Adverbials, with Reference to *Beowulf* and the *Canterbury Tales*', *Eng. Lang. and Ling.* (Seoul) 16, 25–43 [in Korean]

Parry, David, see sect. 10 [OE primer]

Pimenova, Natalia B., 'Zum Konzept der diachron-vergleichenden semantischen Analyse von Wortbildungsmodellen. Schwache *an*-Maskulina mit abstrakter Semantik in altgermanischen Sprachen', *BGDSL* 125, 391–430

Pinto de Lima, José, 'Grammaticalization, Subjectification and the Origin of Phatic Markers', *New Reflections on Grammaticalization*, ed. Ilse Wischer and Gabriele Diewald (Amsterdam, 2002), pp. 363–78 [*þā hwīle þe* and *siððan*, sects. 1 and 7]

Pintzuk, Susan, 'Verb–Object Order in Old English: Variation as Grammatical Competition', *Syntactic Effects*, ed. Lightfoot, pp. 276–99

'Variationist Approaches to Syntactic Change', *The Handbook of Historical Linguistics*, ed. Brian D. Joseph and Richard D. Janda (Oxford), pp. 509–28 ['The Position of the Finite Verb in Old English: a Case Study', sect. 3]

Polo, Chiara, 'Double Objects and Morphological Triggers for Syntactic Case', *Syntactic Effects*, ed. Lightfoot, pp. 124–42

Poppe, Erich, 'Progress on the Progressive? A Report', *The Celtic Englishes III*, ed. Hildegard L. C. Tristram (Heidelberg), pp. 65–84

Pounder, Amanda, 'Adverb-Marking in German and English: System and Standardization', *Diachronica* 18 (2001), 301–58 [*-lic(e)*, sect. 5.1]

Restle, David, and Dietmar Zaefferer, ed., *Sounds and Systems: Studies in Structure and Change – a Festschrift for Theo Vennemann*, Trends in Ling., Stud. and Monographs 141 (Berlin, 2002)

Rissanen, Matti, '"Without except(ing) unless . . .": on the Grammaticalization of Expressions Indicating Exception in English', *Of dyuersitie*, ed. Lenz and Möhlig, pp. 77–87

Rowe, Charley, 'The Problematic Holtzmann's Law in Germanic', *IF* 108, 258–66

Schreiber, Carolin, 'Dialects in Contact in Ninth-Century England', *Bookmarks from the Past*, ed. Kornexl and Lenker, pp. 1–31

Siemund, Peter, 'Varieties of English from a Cross-Linguistic Perspective: Intensifiers and Reflexives', *Determinants of Grammatical Variation in English*, ed. Günther Rohdenburg and Britta Mondorf (Berlin), pp. 479–506 [dative forms of pronouns, esp. in sects. 4–5]

Sørensen, Knud, 'Particle + Verb-Stem Nouns', *Of dyuersitie*, ed. Lenz and Möhlig, pp. 47–54

Spriggs, Matthew, 'Where Cornish was Spoken and When: a Provisional Synthesis', *Cornish Stud.* 2nd ser. 11, 228–69 [interaction with OE]

Stahlke, Herbert F. W., 'Fortis and Lenis Obstruents in English', *Word* 54, 191–216 [esp. in sects. 5.1–2]

Stenbrenden, Gjertrud F., 'On the Interpretation of Early Evidence for ME Vowel-Change', *Historical Linguistics 2001*, ed. Barry J. Blake and Kate Burridge (Amsterdam), pp. 403–15

Stenroos, Merja, 'Free Variation and Other Myths: Interpreting Historical English Spelling', *Studia Anglica Posnaniensia* 38 (2002), 445–68

Stockwell, Robert P., 'Retraction and Rounding in Old English Breaking', *Sounds and Systems*, ed. Restle and Zaefferer, pp. 121–37

Swan, Toril, 'Present Participles in the History of English and Norwegian', *NM* 104, 179–95

Tanaka, Tomoyuki, 'Synchronic and Diachronic Aspects of Overt Subject Raising in English', *Lingua* 112 (2002), 619–46

Terasawa, Jun, 'A Sociohistorical Study of Periphrastic Comparison in English: Foreign Influence, Text Type and Individual Style', *Current Issues in English Linguistics*, ed. Masatomo Ukaji, Masayuki Ike-Uchi and Yoshiki Nishimura, Special Publ. of the Eng. Ling. Soc. of Japan 2 (Tokyo), pp. 191–207 [esp. on degree of comparison in OE and Middle Eng.]

Thórhallur Eythórsson, 'The Syntax of Verbs in Early Runic', *Working Papers in Scandinavian Syntax* (Lund) 67 (2001), 1–55

'Negation in C: the Syntax of Negated Verbs in Old Norse', *Nordic Jnl of Ling.* 25 (2002), 190–224 [esp. in sect. 4]

Thórhallur Eythórsson and Jóhanna Barðdal, 'Oblique Subjects: a Germanic Inheritance!', *Working Papers in Scandinavian Syntax* (Lund) 71, 145–202

Traugott, Elizabeth Closs, ' "Unless" and "But" Conditionals: a Historical Perspective', *On Conditionals Again*, ed. Angeliki Athanasiadou and René Dirven (Amsterdam, 1997), pp. 145–67 [*butan* and similar, sect. 2]

'From Subjectification to Intersubjectification', *Motives for Language Change*, ed. Raymond Hickey (Cambridge), pp. 124–39 [sects. 4–5]

Trips, Carola, *From OV to VO in Early Middle English*, Linguistik aktuell 60 (Amsterdam, 2002)

Tristram, Hildegard L. C., 'Aspect in Contact', *Anglistentag 1994 Graz: Proceedings*, ed. Wolfgang Riehle and Hugo Keiper (Tübingen, 1995), pp. 269–94 [sect. 4]

van Bergen, Linda, *Pronouns and Word Order in Old English, with Particular Reference to the Indefinite Pronoun 'man'*, Outstanding Dissertations in Ling. (London)

van Gelderen, Elly, 'Bound Pronouns and Non-Local Anaphors: the Case of Earlier

English', *Reflexives: Forms and Functions*, ed. Zygmunt Frajzyngier and Traci S. Curl (Amsterdam, 2000), pp. 187–225

'ASP(ect) in English Modal Complements', *Studia Linguistica* (Lund) 57, 27–43

van Kemenade, Ans, 'Old and Middle English', *The Germanic Languages*, ed. Ekkehard König and Johan van der Auwera (London, 2002), pp. 110–41

Weinstock, Horst, *Kleine Schriften. Ausgewählte Studien zur alt-, mittel- und frühneuenglischen Sprache und Literatur*, Anglistische Forschungen 328 (Heidelberg) [reissued and newly ptd papers]

'Medieval English and German: a Guide to Modern Similarities and Dissimilarities', Weinstock, *Kleine Schriften*, pp. 243–59

Wełna, Jerzy, 'Metathetic and Non-Metathetic Form Selection in Middle English', *Studia Anglica Posnaniensia* 38 (2002), 501–18

White, David L., 'Brittonic Influence in the Reductions of Middle English Nominal Morphology', *The Celtic Englishes III*, ed. Hildegard L. C. Tristram (Heidelberg), pp. 29–45

Woodhouse, Robert, 'Gothic *siuns*, the Domain of Verner's Law and the Relative Chronology of Grimm's, Verner's and Kluge's Laws in Germanic', *BGDSL* 125, 207–22

Yang, Seon-Ki, 'An Optimality-Theoretic Analysis of *h*-deletion in Old English', *Hist. of Eng.* (Seoul) 13 (2002), 91–115 [in Korean]

Yoon, Hee-Cheol, 'Economy Considerations and the Derivation of DP in Old English', *Hist. of Eng.* (Seoul) 13 (2002), 201–26

3. OLD ENGLISH LITERATURE

a. General

Amodio, Mark C., and Katherine O'Brien O'Keeffe, ed., *Unlocking the 'wordhord': Anglo-Saxon Studies in memory of Edward B. Irving, Jr* (Toronto)

Anderson, Earl R., *Folk-Taxonomies in Early English* (Madison, NJ)

Bammesberger, Alfred, see sect. 9*l* [editing OE runic inscriptions]

Bammesberger, Alfred, David Parsons and Karin Fjellhammer Seim, 'Runenreihen', *RGA* XXV, 562–71 ['History of the Anglo-Saxon and Frisian *fuþorc*', sect. 2, by Parsons]

Bauer, Alessia, '*Runica manuscripta*', *RGA* XXV, 600–4

Bauer, Renate, *Adversus Judaeos. Juden und Judentum im Spiegel alt- und mittelenglischer Texte*, Münchener Universitätsschriften, Texte und Untersuchungen zur englischen Philologie 29 (Frankfurt am Main)

Beck, Wolfgang, *Die Merseburger Zaubersprüche*, Imagines Medii Aevi 16 (Wiesbaden) [charms, esp. in chs. VII–VIII; 'Angelsächsische Quellen', sect. X.ii.3]

Bergmann, Rolf, ed., *Volkssprachig–lateinische Mischtexte und Textensembles in der althochdeutschen, altsächsischen und altenglischen Überlieferung. Mediävistisches Kolloquium des Zentrums für Mittelalterstudien der Otto-Friedrich-Universität Bamberg am 16. und 17. November 2001*, Germanistische Bibliothek 17 (Heidelberg)

Berlin, Gail Ivy, 'The Fables of the Bayeux Tapestry: an Anglo-Saxon Perspective', *Unlocking the 'wordhord'*, ed. Amodio and O'Keeffe, pp. 191–216

Bozóky, Edina, *Charmes et prières apotropaïques*, Typologie des sources du Moyen Âge occidental 86 (Turnhout)

Charles-Edwards, Thomas, ed., see sect. 6

Christie, Edward, 'The Image of the Letter: from the Anglo-Saxons to the *Electronic "Beowulf"*', *Culture, Theory and Critique* 44, 129–50

Clunies Ross, Margaret, 'Two Old Icelandic Theories of Ritual', *Old Norse Myths, Literature and Society*, ed. Margaret Clunies Ross (Odense), pp. 279–99 [AS euhemerism; also on Bede, Ælfric and pre-Christian calendar]

Conrad-O'Briain, Helen, 'Grace and Election in Adomnán's *Vita S. Columbae*', *Hermathena* 172 (2003 for 2002), 25–38 [advancing Roman and Celtic links to OE lit., including *Beowulf*]

Damon, John Edward, *Soldier Saints and Holy Warriors: Warfare and Sanctity in the Literature of Early England* (Aldershot)

Daniell, David, *The Bible in English: its History and Influence* (New Haven, CT) ['The Anglo-Saxon Bible, 850–1066', sect. I.3]

Düwel, Klaus, ed., see sect. 9*l* [on *runische Schriftkultur*]

Frantzen, Allen J., 'The Form and Function of the Preface in the Poetry and Prose of Alfred's Reign', *Alfred the Great*, ed. Reuter, pp. 121–36

Fried, Johannes, 'Awaiting the End of Time around the Turn of the Year 1000', *The Apocalyptic Year*, ed. Landes *et al.*, pp. 17–63 [Bede, Abbo, Ælfric *et al.*; also on *Regularis concordia*]

Georgianna, Linda, 'Periodization and Politics: the Missing Twelfth Century in English Literary History', *Mod. Lang. Quarterly* 64, 153–68 [periodization of OE lit.]

Godden, Malcolm, 'The Millennium, Time and History for the Anglo-Saxons', *The Apocalyptic Year*, ed. Landes *et al.*, pp. 155–80 [esp. for Ælfric; also on Æthelweard, *Chronicon*, other prose and verse]

Goyens, Michèle, and Werner Verbeke, ed., *The Dawn of the Written Vernacular in Western Europe*, Mediaevalia Lovaniensia, ser. 1: Studia 33 (Louvain)

Gustavson, Helmer, 'The ISO Runes Project', *Nytt om runer* 17 (2002), 45–6 [runic characters in Unicode]

Harris, Stephen J., *Race and Ethnicity in Anglo-Saxon Literature*, Stud. in Med. Hist. and Culture 24 (London)

Hart, Cyril, *Learning and Culture in Late Anglo-Saxon England and the Influence of Ramsey Abbey on the Major English Monastic Schools*, 2 vols. in 3, Med. Stud. 17, 18a and 18b (Lampeter) [*The New Curriculum in Monastic Schools*, vol. 1, and *A Survey of the Development of Mathematical, Medical and Scientific Studies in England before the Norman Conquest*, vol. 2 (in 2)]

Harte, Jeremy, 'Hell on Earth: Encountering Devils in the Medieval Landscape', *The Monstrous Middle Ages*, ed. Bettina Bildhauer and Robert Mills (Toronto), pp. 177–95 [*Beowulf*, other verse and Felix, *Vita S. Guthlaci*]

Haubrichs, Wolfgang, '"Heroische Zeiten?" Wanderungen von Heldennamen und Heldensagen zwischen den germanischen *gentes* des frühen Mittelalters',

Circolazione di uomini, di idee e di testi nel Medioevo germanico, ed. Franco De Vivo (Cassino, 2002), pp. 77–99

Heizmann, Wilhelm, and Astrid van Nahl, ed., *Runica – Germanica – Mediaevalia*, Ergänzungsbände zum *RGA* 37 (Berlin)

Iamartino, Giovanni, ed., see sect. 3*c*

Jolly, Karen, Catharina Raudvere, and Edward Peters, *Witchcraft and Magic in Europe: the Middle Ages*, ed. Bengt Ankarloo and Stuart Clark (Philadelphia) [esp. in pts. 1 and 3]

Keefer, Sarah Larratt, 'In Closing: Amen and Doxology in Anglo-Saxon England', *Anglia* 121, 210–37

Kornexl, Lucia, and Ursula Lenker, ed., *Bookmarks from the Past: Studies in Early English Language and Literature in honour of Helmut Gneuss*, Münchener Universitätsschriften, Texte und Untersuchungen zur englischen Philologie 30 (Frankfurt am Main)

Landes, Richard, Andrew Gow and David C. Van Meter, ed., *The Apocalyptic Year 1000: Religious Expectation and Social Change, 950–1050* (Oxford)

Murdoch, Brian, *The Medieval Popular Bible: Expansions of Genesis in the Middle Ages* (Woodbridge) [esp. for Ælfric, *Hexameron*, and for *Genesis A* and *B*, in chs. 1 and 4–5]

Niles, John D., 'Prizes from the Borderlands', *Oral Tradition* 18, 223–4 [OE lit. and oral tradition]

Ono, Shigeru, 'Old English and Anglo-Saxon England in History', *Gakuen for Eng.–Amer. Lang. and Lit.* (Showa Women's Univ.) 752, 178–88 [in Japanese]

Orchard, Andy, 'Latin and the Vernacular Languages: the Creation of a Bilingual Textual Culture', *After Rome*, ed. Charles-Edwards, pp. 190–219

'Looking for an Echo: the Oral Tradition in Anglo-Saxon Literature', *Oral Tradition* 18, 225–7

Parsons, David, 'Anglo-Saxon Runes in Continental Manuscripts', *Runische Schriftkultur*, ed. Düwel, pp. 195–220

Pasternack, Carol Braun, 'Negotiating Gender in Anglo-Saxon England', *Gender and Difference in the Middle Ages*, ed. Sharon Farmer and Carol Braun Pasternack (Minneapolis), pp. 107–42

Polia, Mario, *Le rune e gli dèi del Nord*, 2nd ed. (Rimini, 1994) [also for OE charms]

Pollington, Stephen, *The Mead Hall: the Feasting Tradition in Anglo-Saxon England* (Hockwold-cum-Wilton)

Powell, Kathryn, and Donald Scragg, ed., *Apocryphal Texts and Traditions in Anglo-Saxon England*, Publ. of the Manchester Centre for AS Stud. 2 (Cambridge)

Prideaux-Collins, William, '"Satan's bonds are extremely loose": Apocalyptic Expectation in Anglo-Saxon England During the Millennial Era', *The Apocalyptic Year*, ed. Landes *et al.*, pp. 289–310 [esp. for works of Ælfric, other OE prose and Anglo-Latin sources]

Reuter, Timothy, ed., see sect. 6

Richmond, Colleen D., 'Hrotsvit's *Sapientia*: Rhetorical Power and Women of Wisdom', *Renascence* 55 (2002–3), 133–44 [female personages in OE lit.]

Richter, Michael, 'Vom beschränkten Nutzen des Schreibens im Frühmittelalter', *Vom Nutzen des Schreibens*, ed. Walter Pohl and Paul Herold (Vienna, 2002), pp. 193–202 [Gildas, *Historia Brittonum*, *Beowulf* and other sources]

Roberts, Jane, 'Anglo-Saxon Translation: Some *wise wealhstodas*', *English Diachronic Translation*, ed. Iamartino, pp. 19–46

Scarfe Beckett, Katharine, *Anglo-Saxon Perceptions of the Islamic World*, CSASE 33 (Cambridge)

Scheil, Andrew P., 'Babylon and Anglo-Saxon England', *SLI: Stud. in the Lit. Imagination* 36.1, 37–58

Schulman, Jana K., 'Hrotsvit and the Germanic Warrior Hero', *Germanic Notes and Reviews* 34, 13–26

Schwab, Ute, 'Runentituli, narrative Bildzeichen und biblisch-änigmatische Gelehrsamkeit auf der Bargello-Seite des Franks Casket', *Runica – Germanica – Mediaevalia*, ed. Heizmann and van Nahl, pp. 759–803

Scragg, Donald, ed., *Textual and Material Culture in Anglo-Saxon England: Thomas Northcote Toller and the Toller Memorial Lectures* (Cambridge) [lectures for 1987–90, 1992–7 and 2002, some rev., with additional essays]

Solli, Brit, *Seid: myter, sjamanisme og kjønn i vikingenes tid* (Oslo, 2002) [esp. for *Beowulf*; also on Alfredian prose]

Staiti, C., H. Sauer and Ásdís Egilsdóttir, 'Pastorale Literatur', *RGA* XXII, 503–16 ['Angelsächsisches England', sect. 2, by Sauer]

Stanley, Eric G., 'Did the Anglo-Saxons Have a Social Conscience Like Us?', *Anglia* 121, 238–64

Strickland, Debra Higgs, *Saracens, Demons and Jews: Making Monsters in Medieval Art* (Princeton, NJ) [*Marvels of the East*, *Beowulf* and other sources, esp. in chs. 1–2]

Thompson, Victoria, 'The View from the Edge: Dying, Power and Vision in Late Saxon England', *ASSAH* 12, 92–7

Van Uytfanghe, Marc, 'Le latin et les langues vernaculaires au Moyen Âge: un aperçu panoramique', *The Dawn of the Written Vernacular in Western Europe*, ed. Michèle Goyens and Werner Verbeke (Louvain), pp. 1–38

Walker, Jonathan, 'The Transtextuality of Transvestite Sainthood: or, How to Make the Gendered Form Fit the Generic Function', *Exemplaria* 15, 73–110

Wårvik, Brita, '"When you read or hear this story read": Issues of Orality and Literacy in Old English Texts', *Discourse Perspectives on English*, ed. Risto Hiltunen and Janne Skaffari (Amsterdam), pp. 13–55

Wilcox, Jonathan, 'Naked in Old English: the Embarrassed and the Shamed', *Naked before God*, ed. Withers and Wilcox, pp. 275–309

Withers, Benjamin C., and Jonathan Wilcox, ed., *Naked before God: Uncovering the Body in Anglo-Saxon England*, Med. Eur. Stud. 3 (Morgantown, WV)

b. Poetry

i. General

Amodio, Mark C., and Katherine O'B. O'Keeffe, ed., see sect. 3*a*

Biggam, C. P., ed., see sect. 1

Bredehoft, Thomas A., 'Secondary Stress in Compound Germanic Names in Old English Verse', *Jnl of Eng. Ling.* 31, 199–220

'The Three Varieties of Old English Hypermetric Versification', *N&Q* 50, 152–6

Cable, Thomas, 'Kaluza's Law and the Progress of Old English Metrics', *Development in Prosodic Systems*, ed. Paula Fikkert and Haike Jacobs (Berlin), pp. 145–58

Clarke, Catherine A. M., 'Envelope Pattern and the *locus amoenus* in Old English Verse', *N&Q* 50, 263–4

Cronan, Dennis, 'Poetic Meanings in the Old English Poetic Vocabulary', *ES* 84, 397–425

Dronke, Peter, *Imagination in the Late Pagan and Early Christian World: the First Nine Centuries AD*, Millennio medievale 42 [= Strumenti e studi ns 4] (Florence) [esp. in chs. 2–4]

Faraci, Mary, '"I wish to speak": Tolkien's Voice in His *Beowulf* Essay', *Tolkien the Medievalist*, ed. Jane Chance (London), pp. 50–62

Foley, John Miles, *How to Read an Oral Poem* (Urbana, IL, 2002) [esp. in sects. 3–6]

'How Genres Leak in Traditional Verse', *Unlocking the 'wordhord'*, ed. Amodio and O'Keeffe, pp. 76–108

Fulk, R. D., and Kari Ellen Gade, 'A Bibliography of Germanic Alliterative Meters: Comparative and Prehistoric – Old Norse – Old English – Middle English – Old Saxon – Old High German', *Jahrbuch für internationale Germanistik* 34.1 (2002), 87–186

Guerrieri, Anna Maria, 'Coincidenze di strutture mentali o circolazione di idee? Osservazioni a margine di uno stilema della poesia germanica', *Circolazione di uomini, di idee e di testi nel Medioevo germanico*, ed. Franco De Vivo (Cassino, 2002), pp. 157–75

Gvozdetskaya, N. Y., 'The Birth of the Old English Poetical Word (on Resolution of Cultural Conflict in Anglo-Saxon Verse)', *Norna u istochnika Sudby. Sbornik statei v chest Eleny Aleksandrovny Melnikovoi*, ed. T. N. Dzhakson (Moscow, 2001), pp. 44–52 [in Russian]

Harris, Joseph, '"Ethnopaleography" and Recovered Performance: the Problematic Witnesses to "Eddic Song"', *Western Folklore* 62, 97–117

Haubrichs, Wolfgang, 'Emotionen vor dem Tode und ihre Ritualisierung', *Codierungen von Emotionen im Mittelalter*, ed. C. Stephen Jaeger and Ingrid Kasten (Berlin), pp. 70–97 [esp. in *Beowulf* and *Battle of Maldon*]

Hill, John M., 'The Sacrificial Synecdoche of Hands, Heads and Arms in Anglo-Saxon Heroic Story', *Naked before God*, ed. Withers and Wilcox, pp. 116–37

Holderness, Graham, *Cræft: Poems from the Anglo-Saxon* (Nottingham, 2002)

Holsinger, Bruce W., 'Analytical Survey 6: Medieval Literature and Cultures of Performance', *New Med. Literatures* 6, 271–311 [work of K. O'B. O'Keeffe]

Ingham, Patricia Clare, 'From Kinsip to Kingship: Mourning, Gender and Anglo-Saxon Community', *Grief and Gender, 700–1700*, ed. Jennifer C. Vaught (Basingstoke), pp. 17–31

Insley, J., 'Hocingas', *RGA* XV, 24–5 [esp. for *Beowulf* and *Widsith*]

'Hronas', *RGA* XV, 162–3 [*Widsith*]

'Hundingas', *RGA* XV, 240–1 [*Widsith*]

Karasawa, Kazutomo, see sect. 2*a* [*dream* in verse]
Karkov, Catherine E., and George Hardin Brown, ed., see sect. 1
Keefer, Sarah Larratt, '"Either/and" as "Style" in Anglo-Saxon Christian Poetry', *Anglo-Saxon Styles*, ed. Karkov and Brown, pp. 179–200
Kristján Árnason, 'Ferhend hrynjandi í fornyrðislagi og ljóðahætti', *Gripla* 13, 33–60 [comparison of OE and Eddic verse]
McGowan, Joseph, 'Heaney, Cædmon, *Beowulf*', *New Hibernia Rev.* 6.2 (2002), 25–42
MacKenzie, Ian, 'Poetry and Formulaic Language', *Belgian Jnl of Ling.* 15 (2001), 75–86
Maring, Heather, 'Oral Traditional Approaches to Old English Verse', *Oral Tradition* 18, 219–22
Marold, E., 'Kenning', *RGA* XVI, 432–42
'Preislied', *RGA* XXIII, 398–408
Minkova, Donka, *Alliteration and Sound Change in Early English*, Cambridge Stud. in Ling. 101 (Cambridge)
Neville, Jennifer, 'Leaves of Glass: Plant-Life in Old English Poetry', *From Earth to Art*, ed. Biggam, pp. 287–300
Niles, John D., 'The Myth of the Anglo-Saxon Oral Poet', *Western Folklore* 62, 7–61
Salvato, Nick, 'Louis Zukofsky's Old English Sources for *"A"–23*', *N&Q* 49 (2002), 85–8 [*Beowulf*, *Deor* and other verse]
Sävborg, Daniel, 'Medelhavskulturen och eddadiktningens förhistoria', *Maal og minne*, 121–37 [*Beowulf*, *Waldere* and *Deor*]
Scardigli, Piergiuseppe, 'Die europäische Stabreimdichtung', *Jahrbuch für internationale Germanistik* 34.1 (2002), 59–74
Tolley, Clive, 'Oral Assumptions: a Warning from Old Norse', *The 'Kalevala' and the World's Traditional Epics*, ed. Lauri Honko (Helsinki, 2002), pp. 128–35 [work of K. O'B. O'Keeffe, A. Renoir *et al.*]
Tornaghi, Paola, 'Partènza, transito, arrivo: aspetti del viaggio nella poesia anglo-sassone', *Tipologia dei testi e tecniche espressive*, ed. Giovanni Gobber and Celestina Milani (Milan, 2002), pp. 47–76
Treitler, Leo, *With Voice and Pen: Coming to Know Medieval Song and How It Was Made* (Oxford) [esp. in ch. 10]
Watson, Jonathan, 'The Minim-istic Imagination: Scribal Invention and the Word in the Early English Alliterative Tradition', *Oral Tradition* 17 (2002), 290–309
Wilcox, Miranda, 'Exilic Imagining in *The Seafarer* and *The Lord of the Rings*', *Tolkien the Medievalist*, ed. Jane Chance (London), pp. 133–54
Withers, Benjamin C., and Jonathan Wilcox, ed., see sect. 3*a*
Zimmerman, Harold C., 'Continuity and Innovation: Scholarship on the Middle English Alliterative Revival', *Jahrbuch für internationale Germanistik* 35.1 (2002), 107–23

ii. 'Beowulf'

Amodio, Mark C., and Katherine O'B. O'Keeffe, ed., see sect. 3*a*
Bammesberger, Alfred, 'OE *befeallen* in *Beowulf*, line 1126a', *N&Q* 50, 156–8
'The Sequence *sib ge mænum* in *Beowulf* line 1857a', *ANQ* 16.4, 3–5

Bately, Janet, 'Bravery and the Vocabulary of Bravery in *Beowulf* and the *Battle of Maldon*', *Unlocking the 'wordhord'*, ed. Amodio and O'Keeffe, pp. 274–301

Bazelmans, Jos, 'Beowulf: a Man of Worth', *Kings of the North Sea*, ed. Kramer *et al.*, pp. 33–40

Beal, Timothy K., *Religion and its Monsters* (London, 2002) [esp. in ch. 6]

Biggs, Frederick M, '*Beowulf* and Some Fictions of Geatish Succession', *ASE* 32, 55–77

'Hondscioh and Æschere in *Beowulf*', *Neophilologus* 87, 635–52

Blamires, David, 'The Survival of the Middle Ages in British Children's Books', *Anglistentag 2000 Berlin: Proceedings*, ed. Peter Lucko and Jürgen Schlaeger (Tübingen, 2001), pp. 287–300 [adaptations of *Beowulf*]

Bolens, Guillemette, *La logique du corps articulaire. Les articulations du corps humain dans la littérature occidentale* (Rennes, 2000) ['*Beowulf* et les anneaux du squelette', ch. 4]

'The Limits of Textuality: Mobility and Fire Production in Homer and *Beowulf*', *Oral Tradition* 16 (2001), 107–28

Brogyanyi, Bela, ed., see sect. 2*a*

Clark, Tom, *A Case for Irony in 'Beowulf', with Particular Reference to its Epithets*, European Univ. Stud., ser. 14: AS Lang. and Lit. 402 (Bern)

Cooke, William, 'Three Notes on Swords in *Beowulf*', *MÆ* 72, 302–7

'Two Notes on *Beowulf* (with Glances at *Vafþrúðnismál*, Blickling Homily 16 and *Andreas*, lines 839–46)', *MÆ* 72, 297–301

Cosman, Bard C., 'Rikki-Tikki-Tavi as Beowulf', *Kipling Jnl* 75.4 (2001), 16–27

Creed, Robert Payson, 'How the *Beowulf* Poet Composed His Poem', *Oral Tradition* 18, 214–15

Doane, A. N., '*Beowulf* and Scribal Performance', *Unlocking the 'wordhord'*, ed. Amodio and O'Keeffe, pp. 62–75

Fischer, Ron, 'The Loved and the Honored: the Medieval Altars of Atonement', *Proceedings of the 11th Annual Northern Plains Conference on Early British Literature*, ed. Michelle M. Sauer (Minot, ND), pp. 218–31 ['*Beowulf*: the Battle of Order against Chaos', in sect. 2]

Golston, Chris, and Thomas Riad, 'Scansion and Alliteration in *Beowulf*', *Jahrbuch für internationale Germanistik* 35.1 (2002), 77–105

Haines, Simon, 'Dante and Medieval Romanticism', *Critical Rev.* 42 (2002), 111–30 [*Beowulf* as archetypal European epic]

Herman, David, and Becky Childs, 'Narrative and Cognition in *Beowulf*', *Style* 37, 177–203

Hill, John M., 'The Social and Dramatic Functions of Oral Recitation and Composition in *Beowulf*', *Oral Tradition* 17 (2002), 310–24

Hill, Thomas D., '*Consilium et auxilium* and the Lament for Æschere: a Lordship Formula in *Beowulf*', *Haskins Soc. Jnl* 12 (2003 for 2002), 71–82

Karasawa, Kazutomo, 'Hrothgar's Sermon on Pride in *Beowulf* 1724–68 in Comparison with *Vainglory*', *Bull. of Yokohama City Univ.* 54, 281–306 [in Japanese]

King, Judy, 'Launching the Hero: the Case of Scyld and Beowulf', *Neophilologus* 87, 453–71

Kornexl, Lucia, and Ursula Lenker, ed., see sect. 3*a*

Kosacheva, E. V., 'English Literature from *Beowulf* to the Present (for the Hundredth Anniversary of the Birth of E. I. Klimenko)', *Vestnik Moskovskogo universiteta*, ser. 9: *Filologiya*, no. 6, 170–6 [in Russian]

Kramer, Evert, *et al.*, ed., see sect. 6

Kries, Susanne, 'Linking Past and Present: *Beowulf* and the House of Wessex', *Germanisches Altertum und christliches Mittelalter*, ed. Brogyanyi, pp. 137–58

Landolt, C., 'Ingeld', *RGA* XV, 418–20

Lin, Lidan, 'The Narrative Strategy of Double Voicing in *Beowulf*', *North Dakota Quarterly* 69.2 (2002), 40–9

Marvin, William Perry, 'Heorot, Grendel and the Ethos of the Kill', *In Geardagum* 24, 1–39

Mizuno, Tomoaki, 'The Conquest of a Dragon by the Stranger in Holy Combat: Focussing on the Mighty Hero Beowulf and Thor', *Stud. in Humanities* (Shinshu Univ.) 36, 39–66

Pekonen, Osmo, 'How Beowulf Sailed to Finland', *The 'Kalevala' and the World's Traditional Epics*, ed. Lauri Honko (Helsinki, 2002), pp. 149–54

Roberts, Jane, 'Hrothgar's "Admirable Courage"', *Unlocking the 'wordhord'*, ed. Amodio and O'Keeffe, pp. 240–51

Sauer, Hans, and Inge B. Milfull, 'Seamus Heaney: Ulster, Old English and *Beowulf*', *Bookmarks from the Past*, ed. Kornexl and Lenker, pp. 81–141

Saur, Pamela S., 'Proto-Christian Heroes and the Beginnings of National Literatures in Europe', *CLA Jnl* (Baltimore, College Lang. Assoc.), 75–92 [syncretism]

Steele, Felicia Jean, '*Grendel*: Another Dip into the Etymological Mere', *ELN* 40.1, 1–13

Stein, Ron, 'Royal Name, Hero's Deeds: a Pattern in *Beowulf*', *A Garland of Names: Selected Papers of the Fortieth Names Institute*, ed. Wayne H. Finke and Leonard R. N. Ashley (East Rockaway, NY), pp. 126–39

Steinberg, Theodore L., *Reading the Middle Ages: an Introduction to Medieval Literature* (Jefferson, NC) ['*Beowulf*', ch. 1]

Susanek, C., 'Hygelac', *RGA* XV, 298–300

Thayer, James D., 'Fractured Wisdom: the Gnomes of *Beowulf*', *ELN* 41.2, 1–18

Tripp, Raymond P., Jr, 'The Role of God in the Semantics of *ðryðswyð*: *Beowulf* 131a and 736b', *In Geardagum* 24, 67–80

Wallerstein, Nicholas, 'The *ubi sunt* Problem in Beowulf's Lay of the Last Survivor', *In Geardagum* 24, 41–55

iii. Other poems

Amodio, Mark C., and Katherine O'B. O'Keeffe, ed., see sect. 3*a*

Anlezark, Daniel, 'The Fall of the Angels in *Solomon and Saturn II*', *Apocryphal Texts and Traditions*, ed. Powell and Scragg, pp. 121–33

Bammesberger, Alfred, 'Zu *fusæ* in der Runeninschrift auf dem Ruthwell-Kreuz', *Runica – Germanica – Mediaevalia*, ed. Heizmann and van Nahl, pp. 28–34

'A Note on *Genesis A*, line 22a', *N&Q* 50, 7–8

'Die Runeninschrift auf dem Ruthwellkreuz', *Anglia* 121, 265–73

Bauer, Alessia, *Runengedichte. Texte, Untersuchungen und Kommentare zur gesamten Überlieferung*, Studia Medievalia Septentrionalia 9 (Vienna) ['Das angelsächsische Runengedichte', ch. 3]

'Runengedichte', *RGA* XXV, 519–24

Bergmann, Rolf, ed., see sect. 3*a*

Bjork, Robert E., 'N. F. S. Grundtvig's 1840 Edition of the Old English *Phoenix*: a Vision of a Vision of Paradise', *Unlocking the 'wordhord'*, ed. Amodio and O'Keeffe, pp. 217–39

Borysławski, Rafał, 'The Elements of Anglo-Saxon Wisdom Poetry in the Exeter Book Riddles', *Studia Anglica Posnaniensia* 38 (2002), 35–47

Bueno Alonso, Jorge Luis, '"Less epic than it seems": *Deor*'s Historical Approach as a Narrative Device for Psychological Expression', *Revista canaria de estudios ingleses* 46, 161–72

Buzzoni, Marina, 'Per una sintassi del testo iconico: il caso delle iniziali maiuscole nella "Battaglia di Brunanburh"', *Testo e immagine nel Medioevo germanico*, ed. Maria Grazia Saibene and Marina Buzzoni (Milan, 2001), pp. 281–95

Cathey, James E., ed., *Hêliand: Text and Commentary*, Med. Eur. Stud. 11 (Morgantown, WV, 2002) [esp. on *Genesis B*]

Cometta, Marina, 'Observations on the Old English Version of Codex Vaticanus Palatinus Latinus 1447, First Fragment', *English Diachronic Translation*, ed. Iamartino, pp. 39–46 [*Genesis B*]

Conde-Silvestre, Juan Camilo, 'Discourse and Ideology in the Old English *The Wanderer*: Time and Eternity', *Time and Eternity*, ed. Jaritz and Moreno-Riaño, pp. 331–53

Del Pezzo, Raffaella, 'Lc 1, 27: . . . *in fragiftim abin* . . . – "promessa ad un uomo"', *AUON* 10.2 (2003 for 2000), 7–11 [*Christ I*]

Dendle, Peter, 'Pain and Saint-Making in *Andreas*, Bede and the Old English Lives of St Margaret', *Varieties of Devotion in the Middle Ages and Renaissance*, ed. Susan C. Karant-Nunn (Turnhout), pp. 39–52

Dockray-Miller, Mary, 'The Maternal Performance of the Virgin Mary in the Old English *Advent*', *NWSA Jnl* (Norwood, NJ, National Women's Stud. Assoc.) 14.2 (2002), 38–55

'Breasts and Babies: the Maternal Body of Eve in the Junius *Genesis*', *Naked before God*, ed. Withers and Wilcox, pp. 221–56

Ericksen, Janet S., 'Penitential Nakedness and the Junius 11 *Genesis*', *Naked before God*, ed. Withers and Wilcox, pp. 257–74

Estes, Heide, 'Feasting with Holofernes: Digesting Judith in Anglo-Saxon England', *Exemplaria* 15, 325–50

Geith, Karl-Ernst, '*Juliana*', *Die deutsche Literatur des Mittelalters: Verfasserlexikon* 11.3 (2002), 817–18

Grosskopf, John Dennis, 'Time and Eternity in the Anglo-Saxon Elegies', *Time and Eternity*, ed. Jaritz and Moreno-Riaño, pp. 323–30

Hall, Alaric, 'The Images and Structure of *The Wife's Lament*', *Leeds Stud. in Eng.* ns 33 (2003 for 2002), 1–29

Harbus, Antonina, 'The Situation of Wisdom in *Solomon and Saturn II*', *SN* 75, 97–103
Harris, Joseph, 'Cursing with the Thistle: *Skírnismál* 31, 6–8 and OE Metrical Charm 9, 16–17', *The Poetic Edda: Essays on Old Norse Mythology*, ed. Paul Acker and Carolyne Larrington (London, 2002), pp. 79–93
Hawkes, J., and J. McKinnell, 'Ruthwell Cross', *RGA* XXV, 622–9
Heizmann, Wilhelm, and Astrid van Nahl, ed., see sect. 3*a*
Higley, Sarah L., 'The Wanton Hand: Reading and Reaching into Grammars and Bodies in Old English Riddle 12', *Naked before God*, ed. Withers and Wilcox, pp. 29–59
Hough, Carole, 'The Riddle of *The Wife's Lament* line 34b', *ANQ* 16.4, 5–8
Howe, Nicholas, 'Falling into Place: Dislocation in the Junius Book', *Unlocking the 'word-hord'*, ed. Amodio and O'Keeffe, pp. 14–37
Iamartino, Giovanni, ed., see sect. 3*c*
Jacobs, Christina, 'Poetische Umsetzung des angelsächsischen Weltbildes in *Maxims I*', *Übersetzung, Adaptation und Akkulturation im insularen Mittelalter*, ed. Erich Poppe and Hildegard L. C. Tristram (Münster, 1999), pp. 161–84
Jaritz, Gerhard, and Gerson Moreno-Riaño, ed., see sect. 4
Karkov, Catherine E., and George Hardin Brown, ed., see sect. 1
Keefer, Sarah Larratt, '*Ic* and *we* in Eleventh-Century Old English Liturgical Verse', *Unlocking the 'wordhord'*, ed. Amodio and O'Keeffe, pp. 123–46
Klein, Stacy S., 'Reading Queenship in Cynewulf's *Elene*', *Jnl of Med. and Early Mod. Stud.* 33 (2002), 47–89
Klinck, Anne L., 'Poetic Markers of Gender in Medieval "Woman's Song": Was Anonymous a Woman?', *Neophilologus* 87, 339–59 [*Wulf and Eadwacer* and *Wife's Lament*]
Korhammer, Michael, 'The Last of the Exeter Book Riddles', *Bookmarks from the Past*, ed. Kornexl and Lenker, pp. 69–80
Kornexl, Lucia, and Ursula Lenker, ed., see sect. 3*a*
Lapidge, Michael, 'Cynewulf and the *Passio S. Iulianae*', *Unlocking the 'wordhord'*, ed. Amodio and O'Keeffe, pp. 147–71
Leasure, T. Ross, see sect. 1 [Junius 11]
Lendinara, Patrizia, 'La poesia anglosassone alla fine del X secolo e oltre', *AUON* 11 (2001), 7–46
Liuzza, R. M., 'The Tower of Babel: *The Wanderer* and the Ruins of History', *SLI: Stud. in the Lit. Imagination* 36.1, 1–35
Luiselli Fadda, Anna Maria, 'La Croce nella tradizione poetica anglosassone (secc. VIII–X)', *Romanobarbarica* 17 (2000–2), 333–59
Milfull, Inge B., 'Formen und Inhalte lateinisch–altenglischer Textensembles und Mischtexte: Durham Cathedral B. III. 32 und *The Phoenix*', *Volkssprachig–lateinische Mischtexte*, ed. Bergmann, pp. 467–91
Milfull, Inge B., and Ásdís Égilsdóttir, 'Religiöse Dichtung', *RGA* XXIV, 418–29 ['Altenglische religiöse Dichtung', sect. 1, by Milfull]
Momma, Haruko, 'Epanalepsis: a Retelling of the Judith Story in the Anglo-Saxon Language', *SLI: Stud. in the Lit. Imagination* 36.1, 59–73
Naumann, H.-P., 'Runendichtung', *RGA* XXV, 512–18

Niles, John D., 'The Problem of the Ending of *The Wife's Lament*', *Speculum* 78, 1107–50
'The Trick of the Runes in *The Husband's Message*', *ASE* 32, 189–223
Norris, Robin, 'The Augustinian Theory of Use and Enjoyment in *Guthlac A* and *B*', *NM* 104, 159–78
Olsen, Alexandra H., 'Subtractive Rectification and the Old English *Riming Poem*', *In Geardagum* 24, 57–66
Orchard, Andy, 'Both Style and Substance: the Case for Cynewulf', *Anglo-Saxon Styles*, ed. Karkov and Brown, pp. 271–305
Osborn, Marijane, 'Norse Ships at Maldon: the Cultural Context of *æschere* in the Old English Poem *The Battle of Maldon*', *NM* 104, 261–80
'Tir as Mars in the Old English *Rune Poem*', *ANQ* 16.1, 3–13
Petzoldt, L., R. Poole and Jón Hnefill Aðalsteinsson, 'Rätsel und Rätseldichtung', *RGA* XXIV, 88–98 ['Riddles in Old English', sect. 2, by Poole]
Powell, Kathryn, and Donald Scragg, ed., see sect. 3*a*
Raw, Barbara, 'Two Versions of Advent: the Benedictional of Æthelwold and *The Advent Lyrics*', *Leeds Stud. in Eng.* ns 33, 1–28
Salvador, Mercedes, 'The Key to the Body: Unlocking Riddles 42–46', *Naked before God*, ed. Withers and Wilcox, pp. 60–96
Schulz, Monika, '*Nigon wyrta galdor*. Zur Rationalität der *ars magica*', *Zeitschrift für Literaturwissenschaft und Lingusitik: LiLi* 130, 8–24 ['Nine Herbs Charm']
Schweighauser, Philipp, 'Concepts of Masculinity in *The Wife's Lament* and its Critical Literature', *Masculinities – Maskulinitäten: Mythos, Realität, Repräsentation, Rollendruck*, ed. Therese Steffen (Stuttgart, 2002), pp. 177–85
Scragg, Donald, 'A Reading of *Brunanburh*', *Unlocking the 'wordhord'*, ed. Amodio and O'Keeffe, pp. 109–22
Stanley, E. G., 'Old English *The Fortunes of Men*, lines 80–84', *N&Q* 50, 265–8
Terasawa, Jun, 'Old English *Exodus* 118a: the Use of Wolf Imagery', *N&Q* 50, 259–61
Tiffany, Daniel, 'Lyric Substance: on Riddles, Materialism and Poetic Obscurity', *Critical Inquiry* 28 (2001–2), 72–98 [esp. at pp. 77–87]
Wilcox, Jonathan, 'Eating People Is Wrong: Funny Style in *Andreas* and its Analogues', *Anglo-Saxon Styles*, ed. Karkov and Brown, pp. 201–22
Wisniewski, Roswitha, *Deutsche Literatur vom achten bis elften Jahrhundert*, Germanistische Lehrbuchsammlung 28 (Berlin) ['Altsächsische *Genesis*', in ch. 4]
Withers, Benjamin C., and Jonathan Wilcox, ed., see sect. 3*a*
Yoshimi, Akinori, 'On the Anglo-Saxon Poem *Deor*: a Portrait of the Skald', *Meiji Gakuin Univ. Rev.* 701, 1–50 [in Japanese]
Zacher, Samantha, 'Cynewulf at the Interface of Literacy and Orality: the Evidence of the Puns in *Elene*', *Oral Tradition* 17 (2002), 346–87

c. Prose

Amodio, Mark C., and Katherine O'B. O'Keeffe, ed., see sect. 3*a*
Atkinson, Nancy E., and Dan E. Burton, 'Harrowing the Houses of the Holy: Images of Violation in Wulfstan's Homilies', *The Year 1000*, ed. Michael Frassetto (Basingstoke, 2002), pp. 49–62

Baraz, Daniel, *Medieval Cruelty: Changing Perceptions, Late Antiquity to the Early Modern Period* (Ithaca, NY) [esp. for Chronicle, ch. 3 with appendix 4]

Bately, Janet, 'The Alfredian Canon Revisited: One Hundred Years On', *Alfred the Great*, ed. Reuter, pp. 107–20

Battista, Simonetta, 'Interpretations of the Roman Pantheon in the Old Norse Hagiographical Sagas', *Old Norse Myths, Literature and Society*, ed. Margaret Clunies Ross (Odense), pp. 175–97 [Ælfric, *De falsis deis*]

Bremmer, Rolf H., Jr, 'The Reception of the Acts of John in Anglo-Saxon England', *The Apocryphal Acts of John*, ed. Jan N. Bremmer (Kampen, 1995), pp. 183–96

'The Final Countdown: Apocalyptic Expectations in Anglo-Saxon Charters', *Time and Eternity*, ed. Jaritz and Moreno-Riaño, pp. 501–14

Butcher, Carmen Acevedo, 'Recovering Unique Ælfrician Texts Using the Fiber Optic Light Cord: Pope XVII in London, BL Cotton Vitellius C. v', *OEN* 36.3, 13–22

Cavill, Paul, 'Analogy and Genre in the Legend of St Edmund', *Nottingham Med. Stud.* 47, 21–45 [Ælfric]

Corsi Mercatanti, Gloria, 'Redazione E (Peterborough) della Cronaca Sassone: appunti stilistici', *International Scandinavian and Medieval Studies*, ed. Dallapiazza *et al.*, pp. 307–22

Crépin, André, 'Peuples scandinaves dans l'"Orose" vieil-anglais', *Hugur. Mélanges d'histoire, de littérature et de mythologie offerts à Régis Boyer pour son 65e anniversaire*, ed. Claude Lecouteux (Paris, 1997), pp. 39–50

Cubitt, Catherine, ed., see sect. 4

Dallapiazza, Michael, Olaf Hansen, Preben Meulengracht Sørensen and Yvonne S. Bonnetain, ed., *International Scandinavian and Medieval Studies in memory of Gerd Wolfgang Weber*, Hesperides 12 (Trieste, 2000)

D'Aronco, M. A., 'Le conoscenze mediche nell'Inghilterra anglosassone: il ruolo del mondo carolingio', *International Scandinavian and Medieval Studies*, ed. Dallapiazza *et al.*, pp. 129–46

DeGregorio, Scott, '*þegenlic* or *flæsclic*: the Old English Prose Legends of St. Andrew', *JEGP* 102, 449–64

Drout, Michael, 'Anglo-Saxon Wills and the Inheritance of Tradition in the English Benedictine Reform', *SELIM: Jnl of the Spanish Soc. for Med. Eng. Lang. and Lit.* 10 (2002 for 2000), 5–53

Faraci, Dora, 'Narrative Patterns in the Medieval Charm Tradition: the German Worm Charm of Codex Vaticanus, Pal. lat. 1227', *Zeitschrift für Literaturwissenschaft und Lingusitik: LiLi* 130, 48–71 [esp. for Alfred, Ælfric and *Adrian and Ritheus*]

Frankis, John, 'Towards a Regional Context for Lawman's *Brut*: Literary Activity in the Dioceses of Worcester and Hereford in the Twelfth Century', *Laȝamon: Contexts, Language and Interpretation*, ed. Rosamund Allen, Lucy Perry and Jane Roberts (London, 2002), pp. 53–78 [esp. on knowledge of Ælfric]

Franzen, Christine, 'The Tremulous Hand of Worcester and the Nero Scribe of the *Ancrene Wisse*', *MÆ* 72, 13–31 [esp. for Ælfric; also on prose in Worcester fragments of *Soul's Address to the Body* and 'The St Bede Lament' (*HomU* 5.1–7 and 13)]

Giordano, Carmela, 'Die *Elucidarium*-Rezeption in den germanischen Literaturen des Mittelalters. Ein Überblick', *Mittellateinisches Jahrbuch* 38, 171–87

Gneuss, Helmut, 'Ælfrics "Grammatik" und "Glossar": Sprachwissenschaft um die Jahrtausendwende in England', *Heilige und profane Sprachen*, ed. Werner Hüllen and Friederike Klippel (Wiesbaden, 2002), pp. 77–92

Godden, Malcolm R., 'King Alfred's Preface and the Teaching of Latin in Anglo-Saxon England', *EHR* 117 (2002), 596–604

'The Player King: Identification and Self-Representation in King Alfred's Writings', *Alfred the Great*, ed. Reuter, pp. 137–50

'Text and Eschatology in Book III of the Old English "Soliloquies"', *Anglia* 121, 177–209

see also sect. 1 [Alfredian Boethius]

Graham, Timothy, 'King Cnut's Grant of Sandwich to Christ Church, Canterbury: a New Reading of a Damaged Annal in Two Copies of the Anglo-Saxon Chronicle', *Unlocking the 'wordhord'*, ed. Amodio and O'Keeffe, pp. 172–90

Gulley, Alison, '"Seo fæmne þa lærde swa lange þone cniht oðþæt he ge-lyfde on þone lifigendan god": the Christian Wife as Converter and Ælfric's Anglo-Saxon Audience', *Parergon* ns 19.2 (2002), 39–51

Hall, Thomas N., 'Ælfric and the Epistle to the Laodicians', *Apocryphal Texts and Traditions*, ed. Powell and Scragg, pp. 65–83

'The Psychedelic Transmogrification of the Soul in Vercelli Homily IV', *Time and Eternity*, ed. Jaritz and Moreno-Riaño, pp. 309–22

Harris, Stephen J., 'Ælfric's *Colloquy*', *Medieval Literature for Children*, ed. Daniel T. Kline (London), pp. 112–30

Heizmann, Wilhelm, 'Gefjon: Metamorphosen einer Göttin', *Mythological Women*, ed. Rudolf Simek and Wilhelm Heizmann (Viennna, 2002), pp. 197–255 [Ælfric on Herodias]

Hewish, Juliet, 'Eastern Asceticism versus Western Monasticism: a Conflict of Ideals in the Old English Translations of the Works of Sulpicius Severus', *Quaestio Insularis* (Cambridge) 4, 115–28

Hill, Joyce, 'Learning Latin in Anglo-Saxon England: Traditions, Texts and Techniques', *Learning and Literacy in Medieval England and Abroad*, ed. Sarah Rees Jones (Turnhout), pp. 7–29 [esp. on Ælfric]

Iamartino, Giovanni, ed., *English Diachronic Translation. Atti del VII Convegno nazionale di storia della lingua inglese*, Quaderni di libri e riviste d'Italia 35 (Rome, 1998)

Irvine, Susan, 'The *Anglo-Saxon Chronicle* and the Idea of Rome in Alfredian Literature', *Alfred the Great*, ed. Reuter, pp. 63–77

'Wrestling with Hercules: King Alfred and the Classical Past', *Court Culture*, ed. Cubitt, pp. 171–88

Jaritz, Gerhard, and Gerson Moreno-Riaño, ed., see sect. 4

Jayatilaka, Rohini, 'The Old English Benedictine Rule: Writing for Women and Men', *ASE* 32, 147–87

Karkov, Catherine E., and George Hardin Brown, ed., see sect. 1

Kelly, Richard J., ed., *The Blickling Homilies* (London)

Kilburn, Jasmine A. L., 'The Contrasted "Other" in the Old English Apocryphal Acts of Matthew, Simon and Jude', *Neophilologus* 87, 137–51

Kim, Susan M., 'The Donestre and the Person of Both Sexes', *Naked before God*, ed. Withers and Wilcox, pp. 162–80 [*Marvels of the East*]

Kleist, Aaron J., 'The Influence of Bede's *De temporum ratione* on Ælfric's Understanding of Time', *Time and Eternity*, ed. Jaritz and Moreno-Riaño, pp. 81–97

Knebel, Tim, 'The Anglicising of Apollonius', *Offa* 58 (2003 for 2001), 287–91

Kobayashi, Ayako, 'Some Discrepancies in the Annual Numbers in the Anglo-Saxon Chronicle', *Bull. of Tokyo Kasei Univ.* 43.1, 133–7 [in Japanese]

Kornexl, Lucia, 'From Ælfric to John of Cornwall: Evidence for Vernacular Grammar Teaching in Pre- and Post-Conquest England', *Bookmarks from the Past*, ed. Kornexl and Lenker, pp. 229–59

Kornexl, Lucia, and Ursula Lenker, ed., see sect. 3*a*

Lainé, Ariane, 'L'Antéchrist dans les homélies eschatologiques de Wulfstan: un mal du siècle', *Hist. Reflections* 26 (2000), 173–87

Langefeld, Brigitte, ed., *The Old English Version of the Enlarged Rule of Chrodegang, edited together with the Latin Text and an English Translation*, Münchener Universitätsschriften, Texte und Untersuchungen zur englischen Philologie 26 (Frankfurt am Main)

Lazzari, Loredana, 'Il glossario latino–inglese antico nel manoscritto di Anversa e Londra ed il "Glossario" di Ælfric: dipendenza diretta o derivazione comune?', *Linguistica e filologia* (Bergamo) 16, 159–90

Lendinara, Patrizia, 'Di meraviglia in meraviglia', *Circolazione di uomini, di idee e di testi nel Medioevo germanico*, ed. Franco De Vivo (Cassino, 2002), pp. 177–229 [*Marvels of the East* and *Alexander's Letter*]

Lopez, David A., 'Translation and Tradition: Reading the "Consolation of Philosophy" through King Alfred's *Boethius*', *The Politics of Translation in the Middle Ages and the Renaissance*, ed. Renate Blumenfeld-Kosinski, Luise von Flotow and Daniel Russell (Ottawa, ON, and Tempe, AZ, 2001), pp. 69–84

Lowe, Kathryn A., 'The Anglo-Saxon Contents of a Lost Register from Bury St Edmunds', *Anglia* 121, 515–34 [vernacular charters]

Mele Marrero, Margarita, 'Two Extremes of English out of the Standards: Cant and Old English', *Revista canaria de estudios ingleses* 46, 85–98 [esp. on Ælfric and standardization of OE]

Mengato, Simonetta, 'The Old English Translations of Bede's *Historia ecclesiastica* and Orosius' *Historiuarum* [sc. *Historia(e)*] *adversus paganos*: a Comparison', *Linguistica e filologia* (Bergamo) 16, 191–213

Menzer, Melinda J., 'Speaking *brittonice*: Vowel Quantities and Musical Length in Ælfric's *Grammar*', *Peritia* 16 (2002), 26–39

Momma, Haruko, 'Rhythm and Alliteration: Styles of Ælfric's Prose up to the *Lives of Saints*', *Anglo-Saxon Styles*, ed. Karkov and Brown, pp. 253–69

Morini, Carla, 'La versione anglosassone del romanzo di *Apollonio* nel contesto del suo manoscritto', *AUON* 10.2 (2003 for 2000), 13–26

O'Keeffe, Katherine O'Brien, ed., see sect. 5 [Chronicle]

Orton, Peter, 'Sticks or Stones? The Story of Imma in Cambridge, Corpus Christi College, MS 41 of the *Old English Bede* and Old English *tān* ("Twig")', *MÆ* 72, 1–12

Papahagi, Adrian, '*Res paene inusitata*: les traductions de la *Consolatio Philosophiae* du Roi Alfred et de Notker Labeo', *Med. Translator* (Turnhout) 8, 71–87

Powell, Kathryn, and Donald Scragg, ed., see sect. 3*a*

Pratt, David, 'Persuasion and Invention at the Court of King Alfred the Great', *Court Culture*, ed. Cubitt, pp. 189–221

Rauer, Christine, 'The Sources of the *Old English Martyrology*', *ASE* 32, 89–109

Reuter, Timothy, ed., see sect. 6

Richards, Mary P., 'Wulfstan and the Millennium', *The Year 1000*, ed. Michael Frassetto (Basingstoke, 2002), pp. 41–8

'The Body as Text in Early Anglo-Saxon Law', *Naked before God*, ed. Withers and Wilcox, pp. 97–115

Rowley, Sharon, '"A wese\n/dan nacodnisse and þa ecan þistru": Language and Mortality in the Homily for Doomsday in Cambridge, Corpus Christi College MS 41', *ES* 84, 493–510

Schreiber, Carolin, *King Alfred's Old English Translation of Pope Gregory the Great's 'Regula pastoralis' and its Cultural Context: a Study and Partial Edition according to All Surviving Manuscripts Based on Cambridge, Corpus Christi College 12*, Münchener Universitätsschriften, Texte und Untersuchungen zur englischen Philologie 25 (Frankfurt am Main)

Scragg, Donald, 'Editing Ælfric's *Catholic Homilies*', *Anglia* 121, 610–18 [on *Ælfric's Catholic Homilies* I and III, ed. P. Clemoes and M. Godden (1997–2000)]

Semper, Philippa J., 'Going Round in Circles? Time and the Old English *Apollonius of Tyre*', *Time and Eternity*, ed. Jaritz and Moreno-Riaño, pp. 297–308

Sinisi, Lucia, '*Worde be worde* or *andgit of andgite*? Alfred and Chaucer Translate Boethius', *English Diachronic Translation*, ed. Iamartino, pp. 71–9

Smith, Liesl, '"Ic augt þolye more": Models of Sanctity in Two Legends of Saints Chrysanthus and Daria', *Florilegium* 19 (2003 for 2002), 163–88 [Ælfric]

Smythe, Ross, 'King Alfred's Translations: Authorial Integrity and the Integrity of Authority', *Quaestio Insularis* (Cambridge) 4, 98–114

Stace, Christopher, *St George: Patron Saint of England* (London, 2002) [Ælfric and AS cult, pp. 26–30]

Stalmaszczyk, Piotr, 'Cornish Language and Literature: a Brief Introduction', *Stud. in Eng. and Amer. Lit.* 7 [= *Acta Universitatis Lodziensis, Folia Litteraria Anglica* 3] (1999), 117–27 [Ælfric, *Glossary*]

Szarmach, Paul E., 'Ælfric Revises: the Lives of Martin and the Idea of the Author', *Unlocking the 'wordhord'*, ed. Amodio and O'Keeffe, pp. 38–61

Taylor, Claire, 'The Year 1000 and Those Who Labored', *The Year 1000*, ed. Michael Frassetto (Basingstoke, 2002), pp. 187–236 [Ælfric and Wulfstan]

Tornaghi, Paola, 'Byrhtferth's *Manual*: Knowledge and Translation of the Rhetorical Figures and Grammatical Terminology', *English Diachronic Translation*, ed. Iamartino, pp. 47–70

Treharne, Elaine M., 'The Form and Function of the Twelfth-Century Old English *Dicts of Cato*', *JEGP* 102, 465–85

Tristram, Hildegard L. C., 'Bedas *Historia ecclesiastica gentis anglorum* im Altenglischen und Altirischen: ein Vergleich', *Übersetzung, Adaptation und Akkulturation im insularen Mittelalter*, ed. Erich Poppe and Hildegard L. C. Tristram (Münster, 1999), pp. 51–72

Wellman, Tennyson J., 'Apocalyptic Concerns and Mariological Tactics in Eleventh-Century France', *The Year 1000*, ed. Michael Frassetto (Basingstoke, 2002), pp. 133–63 [Ælfric]

Withers, Benjamin C., and Jonathan Wilcox, ed., see sect. 3*a*

Wright, Charles D., 'Vercelli Homilies XI–XIII and the Anglo-Saxon Benedictine Reform: Tailored Sources and Implied Audiences', *Preacher, Sermon and Audience in the Middle Ages*, ed. Carolyn Muessig (Leiden, 2002), pp. 203–27

'The Apocalypse of Thomas: Some New Latin Texts and Their Significance for the Old English Versions', *Apocryphal Texts and Traditions*, ed. Powell and Scragg, pp. 27–64

Zott, Lynn M., ed., *Classical and Medieval Literature Criticism* XLIX (Detroit) ['Wulfstan, *c.* Mid–Late Tenth Century–1023', pp. 261–350]

4. ANGLO-LATIN, LITURGY AND OTHER LATIN ECCLESIASTICAL TEXTS

Alberi, Mary, '"The sword which you hold in your hand": Alcuin's Exegesis of the Two Swords and the Lay *miles Christi*', *The Study of the Bible*, ed. Chazelle and Edwards, pp. 117–31

Alibert, Dominique, 'Figures du David carolingien', *Apocryphité. Histoire d'un concept transversal aux religions du livre*, ed. Simon Claude Mimouni (Turnhout, 2002), pp. 203–27 [Alcuin]

Allan, Verity, 'Bede: Educating the Educators of Barbarians', *Quaestio* (Cambridge) 3 (2002), 28–44

Allen, Michael I., 'Universal History 300–1000: Origins and Western Developments', *Historiography in the Middle Ages*, ed. Deborah Mauskopf Deliyannis (Leiden), pp. 17–42 [Bede]

Arweiler, Alexander, 'Zu Text und Überlieferung einer gekürzten Fassung von Macrobius *Saturnalia* I, 12, 2–1, 15, 20', *Zeitschrift für Papyrologie und Epigraphik* 131 (2000), 45–57 [Bede]

Bachrach, David, 'Confession in the *regnum Francorum* (742–900): the Sources Revisited', *JEH* 54, 3–22 [penitentials; also on Boniface]

Basic, Rozmeri, *St Donat and Alcuin's Acrostics: Case Studies in Carolingian Modulation*, Nexus: Architecture and Mathematics (Florence)

Beare, Rhona, 'Is the Barnacle Goose Selfish, and Is It Harold?', *N&Q* 50, 10–11 [*Vita Edwardi regis*]

Bergmann, Rolf, ed., see sect. 3*a*

Berndt, Rainer, '*Scientia* und *disciplina* in der lateinischen Bibel und in der Exegese des hohen Mittelalters', *'Scientia' und 'disciplina'. Wissenstheorie und Wissenschaftspraxis im 12. und 13. Jahrhundert*, ed. Berndt, Matthias Lutz-Bachmann and Ralf M. W. Stammberger (Berlin, 2002), pp. 9–36 [Bede]

Berndt, Rainer, ed., *Das Frankfurter Konzil von 794: Kristallisationspunkt karolingischer Kultur. Akten zweier Symposien (vom 23. bis 27. Februar und vom 13. bis 15. Oktober 1994) anlässlich der 1200-Jahrfeier der Stadt Frankfurt am Main*, 1 vol. in 2, Quellen und Abhandlungen zur mittelrheinischen Kirchengeschichte 80 (Mainz, 1997)

Beutler, Christian, 'Der Kruzifixus des Bonifatius', *Das Frankfurter Konzil*, ed. Berndt, pp. 549–53

Black, Jonathan, 'Psalm Uses in Carolingian Prayerbooks: Alcuin's *Confessio peccatorum pura* and the Seven Penitential Psalms (Use 1)', *MS* 65, 1–56

Bonnery, André, 'A propos du Concile de Francfort (794). L'action des moines de Septimanie dans la lutte contre l'adoptianisme', *Das Frankfurter Konzil*, ed. Berndt, pp. 767–86 [Alcuin]

Bovon, François, 'Beda Venerabilis, *In Lucae euangelium expositio*', *Corpus Christianorum, 1953–2003: Xenium Natalicium – Fifty Years of Scholarly Editing*, ed. Johan Leemans (Turnhout), pp. 259–65

Breeze, Andrew, 'A Welsh Crux in an Æthelwoldian Poem', *N&Q* 50, 262–3

Brunhölzl, Franz, 'Über die Verse *De Karolo rege et Leone papa*', *Historisches Jahrbuch* 120 (2000), 274–83 [Alcuin; also on Bede]

Bullough, Donald, 'Alcuin before Frankfort', *Das Frankfurter Konzil*, ed. Berndt, pp. 571–85 [also for Bede]

'Unsettled at Aachen: Alcuin between Frankfort and Tours', *Court Culture*, ed. Cubitt, pp. 17–38

'York, Bede's Calendar and a Pre-Bedan English Martyrology', *AB* 121, 329–55 [also for Alcuin]

Butzer, Paul L., and Karl W. Butzer, 'Mathematics at Charlemagne's Court and its Transmission', *Court Culture*, ed. Cubitt, pp. 77–89 [Alcuin]

Caldwell, John, 'Winchester Troper', *Die Musik in Geschichte und Gegenwart. Allgemeine Enzyklopädie der Musik. Sachteil*, ed. Ludwig Finscher, 2nd ed., 10 vols. (Kassel, 1994–9) IX, 2047–8

Callebat, Louis, and Olivier Desbordes, ed., *Science antique, science médiévale (autour d'Avranches 235)* (Hildesheim, 2000)

Carver, Martin, ed., see sect. 6

Casiday, Augustine, 'Thomas Didymus from India to England', *Quaestio Insularis* (Cambridge) 4, 70–81 [Aldhelm]

Castro, Eva, 'De San Agustín a Beda: la estética de la poesía rítmica', *Cuadernos de filología clásica, estudios latinos* ns 13 (1997), 91–106

Cavadini, John, 'Elipandus and His Critics at the Council of Frankfort', *Das Frankfurter Konzil*, ed. Berndt, pp. 787–807 [Alcuin]

'A Carolingian Hilary', *The Study of the Bible*, ed. Chazelle and Edwards, pp. 133–40 [Alcuin]

Chadwick, Henry, *East and West: the Making of a Rift in the Church – from Apostolic Times until the Council of Florence*, Oxford Hist. of the Christian Church (Oxford) [Bede and Alcuin, esp. in chs. 12–15]

Charles-Edwards, T. M., '*Dliged*: its Native and Latinate Usages', *Celtica* 24, 65–78 [Bede, *De natura rerum* and *De temporum ratione*, sect. ii]

Chazelle, Celia, and Burton Van Name Edwards, ed., *The Study of the Bible in the Carolingian Era*, Med. Church Stud. 3 (Turnhout)

Chiesa, Paolo, ed., *Paolino d'Aquileia e il contributo italiano all'Europa carolingia. Atti del convegno internazionale di studi, Cividale del Friuli – Premariacco, 10–13 ottobre 2002*, Libri e biblioteche 12 (Udine)

Clark, Francis, *The '"Gregorian" Dialogues' and the Origins of Benedictine Monasticism*, Stud. in the Hist. of Christian Thought 108 (Leiden) [Aldhelm, Bede *et al.*, esp. in pt. iii, for early Eng. reception of Benedict's *Regula*]

Contreni, John, 'John Scottus and Bede', *History and Eschatology*, ed. McEvoy and Dunne, pp. 91–140

'Glossing the Bible in the Early Middle Ages: Theodore and Hadrian of Canterbury and John Scottus (Eriugena)', *The Study of the Bible*, ed. Chazelle and Edwards, pp. 19–38

'"Building mansions in Heaven": the *Visio Baronti*, Archangel Raphael and a Carolingian King', *Speculum* 78, 673–706 [Bede, esp. on visions]

Corradini, Richard, 'Zeiträume – Schriftträume. Überlegungen zur Komputistik und Marginalchronographie am Beispiel der *Annales Fuldenses antiquissimi*', *Vom Nutzen des Schreibens*, ed. Walter Pohl and Paul Herold (Vienna, 2002), pp. 113–66 [Bede and Alcuin]

'The Rhetoric of Crisis: *computus* and *liber annalis* in Early Ninth-Century Fulda', *The Construction of Communities in the Early Middle Ages*, ed. Corradini, Max Diesenberger and Helmut Reimitz (Leiden), pp. 269–321 [Bede, Boniface and Alcuin]

Crouch, David, 'The Origin of Chantries: Some Further Anglo-Norman Evidence', *JMH* 27 (2001), 159–80 [pre-Conquest intercessory masses]

Cubitt, Catherine, ed., *Court Culture in the Early Middle Ages: the Proceedings of the First Alcuin Conference*, Stud. in the Early Middle Ages 3 (Turnhout)

Cünnen, Janina, '"Oro pro te sicut pro me": Berthgyths Briefe an Balthard als Beispiele produktiver Akkulturation', *Übersetzung, Adaptation und Akkulturation im insularen Mittelalter*, ed. Erich Poppe and Hildegard L. C. Tristram (Münster, 1999), pp. 185–203

Delierneux, Nathalie, 'Pratiques et vénération orientales et occidentales des images chrétiennes dans l'Antiquité tardive: à propos de quelques ambiguïtes', *Revue belge de philologie et d'histoire* 79 (2001), 373–420 [Bede, pp. 405–11]

Dempsey, G. T., '*Claviger aetherius*: Aldhelm of Malmesbury between Ireland and Rome', *Jnl of the R. Soc. of Antiquaries of Ireland* 131 (2002 for 2001), 5–18

De Rubeis, Flavia, 'Sillogi epigrafiche: le vie della pietra in èta carolingia', *Paolino d'Aquileia*, ed. Chiesa, pp. 93–114 [Alcuin]

Diebold, William J., 'The New Testament and the Visual Arts in the Carolingian Era, with Special Reference to the *sapiens architectus* (I Cor. 3. 10)', *The Study of the Bible*, ed. Chazelle and Edwards, pp. 141–53 [Alcuin's use of Chrysostom; also on Bede] di Sciacca, Claudia, 'Isidorian Scholarship at the School of Theodore and Hadrian: the Case of the *Synonyma*', *Quaestio* (Cambridge) 3 (2002), 76–106

Dolbeau, François, 'Documents du XVIe siècle relatifs aux manuscrits de Saint-Remi de Reims', *La tradition vive*, ed. Lardet, pp. 59–82 [Aldhelm, Bede and Alcuin]

Domínguez Domínguez, Juan Francisco, and Raúl Manchón Gómez, 'Recherches sur les mots *campidoctor* et *campiductor*: de l'Antiquité au Moyen Âge tardif', *Bulletin Du Cange / Archivum Latinitatis Medii Aevi* 58 (2000), 5–44 [Bede, *Martyrologium*, sect. III.i.1]

Dulaey, Martine, 'Les combats de David contre les monstres. 1 Samuel 17 dans l'interprétation patristique', *Rois et reines de la Bible au miroir des Pères* [= Cahiers de *Biblia Patristica* 6] (Strasbourg, 1999), pp. 7–51 [Bede]

Eastwood, Bruce, *The Revival of Planetary Astronomy in Carolingian and Post-Carolingian Europe*, Collected Stud. Ser. 729 (Aldershot, 2002) [esp. for Bede and Alcuin; repr. papers]

Elm, Eva, *Die Macht der Weisheit. Das Bild des Bischofs in der 'Vita Augustini' des Possidius und anderen spätantiken und frühmittelalterlichen Bischofsviten*, Stud. in the Hist. of Christian Thought 109 (Leiden) [Alcuin, *Vita S. Willibrordi*, ch. 7; also on Bede]

Englisch, Brigitte, *Zeiterfassung und Kalenderprogrammatik in der frühen Karolingerzeit. Das Kalendarium der Hs. Köln DB 83–2 und die Synode von Soissons 744*, Instrumenta 8 (Stuttgart, 2002) [Bede, Boniface and Alcuin]

Esmyol, Andrea, *Geliebte oder Ehefrau? Konkubinen im frühen Mittelalter*, Beihefte zum *Archiv für Kulturgeschichte* 52 (Cologne, 2002) [penitentials; also on Bede, Boniface *et al.*]

Favreau, Robert, '*Rex*, *lex*, *lux*, *pax*: jeux de mots et jeux de lettres dans les inscriptions médiévales', *Bibliothèque de l'École des chartes* 161, 625–35 [Anglo-Latin analogues]

Ferrari, Michele Camillo, 'Schulfragmente: Text und Glosse im mittelalterlichen Echternach', *Die Abtei Echternach*, ed. Michele Camillo Ferrari, Jean Schroeder and Henri Traffler (Echternach, 1999), pp. 123–64 [esp. on *Kalendarium Willibrordi*; also on Alcuin]

Firey, Abigail, 'The Letter of the Law: Carolingian Exegetes and the Old Testament', *With Reverence for the Word*, ed. Jane Dammen McAuliffe, Barry D. Walfish and Joseph W. Goering (Oxford), pp. 204–24 [esp. on Theodore and Boniface]

Folkerts, Menso, '*De arithmeticis propositionibus*: a Mathematical Treatise ascribed to the Venerable Bede', Folkerts, *Essays* III, 1–30 [expansion and Eng. trans. of stud. publ. in 1972]

'Die älteste mathematische Aufgabensammlung in lateinischer Sprache: die Alkuin zugeschriebenen *Propositiones ad acuendos iuvenes* – Überlieferung, Inhalt, kritische Edition', Folkerts, *Essays* V, 14–78 [repr. of work publ. in 1978; new to *ASE*]

'The *Propositiones ad acuendos iuvenes* ascribed to Alcuin', Folkerts, *Essays* IV, 1–9 [Eng. trans. of stud. publ. in 1993]

'Frühe westliche Benennungen der indisch–arabischen Ziffern und ihr Vorkommen', *'Sic itur ad astra'. Studien zur Geschichte der Mathematik und Naturwissenschaften*, ed. Folkerts and Richard Lorch (Wiesbaden, 2000), pp. 216–33 [Abbo, esp. in Oxford, St John's College 17]

'The Names and Forms of the Numerals on the Abacus in the Gerbert Tradition', Folkerts, *Essays* VI, 1–17 [Abbo; also on Bede: rev. reissue of stud. publ. in 2001]

Essays on Early Medieval Mathematics: the Latin Tradition, Collected Stud. 751 (Aldershot) [collected papers, many rev.]

Forse, James H., 'Religious Drama and Ecclesiastical Reform in the Tenth Century', *Early Theatre* 5.2 (2002), 47–70 [*Regularis concordia*]

Forte, Anthony J., 'Bengt Löfstedt's "Fragmente eines Matthäus-Kommentars": Reflections and Addenda', *Sacris erudiri* 42, 327–68 [Bede]

Fouracre, Paul, 'Why Were so Many Bishops Killed in Merovingian France?', *Bischofsmord im Mittelalter*, ed. Natalie Fryde und Dirk Reitz (Göttingen), pp. 13–35 [Boniface; also on Stephen of Ripon]

Fox, Michael, 'Alcuin the Exegete: the Evidence of the *Quaestiones in Genesim*', *The Study of the Bible*, ed. Chazelle and Edwards, pp. 39–60

Frank, R., 'Ongendus', *RGA* XXII, 104–5 [Alcuin, esp. in his treatment of Willibrord]

Fransen, Paul-Irénée, 'Extraits non encore repérés dans la compilation augustinienne de Florus sur l'Apôtre', *RB* 113, 80–9 [Bede, *Collectio ex opusculis S. Augustini in epistulas Pauli apostoli*]

Fulton, Rachel, *From Judgment to Passion: Devotion to Christ and the Virgin Mary, 800–1200* (New York, 2002) [Aldhelm, Bede *et al.*, esp. in chs. 3–5 and 7–8]

Gamberini, Roberto, ed., *BISLAM: Bibliotheca Scriptorum Latinorum Medii Recentiorisque Aevi – Repertory of Medieval and Renaissance Latin Authors*, I: *Gli autori in 'Medioevo latino'* (Florence) [CD-ROM]

Garrison, Mary, 'The Bible and Alcuin's Interpretation of Current Events', *Peritia* 16 (2002), 68–84

Gautier Dalché, Pierre, 'Connaissance et usages géographiques des coordonnées dans le Moyen Âge latin (du vénérable Bède à Roger Bacon)', *Science antique*, ed. Callebat and Desbordes, pp. 401–36

'Principes et modes de la représentation de l'espace géographique durant le haut Moyen Âge', *SettSpol* 50, 117–50 [Bede]

Gazzo, Natalia, 'Simmetria, classicismo e virtuosismo versificatorio negli *Aenigmata* di Bonifacio', *Maia* 50 (1998), 329–48

Ghilardi, Massimiliano, '"Egregium Albanum fecunda Britannia profert." Albano e i primi santi della Britannia romana', *Romanobarbarica* 17 (2000–2), 1–18 [Gildas and Bede]

Giannarelli, Elena, 'I cristiani, la medicina, Cosma e Damiano', *Cosma e Damiano, dall'Oriente a Firenze*, ed. Elena Giannarelli (Florence, 2002), pp. 7–65 [Aldhelm; also on Bede, *Martyrologium*]

Gittos, Helen, see sect. 9*e* [architecture and liturgy]

Gleason, Michael, 'Water, Water, Everywhere: Alcuin's Bede and Balthere', *Mediaevalia* 24, 75–100

Gneuss, Helmut, and Michael Lapidge, see sect. 5 [Bede, *Vita S. Cuthberti metrica*]

Goetz, Hans-Werner, *Frauen im frühen Mittelalter. Frauenbild und Frauenleben im Frankenreich* (Weimar, 1995) ['Teilhabe an theologischer Bildung: der Brief Gislas und Rodtruds an Alcuin', in ch. 10; esp. also on circle of Boniface]

Gómez Pallarés, Joan, *Studia Chronologica. Estudios sobre manuscritos latinos de cómputo*, ed. Gemma Puigvert and Rosario Perea (Madrid, 1999) [esp. for Bede; reissued papers]

Gregory, Tullio, 'Lo spazio come geografia del sacro nell'Occidente altomedievale', *SettSpol* 50, 27–68 [Bede; 'Discussione sulla lezione Gregory', pp. 61–8]

Gryson, Roger, ed., *Commentaria minora in Apocalypsin Johannis*, CCSL 107 (Turnhout) [Bede, esp. in introd. to the anon. *Commemoratorium*; also for pseudo-Bede]

Harmon, Steven R., 'A Note on the Critical Use of *instrumenta* for the Retrieval of Patristic Biblical Exegesis', *Jnl of Early Christian Stud.* 11, 95–107 [Bede and Alcuin]

Harris, Stephen J., 'Bede and Gregory's Allusive Angles', *Criticism* 44 (2002), 271–89

Heffernan, Thomas J., 'Christian Biography: Foundation to Maturity', *Historiography in the Middle Ages*, ed. Deborah Mauskopf Deliyannis (Leiden), pp. 115–54 [Bede]

Hehle, Christine, *Boethius in St. Gallen. Die Bearbeitung der 'Consolatio Philosophiae' durch Notker Teutonicus zwischen Tradition und Innovation*, Münchener Texte und Untersuchungen zur deutschen Literatur des Mittelalters 122 (Tübingen, 2002) [Alcuin, esp. in chs. 3–4 and 7; also on Aldhelm, Bede *et al.*]

Heil, Johannes, *Kompilation oder Konstruktion? Die Juden in den Pauluskommentaren des 9. Jahrhunderts*, Forschungen zur Geschichte der Juden, Abteilung A: Abhandlungen 6 (Hannover, 1998) [esp. for Bede, Alcuin and pseudo-Bede]

'Labourers in the Lord's Quarry: Carolingian Exegetes, Patristic Authority and Theological Innovation: a Case Study in the Representation of Jews in Commentaries on Paul', *The Study of the Bible*, ed. Chazelle and Edwards, pp. 76–95 [Alcuin; also on pseudo-Bede]

Hiley, David, 'The Repertory of Sequences at Winchester', *Essays on Medieval Music in honor of David G. Hughes*, ed. Graeme M. Boone (Cambridge, MA, 1995), pp. 153–93

'The English Benedictine Version of the *Historia Sancti Gregorii* and the Date of the "Winchester Troper" (Cambridge, Corpus Christi College, 473)', *Cantus Planus: Papers Read at the Seventh Meeting*, ed. László Dobszay (Budapest, 1998), pp. 287–303

Hill, Joyce, 'Coping with Conflict: Lunar and Solar Cycles in the Liturgical Calendars', *Time and Eternity*, ed. Jaritz and Moreno-Riaño, pp. 99–108

Holder, Arthur G., 'The Patristic Sources of Bede's Commentary on the Song of Songs', *Studia Patristica* (Louvain) 34 (2001), 370–5

Holtz, Louis, 'Priscien dans la pédagogie d'Alcuin', *Manuscripts and Tradition of Grammatical Texts from Antiquity to the Renaissance*, ed. Mario De Nonno, Paolo De Paolis and Louis. Holtz, 1 vol. in 2 (Cassino, 2000), pp. 289–326

'Arti liberali ed enciclopedismo da Cassiodoro a Alcuino', *Giornate filologiche 'Francesco Della Corte' – II*, ed. Ferruccio Bertini (Genoa, 2001), pp. 213–30

Hornby, Emma, 'The Transmission History of the Proper Chant for St Gregory: the Eighth-Mode Tract *Beatus vir*', *Plainsong and Med. Music* 12, 97–127

Huglo, Michel, 'Division de la tradition monodique en deux groupes "est" et "ouest"', *Revue de musicologie* 85 (1999), 5–28 [Alcuin, esp. in his *comes*]

Hurst, David, ed., Vuillaume, Christophe, trans., *Bède le vénérable. Le tabernacle*, Sources chrétiennes 475 (Paris)

I Deug-Su, 'Lioba, *dilecta Bonifatii*: die Eloquenz des Schweigens in lateinischen Quellen des Mittelalters', *Jahrbuch für internationale Germanistik* 33.2 (2001), 189–219

'Tipi di rifacimento agiografico: alcuni esempi in epoca carolingia e ottoniana', *Hagiographica* 10, 123–37 [esp. on Hygeburh, Willibald and Alcuin]

Jaeger, C. Stephen, *Scholars and Courtiers: Intellectuals and Society in the Medieval West*, Collected Stud. Ser. 753 (Aldershot, 2002) [esp. on Alcuin, in items I, III and VIII; repr. papers]

Jaritz, Gerhard, and Gerson Moreno-Riaño, ed., *Time and Eternity: the Medieval Discourse*, International Med. Research 9 (Turnhout)

Jarnut, Jörg, 'Bonifatius und Bayern', *Der weite Blick des Historikers*, ed. Wilfried Ehbrecht, Angelika Lampen, Franz-Joseph Post and Mechthild Siekmann (Cologne, 2002), pp. 269–81

Jones, Christopher A., 'Monastic Custom in Early Norman England: the Significance of Bodleian MS. Wood empt. 4', *RB* 113, 135–68 and 302–36 [esp. for Ælfric, *Epistola ad monachos*]

Jun, Nathan J., 'The Letter of Fredegisus of Tours on Nothingness and Shadow: a New Translation and Commentary', *Comitatus* 34, 150–69

Karkov, Catherine E., and George Hardin Brown, ed., see sect. 1

Kelly, Joseph F., 'Bede's Use of the Fathers to Interpret the Infancy Narratives', *Studia Patristica* (Louvain) 34 (2001), 388–94

Koal, Valeska, *Studien zur Nachwirkung der Kapitularien in den Kanonessammlungen des Frühmittelalters*, Freiburger Beiträge zur mittelalterlichen Geschichte 13 (Frankfurt, 2001) [Alcuin and Abbo, esp. in sect. *b*]

Kroesen, Justin E. A., *The 'sepulchrum Domini' through the Ages: its Form and Function*, Liturgia Condenda 10 (Louvain, 2000) [*Regularis concordia*, sect. ii*b*]

Krstovič, Jelena O., and Daniel G. Marowski, ed., *Classical and Medieval Literature Criticism* XX (Detroit, 1997) ['Bede, *c.* 673–735', pp. 1–128]

Lake, Stephen, 'Knowledge of the Writings of John Cassian in Early Anglo-Saxon England', *ASE* 32, 27–41

Lapidge, Michael, *The Cult of St Swithun*, Winchester Stud. 4: the AS Minsters of Winchester, pt. ii (Oxford)

'Rufinus at the School of Canterbury', *La tradition vive*, ed. Lardet, pp. 119–29

see also sect. 6 [latinity of Asser]

Lapidge, Michael, Gian Carlo Garfagnini and Claudio Leonardi, ed., *CALMA. Compendium Auctorum Latinorum Medii Aevi (500–1500)*, I: *Abaelardus Petrus – Bartholomaeus de Forolivio* (Florence, 2000–3) [vol. 1 now complete in 6 fascs.; *index chronologicus auctorum* for s. vii–xi, pp. 817–18]

Lardet, Pierre, ed., *La tradition vive. Mélanges d'histoire des textes en l'honneur de Louis Holtz*, Bibliologia 20 (Turnhout)

Law, Vivien, 'Memory and the Structure of Grammars in Antiquity and the Middle Ages', *Manuscripts and Tradition of Grammatical Texts from Antiquity to the Renaissance*, ed. Mario De Nonno, Paolo De Paolis and Louis. Holtz, 1 vol. in 2 (Cassino, 2000), pp. 9–57 [German trans. now publ. as 'Gedächtnis und Grammatikschreibung im Mittelalter', *Heilige und profane Sprachen*, ed. Werner Hüllen and Friederike Klippel (Wiesbaden, 2002), pp. 31–75]

The History of Linguistics in Europe from Plato to 1600 (Cambridge) [Aldhelm, Tatwine, Bede *et al.*, esp. in chs. 6–7 and 9]

Lazzari, Loredana, 'I *colloquia* nelle scuole monastiche anglosassoni tra la fine del X e la prima metà dell'XI secolo', *SM* 44, 147–77

Lendinara, Patrizia, 'Presenza e collocazione dei componimenti poetici di Paolino d'Aquileia nei codici medievali', *Paolino d'Aquileia*, ed. Chiesa, pp. 329–71 [esp. for Bede; also on Aldhelm and Alcuin]

'Un ritmo dei *Carmina Cantabrigiensia*', *Poetry of the Early Medieval Europe*, ed. Edoardo D'Angelo and Francesco Stella (Florence), pp. 63–73

'The *Versus Sibyllae de die iudicii* in Anglo-Saxon England', *Apocryphal Texts and Traditions*, ed. Powell and Scragg, pp. 85–101 [Canterbury school, Bede, Milred and pseudo-Bede]

Luff, Robert, '*Philomena – roussignol – nahtigal.* Anmerkungen zum Umgang mit der Nachtigall in mittelalterlicher Lyrik und Naturkunde', *Mystik – Überlieferung – Naturkunde*, ed. Luff and Rudolf Kilian Weigand (Hildesheim, 2002), pp. 37–76 [Alcuin]

Luhtala, Anneli, 'A Priscian Commentary Attributed to Eriugena', *History of Linguistics 1999*, ed. Sylvain Auroux (Amsterdam), pp. 19–30 [Alcuin]

Lutterbach, Hubertus, 'Die Fastenbusse im Mittelalter', *Frömmigkeit im Mittelalter*, ed. Klaus Schreiner (Munich, 2002), pp. 399–437 [Alcuin]

McCarthy, Daniel P., 'The Emergence of *anno Domini*', *Time and Eternity*, ed. Jaritz and Moreno-Riaño, pp. 31–53

'On the Shape of the Insular Tonsure', *Celtica* 24, 140–67 [Aldhelm, Ceolfrith *et al.*]

McCarthy, Daniel P., and Aidan Breen, ed., *The Ante-Nicene Christian Pasch: De Ratione Paschali – the Paschal Tract of Anatolius, Bishop of Laodicea* (Dublin) [esp. for Bede; also on Aldhelm *et al.*]

McDaniel, Rhonda L., 'An Unidentified Passage from Jerome in Bede', *N&Q* 50, 375

McEvoy, James, and Michael Dunne, ed., *History and Eschatology in John Scottus Eriugena and His Time*, Ancient and Med. Philosophy, ser. 1, 30 (Louvain, 2002) [esp. for Alcuin; also on Aldhelm *et al.*]

MacGinty, G., ed., *The Reference Bible – Das Bibelwerk: inter Pauca problesmata de enigmatibus ex tomis canonicis, nunc prompta sunt Praefatio et libri de Pentateucho Moysi*, 2 vols., Corpus Christianorum, Continuatio Medievalis 173–173A [= Scriptores Celtigenae 3] (Turnhout, 2000–2) [for Bede and pseudo-Bede, *Collectanea*]

Mackay, Thomas W., 'Apocalypse Comments by Primasius, Bede and Alcuin: Interrelationship, Dependency and Individuality', *Studia Patristica* (Louvain) 36 (2001), 28–34

McNamara, Martin, 'Christ Forty Hours in the Tomb and the Forty Hours Devotion', *Celtica* 24, 205–12 [*Collectanea pseudo-Bedae*]

MacQuarrie, Charles W., 'Insular Celtic Tattooing: History, Myth and Metaphor',

Written on the Body: the Tattoo in European and American History, ed. Jane Caplan (Princeton, NJ, 2000), pp. 32–45 [Canterbury Commentaries]

Mara, Maria Grazia, 'L'epistolario apocrifo di Seneca e San Paolo', *Seneca e i cristiani*, ed. Antonio P. Martina (Milan, 2001), pp. 41–54 [Alcuin]

Marenbon, John, 'Alcuin, the Council of Frankfort and the Beginnings of Medieval Philosophy', *Das Frankfurter Konzil*, ed. Berndt, pp. 603–15

Marina Sáez, Rosa María, 'Acerca de algunas observaciones de los metricólogos antiguos sobre la disposición de las palabras en el hexámetro dactílico', *Cuadernos de filología clásica, estudios latinos* ns 12 (1997), 87–106 [Bede]

Martín, José Carlos, 'La traduction indirecte de la "Chronique" d'Isidore de Séville', *Revue d'histoire des textes* 31 (2001), 167–225 [Bede; also on Chronicle, and on *Historia Brittonum*]

Martínez Pizarro, Joaquín, 'Ethnic and National History *ca.* 500–1000', *Historiography in the Middle Ages*, ed. Deborah Mauskopf Deliyannis (Leiden), pp. 43–87 [Bede; also on Chronicle]

Matter, E. Ann, 'Exegesis of the Apocalypse in the Early Middle Ages', *The Year 1000*, ed. Michael Frassetto (Basingstoke, 2002), pp. 29–40 [Bede and Alcuin]

Mazza, Enrico, 'La celebrazione della penitenza nella liturgia bizantina e in Occidente: due concezioni a confronto', *Ephemerides Liturgicae* 115 (2001), 385–440 [Theodore, pseudo-Bede *et al.*, sect. 2.6]

Mazzini, Innocenzo, 'Lingua e linguaggi dell'evangelizzazione nell'Occidente latino dal terzo all'ottavo secolo', *Evangelizzazione dell'Occidente dal terzo all'ottavo secolo*, ed. Innocenzo Mazzini and Lucia Bacci (Rome, 2001), pp. 9–74 [Augustine of Canterbury, Bede and Alcuin]

Meens, Rob, 'The Frequency and Nature of Early Medieval Penance', *Handling Sin: Confession in the Middle Ages*, ed. Peter Biller and A. J. Minnis (Woodbridge, 1998), pp. 35–61

'The Oldest Manuscript Witness of the *Collectio canonum Hibernensis*', *Peritia* 14 (2000), 1–19 [Theodore, Boniface *et al.*]

Mehtonen, Päivi, 'Scriptural Difficulty and the Obscurity of *historia*', *Historia: the Concept and Genres*, ed. Tuomas M. S. Lehtonen and Päivi Mehtonen (Helsinki, 2000), pp. 51–67 [Aldhelm]

Meyer, Ann R., *Medieval Allegory and the Building of the New Jerusalem* (Woodbridge) ['Sacred Architecture of the Hebrew Bible and the Exegesis of Bede', pp. 16–23]

Meyvaert, Paul, and Anselme Davril, 'Théodulfe et Bède au sujet des blessures du Christ', *RB* 113, 71–9 [Bede, *Collectio ex opusculis S. Augustini in epistulas Pauli apostoli*]

Milani, Celestina, 'La continuità della tradizione classica negli *itineraria ad loca sancta* (IV–VIII secolo)', *La diffusione dell'eredità classica nell'età tardoantica e medievale*, ed. Rosa Bianca Finazzi and Alfredo Valvo (Alessandria, 1998), pp. 109–23 [Bede]

'Gli *itineraria ad loca sancta*', *Tipologia dei testi e tecniche espressive*, ed. Giovanni Gobber and Milani (Milan, 2002), pp. 37–45 [Bede and Alcuin, esp. in relation to *Itinerarium Antonini Placentini*]

Mosetti Casaretto, Francesco, 'Sankt Gallen, Stiftsbibliothek, 265: *Ad Grimaldum abbatem*?', *Maia* 51 (1999), 471–83 [Bede, *Vita S. Cuthberti metrica* and other verse]

'"Intuere caelum apertum": l'esordio dell'*Epistola ad Grimaldum abbatem* di Ermenrico di Ellwangen fra Ilduino di Saint-Denis e Giovanni Scoto', *History and Eschatology*, ed. McEvoy and Dunne, pp. 203–25 [Bede, pseudo-Bede, Alcuin and Wigbod]

Mostert, Marco, 'Gerbert d'Aurillac, Abbon de Fleury et la culture de l'An Mil: étude comparative de leurs œuvres et de leur influence', *Gerberto d'Aurillac da abate di Bobbio a papa dell'anno 1000*, ed. Flavio G. Nuvolone (Bobbio, 2001), pp. 397–431

Munzi, Luigi, 'Testi grammaticali e *renovatio studiorum* carolingia', *Manuscripts and Tradition of Grammatical Texts from Antiquity to the Renaissance*, ed. Mario De Nonno, Paolo De Paolis and Louis. Holtz, 1 vol. in 2 (Cassino, 2000), pp. 351–88 [Alcuin; also on Aldhelm *et al.*]

Murano, Giovanna, 'Un *ordo Romanus* di provenienza vallombrosana (Firenze, Bibl. nazionale centrale, Conv. Soppr. B. II. 406)', *Aevum* 77, 249–62 [Alcuin]

Ohashi, Masako, '"Sexta aetas continet annos praeteritos DCCVIIII" (Bede, *De temporibus*, 22): a Scribal Error?', *Time and Eternity*, ed. Jaritz and Moreno-Riaño, pp. 55–61

O'Leary, Aideen M., 'Apostolic *passiones* in Early Anglo-Saxon England', *Apocryphal Texts and Traditions*, ed. Powell and Scragg, pp. 103–19 [Aldhelm and Bede]

Ó Néill, Pádraig, 'Irish Transmission of Late Antique Learning: the Case of Theodore of Mopsuestia's Commentary on the Psalms', *Ireland and Europe in the Early Middle Ages: Texts and Transmission*, ed. Próinséas Ni Chatháin and Michael Richter (Dublin, 2002), pp. 68–77 [AS psalters; also on Theodore, Aldhelm and pseudo-Bede]

Orchard, Nicholas, 'The Ninth- and Tenth-Century Additions to Cambrai, Mediathèque municipale, 164', *RB* 113, 285–97 [esp. on benedictionals and 'Durham collectar']

'A Supplementary Note on *Pater sancte*', *RB* 113, 298–301

O'Sullivan, Sinead, 'Aldhelm's *De virginitate* and the Psychomachian Tradition', *Mediaevalia* 20 (2001 for *c.* 1996), 313–37

Partoens, Gert, 'La collection de sermons augustiniennes *De verbis Apostoli*. Introduction et liste des manuscrits les plus anciens', *RB* 111 (2001), 317–52 [Bede, *Collectio ex opusculis S. Augustini in epistulas Pauli apostoli*]

'Le sermon 151 de saint Augustin. Introduction et édition', *RB* 113, 18–70 [Bede, in cited *Collectio*]

Passalacqua, Marina, 'Terminologia filologica negli epistolari carolingi: intellettuali e testi', *Paolino d'Aquileia*, ed. Chiesa, pp. 405–20 [Alcuin; also on Aldhelm and Tatwine]

Peden, A. M., ed., *Abbo of Fleury and Ramsey: Commentary on the 'Calculus' of Victorius of Aquitaine*, Auctores Britannici Medii Aevi 15 (Oxford)

Petersen, Nils-Holger, 'Les textes polyvalents du *Quem quaeritis* à Winchester au xe siècle', *Revue de musicologie* 86 (2000), 105–18

'The Representational Liturgy of the *Regularis concordia*', *The White Mantle of Churches: Architecture, Liturgy and Art around the Millennium*, ed. Nigel Hiscock (Turnhout), pp. 107–17

Petersen, William L., 'Ephrem Syrus and the Venerable Bede: Do East and West Meet?', *Studia Patristica* (Louvain) 34 (2001), 443–52

Picker, Hanns-Christoph, *Pastor Doctus: Klerikerbild und karolingische Reformen bei Hrabanus Maurus*, Veröffentlichungen des Instituts für europäische Geschichte, Mainz: Abteilung für abendländische Religionsgeschichte 186 (Mainz, 2001) [Alcuin, esp. in chs. 1 and 3; also on Aldhelm, Bede *et al.*]

Plötz, Robert, '"De hoc quod apostolus Karolo apparuit". Die Traumvision Karls des Grossen: ein typisch mittelalterliche Vision?', *Jakobus und Karl der Grosse*, ed. Klaus Herbers (Tübingen), pp. 39–78 [Bede and other AS links, sect. vi]

Pollmann, Karla, 'Apocalypse Now? Der Kommentar des Tyconius zur Johannesoffenbarung', *Der Kommentar in Antike und Mittelalter*, ed. Wilhelm Geerlings and Christian Schulze (Leiden, 2002), pp. 33–54 [Bede, *Commentarius in Apocalypsim*]

Powell, Kathryn, and Donald Scragg, ed., see sect. 3*a*

Puigvert i Planagumà, Gemma, 'Textes communs au manuscrit ACA Ripoll 225 et au manuscrit Avranches 235', *Science antique*, ed. Callebat and Desbordes, pp. 171–87 [Bede, *De temporum ratione*]

Rambridge, Kate, 'Alcuin's Narratives of Evangelism: the Life of St Willibrord and the Northumbrian Hagiographical Tradition', *The Cross Goes North*, ed. Carver, pp. 371–81

Repsher, Brian, 'The *abecedarium*: Catechetical Symbolism in the Rite of Church Dedication', *Mediaevalia* 24, 1–18 [Bede]

Rosier, Irène, Colette Jeudy, Vivien Law, *et al.*, 'Moyen Âge', *Corpus représentatif des grammaires et des traditions linguistiques*, ed. Bernard Colombat, 2 vols. (Paris, 1998–2000) I, 54–74 ['Bède le Vénérable' and 'Alcuin', by Rosier, and 'Ælfric', by Rosier and Law]

Rowley, Sharon M., 'Reassessing Exegetical Interpretations of Bede's *Historia ecclesiastica gentis Anglorum*', *Lit. and Theol.* 17, 227–43

Ruff, Carin, 'Aldhelm's Jewel Tones: Latin Colors through Anglo-Saxon Eyes', *Anglo-Saxon Styles*, ed. Karkov and Brown, pp. 223–38

Saxer, Victor, *Saint Vincent, diacre et martyr. Culte et légendes avant l'An Mil*, Subsidia Hagiographica 83 (Brussels, 2002) [esp. for Bede and on Cotton–Corpus archetype, chs. 7–8; reissued papers]

Scharff, Thomas, *Die Kämpfe der Herrscher und der Heiligen. Krieg und historische Erinnerung in der Karolingerzeit*, Symbolische Kommunikation in der Vormoderne (Darmstadt, 2002) [Alcuin, esp. in pt. I; also on Bede]

Schmidt, Michael, *Germanien unter den Merowingern und frühen Karolingern. Auf den Spuren der ersten Herzöge, Bischöfe und Missionare, von 482 bis 755* (Frankfurt am Main, 2001) [Willibrord, Boniface *et al.*, esp. in chs. 4–5]

Schmidt, Paul Gerhard, 'Die Gegenwelt im Jenseits', *Literaturwissenschaftliches Jahrbuch* 44, 9–17 [Bede, esp. on Dryhthelm's vision]

Schneider, Jens, 'Latein und Althochdeutsch in der Cambridger Liedersammlung: *De Heinrico, Clericus et nonna*', *Volkssprachig–lateinische Mischtexte*, ed. Bergmann, pp. 297–314 [also on OE verse]

Schreiner, Klaus, '"Göttliche Schreib-Kunst": eigenhändige Aufzeichen Gottes, Jesu und Maria. Schriftlichkeit in heilsgeschichtlichen Kontexten', *FS* 36 (2002), 95–132 [Alcuin]

Schuler, Stefan, 'Pourquoi lire Vitruve au Moyen Âge? Un point de rencontre entre savoir antique et savoir médiéval', *Science antique*, ed. Callebat and Desbordes, pp. 319–41 [Alcuin]

Semmler, Josef, 'Bonifatius, die Karolinger und "die Franken"', *Mönchtum – Kirche – Herrschaft, 750–1000*, ed. Dieter R. Bauer, Rudolf Hiestand, Brigitte Kasten and Sönke Lorenz (Sigmaringen, 1998), pp. 3–49

Sharpe, Richard, 'The Naming of Bishop Ithamar', *EHR* 117 (2002), 889–94 [Bede, *Historia ecclesiastica*]

Titulus: Identifying Medieval Latin Texts, an Evidence-Based Approach (Turnhout) [esp. on *CALMA*, ed. M. Lapidge *et al.* (Florence, 2000–), and on Sharpe's *Handlist*, in chs. 11–12]

Siewers, Alfred K., 'Landscapes of Conversion: Guthlac's Mound and Grendel's Mere as Expressions of Anglo-Saxon Nation-Building', *Viator* 34, 1–39 [Felix; also on Bede]

Simonetti, Giuseppina Abbolito, trans., *Venerabile Beda, Esposizione e revisione degli Atti degli Apostoli. Introduzione, traduzione e note*, Collana di testi patristici 121 (Rome, 1995)

Simoni, Fiorella, 'La memoria del regno ostrogoto nella tradizione storiografica carolingia', *Le invasioni barbariche nel meridione dell'impero*, ed. Paolo Delogu (Catanzaro, 2001), pp. 351–75 [Bede, *De temporibus* and *Chronica maiora* (in *De temporum ratione*)]

Smyth, Matthieu, *La liturgie oubliée. La prière eucharistique en Gaule antique et dans l'Occident non romain* (Paris) [esp. in chs. I.4–6]

Sorbi, Luca, 'Il *Parmenide* di Platone e la sua funzione nella filosofia di Aristotele e in quella dei filosofi cristiani', *Atti e memorie dell'Accademia toscana di scienze e lettere 'La Colombaria'* 68, 55–110 [pseudo-Bede, *De arithmeticis propositionibus*]

Springsfeld, Kerstin, *Alkuins Einfluss auf die Komputistik zur Zeit Karls des Grossen*, *Sudhoffs Archiv* Beihefte 48 (Stuttgart, 2002)

Thunø, Erik, *Image and Relic: Mediating the Sacred in Early Medieval Rome*, Analecta Romana Instituti Danici, Supplementa 32 (Rome, 2002) [Bede and Alcuin, esp. in chs. 4–7]

Tugene, Georges, *L'image de la nation anglaise dans l''Histoire ecclésiastique' de Bède le Vénérable* (Strasbourg, 2001)

'Reflections of "Ethnic" Kingship in Bede's "Ecclesiastical History"', *Romanobarbarica* 17 (2000–2), 309–31

Vaciago, Paolo, 'From Canterbury to Sankt Gallen: on the Transmission of Early Medieval Glosses to the Octateuch and the Books of Kings', *Romanobarbarica* 17 (2000–2), 237–308

Verbist, Peter, 'Abbo of Fleury and the Computational Accuracy of the Christian Era', *Time and Eternity*, ed. Jaritz and Moreno-Riaño, pp. 63–80

Vessey, Mark, 'From *cursus* to *ductus*: Figures of Writing in Western Late Antiquity (Augustine, Jerome, Cassiodorus, Bede)', *European Literary Careers: the Author from Antiquity to the Renaissance*, ed. Patrick Cheney and Frederick A. de Armas (Toronto, 2002), pp. 47–103

Veyrard-Cosme, Christiane, 'Typologie et hagiographie en prose carolingienne: mode de pensée et réécriture. Étude de la *Vita Willibrordi*, de la *Vita Vedasti* et de la *Vita Richarii* d'Alcuin', *Écriture et modes de pensée au Moyen Âge (VIIIe–XVe siècles)*, ed. Dominique Boutet and Laurence Harf-Lancner (Paris, 1993), pp. 157–86

'L'image de Charlemagne *dans* la correspondance d'Alcuin', *L'Éloge du prince. De l'Antiquité au temps des lumières*, ed. Isabelle Cogitore and Francis Goyet (Grenoble), pp. 137–67

'Saint Jérôme dans les lettres d'Alcuin: de la source matérielle au modèle spirituel', *Revue des études augustiniennes* 49, 323–51

Veyrard-Cosme, Christiane, ed., *L'Œuvre hagiographique en prose d'Alcuin. Vitae Willibrordi, Vedasti, Richarii: édition, traduction, études narratologiques*, Per Verba: Testi mediolatini con traduzione 21 (Florence)

Vinay, Gustavo, with Corinna Bottiglieri and Iolanda Ventura, *Alto Medioevo latino. Conversazioni e no*, ed. Ileana Pagani and Massimo Oldoni, Nuovo Medioevo 14 (Naples) ['Beda o la storia della disponibilità', ch. 5; also on Alcuin *et al.*: rev. reissue of work publ. in 1978]

von Euw, Anton, 'Der *Aratus Latinus* in Hs. 83^{II} der Kölner Dombibliothek', *Romische historische Mitteilungen* 41 (1999), 405–22 [Bede and Alcuin]

Wagner, Heinrich, *Bonifatiusstudien*, Quellen und Forschungen zur Geschichte des Bistums und Hochstifts Würzburg 60 (Würzburg)

Waldhoff, Stephan, *Alcuins Gebetbuch für Karl den Grossen. Seine Rekonstruktion und seine Stellung in der frühmittelalterlichen Geschichte der 'libelli precum'*, Liturgiewissenschaftliche Quellen und Forschungen 89 (Münster)

Ward, Anthony, 'Dom Alban Dold's Proposed Selection of Ancient Prefaces', *Ephemerides Liturgicae* 117, 449–503 ['Leofric' missal, sect. I.39]

White, Caroline, 'Medieval Senses of Classical Words', *Peritia* 16 (2002), 131–43 [esp. on penitentials; also on Alcuin]

Winterbottom, Michael, 'The Earliest Life of St Dunstan', *Scripta Classica Israelica* 19 (2000), 163–79

Wollasch, Joachim, 'Frühe Bildzeugnisse für das Nachleben Papst Gregors des Grossen in Rom?', *FS* 36 (2002), 159–70 [Bede]

Woods, David, 'Arculf's Luggage: the Sources for Adomnán's *De locis sanctis*', *Ériu* 52 (2002), 25–52 [Bede]

Wright, Roger, 'Rhythmic Poetry and the Author's Vernacular', *Poetry of the Early Medieval Europe*, ed. Edoardo D'Angelo and Francesco Stella (Florence), pp. 343–55 [esp. for Aldhelm and Alcuin]

'La période de transition du latin, de la *lingua Romana* et du français', *Médiévales* 45, 11–23 [Alcuin]

Zanna, Paolo, ed., *Responsa contra Claudium: a Controversy on Holy Images*, Per Verba: Testi mediolatini con traduzione 17 (Florence, 2002) [Alcuin; also on Gildas, Aldhelm, *et al.*]

Zelzer, Michaela, 'Das ambrosianische Corpus *De virginitate* und seine Rezeption im Mittelalter', *Studia Patristica* (Louvain) 38 (2001), 510–23 [Bede]

'Buch und Text von Augustus zu Karl dem Grossen', *Mitteilungen der Österreichischen Gesellschaft für Wissenschaftsgeschichte* 109 (2001), 291–314 [Alcuin]

5. PALAEOGRAPHY, DIPLOMATIC AND ILLUMINATION

Bicchieri, Marina, Francesco Paolo Romano, Lighea Pappalardo, Luigi Cosentino, Nardone Michele and Armida Sodo, 'Non-Destructive Analysis of the *Bibbia Amiatina* by XRF, PIXE–[GK LC ALPHA] and Raman', *Quinio* (Rome) 3 (2001), 169–79

Bierbrauer, Katharina, 'Insulares in der kontinentalen Buchmalerei des 8. Jahrhunderts', *Tiere, Menschen, Götter*, ed. Müller-Wille and Larsson, pp. 63–87

Biggam, C. P., ed., see sect. 1

Bouet, Pierre, and Monique Dosdat, ed., *Manuscrits et enluminures dans le monde normand (X^e–XVe siècles)* (Caen, 1999)

Bräm, Andreas, 'Bilder der Liturgie in liturgischen Handschriften bis in ottonische Zeit', *Art, cérémonial et liturgie au Moyen Âge*, ed. Nicolas Bock, Peter Kurmann, Serena Romano and Jean-Michel Spieser (Rome, 2002), pp. 141–68 [esp. for Gneuss nos. 301, 879 and 922]

British Library, with the assistance of Janet Backhouse, Karen Brookfield, Michelle Brown, Robin Herford, Clive Izard and David Way, *The Lindisfarne Gospels* (London, 2000) [CD-ROM]

Brown, Michelle P., *Das Buch von Lindisfarne. Cotton MS Nero D. iv in der British Library, London. Kommentarband I* (Lucerne, 2002), now publ. with separate ed. of Brown, *The Lindisfarne Gospels* (cited below), as 2nd vol. of commentary, augmented by a new appendix, for 3 vols. in 2 (Lucerne, 2002–3) [includes 149-page, discretely paginated 'Appendix 2: the Contents of the Lindisfarne Gospels']

The Lindisfarne Gospels: Society, Spirituality and the Scribe, Brit. Lib. Stud. in Med. Culture (London) [also issued with commentary vols. for Brown, ed., *Das Buch von Lindisfarne* (2002–3; as cited above); see further *ASE* 32 (2002), p. 358]

Painted Labyrinth: the World of the Lindisfarne Gospels (London) [adjunct to British Library exhibition]

The World of the Lindisfarne Gospels (London) [DVD and videocassette]

'House Style in the Scriptorium: Scribal Reality and Scholarly Myth', *Anglo-Saxon Styles*, ed. Karkov and Brown, pp. 131–50 [scriptoria at Monkwearmouth–Jarrow and Lindisfarne]

'Exhibiting the Lindisfarne Gospels', *Hist. Today* 53.5, 4–6

Caldini Montanari, Roberta, *Tradizione medievale ed edizione critica del 'Somnium Scipionis'*, Millennio medievale 33 [= Testi 10] (Florence, 2002) [Gneuss nos. 1.5 and 536]

Chabries, D. M., S. W. Booras and G. H. Bearman, 'Imaging the Past: Recent Applications of Multispectral Imaging Technology to Deciphering Manuscripts', *Antiquity* 77, 359–72

Chaplais, Pierre, see sect. 6

Charles-Edwards, Thomas, ed., see sect. 6

Chazelle, Celia, 'Ceolfrid's Gift to St Peter: the First Quire of the Codex Amiatinus and the Evidence of its Roman Destination', *EME* 12, 129–58

Chedzey, Jane, 'Manuscript Production in Medieval Winchester', *Reading Med. Stud.* 29, 1–18 [esp. on pre-Conquest evidence]

Cichoń, Krzysztof, 'Tablice kanonów: symbolika dekoracji architektonicznej [Canon Tables: the Symbolism of the Architectural Iconography]', *Acta Universitatis Lodziensis, Folia Historica* 74 (2002), 87–108 [CCCC 286]

Clarke, Mark, 'L'analyse de pigments *in situ*, et sans prélèvement, dans les manuscrits médiévaux: l'exemple des manuscrits anglo-saxons', *L'archéometrie au service des monuments et des œuvres d'art*, ed. D. Allart and P. Hoffsummer, Dossier de la Commission royale des monuments, sites et fouilles 10 (Liège), pp. 187–94

Clegg, Justin, *The Medieval Church in Manuscripts* (London) [Benedictional of Æthelwold and New Minster *Liber vitae*, sect. 2]

Coatsworth, Elizabeth, 'The Book of Enoch and Anglo-Saxon Art', *Apocryphal Texts and Traditions*, ed. Powell and Scragg, pp. 135–50

Cohen, Adam S., *The Uta Codex: Art, Philosophy and Reform in Eleventh-Century Germany* (University Park, PA, 2000) [AS links, esp. in ch. 8]

Collins, Minta, introd., with Sandra Raphael, *A Medieval Herbal: a Facsimile of British Library Egerton MS 747* (London) [esp. on OE version of pseudo-Apuleius, *Herbarius*, in witness of Brit. Lib., Cotton Vitellius C. iii]

D'Aronco, Maria Amalia, 'Interazione fra testo e illustrazione: il caso di London, BL, Cotton Vitellius C. iii', *Testo e immagine nel Medioevo germanico*, ed. Maria Grazia Saibene and Marina Buzzoni (Milan, 2001), pp. 103–14

'Anglo-Saxon Plant Pharmacy and the Latin Medical Tradition', *From Earth to Art*, ed. Biggam, pp. 133–51

Davies, Wendy, ed., see sect. 6

Ebersperger, Birgit, 'BSG, MS 2409 + Arsenal, MS 933, ff. 128–334: an Anglo-Saxon Manuscript from Canterbury?', *Bookmarks from the Past*, ed. Kornexl and Lenker, pp. 177–93

Englisch, Brigitte, *Ordo Orbis Terrae: die Weltsicht in den 'mappae mundi' des frühen und hohen Mittelalters*, Orbis Mediaevalis 3 (Berlin, 2002) [esp. for BL, Cotton Tiberius B. v, fol. 56v]

Farr, Carol, 'Style in Late Anglo-Saxon England: Questions of Learning and Intention', *Anglo-Saxon Styles*, ed. Karkov and Brown, pp. 115–30 [esp. on BL, Additional 40618; on Copenhagen, Kongelige Bibliotek, G. K. S. 10 (2°); and on the work of Eadwig Basan]

Foot, Mirjam, *The History of Bookbinding as a Mirror of Society*, Panizzi Lectures 1997 (London, 1998) [esp. for early AS binding in BL, Loan 74 ('St Cuthbert Gospel of John', s. vii/viii)]

Gameson, Richard, 'Manuscrits normands à Exeter aux XIe et XIIe siècles', *Manuscrits et enluminures*, ed. Bouet and Dosdat, pp. 107–27

'La Normandie et l'Angleterre au XIe siècle: le témoinage des manuscrits', *La Normandie et l'Angleterre au Moyen Âge*, ed. P. Bouet and V. Gazeau (Caen), pp. 129–59

Gilbert, B., S. Denoel, G. Weber and D. Allart, 'Analysis of Green Copper Pigments in Illuminated Manuscripts by Micro-Raman Spectroscopy', *Analyst* 128, 1213–17

Gneuss, Helmut, 'Addenda and Corrigenda to the *Handlist of Anglo-Saxon Manuscripts*', *ASE* 32, 293–305

Gneuss, Helmut, and Michael Lapidge, 'The Earliest Manuscript of Bede's Metrical *Vita S. Cudbercti*', *ASE* 32, 43–54

Gorman, Michael M., 'The Codex Amiatinus: a Guide to the Legends and Bibliography', *SM* 44, 863–910

Gretsch, Mechthild, 'Cambridge, Corpus Christi College 57: a Witness to the Early Stages of the Benedictine Reform in England?', *ASE* 32, 111–46

Grimmer, Martin, 'The Early History of Glastonbury Abbey: a Hypothesis Regarding the "British Charter"', *Parergon* ns 20.2, 1–20

Grossi, Ada, 'Borsa o chirografo? Le diverse tradizioni del libro di Tobia nella ricerca delle origini del documento bipartito', *SM* 44, 755–94 [ninth-century AS witness, esp. in sect. 2.2]

Gullick, Michael, 'Manuscrits et copistes normands en Angleterre (XIe–XIIe siècles)', *Manuscrits et enluminures*, ed. Bouet and Dosdat, pp. 83–93 ['Liste préliminaire des manuscrits importés de Normandie en Angleterre (XIe–XIIe siècles)', appendix]

Gumbert, J. P., 'On Folding Skins, According to Gilissen', *Gazette du livre médiéval* 43, 47–51

Hahn, Cynthia, *Portrayed on the Heart: Narrative Effect in Pictorial Lives of Saints from the Tenth through the Thirteenth Century* (Berkeley, CA, 2001) [esp. in chs. 3 and 7]

Haney, Kristine, *The St Albans Psalter: an Anglo-Norman Song of Faith*, Stud. in the Humanities 60 (Frankfurt am Main, 2002) [treatment of Utrecht Psalter, and of Gneuss nos. 171, 422 and 912, with plates]

Harbison, Peter, 'Der Einfluss des Mittelmeerraumes auf die Kunst Britanniens und Irlands', *Von Mohammed zu Karl dem Grossen*, ed. Eduard Carbonell and Roberto Cassanelli (Stuttgart, 2001), pp. 100–15

Hawkes, Jane, see sect. 9*g* [plants and AS art]

Heintzelman, Matthew Z., 'English Resources at the Hill Monastic Manuscript Library', *OEN* 36.1 (2003 for 2002), 24–31

Hilmo, Maidie, *Medieval Images: Icons and Illustrated English Literary Texts from the Ruthwell Cross to the Ellesmere Chaucer* (Aldershot)

Hornby, Emma, see sect. 4 [transmission of chant]

Hull, Derek, *Celtic and Anglo-Saxon Art: Geometric Aspects* (Liverpool)

John, James J., 'The Named (and Namable) Scribes in *Codices Latini Antiquiores*', *Scribi e colofoni*, ed. Emma Condello and Giuseppe De Gregorio (Spoleto, 1995), pp. 107–21 [scribes with AS links, *ad indicem*, pp. 115–21]

Karkov, Catherine E., 'Exiles from the Kingdom: the Naked and the Damned in Anglo-Saxon Art', *Naked before God*, ed. Withers and Wilcox, pp. 181–220

'Judgement and Salvation in the New Minster *Liber vitae*', *Apocryphal Texts and Traditions*, ed. Powell and Scragg, pp. 151–63

Karkov, Catherine E., and George Hardin Brown, ed., see sect. 1

Kasper, Muriel, 'Angebot und Nachfrage. Der mittelalterliche englische Schreiber auf dem Weg vom Skriptorium zum *bookshop*', *Das Mittelalter* 7.2 (2002), 33–47 ['Altenglisch', sect. 3]

Kauffmann, C. M., *Biblical Imagery in Medieval England, 700–1550* (London) ['The Old Testament in Anglo-Saxon Art', ch. 2; also in ch. 1]

Kitzinger, Ernst, *Studies in Late Antique, Byzantine and Medieval Western Art*, 2 vols. (London, 2002–3) ['Anglo-Saxon Art', sects. xx–xxiii; reissued papers]

Kornexl, Lucia, and Ursula Lenker, ed., see sect. 3*a*

Lawrence-Mathers, Anne, *Manuscripts in Northumbria in the Eleventh and Twelfth Centuries* (Woodbridge)

Lemoine, Louis, 'Contribution à la reconstitution des scriptoria bretons du haut Moyen Âge', *Bulletin Du Cange / Archivum Latinitatis Medii Aevi* 59 (2001), 261–8 [esp. for Gneuss nos. 279, 295, 362, 530 and 866.5]

Lowden, John, 'Illuminated Books and the Liturgy: Some Observations', *Objects, Images and the Word: Art in the Service of the Liturgy*, ed. Colum Hourihane (Princeton, NJ), pp. 17–53 [Lindisfarne Gospels and Benedictional of Æthelwold]

Lowe, Kathryn A., see sect. 6 [Sawyer 1070]

Magrini, Sabina, '"Per difetto del legatore . . ." Storia delle rilegature della Bibbia Amiatina in Laurenziana', *Quinio* (Rome) 3 (2001), 137–67

Manion, Margaret, 'The Early Illuminated Gospel Book: Liturgical Sources and Influences', *Prayer and Spirituality in the Early Church*, ed. Pauline Allen, Raymond Canning and Lawrence Cross, 2 vols. (Brisbane, 1998–9) II, 155–71

Marchesin, Isabelle, *L'image 'organum', la représentation de la musique dans les psautiers médiévaux, 800–1200* (Turnhout, 2000) [esp. in chs. 1–3, 6 and 10]

Matthews, Karen Rose, see sect. 9*k* [Bayeux 'tapestry' and AS art]

Mortimer, Richard, 'Anglo-Norman Lay Charters, 1066–*c.* 1100: a Diplomatic Approach', *ANS* 25, 153–75

Müller-Wille, Michael, and Lars Olof Larsson, ed., *Tiere, Menschen, Götter: wikingerzeitliche Kunststile und ihre neuzeitliche Rezeption*, Veröffentlichung der Joachim Jungius-Gesellschaft der Wissenschaften Hamburg 90 (Göttingen, 2001)

Nees, Lawrence, 'Reading Aldred's Colophon for the Lindisfarne Gospels', *Speculum* 78, 333–77

Ó Cróinín, Dáibhí, 'Writing', *From the Vikings to the Normans*, ed. Davies, pp. 168–200

O'Keeffe, Katherine O'Brien, ed., *Manuscripts Containing the Anglo-Saxon Chronicle, Works by Bede and Other Texts*, AS Manuscripts in Microfiche Facsimile 10 (Tempe, AZ)

Olson, Mary, *Fair and Varied Forms: Visual Textuality in Medieval Illuminated Manuscripts*, Stud. in Med. Hist. and Culture 15 (London) [esp. on Harley Psalter, Claudius Hexateuch and *Marvels of the East*]

Ó Néill, Pádraig P., *Biblical Study and Mediaeval Gaelic History*, Quiggin Pamphlets on the Sources of Med. Gaelic Hist. 6 (Cambridge) [esp. on AS use of Celtic biblical manuscripts]

Orchard, Nicholas, see sect. 4 [AS codices and continental liturgy]

O'Reilly, Jennifer, 'The Art of Authority', *After Rome*, ed. Charles-Edwards, pp. 140–89 [Insular art]

Orton, P., see sect. 3*c* [CCCC 41]

Palazzo, Eric, 'La liturgie épiscopale au Moyen Âge. Réflexions sur sa signification théologique et politique', *Das Mittelalter* 7.1 (2002), 71–8 [Benedictional of Æthelwold and Sherborne Pontifical]

Pirotte, Emmanuelle, 'La *parole* est aux images. La lettre, l'espace et la voix dans les évangéliaires insulaires', *Les images dans les sociétés médiévales*, ed. Jean-Marie Sansterre and Jean-Claude Schmitt (Brussels, 1999), pp. 61–5

Powell, Kathryn, and Donald Scragg, ed., see sect. 3*a*

Pulsiano, Phillip, 'Jaunts, Jottings and Jetsam in Anglo-Saxon Manuscripts', *Florilegium* 19 (2003 for 2002), 189–97 with figs. 1–12

Rittmueller, Jean, ed., *Liber questionum in Evangeliis*, CCSL 108F (Turnhout) [AS transmission, sects. II.2, II.5, III.2 and III.5]

Robinson, Pamela, *Catalogue of Dated and Datable Manuscripts* c. *888–1600 in London Libraries*, 2 vols. (London)

Rosenfeld, Randall A., 'Iconographical Sources of Scribal Technology: Select Catalogue of Non-Formulaic Depictions of Scribes and Allied Craftsmen (Western Europe, s. vii ex.–xiv in.)', *MS* 65, 319–63 [esp. for Codex Amiatinus]

Schipper, William, 'Style and Layout of Anglo-Saxon Manuscripts', *Anglo-Saxon Styles*, ed. Karkov and Brown, pp. 151–68

Scholla, Agnes, 'Early Western Limp Bindings: Report on a Study', *Care and Conservation of Manuscripts 7*, ed. Gillian Fellows-Jensen and Peter Springborg (Copenhagen), pp. 132–58

Seales, W. Brent, James Griffioen, Kevin Kiernan, Cheng Jiun Yuan and Linda Cantara, 'The Digital Athenaeum: Preserving Old Documents', *Computers in Libraries* 20.2 (2000), 26–30 [Cottonian manuscripts]

Semple, Sarah, 'Illustrations of Damnation in Late Anglo-Saxon Manuscripts', *ASE* 32, 231–45

Stammberger, Ralf M. W., *Scriptor und Scriptorium. Das Buch im Spiegel mittelalterlicher Handschriften*, Lebensbilder des Mittelalters (Graz) [Lindisfarne Gospels, no. 41]

Stévanovitch, Colette, 'La représentation de l'enfer et du ciel dans les illustrations de manuscrits anglo-saxons (*Liber Vitae*, Junius XI)', *Enfer et paradis. L'au-delà dans l'art et la littérature en Europe*, ed. Centre européen d'art et de civilisation médiévale (Conques, 1995), pp. 177–93

Tite, Colin G. C., *The Early Records of Sir Robert Cotton's Library: Formation, Cataloguing, Use* (London)

Treharne, Elaine M., 'Producing a Library in Late Anglo-Saxon England: Exeter, 1050–1072', *RES* 54, 155–72

Watson, Rowan, *Illuminated Manuscripts and Their Makers: an Account Based on the Collection of the Victoria and Albert Museum* (London)

Werner, Martin, 'The Beginning of Insular Book Illumination', *Making Medieval Art*, ed. Phillip Lindley (Donington), pp. 91–103

Withers, Benjamin C., and Jonathan Wilcox, ed., see sect. 3*a*

6. HISTORY

Abels, Richard, 'Royal Succession and the Growth of Political Stability in Ninth-Century Wessex', *Haskins Soc. Jnl* 12 (2003 for 2002), 83–97

'Alfred the Great, the *micel hæðen here* and the Viking Threat', *Alfred the Great*, ed. Reuter, pp. 265–79

Alcock, Leslie, *Kings and Warriors, Craftsmen and Priests in Northern Britain, AD 550–850*, Soc. of Antiquaries of Scotland Monograph Ser. 24 (Edinburgh) [treats England north of the Tees]

see also sect. 9*a* [Angles, Britons and Scots]

Annett, D. M., *Saints in Herefordshire: a Study of Dedications* (Almeley, Herts., 1999)

Anton, H., *et al.*, '*Origo gentis*', *RGA* XXII, 174–88 ['Angelsachsen', sect. 6, by I. N. Wood]

Bailey, Keith A., 'The Population of Buckinghamshire in 1086', *Records of Buckinghamshire* 42 (2002), 1–14

'The Church in Anglo-Saxon Buckinghamshire *c.* 650–*c.* 1100', *Records of Buckinghamshire* 43, 61–76

Bailey, Richard N., 'Bede's Bones', *New Offerings, Ancient Treasures: Studies in Medieval Art for George Henderson*, ed. Paul Binski and William Noel (Stroud, 2001), pp. 165–86

Banham, Debby, '*Be hlafum and wyrtum*: Food Plants in Anglo-Saxon Society and Economy', *From Earth to Art*, ed. Biggam, pp. 119–31

Barnwell, Paul S., 'Britons and Warriors in Post-Roman South-East England', *ASSAH* 12, 1–8

Barnwell, Paul S., L. A. S. Butler and C. J. Dunn, 'The Confusion of Conversion: *Streanaeshalch*, Strensall and Whitby and the Northumbrian Church', *The Cross Goes North*, ed. Carver, pp. 311–26

Barrow, G. W. S., 'Companions of the Atheling', *ANS* 25, 35–45 [Edgar, grandson of Edmund Ironside]

Beaumont-James, Thomas, 'Les palais anglais: le terme *palatium* et sa signification dans l'Angleterre médiévale (1000–1600)', *'Aux marches du palais'. Qu'est-que-ce-qu'un palais médiéval? Données historiques et archéologiques*, ed. Annie Renoux (Le Mans, 2001), pp. 135–43

Bevan-Jones, Robert, *The Ancient Yew: a History of 'Taxus baccata'* (Macclesfield, 2002) [charter evidence; also on surviving pre-Conquest yews, ch. 6]

Biggam, C. P., ed., see sect. 1

Bond, James, 'Medieval Nunneries in England and Wales: Buildings, Precincts and Estates', *Women and Religion*, ed. Wood, pp. 46–90 [esp. on Romsey]

Breeze, Andrew, 'The *Anglo-Saxon Chronicle* for 1053 and the Killing of Rhys ap Rhydderch', *Trans. of the Radnorshire Soc.* 71 (2001), 168–9 [with discussion of place-name Bulendun]

Bridgeford, Andrew, *1066: the Hidden History of the Bayeux Tapestry* (London, 2002)

Brookes, Stuart, 'The Early Anglo-Saxon Framework for Middle Anglo-Saxon Economics: the Case of East Kent', *Markets in Early Medieval Europe*, ed. Pestell and Ulmschneider, pp. 84–96

Brooks, Nicholas, 'Romney Marsh in the Early Middle Ages', *Romney Marsh*, ed. Eddison and Green, pp. 90–104

Church, State and Access to Resources in Early Anglo-Saxon England, Brixworth Lectures, 2nd ser. 2 (Brixworth)

'Alfredian Government: the West Saxon Inheritance', *Alfred the Great*, ed. Reuter, pp. 153–73

Brown, A. E., 'The Lost Village of Andreschurch', *Leicestershire Archaeol. and Hist. Soc. Trans.* 77, 1–11

Brown, Andrew, *Church and Society in England, 1000–1500*, Social Hist. in Perspective (Basingstoke) ['Anglo-Saxon Church and Society *c.* 1000', ch. 1]

Burns, David, 'The Continental Homelands of the Anglo-Saxons', *Contemporary Rev.* 281 (2002), 354–9

Busse, Wilhelm, 'Englische Bischofshöfe als Kulturzentren', *Das Mittelalter* 7.1 (2002), 147–64

Campbell, James, 'Anglo-Saxon Courts', *Court Culture*, ed. Cubitt, pp. 156–69

'Placing King Alfred', *Alfred the Great*, ed. Reuter, pp. 3–23

'Production and Distribution in Early and Middle Anglo-Saxon England', *Markets in Early Medieval Europe*, ed. Pestell and Ulmschneider, pp. 12–19

Carver, Martin, ed., *The Cross Goes North: Processes of Conversion in Northern Europe, AD 300–1300* (York)

Chaplais, Pierre, *English Diplomatic Practice in the Middle Ages* (London) [ch. 1]

Chapman, Anna, 'King Alfred and the Cult of St Edmund', *Hist. Today* 53.7, 37

Charles-Edwards, Thomas, ed., *After Rome*, Short Oxford Hist. of the Brit. Isles (Oxford)

Cholakian, Rouben C., *The Bayeux Tapestry and the Ethos of War* (Delmar, NY, 1998)

'Prefigurations of Courtliness in the Bayeux Tapestry', *The Court Reconvenes: Courtly Literature Across the Disciplines*, ed. Barbara K. Altmann and Carleton W. Carroll (Cambridge), pp. 241–53

Clancy, John, 'The 1500 Year History of Holy Trinity Church, Milton Regis', *Kent Archaeol. Rev.* 154, 73–6

Combes, Pamela, 'Bishopstone: a Pre-Conquest Minster Church', *Sussex Archaeol. Collections* 140 (2003 for 2002), 49–56

Cooper, Alan, 'The Rise and Fall of the Anglo-Saxon Law of the Highway', *Haskins Soc. Jnl* 12 (2003 for 2002), 39–69

Corning, Caitlin, 'The Baptism of Edwin, King of Northumbria: a New Analysis of the British Tradition', *Northern Hist.* 36 (2000), 1–15

Coss, Peter, *The Origins of the English Gentry*, Past and Present Publ. (Cambridge) [ch. 2]

Crawford, Sally, see sect. 9*d* [women and burial practices]

Crick, Julia, 'St Albans, Westminster and Some Twelfth-Century Views of the Anglo-Saxon Past', *ANS* 25, 65–83 [esp. on charters; 'The Pre-Conquest Evidence', sect. 3]

Cubitt, Catherine, ed., see sect. 4

Dark, K. R., 'Large-Scale Population Movements into and from Britain South of Hadrian's Wall in the Fourth to Sixth Centuries AD', *Reading Med. Stud.* 29, 31–49

Davies, Wendy, ed., *From the Vikings to the Normans*, Short Oxford Hist. of the Brit. Isles (Oxford) [esp. in chs. 1 and 3–6]

Donaldson, Christopher, *In the Footsteps of Saint Augustine: the Great English Pilgrimage from Rome to Canterbury, 1400th Anniversary AD 597–1997* (Norwich, 1995)

Draper, Simon, see sect. 7 [post-Roman Wilts.]

Eagles, Bruce, 'Augustine's Oak', *Med. Archaeol.* 47, 175–8 [on site of his meeting with Brit. ecclesiastics]

Eddison, Jill, and Christopher Green, ed., *Romney Marsh: Evolution, Occupation, Reclamation*, Oxford Univ. Committee for Archaeol. Monograph 24 (Oxford, 1988)

Ehlers, Joachim, 'Die Königin aus England. Ottos des Grossen erste Gemahlin', *Sachsen und Anhalt* 22 (1999–2000), 27–55

Enright, Michael J., 'Further Reflections on Royal Ordinations in the *Vita Columbae*', *Ogma: Essays in Celtic Studies in honour of Próinséas Ní Chatháin*, ed. Michael Richter and Jean-Michel Picard (Dublin, 2002), pp. 20–35 [treatment of Oswald]

Evans, Michael, *The Death of Kings: Royal Deaths in Medieval England* (London) [Edward the Confessor and Harold, ch. 1; also on Æthelberht, Alfred *et al.*]

Fairclough, John, 'The Bounds of Stoke and the Hamlets of Ipswich', *Proc. of the Suffolk Inst. of Archaeol. and Hist.* 40, 262–77

Fernie, Eric, 'History and Architectural History', *TRHS* 13, 199–206 [discussion of AS examples]

Fjalldal, Magnús, 'Anglo-Saxon History in Medieval Iceland: Actual and Legendary Sources', *Leeds Stud. in Eng.* ns 33, 77–108

Foot, Sarah, 'Unveiling Anglo-Saxon Nuns', *Women and Religion*, ed. Wood, pp. 13–31

Forsman, Deanna, 'An Appeal to Rome: Anglo-Saxon Dispute Settlement, 800–810', *Heroic Age* 6 [online]

Foys, Martin K., ed., *The Bayeux Tapestry: Digital Edition* (Leicester) [CD-ROM]
see also sect. 9*k*

Fraesdorff, David, 'The Power of Imagination: the *christianitas* and the Pagan North During Conversion to Christianity (800–1200)', *Med. Hist. Jnl* (New Delhi) 5 (2002), 309–32

Friel, Ian, *The British Museum Maritime History of Britain and Ireland,* c. *400–2001* (London) ['*Wic*s, Wars and "Heathen Men", 700–1066', ch. 2]

Gade, Kari Ellen, 'Norse Attacks on England and Arnórr Jarlaskald's *Þórfinnsdrápa*', *Skandinavistik* 33, 1–14

Garnett, George, 'The Third Recension of the English Coronation *ordo*: the Manuscripts', *Haskins Soc. Jnl* 11 (2003 for 1998), 43–71

Giannarelli, Elena, 'La stranezze degli antichi santi', *Cosma e Damiano, dall'Oriente a Firenze*, ed. Elena Giannarelli (Florence, 2002), pp. 132–48 [cult of Rumwold]

Gittos, Brian, and Moira Gittos, 'The Evidence for the Saxon Minster at Yeovil', *Chronicle* 4 (1989), 95–104

Gough, Harold, 'Was Reculver's Black Rock an Offshore Island?', *Kent Archaeol. Rev.* 154, 90–2

Grassi, J. L., 'The Lands and Revenues of Edward the Confessor', *EHR* 117 (2002), 251–83

Gray, Stephen, 'Walking through Anglo-Saxon England', *Hampshire Field Club and Archaeol. Soc. Section Newsletters* ns 12 (1989), 28–9 [tracing the tenth-century bounds of Kilmeston]

Green, Dennis H., and Frank Siegmund, ed., *The Continental Saxons from the Migration Period to the Tenth Century: an Ethnographic Perspective*, Stud. in Hist. Archaeoethnology 6 (Woodbridge)

Green, Michael A., *St Augustine of Canterbury: Celebrating 1400 Years of His Arrival in England* (London, 1997)

Griffiths, David, Andrew Reynolds and Sarah Semple, ed., *Boundaries in Early Medieval Britain* [= *ASSAH* 12] (Oxford)

Hadley, D. M., 'Burial Practices in the Northern Danelaw, *c.* 650–1100', *Northern Hist.* 36 (2000), 199–216

Halliday, Robert, 'St. Walstan of Bawburgh', *Norfolk Archaeol.* 44.2, 316–25

Halsall, Guy, *Warfare and Society in the Barbarian West, 450–900*, Warfare and Hist. (London) [esp. in chs. 5–9]

Hart, Cyril, see sect. 3*a*

Hayashi, Hiroshi, 'A Study of the Charter-Criticism of the Anglo-Saxon Period (15)', *Gakushuin Rev. of Law and Politics* 38.1 (2002), 327–36

Hayter, Deborah, 'King's Sutton: an Early Anglo-Saxon Estate?', *Northamptonshire Past and Present* 56, 7–21

Helle, Knut, ed., *The Cambridge History of Scandinavia,* I: *Prehistory to 1520* (Cambridge) [esp. in pt. ii]

Higgins, David H., 'The Anglo-Saxon Charters of Stoke Bishop: a Study of the Boundaries of *Bisceopes stoc*', *Trans. of the Bristol and Gloucestershire Archaeol. Soc.* 120 (2003 for 2002), 107–31

Higgitt, John, 'From Bede to Rabelais: or How St Ninian Got His Chain', *New Offerings, Ancient Treasures: Studies in Medieval Art for George Henderson*, ed. Paul Binski and William Noel (Stroud, 2001), pp. 187–209

Higham, N. J., 'Bucklow Hundred: the Domesday Survey and the Rural Community', *Cheshire Archaeol. Bull.* 8 (1982), 15–21

'Bishop Wilfrid in Southern England: a Review of His Political Objectives', *Studien zur Sachsenforschung* 13 (1999), 207–17

Hill, David, 'Mercians: the Dwellers on the Boundary', *Mercia: an Anglo-Saxon Kingdom in Europe*, ed. Michelle P. Brown and Carol A. Farr (London, 2001), pp. 173–82

'The Origin of Alfred's Urban Policies', *Alfred the Great*, ed. Reuter, pp. 219–33

Hill, David, and Margaret Worthington, *Offa's Dyke: History and Guide* (Stroud)

'Offa's Dyke', *RGA* XXII, 24–8

Hines, John, 'Culture Groups and Ethnic Groups in Northern Germany in and around the Migration Period', *Studien zur Sachsenforschung* 13 (1999), 219–32

'Welsh and English: Mutual Origins in Post-Roman Britain?', *Studia Celtica* 34 (2000), 81–104

Holdsworth, Christopher, 'Tavistock Abbey in its Late Tenth Century Context', *Devonshire Assoc. for the Advancement of Science, Lit. and the Arts. Report and Trans.* 135, 31–58

Honegger, T., and A. Scharer, 'Offa', *RGA* XXII, 17–24

Hooke, Della, 'Mercia: Landscape and Environment', *Mercia: an Anglo-Saxon Kingdom in Europe*, ed. Michelle P. Brown and Carol A. Farr (London, 2001), pp. 160–72

'Trees in the Anglo-Saxon Landscape: the Charter Evidence', *From Earth to Art*, ed. Biggam, pp. 17–39

Howard, Ian, *Swein Forkbeard's Invasions and the Danish Conquest of England, 991–1017* (Woodbridge)

Hunter Blair, Peter, *An Introduction to Anglo-Saxon England*, 3rd ed., with a new introd. by Simon Keynes (Cambridge) [Keynes, 'Changing Perceptions of Anglo-Saxon History', introd.]

Hurley, Christopher, 'Landscapes of Gwent and the Marches as Seen through Charters of the Seventh to Eleventh Centuries', *Landscape and Settlement in Medieval Wales*, ed. Nancy Edwards (Oxford, 1997), pp. 31–40 [esp. on agriculture in two estates, extending into Herefords.]

Hyams, Paul R., *Rancor and Reconciliation in Medieval England*, Conjunctions of Religion and Power in the Med. Past (Ithaca, NY) [esp. in chs. 1–3]

Insley, Charles, 'Assemblies and Charters in Late Anglo-Saxon England', *Political Assemblies in the Earlier Middle Ages*, ed. P. S. Barnwell and Marco Mostert (Turnhout), pp. 47–59

Insley, J., 'Hwicce', *RGA* XV, 287–95

'Iclingas', *RGA* XV, 320–3

'Oswald', *RGA* XXII, 360–70

'Oswiu', *RGA* XXII, 370–6

'Penda', *RGA* XXII, 551–3

'Rædwald', *RGA* XXIV, 65–8

Insley, J., and M. G. Welch, 'Kent', *RGA* XVI, 444–52

Jones, Glanville R. J., 'The Ripon Estate: Landscape into Townscape', *Northern Hist.* 37 (2000), 13–30

Jones, Lynn, 'From *Anglorum basileus* to Norman Saint: the Transformation of Edward the Confessor', *Haskins Soc. Jnl* 12 (2003 for 2002), 99–120

Jurasinski, Stefan, '*Reddatur parentibus*: the Vengeance of the Family in Cnut's Homicide Legislation', *Law and Hist. Rev.* 20 (2002), 157–80

Kaiser, Reinhold, with Marie-Thérèse Kaiser-Guyot, *Trunkenheit und Gewalt im Mittelalter* (Cologne, 2002) [laws, in 'Angelsächsische Gilden', sect. III.2; also on *Beowulf*, and on Aldhelm and Bede]

Karkov, Catherine E., 'The Body of St Æthelthryth: Desire, Conversion and Reform in Anglo-Saxon England', *The Cross Goes North*, ed. Carver, pp. 397–411

Keene, Derek, 'Alfred and London', *Alfred the Great*, ed. Reuter, pp. 235–49

Keynes, Simon, *Anglo-Saxon England: a Bibliographical Handbook for Students of Anglo-Saxon History*, 4th ed., ASNC Guides, Texts and Stud. 1 (Cambridge)

'Ely Abbey 672–1109', *A History of Ely Cathedral*, ed. Nigel Ramsay and Peter Meadows (Woodbridge), pp. 3–58

'The Power of the Written Word: Alfredian England 871–899', *Alfred the Great*, ed. Reuter, pp. 175–97

see also above, with Hunter Blair, Peter, and in sect. 9*a*

Klaniczay, Gábor, *Holy Rulers and Blessed Princesses: Dynastic Cults in Medieval Central Europe*, trans. Eva Pálmai, Past and Present Publ. (Cambridge, 2002) ['The Anglo-Saxon Model', in ch. 2]

Kramer, Evert, Ingrid Stoumann and Andrew Greg, ed., *Kings of the North Sea, AD 250–850* (Newcastle upon Tyne, 2000) [esp. in sects. 3–6; exhibition catalogue]

Krier, Jean, 'Von Epternus zu Willibrord. Die Vor- und Frühgeschichte Echternachs aus archäologischer Sicht', *Die Abtei Echternach*, ed. Michele Camillo Ferrari, Jean Schroeder and Henri Traffler (Echternach, 1999), pp. 29–46

Lapidge, Michael, 'Asser's Reading', *Alfred the Great*, ed. Reuter, pp. 27–47 ['The Authenticity of Asser', appendix]

Leamon, Rosemary, 'Anglo-Saxon Charter Bounds for Ecchinswell and Sydmonton', *Hampshire Field Club and Archaeol. Soc. Newsletter* 31 (1999), 12–17

Lee, Christina, 'Eclectic Memories: in Search of Eadgyth', *Offa* 58 (2003 for 2001), 277–85

Lenz, Katja, and Ruth Möhlig, ed., see sect. 2*b*

Lepelley, René, 'Sur le nom du bateau de Guillaume', *Annales de Normandie* 53, 1–19

Lepine, David, and Nicholas Orme, ed., *Death and Memory in Medieval Exeter*, Devon and Cornwall Record Soc. ns 47 (Exeter) ['Obits from the Leofric Missal, Tenth and Eleventh Centuries', sect. 24]

Liddiard, Robert, 'The Deer Parks of Domesday Book', *Landscapes* 4.1, 4–23

Little, Brian, *Banbury: a History* (Chichester) [in ch. 1]

Lowe, Kathryn A., 'Sawyer 1070: a Ghost Writ of King Edward the Confessor', *N&Q* 50, 150–2

Loyn, H. R., and S. C. Saar, 'Ine von Wessex', *RGA* XV, 413–16

Luxford, Julian M., 'The Anglo-Saxon Nunnery at Chichester: a Further Source', *Sussex Archaeol. Collections* 140 (2003 for 2002), 150–1

'The Cranborne Abbey Relic List', *Dorset and Somerset Notes and Queries* 35, 239–42

McKitterick, Rosamond, 'Kulturelle Verbindungen zwischen England und den fränkischen Reichen in der Zeit der Karolinger: Kontexte und Implikationen', *Deutschland und der Westen Europas im Mittelalter*, ed. Joachim Ehlers (Stuttgart, 2002), pp. 121–48

Meier, Dirk, 'The North Sea Coastal Area: Settlement History from Roman to Early Medieval Times', *The Continental Saxons*, ed. Green and Siegmund, pp. 37–76 ['Discussion', pp. 67–76]

Mills, Sally, 'Alfred, Bede and the Mercians: the Creation of Anglo-Saxon Histories', *Chronicle* 8 (1999), 12–15

Moore-Scott, Terry, 'Edmund Ironside and Minsterworth: Fact or Fiction?', *Glevensis* 36, 28

Musset, Lucien, *La tapisserie de Bayeux*, new ed. (Paris, 2002)

Nelson, Janet L., 'Les douaires des reines anglo-saxonnes', *Dots et douaires dans le haut Moyen Âge*, ed. François Bougard, Laurent Feller and Régine Le Jan (Rome, 2002), pp. 527–34

'Alfred's Carolingian Contemporaries', *Alfred the Great*, ed. Reuter, pp. 293–310

'England and the Continent in the Ninth Century, II: the Vikings and Others', *TRHS* 13, 1–28

Neumann, G., M. Eggers and N. Hardt, 'Jüten', *RGA* XVI, 92–100

O'Brien, Bruce, 'The *Instituta Cnuti* and the Translation of English Law', *ANS* 25, 177–97

Oosthuizen, Susan, 'The Roots of the Common Fields: Linking Prehistoric and Medieval Field Systems in West Cambridgeshire', *Landscapes* 4.1, 40–64

Ossa, Suzanne Nicole, 'An Unholy Alliance? Olaf Guthfrithsson and the Northumbrian Church', *Offa* 58 (2003 for 2001), 293–7

Palmer, Ben, 'The Hinterlands of Three Southern English *emporia*: Some Common Themes', *Markets in Early Medieval Europe*, ed. Pestell and Ulmschneider, pp. 48–60

Palmer, John, Matthew Palmer and George Slater, *Domesday Explorer: Great Domesday Book on CD-ROM, Version 1.0* (Chichester, 2000)

Pantos, Aliki, '"On the Edge of Things": the Boundary Location of Anglo-Saxon Assembly Sites', *ASSAH* 12, 38–49

Paxton, Jennifer, 'Monks and Bishops: the Purpose of the *Liber Eliensis*', *Haskins Soc. Jnl* 11 (2003 for 1998), 17–30

Pearce, Susan, *South-Western Britain in the Early Middle Ages*, Stud. in the Early Hist. of Britain (London)

Pestell, Tim, 'The Afterlife of "Productive" Sites in East Anglia', *Markets in Early Medieval Europe*, ed. Pestell and Ulmschneider, pp. 122–36 [esp. on late Saxon landscape hist.]

Pestell, Tim, and Katharina Ulmschneider, ed., *Markets in Early Medieval Europe: Trading and 'Productive' Sites, 650–850* (Macclesfield)

Pitt, Jonathan, 'Malmesbury Abbey and Late Saxon Parochial Development in Wiltshire', *Wiltshire Archaeol. and Nat. Hist. Mag.* 96, 77–88

'Minster Churches and Minster Territories in Wiltshire', *ASSAH* 12, 58–71

Pottrell, A. L., 'Some Problems in Using Saxon Charters', *Hampshire Field Club and Archaeol. Soc. Section Newsletter* 1 (1984), 2–3

Reuter, Timothy, ed., *Alfred the Great: Papers from the Eleventh-Centenary Conferences*, Stud. in Early Med. Britain 3 (Aldershot)

Roberts, Edward, 'The Saxon Bounds of *Ticceburn*', *Hampshire Field Club and Archaeol. Soc. Section Newsletters* 18 (1992), 29–33

Roberts, Edward, with Gary Allam, 'Saxon Alresford and Bighton', *Hampshire Field Club and Archaeol. Soc. Section Newsletters* 20 (1993), 9–13 [charter bounds]

Rollason, David, *Northumbria, 500–1100: Creation and Destruction of a Kingdom* (Cambridge)

Rose, Susan, *Medieval Naval Warfare, 1000–1500*, Warfare and Hist. (London, 2001) ['Invaders and Settlers: Operations in the Channel and the North Sea *c.* 1000–*c.* 1250', ch. 2]

Sauer, Hans, 'The English Kings and Queens and the English Language', *Of dyuersitie*, ed. Lenz and Möhlig, pp. 180–98 [esp. on Alfred and Cnut]

Scharer, Anton, 'Alfred the Great and Arnulf of Carinthia: a Comparison', *Alfred the Great*, ed. Reuter, pp. 311–21

Sharpe, Richard, 'The Use of Writs in the Eleventh Century', *ASE* 32, 247–91

see also sect. 4

Sheppard, Alice, 'The King's Family: Securing the Kingdom in Asser's *Vita Ælfredi*', *PQ* 80 (2003 for 2001), 409–39

Shirai, Naomi, and Shigeki Toyama, 'The Origin of the Cult of St Cuthbert: a Study', *Tohoku Koeki Bunka Univ. General Stud.* 6, 121–39 [in Japanese]

Sivier, David, *Anglo-Saxon and Norman Bristol* (Stroud, 2002)

Smith, Mary Frances, Robin Fleming and Patricia Halpin, 'Court and Piety in Late Anglo-Saxon England', *Catholic Hist. Rev.* 87 (2001), 569–602

Stafford, Pauline, 'Kings, Kingships and Kingdoms', *From the Vikings to the Normans*, ed. Davies, pp. 10–39

'Succession and Inheritance: a Gendered Perspective on Alfred's Family History', *Alfred the Great*, ed. Reuter, pp. 251–64

Stagg, David, 'Sydmonton: the Suggested Identification of a Saxon Charter', *Hampshire Field Club and Archaeol. Soc. Section Newsletters* 4 (1985), 8–11

Stevenson, E. M., 'Saxon Curdridge', *Hampshire Field Club and Archaeol. Soc. Section Newsletters* 20 (1993), 18–19 [charter bounds]

Stokes, Kaele, 'The Educated Barbarian? Asser and Welsh Learning in Anglo-Saxon England', *Quaestio* (Cambridge) 3 (2002), 45–58

Story, Joanna, *Carolingian Connections: Anglo-Saxon England and Carolingian Francia,* c. *750–870*, Stud. in Early Med. Britain (Aldershot)

Sundqvist, O., 'Priester und Priesterinnen', *RGA* XXIII, 424–35 ['Kontinentale und angelsächsische Verhältnisse', sect. 3]

Syrett, Martin, *Scandinavian History in the Viking Age: a Select Bibliography*, rev. ed., ASNC Guides, Texts and Stud. 2 (Cambridge)

Thomas, Hugh M., *The English and the Normans: Ethnic Hostility, Assimilation and Identity 1066–*c.*1220* (Oxford) ['English Identity before the Conquest', ch. 2]

'The Significance and Fate of the Native English Landholders of 1086', *EHR* 118, 303–33

Tinti, Francesca, 'From Episcopal Conception to Monastic Compilation: Hemming's Cartulary in Context', *EME* 11 (2002), 233–61

'Dal *church-scot* alla decima: origine, natura e sviluppo dei tributi ecclesiastici nell'Inghilterra altomedievale', *SM* 44, 219–51

Todd, John M., 'The Pre-Conquest Church in St Bees, Cumbria: a Possible Minster?', *Trans. of the Cumberland and Westmorland Ant. and Archaeol. Soc.* 3, 97–108

Toy, John, 'St Botulph: an English Saint in Scandinavia', *The Cross Goes North*, ed. Carver, pp. 565–70

Webb, Diana, 'Freedom of Movement? Women Travellers in the Middle Ages', *Studies on Medieval and Early Modern Women: Pawns or Players?*, ed. Christine Meek and Catherine Lawless (Dublin), pp. 75–89 [itineraries of Leoba *et al.*]

Wheeler, R. C., 'Domesday Ploughlands in Boothby Wapentake', *Lincolnshire Past and Present* 53, 9–10

Wileman, Julie, 'The Purpose of the Dykes: Understanding the Earthworks of Early Medieval Britain', *Landscapes* 4.2, 59–66

Williams, Ann, *Æthelred the Unready: the Ill-Counselled King* (London)

'England in the Eleventh Century', *A Companion to the Anglo-Norman World*, ed. Christopher Harper-Bill and Elisabeth van Houts (Woodbridge), pp. 1–18

Wood, Diana, ed., *Women and Religion in Medieval England* (Oxford)

Wood, Ian, *The Missionary Life: Saints and the Evangelisation of Europe, 400–1050*, Med. World (Harlow, 2001) [esp. in chs. 2–5]

see also above, with Anton, H., *et al.* [AS '*origo gentis*']

Woolf, Alex, 'An Interpolation in the Text of Gildas's *De excidio Britanniae*', *Peritia* 16 (2002), 161–7 [*adventus Saxonum*]

Wormald, Patrick, 'The *leges barbarorum*: Law and Ethnicity in the Post-Roman West', *'Regna' and 'gentes'*, ed. Hans-Werner Goetz, Jörg Jarnut and Walter Pohl (Leiden), pp. 21–53

Yorke, Barbara, 'The Legitimacy of St Edith', *Haskins Soc. Jnl* 11 (2003 for 1998), 97–113

Nunneries and the Anglo-Saxon Royal Houses, Women, Power and Politics (London)

'The Adaptation of the Anglo-Saxon Royal Courts to Christianity', *The Cross Goes North*, ed. Carver, pp. 243–57

'Anglo-Saxon *gentes* and *regna*', *'Regna' and 'gentes'*, ed. Hans-Werner Goetz, Jörg Jarnut and Walter Pohl (Leiden), pp. 381–407

Ziegler, Michelle, 'The Ripon Connection? Willibrord, Wilfrid and the Mission to Frisia', *Heroic Age* 6 [online]

Zimmermann, C., 'Primsigning', *RGA* XXIII, 445–53 ['Angelsächsische und fränkische Zeugnisse', sect. 3]

7. NUMISMATICS

Abdy, Richard, Martin Allen and Anna Gannon, ed., 'Coin Register 2002', *BNJ* 72 (2002), 189–212 [includes 142 finds of the AS period]

Alfaro, Carmen, and Andrew Burnett, ed., *A Survey of Numismatic Research 1996–2001*, International Assoc. of Professional Numismatists, Special Publ. 14 (Madrid)

Allan, John, 'The Anglo-Saxon Mint at Lydford', *Devonshire Assoc. for the Advancement of Science, Lit. and the Arts. Report and Trans.* 134 (2002), 9–32

Allen, Martin, 'England, Wales and Scotland: Medieval', *A Survey of Numismatic Research*, ed. Alfaro and Burnett, pp. 405–22

[Anon.], see sect. 9*i* [silver sceat and silver penny; two entries]

Blackburn, Mark, 'Alfred's Coinage Reforms in Context', *Alfred the Great*, ed. Reuter, pp. 199–217

'"Productive" Sites and the Pattern of Coin Loss in England, 600–1180', *Markets in Early Medieval Europe*, ed. Pestell and Ulmschneider, pp. 20–36

Blackburn, Mark, and Hugh Pagan, 'The St Edmund Coinage in the Light of a Parcel from a Hoard of St Edmund Pennies', *BNJ* 72 (2002), 1–14

Blanchard, Ian, *Mining, Metallurgy, and Minting in the Middle Ages*, I: *Asiatic Supremacy, 425–1125* (Stuttgart, 2001) [in pt. 3]

Clunies Ross, Margaret, 'An Anglo-Saxon Runic Coin and its Adventures in Sweden', *ASE* 32, 79–88

Department for Culture, Media and Sport, see sect. 9*i*

de Wit, G. W., 'Series F', *NCirc* 111, 309 [early eighth-century pennies]

Eaglen, Robin J., 'Further Coins from the Mint of Huntingdon', *BNJ* 72 (2002), 14–23 [addenda to the author's corpus, as publ. in *BNJ* 69 (1999), 47–145]

Gannon, Anna, *The Iconography of Early Anglo-Saxon Coinage: Sixth to Eighth Centuries*, Med. Hist. and Archaeol. (Oxford)

Holt, Anton, 'Fynd av mynt från vikingatiden på Island', *Ord med Mening*, ed. Jens Christian Moesgaard and Preben Nielsen (Copenhagen, 1998), pp. 45–7 [AS coins in Iceland, including a penny of Eadwig]

Lafaurie, Jean, and Jacqueline Pilet-Lemière, *Monnaies du haut Moyen Âge découvertes en France, Ve–VIIIe siècle*, Cahiers Ernest-Babelon 8 (Paris)

Laing, Lloyd, and Mathew Ponting, 'An Unpublished Early Penny from Lincolnshire and its Significance', *BNJ* 72 (2002), 164–7

Lessen, Marvin, 'A Presumed "Hampshire" Hoard of Edgar CC Coins', *NCirc* 111, 61–2

Lyon, Stewart, 'Anglo-Saxon Numismatics', *BNJ* 73, 58–75 [survey of developments over the last century]

Malmer, Brita, 'Felande länk funnen i Trondheim', *Svensk numismatisk tidskrift* 1999/5 (1999), 100–1 [esp. on die link observed recently among Anglo-Scandinavian coins]

Marsden, Adrian, 'Coin Finds from Norfolk, July–December 2002', *Norfolk Archaeol.* 44.2, 345–8 [penny of Eadred and cut quarter of Cnut]

Matzke, M., 'Pfennig', *RGA* XXIII, 13–19

Metcalf, D. Michael, 'Financial Support for Outlying Churches? A Perspective on the Uses of Money in Eighth-Century Northumbria', *BNJ* 72 (2002), 167–9

'Variations in the Composition of the Currency at Different Places in England', *Markets in Early Medieval Europe*, ed. Pestell and Ulmschneider, pp. 37–47

Newman, J., and D. M. Metcalf, see sect. 9*i* [coin-derived decoration]

Page, R. I., and M. L. Nielsen, 'Runenmünzen', *RGA* XXV, 546–56 ['England', sect. 1, by Page]

Pestell, Tim, and Katharina Ulmschneider, ed., see sect. 6

Pirie, Elizabeth J. E., '*Styca* or *sceat*: Another Conundrum for Northumbria', *NCirc* 111, 129–30

Pons Sanz, Sara, see sect. 2*a* [OE numismatic terminology]

Reuter, Timothy, ed., see sect. 6

Smith, Caroline, 'A Barbarized Coinage? Copper Alloy in Pre-Viking Age Northumbrian Coinage', *Quaestio* (Cambridge) 3 (2002), 59–75

Story, Joanna, see sect. 6 [continental links]

Wise, Philip J., see sect. 9*i* [finds from Essex]

8. ONOMASTICS

Anderson, John, 'On the Structure of Names', *Folia Linguistica* (The Hague) 37, 347–98 [sect. 2.2]

Biggam, C. P., ed., see sect. 1

Bourne, Jill, *Understanding Leicestershire and Rutland Place Names* (Loughborough)

Breeze, Andrew, 'The *Anglo-Saxon Chronicle* for 1055 and Bishop Tramerin of St Davids', *Trans. of the Woolhope Naturalists' Field Club, Herefordshire* 50.1 (2003 for 2000), 90–1

'Chaceley, Meon, Prinknash and Celtic Philology', *Trans. of the Bristol and Gloucestershire Archaeol. Soc.* 120 (2003 for 2002), 103–6
'Celtic Philology and Chickerell, Dorset', *Dorset and Somerset Notes and Queries* 35, 248–9
see also sect. 5 [Bulendun]
Brooke, Leslie, 'Why was it called that? A Study of Some Yeovil Field-Names', *Chronicle* 7 (1996–7), 8–16 and 33–42
Charles-Edwards, Gifford, see sect. 9*l* [Osgyd]
Cole, Ann, 'The Use of *netel* in Place-Names', *JEPNS* 35 (2002–3), 49–58
Conisbee, L. R., 'Animals in Bedfordshire Place-Names', *Bedfordshire Mag.* 16.125 (1978), 191–3
Crisp, Barry, Brian Rich, Mary Wiltshire and Sue Woore, 'Hough and Hoon, Derbyshire', *JEPNS* 35 (2002–3), 45–8
Dawson, Graham, 'Southwark or Southburgh', *Surrey Archaeol. Soc. Bull.* 365, 13
Dodgson, John, 'Addenda and Corrigenda to Tengvik', *Names, Time and Place*, ed. Hooke and Postles, pp. 23–40 [on G. Tengvik, *Old English Bynames* (Uppsala, 1938)]
Draper, Simon, 'Old English *wīc* and *walh*: Britons and Saxons in Post-Roman Wiltshire', *Landscape Hist.* 24 (2002), 29–43 [with gazetteer of these elements in Wilts.]
English, Judie, 'Worths in a Landscape Context', *Landscape Hist.* 24 (2002), 45–51
Fellows-Jensen, Gillian, 'From *Durobrivae* to the *Hundred Acre Wood*: Analogical Naming in Great Britain', *You Name It: Perspectives on Onomastic Research*, ed. Ritva Liisa Pitkänen and Kaija Mallat (Helsinki, 1997), pp. 63–71
'In Quest of Lost Danes: the Scandinavian Element in English Surnames', *Names, Time and Place*, ed. Hooke and Postles, pp. 41–57
Gelling, Margaret, 'English Place-Name Studies: Some Reflections. Being the First Cameron Lecture, Delivered 11th December 2002, Inaugurating the Institute for Name-Studies', *JEPNS* 35 (2002–3), 5–16
see also with Udolph, Jürgen, *et al.*, below
Hayward, Geoffrey, 'The Hayward: a Manorial Official', *Dorset and Somerset Notes and Queries* 35, 249–53 [possible pre-Conquest origin]
Heizmann, Wilhelm, and Astrid van Nahl, ed., see sect. 3*a*
Higham, Mary C., 'Place-Names and Local History', *Trans. of the Lancashire and Cheshire Antiquarian Soc.* 99, 205–13
Hooke, Della, 'Names and Settlement in the Warwickshire Arden', *Names, Time and Place*, ed. Hooke and Postles, pp. 67–99
Hooke, Della, and David Postles, ed., *Names, Time and Place: Essays in memory of Richard McKinley* (Oxford)
Horovitz, David, Richard Coates and Stephen Potter, 'Ingestre, Staffordshire', *Nomina* 26, 65–82
Hough, Carole, 'Place-Name Evidence for Anglo-Saxon Plant-Names', *From Earth to Art*, ed. Biggam, pp. 41–78
Hough, Carole, 'Bibliography 2002', *JEPNS* 35 (2002–3), 61–6
'Strensall, *Streanaeshalch* and Stronsay', *JEPNS* 35 (2002–3), 17–24
'Bibliography for 2002', *Nomina* 26, 143–56

'Dwerryhouse in Lancashire', *N&Q* 50, 3–5
'Onomastic Uses of the Term "White"', *Nomina* 26, 83–92
'Wilsill in Yorkshire and Related Place-Names', *N&Q* 50, 253–7
Insley, John, '*Hwinca*', *RGA* XV, 296
'Oiscingas', *RGA* XXII, 33–8
'*Otlinga Saxonia*', *RGA* XXII, 387–91
'Penselwood', *RGA* XXII, 558–9
'Portesmutha', *RGA* XXIII, 290–2
'Pre-Conquest Personal Names', *RGA* XXIII, 367–96
see also sect. 9*b* [Ipswich]
Insley, John, and Rosemary Cramp, see sect. 9*e* [Insley on Jarrow]
Insley, John, and D. M. Wilson, see sects. 9*e* and 9*i* [Insley on Pentney and Reculver]
Kemble, James, 'Place-Names of Early Essex River-Crossings', *Essex Jnl* 38.1, 23–5
Kristensson, Gillis, 'The Place-Name Lackford (Suffolk)', *N&Q* 50, 257–8
'The Place-Name Thremhall (Essex)', *N&Q* 50, 149–50
Laflin, Susan, 'Roman Roads and Ford Place-Names in Shropshire', *Shropshire Hist. and Archaeol.* 76 (2001), 1–10
'Do *-ingas* Place-Names Occur in Pairs?', *JEPNS* 35 (2002–3), 31–40
Lewis, Jennifer, see sect. 9*a* [Sefton rural fringes]
Luscombe, Paul, 'A Trio – and More – of South Hams Place-Names', *Devon and Cornwall Notes and Queries* 39 (2002), 38–41
Mills, A. D., *A Dictionary of British Place-Names*, rev. ed. (Oxford)
Owen-Crocker, Gale R., 'Anglo-Saxon Women: the Art of Concealment', *Leeds Stud. in Eng.* ns 33 (2003 for 2002), 31–51 [concealment of women's names]
Parsons, David N., 'Ellough: a Viking Temple in Suffolk?', *JEPNS* 35 (2002–3), 25–30
Reichert, Hermann, 'Vier Miszellen zum Urgermanischen und "Altrunischen"', *ZDA* 132, 335–56 [OE theme **-wini*, sect. 1]
Room, Adrian, *The Penguin Dictionary of British Place Names* (London)
Rowley, Anthony R., 'Elslack – Olenacum: an Onomastic Relic of Pre-Roman Britain?', *Nomina* 26, 5–14
Rutledge, Paul, 'Colkirk Settlement Pattern: a Reappraisal and a Question', *Norfolk Archaeol.* 44.2, 331–5
Schwab, Ute, and René Derolez, see sect. 9*l*
Tranter, Margery, 'Name, Race, Terrain: the Making of a Leicestershire Boundary', *Names, Time and Place*, ed. Hooke and Postles, pp. 209–41
Udolph, Jürgen, 'Sachsenproblem und Ortsnamenforschung', *Studien zur Sachsenforschung* 13 (1999), 427–48 ['Übersiedlung nach England', sect. 3]
'Holtsati', *RGA* XV, 84–90 [names in *-sæt-*, sect. *c*]
Udolph, Jürgen, *et al.*, 'Orts- und Hofnamen', *RGA* XXII, 233–304 ['England', sect. 13, by Margaret Gelling]
Vennemann, Theo, 'Remarks on Some British Place Names', Vennemann, *Europa Vasconica*, pp. 479–515 [esp. for Arundel, Bedford (and similar) and Thames; reissue of stud. publ. in 1998]
see also sect. 2*a*

Wagner, Norbert, 'Zu einigen Germanennamen bei Papst Gregor dem Grossen', *BN* 34 (1999), 255–67 [esp. on *Æðelberht* and *Hondsciōh*]

Watts, Victor, 'Some Ryedale Place-Names', *Ryedale Historian* 20 (2000–1), 11–14

Waxenberger, Gaby, 'The Non-Latin Personal Names on the Name-Bearing Objects in the Old English Runic Corpus (Epigraphical Material): a Preliminary List', *Runica – Germanica – Mediaevalia*, ed. Heizmann and van Nahl, pp. 932–68

9. ARCHAEOLOGY

a. General

Addyman, Peter, 'John Gilbert Hurst (1927–2003)', *Med. Archaeol.* 47, 195–7

Albone, James, and Naomi Field, ed., 'Archaeology in Lincolnshire 2001–2002', *Lincolnshire Hist. and Archaeol.* 37 (2003 for 2002), 44–61 [includes AS]

Alcock, Leslie, *The Neighbours of the Picts: Angles, Britons and Scots at War and at Home* ([Rosemarkie, Fortrose], 1993)

see also sect. 6 [England north of the Tees]

Ambers, J., and S. Bowman, 'Radiocarbon Measurements from the British Museum: Datelist XXVI', *Archaeometry* 45, 531–40 [includes dates from AS settlements at Barking, Riverdene and Collingbourne Ducis]

Androschchuk, Fedir, 'The Hvoshcheva Sword: an Example of Contacts between Britain and Scandinavia in the Late Viking Period', *Fornvännen* 98, 35–43

[Anon.], 'Main Report', *Portable Antiquities Scheme Ann. Report* 5 (2003 for 2001–3), 18–58 [includes AS sites and finds]

'Excavation and Fieldwork in Wiltshire 2001', *Wiltshire Archaeol. and Nat. Hist. Mag.* 96, 229–37 [includes AS]

Austin, David, 'The "Proper Study" of Medieval Archaeology', *From the Baltic to the Black Sea: Studies in Medieval Archaeology*, ed. Austin and Leslie Alcock, One World Archaeol. 18 (London, 1990), pp. 9–42

Bennett, A., ed., 'Archaeology in Essex 2001', *Essex Archaeol. and Hist.* 33 (2002), 390–413 [includes AS, as listed on p. 390]

Biggam, C. P., ed., see sect. 1

Bird, D. G., Glenys Crocker and J. S. McCracken, 'Archaeology in Surrey 1990', *Surrey Archaeol. Collections* 81 (1991–2), 147–67 [includes AS]

Blackford, J. J., and F. M. Chambers, 'Proxy Records of Climate from Blanket Mires: Evidence for a Dark Age (1400 BP) Climatic Deterioration in the British Isles', *Holocene* 1.1 (1991), 63–7

Bradley, John, and Märit Gaimster, comp. and ed., 'Medieval Britain and Ireland 2002', gen. ed. Tom Beaumont James, *Med. Archaeol.* 47, 199–339 [includes Portable Antiquities Scheme report, compiled and ed. by Helen Geake]

Braithwaite, Rosemary, and Susan Smith, ed., *Archaeology in Hampshire: Annual Report for 94/95* ([Winchester], 1995) [includes AS]

Brooks, Catherine, Robin Daniels and Anthony Harding, ed., *Past, Present and Future: the*

Archaeology of Northern England. Proceedings of a Conference Held in Durham in 1996, Archit. and Archaeol. Soc. of Durham and Northumberland Research Report 5 (Durham, 2002)

Buckley, Richard, and Sam George, ed., 'Archaeology in Leicestershire and Rutland 2002', *Leicestershire Archaeol. and Hist. Soc. Trans.* 77, 125–56 [includes AS]

[Canterbury Archaeological Trust], 'Interim Reports on Recent Work Carried out by the Canterbury Archaeological Trust', *AC* 123, 291–307 [esp. on two early cemeteries north of Saltwood Tunnel]

Chitty, Gill, 'St Helens Rural Fringes', ed. Jennifer Lewis, *Jnl of the Merseyside Archaeol. Soc.* 11 (2002), 167–206 [archaeol. and hist. review, including AS]

Clarke, Pamela V., 'John Gilbert Hurst, 1927–2003', *Rescue News* 90, 8

Clough, T. H. McK., ed., 'Rutland History and Archaeology in 2000', *Rutland Record* 21 (2001), 38–48 [includes AS]

Coulson, Charles L. H., *Castles in Medieval Society: Fortresses in England, France and Ireland in the Central Middle Ages* (Oxford) [esp. in sects. I.1–2 and II.1–2]

Council for British Archaeology, Group 6 (Norfolk and Suffolk), *Bulletin of Archaeological Discoveries 21* ([Norwich], *c.* 1975 for 1974) [includes AS]

Bulletin of Archaeological Discoveries 22 ([Norwich], *c.* 1976 for 1975) [includes AS]

Bulletin of Archaeological Discoveries 23 ([Norwich], *c.* 1977 for 1976) [includes AS]

Bulletin 27 ([Norwich], 1982) [esp. on AS pottery kiln in Norwich]

Cowell, R. W, 'Knowsley Rural Fringes', *Jnl of the Merseyside Archaeol. Soc.* 11 (2002), 123–66 [archaeol. and hist. survey, including AS]

'Liverpool Urban Fringes', *Jnl of the Merseyside Archaeol. Soc.* 11 (2002), 89–122 [archaeol. and hist. survey, including AS]

Cowell, R. W., and J. B. Innes, *The Wetlands of Merseyside*, North West Wetlands Survey 1 (Lancaster, 1994) [includes AS]

Crabtree, Pam J., ed., *Medieval Archaeology: an Encyclopedia* (London, 2001) ['England', pp. 97–101, with cross-references]

Cramp, Rosemary, 'Introduction', *Past, Present and Future*, ed. Brooks *et al.*, pp. 123–5 ['Anglo-Saxon', sect. 4]

Cunliffe, Barry W., 'The Evolution of Romney Marsh: a Preliminary Statement', *Romney Marsh*, ed. Eddison and Green, pp. 37–55 [includes AS]

Wessex to AD 1000 (London and New York, 1993)

Darvill, Timothy, Paul Stamper, and Jane Timby, *England: an Oxford Archaeological Guide to Sites from Earliest Times to AD 1600* (Oxford, 2002)

Davison, Alan, 'The Archaeology of the Parish of West Acre, Part 1: Field Survey Evidence', *Norfolk Archaeol.* 44.2, 202–21 [includes AS]

Eddison, Jill, and Christopher Green, ed., see sect. 6

Faulkner, Neil, 'The Debate about the End: a Review of Evidence and Methods', with a contribution by Richard Reece, *ArchJ* 159 (2003 for 2002), 59–76 [decline of Roman Britain]

Flitcroft, Myk, 'Archaeology in Northamptonshire 2002', *Northamptonshire Archaeol.* 30 (2002), 145–54 [includes AS]

Ford, Steve, *East Berkshire Archaeological Survey*, Dept. of Highways and Planning,

Berkshire County Council, Occasional Paper 1 ([Reading], 1987) [includes AS, with list of stray finds]

Gerrard, Christopher M., *Medieval Archaeology: Understanding Traditions and Contemporary Approaches* (London)

Gilchrist, Roberta, *Gender and Archaeology: Contesting the Past* (London, 1999) [esp. in ch. 4]

Gurney, David, 'Excavations and Surveys in Norfolk', *CBA East Anglia Bull.* 37 (1995), 2–9 [includes AS]

Gurney, David, and Kenneth Penn, ed., 'Excavations and Surveys in Norfolk, 2002', *Norfolk Archaeol.* 44.2, 368–85 [includes AS]

Hall, Allan R., 'Investigating Anglo-Saxon Plant Life and Plant Use: the Archaeobotanical Angle', *From Earth to Art*, ed. Biggam, pp. 101–18

Hall, Allan R., and Jacqueline P. Huntley, 'Environmental Archaeology: the Post-Roman Period', *Past, Present and Future*, ed. Brooks *et al.*, pp. 155–9

Hall, R. A., 'Yorkshire AD 700–1066', *The Archaeology of Yorkshire*, ed. T. G. Manby *et al.*, pp. 171–80

Hamerow, Helena, 'BAR: the Early Medieval Volumes', *British Archaeological Reports Past, Present and Future: Proceedings of a Conference Held in Oxford in June 1994 to Mark the Twentieth Anniversary of BAR*, ed. David Davison and Martin Henig (Oxford, 1996), pp. 29–31

Härke, Heinrich, 'Population Replacement or Acculturation? An Archaeological Perspective on Population and Migration in Post-Roman Britain', *The Celtic Englishes III*, ed. Hildegard L. C. Tristram (Heidelberg), pp. 13–28 ['Archaeological Evidence for Britons in Anglo-Saxon England', sect. 4]

Harris, Anthea, *Byzantium, Britain and the West: the Archaeology of Cultural Identity, AD 400–650* (Stroud) [esp. in ch. 6, on 'Byzantine Objects in Anglo-Saxon Graves' and related evidence]

Heslop, David, 'Archaeology and the Planning Process in the North-East of England', *Kings of the North Sea*, ed. Kramer *et al.*, pp. 123–8

Higham, Robert, 'Dating in Medieval Archaeology: Problems and Possibilities', *Problems and Case Studies in Archaeological Dating*, ed. Bryony Orme, Exeter Stud. in Hist. 4 [= Exeter Stud. in Archaeol. 1] (Exeter, 1982), pp. 83–107 [includes AS]

Hills, Catherine, *Origins of the English*, Duckworth Debates in Archaeol. (London)

Hines, John, 'På tvers av Nordsjøen. Britiske perspektiv på Skandinaviens senere jernalder', *Universitetets Oldsaksamling Årbok* 1991–2 (1993), 103–24 [esp. on metalwork, craftsmen and markets before Viking Age]

Hinton, David A., and Michael Hughes, ed., *Archaeology in Hampshire: a Framework for the Future* ([?Winchester], 1996)

Holroyd, Isabel, and Robert Bath, ed., *British and Irish Archaeological Bibliography, Volume 7*, 2 vols. (London)

Hopkins, David, ed., *Archaeology in Hampshire: Annual Report for 1999* (Winchester, 2000) [includes AS]

Archaeology in Hampshire: Annual Report for 2000 (Winchester, 2001) [includes AS]

Archaeology in Hampshire: Annual Report for 2001 (Winchester, 2002) [includes AS]

Howard, Bruce, and Rosemary Braithwaite, ed., *Archaeology in Hampshire: Annual Report for 1996* ([Winchester], 1997) [includes AS]

Hughes, Mike, ed., *Archaeological Excavation, Fieldwork and Finds in Hampshire 1977* ([Winchester], 1979) [AS reports, pp. 9–10]

Archaeology in Hampshire: Annual Report for 1981 ([Winchester], 1982) [treats AS excavations and finds, notably brooches and a hook]

Archaeology in Hampshire: Annual Report for 1982 ([Winchester], 1983) [AS period *ad indicem*, pp. 30–4]

Archaeology and Historic Buildings in Hampshire ([Winchester], 1986) [ann. report for 1984–5; AS period *ad indicem*, pp. 31–7]

Archaeology in Hampshire: Annual Report for 1986 ([Winchester], 1987) [AS period *ad indicem*, pp. 16–22]

Archaeology in Hampshire: Annual Report for 1987 ([Winchester], 1988) [AS period *ad indicem*, pp. 19–20]

Archaeology in Hampshire: Annual Report for 1988 ([Winchester], 1989) [AS period *ad indicem*, pp. 12–16]

Archaeology in Hampshire: Annual Report for 1989 ([Winchester], 1990) [AS period *ad indicem*, pp. 20–2]

Archaeology in Hampshire: Annual Report for 1990 ([Winchester], 1991) [AS period *ad indicem*, pp. 38–9]

Archaeology in Hampshire: Annual Report for 1991 ([Winchester], *c.* 1992) [includes AS]

Archaeology in Hampshire: Annual Report for 1992 ([Winchester], 1993) [includes AS]

Archaeology in Hampshire: Annual Report for 1993 ([Winchester], 1994) [includes AS]

Kennett, David H., 'An Elusive Antiquary', *Bedfordshire Mag.* 16.122 (1977), 76–9 [Samuel Edward Fitch and AS cemetery at Kempston, Beds.]

Keynes, Simon, 'The Discovery of the Bones of the Saxon "Confessors" 1769: William Cole's Account of the Discovery of the Bones of Ealdorman Byrhtnoth and Others at Ely', *A History of Ely Cathedral*, ed. Nigel Ramsay and Peter Meadows (Woodbridge), pp. 401–4

Koo, Tsai Kee, 'Applying Close-Range Photogrammetry to Wood Archaeology', *Land and Minerals Surveying* 4 (1986), 645–54 [technique to show deformation of wood, as applied to tenth-century material from York]

Kramer, Evert, *et al.*, ed., see sect. 6

Lang, James T., *et al.*, see sect. 9*h* [northern Yorks.]

Leahy, Kevin, 'Middle Anglo-Saxon Lincolnshire: an Emerging Picture', *Markets in Early Medieval Europe*, ed. Pestell and Ulmschneider, pp. 138–54 [esp. on 'productive' site at Melton Ross]

Lewis, Jennifer, 'Sefton Rural Fringes', *Jnl of the Merseyside Archaeol. Soc.* 11 (2002), 5–88 [archaeol. and hist. review, including AS]

Loveluck, Chris, '"The Romano-British to Anglo-Saxon Transition": Social Transformations from the Late Roman to Early Medieval Period in Northern England, AD 400–700', *Past, Present and Future*, ed. Brooks *et al.*, pp. 127–48

'The Archaeology of Post-Roman Yorkshire, AD 400–700: Overview and Future

Directions for Research', *The Archaeology of Yorkshire*, ed. Manby *et al.*, pp. 151–70

Maloney, Cath, and Isabel Holroyd, *London Fieldwork and Publication Round-Up 1999*, London Archaeologist 9, suppl. 2 (Tonbridge, 2000)

London Fieldwork and Publication Round-Up 2002, London Archaeologist 10, suppl. 2 (Tonbridge)

Manby, T. G., Stephen Moorhouse and Patrick Ottaway, ed., *The Archaeology of Yorkshire: an Assessment at the Beginning of the Twenty-First Century. Papers Arising out of the Yorkshire Archaeological Resource Framework Forum Conference at Ripon, September 1998*, Yorkshire Archaeol. Soc. Occasional Paper 3 (Leeds)

Martin, Edward, Colin Pendleton and Judith Plouviez, 'Archaeology in Suffolk, 1993', *CBA East Anglia Bull.* 37 (1995), 15–42 [includes AS]

'Archaeology in Suffolk 2002', *Proc. of the Suffolk Inst. of Archaeol. and Hist.* 40, 337–70 [includes AS]

Mays, Simon, 'Bone Strontium: Calcium Ratios and Duration of Breastfeeding in a Mediaeval Skeletal Population', *Jnl of Archaeol. Science* 30, 731–41 [from Wharram Percy, tenth-century and later]

Mays, Simon, G. M. Taylor, A. J. Legge, D. B. Young and G. Turner-Walker, 'Paleopathological and Biomolecular Study of Tuberculosis in a Medieval Skeletal Collection from England', *Amer. Jnl of Physical Anthropology* 114 (2001), 298–311 [from Wharram Percy, late Saxon and later]

Miket, Roger, 'Current Work and Problems, III: Pagan Anglo-Saxon Bernicia', *Archaeol. Newsbulletin for CBA Regional Group 3* 2 (1972), 2–4

O'Connor, T. P., 'Pets and Pests in Roman and Medieval Britain', *Mammal Rev.* 22.2 (1992), 107–13

Olivier, A. C. H., 'Archaeological Activities Undertaken by English Heritage', *Archaeol. Rev.* 1993–4, 8–60 [esp. on Flixborough, pp. 57–9]

Pearce, Susan, see sect. 6 [south-western Britain]

Pearson, Andrew, *The Construction of the Saxon Shore Forts*, BAR Brit. Ser. 349 (Oxford)

Pennick, Nigel, *Masterworks: the Arts and Crafts of Traditional Buildings in Northern Europe* (Loughborough, 2002) [esp. in ch. 2]

Pestell, Tim, and Katharina Ulmschneider, ed., see sect. 6

Purdy, Anna, and David Hopkins, ed., *Archaeology in Hampshire: Annual Report for 1998* (Winchester, 1999) [includes AS]

Rahtz, Philip, 'John Hurst', *The Antiquary* 8, 1

'Obituary: John Hurst 1927–2003', *Antiquity* 77, 880–1

Russel, Andy, 'Work by Southampton City Council Archaeology Unit', *CBA Wessex News* April 2003, 17–18 [includes AS]

Sermon, Richard, 'Britons and Saxons in Gloucestershire: Migration or Assimilation?', *CBA South West* 7 (2001), 37–40

Shoesmith, R., 'Reports of the Sectional Recorders: Archaeology, 2000', *Trans. of the Woolhope Naturalists' Field Club, Herefordshire* 50.1 (2003 for 2000), 93–116 [includes AS]

Thompson, F. H., ed., *Archaeology and Coastal Change*, Soc. of Antiquaries of London Occasional Paper 1 (London, 1980)

[Various], 'Anglo-Saxon and Medieval', *Group 9 CBA Newsletter* 1 (1971), 13–20

'Anglo-Saxon and Medieval', *CBA Regional Group 9 Newsletter* 2 (1972), 16–20

'Anglo-Saxon, Medieval and Post-Medieval', *CBA Regional Group 9 Newsletter* 4 (1974), 12–19

'Anglo-Saxon, Medieval and Post-Medieval', *CBA Regional Group 9 Newsletter* 5 (1975), 19–23

'Fieldwork, Watching Briefs and Documentary Research', *Archaeol. in Hampshire* 1987 (1988), 39–49 [includes AS]

'Fieldwork and Excavation in 2002', *Med. Settlement Research Group Ann. Report* 17 (2002), 48–69 [includes AS]

'Fieldwork in Cambridgeshire 2002', *Proc. of the Cambridge Ant. Soc.* 92, 215–24 [includes AS]

Webster, C. J., 'Somerset Archaeology, 2002', *Somerset Archaeol. and Nat. Hist.* 146, 131–73 [includes AS, esp. at p. 151]

Welch, Martin G., 'Anglo-Saxon Hampshire', *Archaeology in Hampshire*, ed. Hinton and Hughes, pp. 35–9

'The Archaeology of Mercia', *Mercia: an Anglo-Saxon Kingdom in Europe*, ed. Michelle P. Brown and Carol A. Farr (London, 2001), pp. 147–59

White, Roger H., 'Mayer and British Archaeology', *Joseph Mayer of Liverpool, 1803–1886*, ed. Margaret Gibson and Susan M. Wright, Soc. of Antiquaries of London Occasional Paper 11 (London, 1988), pp. 118–36 [esp. on Mayer's purchase of the Faussett Collection, other AS artefacts]

Wilson, David M., *The British Museum: a History* (London, 2002) [AS antiquities, esp. in chs. 3–7]

Woodcock, Andrew, 'Gazetteer of Prehistoric, Roman and Saxon Sites in Romney Marsh and the Surrrounding Area', *Romney Marsh*, ed. Eddison and Green, pp. 177–85

Zeepvat, Bob, 'Archaeological Notes', *Records of Buckinghamshire* 42 (2002), 147–60 [includes AS]

'Archaeological Notes', *Records of Buckinghamshire* 43, 220–33 [includes AS]

b. Towns and other major settlements

Addyman, Peter V., 'Reconstruction as Interpretation: the Example of the Jorvik Viking Centre, York', *The Politics of the Past*, ed. Peter Gathercole and David Lowenthal, One World Archaeol. 12 (London, 1990), pp. 257–64

'The Public Role of Environmental Archaeology: Presentation and Interpretation', *Issues in Environmental Archaeology: Perspectives on its Archaeological and Public Role. Papers from the Tenth Anniversary Conference of the Association for Environmental Archaeology Held at the Institute of Archaeology, UCL, July 1989*, ed. Nicholas Balaam and James Rackham (London, 1992), pp. 63–9 [mainly on Jorvik]

Allan, John, see sect. 7 [Lydford]

[Anon.], 'Sites Review: Coppergate', *Interim* 5.2 (1978), 19–31

Bateman, Nick, *Gladiators at the Guildhall: the Story of London's Roman Amphitheatre and Medieval Guildhall* (London, 2000) [includes AS]

Bayley, Justine, see sect. 9*i* [Cheapside]

Blair, John, 'Anglo-Saxon Bicester: the Minster and the Town', *Oxoniensia* 67 (2003 for 2002), 133–40

Boulter, Stuart, 'Flixton Park Quarry: a Royal Estate of the First Anglo-Saxon Kings?', *CA* 187, 280–5 [discusses several halls, a possible shrine and a cemetery]

Bourdillon, Jennifer, 'The Animal Bone of Hamwih: Some Comparisons', *Archaeozoology, vol. 1: Proceedings of the IIIrd International Archaeozoological Conference held 23–26th April 1978 at The Agricultural Academy, Szczecin, Poland*, ed. Marian Kubasiewicz (Szczecin, 1979), pp. 515–24

Animal Bones from Late Saxon Sites in Winchester, Hampshire, Ancient Monuments Laboratory Report 42/92 (London, 1992)

Canterbury Archaeological Trust, *Third Annual Report, April 1978–April 1979* (Canterbury, 1979) [esp. on *Grubenhäuser* from 16 Watling Street]

Annual Report 2000–2001, ed. John Willson, Jane Elder and Paul Bennett (Canterbury) [esp. on two AS cemeteries north of Saltwood Tunnel; *Canterbury's Archaeology 25*, cover title]

Carrington, Peter, *English Heritage Book of Chester* (London, 1994) [includes ch. on Dark Age and Saxon Chester]

see also sect. 9*j* [Chester]

Carrott, J., *et al.*, *Assessment of Biological Remains from Excavations at 12–18 Swinegate, 8 Grape Lane, and 14, 18, 20 and 22 Back Swinegate/Little Stonegate, York*, Reports from the Environmental Archaeol. Unit 94/13 (York, 1994) [includes AS]

Assessment of Biological Remains from Excavations at Wellington Row, York, Reports from the Environmental Archaeol. Unit 95/14 (York, 1995) [includes AS]

Assessment of Biological Remains from Excavations at 22 Piccadilly (ABC Cinema), York, Reports from the Environmental Archaeol. Unit 95/53 (York, 1995) [includes AS]

An Evaluation of Biological Remains from Excavations at 44–45 Parliament Street, York, Reports from the Environmental Archaeol. Unit 95/8 (York, 1995) [includes AS]

Archaeological Excavations at Layerthorpe Bridge and in Peasholme Green, York (96–7.345): Assessment of the Interpretative Potential of Biological Remains, Reports from the Environmental Archaeol. Unit 97/25 (York, 1997) [includes AS]

An Assessment of Biological Remains from Excavations at St Saviourgate, York, Reports from the Environmental Archaeol. Unit 98/14 (York, 1998) [includes AS]

Report on the Biological Remains from the Former Female Prison, York, Reports from the Environmental Archaeol. Unit 98/21 (York, 1998) [includes Anglo-Scandinavian]

Cowie, Robert, 'Mercian London', *Mercia: an Anglo-Saxon Kingdom in Europe*, ed. Michelle P. Brown and Carol A. Farr (London, 2001), pp. 194–209

Cowie, Robert, with Charlotte Harding, see sect. 9*c*

Coy, Jennie, 'Medieval Records versus Excavation Results: Examples from Southern England', *Archaeofauna* 5 (1996), 55–63 [mid-Saxon to late Med. evidence from Southampton for fish]

Creighton, Oliver, Neil Christie, Deirdre O'Sullivan and Helena Hamerow, 'The Wallingford Burgh [sc. *burh*] to Borough Research Project', *Med. Settlement Research Group Ann. Report* 17 (2002), 43–6

Davenport, Peter, *Medieval Bath Uncovered* (Stroud, 2002) [includes AS]

Dobney, K., A. Hall, D. Jaques, H. Kenward, F. Large, and T. Shaw, *An Evaluation of Biological Remains from Excavations at Flemingate, Beverley*, Reports from the Environmental Archaeol. Unit 95/48 (York, 1995)

Dodd, Anne, ed., *Oxford before the University: the Late Saxon and Norman Archaeology of the Thames Crossing, the Defences and the Town*, with major contributions by Maureen Mellor, Julian Munby, Mark Robinson and David R. P. Wilkinson, Thames Valley Landscapes Monograph 17 (Oxford)

Driver, J. C., J. Rady, and M. Sparks, *Excavations in the Cathedral Precincts, 2: Linacre Garden, 'Meister Omers' and St Gabriel's Chapel*, ed. E. C. Edwards, Archaeol. of Canterbury 4 (Maidstone, 1990) [evidence for AS settlement and, possibly, the cathedral]

Elsden, Nicholas J., *Excavations at 25 Cannon Street, City of London: from the Middle Bronze Age to the Great Fire*, MoLAS Archaeol. Stud. Ser. 5 (London, 2002) [includes AS, with a pottery report by Lyn Blackmore; publ. of Museum of London Archaeol. Service]

Frere, S. S., P. Bennett, J. Rady, and S. Stow, *Canterbury Excavations: Intra- and Extra-Mural Sites, 1949–55 and 1980–84*, Archaeol. of Canterbury 8 (Maidstone, 1987) [includes AS finds]

Garner, M. F., 'Excavation at St Mary's Road, Southampton (SOU 379 and SOU 1112)', *Proc. of the Hampshire Field Club and Archaeol. Soc.* 58, 106–29 [sites on the edge of middle Saxon Hamwic]

Goodburn, Damian M., see sect. 9*f* [London]

Greig, J. R. A., *Pollen and Charred Seeds from Saxon and Medieval Material connected with the Rampart at Newark on Trent, Slaughterhouse Lane*, Ancient Monuments Laboratory Report 63/92 (London, 1992)

Griffiths, David, 'Markets and "Productive" Sites: a View from Western Britain', *Markets in Early Medieval Europe*, ed. Pestell and Ulmschneider, pp. 62–72 [includes AS]

Groves, Cathy, *Tree-Ring Analysis of Oak Timbers from Queen's Hotel, York, Yorkshire, 1988–89, Part 2*, Ancient Monuments Laboratory Report 38/93 (London, 1993) [esp. on tree-ring master curve for mid-eighth to mid-eleventh centuries]

Hall, Allan R., *Anglo-Scandinavian 16–22 Coppergate: Timber Identifications*, Reports from the Environmental Archaeol. Unit 97/23 (York, 1997)

'An Embarrassment of Riches? Some Thoughts on the Study of Plant and Invertebrate Remains from Richly Organic Medieval Urban Archaeological Deposits from the Perspective of Analyses on Anglo-Scandinavian York', *History of Medieval Life and the Sciences: Proceedings of an International Round-Table-Discussion, Krems an der Donau, September 28–29, 1998*, ed. Gerhard Jaritz with Mark Peterson, Forschungen des Instituts für Realienkunde des Mittelalters und der frühen Neuzeit, Diskussionen und Materialien 4 (Vienna, 2000), pp. 93–104

Hall, Allan R., and Harry Kenward, *Data Archive for Biological Samples from Anglo-Scandinavian 16–22: Coppergate, York (Sitecode 1976–81.7), 1. Sample Concordance*, Reports from the Environmental Archaeol. Unit 97/33 (York, 1997)

Plant and Invertebrate Remains from Anglo-Scandinavian Deposits at 16–22 Coppergate, York: Technical Report, Part 1, Period 3, Reports from the Environmental Archaeol. Unit 99/30 (York, 1999)

Plant and Invertebrate Remains from Anglo-Scandinavian Deposits at 16–22 Coppergate, York: Technical Report, Part 2, Periods 4A and 4B, Reports from the Environmental Archaeol. Unit 99/38 (York, 1999)

Plant and Invertebrate Remains from Anglo-Scandinavian Deposits at 16–22 Coppergate, York: Technical Report, Part 3, Period 5A, Reports from the Environmental Archaeol. Unit 99/47 (York, 1999)

Plant and Invertebrate Remains from Anglo-Scandinavian Deposits at 16–22 Coppergate, York: Technical Report, Part 4, Period 5B, Reports from the Environmental Archaeol. Unit 99/49 (York, 2000)

Plant and Invertebrate Remains from Anglo-Scandinavian Deposits at 16–22 Coppergate, York: Technical Report, Part 5, Period 5C, Reports from the Environmental Archaeol. Unit 99/63 (York, 2000)

Technical Report: Plant and Invertebrate Remains from Anglo-Scandinavian Deposits at 4–7 Parliament Street (Littlewoods Store), York (Site Code 99.946), Reports from the Environmental Archaeol. Unit 2000/22 (York, 2000)

Harding, P. A., and Phil Andrews, 'Anglo-Saxon and Medieval Settlement at Chapel Street, Bicester: Excavations 1999–2000', *Oxoniensia* 67 (2003 for 2002), 141–79

Haslam, Jeremy, 'Excavations at Cricklade, Wiltshire, 1975', *Internet Archaeol.* 14 [online] [reassessment of AS defences]

Hawkins, Duncan, Frank Meddens and Peter Moore, 'Archaeological Investigations at North Street / George Street, Barking', *London Archaeologist* 10, 148–53 [indications of secular settlement contemporary with AS abbey]

Heighway, Carolyn, 'Christian Continuity and the Early Medieval Topography of Gloucester', *Glevensis* 36, 3–12

Henderson, C. G., 'The Development of the South Gate of Exeter and its Role in the City's Defences', *Devon Archaeol. Soc. Proc.* 59 (2001), 45–123 [includes sub-Roman, late Saxon and Saxo-Norman phases]

Hicks, Alison, and Mark Houliston, 'Whitefriars', *Canterbury's Archaeol.* 26 (2003 for 2001–2), 4–7 [treats an AS occupation phase; also has a report on ninth-century grain, p. 78]

Hillam, Jennifer, *Tree-Ring Analysis of Oak Timbers from the Coppergate Helmet Pit, York*, Ancient Monuments Laboratory Report 70/92 (London, 1992)

Tree-Ring Analysis of Timbers from The Brooks, Winchester, Hampshire, Ancient Monuments Laboratory Report 69/92 (London, 1992) [series of felling date ranges within AS period]

Hillam, Jennifer, and Dan Miles, *Tree-Ring Analysis of Timbers from the Oxford Shire Lake Project*, Ancient Monuments Laboratory Report 75/92 (London, 1992) [several felling date ranges within AS period]

Hoffmann, Per, ed., *Proceedings of the 4th ICOM–Group on Wet Organic Archaeological Materials Conference, Bremerhaven 1990* (Bremerhaven, 1991) [group assoc. with International Council of Museums]

Hull, Graham, and Steve Preston, 'Excavation of Late Saxon, Medieval and Post-Medieval Deposits on Land at Proctor's Yard, Bicester', *Oxoniensia* 67 (2003 for 2002), 181–98

Insley, J., 'Ipswich', *RGA* XV, 476–83

Insley, J., and D. M. Wilson, see sect. 9*i* [Pentney]

Jaques, D., J. Carrott, A. Hall, H. Kenward, and S. Rowland, *Evaluation of Biological Remains from Excavations in the Hungate Area, York*, Reports from the Environmental Archaeol. Unit 2000/29 (York, 2000) [includes AS]

Kamash, Zena, David R. P. Wilkinson, Ben M. Ford and Jonathan Hiller, 'Late Saxon and Medieval Occupation: Evidence from Excavations at Lincoln College, Oxford 1997–2000', *Oxoniensia* 67 (2003 for 2002), 199–286

Keene, Derek, 'Issue of Water in Medieval London to *c.* 1300', *Urban Hist.* 28 (2001), 161–79

Kenward, H., *Data Archive: Insect Assemblages from 6–8 Pavement (the Lloyds Bank Site), York*, Reports from the Environmental Archaeol. Unit 2000/39 (York, 2000) [includes AS]

Kenward, H., and A. Hall, *Technical Report: Plant and Invertebrate Remains from Anglo-Scandinavian Deposits at the Queen's Hotel Site, 1–9 Micklegate, York (Site Code 88–9.17)*, Reports from the Environmental Archaeol. Unit 2000/14 (York, 2000)

King, Roy, and Graeme Walker, '113–119 High Street, Oxford', *Cotswold Archaeol. Trust Ann. Rev.* 5 (1995 for 1994), 13–14

Koo, Tsai Kee, see sect. 9*a* [York]

Lavelle, Ryan, *Fortifications in Wessex* c. *800–1066*, Fortress 14 (Botley) [esp. on *burh*s and linear earthworks; includes reconstruction drawings by D. Spedaliere and S. S. Spedaliere]

Leahy, Kevin, see sect. 9*a* [Melton Ross]

Little, Brian, see sect. 6 [Banbury]

Lyle, Marjorie, *English Heritage Book of Canterbury* (London, 1994) [ch. on '*Cantwaraburh*' and its churches]

McDonnell, J. G., *et al.*, see sect. 9*i* [Hamwih, Southampton]

Macnab, Neil, *Anglo-Scandinavian, Medieval and Post-Medieval Urban Occupation at 41–49 Walmgate, York, UK*, Archaeol. of York Web Ser. 1 ([York]) [online: www.yorkar-chaeology.co.uk/wgate/main/]

Macnab, Neil, and Jane McComish, 'Low Life in High Ousegate', *Yorkshire Archaeol. Today* 5, 14–15 [Anglo-Scandinavian York]

Macphail, Richard I., *Soil Report on the Deansway Archaeology Project, Worcester*, Ancient Monuments Laboratory Report 82/91 (London, 1991) [Roman to late Saxon period]

Macphail, Richard I., Henri Galinié and Frans Verhaeghe, 'A Future for Dark Earth?', *Antiquity* 77, 349–58

Malcolm, Gordon, and David Bowsher, with Robert Cowie, *Middle Saxon London:*

Excavations at the Royal Opera House 1989–99, MoLAS Monograph 15 (London) [publ. of Museum of London Archaeol. Service]

Mason, D., 'Pre-Conquest Chester: the Archaeological Evidence', *Cheshire Archaeol. Bull.* 3 (1975), 11–13

Milne, Gustav, with Nathalie Cohen, *Excavations at Medieval Cripplegate, London: Archaeology after the Blitz, 1946–68, based on the Work of Professor W. F. Grimes for the Roman and Mediaeval London Excavation Council, and Related Research by the Museum of London and by University College London* (Swindon, 2002) [esp. on AS defences, buildings and street pattern]

Moffett, L. C., *Botanical Remains from Worcester Deansway*, Ancient Monuments Laboratory Report 123/91 (London, 1991) [evidence for fruit and cereals from late Saxon period]

Moloney, Colm, 'New Evidence for the Origins and Evolution of Dunbar: Excavations at the Captain's Cabin, Castle Park, Dunbar, East Lothian', *Proc. of the Soc. of Antiquaries of Scotland* 131 (2001), 283–317 [treats an Anglian phase]

Murphy, Peter, *Calvert Street, Norwich, Norfolk (84ON): Plant Remains from Late Saxon to Early Medieval Deposits*, Ancient Monuments Laboratory Report 67/91 (London, 1991)

Ipswich, Suffolk: Plant Macrofossils from Sites 1AS 3104 (Buttermarket), 1AS 3201 (ABC Cinema) and 1AS 5203 (Greyfriars Road), Ancient Monuments Laboratory Report 33/91 (London, 1991)

Murray, Jon, '17 Dean's Yard, Westminster: Archaeological Investigations', *Med. Archaeol.* 47, 41–52 [discusses a late Saxon partial donkey skeleton]

Newman, John, 'Exceptional Finds, Exceptional Sites? Barham and Coddenham, Suffolk', *Markets in Early Medieval Europe*, ed. Pestell and Ulmschneider, pp. 97–109

Nicholas, M., see sect. 9*i* [London]

Nixon, Taryn, Ellen McAdam, Roberta Tomber and Hedley Swain, ed., *A Research Framework for London Archaeology* (London, 2002) [includes AS]

Ottaway, Patrick, 'New Streets for Old? Recent Work in the Sewers of York', *Interim* 21.4 (1996), 12–21

Pestell, Tim, and Katharina Ulmschneider, ed., see sect. 6

Philp, Brian, *The Discovery and Excavation of Anglo-Saxon Dover: the Detailed Report on Fourteen of the Major Anglo-Saxon Structures and Deposits discovered in the Centre of Ancient Dover, During Large Scale Rescue-Excavation 1970–1990*, with substantial contributions by John Willson, Maurice Chenery, Peter Keller and Wendy Williams, Kent Monograph Ser. 9 (Dover)

Rady, Jonathan, 'Canterbury City Sites, 1: Market Way', *Canterbury's Archaeol.* 23 (2001 for 1998–9), 4–7 [includes AS settlement]

Richards, Julian D., 'The Anglian and Anglo-Scandinavian Sites at Cottam, East Yorkshire', *Markets in Early Medieval Europe*, ed. Pestell and Ulmschneider, pp. 155–66

Rogerson, Andrew, 'Six Middle Anglo-Saxon Sites in West Norfolk', *Markets in Early Medieval Europe*, ed. Pestell and Ulmschneider, pp. 110–21 [Bawsey, Burnham, Congham, Rudham, West Walton and Wormegay]

Rowsome, Peter, *Heart of the City: Roman, Medieval and Modern London Revealed by Archaeology at 1 Poultry* (London, 2000) [includes AS]

Sidell, Jane, 'Environmental Archaeology in London 1995–1998, Part 3', *London Archaeologist* 9 (2000), 188–94 [evidence from AS and Med. periods]

Sivier, David, see sect. 6 [Bristol]

Spriggs, James A., 'The Treatment, Monitoring and Display of Viking Structures at York', *Proceedings*, ed. Hoffmann, pp. 49–60

Thompson, Victoria, see sect. 9*h* [York]

Ulmschneider, Katharina, 'Markets around the Solent: Unravelling a "Productive" Site on the Isle of Wight', *Markets in Early Medieval Europe*, ed. Pestell and Ulmschneider, pp. 73–83

Vince, Alan, 'The Growth of Market Centres and Towns in the Area of the Mercian Hegemony', *Mercia: an Anglo-Saxon Kingdom in Europe*, ed. Michelle P. Brown and Carol A. Farr (London, 2001), pp. 183–93

Wallsgrove, S. G., 'Warwick: an Analysis of the Layout of the Anglo-Saxon *burh*', *Warwickshire Hist.* 12, 147–53

Ward, Alan, see sect. 9*e* [Rochester]

Watson, Bruce, Trevor Brigham, and Tony Dyson, *London Bridge: 2000 Years of a River Crossing*, MoLAS Monograph 8 (London, 2001) [includes late Saxon and Saxo-Norman phases; publ. of Museum of London Archaeol. Service]

Wilson, D. M., 'Portchester', *RGA* XXIII, 289–90

York Archaeological Trust, *The Archaeology of York, Volume 14: the Past Environment of York* (York, 1998)

Young, Graeme, *Bamburgh Castle: the Archaeology of the Fortress of Bamburgh, AD 500 to AD 1500*, ed. Paul Gething ([Bamburgh])

c. Rural settlements, agriculture and the countryside

Adams, Max, 'Archaeological Evaluations at Milfield', *Archaeol. in Northumberland* 1992–3, 28

Ambers, J., and S. Bowman, see sect. 9*a* [Barking, Riverdene and Collingbourne Ducis]

Ashbee, Paul, 'Mawgan Porth Remembered', *Cornish Archaeol.* 37–8 (2002 for 1998–9), 224–31 [review article]

Bagshaw, Steve, 'Deerhurst: Resistivity Survey South of Abbot's Court, 2002', *Glevensis* 36, 37–42 [signs of settlement adjacent to Odda's Chapel]

Baile, Jane, 'The Prebendal Manor Research Project, Nassington', *Northamptonshire Archaeol.* 30 (2002), 116–18 [treats an AS settlement]

Bamford, Helen M. *et al.*, *Briar Hill Excavation 1974–1978*, Northampton Development Corporation, Archaeol. Monograph 3 (Northampton, 1985) [esp. on AS sunken-featured buildings; with a pottery report by Varian Denham]

Bateman, Clifford, and Dawn Enright, 'Lechlade, Gloucestershire', *Cotswold Archaeol. Trust Ann. Rev.* 8 (1998 for 1997), 9–10 [discovery of six AS buildings]

Bettey, Joseph, 'Downlands', *The English Rural Landscape*, ed. Thirsk, pp. 27–49 ['The Anglo-Saxon Invasions', sect. 4]

Bradley, Jeremy, 'Excavations at Barrow Road, Barton-on-Humber, 1999–2000',

Lincolnshire Hist. & Archaeol. 37 (2003 for 2002), 5–20 [includes several AS settlement phases]

Brooks, Howard, 'A Bronze Age and Saxon Occupation Site at Frog Hall Farm, Fingringhoe', *Essex Archaeol. and Hist.* 33 (2002), 54–62

Cabot, Sophie, 'Sedgeford Historical and Archaeological Research Project: Interim Report 2002', *Norfolk Archaeol.* 44.2, 354–6 [includes AS]

Canti, Matthew, *Research into Natural and Anthropogenic Deposits from the Excavations at Flixborough, Humberside*, Ancient Monuments Laboratory Report 53/92 (London, 1992) [wind-blown sand deposits at middle Saxon settlement site]

Carr, Robert, 'The Middle-Saxon Settlement at Staunch Meadow, Brandon, Suffolk: a Final Up-Date', *The Quarterly* 5 (1992), 16–22

Carrott, J., A. Hall, M. Issitt, H. Kenward, F. Large, and A. Milles, *An Assessment of Biological Remains from Excavations at the Anglian Site at Cottam, North Humberside (Site Code COT93)*, Reports from the Environmental Archaeol. Unit 94/32 (York, 1994)

Carruthers, Wendy, *Charred and Mineralised Plant Macrofossils from Paddock Hill, Octon, Thwing, Yorkshire*, Ancient Monuments Laboratory Report 14/93 (London, 1993) [evidence for AS cultivation of barley and wheat]

Cohen, Nathalie, 'Boundaries and Settlement: the Role of the River Thames', *ASSAH* 12, 9–20 [treats period *c.* 500–1100]

Cowie, Robert, and Charlotte Harding, 'Saxon Settlement and Economy from the Dark Ages to Domesday', *The Archaeology of Greater London*, ed. Frederick *et al.*, pp. 171–206

Dacre, Max, 'Saxon Site at Charlton, Andover', *Hampshire Field Club and Archaeol. Soc. News Letter* 7 (1977), 22

Davis, Simon J. M., *Faunal Remains from the Late Saxon–Mediaeval Farmstead at Eckweek in Avon, 1988–1989 Excavations*, Ancient Monuments Laboratory Report 35/91 (London, 1991)

Saxon and Medieval Animal Bones from Burystead and Langham Road, Northants, 1984–1987 Excavations, Ancient Monuments Laboratory Report 71/92 (London, 1992)

Dix, Brian, 'Saxon Wells Near Harrold', *Bedfordshire Mag.* 18.138 (1981), 69–71

Dobney, K., A. Hall, H. Kenward, and A. Milles, *Integrated Assessment of Biological Remains from Excavations at Flixborough, S. Humberside*, Reports from the Environmental Archaeol. Unit 94/9 (York, 1994)

Dobney, K., D. Jaques, and D. Brothwell, *Assessment of the Middle Saxon Bone Assemblage from Cottam, North Yorkshire (Site Code COT93)*, Reports from the Environmental Archaeol. Unit 94/33 (York, 1994)

Dobney, K., A. Milles, D. Jaques, and B. Irving, *Material Assessment of the Animal Bone Assemblage from Flixborough*, Reports from the Environmental Archaeol. Unit 94/6 (York, 1994)

Dyer, Christopher, 'Villages and Non-Villages in the Medieval Cotswolds', *Trans. of the Bristol and Gloucestershire Archaeol. Soc.* 120 (2003 for 2002), 11–35 [includes AS]

Dyer, Christopher, Richard Jones and Mark Page, 'The Whittlewood Project', *Soc. for Med. Archaeol. Newsletter* 28, [8–9] [early Med. evidence from fieldwork]

Enright, Dawn, and David Kenyon, 'Lower Slaughter, Gloucestershire', *Cotswold Archaeol. Ann. Rev.* 10 (2000 for 1999) [online]

Enright, Dawn, and Martin Watts, *A Romano-British and Medieval Settlement Site at Stoke Road, Bishop's Cleeve, Gloucestershire*, Bristol and Gloucestershire Archaeol. Report 1 (Cirencester, 2002) [esp. on postholes for structure of seventh- to ninth-century date]

Faulkner, Neil, 'The Sedgeford Project, Norfolk: an Experiment in Popular Participation and Dialectal Method', *Archaeol. International* 2001/2002, 16–20

Fenton-Thomas, Chris, *Late Prehistoric and Early Historic Landscapes of the Yorkshire Chalk*, BAR Brit. Ser. 350 (Oxford)

Finneran, Niall, and Sam Turner, 'An Archaeological History of the Landscape of Little Haldon, Teignmouth, South Devon', *Devonshire Assoc. for the Advancement of Science, Lit. and the Arts. Report and Trans.* 135, 235–59

Ford, W. J., 'The Romano-British and Anglo-Saxon Settlement and Cemeteries at Stretton-on-Fosse, Warwickshire', *Birmingham and Warwickshire Archaeol. Soc. Trans.* 106 (2003 for 2002), 1–116

Fox, Harold, 'Wolds: the Wolds before *c.* 1500', *The English Rural Landscape*, ed. Thirsk, pp. 50–61 [esp. in sect. 2]

Frederick, Katie, Paul Garwood, Peter Hinton, Monica Kendall and Ellen McAdam, ed., *The Archaeology of Greater London: an Assessment of Archaeological Evidence for Human Presence in the Area Now Covered by Greater London* (London, 2000) [includes gazetteer of sites and finds]

Fuller, B. T., M. P. Richards and S. A. Mays, 'Stable Carbon and Nitrogen Isotope Variations in Tooth Dentine Serial Sections from Wharram Percy', *Jnl of Archaeol. Science* 30.12, 1673–84 [evidence for breastfeeding, diet, and so on, in teeth dating from tenth century on]

Gale, Rowena M. O., *Thwing, Yorkshire: Charcoal Identification*, Ancient Monuments Laboratory Report 23/91 (London, 1991)

Old Windsor: Charcoal Identification, Ancient Monuments Laboratory Report 11/91 (London, 1991) [sites dated to *c.* 650–*c.* 1150; discusses evidence for coppicing]

Gardiner, Mark, 'Economy and Landscape Change in Post-Roman and Early Medieval Sussex, 450–1175', *The Archaeology of Sussex to AD 2000*, ed. David Rudling (Great Dunham, Norf.), pp. 151–60

Gibson, C., with J. Murray, 'An Anglo-Saxon Settlement at Godmanchester, Cambridgeshire', *ASSAH* 12, 137–217

Gittos, Brian, and Moira Gittos, 'Notes on Alvington's Archaeological Potential', *Chronicle* 5 (1991), 94 [site of an AS settlement]

Hadley, Dawn, see sect. 9*e* [Whitton, Lincs.]

Hall-Torrance, Melanie, and Steven D. G. Weaver, 'The Excavation of a Saxon Settlement at Riverdene, Basingstoke, Hampshire, 1995', *Proc. of the Hampshire Field Club and Archaeol. Soc.* 58, 63–105

Hamerow, Helena, 'Angles, Saxons and Anglo-Saxons: Rural Centres, Trade and Production', *Studien zur Sachsenforschung* 13 (1999), 189–205

Harward, Chiz, 'Saxo-Norman Occupation at Beckenham, Kent?', *London Archaeologist* 10.7, 171–8

Hawkes, Sonia Chadwick, 'Gazetteer of Early Anglo-Saxon Sites in Hampshire, Fifth to Seventh Century', Hawkes, *The Anglo-Saxon Cemetery at Worthy Park*, pp. 201–7

see also sect. 9*d* [two items, publ. with G. Grainger and C. Wells]

Hepple, Leslie W., and Alison M. Doggett, 'Stonor: a Chilterns Landscape', *The English Rural Landscape*, ed. Thirsk, pp. 265–75 ['The Anglo-Saxon Charter Boundary', sect. 2]

Hesse, Mary, 'Domesday Settlement in Suffolk', *Landscape Hist.* 25, 45–57

Hill, David, and Margaret Worthington, see sect. 6 [Offa's Dyke; two items]

Hillam, Jennifer, *Tree-Ring Dating of Oak Timbers from Warren Villas, Sandy, Bedfordshire, 1990*, Ancient Monuments Laboratory Report 44/91 (London, 1991) [hurdle structures dated to 960–*c.* 1150]

Tree-Ring Analysis of Well Timbers from Godmanchester, Cambridgeshire, Ancient Monuments Laboratory Report 97/93 (London, 1993) [includes AS]

Hodges, Richard, 'Notes on the Medieval Archaeology of the White Peak', *Recent Developments in the Archaeology of the Peak District*, ed. Richard Hodges and Ken Smith, Sheffield Archaeol. Monograph 2 (Sheffield, 1991), pp. 111–21

Hooke, Della, 'Early Forms of Open-Field Agriculture in England', *Geografiska Annaler*, ser. B, 70B.1 (1988), 123–31

Hughes, Mike, 'The Excavations of a Roman and Saxon Settlement and Cemetery at Shavards Farm, Meonstoke, 1984/5', *Archaeology and Historic Buildings*, ed. Hughes, pp. 2–8

Hughes, Mike, ed., see sect. 9*a*

Hull, Graham, and Melanie Hall, 'Excavations of Medieval Features at St Andrews Church Vicarage, Sonning, Berkshire', *Berkshire Archaeol. Jnl* 76 (2003 for 1998–2003), 73–93 [settlement dating from the tenth century]

James, Richard, 'The Excavation of a Saxon *Grubenhaus* at Itford Farm, Beddingham, East Sussex', with major contributions by Luke Barber and Lucy Sibun, *Sussex Archaeol. Collections* 140 (2003 for 2002), 41–7

Johnson, Stephen, 'Excavations at Hayton Roman Fort, 1975', *Britannia* 9 (1978), 57–114 [treats an AS settlement, with finds report by Alison Cook, pp. 73–5 and 103–13]

Jones, Richard, and Mark Page, 'Characterizing Rural Settlement and Landscape: Whittlewood Forest in the Middle Ages', *Med. Archaeol.* 47, 53–83 [includes AS]

Lewis, Carenza, 'Medieval Settlement in Hampshire and the Isle of Wight', *Townships to Farmsteads: Rural Settlement Studies in Scotland, England and Wales*, ed. John A. Atkinson, Iain Banks and Gavin MacGregor, BAR Brit. Ser. 293 (Oxford, 2000), pp. 78–89

Linford, P. K., *Whitby Abbey Cliff, Whitby, North Yorkshire: Archaeomagnetic Dating Report 2002*, Centre for Archaeol. Report 98/2002 (Portsmouth, 2002) [two fired-clay features from settlement assoc. with AS abbey]

Linford, P. K., and N. Linford, *Archaeomagnetic Dating: Flixborough, Humberside, 1991*, Ancient Monuments Laboratory Report 62/91 (London, 1991) [floor of a clay oven]

Lott, Beryl, 'Seigneurial Hierarchy and Medieval Buildings in Westmorland', *The Seigneurial Residence in Western Europe AD* c. *800–1600*, ed. Gwyn Meirion-Jones, Edward Impey and Michael Jones, BAR International Ser. 1088 (Oxford, 2002), pp. 101–11 [includes AS]

Lovell, Julie, 'Excavations on a Medieval Site at Little High Street, Worthing, West Sussex, 1997', *Sussex Archaeol. Collections* 139 (2003 for 2001), 133–45 [earliest phase probably in tenth century]

McDonnell, J. G., see sect. 9*i* [Mucking, Essex]

McHugh, Maureen, *Soils, Vegetation and Landuse Change in the Stainmore Area of the Northern Pennines*, Ancient Monuments Laboratory Report 45/92 (London, 1992) [esp. on renewal of agriculture in seventh and tenth centuries]

Mire Development and Spring Activity at Grange Farm, Long Lane, Beverley, Ancient Monuments Laboratory Report 62/93 (London, 1993) [treats early Med. peat, change in vegetation]

Manby, Terry G., 'Excavation and Field Archaeology in Eastern Yorkshire: the Thwing Project 1973–1987', *CBA Forum* 1988, 16–18 [esp. on re-use of ring earthwork from *c.* 700]

Manby, Terry G., *et al.*, ed., see sect. 9*a*

Margham, John, 'Charters, Landscapes and Hides on the Isle of Wight', *Landscape Hist.* 25, 17–43

Mays, Simon, *et al.*, see sect. 9*a* [Wharram Percy; two items]

Murphy, Peter, *Plant Macrofossils from Multi-Period Excavations at Slough House Farm and Chigborough Farm Near Heybridge, Essex*, Ancient Monuments Laboratory Report 64/91 (London, 1991) [esp. on contents of two AS wells]

Norwich Southern By-Pass: Plant Remains from Beaker, Bronze Age, Iron Age, Romano-British and Late Saxon Contexts; River Valley Sediments, Ancient Monuments Laboratory Report 20/92 (London, 1992)

Cambridgeshire Dykes Project: Mollusca and Other Macrofossils, Ancient Monuments Laboratory Report 109/93 (London, 1993)

Olivier, A. C. H., see sect. 9*a* [Flixborough]

Oosthuizen, Susan, 'Medieval Greens and Moats in the Central Province: Evidence from the Bourn Valley, Cambridgeshire', *Landscape Hist.* 24 (2002), 73–88 [considers survival of certain AS features]

Partridge, Clive, *Foxholes Farm: a Multi-Period Gravel Site* (Hertford, 1989) [includes AS]

Pelling, Ruth, 'Early Saxon Cultivation of Emmer Wheat in the Thames Valley and its Cultural Implications', *Archaeological Sciences 1999: Proceedings of the Archaeological Sciences Conference, University of Bristol, 1999*, ed. Kate A. Robson Brown, BAR International Ser. 1111 (Oxford), pp. 103–10

Pine, Jo, 'Excavation of a Medieval Settlement, Late Saxon Features and a Bronze Age Cremation Cemetery at Loughton, Milton Keynes', *Records of Buckinghamshire* 43, 77–126

'Excavation of Roman and Medieval Deposits at the Rear of 29–55 High Street, Dorking', *Surrey Archaeol. Collections* 90, 261–71 [AS phase indicated by pottery and a bone pinbeater]

Ponsford, Michael, 'Excavations at a Saxo-Norman Settlement, Bickley, Cleeve, 1982–89', *Somerset Archaeol. and Nat. Hist.* 146, 47–112

Powlesland, Dominic, 'The Heslerton Parish Project: 20 Years of Archaeological Research in the Vale of Pickering', *The Archaeology of Yorkshire*, ed. T. G. Manby *et al.*, pp. 275–91 [includes AS]

Reynolds, Andrew, 'Boundaries and Settlements in Later Sixth to Eleventh-Century England', *ASSAH* 12, 98–136

Rippon, Stephen, 'Landscapes in Context: the Exploration and Management of Coastal Resources in Southern and Eastern Britain During the First Millennium AD', *Settlement and Landscape: Proceedings of a Conference in Århus, Denmark, May 4–7 1998*, ed. Charlotte Fabech and Jytte Ringtved, Jutland Archaeol. Soc. Publ. (Moesgård, 1999), pp. 225–36

'Infield and Outfield: the Early Stages of Marshland Colonisation and the Evolution of Medieval Field Systems', *Through Wet and Dry: Essays in honour of David Hall*, ed. Tom Lane and John Coles, Lincolnshire Archaeol. and Heritage Reports Ser. 5 [= WARP Occasional Paper 17] (Sleaford, Lincs., and Exeter, 2002), pp. 54–70 [includes early Med.]

Roberts, Brian K., and Stuart Wrathmell, *Region and Place: a Study of English Rural Settlement* (London, 2002)

Robertson, David, 'A Neolithic Enclosure and Early Saxon Settlement: Excavations at Yarmouth Road, Broome, 2001', *Norfolk Archaeol.* 44.2, 222–50

Royal Commission on the Historical Monuments of England, *An Inventory of Historical Monuments in the County of Cambridge, Volume 2: North-East Cambridgeshire* ([London], 1972) [Devil's Dyke and Fleam Dyke, in appendix, pp. 139–47]

Rushton, Sara, 'Evaluation at Whitton Park, Milfield', *Archaeol. in Northumberland* 1993–4, 12

Samuel, Jens, 'Excavations at "Matford", Bradley Stoke Way, Bradley Stoke, South Gloucestershire, 2001', *Bristol and Avon Archaeol.* 18 (2003 for 2001), 41–100 [includes a Saxo-Norman phase, 1000–1120]

Short, Brian, 'Forests and Wood-Pasture in Lowland England', *The English Rural Landscape*, ed. Thirsk, pp. 122–49 ['Saxon Woodland Landscapes', sect. 4]

Snape, Margaret E., 'The Roman Bridge and an Anglo-Saxon Watermill at Corbridge', *Archaeol. North* 10 (1995), 8–12

'A Horizontal-Wheeled Watermill of the Anglo-Saxon Period at Corbridge, Northumberland, and its River Environment', with a contribution by David G. Passmore, *AAe* 32, 37–72

Stocker, David, and Paul Everson, see sect. 9*e* [Witham Valley, Lincs.]

Symonds, L. A., 'Territories in Transition: the Construction of Boundaries in Anglo-Scandinavian Lincolnshire', *ASSAH* 12, 28–37

Taylor, Christopher C., 'Fenlands', *The English Rural Landscape*, ed. Thirsk, pp. 167–87 ['The Saxon Fenlands', sect. 4]

'Nucleated Settlement: a View from the Frontier', *Landscape Hist.* 24 (2002), 53–71

Taylor, Gary, with Carol Allen *et al.*, 'An Early to Middle Saxon Settlement at Quarrington, Lincolnshire', *AntJ* 83, 231–80

Thirsk, Joan, ed., *The English Rural Landscape* (Oxford, 2000) [summaries of AS evidence in many chs.]

Thomas, Gabor, 'Mapping the Origins of Bishopstone, East Sussex', *Soc. for Med. Archaeol. Newsletter* 28, [6–7] [discovery of late Saxon occupation]

Upex, Stephen G., 'Landscape Continuity and the Fossilization of Roman Fields into Saxon and Medieval Landscapes', *ArchJ* 159 (2003 for 2002), 77–108

Vyner, Blaise, 'Excavations at Low Farm, Thornton, Cleveland', *Durham Archaeol. Jnl* 17, 17–24 [includes an early Med. settlement phase]

Weekes, Jake, 'Church Lane Meadows, Seasalter', *Canterbury's Archaeol.* 26 (2003 for 2001–2), 31–2 [an AS hollow way]

Wileman, Julie, 'The Purpose of the Dykes: Understanding the Linear Earthworks of Early Medieval Britain', *Landscapes* 4.2, 59–66

Williamson, Tom, *Shaping Medieval Landscapes: Settlement, Society, Environment* (Macclesfield) [esp. in chs. 2–5]

Wilson, D. M., 'Ribblehead', *RGA* XXIV, 548–9

Wiltshire, Patricia E. J., *Palynological Analysis of Sediments from a Series of Waterlogged Features at Slough House Farm, near Heybridge, Essex*, Ancient Monuments Laboratory Report 25/92 (London, 1992) [esp. on sediments from two AS wells]

Wiltshire, Patricia E. J., and P. Murphy, *An Analysis of Microfossils and Macrofossils from Waterlogged Deposits at Slough House and Chigborough Farms, near Heybridge, Essex*, Ancient Monuments Laboratory Report 66/93 (London, 1993) [treats evidence for AS vegetation]

Wright, L. W., 'Woodland Continuity and Change: Ancient Woodland in Eastern Hertfordshire', *Landscape Hist.* 25, 67–82 [contribution to the 'clearing of the forest' debate]

d. Pagan and conversion-period burials, including Sutton Hoo

Anderson, S., *The Human Skeletal Remains from Caister-on-Sea, Norfolk*, with data produced by C. Wells and D. Birkett, Ancient Monuments Laboratory Report 9/91 (London, 1991)

Anderson, S., and D. Birkett, *The Human Skeletal Remains from Burgh Castle, Norfolk, 1960: Additional Data*, Ancient Monuments Laboratory Report 6/91 (London, 1991) [suppl. to Report 27/89, S. M. Anderson and D. A. Birkett, *The Human Skeletal Remains* (1989): see *ASE* 32 (2002), 385]

[Anon.], 'Summary Report', *Portable Antiquities Scheme Ann. Report* 5 (2003 for 2001–3), 9–17 [esp. on four new AS sites in Kent, including at least two cemeteries]

see also sect. 9*i* [cemeteries in Hants. and Lincs.]

Boulter, Stuart, see sect. 9*b* [Flixton Park Quarry]

Canterbury Archaeological Trust, see sects. 9*a* and 9*b* [cemeteries north of Saltwood Tunnel]

Carver, Martin, ed., see sect. 6

Chichester District Council Archaeological Advisory Committee, ed., *The Archaeology of Chichester and District 1985* ([?Chichester], *c.* 1985)

The Archaeology of Chichester and District 1987 ([?Chichester], *c.* 1987)

The Archaeology of Chichester and District 1988 ([?Chichester], *c.* 1988)

Clarke, Bob, 'Outcast? A Dated Roadside Burial', *Antiquity* 77.296, [online] [burial at Broad Town, Wilts., dated to 540–680; possibly witnessing an execution]

Crawford, Sally, 'Anglo-Saxon Women, Furnished Burial and the Church', *Women and Religion*, ed. Wood, pp. 1–12

Crowfoot, Elisabeth, see sect. 9*k* [two items, one on Wakerley, Northants.]

Davis, Simon J. M., and Peter King, *Small Mammal Remains Found in a Saxon Bucket at Carisbrooke Castle, Isle of Wight, 1981 Excavations*, Ancient Monuments Laboratory Report 17/92 (London, 1992) [six shrews and a wood-mouse in an AS grave]

Down, Alec, and Martin G. Welch, 'Compton: the Anglo-Saxon Cemetery at Appledown (SU 793153)', *The Archaeology of Chichester and District 1985*, ed. Chichester District Council Archaeological Advisory Committee, pp. 28–30

'Compton: the Anglo-Saxon Cemetery at Appledown (SU 793153)', *The Archaeology of Chichester and District 1987*, ed. Chichester District Council Archaeological Advisory Committee, pp. 40–2

Duncan, Holly, Corinne Duhig and Mark Phillips, 'A Late Migration/Final Phase Cemetery at Water Lane, Melbourn', *Proc. of the Cambridge Ant. Soc.* 92, 57–134

Eckardt, Hella, and Howard Williams, 'Objects without a Past? The Use of Roman Objects in Early Anglo-Saxon Graves', *Archaeologies of Remembrance*, ed. Williams, pp. 141–70

see also sect. 9*g* [Roman objects in early AS graves]

Effros, Bonnie, *Merovingian Mortuary Archaeology and the Making of the Early Middle Ages*, Transformation of the Classical Heritage 35 (Berkeley, CA) [in chs. 3–4]

Fiorato, Veronica, 'Archaeology in West Berkshire', *CBA Wessex News* April 2003, 27–8 [discusses traces of previously unknown AS cemetery]

Ford, W. J., see sect. 9*c* [Stretton-on-Fosse, Warwicks.]

Geake, Helen, 'The Control of Burial Practice in Anglo-Saxon England', *The Cross Goes North*, ed. Carver, pp. 259–69

'Plough Damage on Anglo-Saxon Cemeteries', *The Archaeologist* 47, 16–17

Green, Charles, *Sutton Hoo: the Excavation of a Royal Ship-Burial*, 2nd ed. (London, 1986)

Hadley, D. M., see sect. 6 [Danelaw]

Halsall, Guy, 'Burial Customs around the North Sea, *c.* 350–700', *Kings of the North Sea*, ed. Kramer *et al.* (Newcastle upon Tyne, 2000), pp. 93–104

Härke, Heinrich, and Roy Entwistle, 'An Anglo-Saxon Quadruple Weapon Burial at Tidworth: a Battle-Site Burial on Salisbury Plain?', *Proc. of the Hampshire Field Club and Archaeol. Soc.* 57 (2002), 38–52

Harp, Peter, and John Hines, 'An Anglo-Saxon Cemetery at Headley Drive, Tadworth, Near Banstead', *Surrey Archaeol. Collections* 90, 117–45

Hawkes, Sonia Chadwick, with Guy Grainger, *The Anglo-Saxon Cemetery at Worthy Park, Kingsworthy, near Winchester, Hampshire*, Oxford Univ. School of Archaeol. Monograph 59 (Oxford)

Hawkes, Sonia Chadwick, and Calvin Wells, 'Absence of the Left Upper Limb and Pectoral Girdle in a Unique Anglo-Saxon Burial', *Bull. of the New York Acad. of Medicine*, 2nd ser. 52 (1976), 1229–35 [Grave 38, Worthy Park, Hants.]

Hayman, Graham N., 'Further Excavations at the Former Goblin Works, Ashtead (TQ 182 567)', *Surrey Archaeol. Collections* 81 (1991–2), 1–18 [an AS pagan cemetery]

Hill, Paul, and Logan Thompson, see sect. 9*i* [Mitcham]

Hines, John, 'Finds from the Anglo-Saxon Cemetery at Tadworth', *Surrey Archaeol. Soc. Bull.* 353 (2001), 4

Hughes, Mike, see sect. 9*c* [Shavards Farm, Meonstoke, Hants.]

Hutchinson, M. E., see sect. 9*h* [Sancton, Humberside]

Kennett, David H., see sect. 9*a* [Kempston, Beds.]

Kramer, Evert, *et al.*, ed., see sect. 6

McAndrew, Duncan, 'Whose Hoo? A Review and Critique of "Sutton Hoo", Sutton Hoo National Trust Visitor Centre, Sutton Hoo, Suffolk', *Papers from the Inst. of Archaeol.* 14, 136–43

McKinley, Jacqueline I., 'The Early Saxon Cemetery at Park Lane, Croydon', *Surrey Archaeol. Collections* 90, 1–116

'A Wiltshire "Bog Body"? Discussion of a Fifth/Sixth Century AD Burial in the Woodford Valley', *Wiltshire Archaeol. and Nat. Hist. Mag.* 96, 7–18

Mainman, Ailsa, see sect. 9*j* [Heslington Hill, near York]

Mays, S. A., *Anglo-Saxon Human Remains from Mucking, Essex*, Ancient Monuments Laboratory Report 18/92 (London, 1992)

Cremated Human Bone from Park Road, Raunds, Northamptonshire (Excavated 1989), Ancient Monuments Laboratory Report 7/93 (London, 1993)

Meaney, Audrey L., 'Anglo-Saxon Pagan and Early Christian Attitudes to the Dead', *The Cross Goes North*, ed. Carver, pp. 229–41

Mortimer, Catherine, see sect. 9*i* [Edix Hill, Cambs.]

Mortimer, Catherine, and Paul Wilthew, see sect. 9*g* [Castle Dyke, Barton on Humber]

Newman, John, 'The Boss Hall Anglo-Saxon Cemetery', *The Quarterly* 2 (1991), 16–23

Nurse, Keith, 'Digging up Dark Deeds: the Sutton Hoo Excavation', *Country Life* 184 (1990), 113

O'Connor, Terence, 'A Horse Skeleton from Sutton Hoo, Suffolk, U.K.', *ArchaeoZoologia* 7 (1994), 29–37

Parfitt, Keith, see sect. 9*g* [Mill Hill, Deal, Kent]

Penn, Kenneth J., 'The Anglo-Saxon Cemetery at Oxborough and the Master of the Gliding Gouge', *The Quarterly* 4 (1991), 7–10 [includes discussion of a surgical technique]

Penn, Kenneth J., with Steven Ashley, 'Two Early Saxon Cemeteries in South Norfolk', *Norfolk Archaeol.* 44.2, 304–15

Philp, Brian, *The Anglo-Saxon Cemetery at Polhill near Sevenoaks, Kent 1964–1986*, Kent Special Subject Ser. 15 (West Wickham, 2002)

Archaeology in the Front Line: 50 Years of Kent Rescue 1952–2002. Discovery, Excavation, Publication, Preservation, Presentation, Education (Dover, 2002) [treats AS cemeteries at Polhill and Eastry]

Richards, Julian D., 'Pagans and Christians at a Frontier: Viking Burial in the Danelaw', *The Cross Goes North*, ed. Carver, pp. 383–95

'Heath Wood, Ingleby', *CA* 184, 170–3 [ninth-century pagan Viking cemetery in Derbys.]

Semple, Sarah, 'Burials and Political Boundaries in the Avebury Region, North Wiltshire', *ASSAH* 12, 72–91

Sparey-Green, Christopher, 'Horton Pipe-Line, Chartham', *Canterbury's Archaeol.* 26 (2003 for 2001–2), 27–9 [discusses previously unknown AS cemetery]

Stead, I. M., 'Iron Age and Anglian Cemeteries near Garton Station, Garton-on-the-Wolds, East Yorkshire', *CBA Forum* 1986, 2–5

Stoodley, Nick, and Chris Fern, 'The Anglo-Saxon Cemetery at Micheldever – Rediscovered', *Soc. for Med. Archaeol. Newsletter* 29, [3–4]

Strongman, S. R., *Three Early Anglo-Saxon Burials from Carisbrooke Castle, Isle of Wight, Excavated 1976–1981*, Ancient Monuments Laboratory Report 101/91 (London, 1991)

Taylor, Tim, *The Time Team Reports*, ed. Derek Jones (London, 1995) [esp. on AS cemetery at Winterbourne, Wilts.]

Thomas, Gabor, 'Teeth Worn Down Like Iguanodons: New Evidence for Early Anglo-Saxon Lewes', *Sussex Past and Present* 96 (2002), 4–5 [five fifth- to sixth-century graves]

Warren, Dave, '"Saxon" Skeleton Found on Puddlehill, June 1994', *Manshead* 41 (2001), 25–7 [undated burial found close to AS cemetery]

Watson, Jacqui, *Mineral Preserved Organic Material Associated with Metalwork from Harford Farm, Norfolk*, Ancient Monuments Laboratory Report 66/92 (London, 1992) [material from AS cemetery]

see also sect. 9*g* [Edix Hill, Cambs., and Gunthorpe, Cambs.; two items]

Watson, Jacqui, and Glynis Edwards, *Organic Material Associated with Metalwork from the Anglo-Saxon Cemetery at Beckford, Hereford and Worcester*, Ancient Monuments Laboratory Report 59/91 (London, 1991)

Welch, M. G., 'Kingston', *RGA* XVI (2000), 551–3

Williams, D. F., see sect. 9*j* [Sancton, Humberside]

Williams, Howard, 'Material Culture as Memory: Combs and Cremation in Early Medieval Britain', *EME* 12, 89–128

Williams, Howard, ed., *Archaeologies of Remembrance: Death and Memory in Past Societies* (New York)

Wilson, D. M., 'Ingleby', *RGA* XV (2000), 424–5

Wood, Diana, ed., see sect. 6

e. Churches, monastic sites and Christian cemeteries

Ahrens, Claus, *Die frühen Holzkirchen Europas*, 2 vols., Schriften des Archäologischen Landesmuseums 7 (Stuttgart, 2001) ['Britische Holzkirchen in sächsischer und normannischer Zeit', vol. 1, sect. 2.3, with vol. 2, sect. 10]

Aldsworth, Fred, 'Deerhurst Church: the Problems of Survey', *Bull. of the CBA Churches Committee* 4 (1976), 12–14 with 2 figs.

'Singleton: Survey of Church Tower (SU 878130)', *The Archaeology of Chichester and District 1987*, ed. Chichester District Council Archaeological Advisory Committee, pp. 48–9

'Bosham: the Tower of Holy Trinity Church', *The Archaeology of Chichester and District 1988*, ed. Chichester District Council Archaeological Advisory Committee, pp. 18–20

Andrews, R. D., 'St Patrick's Chapel, Heysham, Lancs', *Bull. of the CBA Churches Committee* 8 (1978), 2

[Anon.], 'An Early Christian Cemetery at Bishopsmill School, Norton, Stockton-on-Tees', *Tees Archaeol.* 2, [1]

'New Anglo-Saxon Discoveries in Hartlepool', *Tees Archaeol.* 3, [3] [a new area of the AS monastery]

Archer, Lucy, *Architecture in Britain and Ireland 600–1500* (London, 1999) [esp. for photographs by Edwin Smith and on AS churches and sculpture]

Bagshaw, Steve, see sect. 9*c* [Deerhurst]

Bailey, Richard N., 'Hexham Abbey', *Bull. of the CBA Churches Committee* 11 (1979), 4–6 with fig. 1

Biddle, Martin, 'Excavations at St Wystan's Church, Repton, 1974–5', *Bull. of the CBA Churches Committee* 2 (1975), 18–20

'Little Somborne', *Bull. of the CBA Churches Committee* 2 (1975), 17

Biddle, Martin, B. Kjølbye-Biddle and H. M. Taylor, 'St Wystan, Repton', *Bull. of the CBA Churches Committee* 7 (1977), 7–9

Bidwell, P. T., 'The Cathedral Close, Exeter', *Bull. of the CBA Churches Committee* 9 (1978), 8–11 [excavation of four cemeteries and the minster]

Blair, John, see sect. 9*b* [Bicester]

Blockley, Kevin, 'La cathédrale de Canterbury', *Archéologia* 302 (1994), 54–61 [recent excavations, including foundations of the AS cathedral]

Boddington, A., 'Raunds (SP999733)', *Bull. of the CBA Churches Committee* 11 (1979), 7–8 with figs. 2–3 [two AS phases in the church, and a cemetery]

Bond, C. J., see sect. 9*i* [Fladbury, Worcs.]

Brain, Derek, and P. M. Welford, see sect. 9*h* [Canterbury]

Brooks, Catherine, *et al.*, ed., see sect. 9*a*

Butler, Lawrence, 'Excavations at Medieval Parish Churches: a Bibliography', *Bull. of the CBA Churches Committee* 3 (1976), 15–20 [includes AS]

Carver, Martin, ed., see sect. 6

Chichester District Council Archaeological Advisory Committee, ed., see sect. 9*d* [two items, publ. *c.* 1987 and *c.* 1988]

Coggins, D., and K. J. Fairless, 'The Old Church of St Mary, Brignall, near Barnard Castle', *Durham Archaeol. Jnl* 17, 25–41 [site of an early Med. burial ground; includes report on a decorated stone, by R. J. Cramp]

Colyer, Christina, 'Excavations at St Mark, Lincoln', *Bull. of the CBA Churches Committee* 5 (1976), 5–9 [a late eleventh-century church with pre-Conquest burials and sculpture]

Coppack, G., 'St Lawrence, Burnham, South Humberside', *Bull. of the CBA Churches Committee* 8 (1978), 5–6 with 1 fig.

Cramp, Rosemary J., 'The Anglo-Saxon and Medieval Monastery of Jarrow, Co. Durham', *Archaeol. Newsbulletin for CBA Regional Group 3* [1] ([1972]), 5–6

'The Anglo-Saxon and Medieval Monastery of Monkwearmouth, Co. Durham', *Archaeol. Newsbulletin for CBA Regional Group 3* [1] ([1972]), 6

Crowe, Christopher, 'Early Medieval Parish Formation in Dumfries and Galloway', *The Cross Goes North*, ed. Carver, pp. 195–206

Dickinson, Steve, *The Beacon on the Bay: the Discovery of an Early Christian Church and Monastic Site at Great Urswick, Low Furness, Cumbria, and the Case for its Connections with St Ninian, St Patrick, St Hild and St Columba* (Ulverston, 2002) [offers major re-evaluation of AS runic inscription on a cross fragment]

Dunning, Robert, *Somerset Monasteries* (Stroud, 2001) [esp. in chs. 2–4]

Driver, J. C., J. Rady, and M. Sparks, see sect. 9*b* [Canterbury]

Gem, Richard, *Studies in English Pre-Romaneque and Romanesque Architecture* I (London, *c.* 2003) [reissued papers]

Gittos, Brian, and Moira Gittos, 'Further Observations on the Anglo-Saxon Work at East Coker', *Chronicle* 5 (1991), 95–6

'The Surviving Anglo-Saxon Fabric of East Coker Church', *Chronicle* 5 (1991), 58–9

Gittos, Helen, 'Architecture and Liturgy in England *c.* 1000: Problems and Possibilities', *The White Mantle of Churches: Architecture, Liturgy and Art around the Millennium*, ed. Nigel Hiscock (Turnhout), pp. 91–105

Graham-Campbell, James, *Whithorn and the Viking World* (Whithorn, 2001)

Grounds, Douglas, *A History of the Church of St Laurence, Church Stretton: a Rural Parish through a Thousand Years* (Little Logaston, 2002) ['The Saxon and Norman Churches', ch. 1]

Hadley, Dawn, 'Whitton, Lincolnshire', *CA* 186, 234–7 [a middle Saxon cemetery with evidence for late Saxon occupation]

Hall, Richard, 'St Mary's Castlegate, York: a Watching Brief', *Bull. of the CBA Churches Committee* 3 (1976), 11–14 [on the church and sculpture]

Hardie, Caroline, 'St Ebba's Chapel, Beadnell', *Archaeol. in Northumberland* 1993–4 (*c.* 1994), 24

Hardy, Alan, Anne Dodd, and Graham D. Keevill, *Ælfric's Abbey: Excavations at Eynsham Abbey, Oxfordshire, 1989–92*, Thames Valley Landscapes 16 (Oxford)

Hawkins, Duncan, *et al.*, see sect. 9*b* [Barking]

Heighway, C., 'St Oswald's Priory, Gloucester', *Bull. of the CBA Churches Committee* 8 (1978), 3–4 with 1 fig.

Hill, Peter, and Dave Pollock, *The Whithorn Dig* (Whithorn, 1992)

Hinton, David A., 'The Archaeology of the Church in Hampshire', *Archaeology in Hampshire*, ed. Hinton and Hughes, pp. 86–9

'Debate: the Dating of Ferruginously-Cemented Gravel as Building Material', *Landscape Hist.* 24 (2002), 121–2 [discusses view that such material will often indicate an AS date]

'Recent Work on St Lawrence's Chapel, Bradford-on-Avon: an Interim Report', *Wiltshire Archaeol. and Nat. Hist. Mag.* 96, 206–7

Hinton, David A., and Michael Hughes, ed., see sect. 9*a*

Hull, Graham, 'Barkingwic? Saxon and Medieval Features Adjacent to Barking Abbey', *Essex Archaeol. and Hist.* 33 (2002), 157–90 [evidence of river landing-stage and industrial processes]

Insley, J., and R. J. Cramp, 'Jarrow', *RGA* XVI, 37–41

Insley, J., and D. M. Wilson, 'Reculver', *RGA* XXIV, 297–303 [sect. 3, by Wilson]

Lyle, Marjorie, see sect. 9*b* [Canterbury]

MacBeth, Nigel, 'Creeting St Olave', *CA* 189, 406–9 [search for Creeting St Mary's third Domesday Book church]

Newman, R. M., 'Anglo-Saxon Christianity', *Past, Present and Future*, ed. Brooks *et al.*, pp. 149–54 [church archaeol. in the north]

Norton, Christopher, 'The Luxury Pavement in England before Westminster', *Westminster Abbey: the Cosmati Pavements*, ed. Lindy Grant and Richard Mortimer, Courtauld Research Papers 3 (Aldershot, 2002), 7–36 [limitations of AS evidence]

Parsons, David, 'All Saints' Church, Brixworth', *Bull. of the CBA Churches Committee* 7 (1977), 10–12 with figs. 1–2

'The Mercian Church: Archaeology and Topography', *Mercia: an Anglo-Saxon Kingdom in Europe*, ed. Michelle P. Brown and Carol A. Farr (London, 2001), pp. 50–68

Rahtz, Philip, and Lorna Watts, 'Three Ages of Conversion at Kirkdale, North Yorkshire', *The Cross Goes North*, ed. Carver, pp. 289–309

Reynolds, Andrew, and Sam Turner, 'Excavations at Holy Trinity, Buckfastleigh, Spring 2002', *R. Archaeol. Inst. Newsletter* 26, 3–5 [AS burials as evidence for an early monastic settlement]

Rigold, S. E., *North Elmham Saxon Cathedral*, 2nd ed. (London, 1978)

Rodwell, Kirsty, and Warwick Rodwell, 'St Peter, Barton-on-Humber', *Bull. of the CBA Churches Committee* 10 (1979), 5–7

Rodwell, Warwick, 'Wells Cathedral', *Bull. of the CBA Churches Committee* 11 (1979), 10–12 with figs. 5–6

'The Windows of Hadstock', *Essex Archaeol. News* 71 (1980), 11–13

Rogan, John, ed., see sect. 9*h* [Bristol]

Sills, John, 'A Re-Examination of Holton-le-Clay Church', *Bull. of the CBA Churches Committee* 2 (1975), 10–12 with figs. 1–5 [evidence for AS churches]

Sparey-Green, Christopher, 'St Martin's Priory', *Canterbury's Archaeol.* 26 (2003 for 2001–2), 18–20 [an AS cemetery and settlement phase]

Sparks, Margaret, *St Augustine's Abbey, Canterbury, Kent*, 2nd ed. (London, 1990)

Stocker, David, and Paul Everson, 'The Straight and Narrow Way: Fenland Causeways and the Conversion of the Landscape in the Witham Valley, Lincolnshire', *The Cross Goes North*, ed. Carver, pp. 271–88

Tatton-Brown, Tim, *Great Cathedrals of Britain* (London, 1989) [esp. for AS period; useful illustrations, some from Soc. of Antiquaries' Lib.]

Thurlby, Malcolm, 'Anglo-Saxon Architecture beyond the Millennium: its Continuity in Norman Building', *The White Mantle of Churches: Architecture, Liturgy and Art around the Millennium*, ed. Nigel Hiscock (Turnhout), pp. 119–37

Turner, Sam, 'Making a Christian Landscape: Early Medieval Cornwall', *The Cross Goes North*, ed. Carver, pp. 171–94

'Boundaries and Religion: the Demarcation of Early Christian Settlements in Britain', *ASSAH* 12, 50–7

Ward, Alan, 'Kent Sites, 27: Boley Hill Repaving, Rochester', *Canterbury's Archaeol.* 23 (2001 for 1998–9), 33–42 [discusses an early AS church]

Whitwell, J. B., and J. M. Boden, 'Barrow-on-Humber, South Humberside', *Bull. of the CBA Churches Committee* 10 (1979), 7–9

Willson, John, and Andrew Linklater, 'St Mary's Church, Chartham', *Canterbury's Archaeol.* 26 (2003 for 2001–2), 29–31 [discusses foundations of late Saxon church]

Wilson, D. M., 'Repton', *RGA* XXIV, 512–14

'Ripon', *RGA* XXV, 28–9

Zadora-Rio, Elisabeth, 'The Making of Churchyards and Parish Territories in the Early Medieval Landscape of France and England in the Seventh–Twelfth Centuries: a Reconsideration', *Med. Archaeol.* 47, 1–19

f. Ships and seafaring

Bacon, Stuart R., 'Buss Creek, Southwold, Suffolk', *The Quarterly* 5 (1992), 23–4 [discovery of timbers from early Med. ship]

Bill, Jan, 'Iron Nails in Iron Age and Medieval Shipbuilding', *Crossroads in Ancient Shipbuilding: Proceedings of the Sixth International Symposium on Boat and Ship Archaeology, Roskilde 1991*, ed. Christer Westerdahl, Oxbow Monograph 40 (Oxford, 1994), pp. 55–63 [includes AS material]

Crumlin-Pedersen, Ole, 'Ships as Indicators of Trade in Northern Europe 600–1200', *Maritime Topography and the Medieval Town: Papers from the Fifth International Conference on Waterfront Archaeology in Copenhagen, 14–16 May 1998*, ed. Jan Bill and Birthe L. Clausen, PNM: Publ. from the National Museum, Stud. in Archaeol. and Hist. 4 (Copenhagen, 1999), pp. 11–20

Detalle, Michel-Pierre, *La piraterie en Europe du Nord-Ouest à l'époque Romaine*, BAR International Ser. 1086 (Oxford, 2002) [treats AS ships]

Gifford, Edwin, and Joyce Gifford, 'Alfred's New Longships', *Alfred the Great*, ed. Reuter, pp. 281–9

Goodburn, Damian M., 'Some Unfamiliar Aspects of Early Woodworking revealed by Recent Rescue Excavations in London', *Proceedings*, ed. Hoffmann, pp. 143–55 [includes sect. on 'Saxon Boatbuilding']

Hoffmann, Per, ed., see sect. 9*b*

Reuter, Timothy, ed., see sect. 6

Rose, Susan, see sect. 6

g. Miscellaneous artefacts

Ashwin, Trevor, Mary Davis and Kenneth Penn, 'A Silver Composite Disc Brooch from Harford Farm, Caistor St Edmund', *The Quarterly* 5 (1992), 12–16 [discusses garnet and glass decoration]

Aston, M. A., ed., *The Shapwick Project: a Topographical and Historical Study, 1989. 2nd Report* (Bristol, 1989)

Beilke-Voigt, Ines, *Frühgeschichtliche Miniaturobjekte mit Amulettcharakter zwischen Britischen Inseln und Schwarzem Meer*, Universitätsforschungen zur prähistorischen Archäologie 51 [= Schriften zur Archäologie der germanischen und slawischen Frühgeschichte 3] (Bonn, 1998) [finds from thirty-seven AS sites]

Bierbrauer, Volker, 'Kontinentaler und insularer Tierstil im Kunsthandwerk des 8. Jahrhunderts', *Tiere, Menschen, Götter*, ed. Müller-Wille and Larsson, pp. 89–130

Biggam, C. P., ed., see sect. 1

Brown, David, 'Data Sheet 1: Anglo-Saxon Shields', *United Kingdom Inst. for Conservation Occasional Papers* 1 (1980), 11–12 and 14–15 [parts of shields and their interpretation]

Eckardt, Hella, and Howard Williams, 'Objects without a Past? The Use of Roman Objects in Early Anglo-Saxon Graves', *Archaeologies of Remembrance*, ed. Williams, pp. 141–70

Fuglesang, Signe Horn, 'Animal Ornament: the Late Viking Period', *Tiere, Menschen, Götter*, ed. Müller-Wille and Larsson, pp. 157–94

Geber, Øystein, 'Over Nordsjøen etter gull? Handel og plyndring, import til Vestlandet i vikingetid', *Arkeologiske skrifter* 10 (1999), 61–83 [Insular artefacts found in Norway as evidence for the Vik voyages]

Gerrard, Christopher, 'Fieldwalking Results, Methodological Experiments and Future Strategy', *The Shapwick Project: a Topographical and Historical Study, 1989. 2nd Report*, ed. M. A. Aston (Bristol, 1989), pp. 21–57 [includes AS finds]

Gurney, David, ed., 'Archaeological Finds in Norfolk 2002', *Norfolk Archaeol.* 44.2, 356–68 [includes AS]

Hawkes, Jane, 'The Plant-Life of Early Christian Anglo-Saxon Art', *From Earth to Art*, ed. Biggam, pp. 263–86

Karkov, Catherine E., and George Hardin Brown, ed., see sect. 1

Lamm, Jan Peder, 'Some Scandinavian Art Styles', *From Attila to Charlemagne: Arts of the Early Medieval Period in The Metropolitan Museum of Art*, ed. Katharine Reynolds Brown, Dafydd Kidd and Charles T. Little, Metropolitan Museum of Art Symposia (New York, 2000), pp. 308–21 [styles occurring also in England]

Lawson, Graeme, 'Data Sheet 2: Stringed Musical Instruments', *United Kingdom Inst. of Conservation Occasional Papers* 1 (1980), 12–13 and 16–20 [parts of musical instruments, and their interpretation; includes AS]

Leahy, Kevin, *Anglo-Saxon Crafts* (Stroud)

Michelli, Perette E., 'Beckwith Revisited: Some Ivory Carvings from Canterbury', *Anglo-Saxon Styles*, ed. Karkov and Brown, pp. 101–13

Mortimer, Catherine, and Paul Wilthew, *X-Ray Fluorescent Analysis of Grave Goods from the Anglian Cemetery at Castle Dyke, Barton on Humber, Excavated 1982–83*, Ancient Monuments Laboratory Report 21/91 (London, 1991)

Müller-Wille, Michael, and Lars Olof Larsson, ed., see sect. 5

Parfitt, Keith, 'Scientific Examination of Anglo-Saxon Grave-Goods from Mill Hill, Deal, Kent', *Archaeol. Rev.* 154, 76–81

Smith, Andrea N., 'Material Culture and North Sea Contacts in the Fifth to Seventh Centuries AD', *The Prehistory and Early History of Atlantic Europe: Papers from a Session Held at the European Association of Archaeologists' Fourth Annual Meeting in Göteborg 1998*, ed. Jon C. Henderson, BAR International Ser. 861 (Oxford, 2000), pp. 181–8

Watson, Jacqui, *Organic Material Associated with Metalwork from the Anglo-Saxon Cemetery at Gunthorpe, Cambridgeshire*, Ancient Monuments Laboratory Report 41/92 (London, 1992)

Organic Material Associated with Metalwork from the Anglo-Saxon Cemetery at Edix Hill, Barrington, Cambridgeshire, Centre for Archaeol. Report 88/2002 (Portsmouth, 2002)

Webster, Leslie, 'Encrypted Visions: Style and Sense in the Anglo-Saxon Minor Arts, AD 400–900', *Anglo-Saxon Styles*, ed. Karkov and Brown, pp. 11–30

Williams, Howard, ed., see sect. 9*d*

Wilson, David M., 'The Earliest Animal Styles of the Viking Age', *Tiere, Menschen, Götter*, ed. Müller-Wille and Larsson, pp. 131–56

h. Bone, stone and wood

Adams, Noël, 'Garnet Inlays in the Light of the Armaziskhevi Dagger Hilt', *Med. Archaeol.* 47, 167–75

[Anon.], ed., *A Bewcastle Miscellany: a Collection of Articles Published with the Aid of a Millennium Award Grant by Voluntary Action Cumbria to Ian James of the Bewcastle Heritage Society* (Carlisle, 2000)

Bailey, Richard N., '"Innocent from the Great Offence"', *Theorizing Anglo-Saxon Stone Sculpture*, ed. Karkov and Orton, pp. 93–103 [reply to Orton's criticism of 'corpus scholarship' in sculpture stud.]

Bourdillon, Jennifer, 'Bias from Bone Working at Middle Saxon Hamwic, Southampton', *Materials of Manufacture*, ed. Riddler, pp. 49–64

Brain, Derek, and P. M. Welford, *The Conservation of a Stone Capital from St Augustine's Abbey, Canterbury*, Ancient Monuments Laboratory Report 121/91 (London, 1991)

Brugmann, Birte, *Corpus of Anglo-Saxon Buckets: Database of the Archive of Jean M. Cook* ([Oxford], *c.* 2003) [online: www.arch.ox.ac.uk/archives/asbuckets/; adjunct to forthcoming monograph by Cook, ed. Brugmann; design and programming by Deborah Harlan]

Carver, Martin, ed., see sect. 6

Cook, Jean Mary, see with Brugmann, Birte, above [buckets]

Cramp, Rosemary J., 'The Anglian Sculptures from Jedburgh', *From the Stone Age to the 'Forty-Five'*, ed. O'Connor and Clarke, pp. 269–84

'The Pre-Conquest Sculptures of Glastonbury Monastery', *New Offerings, Ancient Treasures: Studies in Medieval Art for George Henderson*, ed. Paul Binski and William Noel (Stroud, 2001), pp. 148–62

see also with Coggins, D., and K. J. Fairless, sect. 9*e* [stone at Brignall, Yorks.]

Ewing, Thor, 'Understanding the Heysham Hogback: a Tenth-Century Sculpted Stone Monument and its Context', *Trans. of the Hist. Soc. of Lancashire and Cheshire* 152, 1–20

Galloway, Patricia, and Mark Newcomer, 'The Craft of Comb-Making: an Experimental Enquiry', *BIAL* 18 (1981), 73–90 [esp. on early Med. combs]

Gittos, Brian, and Moira Gittos, 'Anglo-Scandinavian(?) Beast Head in Hardington Mandeville Church', *Chronicle* 7 (1997), 64–6

Hart, Clive R., and Elisabeth Okasha, 'Early Medieval Stone Bowls from Sunderland, Dalden and Durham', *Durham Archaeol. Jnl* 17, 13–15 [one with incised lettering; possible ecclesiastical function]

Hawkes, Jane, 'Constructing Iconographies: Questions of Identity in Mercian Sculpture', *Mercia: an Anglo-Saxon Kingdom in Europe*, ed. Michelle P. Brown and Carol A. Farr (London, 2001), pp. 230–45

'*Iuxta morem Romanorum*: Stone and Sculpture in Anglo-Saxon England', *Anglo-Saxon Styles*, ed. Karkov and Brown, pp. 69–99

'Reading Stone', *Theorizing Anglo-Saxon Stone Sculpture*, ed. Karkov and Orton, pp. 5–30 [interpretation of Sandbach cross by mod. – and AS – observers]

'Sacraments in Stone: the Mysteries of Christ in Anglo-Saxon Sculpture', *The Cross Goes North*, ed. Carver, pp. 351–70

Henderson, Isabel, 'Pictish Vine-Scroll Ornament', *From the Stone Age to the 'Forty-Five'*, ed. O'Connor and Clarke, pp. 243–68 [possible Anglian influence]

Hodges, Richard, 'Dark Age Handled Combs in North-West Europe', *Archaeologia Atlantica* 3 (1981 for 1980), 145–6

Hutchinson, M. E., *Identification of Two Gemstones from Sancton, Humberside (AML Site Number 1251)*, Ancient Monuments Laboratory Report 119/91 (London, 1991) [almandine garnets from AS cremation]

Identification of a Red Stone in an Anglo-Saxon Buckle Plate from Mucking, Essex, AML Site No. 239, Ancient Monuments Laboratory Report 10/92 (London, 1992) [almandine garnet]

Identification of a Red Stone Set in an Anglo-Saxon Buckle from Market Lavington, Wiltshire, AML Site No. 2245, Ancient Monuments Laboratory Report 9/92 (London, 1992) [almandine garnet of unusual tint]

Jewell, Richard, 'Classicism of Southumbrian Sculpture', *Mercia: an Anglo-Saxon Kingdom in Europe*, ed. Michelle P. Brown and Carol A. Farr (London, 2001), pp. 246–62

Karkov, Catherine E., 'Naming and Renaming: the Inscription of Gender in Anglo-Saxon Sculpture', *Theorizing Anglo-Saxon Stone Sculpture*, ed. Karkov and Orton, pp. 31–64

Karkov, Catherine E., and George Hardin Brown, ed., see sect. 1

Karkov, Catherine E., and Fred Orton, ed., *Theorizing Anglo-Saxon Stone Sculpture*, Med. European Stud. 4 (Morgantown, VA)

Lang, James T., *et al.*, *Corpus of Anglo-Saxon Stone Sculpture*, VI: *Northern Yorkshire* (Oxford, 2001)

Michelli, Perette E., 'Beckwith Revisited: Some Ivory Carvings from Canterbury', *Anglo-Saxon Styles*, ed. Karkov and Brown, pp. 101–13

Mitchell, John, 'The High Cross and Monastic Strategies in Eighth-Century Northumbria', *New Offerings, Ancient Treasures: Studies in Medieval Art for George Henderson*, ed. Paul Binski and William Noel (Stroud, 2001), pp. 88–114

Morgan, Ruth A., *The Stakes from Upwich, Droitwich (HWCM 4575): an Analysis of Woodworking Techniques and Woodland Origins through Tree-Ring Study*, Ancient Monuments Laboratory Report 32/91 (London, 1991) [emphasis on AS period]

Morris, Chris, 'Notes on Pre-Norman Sculpture from Co. Durham', *Archaeol. Newsbulletin for CBA Regional Group 3* 10 (1975), 15–18 [for two additional sites, see notice in later no. of this bull., vol. 15 (1977), p. 16]

Neuman de Vegvar, Carol, 'A Feast to the Lord: Drinking Horns, the Church and the

Liturgy', *Objects, Images and the Word: Art in the Service of the Liturgy*, ed. Colum Hourihane (Princeton, NJ), pp. 231–56

Newman, R., 'The Bewcastle Cross', *A Bewcastle Miscellany*, ed. [Anon.], pp. 22–7

Norton, Christopher, see sect. 9*e* [luxury pavements]

Oakes, Catherine M., 'Romanesque Architecture and Sculpture', *Bristol Cathedral*, ed. Rogan, pp. 64–87 [esp. on 'Harrowing of Hell' sculpture]

Oakes, Catherine M., and Michael Costen, 'The Congresbury Carvings: an Eleventh-Century Saint's Shrine?', *AntJ* 83, 281–309 [carvings comparable in style with AS sculpture and figures drawn in AS manuscripts]

Ó Carragáin, Éamonn, 'Between Annunciation and Visitation: Spiritual Birth and the Cycles of the Sun on the Ruthwell Cross. A Response to Fred Orton', *Theorizing Anglo-Saxon Stone Sculpture*, ed. Karkov and Orton, pp. 131–87

O'Connor, Anne, and D. V. Clarke, ed., *From the Stone Age to the 'Forty-Five': Studies presented to R. B. K. Stevenson, Former Keeper, National Museum of Antiquities of Scotland* (Edinburgh, 1983)

Orton, Fred, 'Rethinking the Ruthwell and Bewcastle Monuments: Some Deprecation of Style; Some Consideration of Form and Ideology', *Anglo-Saxon Styles*, ed. Karkov and Brown, pp. 31–67

'Rethinking the Ruthwell and Bewcastle Monuments: Some Strictures on Similarity; Some Questions of History', *Theorizing Anglo-Saxon Stone Sculpture*, ed. Karkov and Orton, pp. 65–92

Pine, Jo, see sect. 9*c* [bone pinbeater]

Riddler, Ian, 'A Lesser Material: the Working of Roe Deer Antler in England During the Anglo-Saxon Period', *Materials of Manufacture*, ed. Riddler, pp. 41–8

Riddler, Ian, ed., *Materials of Manufacture: the Choice of Materials in the Working of Bone and Antler in Northern and Central Europe during the First Millennium AD*, BAR International Ser. 1193 (Oxford)

Riddler, Ian, and Nicola Trzaska-Nartowski, 'Late Saxon Worked Antler Waste from Holy Rood, Southampton (SOU106)', *Materials of Manufacture*, ed. Riddler, pp. 65–75

Roesdahl, Else, 'Walrus Ivory in the Viking Age – and Ohthere (Ottar)', *Offa* 58 (2003 for 2001), 33–7 [includes brief discussion of location of Ohthere's farm]

Rogan, John, ed., *Bristol Cathedral: History and Architecture* (Stroud, 2000)

Schwab, Ute, 'Bekannte und unbekannte mythische Frauen im Bildprogramm des "Franks Casket"', *Mythological Women*, ed. Rudolf Simek and Wilhelm Heizmann (Viennna, 2002), pp. 125–81 [with eleven plates]

Tatton-Brown, Tim, ed., *Building with Stone in Wessex over 4000 Years* [= *Hatcher Rev.* 5, no. 45] (Winchester, 1998)

Thompson, Victoria, 'Memory, Salvation and Ambiguity: a Consideration of Some Anglo-Scandinavian Grave-Stones from York', *Archaeologies of Remembrance*, ed. Williams, pp. 215–26

Watson, Jacqui, *Basketry from Anslow's Cottages, Berkshire (AM Lab. No. 886119)*, Ancient Monuments Laboratory Report 30/91 (London, 1991) [early Med. eel trap]

White, Andrew, 'A Previously Unrecorded Anglo-Saxon Cross Fragment from Lancaster', *Contrebis* 27 (2002–3), 7–8

Williams, Howard, ed., see sect. 9*d*

Wood, Ian, 'Ruthwell: Contextual Searches', *Theorizing Anglo-Saxon Stone Sculpture*, ed. Karkov and Orton, pp. 104–30 [monastic context of the monument]

Worssam, B. C., 'Anglo-Saxon Building Stone and Stone Sculpture in Wessex', *Building with Stone*, ed. Tatton-Brown, pp. 27–32 [geological aspects]

i. Metalwork

Androschchuk, Fedir, 'The Hvoshcheva Sword: an Example of Contacts between Britain and Scandinavia in the Late Viking Period', *Fornvännen* 98, 35–43 [sword in the Ukraine, possibly from AS Danish centre]

[Anon.], 'Metallic Finds', *Dean Archaeol.* 10 (1997), 15–37 [esp. on an AS spearhead]

'Achievements of the Portable Antiquities Scheme', *Portable Antiquities Ann. Reports* 2 (1999 for 1997–98), 7–31 [esp. on a silver sceat, early Med. metalwork]

'Portable Antiquities and the Study of Material Culture', *Portable Antiquities Ann. Reports* 4 (2002 for 2000–1), 72–85 [esp. on a silver penny and metalwork; also on two figurines, perhaps of Woden]

'Portable Antiquities and the Treasure Act', *Portable Antiquities Ann. Reports* 4 (2002 for 2000–1), 48–55 [esp. on a gold zoomorphic fitting from Yorks.]

'Portable Antiquities as a Source for Understanding the Historic Environment: the Scheme and Sites and Monuments Records', *Portable Antiquities Ann. Reports* 4 (2002 for 2000–1), 60–71 [metalwork finds; also on early cemeteries in Hants. and Lincs.]

'A Viking Ring from Norton', *Tees Archaeol.* 3, [1]

Ashwin, Trevor, *et al.*, see sect. 9*g* [disc brooch]

Axboe, Morten, 'Amulet Pendants and a Darkened Sun: on the Function of the Gold Bracteates and a Possible Motivation for the Large Gold Hoards', *Roman Gold*, ed. Magnus, pp. 119–36 [esp. on bracteates found in England]

Ball, Robert, *Technological Samples from Slough House Farm and Chigborough Farm, Essex*, Ancient Monuments Laboratory Report 12/92 (London, 1992) [evidence for iron-smelting at Slough House Farm in Saxon period]

Bayley, Justine, *Evidence for Anglian Metalworking from Warram Percy, Yorkshire (Sites 94 and 95)*, Ancient Monuments Laboratory Report 26/91 (London, 1991)

Assessment of Slag from Cheapside (Site CID90), Ancient Monuments Laboratory Report 44/92 (London, 1992) [evidence for tenth-century blacksmithing]

Assessment of Metalworking Debris from the Castle Mall Excavations, Norwich, Norfolk, Ancient Monuments Laboratory Report 111/93 (London, 1993) [discusses late Saxon material]

Bierbrauer, Volker, see sect. 9*g* [Insular *Tierstil*]

Bill, Jan, see sect. 9*f* [iron nails]

Blanchard, Ian, see sect. 7 [metallurgy]

Bond, C. J., 'Two Recent Saxon Discoveries in Fladbury', *Vale of Evesham Hist. Soc. Research Papers* 5 (1976), 17–24 [saucer brooch and unassociated burial without grave goods, possibly AS]

Brugmann, Birte, see sect. 9*h* [buckets in archive of J. M. Cook]

Bruns, Dorothee, *Germanic Equal Arm Brooches of the Migration Period: a Study of Style, Chronology and Distribution Including a Full Catalogue of Finds and Contexts*, BAR International Ser. 1113 (Oxford)

Clement, Morag, 'Recent Acquisitions and Reported Finds to Kendal Museum', *Trans. of the Cumberland and Westmorland Ant. and Archaeol. Soc.* 3, 233–7 [esp. on an eighth-century copper alloy object, probably AS]

Corfield, M., 'Radiography of Archaeological Ironwork', *Conservation of Iron*, ed. R. W. Clarke and S. M. Blackshaw, Maritime Monographs and Reports 53 (London, 1982), pp. 8–14 [treats several AS artefacts; discussion, pp. 13–14]

Department for Culture, Media and Sport, *Treasure Annual Report 2001, 1 January–31 December 2001* (London) [items reported as potential treasure, gold or silver; early Med. catalogue, pp. 26–52, lists coins, items 42 and 73]

Edwards, B. J. N., 'An Anglo-Saxon Strap-End from Shap', *Trans. of the Cumberland and Westmorland Ant. and Archaeol. Soc.* 3, 231–3

Gerrard, James, and Sally Mills, 'An Anglo-Saxon Spur from Yeovil', *Chronicle* 8 (2002), 76–7

Gilmour, B., *A Snake Patterned Sword Blade from West Heslerton, North Yorkshire*, Ancient Monuments Laboratory Report 129/91 (London, 1991)

Gittos, Brian, and Moira Gittos, 'Archaeological Unit Report', *Chronicle* 4 (1990), 176–8 [esp. on an AS strap-end]

Gosling, Kevin, see sect. 9*l* [two entries]

Graham-Campbell, James, *Pictish Silver: Status and Symbol*, H. M. Chadwick Memorial Lecture 13 (Cambridge, 2002) [discussion of AS parallels]

Hill, Paul, and Logan Thompson, 'The Swords of the Saxon Cemetery at Mitcham', *Surrey Archaeol. Collections* 90, 147–61

Hillam, Jennifer, see sect. 9*b* [Coppergate]

Hines, John, see sects. 9*a* [early metalwork] and 9*l* [esp. on inscribed disc; three entries]

Hinton, David A., 'A Mid Saxon Disc-Brooch from Upavon', *Wiltshire Archaeol. and Nat. Hist. Mag.* 96, 218–19

Hughes, Mike, ed., see sect. 9*a* [brooches and a hook]

Hutchinson, M. E., see sect. 9*h* [buckle and plate; two entries]

Insley, J., and D. M. Wilson, 'Pentney', *RGA* XXII, 559–61 [six silver openwork disc brooches, discussed by Wilson]

Jewell, Richard, 'An English Romanesque Mount and Three Ninth-Century Strap-Ends', *AntJ* 83, 433–41

Jones, Howard, and David Knight, 'An Anglo-Saxon *seax* from Rampton, Nottinghamshire', *Trans. of the Thoroton Soc. of Nottinghamshire* 106, 47–51

Lindahl, Fritze, 'Some Late Tenth- and Eleventh-Century *cloisonné* Enamel Brooches and Finger-Rings from Denmark', *Through a Glass Brightly: Studies in Byzantine and Medieval Art and Archaeology, presented to David Buckton*, ed. Chris Entwistle (Oxford), pp. 163–70 [AS goldsmiths abroad]

McCulloch, Paul, 'Excavations at Monk Sherborne', *Hampshire Field Club and Archaeol. Soc. Newsletter* 27 (1997), 2–4 [esp. on an AS buckle and plate from site of this Roman villa]

McDonnell, J. G., *Metallurgical Analysis of the Coppergate Weaving Sword*, Ancient Monuments Laboratory Report 95/91 (London, 1991)

The Examination of the Slags and Residues from Mucking, Essex, Ancient Monuments Laboratory Report 4/93 (London, 1993)

McDonnell, J. G., Vanessa Fell, and Phil Andrews, *The Typology of Saxon Knives from Hamwih*, Ancient Monuments Laboratory Report 96/91 (London, 1991)

Magnus, Bente, ed., *Roman Gold and the Development of the Early Germanic Kingdoms: Aspects of Technical, Socio-Political, Socio-Economic, Artistic and Intellectual Development, AD 1–550. Symposium in Stockholm 14–16 November 1997*, Kungl. vitterhets, historie och antikvitets akademien, Konferenser 51 (Stockholm, 2001) [treats bracteates found in England]

Margeson, Sue, 'Viking Mount from Bylaugh', *The Quarterly* 3 (1991), 16–17

Marzinzik, Sonja, *Early Anglo-Saxon Belt Buckles (Late Fifth to Early Eighth Centuries AD): Their Classification and Context*, BAR Brit. Ser. 357 (Oxford)

Mortimer, Catherine, *Metalworking Debris from Thwing, Yorkshire*, Ancient Monuments Laboratory Report 34/92 (London, 1992) [Late Saxon]

Assessment of Non-Ferrous Metal Artefacts from Barrington (Edix Hill Hole), Cambridgeshire Excavations, 1987–1991, Ancient Monuments Laboratory Report 76/93 (London, 1993) [material from AS cemetery]

Mortimer, Catherine, and Brian Gilmour, *Compositional Analysis of Four Early Anglo-Saxon Copper-Alloy Vessels from Loveden Hill, Lincolnshire*, Ancient Monuments Laboratory Report 85/91 (London, 1991)

Müller-Wille, Michael, and Lars Olof Larsson, ed., see sect. 5

Newman, J., and D. M. Metcalf, 'A Gold Bracteate or Uniface from Martlesham, Suffolk', *Proc. of the Suffolk Inst. of Archaeol. and Hist.* 40, 334–5 [inscribed with fictive alphabetic characters and coin-derived decoration]

Nicholas, M., *Copper Alloy Objects from Seven Sites within Mid Saxon London (Lundenwic)*, Centre for Archaeol. Report 36/2003 (Portsmouth)

Northover, Peter, and Kilian Anheuser, 'Gilding in Britain: Celtic, Roman and Saxon', *Gilded Metals: History, Technology and Conservation*, ed. Terry Drayman-Weisser (London, 2000), pp. 109–21

Nurse, Keith, 'Not so Dark Ages: East Anglian Jewellery Finds', *Country Life* 185 (1991), 75 [items from Boss Hall, Ipswich]

Okasha, Elisabeth, see sect. *9l* [inscribed rings]

Okasha, Elisabeth, and Susan Youngs, 'A Late Saxon Inscribed Pendant from Norfolk', *ASE* 32, 225–30

O'Leary, T. J., 'Excavations at Orange Grove and Related Studies', *Archaeology in Bath 1976–1985*, ed. Peter Davenport, Oxford Univ. Committee for Archaeol. Monograph 28 (Oxford, 1991), pp. 1–39 [includes report on a Viking-period sword by Sarah Watkins and David Brown, pp. 1–4]

Page, R. I., see sect. 9*l* [three entries, in items publ. for 1990, 1997 and 2000]

Parsons, David, see sect. 9*l* [two entries]

Plunkett, Steven J., 'Some Recent Metalwork Discoveries from the Area of the Gipping Valley and Their Local Context', *New Offerings, Ancient Treasures: Studies in Medieval*

Art for George Henderson, ed. Paul Binski and William Noel (Stroud, 2001), pp. 61–87

Read, Brian, *Metal Artefacts of Antiquity: a Catalogue of Small Finds from Specific Areas of the United Kingdom, Volume One* (Huish Episcopi, Somerset, 2001) [illustrates finds of metal detectorists; includes AS]

Reuter, Timothy, ed., see sect. 6

Stedman, Mark, 'Two Anglo-Saxon Metalwork Pieces from Shawford, Compton and Shawford Parish, Winchester', *Proc. of the Hampshire Field Club and Archaeol. Soc.* 58, 59–62

Stokes, Michael A., 'An Anglo-Saxon Disc from Shropshire', *West Midlands Archaeol.* 44 (2001), 76–7

'Archaeology in Shrewsbury Museums Service', *Shropshire Hist. and Archaeol.* 76 (2001), 89–90 [esp. on an AS gilt-bronze disc of sixth-century type]

Thomas, Gabor, 'Hamsey near Lewes, East Sussex: the Implications of Recent Finds of Late Anglo-Saxon Metalwork for its Importance in the Pre-Conquest Period', *Sussex Archaeol. Collections* 139 (2003 for 2001), 123–32

[Various], 'Stray Finds', *Cheshire Archaeol. Bull.* 9 (1983), 98–112 [esp. on an AS bronze mount]

'Archaeological Contributions', *Discovery and Excavation in Scotland* 3 (2003 for 2002), 7–125 [esp. on metal-detectorist finds of an AS strap-end and sword-pommel]

Walters, Bryan, ed., 'Summary Observations and Additions to the Archaeological Record', *Dean Archaeol.* 4 (1992 for 1991), 38–47 [discusses an AS silver pin with filigree decoration]

Watkins, Sarah, and David Brown, see above with O'Leary, T. J. [sword]

Watson, Jacqui, see sects. 9*d* [two items, one with G. Edwards] and 9*g* [two items]

Wear, Sara, 'Recent Finds from Warwickshire', *West Midlands Archaeol.* 44 (2001), 105–7 [AS gold terminal, gilded brooch and gold disc]

Webster, Leslie, 'The Anglo-Saxon *Hinterland*: Animal Style in Southumbrian Eighth-Century England, with Particular Reference to Metalwork', *Tiere, Menschen, Götter*, ed. Müller-Wille and Larsson, pp. 39–62

'Metalwork of the Mercian Supremacy', *Mercia: an Anglo-Saxon Kingdom in Europe*, ed. Michelle P. Brown and Carol A. Farr (London, 2001), pp. 263–77

'*Ædificia nova*: Treasures of Alfred's Reign', *Alfred the Great*, ed. Reuter, pp. 79–103

Whitfield, Niamh, 'Round Wire in the Early Middle Ages', *Jewellery Stud.* 4 (1990), 13–28 [includes AS material]

Wilson, D. M., 'Ormside Bowl', *RGA* XXII, 218–20

Wise, Philip J., 'Recent Finds from Essex Reported to Colchester Museums 1998–2000', *Essex Archaeol. and Hist.* 33 (2002), 385–9 [esp. on AS metalwork and coins]

Worrell, Sally, 'Recent Metalwork Discoveries in Hampshire', *Proc. of the Hampshire Field Club and Archaeol. Soc.* 57 (2002), 89–95 [esp. on AS strap-end and stirrup terminal]

Youngs, Susan, '"The Celtic Fringe": Two Enamelled Mounts', *Through a Glass Brightly: Studies in Byzantine and Medieval Art and Archaeology, presented to David Buckton*, ed. Chris Entwistle (Oxford), pp. 155–62 [AS *comparanda*] *j. Pottery and glass*

Allen, Stephen, 'A New Saxon Site in the Kennet Valley, Berkshire: Some Chaff Tempered Ware, its Character and Distant Provenance', *Berkshire Archaeol. Jnl* 76 (2003 for 1998–2003), 68–72

Bacon, Louise, and Barry Knight, ed., *From Pinheads to Hanging Bowls: the Identification, Deterioration and Conservation of Applied Enamel and Glass Decoration on Archaeological Artefacts. The Proceedings of a Conference Held by UKIC Archaeology Section, May 1984*, United Kingdom Inst. for Conservation Occasional Paper 7 (London, 1987)

Bateson, J. D., 'Enamels from Britain to AD 1500', *From Pinheads to Hanging Bowls*, ed. Bacon and Knight, pp. 3–6 [includes AS]

Bayley, Justine, *Crucibles from Minstergate, Thetford, Norfolk*, Ancient Monuments Laboratory Report 15/91 (London, 1991) [mainly early eleventh-century Stamford Ware]

'Glass Bead-Making in Viking York', *CA* 186, 252–3

Blackmore, Lyn, see with Elsden, Nicholas J., in sect. 9*b* [pottery]

Blinkhorn, Paul, *The Ipswich Ware Project Pilot Study* (Northampton, 1994)

Brooks, Catherine, 'Pot Spot: Pingsdorf Ware', *Interim* 6.2 (1979), 40–2

Brown, Duncan H., 'Bound by Tradition: a Study of Pottery in Anglo-Saxon England', *ASSAH* 12, 21–7

Brugmann, Birte, '"Traffic Light Beads" in Early Anglo-Saxon England', *CA* 185, 223–5

Carrington, P., 'Some Types of Late Saxon Pottery from Chester', *Cheshire Archaeol. Bull.* 3 (1975), 3–10

Council for British Archaeology, Group 6 (Norfolk and Suffolk), see sect. 9*a* [kiln]

Cramp, Rosemary J., 'Seventh–Tenth-Century Window Glass from the British Isles', *Glass News* 11 (2002), 2–3

Denham, Varian, see with Bamford, Helen M., *et al.*, in sect. 9*c* [pottery]

Eagles, Bruce, and Diana Briscoe, 'Animal and Bird Stamps on Early Anglo-Saxon Pottery in England', *Studien zur Sachsenforschung* 13 (1999), 99–111

Gerrard, Chris, and Phil Marter, 'Database of Medieval Pottery Production Centres in England: a New Resource for Archaeology', *Soc. for Med. Archaeol. Newsletter* 28, [10–11] [pottery dated from *c.* 850 on]

Hughes, M. J., 'Enamels: Materials, Deterioration and Analysis', *From Pinheads to Hanging Bowls*, ed. Bacon and Knight, pp. 10–12 [esp. on Dark Age reds and yellows]

Hunter, Kate, and Kate Foley, 'The Lincoln Hanging Bowl', *From Pinheads to Hanging Bowls*, ed. Bacon and Knight, pp. 16–18 [esp. on enamelled escutcheons]

Leary, Jim, and Kim Stabler, 'The Kingston Rotunda: Further Evidence for Early Medieval Pottery Production in Kingston', *Surrey Archaeol. Soc. Bull.* 353 (2001), 13

Linford, P. K., and N. Linford, see sect. 9*c* [clay oven]

Mainman, Ailsa, 'Pagan Pottery', *Yorkshire Archaeol. Today* 5, 13 [pottery and glass beads as evidence for a third AS cemetery on Heslington Hill, near York]

Maul, Birgit, *Frühmittelalterliche Gläser des 5.–7./8. Jahrhunderts n. Chr: Sturzbecher, glocken-*

förmige Becher, Tummler und Glockentummler, 2 vols., Universitätsforschungen zur prähistorischen Archäologie 84 (Bonn, 2002) [includes AS]

Mortimer, Catherine, *Chemical Analysis of Fragments from Two Early Saxon Glass Vessels from Carisbrooke Castle, Isle of Wight*, Ancient Monuments Laboratory Report 22/91 (London, 1991)

X-Ray Fluorescence Analysis of Early Anglo-Saxon Glass Beads from Market Lavington, Wiltshire, Ancient Monuments Laboratory Report 30/92 (London, 1992)

Noël Hume, Ivor, *'If these pots could talk': Collecting 2,000 Years of British Household Pottery* (Milwaukee, WI, 2001) [in ch. 2]

Pine, Jo, see sect. 9*c* [pottery]

Riddler, Ian, 'The Finds Department, 3: Anglo-Saxon Ceramic Weights from the Ramsgate Harbour Approach Road', *Canterbury's Archaeol.* 23 (2001 for 1998–9), 64–5

Steppuhn, Peter, 'Der mittelalterliche Gniedelstein: Glättglas oder Glasbarren? Zu Primärfunktion und Kontinuität eines Glasobjektes vom Frühmittelalter bis zur Neuzeit', *Nachrichten aus Niedersachsens Urgeschichte* 68 (1999), 113–39 [includes AS examples]

Stiff, Matthew, 'Anglo-Saxon Vessel Glass', *CA* 186, 250–1

Symonds, Leigh Andrea, *Landscape and Social Practice: the Production and Consumption of Pottery in Tenth Century Lincolnshire*, BAR Brit. Ser. 345 (Oxford)

Träger, Angelika, 'Die Verbreitung der Stempelverzierung auf der Keramik des 5.–8. Jh. zwischen Oder/Neisse und Weser', *Arbeits- und Forschungsberichte zur sächsischen Bodendenkmalpflege* 29 (1985), 159–225 [includes AS material]

Vierck, H., 'Noel Myres und die Besiedlung Englands', *Praehistorische Zeitschrift* 51 (1976), 43–55

Williams, D. F., *A Note on the Petrology of Mediaeval Pottery from the 1988–89 Excavations at Eckweek Farmstead, Avon*, Ancient Monuments Laboratory Report 7/91 (London, 1991) [late Saxon to late Med. pottery]

A Note on the Petrology of Some Late Saxon/Early Mediaeval Pottery from West Cotton, Northamptonshire, Ancient Monuments Laboratory Report 59/92 (London, 1992)

A Petrological Examination of Some Early Saxon Pottery from Leicester, Ancient Monuments Laboratory Report 13/92 (London, 1992)

A Petrological Note on Pottery from Sancton Anglo-Saxon Cemetery, Humberside, Ancient Monuments Laboratory Report 15/92 (London, 1992)

k. Textiles and leather

Boardman, Kate L., 'John Collingwood Bruce and His Bayeux Tapestry Facsimile', *AAe* 32, 179–88

Brooks, Mary M., *et al.*, ed., *Textiles Revealed: Object Lessons in Historic Textile and Costume Research* (London, 2000) [ed. Brooks, with Joanna M. Marschner and Philip A. Sykas serving as 'editorial panel']

Crowfoot, Elisabeth, *Textiles: Wakerley, Northants. Anglo-Saxon Cemetery*, Ancient Monuments Laboratory Report 44/88 (London, 1988)

Textile: Carisbrooke Castle, Isle of Wight, Ancient Monuments Laboratory Report 75/91 (London, 1991) [from early AS burials]

Crummy, Nina, 'From Self-Sufficiency to Commerce: Structural and Artifactual Evidence for Textile Manufacture in Eastern England in the Pre-Conquest Period', *Encountering Medieval Textiles and Dress: Objects, Texts, Images*, ed. Désirée G. Koslin and Janet E. Snyder (Basingstoke, 2002), pp. 25–43

Foys, Martin K., '"All's well that ends": Closure, Hypertext and the Missing End of the Bayeux Tapestry', *Exemplaria* 15, 39–72

see also sect. 6

Granger-Taylor, Hero, 'The Earth and Ocean Silk from the Tomb of St Cuthbert at Durham; Further Details', *Ancient and Medieval Textiles: Studies in honour of Donald King*, ed. Lisa Monnas and Hero Granger-Taylor (London, [1989]), pp. 151–66

Jenkins, David, ed., *The Cambridge History of Western Textiles*, 1 vol. in 2 (Cambridge)

King, Donald, 'English Embroidery before Alfred the Great', *Textiles Revealed*, ed. Brooks *et al.*, pp. 33–7

Ling, Lesley A., 'The Bayeux Tapestry', *Making Medieval Art*, ed. Phillip Lindley (Donington), pp. 104–19

Matthews, Karen Rose, 'Nudity on the Margins: the Bayeux Tapestry and its Relationship to Marginal Architectural Sculpture', *Naked before God*, ed. Withers and Wilcox, pp. 138–61 [also on links to AS art]

Mould, Quita, Ian Carlisle, and Esther Cameron, *Craft, Industry and Everyday Life: Leather and Leatherworking in Anglo-Scandinavian and Medieval York*, Archaeol. of York 17.16 (York)

Musset, Lucien, see sect. 6 [Bayeux 'tapestry']

Muthesius, Anna, 'A Previously Unrecognised Lion Silk at Canterbury Cathedral', *The Roman Textile Industry*, ed. Rogers *et al.*, pp. 148–57 [of ninth- or tenth-century date; early provenance not stated]

Rogers, Walton Penelope, 'The Re-Appearance of an Old Roman Loom in Medieval England', *The Roman Textile Industry*, ed. Rogers *et al.*, pp. 158–71

'The Anglo-Saxons and Vikings in Britain, AD 450–1050', *The Cambridge History of Western Textiles*, ed. Jenkins, pp. 124–32

Rogers, Penelope Walton, Lise Bender Jørgensen and Antoinette Rast-Eicher, ed., *The Roman Textile Industry and its Influence: a Birthday Tribute to John Peter Wild* (Oxford, 2001)

Watson, Jacqui, see sect. 9*d* [material from cemetery]

Withers, Benjamin C., and Jonathan Wilcox, ed., see sect. 3*a*

l. Inscriptions

Åhfeldt, Laila Kitzler, *Work and Worship: Laser Scanner Analysis of Viking Age Rune Stones*, Theses and Papers in Archaeol. B:9 (Stockholm, 2002) ['Workshops for English Stone Sculpture', in ch. I.7]

[Anon.], 'Runic Research in the British Isles, the Netherlands, and Belgium', *Nytt om runer* 5 (1991 for 1990), 27–31

'Roman and Medieval Inscriptions Found in Norfolk', *Brit. Archaeol.* 72, 7 [discusses two lead plaques, one certainly AS, the other displaying Norse runes]

Axelson, Jan, James E. Knirk and K. Jonas Nordby, 'Runic Bibliography for 2001', *Nytt om runer* 17 (2002), 47–66

'Supplements to the Runic Bibliographies for 1999 and 2000', *Nytt om runer* 17 (2002), 66–72

Bammesberger, Alfred, 'Editing Old English Runic Inscriptions', *Anglistentag 1993 Eichstätt: Proceedings*, ed. Günther Blaicher and Brigitte Glaser (Tübingen, 1994), pp. 503–15

Bammesberger, Alfred, and Gaby Waxenberger, 'Old English and Old Frisian Runic Inscriptions Databank at Katholische Universität Eichstatt, Germany', *Nytt om runer* 10 (1996 for 1995), 20–1

Bauer, Alessia, see sect. 3*a* [*runica manuscripta*]

Carver, Martin, ed., see sect. 6

Charles-Edwards, Gifford, 'The East Cross Inscription from Toureen Peacaun: Letterform Analysis and a Suggested Reading', *Archaeol. Ireland* 17.1, 13–15 [includes an AS name, Osgyd]

Clunies Ross, Margaret, see sect. 7 [coin]

Derolez, René, 'Some New Runes and the Problem of Runic Unity', *Runor och runinskrifter*, ed. Kungl. vitterhets, historie och antikvitets akademien, pp. 55–72 [esp. on Eng. evidence; includes discussion, pp. 67–72, addressing Spong Hill runes]

Dickinson, Steve, see sect. 9*e* [inscription on cross fragment from Cumbria]

Düwel, Klaus, 'Runeninschriften', *RGA* XXV, 525–37

'Runenschrift', *RGA* XXV, 571–85

'Runen und Runendenkmäler', *RGA* XXV, 499–512

Düwel, Klaus, ed., with Hannelore Neumann and Sean Nowak, *Runische Schriftkultur in kontinental–skandinavischer und -angelsächsischer Wechselbeziehung. Internationales Symposium in der Werner-Reimers-Stiftung vom 24.–27. Juni 1992 in Bad Homburg*, Ergänzungsbände zum *RGA* 10 (Berlin, 1994)

Düwel, Klaus, and R. I. Page, 'Inschriften', *RGA* XV, 445–50 ['England, Runic and Latin Inscriptions', sect. 3, by Page]

Gosling, Kevin, 'An Anglo-Saxon Runic Inscription from Leicestershire, England', *Nytt om runer* 3 (1989 for 1988), 14 [also for metalwork]

'Runic Finds from London', *Nytt om runer* 4 (1989), 12–13 [also for metalwork]

Gräslund, A.-S., and K. Düwel, 'Runensteine', *RGA* XXV, 585–96

Hart, Clive R., and Elisabeth Okasha, see sect. 9*h* [stone bowl]

Higgitt, John, 'Design and Meaning in Early Medieval Inscriptions in Britain and Ireland', *The Cross Goes North*, ed. Carver, pp. 327–38

Hines, John, 'A New Runic Inscription from South Humberside, England', *Nytt om runer* 4 (1989), 14 [also for metalwork]

'A New Runic Inscription from Norfolk', *Nytt om runer* 6 (1991), 6–7 [also for metalwork]

'An Inscribed Disc from the River Yare near Norwich', *Nytt om runer* 12 (1998 for 1997), 13–15

Isakson, Bo, 'The Problematic *ga:sric* on the Franks Casket', *North-Western European Lang. Evolution* 43, 65–70

Kornexl, Lucia, and Ursula Lenker, ed., see sect. 3*a*

Kungl. vitterhets, historie och antikvitets akademien, ed., *Runor och runinskrifter. Föredrag vid Riksantikvarieämbetets och Vitterhetsakademiens symposium 8–11 September 1985*, Kungl. vitterhets, historie och antikvitets akademien, Konferenser 15 (Stockholm, 1987) [papers from Second International Symposium on Runes and Runic Inscriptions]

Looijenga, Tineke, *Texts and Contexts of the Oldest Runic Inscriptions*, Northern World 4 (Leiden) ['Early Runic Inscriptions in England', ch. 8; also esp. in sects. 1.6 and 2.9]

McKinnell, John, 'A Runic Fragment from Lincoln', *Nytt om runer* 10 (1996 for 1995), 10–11

MacLeod, Mindy, *Bind-Runes: an Investigation of Ligatures in Runic Epigraphy*, Runrön 15 (Uppsala, 2002) [esp. in sects. 2.3 and 4.7.1]

Nedoma, R., see sect. 2*a* [on *Runennamen*]

Newman, J., and D. M. Metcalf, see sect. 9*i* [fictive alphabetic characters on bracteate]

Odenstedt, Bengt, 'The Runic Inscription on the Undley Bracteate', *SN* 72 (2000), 113–20

Okasha, Elisabeth, 'Spaces between Words: Word Separation in Anglo-Saxon Inscriptions', *The Cross Goes North*, ed. Carver, pp. 339–49

'Anglo-Saxon Inscribed Rings', *Leeds Stud. in Eng.* ns 33, 29–45

Okasha, Elisabeth, and Susan Youngs, see sect. 9*i* [pendant]

Owen-Crocker, Gale R., see sect. 8 [names of women]

Page, R. I., 'New Runic Finds in England', *Runor och runinskrifter*, ed. Kungl. vitterhets, historie och antikvitets akademien, pp. 185–97

'A New Find from Cumbria, England', *Nytt om runer* 5 (1991 for 1990), 13 [also for metalwork]

'English Runes Imported into the Continent', *Runische Schriftkultur*, ed. Düwel, pp. 176–94

'Epigraphical Runes in Worcester', *Nytt om runer* 9 (1994), 17

'An Anglo-Saxon Runic Ring', *Nytt om runer* 12 (1998 for 1997), 11–12

'Runes at the Royal Opera House, London', *Nytt om runer* 12 (1998 for 1997), 12–13

'New Anglo-Saxon Rune Finds', *Nytt om runer* 15 (2001 for 2000), 10–11 [also for metalwork]

Page, R. I., and M. L. Nielsen, see sect. 7 [on *Runenmünzen*]

Parsons, David, 'New Runic Finds from Brandon, Suffolk', *Nytt om runer* 6 (1991), 8–11 [also for metalwork]

'German Runes in Kent?', *Nytt om runer* 7 (1992), 7–8 [also for metalwork]

see also in sect. 3*a* [on *runica manuscripta*] and also there with Bammesberger, A., *et al.* [on *Runenreihen*]

Quak, Arend, 'Die friesischen Inschriften im Spiegel kontinental–angelsächsischer Wechselbeziehung', *Runische Schriftkultur*, ed. Düwel, pp. 221–8

Schwab, Ute, 'Weitere angelsächsische Runen in Rom', *Nytt om runer* 17 (2002), 17–18

'More Anglo-Saxon Runic Grafitti in Roman Catacombs', *OEN* 37.1, 36–9

Schwab, Ute, and René Derolez, 'More Runes at Monte Sant'Angelo', *Nytt om runer* 9 (1994), 18–19 [discussion of Eng. names]

Waxenberger, Gaby, 'The Intriguing Inscription of the Gandersheim Runic Casket Revisited', *Bookmarks from the Past*, ed. Kornexl and Lenker, pp. 143–76

see also sect. 8 [corpus of non-Latin personal names]

10. REVIEWS

Anderson, Earl R., *Folk-Taxonomies in Early English* (Madison, NJ): P. Augustyn, *Jnl of Indo-European Stud.* 31, 483–91

Baker, Peter S., *Introduction to Old English* (Oxford): R. D. Stevick, *Envoi* 10, 100–3

Baker, Peter S., ed., *MS F*, The Anglo-Saxon Chronicle: a Collaborative Edition 8 (Woodbridge, 2000): E. G. Stanley, *EHR* 117, 676–7

Barlow, Frank, *The Godwins: the Rise and Fall of a Noble Dynasty* (Harlow, 2002): L. Abrams, *TLS* 8 March 2002, 30

Barnhouse, Rebecca, and Benjamin C. Withers, ed., *The Old English Hexateuch: Aspects and Approaches* (Kalamazoo, MI, 2000): C. Hough, *MLR* 98, 436–8

Bassett, Steven, *Anglo-Saxon Coventry and its Churches* (Stratford-upon-Avon, 2001): M. J. Franklin, *JEH* 113, 532–3; K. Lilley, *Landscape Hist.* 24, 148–9; A. Reynolds, *History* 88, 115–16; B. Yorke, *Midland Hist.* 27, 183

Bedingfield, M. Bradford, *The Dramatic Liturgy of Anglo-Saxon England* (Woodbridge, 2002): R. Pfaff, *Med. Rev.* [online]; M. Swan, *MÆ* 72, 321–3

Bergmann, Rolf, Elvira Glaser and Claudine Moulin-Fankhänel, ed., *Mittelalterliche volkssprachige Glossen* (Heidelberg, 2001): J. C. Frakes, *JEGP* 102, 295–7; A. Poppenborg, *Niederdeutsches Jahrbuch* 126, 165–8

Binski, Paul, and William Noel, ed., *New Offerings, Ancient Treasures: Studies in Medieval Art for George Henderson* (Stroud, 2001): N. Saul, *JEH* 54, 114–15

Boenig, Robert, trans., *Anglo-Saxon Spirituality: Selected Writings* (New York, 2000): M. Frohlich, *Catholic Lib. World* 72, 167

Bredehoft, Thomas A., *Textual Histories: Readings in the 'Anglo-Saxon Chronicle'* (Toronto, 2001): R. E. Bjork, *Speculum* 78, 841–3

Brooke, Christopher, *The Saxon and Norman Kings*, 3rd ed. (Oxford, 2001): F. Barlow, *EHR* 117, 678–9

Brooks, Nicholas, *Anglo-Saxon Myths: State and Church 400–1066* (London, 2000): S. Foot, *History* 87, 117–18; D. P. Kirby, *JEH* 53, 130–2; J. Story, *EconHR* 55, 349

Communities and Warfare, 700–1400 (London, 2000): S. Foot, *History* 87, 117–18; D. P. Kirby, *JEH* 53, 130–2; J. Story, *EconHR* 55, 349; S. Walton, *Jnl of Military Hist.* 65, 781–2

Brown, Michelle P., and Carol A. Farr, ed., *Mercia: an Anglo-Saxon Kingdom in Europe* (London, 2001): J. Blair, *Landscape Hist.* 24, 147–8; A. Burghart, *EME* 11, 283–4

Browne, Gerald M., ed., *Collectio psalterii Bedae Venerabili adscripta* (Leipzig, 2001): D. Weber, *Zeitschrift für antikes Christentum* 6, 222

Caie, Graham D., *The Old English Poem 'Judgement Day II': a Critical Edition with Editions of 'De die iudicii' and the Hatton 113 Homily 'Be domes dæge'* (Cambridge, 2000): F. M. Biggs, *MLR* 98, 153–4

Campbell, Alistair, ed., *Encomium Emmae Reginae*, with suppl. by Simon Keynes (Cambridge, 1998): H. Tanner, *Med. Rev.* [online]

Campbell, James, *The Anglo-Saxon State* (London, 2000): S. Foot, *JEH* 54, 123–4

Caputa, Giovanni, *Il sacerdozio dei fedeli secondo San Beda. Un itinerario di maturità cristiana* (Vatican City, 2002): A. Haquin, *Revue d'histoire ecclésiastique* 98, 690–1

Cavill, Paul, *Maxims in Old English Poetry* (Cambridge, 1999): K. H. Scholz, *Anglia* 121, 648–50

Clemoes, Peter, ed., *Ælfric's Catholic Homilies: The First Series. Text* (Oxford, 1997): D. G. Scragg, see sect. 3*c*

Coatsworth, Elizabeth, and Michael Pinder, *The Art of the Anglo-Saxon Goldsmith: Fine Metalwork in Anglo-Saxon England, its Practice and Practitioners* (Woodbridge, 2002): M. Welch, *Med. Archaeol.* 47, 359–60

Conrad O'Briain, Helen, Anne Marie D'Arcy, and John Scattergood, ed., *Text and Gloss: Studies in Insular Learning and Literature* (Dublin, 1999): H. Gneuss, *Anglia* 121, 102–3

de Dreuille, Christophe, ed., *L'église et la mission au VIe siècle. La mission d'Augustin de Cantorbéry et les églises de Gaule sous l'impulsion de Grégoire le Grand* (Paris, 2000): B. Merdrignac, *Revue historique* 303, 760–3

Dendle, Peter, *Satan Unbound: the Devil in Old English Literature* (Toronto, 2001): R. Dance, *MÆ* 72, 131; K. Powell, *Envoi* 10, 132–5; C. Rauer, *N&Q* 50, 87–8

DeVries, Kelly, *The Norwegian Invasion of England in 1066* (Woodbridge, 1999): S. Morillo, *Jnl of Military Hist.* 64, 820–1

Dockray-Miller, Mary, *Motherhood and Mothering in Anglo-Saxon England* (New York, 2000): J. A. Smith, *Parergon* ns 19.2, 184–6

Dodwell, C. R., *Anglo-Saxon Gestures and the Roman Stage* (Cambridge, 2000): J. C. Conde Silvestre, *SELIM: Jnl of the Spanish Soc. for Med. Eng. Lang. and Lit.* 10, 169–75

Donaldson, E. Talbot, trans., Nicholas Howe, ed., *Beowulf: a Prose Translation. Backgrounds and Contexts, Criticism*, 2nd ed. (London, 2002): A. Orchard, *N&Q* 50, 80–1

Düwel, Klaus, ed., *Runeninschriften als Quellen interdisziplinärer Forschung* (Berlin, 1998): H. Birkhan, *Anglia* 121, 633–9; H. Perridon, *IROS: International Rev. of Scandinavian Stud.* 1998–9, 125

Feulner, Anna Helene, *Die griechischen Lehnwörter im Altenglischen*, Texte und Untersuchungen zur englischen Philologie 21 (Frankfurt am Main, 2000): G. H. Brown, *Speculum* 78, 878–9; F. Schleburg, *Kratylos* 48, 227–9

Fischer, Olga, *et al.*, *The Syntax of Early English* (Cambridge, 2000): M. den Dikken, *Lingua* 112, 415–22; S. Pintzuk, *Eng. Lang. and Ling.* 7, 327–33

Fisiak, Jacek, and Peter Trudgill, ed., *East Anglian English* (Cambridge, 2001): F. Chevillet, *EA* 56, 336–7

Foley, W. Trent, and Arthur G. Holder, trans., *Bede: a Biblical Miscellany* (Liverpool, 1999): J. Auwers, *Revue d'histoire ecclésiastique* 98, 124

Foot, Sarah, *Veiled Women*, 2 vols. (Aldershot, 2000): M. Frigge, *Amer. Benedictine Rev.* 54, 104–7; M. Giese, *DAEM* 59, 835; B. L. Venarde, *Speculum* 78, 171–3;

Fulk, R. D., and Christopher M. Cain, *A History of Old English Literature* (Oxford): E. Treharne, *RES* 54, 677–9

Gameson, Richard, ed., *St Augustine and the Conversion of England* (Stroud, 1999): D. Walker, *Welsh Hist. Rev.* 20, 574–5

Gaşiorowski, Piotr, *The Phonology of Old English Stress and Metrical Structure* (Frankfurt am Main, 1997): J. Hitchcock, *Ling. and Lang. Behavior Abstracts: LLBA* 33, 121

Geake, Helen, *The Use of Grave-Goods in Conversion-Period England,* c. *600–*c. *850* (Oxford, 1997): E. O'Brien, *Peritia* 16, 507–10

Gneuss, Helmut, *Handlist of Anglo-Saxon Manuscripts: a List of Manuscripts and Manuscript Fragments Written or Owned in England up to 1100* (Tempe, AZ, 2001): J. Hill, *N&Q* 50, 343–4

Ælfric von Eynsham und seine Zeit, Bayerische Akademie der Wissenschaften, Phil.–Hist. Klasse, Sitzungsberichte 1 (Munich, 2002): R. Schieffer, *DAEM* 59, 852

Godden, Malcolm, ed., *Ælfric's Catholic Homilies: Introduction, Commentary and Glossary*, EETS ss 18 (Oxford, 2000): J. Hill, *RES* 54, 399–400; A. P. Scheil, *Med. Rev.* [online]; D. G. Scragg, see sect. 3*c*

Graham, Timothy, ed., *The Recovery of Old English: Anglo-Saxon Studies in the Sixteenth and Seventeenth Centuries* (Kalamazoo, MI, 2000): T. N. Hall, *Anglia* 121, 124–6; C. Hough, *MLR* 98, 436–8; D. P. O'Donnell, *EME* 11, 93–5

Graham-Campbell, James, *et al.*, ed., *Vikings and the Danelaw: Select Papers from the Proceedings of the Thirteenth Viking Congress* (Oxford, 2001): B. Crawford, *ArchJ* 159, 333–4

Green, Eugene, *Anglo-Saxon Audiences* (New York, 2001): L. Carruthers, *Le Moyen Âge* 109, 615–16; G. Morgan, *Med. Rev.* [online]

Gretsch, Mechthild, *The Intellectual Foundations of the English Benedictine Reform* (Cambridge, 1999): J. Hill, *Anglia* 121, 118–20; P. Wormald, *JEH* 53, 142–3

Gryson, Roger, ed., *Bedae presbyteri Expositio Apocalypseos*, CCSL 121A (Turnhout, 2001): É. Rousseau, *Nouvelle revue théologique* 125, 339; A. Ward, *Ephemerides Liturgicae* 117, 249–50; B. Ward, *JTS* 54, 355–7

Hadley, Dawn M., *The Northern Danelaw: its Social Structure,* c. *800–1100* (London, 2000): D. M. Palliser, *Midland Hist.* 28, 144–6; D. Roffe, *History* 87, 117

Death in Medieval England: an Archaeology (Stroud, 2001): C. Dyer, *EHR* 117, 681–2; B. Sloane, *Antiquity* 76, 588–9

Hadley, Dawn M., and Julian Richards, ed., *Cultures in Contact: Scandinavian Settlement in England in the Ninth and Tenth Centuries* (Turnhout, 2000): M. Clunies Ross, *Parergon* ns 19.2, 200–2; J. Hines, *ArchJ* 159, 332–3; R. Poole, *JEGP* 102, 136–8; S. Yarrow, *EME* 12, 183–5

Hall, Thomas N., ed., *Via Crucis: Essays on Early Medieval Sources and Ideas in memory of J. E. Cross* (Morgantown, WV, 2002): M. Swan, *Anglia* 121, 645–7

Hamerow, Helena, *Early Medieval Settlements: the Archaeology of Rural Communities in Northwest Europe, 400–900* (Oxford, 2002): G. Halsall, *EHR* 118, 1305–6; J. Hines, *Med. Rev.* [online]; D. Hooke, *Landscape Hist.* 25, 97–8

Harbus, Antonina, *The Life of the Mind in Old English Poetry*, Costerus ns 143 (Amsterdam, 2002): R. Dunn, *Parergon* ns 20.2, 200–2

Hatz, Gert, *Der Münzfund vom Goting-Kliff/Föhr*, Numismatische Studien 14 (Hamburg, 2001): D. M. Metcalf, *NChron* 163, 420–1

Heaney, Seamus, trans., *Beowulf* (London, 1999): S. A. J. Bradley, *Cambridge Quarterly* 30, 82–6; J. McGowan, see sect. 3*bi*; H. Sauer and I. B. Milfull, see sect. 3*bii*

Heaney, Seamus, trans., Daniel Donoghue, ed., *Beowulf: a Verse Translation. Authoritative Text, Contexts, Criticism* (New York, 2002): A. Orchard, *N&Q* 50, 80–1

Higgitt, John, Katherine Forsyth and David N. Parsons, ed., *Roman, Runes and Ogham: Medieval Inscriptions in the Insular World and on the Continent* (Donington, 2001): D. J. Waugh, *Nomina* 26, 131–3

Higham, N. J., and D. H. Hill, ed., *Edward the Elder, 899–924* (London, 2000): S. Foot, *History* 88, 114–15; E. James, *Speculum* 78, 1316–18

Hill, John M., *The Anglo-Saxon Warrior Ethic: Reconstructing Lordship in Early English Literature* (Gainesville, FL, 2000): B. Bachrach, *Med. Rev.* [online]; R. E. Bjork, *Speculum* 78, 1318–19; C. Rauer, *MLR* 98, 151

Horner, Shari, *The Discourse of Enclosure: Representing Women in Old English Literature* (Albany, NY, 2001): A. Savage, *Speculum* 78, 520–3

Hough, Carole, and Kathryn A. Lowe, ed., *'Lastworda betst': Essays in memory of Christine E. Fell with her Unpublished Writings* (Donington, 2002): R. Dance, *MÆ* 72, 126–7; G. Fellows-Jensen, *Nomina* 26, 134–7; R. Marsden, *Nottingham Med. Stud.* 47, 239–43; R. Poole, *N&Q* 50, 79; A. Woolf, *JEPNS* 35, 67–9

Houwen, L. A. J. R., and A. A. MacDonald, ed., *Beda Venerabilis*, Mediaevalia Groningana 19 (Groningen, 1996): D. Rollason, *Histos* (Durham) 1 [online]

Alcuin of York, Scholar at the Carolingian Court, Germania Latina 3 [= Mediaevalia Groningana 22] (Groningen, 1998): G. Silagi, *DAEM* 58, 683

Jones, Christopher A., ed., *Ælfric's Letter to the Monks of Eynsham* (Cambridge, 1998): Y. Hen, *Revue belge de philologie et d'histoire* 79, 1421

Kabir, Ananya Jahanara, *Paradise, Death and Doomsday in Anglo-Saxon Literature*, CSASE 32 (Cambridge, 2001): H. Magennis, *N&Q* 50, 85–6; F. C. Robinson, *Albion* 35, 257–8; O. M. Traxel, *Anglia* 121, 305–8

Karkov, Catherine E., *Text and Picture in Anglo-Saxon England: Narrative Strategies in the Junius 11 Manuscript*, CSASE 31 (Cambridge, 2001): R. Gameson and F. Gameson, *N&Q* 50, 83–5; S. J. Harris, *Med. Rev.* [online]; G. Russom, *Speculum* 78, 541–2; M. F. Smith, *Albion* 35, 91–2; O. M. Traxel, *Anglia* 121, 305–8

Keats-Rohan, K. S. B., *Domesday People: a Prosopography of Persons Occurring in English Documents, 1066–1166, I. Domesday Book* (Woodbridge, 1999): M. Gervers, *Med. Rev.* [online]

Kelly, S. E., ed., *Charters of Selsey*, AS Charters 6 (Oxford, 1998): A. R. Rumble, *History* 88, 295

Charters of Abingdon Abbey, Part I, AS Charters 7 (Oxford, 2000): A. J. Kosto, *Med. Rev.* [online]

Charters of Abingdon Abbey, Parts I–II, AS Charters 7–8 (Oxford, 2000–1): R. Faith, *EHR* 117, 945–7; S. Foot, *JEH* 54, 115–17

Kieling, Michał, *Terrena non amare sed coelestia. Theologie der Welt in Alkuins 'Commentaria super Ecclesiasten'* (Frankfurt am Main, 2002): S. Vanderputten, *Revue d'histoire ecclésiastique* 98, 692

Lambdin, Robert Thomas, and Laura Cooner Lambdin, ed., *A Companion to Old and*

Middle English Literature (Westport, CT, 2002): B. L. Eden, *Amer. Reference Books Ann.* 34, 491–2

Lang, James T., *et al.*, *Corpus of Anglo-Saxon Stone Sculpture*, VI: *Northern Yorkshire* (Oxford, 2001): P. Everson, *AntJ* 83, 502–4; J. Graham-Campbell, *SBVS* 27, 104–5; C. E. Karkov, *Med. Archaeol.* 47, 358–9

Lapidge, Michael, *Anglo-Latin Literature, 600–899* (London, 1996): P. Orth, *Mittellateinisches Jahrbuch* 38, 297–8

Lapidge, Michael, Gian Carlo Garfagnini, and Claudio Leonardi, ed., *CALMA Compendium Auctorum Latinorum Medii Aevi (500–1500)*, I.1: *Abaelardus Petrus – Agobardus Lugdunensis archiep.* (Florence, 2000): M. Giovini, *Maia* 55, 196–7, J. M. Ziolkowski, *Speculum* 78, 553–5; I.2: *Agobardus Lugdunensis archiep. – Anastasius Bibliothecarius* (Florence, 2000): A. Bartòla, *Bulletin Du Cange/Archivum Latinitatis Medii Aevi* 59, 297–302; I.1–2 (Florence, 2000): V. Lukas, *DAEM* 58, 590–1; I.3: *Anastasius Montis Sancti Michaelis abb. – Antonius Galatheus* (Florence, 2001): A. Bartòla, *Bulletin Du Cange/Archivum Latinitatis Medii Aevi* 61, 313–17; and I.1–4 (Florence, 2000–1): J. Pycke, *Revue d'histoire ecclésiastique* 98, 540–2

Lapidge, Michael, Simon Keynes and Malcolm Godden, ed., *Anglo-Saxon England* 30 (Cambridge, 2001): R. Dance, *MÆ* 72, 183–4; C. Larrington, *RES* 54, 679–80

Lapidge, Michael, *et al.*, ed., *The Blackwell Encyclopaedia of Anglo-Saxon England* (Oxford, 1999): J. Insley, *Anglia* 121, 639–43

Lavelle, Ryan, *Aethelred II: King of the English, 978–1016* (Stroud, 2002): N. Higham, *History* 88, 670–1

Lawson, M. K., *The Battle of Hastings 1066* (Stroud, 2002): S. Morillo, *Jnl of Military Hist.* 67, 548–9; H. Nicholson, *History* 88, 671–2

Lees, Clare A., and Gillian R. Overing, *Double Agents: Women and Clerical Culture in Anglo-Saxon England* (Philadelphia, 2001): C. S. Cox, *Choice* (Chicago) 39, 1960; V. L. Garver, *EME* 12, 194–5; R. Jayatilaka, *MÆ* 72, 132–3; C. Larrington, *RES* 54, 400–2; M. P. Richards, *Speculum* 78, 940–1; K. Walsh, *DAEM* 59, 366–7

Leimus, Ivar, and Arkadi Molvõgin, *Estonian Collections: Anglo-Saxon, Anglo-Norman and Later British Coins*, SCBI 51 (Oxford, 2001): H. Pagan, *BNJ* 72, 217

Liuzza, R. M., trans., *Beowulf* (Peterborough, ON, 2000): S. Valenzuela, *SELIM: Jnl of the Spanish Soc. for Med. Eng. Lang. and Lit.* 10, 193–200

Lowe, Chris, *Angels, Fools and Tyrants: Britons and Anglo-Saxons in Southern Scotland AD 450–750* (Edinburgh, 1999): D. Gregory, *Scottish Hist. Rev.* 81, 255–7

Loyn, H. R., *The English Church, 940–1154* (2000): H. Vollrath, *DAEM* 59, 410–11

Magennis, Hugh, ed., *The Old English Life of St Mary of Egypt: an Edition of the Old English Text with Modern English Parallel-Text Translation* (Exeter, 2002): F. De Vriendt, *AB* 121, 422–4; A. Harbus, *Parergon* ns 20.2, 210–12; J. Hill, *EME* 12, 191–2; R. Jayatilaka, *MÆ* 72, 323; R. Dance, *ES* 84, 392; P. Shaw, *Leeds Stud. in Eng.* ns 33, 205–7

Marocco Stuardi, Donatella, *Alcuino di York nella tradizione degli 'specula principis'* (Milan, 1999): M. T. Ferrer Mallol, *Anuario de estudios medievales* 33, 981

Miles, David, ed., with Rohini Jayatilaka and Malcolm Godden, *Fontes Anglo-Saxonici: a*

Register of Written Sources Used by Anglo-Saxon Authors. CD-ROM Version I.1 (Oxford, 2002): S. J. Harris, *N&Q* 50, 342–3

Miller, Sean, ed., *Charters of the New Minster, Winchester*, AS Charters 9 (Oxford, 2001): A. J. Kosto, *Med. Rev.* [online]

Minkova, Donka, *Alliteration and Sound Change in Early English* (Cambridge): R. D. Fulk, *Eng. Lang. and Ling.* 7, 347–51

Offer, Clifford, *In Search of 'Clofesho': the Case for Hitchin* (Norwich, 2002): B. Yorke, *History* 88, 670

Ohkado, Masayuki, *Old English Constructions with Multiple Predicates* (Tokyo, 2001): Y. Iyeiri, *Stud. in Med. Eng. Lang. and Lit.* (Tokyo) 18, 21–9; E. van Gelderen, *Jnl of Germanic Ling.* 15, 75–7

O'Keeffe, Katherine O'Brien, ed., *MS C*, The Anglo-Saxon Chronicle: a Collaborative Edition 5 (Cambridge, 2001): T. A. Bredehoft, *Speculum* 78, 579–81; E. G. Stanley, *EHR* 117, 676–7

O'Neill, Patrick P., ed., *King Alfred's Old English Prose Translation of the First Fifty Psalms* (Cambridge, MA, 2001): J. Bately, *MÆ* 72, 127–8; M. K. Ramsey, *South Atlantic Rev.* 68.3, 151–3; F. Schleburg, *Anglia* 121, 469–71; P. E. Szarmach, *Speculum* 78, 239–41

Orchard, Andy, *A Critical Companion to 'Beowulf'* (Cambridge): D. Anlezark, *MÆ* 72, 320–1; J. Bloomfield, *Med. Rev.* [online]

Orton, Peter, *The Transmission of Old English Poetry* (Turnhout, 2000): A. Harbus, *Parergon* ns 20.2, 221–2; R. M. Liuzza, *MLR* 98, 154–5; M. Swan, *Leeds Stud. in Eng.* ns 33, 207–9

Owen-Crocker, Gale R., *The Four Funerals in 'Beowulf' and the Structure of the Poem* (Manchester, 2000): T. A. Shippey, *JEGP* 102, 134–6

Page, R. I., *Runes and Runic Inscriptions* (Woodbridge, 1995): A. Finlay, *The Library* 6th ser. 21, 274–5

An Introduction to English Runes, 2nd ed. (Woodbridge, 1999): J. Hines, *JEGP* 102, 128–30; R. Simek, *Albion* 33, 429–30

Palmer, John, Matthew Palmer and George Slater, *Domesday Explorer: Great Domesday Book on CD-ROM. Version 1.0* (Chichester, 2000): S. Baxter, *EHR* 118, 130–2; D. R. Roffe, *Med. Rev.* [online]

Parry, David, *Englisc: Old English for Beginners* (Harleston): [Anon.], *MÆ* 72, 372

Parsons, David N., *Recasting the Runes: the Reform of the Anglo-Saxon Futhorc* (Uppsala, 1999): S. Fischer, *Fornvännen* 97, 302–4

Peddie, John, *Alfred, Warrior King* (Stroud, 1999): H. R. Loyn, *Welsh Hist. Rev.* 20, 575–6

Pelteret, David A. E., ed., *Anglo-Saxon History: Basic Readings* (New York, 2000): M. Swan, *Med. Rev.* [online]

Pestell, Tim, and Katharina Ulmschneider, ed., *Markets in Early Medieval Europe: Trading and 'Productive' Sites, 650–850* (Macclesfield): M. Redknap, *Landscape Hist.* 25, 99–100

Pirie, Elizabeth J. E., *Coins of Northumbria: an Illustrated Guide to Money from the Years 670 to 867* (Llanfyllin, 2002): C. Barclay, *BNJ* 72, 221

Porter, David W., ed., *Excerptiones de Prisciano: the Source for Ælfric's Latin–Old English*

Grammar, AST 4 (Cambridge, 2002): A. Crépin, *Comptes rendus des séances de l'Académie des inscriptions et belle-lettres* 2002, 1101–3; M. R. Godden, *MÆ* 72, 128–30

Pulsiano, Phillip, ed., *Old English Glossed Psalters: Psalms 1–50* (Toronto, 2001): R. M. Liuzza, *Speculum* 78, 590–2; M. J. Toswell, *N&Q* 50, 86–7

Pulsiano, Phillip, and Elaine Treharne, ed., *A Companion to Anglo-Saxon Literature* (Oxford, 2001): [Anon.], *Historiographia Linguistica* 29, 476; C. P. Jamison, *Choice* (Chicago) 39, 1582

Rauer, Christine, *Beowulf and the Dragon: Parallels and Analogues* (Cambridge, 2000): N. Howe, *Speculum* 78, 592–4; R. P. Tripp, Jr, *MLR* 98, 151–3

Redknap, Mark, *et al.*, ed., *Pattern and Purpose in Insular Art: Proceedings of the Fourth International Conference on Insular Art* (Oxford, 2001): J. Hawkes, *ArchJ* 159, 330–2

Reynolds, Andrew, *Later Anglo-Saxon England: Life and Landscape* (Stroud, 1999): P. Patrick, *Archaeol. Rev. from Cambridge* 18, 183–4

Roberts, Brian K., and Stuart Wrathmell, *Region and Place: a Study of English Rural Settlement* (London, 2002): C. Dyer, *Landscape Hist.* 25, 103–4

Roberts, Jane, and Christian Kay, with Lynne Grundy, *A Thesaurus of Old English*, 2 vols. (1995; as reissued Amsterdam, 2000): H. Momma, *N&Q* 50, 79–80; E. van Gelderen, *Stud. in Lang.* 27, 200–3

Roberts, Jane, and Janet Nelson, ed., *Essays on Anglo-Saxon and Related Themes in memory of Lynne Grundy* (London, 2000): S. Foot, *JEH* 54, 336–7

Rodwell, Warwick, *Wells Cathedral: Excavations and Structural Studies, 1978–93*, 2 vols., English Heritage Archaeol. Report 21 (London, 2001): P. Rahtz, *CBA South West* 8, 29–33

Roffe, David, *Domesday: the Inquest and the Book* (Oxford, 2000): B. R. O'Brien, *Speculum* 78, 988–90; J. Taylor, *Northern Hist.* 36, 165–6; P. Wormald, *Albion* 33, 432–3

Room, Adrian, *The Penguin Dictionary of British Place Names* (London): K. Tucker, *Names* 51, 139–45

Rumble, Alexander R., *Property and Piety in Early Medieval Winchester: Documents Relating to the Topography of the Anglo-Saxon and Norman City and its Minsters*, Winchester Stud. 4.3 (Oxford, 2002): H. E. J. Cowdrey, *JTS* 54, 814–16; D. Misonne, *RB* 113, 462

Russo, Daniel G., *Town Origins and Development in Early England,* c. *400–950 AD* (Westport, CT, 1998): D. M. Palliser, *Northern Hist.* 36, 331–2

Russom, Geoffrey, *'Beowulf' and the Origins of Old Germanic Metre* (Cambridge, 1998): R. Mines, *Nordic Jnl of Ling.* 23, 97–102

Sawyer, P. H., *Anglo-Saxon Lincolnshire*, Hist. of Lincolnshire 3 (Lincoln, 1998): D. M. Palliser, *Northern Hist.* 36, 164–5

Scragg, Donald, and Carole Weinberg, ed., *Literary Appropriations of the Anglo-Saxons from the Thirteenth to the Twentieth Century* (Cambridge, 2000): D. P. O'Donnell, *EME* 11, 184–5; A. Smol, *Dalhousie Rev.* 82, 183–4

Smyth, Alfred P., trans., *The Medieval 'Life' of King Alfred the Great: a Translation and Commentary on the Text Attributed to Asser* (Basingstoke, 2002): S. J. Harris, *Med. Rev.* [online]; A. King, *MÆ* 72, 182

South, Ted Johnson, ed., *Historia de Sancto Cuthberto: a History of Saint Cuthbert and a*

Record of His Patrimony, AST 3 (Cambridge, 2002): B. Aird, *JEH* 113, 329–30; B. Gordon-Taylor, *MÆ* 72, 182–3; D. Rollason, *Albion* 35, 258–9; J. van der Straeten, *AB* 121, 191–2

Springsfeld, Kerstin, *Alkuins Einfluss auf die Komputistik zur Zeit Karls des Grossen* (Stuttgart, 2002): O. de Solan, *Bibliothèque de l'École des chartes* 161, 694–701; G. Schmitz, *DAEM* 59, 718–19

Stanley, Eric Gerald, *Imagining the Anglo-Saxon Past: 'The Search for Anglo-Saxon Paganism' and 'Anglo-Saxon Trial by Jury'* (Cambridge, 2000): J. Campbell, *EHR* 117, 149; T. Honegger, *Anglia* 121, 643–4; C. Larrington, *Med. Rev.* [online]

Stanton, Robert, *The Culture of Translation in Anglo-Saxon England* (Cambridge, 2002): S. Downey, *N&Q* 50, 454–5; M. Drout, *Med. Rev.* [online]; A. Harbus, *Parergon* ns 20.2, 239–41; R. Jayatilaka, *MÆ* 72, 317–19

Suzuki, Seiichi, *The Quoit Brooch Style and Anglo-Saxon Settlement: a Casting and Recasting of Cultural Identity Symbols* (Woodbridge, 2000): J. Campbell, *EHR* 117, 149–50; N. Stoodley, *EME* 11, 185–6

Swan, Mary, and Elaine M. Treharne, ed., *Rewriting Old English in the Twelfth Century* (Cambridge, 2000): K. Davis, *Speculum* 78, 609–12; K. Dietz, *Anglia* 121, 120–3; A. Lawrence, *MLR* 98, 417–18; H. Wilson, *RES* 54, 238–9

Tolkien, J. R. R., *'Beowulf' and the Critics*, ed. Michael D. C. Drout (Tempe, AZ, 2002): D. Anlezark, *MÆ* 72, 319–20

Tugene, Georges, *L'idée de nation chez Bède le Vénérable* (Paris, 2001): S. Fanning, *Speculum* 78, 1007–9; K. Nass, *DAEM* 59, 666; B. Ward, *JTS* 54, 357–8

L'image de la nation anglaise dans l' 'Histoire ecclésiastique' de Bède le Vénérable (Strasbourg, 2001): K. Nass, *DAEM* 59, 262–3; F. P. Terlizzi, *SM* 44, 682–4

Voigts, Linda Ehrsam, and Patricia Deery Kurtz, *Scientific and Medical Writings in Old and Middle English: an Electronic Reference* (Ann Arbor, MI, 2001): M. H. Green, *Speculum* 78, 620–3

Waite, Gregory, *Old English Prose Translations of King Alfred's Reign*, Annotated Bibliographies of Old and Middle Eng. Lit. 6 (Cambridge, 2000): C. Schreiber, *Anglia* 121, 466–8

Walker, Ian W., *Mercia and the Making of England* (Stroud, 2000): A. Burghart, *EME* 11, 294; J. Insley, *DAEM* 59, 834–5

Wilcox, Jonathan, ed., *Humour in Anglo-Saxon Literature* (Cambridge, 2000): P. Dendle, *JEGP* 102, 133–4; A. P. Scheil, *MLR* 98, 946–7

Wilson, H. A., *The Calendar of St Willibrord from MS Paris. Lat. 10837: Facsimile with Transcription, Introduction and Notes*, HBS 15 (1918; as reissued Woodbridge, 1998): M. Klöckener, *Archiv für Liturgiewissenschaft* 45, 93–4

Wood, Michael, *In Search of England: Journeys into the English Past* (London, 1999): M. Hewitt, *Hist.: Reviews of New Books* 29, 116–17

Wormald, Patrick, *The Making of English Law, King Alfred to the Twelfth Century*, I: *Legislation and its Limits* (Oxford, 1999): A. Boureau, *Annales: histoire, sciences sociales* 57, 1650–1

Wright, C. J., ed., *Sir Robert Cotton as Collector* (London, 1997): R. Ovenden, *The Library* 6th ser. 21, 380–2

Wyly, Bryan Weston, *Figures of Authority in the Old English 'Exodus'* (Heidelberg, 1999): R. Bauer, *Anglia* 121, 114–18

Ziolkowski, Jan M., ed., *The Cambridge Songs (Carmina Cantabrigiensia)* (1994; as reissued Tempe, AZ, 1998): D. Di Rienzo, *Bollettino di studi latini* 29, 254–7